STUDIES IN MĪMĀṀSĀ

Dr Mandan Mishra

STUDIES IN MĪMĀṀSĀ

Dr. Mandan Mishra Felicitation Volume

Edited by
R.C. DWIVEDI

MOTILAL BANARSIDASS PUBLISHERS
PRIVATE LIMITED • DELHI

Reprint: Delhi, 2016
First Edition: Delhi, 1994

ISBN: 978-81-208-1109-6

Also available at:
MOTILAL BANARSIDASS
41 U.A. Bungalow Road, Jawahar Nagar, Delhi 110 007
8 Mahalaxmi Chamber, 22 Bhulabhai Desai Road, Mumbai 400 026
203 Royapettah High Road, Mylapore, Chennai 600 004
236, 9th Main III Block, Jayanagar, Bengaluru 560 011
8 Camac Street, Kolkata 700 017
Ashok Rajpath, Patna 800 004
Chowk, Varanasi 221 001

MLBD Cataloging-in-Publication Data
Studies in Mīmāṁsā
Edited by R.C. Dwivedi
Includes Index
ISBN : 978-81-208-1109-6
I. Philosophy/Indian II. Mimamsa
III. Mishra, Mandana IV. Dwivedi, R.C.

Printed in India

by RP Jain at NAB Printing Unit,
A-44, Naraina Industrial Area, Phase I, New Delhi–110028
and published by JP Jain for Motilal Banarsidass Publishers (P) Ltd,
41 U.A. Bungalow Road, Jawahar Nagar, Delhi-110007

CONTENTS

SECTION II

LANGUAGE, MEANING, GRAMMAR

SECTION III

HERMENEUTICAL ESSAYS

INTRODUCTION

Massive and unique contribution of Mīmāṁsā to the philosophy of language, hermeneutics, exegesis and semiology, to the philosophy of religion, epistemology and above all to the philosophy of pragmatic active life affirming continuity of cultural tradition remains important for the intellectual pursuits in the world of knowledge and culture. Its influence on other branches of learning in India is formidable. No system of thought can be properly and comprehensively understood without a reference to Mīmāṁsā.

Research papers by eminent pundits and scholars included in this felicitation volume in honour of my friend Dr. Mandan Mishra, who is known for his basic intellectual interest in Mīmāṁsā, are devoted mainly to analytical and critical exposition of its theories, focusing attention on its relation to other disciplines and presenting a comparative study with similar Indian and Western speculations. This is perhaps the first international intellectual adventure of its kind which is bound to generate fresh thinking and create right perspectives in the field of Mīmāṁsā. Studies in Mīmāṁsā in this volume take it out of its traditionally recognised narrow confines of ritualistic interpretation of the Vedic sentences and make it part of the global philosophy of language and religion. It is difficult to put the papers under neat classification or watertight compartments, yet, broadly speaking, these have been arranged under three Sections: 1. Philosophy, Epistemology, Ethics; 2. Language, Meaning, Grammar; and 3. Hermeneutical Essays.

G.P. Bhatt in his article gives a brief statement of the non-ritualistic and purely philosophical ideas and doctrines found in the works of Mīmāṁsā, more particularly its leading thinkers, Kumārila Bhaṭṭa and Prabhākara.

John A. Taber advances arguments of Kumārila against the Buddhist denial of the existence of objects outside consciousness. He emphasizes Kumārila's assertion that the reality of the external world is revealed directly by our perceptions and other cognitions. This is based on the theory of intrinsic validity of knowledge (*svataḥprāmāṇya*) which is a unique contribution of Mīmāṁsā to the Theory of Knowledge.

Those interested in the philosophy of religion will find certain discussions here quite exciting. Peri Sarveswara Sharma makes a close textual study of the *Sambandhaparīkṣā* section of Kumārila's *Ślokavārtika* denying creation and dissolution of the world along with a refutation of the theories of Vaiśeṣika, Nyāya, Sāṁkhya and Vedānta.

A paper by Lars Göhler in comparative philosophy examining the similarities in the philosophical concepts of Kumārila and K.R. Popper regarding verification and falsity of cognition underlines contemporary significance of Mīmāṁsā epistemology.

The injunctive nature of the Vedic sentence presents a pragmatic paradox, argues Shlomo Biderman, which makes it possible to remain innocuous by opening new possibilities of understanding the role that interpretation plays in religion. He distinguishes it from the 'Semantic Paradox' found in the monotheistic context.

Tomoyasu Takenaka explains the relation between *liṅga* (*vyāpya* or pervaded) and *liṅgin* (*vyāpaka* or pervader) and the *sāhitya-niyama* of the Bhāṭṭa School which establishes this relationship. In his view this notion of the Bhāṭṭa School is larger than that of Vaiśeṣika or Dharmakīrti.

Self-revealed nature of the scriptual knowledge (*Vedāpauruṣeyatva*) which is a basic concept of the epistemology of Mīmāṁsā is critically presented in the light of Buddhist objections in a paper by J.M. Verpoorten.

The philosophy of activism, as expounded by P.T. Raju in a paper reprinted here is a strong rebuttal of the general notion of Indian ethics as life-denying or advocacy of inaction. The paper will prove affirmation of life in Indian thought leading to the national regeneration and international co-operation for global peace.

Hajime Nakamura demonstrates that a Western notion, such as Kantian categorical imperative, could be applied to the idea of *niyoga* in the Prābhākara School. He suggests that *anapekṣo vidhiḥ* or *anapekṣā codanā* found in the philosophy of Prabhākara and the *Nyāyakaṇikā*, a commentary by Vācaspati Miśra on the *Vidhiviveka* of Maṇḍana Miśra, could be an Indian equivalent to the Western idea of categorical imperative. The notion of *Niyoga* in Prabhākara may have been influenced by the spirit of *maitrī* and *karuṇā* set forth in Buddhism as a categorical imperative. This is an important contribution to the study of comparative ethics.

According to Purushottama Bilimoria, the *autpattika* (relation of word with the meaning from the very beginning) thesis offers semiological insights from de Saussure's work and their extension in the writings of the contemporary French philosopher Jacques Derrida.

The problem of getting at the particular meaning of a sentence from the universal and removing incompatibility in the context, is set forth and a solution suggested by K. Kunjunni Raja by expounding two forms of *Abhidhā* according to the Prābhākaras and two operations of *Lakṣaṇā* according to the Bhāṭṭas. He also draws attention of the scholars to the fact that the *Tātparya Śakti* is nothing more than the *saṁsargamaryādā* accepted by the *Navyanyāya* school. The theories of *abhihitānvaya* held by Kumārila and *anvitābhidhāna* are important contributions to semantics. These are variously explored in the papers. Thus, for example, the theory of prior existence of a meaning whole is comparatively brought out by Harold G. Coward. And again how a simple word *Varṇa* standing for phoneme or sound has been wrongly translated as 'Letter' is exposed by Albrecht Wezler with a penetrating and in-depth study of the texts and translations.

Sri Ramachandrudu points out that according to Kumārila grammar cannot intervene to get at the real meaning of a word of a sentence. Its usefulness is restricted to knowing the correct word to be employed in the performance of sacrifice. Purposes of Vyākaraṇa enunciated by Patañjali in his *Mahābhāṣya* are roundly refuted by Kumārila as of no help for the interpretation of the Veda. This is a significant debate to establish independence of exegetics from grammar which is primarily concerned with the determination of correct word and its formation. It cannot govern its meaning, intention or interpretation.

The views of Prabhākara, Pārthasārathi Miśra and Khaṇḍadeva on the meaning of *ākhyāta* are expounded by a great traditional Sanskrit Pundit Peri Suryanarayan Sastri in his paper in

Sanskrit. He favours the opinion of Khaṇḍadeva, according to which fruit and operation, *phala* and *vyāpāra*, are conveyed by the verb root, and *bhāvanā* in the form of action conducive to the meaning of the root is conveyed by *ākhyāta*. Kumārila's postulation of *apūrva* and Bhartṛhari's theory of *Sphoṭa* are compared to discuss how the words convey the meanings in a relation which is unborn and eternal and is not man-made, conventional or even divine.

The paper in Sanskrit by a renowned Mīmāṁsaka, Padma Bhushan Pt. P.N. Pattabhirama Shastri, the guru of Dr. Mandan Mishra and Chairman of the Editorial Advisory Board, who was snatched away from us by the cruel hands of death before he could see the publication of this volume, establishes that the *nyāyas* (maxims, principles, rulings or judgements) developed by Mīmāṁsā to determine meaning of a scriptural sentence are applied by other disciplines and can be significantly used even in the judgement of worldly transactions.

Application and extension of a specific *nyāya*, namely the principle of *apaccheda*, is pinpointed in the texts of *Dvaita*, *Advaita* and *Viśiṣṭādvaita* Vedānta by N.S. Ramanuja Tatacharya in his paper in Sanskrit.

Francis X. Clooney, S.J. presents continuity and difference of Mīmāṁsā in Vedānta by articulation of a properly Vedāntic mode of exegesis in the *Vedānta Sūtra* 3.3. The Vedāntins employ *upasaṁhāra* in their interpretative movement between a reorganisation of Upaniṣadic knowledge based on the Mīmāṁsā functional systematization of the Veda, and one based in part on the fact that *Brahman* is the known object of that knowledge, its referent. They argue from the grammatical sense of the texts and from their reference, and to highlight *upasaṁhāra*, as one of their key *Uttaramīmāṁsā* principles.

Kunio Harikai after a close examination of the text, *Arthasaṁgraha* by Laugākṣibhāskara, concludes that the threefold classification of *arthavāda*, a statement or explanation of the meaning of a formula or prayer (*mantra* and *vidhi*, injunction, in a Brāhmaṇa text) into *Guṇavāda*, *Vidhiśeṣa* and *Niṣedhaśeṣa* would not be derived from the Mīmāṁsā school but from the Vedānta school or some heterodoxical Mīmāṁsakas.

Equally interesting is another paper is Sanskrit where Batuk-nath Shastri Khiste presents the views of an original thinker of 17th century C.E., Bhāskararāya, to show that the Mīmāṁsā exegesis can be applied to the Āgama texts and the worship of *Śrīvidyā* can be explained in the Vedāntic mode of *Brahmavidyā*. The rootedness of the Āgamas in the Vedic tradition is shown here with necessary textual connections and their fresh and novel interpretations.

Yudhishthira Mimamsaka has for the first time given a metaphysical interpretation to the *Aśvamedha* sacrifice.

In his paper 'Mādhava on Mīmāṁsā' Haruo Kurata establishes through an intimate and close study of the relevant texts that Mādhava, the author of the *Sarvadarśana-saṁgraha*, *Jaiminīyanyāyamālā* and *Pārāśara-mādhavīya*, is neutral to both Kumārila and Prabhākara whereas Sāyaṇa, his brother and well-known commentator of the Vedas, is a follower of Kumārila. Such questions, important for the history of Mīmāṁsā, are also incidentally dealt with by other scholars while dealing with the problems and issues of hermeneutics, philosophy of religion, epistemology or inter-relationship of Mīmāṁsā with other disciplines, Vyākaraṇa, Vedānta, Sāṁkhya and so on.

Johannes Bronkhorst adduces textual proof to establish that Bhartṛhari used a text of Mīmāṁsā older than Śabara's Bhāṣya, most probably Bhavadāsa's *Vṛtti* which contained verses found in Bhartṛhari. In the context of ritual details Bhartṛhari draws upon practical manuals of the Maitrāyaṇīyas.

As against this Kiyotaka Yoshimizu argues that although Prabhākara insists that the fulfilment of obligation is the real interest of Vedic injunction, he also admits like Jaimini and Śabara, and unlike Bādari whom he generally follows otherwise, from the viewpoint of human motivation that the act of sacrificing is a means to and therefore subordinated to the desired result.

K.T. Pandurangi illustrates the logic and methodology of Mīmāṁsā followed by Śaṅkara in the field of *dharmajñāna* at the stage of *avidyā* and application of its principles even in the case of *Brahmajñāna*. What is true of Vedānta is also equally true of Tantra, Alaṁkāra, Dharmaśāstra and other disciplines.

There is no branch of learning and no movement of thought and action which did not interact with Mīmāṁsā. Much work still remains to be done in this area of research. Contemporary philosophers of language and theorists of knowledge may discover fresh insights in this system of thought which has remained largely unexplored for its hard-core philosophy. This volume, one should hope, will mark a shift from pure ritualism to speculative, epistemological, hermeneutical concern and inter-disciplinary significance of Mīmāṁsā which would become part of universal thought systems.

R.C. Dwivedi

SECTION ONE

Philosophy
Epistemology
Ethics

1

MĪMĀṀSĀ AS A PHILOSOPHICAL SYSTEM: A SURVEY

G. P. Bhatt

The body of doctrines that goes popularly by the name of Mīmāṁsā but more exactly by that of Pūrvamīmāṁsā is a 'reasoned investigation' of the earlier part of the Veda. *Veda* is the name of a long series of compositions by the ancient Aryans settled in India, in which four stages of growth are clearly discernible. First came the hymns or songs presumably* sung in praise of natural powers. Thereafter came the *Brāhmaṇas* which are liturgical compositions in prose dealing with the performance of Yajñas and discussing their intricacies. The *Āraṇyakas* or 'Forest Books' constitute the third stage interpreting the Karmakāṇḍa rather symbolically and shifting the emphasis from the physical and literal performance of Yajñas etc., to a mental and symbolic performance. And in the last appeared the *Upaniṣads* or esoteric discussions of a philosophical nature between preceptors and disciples. In the *Brāhmaṇa* stage a highly complex system of rituals developed and the simple nature religion of the inspired poets of the earlier stage was superseded by what appears to be more like magic than religion, when the singing of hymns became an essential accompaniment of a complicated ritual performed for its magical effects. As compared to the *Upaniṣads* or Jñānakāṇḍa rituals or Karmakāṇḍa form the earlier portion of the Veda, the word *Karma* generally meaning action having been used exclusively in the sense of sacrificial ritual, with

*They may as well be the expressions, as is believed in several quarters, of profound philosophical and spiritual truths clothed in a language which has become mostly unintelligible at this remote stage.

which the system of Pūrvamīmāṁsā, also known as Karma-mīmāṁsā, concerns itself.

Though Pūrvamīmāṁsā is based on Jaimini's *Mīmāṁsāsūtra*, yet Jaimini was not the first thinker of this system. He himself has referred to some teachers preceding him, e.g. Bādarāyaṇa, Bādari, Aitiśāyana, Kārṣṇājini, Lāmbukāyana, Kāmukāyana, Ātreya and Ālekhana. Besides, there appears to be at least one more Mīmāṁsā thinker bearing the same name Jaimini and referred to by the Sūtrakāra as the holder of a *prima facie* view (Pūrva-pakṣa). Pāṇini has named two more Mīmāṁsā teachers, viz. Kāśakṛtsna and Āpiśāli. Even before these thinkers occasional discussions of the Mīmāṁsā type are found in the *Brāhmaṇas* themselves and somewhat later in the *Śrautasūtras* in a more systematic way. It seems that as the technicalities of the sacrificial ritual became more and more complicated, doubts began to crop up as to the correct method of performing the sacrifices and the correct interpretation of the Vedic texts enjoining sacrifices. In the course of time this led to the formulation of rules according to which the Vedic texts were to be interpreted. Not one but several attempts at the formulation of such rules must have been made in the remote past and as a result several systems must have appeared simultaneously and successively, which were gradually discarded save Jaimini's system which alone survived.

As is usually the case with the ancient Sūtrakāras, the date of Jaimini is not settled. His work has extremely little of what we now understand by the term 'philosophy'. But since it makes an attempt to defend by arguments the supreme authority and eternality of the Veda, it is definite that it belonged to an age when heterodox thinkers, like the Buddha, challenging the claims of the followers of Veda and casting serious doubts about the real spiritual value of sacrifices, had made their appearance and organized themselves into powerful groups, but the highly developed anti-Vedic metaphysical schools like Yogācāra and Mādhyamika had not yet appeared.

The theme of Jaimini's work as declared in the first Sūtra is Dharma, its nature, its Pramāṇa and other details. Dharma is that which is enjoined by the Veda as conducive to human good and it is known exclusively from the Veda, since perception and other common means of knowledge are restricted to the sphere of existing entities only, while Dharma, being that which is to be accomplished in a transcendental sphere, lies beyond their scope. But why should the Veda alone be relied upon in this matter? Jaimini declared that Veda was not a work of any author, human or divine, but was the eternal word with a meaning independent of any convention and hence, by its very nature, of supreme authority. This has been discussed in a very small portion (Adhyāya 1, Pāda 1) of Jaimini's huge work, the rest having been devoted to other details of practically no philosophical importance now.

In the next, the *Bhāṣya* stage, we find much more that is of philosophical interest. Śabara was the author of the *Bhāṣya* on Jaimini's *Sūtra* which has come down to us. From reference occurring in the Bhāṣya itself and the Mīmāṁsā literature of subsequent period Upavarṣa, Bhartṛmitra, Bhavadāsa and Hari are known to have commented on the *Sūtra* before Śabara. The works of all these commentators, except a small portion of Upavarṣa's *Vṛtti* which has been quoted by Śabara, are now lost and so their contribution to the evolution of the system is not known.

From the *Bhāṣya* it is quite evident that by Śabara's time the Buddhist idealistic schools of Vijñānavāda and Śūnyavāda had firmly established themselves and were threatening the very basis of Vedic ritualism which presupposed the reality of the external world along with that of soul, heaven and the efficacy of Yajñas. Under the conditions Mīmāṁsā could not afford to remain a mere liturgical system. So Śabara came forward to meet the idealist challenge and thenceforth Mīmāṁsā gradually took a genuinely philosophical turn. Śabara indicated the way of refuting* the premises from which idealism drew its conclusions by asserting that (1) cognition is formless and momentary, (2) it cann't cognize itself, (3) its object is always something beyond itself, (4) cognition and object are not cognized simultaneonsly, (5) the form that is cognized always belongs to the object, and (6) the knowledge of cognition appears subsequently through presumption.

Idealism also drew its strength from the common fact of illusory perception from which it concluded that cognition which

*The final refutation was yet to be done by Kumārila.

seems to prove the reality of the external world is intrinsically false. Śabara's realism could not ignore this problem and by offering an adequate answer Śabara laid down the foundation of the celebrated Mīmāṁsā doctrine of intrinsic truth. Besides, Śabara also tried to establish the independent reality and permanence of soul and denied the existence of God so far as it conflicted with the eternality and supreme authority of Veda, this latter idea being quite a revolutionary one in the orthodox circles in those times. Śabara's time is followed by what may be said to be the golden period of Mīmāṁsā. This was the period in which the greatest exponents of the system, Kumārila Bhaṭṭa and Prabhākara Miśra flourished, who differed on important issues from each other so that the system of Pūrvamīmāṁsā got divided into two separate schools known as the Bhāṭṭa school and the Prābhākara school.

This was an age of the most vigorous intellectual activity and philosophical fertility, in which the Mīmāṁsā thought touched the loftiest heights in critical and speculative philosophy. Surely the Buddhist idealism which was but the logical continuation of the Upaniṣadic way of thinking and which had by that time completely dominated the philosophical scene in India, had also played an important role by offering an almost irresistible opposition and was responsible for the achievement of the highest order in Mīmāṁsā.

Kumārila and Prabhākara continuing Śabara's line of thought with all its implications, perfected his arguments while keeping fully in view what was going on in the hostile camps and also introduced numerous new ideas into the system, one of the most important of such ideas being that of Mokṣa which made Mīmāṁsā a full-fledged philosophy. Mīmāṁsā till Śabara's time remained content with the original Vedic ideal of Heaven, of which Yajñas were the sole means. As a matter of fact, the ideal of Mokṣa was somewhat foreign to the spirit of Vedic rituals, and the adoption of this ideal at this stage relegates ritualism to a subordinate position in the system. This may create a suspicion in some minds that ritualism was still adhered to for protecting the interest of the priestly class.

Some more new doctrines of this period worth mentioning here are Kumārila's theories of *Jñātatā* and *Viparītakhyāti* and

Prabhākara's theories of *Tripuṭīpratyakṣa* and *Akhyāti* in epistemology.

The last phase in the evolution of Mīmāṁsā thought is characterized by further enrichment as well as deterioration. This phase extends roughly from 9th century to the 17th. Śālikanātha, Pārthasārathi, Cidānanda, Nārāyaṇa Bhaṭṭa, Nārāyaṇa Paṇḍita, Laugākṣibhāskara and Āpadeva are some important names of this period. Now Buddhism had ceased to be the main adversary and Nyāya-Vaiśeṣika had taken its place. Mīmāṁsā got enriched now significantly by borrowing from Nyāya-Vaiśeṣika with minor changes, since realism was common to both. One noteworthy change that characterizes this period was the bringing of God and the idea of periodic creation and destruction in Mīmāṁsā which had so far been uncompromisingly atheistic.

Sūtrakāra Jaimini

The authorship of the *Pūrvamīmāṁsāsūtra* is attributed to Jaimini who in the absence of any biographical details is to us as good as a mythological figure. Strangely enough, the name Jaimini appears in the text of the *Sūtra* itself in five places and in one place the *prima facie* view (Pūrvapakṣa) expressed in the *Sūtra* is attributed by Śabara to one Jaimini though he has not been named by the Sūtrakāra himself. It is believed that in four out of the above places the views expressed are the Sūtrakāra's own, while in the remaining two places the Jaimini referred to is some older teacher of Mīmāṁsā. There has been still another Jaimini who was the author of a *Sūtra* work on Astrology.

No sufficient historical data is available for settling the date of Jaimini. Jacobi thinks that he can't be earlier than 200 A.C. since he seems to be conversant with the Buddhist theory of *Śūnya* which was propounded by Nāgārjuna (200 A.C.). In Keith's opinion he can't be later than 200 A.C. But most of the scholars now believe that he was much earlier than the Christian Era. Probably he belonged to 400 B.C. The reason given by Jacobi applies to the Bhāṣyakāra Śabara rather to Jaimini. Jaimini could not have been very far removed in time from the Buddha (600 B.C.) who was the first powerful critic of the Vedic ritualism with a very large following and who must therfore have simultaneously provoked the champions of Vedic religion to organize themselves and reinterpret and defend their ritualism. A period of 200 years after the Buddha must be more than enough to give rise to various pre-Jaimini systems of Pūrvamīmāṁsā, which proved rather tentative, so we may say, and were ultimately superseded by that of Jaimini which has come down to us.

The *Mīmāṁsāsūtra* of Jaimini is only a comprehensive and systematic work of one school and this is clear from the references he gives to the views of other preceding authors. It may be said with some degree of confidence that this work of Jaimini was deemed so masterly a work that it has survived all other attempts that were made before him. It was probably written about 200 B.C. and is now the groundwork of the Mīmāṁsā system.

Jaimini's work is divided into twelve Adhyāyas and each Adhyāya is divided into several Pādas not necessarily four which is usually the case. Three of the Adhyāyas have eight Pādas each. The work contains more than 2,500 Sūtras. Four additional Adhyāyas going by the name *Saṅkarṣakāṇḍa* are also mentioned, but they have not yet been discovered. Only the first Pāda of the first Adhyāya of this huge work has any philosophical importance, the rest having been devoted to Yajña and the rules regarding the interpretation of the Veda. In this Pāda known as the *Tarkapāda*, the nature and the means of knowing religious duty have been discussed.

Bhāṣyakāra Śabara

Mīmāṁsā as a system in the form in which it has come down to us started with the *Sūtras* of Jaimini, but as a system of Philosophy it may be said to have started with Śabara or Śabarasvāmin who wrote a *Bhāṣya*, a free commentary on Jaimini's work with additions and alterations suited to the needs of contemporary thought. As is the case with Jaimini, nothing is known with certainty about the personality and date of Śabara. This is a very common thing with our ancient thinkers. Perhaps those ancient seekers of truth were so much engrossed in their pursuit that they forgot or out of modesty deliberately ignored their own personality and other things of passing value.

Though it is difficult to say anything about the time in which Śabara flourished, Dr. Ganganatha Jha would have him about

57 B.C. Śabara's *Bhāṣya* has become the basis of the later Mīmāṁsā works. This *Bhāṣya* was commented upon by an unknown person alluded to as Vṛttikāra by Prabhākara and merely referred to as *Yathāhuḥ* ('as they said') by Kumārila.

There is a tradition that Śabara had six sons, viz. Varāhamihira, Bhartṛhari, Vikrama, Hariścandra, Śaṅku and Amara. But since these belonged to widely different periods of time, there seems no truth in this story. However, the phase of the evolution of Mīmāṁsā represented by Śabara must have followed the rise of Yogācāra and Mādhyamika schools of Buddhism and preceded the appearance of the great Buddhist logician Dharmakīrti. So it appears reasonable to think that Śabara might have flourished at a time between 200 and 400 A.C.

The original name of Śabara is said to be Ādityadeva. He came to be known as Śabara after he disguised himself as a forest-dweller to escape from the so called 'Jaina persecution'.

On the basis of certain facts mentioned in the *Bhāṣya* Dr. Jha thinks that Śabara was a resident of Northern India, perhaps of Kāśmīra or Takṣaśilā. But Dr. Umesh Mishra has pointed out a number of facts including certain food practices mentioned in the *Bhāṣya* which suggest rather his being a resident of Mithilā or some other north-eastern region.

Kumārila Bhaṭṭa and His School

In the framework of doctrines supplied by Śabara the details were superbly filled up by Kumārila Bhaṭṭa, also known as Tūtāta Bhaṭṭa, who was one of the biggest philosophers that India produced. Kumārila was born at a time when Buddhism had acquired a widespread influence in India and the Vedic religion was on the verge of being swept away totally. Kumārila appeared at the right moment as the savior of the Vedic religion and it is in this capacity that he will ever be remembered in the religions history of India.

Kumārila was able to defeat the Buddhists by his profound knowledge of Buddhism, which he is said to have acquired by disguising himself as a Buddhist directly from an eminent Buddhist teacher who also was later defeated by him. The story seems to contain a high degree of probability, since a study of

Kumārila's works amply reveals his accurate and extensive knowledge of Buddhist tenets unparalleled in the orthodox systems.

The stories recorded about him also show that he was a contemporary of the great Buddhist logician Dharmakīrti and the great Śaṅkarācārya. The former is said to have defeated him in a debate at an early stage of his philosophical career and the latter met him on the banks of Triveṇī when he was in the process of burning himself as a self-imposed punishment. He had committed a 'great sin' by defeating his Buddhist Guru in a debate and for its expiation he burnt himself to death. It appears that Kumārila was a senior contemporary of Śaṅkara and junior to Dharmakīrti and lived in the 7th century A.C. He was probably a native of Mithilā which was then a big centre of Buddhism.

His great works are *Ślokavārtika*, *Tantravārtika* and *Ṭupṭīkā*. The first is a commentary in verse on the *Tarkapāda* section (Adhyāya 1, Pāda 1) of Śabara's *Bhāṣya*, the second a commentary on the portion of the *Bhāṣya* extending from Adhyāya 1, Pāda 2 to the end Adhyāya 3, and the third covers the remaining portion. Kumārila is also known to have written two more commentaries, viz. *Bṛhaṭṭīkā* and *Madhyamaṭīkā* but these appear to have been lost.

Ślokavārtika is his main philosophical work. In many places in it he differs from Śabara and even criticizes him. The earliest commentary on *Ślokavārtika* is Umbeka's *Tātparyaṭīkā*. According to Vidyāraṇya, Umbeka was a popular name of Maṇḍanamiśra and some identify him with the great poet Bhavabhūti. But none of these equations has been established. Sucaritamiśra's *Kāśikā* is a very good and extensive commentary on the *Ślokavārtika*. But the best commentary is the *Nyāyaratnākara* of Pārathasārathi Miśra who was the greatest Mīmāṁsaka of the Bhāṭṭa school after Kumārila and probably belonged to the 10th century A.C.

Nyāyaratnamālā is another important work of Pārthasārathi. It is an independent treatise on the system. It contains two chapters of philosophical importance, one dealing exhaustively with the theory of intrinsic truth and another with Vyāpti. Pārthasārathi also wrote *Śāstradīpikā*, an independent commentary on the *Bhāṣya* of Śabara, which is the most popular work on the system.

Two more important and independent works of the Bhāṭṭa school are *Nītitattvāvirbhāva* of Cidānanda Paṇḍita and *Mānameyodaya* of two Nārāyaṇas, one Nārāyaṇabhaṭṭa, the writer of the *Māna* section, and the other Nārāyaṇapaṇḍita, the writer of the *Meya* section. Cidānanda's is a very important work. He flourished before the 14th century. It was commented upon by Parameśvara. The Nārāyaṇas belonged to the 16th-17th centuries. Their work is a summary of Cidānanda's *Nītitattvāvirbhāva*. Both of these works are influenced by Navya Nyāya in style and contents.

There have been many more followers of the Bhāṭṭa school, whom we have not named here because they wrote mainly on the non-philosophical topics of Mīmāṁsā.

Prabhākara Miśra and His School

Another great Mīmāṁsaka was Prabhākara Miśra, also known as Guru, who founded a rival school of Pūrvamīmāṁsā and who was not inferior as an original thinker, though not so influential as Kumārila. There is a story about the origin of the name *Guru* which, incidentally, also shows him as a scholar of very keen intellect. Tradition makes him a pupil of Kumārila. Once Kumārila came across a sentence '*atra tu noktaṁ tatrāpi noktaṁ dvidhā proktam*' in the course of his study. The sentence apparently meant that 'it has been said neither here nor there and yet has been said twice'. Kumārila got puzzled but Prabhākara readily explained it as '*atra tunā uktaṁ tatra apinā uktaṁ dvidhā proktam*' meaning 'here it has been expressed by the article *tu* and there by *api* and thus it has been expressed twice'. Thereupon Kumārila was very much pleased and conferred on Prabhākara the title of *Guru*.

About the date of Prabhākara it is now generally agreed that he was a contemporary of Kumārila, but the issue as to who was senior and who junior is not at all settled. Traditionally Kumārila is supposed to be the senior. But some scholars, notably Dr. Jha, have a serious doubt in this matter. There are two main reasons proposed against Prabhākara's juniority: (1) It is said that Prabhākara's commentary on the *Bhāṣya* is a commentary in the strictest sense; that he simply interprets the *Bhāṣya* without criticizing it, while Kumārila has criticized the *Bhāṣya* in several places. (2) It is also said that Prabhākara's style is older and resembles that of Śabara, while Kumārila's is later like that of Śaṅkara. These reasons, however, are not very convincing, because even now a scholar can write a commentary in the so-called strictest sense and can imitate even the style of the Vedas and can adopt their phraseology. One more reason given by Dr. Jha is that Kumārila seems to criticize Prabhākara while Prabhākara does not criticize Kumārila. But there are scholars who hold that Prabhākara does criticize Kumārila. Prof. A. Subrahmanya Shastri, for instance, says that Kumārila has been referred to by Prabhākara by the use of such words as *Ekadeśin* and *Kaścit*.

Prabhākara wrote *Bṛhatī*, also called *Nibandha* or *Nibandhana*. It has been discovered and published in an incomplete form. He also wrote a second commentary on the *Bhāṣya* by the name *Laghvī* or *Vivaraṇa*, but it has not been discovered. Śālikanātha, a very great Mīmāṁsaka of the Prābhākara school, wrote two commentaries on Prabhākara's difficult works, one being *Ṛjuvimalāpañcikā* on *Bṛhatī* and a second *Dīpaśikhāpañcikā* on *Laghvī*.

Śālikanātha is also known as Śālikānātha and Śārikānātha. Vācaspati refers to him as *Navya* ('the new') Prabhākara as distinguished from *Jarat* (old) Prabhākara (i.e. Prabhākara himself). As a matter of fact, Śālikanātha is the main pillar of the Prābhākara school. Much of Prabhākara's work would have remained obscure without Śālikanātha's commentaries.

As Śālikanātha refutes Maṇḍana's view and Vācaspati Miśra refutes those of Śālikanātha, he must have flourished before the 9th century. If Varadarāja's view that the word 'Gauḍamīmāṁsaka' occurring in Udayanācārya's *Nyāyakusumāñjali* refers to Śālikanātha be relied upon, then Śālikanātha was a native of the Gauḍapradeśa or Bengal.

Śālikanātha is the author of two more works, in addition to his *Ṛjuvimalāpañcikā* and *Dīpaśikhāpañcikā*, the two commentaries on Prabhākara's *Bṛhatī* and *Laghvī* respectively. A work named *Mīmāṁsābhāṣyapariśiṣṭa* is also attributed to him. But his main work is the *Prakaraṇapañcikā*. This gives the views of

Prabhākara almost on all the topics and is indispensable for a knowledge of the school. It is an independent treatise containing 14 chapters, out of which chapters 3, 4, 5, 6, 7, 8 and 10 are more important for a student of philosophy. In chapter 3 the nature of illusion is discussed and the theory of *Akhyāti* established. In the 4th the Buddhist theory of universals is refuted. In the 5th the nature of *Pramāṇas* is discussed briefly. In the 6th the five *Pramāṇas* are defined and rival views refuted. The 7th chapter deals with the relationship of word and meaning and the refutation of God's existence. In the 8th the existence of self is established and the nature of liberation as the highest goal is discussed. In the 10th chapter the Buddhist theory of momentariness is refuted.

Prabhākara was an independent thinker. Though he has not criticized Śabara openly like Kumārila, yet in a number of places he has twisted the *Bhāṣya* and his interpretation appears forced and unconvincing. For example, Śabara obviously recognizes *Anupalabdhi* as an independent *Pramāṇa*, but Prabhākara twists the *Bhāṣya* sentence in such a way that it gives exactly the opposite meaning. In another place the *Bhāṣya* plainly says that *Jñāna* (invariably meaning 'cognition') is not self-luminous but knowable through inference. Prabhākara, however, believes that cognition is self-luminous and so to adapt the *Bhāṣya* to his own view he explains the *Bhāṣya* word *Jñāna* in an entirely unusual sense, viz. that of soul-mind contact.

After Śālikanātha an important follower of Prabhākara was Bhavanāthamiśra who lived before the 11th century. His *Nayaviveka* is an independent commentary on Jaimini's *Sūtra*. It is a very important work as is indicated by a number of commentaries on it. Varadarāja's (16th century) *Dīpikā* is a good commentary on Bhavanātha's *Nayaviveka*. Rāmânujācārya's (18th century) *Tantrarahasya* is a very good work of the Prābhākara school dealing with *Mānas* ('means of valid knowledge') and *Prameyas* ('categories').

Metaphysics

The Mīmāṁsā is opposed to idealism and firmly believes in the reality of the external world. Here we state Mīmāṁsā realism only in its barest essentials.

The Buddhist subjective idealism is based mainly on the common experience of dreams and sensory illusions which are definitely false and have no reality corresponding to them, from which it is concluded that cognitions have no real objective counterpart, that cognition is the only reality and that what appears to be the form of an external object really belongs to the cognition itself.

But how, the Mīmāṁsaka asks, does one know that dreams are false? Obviously because they are negated by waking experience which in itself is never negated and hence must be taken as revealing a real external world. The idealist then may say that ultimately waking experience too is negated by the experience of the mystics, anticipating which the Mīmāṁsaka proves the untenability of mystic experience. To the idealist argument that "all waking cognitions are devoid of real external objects, because they are cognitions, like the cognition in a dream" Kumārila has answered that since dream cognitions are contradicted and shown as false by waking congnitions, the idealist has to accept either of them as true. If it be the latter that he accepts as true, then he will have to give up his conclusion; and if it be the former, then he will have to give up his example, and thus his argument stands refuted.

The idealist tenet that cognition is the only reality which cognizes its own form is also rejected by Kumārila on the ground that in that case the variety of forms becomes inexplicable. The Buddhist tries to explain the variety by his theory of *Vāsanā* or sub-conscious impressions. But such impressions always presuppose past perception of external things and so this theory does not help. Moreover, as Pārthasārathi says, if cognition always cognizes its own form, then it should appear as 'I am blue' etc. instead of 'this is blue'. Therefore, the Mīmāṁsaka concludes that cognition truly reveals the form of an external object and that cognition is by itself formless and it never cognizes itself.

Then how is cognition known? Kumārila says that cognition is never known directly but is always inferred from cognizedness (*Jñātatā*) which it produces in its object like *cookedness* produced in rice by the act of cooking. Prabhākara however, thinks that cognition being self-luminous directly reveals itself, though the form belongs to the object. He is the author of what is known as *Tripuṭīpratyakṣavāda* according to which every cognition reveals itself as well as the self as the subject and an external thing as the object.

The existence of the external world having thus been established, it may be asked as to how the Mīmāṁsaka conceives the world. The Mīmāṁsaka is a pluralist. He believes in many ultimate substances, not one. All the Vaiśeṣika substances are accepted. In addition Kumārila accepts Śabda and Darkness also. This whole world is a product of these basic substances. But it was never created. There was no time when the world was not as it is now. There is no God. Production and destruction of things has been going on and will ever go on. It is the merits and demerits of the individual souls that are responsible for this process. Even the soul is conceived by Kumārila as changeable. Modal change is not incompatible with its permanence.

In addition to substances there are other categories also that enter into the constitution of things. Out of the remaining Vaiśeṣika categories Kumārila accepts those of quality, action, universal and negation only, leaving inherence and particularity. Particularity is rejected by Prabhākara also. Negation for Prabhākara is but the presence of the counter-correlate (*Pratiyogin*) alone and hence is not an independent category. But he adds three new categories, viz. *Śakti* ('power'), *Sādṛśya* ('similarity') and *Saṅkhyā* ('number') which are qualities in the Bhāṭṭa school. He accepts inherence but it is not one and eternal.

Epistemology

The best developed aspect of Mīmāṁsā philosophy is its epistemology and the key to the understanding and proper evaluation of Mīmāṁsā theories in this field is the dogma, which however the Mīmāṁsakas have put in their best efforts to establish on a rational basis, that the Veda is the supreme authority. To justify this dogma they had to make a detailed and critical enquiry into the nature and number of *Pramāṇas*, the nature and criteria of valid knowledge and other related problems.

In all *six Pramāṇas* are recognized, viz. *Pratyakṣa*, *Anumāna*, *Śabda*, *Upamāna*, *Arthāpatti* and *Anupalabdhi*, though Prabhākara and his followers refused to recognize the last one.

Pratyakṣa is the basic *Pramāṇa* and enters into the rest in some form. It is a cognition derived from sense-activity in the presence of an object. In the Prābhākara school it is defined as immediate apprehension, but as Cidānanda points out, this definition appears to lack consistency with the other features of Prabhākara's theory, viz. *Tripuṭīpratyakṣavāda*. It is emphasized that perception always apprehends an existing thing and hence those who claim to perceive past and future things are absolutely mistaken. The Mīmāṁsaka also asserts that the powers of our sense-organs are limited and so none can perceive things ordinarily lying beyond their range. Thus the possibility of the so-called supernormal perception is denied.

As in Nyāya so here also there are five types of external perception and one internal perception which is caused by Manas alone. The conception of Manas and its function in the Prābhākara school is broadly the same. But the Bhāṭṭas assume it to be of infinite size and assign to it one function only, viz. the direct apprehension of pleasure, pain etc.

The nature of sense-organs is inferred, as in Nyāya, according to the principle of like apprehending the like, though Sucarita Miśra follows here a different principle, viz. that of analogy, which is illustrated in the case of the eye thus: Since we see that light is the revealer of colour, therefore, the visual sense which also reveals colour must be of the nature of light. The auditory organ is but Dik enclosed within the ear, though according to Prabhākara and Sucarita Miśra it is of the nature of Ākāśa. The perception of sound is explained in terms of waves produced in the surrounding medium, which is a definite improvement upon the Vaiśeṣika explanation.

Pratyakṣa is of two kinds: *Nirvikalpaka* and *Savikalpaka*. These are rather two stages of perception. In the first stage it is like the perception of a child, a bare awareness (*Ālocana*), free from the subjective contributions of the perceiver. That is, the object in it is not determined as belonging to a class, possessing a name and so on. In the next, *Savikalpaka* stage the consciousness of the object becomes more definite and its generic and specific features are apprehended clearly because of the analytic and synthetic activities of the mind. It should be noted that such features are not imagined but discovered by the assimilative and discriminative operations of the mind. They are as much objective as the individual ('*Vyakti*') revealed in the first stage, which is the concrete unity of universals and particulars. In Nyāya also these two stages are recognized. But while there the first stage is a mere hypothetical one assumed to explain the second, here both the stages are equally real and both are capable of prompting practical activity.

But perception is not always valid. Sometimes it misleads us, as when what we see as a snake turns out to be a mere piece of rope. This is a case of illusion. The cause in such cases is some defect in the sense-organ or in the conditions under which perception occurs.

There are two Mīmāṁsā theories offered to explain such phenomena without giving up realism and yielding to idealism. Kumārila's theory is called *Viparītakhyāti* according to which in illusion one real thing existing elsewhere ('snake') is due to some defects identified with another real thing 'this' ('rope'). Another theory which is offered by Prabhākara is called *Akhyāti* or *Vivekākhyāti* according to which an illusion consists of two cognitions, one presentative and the other representative, and since the perceiver forgets the representative character of the latter, he can't apprehend their difference. On the first theory illusion is a misapprehension, while on the second it is a non-apprehension or incomplete apprehension, the former being an error of commission and the latter that of omission only.

The second *Pramāṇa* is *Anumāna* which is discussed separately under *Logic*. The third *Pramāṇa* is *Śabda*. It is knowledge derived from an authoritative statement which is either factual or imperative and again either secular or Vedic, the latter being of an impersonal origin. Kumārila recognizes both these types as *Pramāṇa* while Prabhākara thinks statements of authoritative persons to be reducible to *Anumāna*. The import of Vedic statements is ultimately action and the apparently factual statements, as of the Upaniṣads, are to be construed as *Arthavāda*, i.e. indirectly commending or condemning some action.

The fourth *Pramāṇa* is *Upamāna* which is different from the *Upamāna* of Nyāya. In Nyāya it is identifying a thing by its description in terms of similarity, dissimilarity etc. already known from some person. The Mīmāṁsakas rightly say that it is not different from verbal testimony. According to them it is a knowledge of 'A' being similar to 'B' on perceiving 'B' as similar to 'A'. It is a sort of immediate inference and is definitely not reductible to *Anumāna* or syllogistic inference.

The fifth *Pramāṇa* is *Arthāpatti* which is presuming some fact, e.g. A's existence outside, from the knowledge of two apparently conflicting facts, e.g. A's being alive and his absence in the house. According to Kumārila apparent inconsistency is the peculiar feature in it which makes it different from *Anumāna*. The Prabhākaras think that such feature is the element of doubt in it, which is obviously wrong.

The sixth *Pramāṇa* is *Anupalabdhi* or non-apprehension which yields the knowledge of the absence of something, e.g. that of a jar on the ground. It is not reducible to *Pratyakṣa* or *Anumāna*. To be more accurate, it is *Yogyānupalabdhi* or non-perception of the perceptible. There is undoubtedly sense-functioning involved in it, but it merely refers to the positive locus of absence. The difficulty in trying to reduce *Anupalabdhi* to *Anumāna* is that it leads to the fallacy of infinite regress. Non-recollection of what is fit to be recollected is also included in *Anupalabdhi*. Prabhākara says that non-perception of a jar on the ground is but perception of the ground alone, but he is unable to explain what 'alone' means.

Now we come to the important question of *Prāmāṇya* or validity. Kumārila's view is that it is a definite and true cognition which yields some new information (*Agṛhītagrāhi*), while according to Prabhākara all presentative knowledge (*Anubhūti*) is valid and memory is invalid, since it is born of mere past impressions. As regards truth, the Mīmāṁsakas like all the realists believe that it is what corresponds to reality.

But how is this correspondence known? In other words, what are the tests of truth? Since it is impossible to know reality otherwise than through cognition, the correspondence can't be ascertained directly and so we have to resort to some sort of inference. The other schools of realism, e.g. Nyāya, maintain that if the cause of a cognition is known to possess excellences (*Guṇavatkāraṇajñāna*), or it leads to successful activity (*Pravṛttisāmarthya*), or is in harmony with other cognitions (*Jñānāntarasaṁvāda*), it may be concluded that the cognition is true, otherwise false. This is the theory of *Parataḥ Prāmāṇya* and *Parataḥ Aprāmāṇya*.

The Mīmāṁsakas have critically examined this theory and found it to be totally unsatisfactory. The knowledge of excellences and successful activity cannot prove a cognition to be true, because, it being itself a cognition, stands in need of such a proof, which again has to be similarly verified, leading to an infinite regress. Thus if once the truth of a cognition is doubted, the doubt will never be removed and if we wish to save us from the predicament, knowledge at some stage will have to be assumed as intrinsically true. Then why not do this at the very beginning?

Harmony too can't prove the truth of a cognition. The knowledge with which harmony is sought may be heterogeneous (*Vijātīya*) or homogeneous (*Sajātīya*). For instance, if I see water and X, Y, Z also see the thing as water, and I myself see it as water later on, then these latter cognitions are homogeneous with the first. And if I see water and then use my senses of touch, taste, etc. also, then my tactual and gustatory cognitions will be heterogeneous. Now certainly the additional homogeneous cognitions possess no superiority over the first one and if you decide to doubt the truth of the first, their truth also becomes equally doubtful. Agreement with the heterogeneous cognitions also is of no avail, since their objects, e.g. a particular touch, a particular taste etc., are different from the object of the first, viz. a particular colour. In that case it is absurd to speak of any agreement at all.

The theory of extrinsic truth having thus been refuted the Mīmāṁsaka offers his own theory of intrinsic truth (*Svataḥ Prāmāṇya*) and extrinsic falsehood (*Parataḥ Aprāmāṇya*). According to this theory truth needs no verification. The causes which produce knowledge also produce truth in the knowledge. Truth is not superadded to knowledge by such extrinsic factors as the presence of excellences in the source. Falsehood, however, is extrinsically produced by the defects vitiating the cause of knowledge. Similarly the truth of a cognition is known by itself and it does not depend for its revelation on extraneous factors, while falsehood is known extraneously by the discovery of defects in the source (*Doṣajñāna*) or by the appearance later on of a contradicting cognition (*Bādhaka Pratyaya*) e.g. 'it is not snake but a mere piece of rope'.

Logic

The term *Anumāna* in Mīmāṁsā and also in all the other schools of Indian philosophy stands for inference of the syllogistic type. Immediate inference was not recognized here. Śabara defines *Anumāna* as the knowledge from the perception of one term of a well-known relationship of the other term which is not at the time in contact with the senses. The first term is called *Liṅga, Hetu* etc. and the second one is called *Liṅgin, Sādhya* etc. Their relationship is called *Vyāpti* or *Niyama*. Kumārila adds that the *Sādhya* must not be already known as true or false through some other *Pramāṇa*. Prabhākara says that it must not be such as is remembered by the person, but according to his follower Śālikanātha the only condition is that it must not be already known as false.

Unlike Nyāya in which *Anumāna* has five constituent propositions, viz. *Pratijñā, Hetu, Udāharaṇa, Upanaya* and *Nigamana*, Mīmāṁsā recognizes only three propositions to be enough and they may be stated either in the order of *Pratijñā, Hetu* and *Udāharaṇa* or of *Udāharaṇa, Upanaya* and *Nigamana*, the remaining two considered as redundant.

The problem of ascertaining *Vyāpti*, i.e. the universal major premise, has been dealt with in great detail. But let us first see what its nature is. According to Kumārila only a necessary proposition can justify the conclusion in *Anumāna* and so should be of the form 'this being present that must necessarily be present'. This is generally accepted except by Pārthasārthi who maintains, like J.S. Mill, that *Anumāna* proceeds from particular to particular. Accordingly for inferring, e.g. that 'the hill has fire', it is enough to know that in all the cases observed in the past fire has been seen to accompany smoke. But others think that *Vyāpti* should cover all the observed and unobserved cases.

Now how is *Vyāpti* known? There is much disagreement on this issue. Kumārila says that it is known by frequent observation of the co-presence (*Anvaya*) and co-absence (*Vyatireka*) of the middle and the major together with no observation of any contradictory instance. In addition he recognizes the method of concomitant variation also. Prabhākara thinks that *Vyāpti* is known in the very first observation of two things together and that later observations are useful only for eliminating extraneous conditions (*Upādhi*) if there be any. According to Umbeka it is known through *Arthāpatti*, i.e. it is presumed to avoid the inexplicability involved in two things always seen occurring together without being necessarily related. Sucarita Miśra says that perception is the *Pramāṇa* of *Vyāpti*, but, unlike Prabhākara, he maintains that it is the last perception of two things uniformly happening together and that it makes its appearance like a flash of lightning. Pārthasārathi's view is that the *Pramāṇa* of *Vyāpti* accepted by him can't be specified and that the *Vyāpti* accepted generally by others is proved by *Anumāna*. Nārāyaṇa, a later follower of Kumārila, defines *Vyāpti* as a natural relation which can be discovered by the method of agreement and difference. To insure its freedom from extraneous conditions he adopts the Nyāya method of *Tarka* ('reductio ad absurdum') in addition to eliminate the apprehension of hidden extraneous conditions.

The charge of *Anumāna* being vitiated by the fallacy of *petitio principii* (*Siddhasādhanatā*) is met by Pārthasārathi in a manner exactly like that of J.S. Mill. He says that the charge would apply if the conclusion, e.g. the 'hill has fire', followed from the *Vyāpti* 'all the cases (observed as well as unobserved) of smoke are cases of fire', whereas it actually follows from all the observed cases only. As a matter of fact, Pārthasārathi has adopted this unusual view of *Vyāpti* to save *Anumāna* from this charge. However, he has also met the charge on behalf of those holding the more usual view. He says that while ascertaining the *Vyāpti* 'all cases of smoke are cases of fire', the hill was not at all thought about, that the *Vyāpti* is epistemically independent of the hill having fire and so not open to the charge. Prabhākara on the other hand, accepts the charge and still thinks *Anumāna* to be a *Pramāṇa* as it is not a case of memory.

The usual division of *Anumāna* into *Svārtha* and *Parārtha* is not unanimously accepted in Mīmāṁsā. Śabara and Kumārila do not mention these kinds nor do Kumārila's commentators. Sucarita Miśra has strongly criticized this division. He says that the so-called *Parārthānumāna* is not *Anumāna* at all but verbal testimony and that those who accept this division will have to divide for similar reasons *Pratyakṣa* also into *Svārthapratyakṣa* and *Parārthapratyakṣa*, which they have not actually accepted. The later Bhāṭṭas, e.g. Nārāyaṇa, however have smuggled this division into Bhāṭṭa Mīmāṁsā from Nyāya. And the followers of Prabhākara also accept these two forms of *Anumāna*.

Śabara recognizes only two kinds of *Anumāna*, viz. *Pratyakṣatodṛṣṭasambandha* and *Sāmānyatodṛṣṭasambandha*. The former is exemplified in the inference of fire from smoke and the latter in that of the sun's movement from its changes of position. Kumārila openly finds fault with this nomenclature as well as with the examples. The two kinds of *Anumāna* recognized by him are *Sāmānyatodṛṣṭa* and *Viśeṣatodṛṣṭa*. The latter is exemplified in the inference by a father of his son's presence from hearing his voice and the former in that of the hill having fire on the basis of the general relation of smoke being accompanied by fire. The corresponding two kinds in Prabhākara are *Adṛṣṭasvalakṣaṇaviṣaya* and *Dṛṣṭasvalakṣaṇaviṣaya*, the examples being the same as given by Śabara. In the latter the specific individuality of the terms of *Vyāpti* is perceptible whereas in the former it is imperceptible. It may be noted that movement is supposed to be imperceptible by Prabhākara. The Nyāya division of *Anumāna* into *Kevalānvayi*, *Kevalavyatirekī* and *Anvayavyatireki* is not recognized in Mīmāṁsā.

The list of fallacies accepted in Mīmāṁsā is not much different from that of Nyāya.

Atheism

Paradoxically enough Mīmāṁsā is an orthodox system par excellence believing in no God or gods. Jaimini seems to have ignored God and Śabara denies God as the creator of the relationship between word and its meaning, though the question of the world having ever been created by God has been left untouched by him. But Kumārila and Prabhākara have positively denied God as the creator of the world. They have offered elaborate anti-theistic arguments and refuted the famous cosmological and moral arguments of the Nyāya-Vaiśeṣika and other theistic systems.

The world is made up of parts and is an effect and so presupposes a cause which in view of the vast magnitude of the effect must be intelligent, omniscient and omnipotent. In the logical form the argument is stated thus: The world has an intelligent creator as its cause, because it is an effect, like the pot.

Kumārila refutes the argument by showing the inadmissibility of the example, viz. the pot, which is caused by the potter. If the pot is really created by the potter, then it is not created by God and so it is not proved that everything in the world is created by God; and if the pot is really created by God, then the potter is not its creator and hence the example becomes ineffective. As a matter of fact, the world as a whole has never been created, though the things in it are being continuously produced and destroyed. And the empirical causes, says Prabhākara, are enough to explain their production. For example, children are produced by their parents and not by any transcendental agency. Again, what may be the motive of God in creating the world? The moral argument says that the world is created by God to provide the individual souls (Jīva) enjoyment and suffering in accordance with their *Adṛṣṭa* (merit and demerit) which being non-intelligent is not enough by itself and hence requires the guidance of God.

Prabhākara points out that the relation of God to the *Adṛṣṭa* can't be explained. It can't be conjunction (*Saṁyoga*) because the latter occurs only between two substances, whereas *Adṛṣṭa* is not a substance but a quality of the individual souls. It can't be inherence (*Samavāya*), since *Adṛṣṭa* inheres in the individual souls and not in God. So guidance of *Adṛṣṭa* by God is not possible. The Mīmāṁsakas think that *Adṛṣṭa*, which they call *Apūrva*, is enough by itself for the purpose. *Apūrva* inheres in the soul of the agent and brings about the things causing enjoyment and suffering in accordance with the inexorable law of Karma in due course.

But if there is no God how does the Mīmāṁsaka interpret the Vedic statements which appear to refer to such an entity? The Mīmāṁsakas' answer is that such statements are merely eulogical serving as the indirect means of providing additional incentive for the performance of sacrifices. The Vedic gods such as Agni, Indra etc., too are not real but mere words occurring in the Mantras, which are recited for the sake of their magical effects, as it were, and not for propitiating the deities. The Mīmāṁsā religion thus appears to be more like primitive magic in a rationalized form than a true religion. The Vedic statements apparently describing the powers of deities too are interpreted as mere *Arthavādas*. The statement, for example, that 'Vāyu is verily the swiftest deity' merely says indirectly that the performer of the sacrifice gets the results swiftly.

However, at a still later stage Mīmāṁsakas, e.g. Āpadeva, Khaṇḍadeva, Laṅgākṣibhāskara and Vedāntadeśika got dissatisfied with this position and slowly smuggled in God.

The Good: Secular and Spiritual Goals

Mīmāṁsā is primarily concerned with Dharma, the superstructure of the philosophical theories being a secondary growth aiming at a logical justification of its conception of Dharma. But the ordinary morality is not Dharma, though it certainly is an indispensable first requirement for the practice of Dharma. The ordinary moral values are included in *Artha* and *Kāma* which are distinguished from *Dharma*, the third *Puruṣārtha*. They aim at the good of the individual as a social being and are known empirically. Our common morality is *Ācāra* as distinguished from *Dharma*, and *Śiṣṭavyavahāra* and *Ātmatuṣṭi* (approval by one's own conscience) with certain conditions are our guide here.

Dharma is something transcendental and is concerned with the individual's good in the life beyond. Its aim is the achievement of Heaven and hence it can't be known through ordinary empirical means, not even by mystic intuition. The Veda alone can tell us what is Dharma and what is Adharma, i.e. what action leads to Heaven and what to Hell. Thus Dharma comprises religious values and in it are included compulsory religious duties, viz. *Nityakarmas* which are to be performed daily and *Naimittikakarmas* which are to be performed on special occasions. There are also *Kāmyakarmas* or optional duties which are to be performed by those desirous of particular results. *Pratiṣiddhakarmas* are those actions which are prohibited by the Veda, e.g. injury to animals, though killing an animal in a sacrifice is enjoined, which may create the impression that Mīmāṁsā prescribed a dual system of morality, one set of rules for ordinary conduct and a different set for religious purposes.

In the third stage of Mīmāṁsā thought *Apavarga* or *Mokṣa* also came to be adopted side by side with *Svarga* as the fourth *Puruṣārtha* and transcendental goal of human efforts. It is the highest good, the *summum bonum*, and is very much the same as conceived in the Nyāya-Vaiśeṣika. It is a pain-free state in which the soul has shaken off the worldly appendage and gone forever beyond the miseries of rebirth. Jaimini, Śabara and Prabhākara do not mention it, while Kumārila and the later Mīmāṁsakas have it as an essential part of their ethics, though the inferior goal of Heaven is also retained.

As Dharma in the form of optional duties and Adharma both lead to bondage, one seeking liberation should give them up. But in no case should one give up compulsory duties, because their non-performance leads to sin and renewal of bondage and their performance is a means of destroying the previously accumulated *karmas*. In addition to *karmas* of this type *Jñāna* also is recognized to be a contributory factor in the achievement of *Mokṣa*.

2

KUMĀRILA'S REFUTATION OF THE DREAMING ARGUMENT: THE *NIRĀLMBANAVĀDA-ADHIKARAṆA*

JOHN A. TABER

René Descartes noted that waking experiences are indistinguishable from dream experiences and concluded, if only provisionally, that we cannot know whether our waking experiences are caused by objects outside consciousness. The Buddhist idealist philosopher, making the same observation, concluded from it not merely that we cannot know whether there are objects outside consciousness but, positively, that there are no such objects! That, at least, is how Hindu philosophers represent the Yogācāra Buddhist position. In this paper I shall examine the arguments of one Hindu thinker, the Mīmāṁsā philosopher Kumārilabhaṭṭa, against the Buddhist denial of the existence of objects outside consciousness. Kumārila presents his arguments in the *Nirālambanavāda* chapter (henceforth, NVA) of his great work the *Ślokavārttika.* At first glance his discussion there seems to be wholly negative. He seems merely to want to refute Buddhist idealism without putting forward arguments in favour of his own position. I shall attempt to show, however, that the negative argumentation of the NVA is actually subsidiary to a significant positive claim, namely, that the reality of the external world is revealed directly by our perceptions and other cognitions. The latter claim, in turn, depends upon the Mīmāṁsā epistemological doctrine of *svataḥ prāmāṇya* or 'intrinsic validity.'

Before proceeding to discuss Kumārila's views, however, it will be necessary to address the question of whether the position being criticized was actually held by any Buddhist philosopher.

I

The argument with which we shall be concerned is formulated by Kumārila in the following abbreviated 'syllogism' or *anumāna*:

> *stambhādipratyayo mithyā pratyayatvāt . . . svapnādipratyayo yathā.*
>
> The cognition of a post, etc. [that is, of anything as an external object] is false, because it is a cognition . . . like a cognition occurring in a dream, etc.[1]

Let us refer to this as 'the Dreaming Argument'. In this *anumāna*, 'being a cognition' (*pratyayatva*) is the *hetu* or middle term, the term which connects the subject ('the cognition of a post, etc.') with the major term or the predicate to be proved ('false'). Being a cognition is presumably taken as a mark of falsehood because all illusory experiences, such as those occurring in dreams, are cognitions. Unfortunately, unless one begs the issue by assuming at the outset that all cognitions have the status of dream cognitions, one must concede that there are some cognitions that apprehend real objects. Hence it would hardly seem that the above argument is valid. Some cognitions are true, others are illusory. Just because something is a cognition does not mean that it lacks a real object. The middle term in this inference is a classic example of a *vyabhicārī hetuḥ*, a middle term that is 'deviant' or not invariably associated with the major term, the predicate to be proved (*sādhya*).[2]

The obvious fallaciousness of the argument would seem to cast doubt on the suggestion that anyone ever really believed it. Moreover, the question can be raised why Kumārila, who was apparently aware of the fallacy,[3] would go to such lengths to refute the Dreaming Argument in his NVA. We shall see, however, that Kumārila uses the Dreaming Argument as an opportunity to discuss criticisms that apply to any form of idealism, regardless of the arguments upon which it is based. A specific consideration of the most formidable and interesting Yogācāra arguments for idealism is in fact postponed by Kumārila until the next *adhikaraṇa* of the *Ślokavārttika*, the *Śūnyavādādhikaraṇa*.[4]

It is important to note that we find references to the Dreaming Argument not just in Mīmāṁsā sources but also in Nyāya literature. Uddyotakara, for example, mentions it in his discussion of *Nyāyabhāṣya* 4.2.33.[5] (Buddhist idealism is dealt with in *Nyāyasūtra* 4.2.26-36.) Now in the same passage Uddyotakara makes two clear allusions to Vasubandhu's *Viṁśatikā*.[6] It seems likely, then, that the Dreaming Argument was taken by Uddyotakara and other Hindu philosophers to represent the idealist position of the *Viṁśatikā*. They probably had in mind, specifically, *Viṁśatikā* 1:

> *vijñaptimātram evedam asadarthāvabhāsanāt /*
> *yadvat taimirikasyāsatkeśoṇḍrakādidarśanam //*

> This [world] is merely consciousness, because of the appearance of non-existent objects, as when someone suffering from an eye disease sees non-existent tufts of hair, etc.

Now in fact this argument is not exactly the Dreaming Argument as formulated above. Obviously, the specific example of an illusion mentioned in this text is not a dream but an optical illusion; but that is not crucial. Nor is it particularly important that the subject of inference is different in both cases: 'this world' in *Viṁśatikā* 1, as opposed to 'the cognition of a post, etc.' in the Dreaming Argument. Rather, what is important is that the reason (*hetu*) is different here: 'because of the appearance of nonexistent objects' versus 'because it is a cognition' in the argument of the Hindu texts. In fact, the expression *asadarthāvabhāsanāt* ('because of the appearance of nonexistent objects') in Vasubandhu's argument is not a true reason at all; for it does not state a property of the subject. A reason, *hetu*, as Vasubandhu himself recognized, should be a property of the subject which is invariably connected with the property one wishes to prove—in this case, 'merely consciousness' (*vijñaptimātram eva*).[7] The expression *asadarthāvabhāsanāt*, however, only refers to the fact that experiences of nonexistent objects—i.e. experiences that are 'merely consciousness'—sometimes do occur. In other words, Vasubandhu's statement merely affirms that illusory experiences sometimes happen; the specific example of an optical illusion is mentioned. (Presumably, dreams, which are discussed in subsequent verses, are alluded to by *ādi*, 'etcetera'.) It does not, however, state what property the experience of this world has in common with such illusions that would render it, too, an illusory experience. The true reason of the argument of *Viṁśatikā* 1 is not made explicit!

If that is so, then the reader of Vasubandhu's text is invited to make the *hetu* of the argument explicit as he sees fit. That appears to be what the Hindu philosophers have done in formulating the Dreaming Argument: experiences of things in the world are illusory *just because they are experiences*; for they have that nature in common with illusions such as dreams. It is interesting to note that NS 4.2.31-33 identifies precisely the problem I have pointed out. The Buddhist idealist *pūrvapakṣa* is stated in NS 4.2.31 and 32:

> *svapnaviṣayābhimānavad ayaṁ pramāṇaprameyābhimānaḥ māyāgandharvanagaramṛgatṛṣṇikāvad vā.*

> The notions of means of knowledge and object of knowledge [are false], like the notions of objects in a dream, or like magical illusions, celestial cities, and mirages.

To this *sūtra* 4.2.33 responds:

> *hetvabhāvād asiddhiḥ.*

> That is not established, because of the absence of a reason (*hetu*).

It seems that the author of the *Nyāyasūtra* recognized that, as the Buddhist argument from illusion was typically formulated, only examples without a *hetu* were given. Thus, I believe, the Nyāya philosophers, followed by Śabara and Kumārila, simply postulated in their discussions of the Buddhist idealist position what they thought the *hetu* of the Buddhist argument must have been; and so they formulated the Dreaming Argument as given above.

It is doubtful, then, that the Dreaming Argument was ever seriously put forward by any Buddhist philosopher of repute.[8,8a] Besides, as I have suggested, it is patently false. It seems, rather, that the Dreaming Argument represents the attempt of Hindu thinkers to reconstruct Vasubandhu's reasoning in the *Viṁśatikā*; and in doing so, of course, they were not particularly concerned to make it compellingly forceful. Although the Hindus were attacking a straw man, their charges did draw attention to the shortcomings in Vasubandhu's attempt to base idealism on the fact that we are sometimes presented in experience with objects that do not exist. Not only did he fail to express the *hetu* of his argument; it seems that in the end no valid *hetu* can be formulated for it. This perhaps led later Yogācāras, most prominently Dignāga and Dharmakīrti, to adopt a new approach to idealism, based on an analysis of the relation of subject and object in consciousness. The Dreaming Argument, meanwhile, continued to serve as a whipping boy for the Hindus in their attacks against the Buddhists.[9]

II

We shall now delve into Kumārila's criticisms of the Dreaming Argument in his *Nirālambanavādādhikaraṇa*. As I have already suggested, although his remarks there are specifically directed against the Dreaming Argument, they would seem also to pertain to any form of idealism or skepticism about the external world. The theme that runs through Kumārila's discussion is that, insofar as the idealist denies the existence of real objects, he renders language and discourse meaningless, and so vitiates his own claims. This theme is first announced with *śloka* 35:

> Since [on the idealist's view] neither subject nor predicate can be apprehended as [really] distinct, either one or the other is not established, or both are not established.[10]

Any argument attributes a certain predicate to a subject. For that to be possible, however, subject and predicate must be 'established' (*siddha*), that is to say, they must be known to be real. It is not valid, for example, to argue that a sky lotus is fragrant because it is a flower; for the subject of the statement, the sky lotus, does not exist.[11] An argument cannot be made about a nonexisting thing. Moreover, the subject and predicate of a significant statement must be known to be distinct; otherwise, one's statement will be tautological: it will merely say of the subject that it is itself. The idealist's position, however, is that one's cognitions do not apprehend anything objective about things, neither their real existence nor real differences between them. Therefore, it seems that one cannot make any significant statements—including the statement that all cognitions are without an object! Thus, *ślokas* 36-37 state:

> The speaker's or hearer's cognition of subject and predicate would itself [according to the Dreaming Argument] be without an object. Thus there would be a denial of [the reality of] both [subject and predicate] by your own statement (*svavāgbādha*). . . . Therefore, there is no felicitous way of stating your thesis.[12]

The statement that attributes predicate to subject in this case itself denies that there is any real subject or predicate. The Dreaming Argument is self-refuting: if it were true, it would not be about anything real.[13]

Kumārila proceeds to apply this analysis to the individual elements of the Dreaming Argument. The predicate attributed to the subject in the Dreaming Argument is *nirālambanatā*, 'being without a basis'. What is *nirālambanatā*? Is it, too, merely something illusory? Indeed, the Buddhist freely admits that *nirālambanatā* is not a 'thing' at all (*na kiñ cid vastu*).[14] In that case, Kumārila asks, how do you intend to convey knowledge about that which is nothing (*avastu*)?; how do you even understand anything by your own thought?[15] To the reply that *nirālambanatā* is not really nothing but merely something imagined (*kalpitā*) Kumārila replies that there cannot be any imagination of that which does not really exist somewhere, sometime. This response tacitly appeals to the theory Kumārila will develop later in the NVA that all ideas are ultimately derived from sense experience: in general, it seems that our dreams and other fantasies and illusions are constructed from elements which we have gleaned from our experience of the real world.[16]

Again, what is a *pratyaya* (cognition), which serves as the subject (*pakṣa*) of the Dreaming Argument? Kumārila tries to show that all ways of conceiving a cognition—whether as *karman* (object), *bhāva* (action), *kartṛ* (agent), or *karaṇa* (means)—are blocked by the conclusion of the argument. Of course, if it is considered to be a *karman*, an object, then the Dreaming Argument is once again self-refuting; for its very conclusion asserts that there are no objects. Yet, without anything to be cognized, a cognition cannot be conceived clearly as agent, action, or means, either.[17] If, moreover, it is conceived as a *karaṇa*, a means, then the words of the argument, which are means for conveying the notions of subject and predicate, hence *karaṇas*, would also be 'void of object' or meaningless.[18] And of course if a cognition were truly what the word *pratyaya* etymologically connotes, namely, an act (*bhāva*) of knowing directed toward another thing (*prati* $\sqrt{i}$), it would have to have an object.[19] In short, the very suggestion that there is no object implies that one does not have to do with a cognition, *pratyaya*, at all.

Kumārila sums up these initial criticisms of the idealist position in *ślokas* 69-71.

> No statement results from a word without a connection [with its meaning]; and there is no connection without a difference [between the word and its meaning]. But there is no difference unless there is a cognition that apprehends a difference which [the word] really has. If those who conduct an inquiry do not understand the various elements of an argument—*pakṣa*, *hetu*, *dṛṣṭānta*, the one who holds the theory, and the one who opposes it—then there is no demonstration. However, if one admits the reality of these things, then one's claim is refuted by one's presuppositions.

You can only attempt a proof if you assume the reality of the elements of proof, based on the reality of the differences of things; but insofar as the Buddhist assumes the reality of the elements of proof in propounding the Dreaming Argument, he refutes his own proof. However, the pernicious consequences of denying external reality extend well beyond the Dreaming Argument itself. If there are no real differences, then the very essence of Buddhism is threatened! Buddhism, like other philosophies, presupposes differences between *dharma* and *adharma*, between master and disciple, between bondage and liberation, etc.[20] Similarly, the Buddhist wishes to assert that cognitions exist, that they are distinct from each other and momentary. If one can indeed have true cognitions of these facts, it would seem that the Buddhist's argument that there are no true cognitions, no cognitions that apprehend the real characters of things, is called into question.

It would be too tedious to discuss in detail all the ways in which Kumārila in the NVA attacks the coherence and self-consistency of the Dreaming Argument. The basic point of his critique, applied in various ways, is that the argument itself either appears to undermine the meanings of the terms in which it is stated, or, if the meanings of the terms are allowed to stand, to refute itself.[21] Once again, from a slightly different angle, Kumārila says:

> Asserting such a conclusion [viz., that all cognitions are without objects], you [the Buddhist] are prevented from instructing [anyone about your doctrine] (*pratipādanāt vihataḥ*); for you do not know a [real] proof commensurate with the conclusion you wish to establish. Likewise, the person to be instructed does not know your conclusion [to be true]; for he realizes that the proof, insofar as it seeks to establish a conclusion of this kind, is invalid. If, on the other hand, the proof is considered to be real, then your statement is not comprehended; for given the reality of the proof, the conclusion is impossible.[22]

The idealist ultimately denies that there are any valid means of proof.[23] A valid means of proof must reveal something true about the world. According to the *nirālambanavāda*, however, there is no world, no objective reality, about which true or false statements can be made. Thus, Kumārila points out, the Buddhist has no proof of his position. The essence of his position is that no statement is objectively true of anything.[24]

It should be noted that in developing this critique of the Dreaming Argument Kumārila is obviously building on the discussion of NS 4.2.26-30. There, following a presentation of the atomic theory of matter, the Buddhist *pūrvapakṣin* asserts that we can never truly know the nature of things; for 'analysis by reason' itself reveals to us that we cannot know reality.[25] To this the Nyāyaśāstra replies: If we can come to this conclusion by rational analysis, then it is not true that we can never apprehend the nature of things! If, on the other hand, we really cannot know the nature of things, then we cannot know this![26] Thus the Mīmāṁsā discussion of Buddhist idealism appears to be derivative of the Nyāya discussion, both in how it frames the problem and how it answers it. This dependence on Nyāya thought is evidenced elsewhere in Mīmāṁsā philosophy, as I have shown in another study.[27]

Let us now consider whether all this which Kumārila has brought forward against the Dreaming Argument really constitutes a valid criticism of it. As I noted at the beginning of this essay, the NVA at first glance appears polemical in that it does not seem to attempt seriously to *establish* that there is an external world but simply attacks the idealist position. This is troublesome, because Indian logicians generally do not accept purely negative argumentation. The method of *tarka*, the *reductio ad absurdum* of an opponent's thesis, is generally held to be admissible only in support of a positive proof of one's own thesis; and *vitaṇḍā*, the use of sophistical reasoning merely to attack a position without putting forward one of one's own, is almost unanimously rejected.[28] We shall see shortly that Kumārila indeed does present a positive argument for the reality of the external world in the NVA. For now, however, we want to consider separately the validity of his negative argument and determine whether it indeed succeeds in refuting idealism.

Kumārila claims to have shown that the thesis of idealism either entails its own unintelligibility or amounts to a self-contradiction. Were the former the case, idealism would remain unestablished; for a meaningless statement can be neither true nor false. Were the latter the case, it would be simply false. In short, idealism is incoherent. The refutation of a thesis by showing it to be incoherent has many distinguished examples in the history of philosophy. Descartes attempts to show in his *Meditations* that one cannot doubt the existence of the 'I'; for any denial of it necessarily presupposes it. Aristotle argues in his *Metaphysics* that one cannot coherently deny the principle of non-contradiction: its denial would render all language, including any denial of the principle of non-contradiction, meaningless.[29] Yet one might question whether the truth of a proposition depends on the possibility of stating it intelligibly. I may not be able to utter or even think the denial of a certain proposition, because its truth is a presupposition of discourse or thought. But suppose I do not say or think anything about it? Doesn't it remain a question whether the proposition is true or not? This is a rather radical way of defending an incoherent theory. A more moderate approach would be to suggest that the 'incoherent' proposition, while ultimately incoherent, may nevertheless serve as a means of gaining the position from which one is able to judge its incoherence—like the proverbial ladder one kicks away after having ascended. One may, in short, resort to a theory of two truths.

There is in fact in contemporary analytic philosophy a refutation of skepticism that closely parallels Kumārila's arguments against idealism. I am referring to Hilary Putnam's demonstration of the incoherence of skepticism in his book *Reason, Truth, and History*.[30] Let us consider his argument briefly here in order to gain a broader perspective on this issue and, ultimately, evaluate Kumārila's critique of idealism.

Putnam considers the thesis that one cannot know anything via the senses; for it is possible that one is not actually a human being living in the physical world, but merely a brain which is floating in a vat of nutrient liquid. The brain is being stimulated electronically by a 'mad scientist' to have experiences as if of an external, physical world. Since this possibility cannot be excluded, one cannot know with certainty that one's perceptions represent real things. Thus empirical knowledge is impossible; for to know, one must know that one knows. Putnam argues, however, that the brain-in-a-vat hypothesis—or for that matter, it would seem, any similar skeptical hypothesis, such as Descartes' hypothesis that our experiences might be caused by an 'Evil Genius'—is either nonsense or self-refuting. For the meaning of the hypothesis depends on the meanings of the terms 'brain', 'vat', 'scientist', etc. If the hypothesis were true, those terms would be without reference and the hypothesis would be nonsense. If, on the other hand, the terms had real reference, then the hypothesis would be false. Obviously, this is quite parallel to the approach Kumārila takes in refuting idealism in the NVA.

Is there any way of formulating the idealist's or skeptic's thesis that avoids this sort of *reductio ad absurdum*? Putnam himself suggests the following ploy. The skeptic could argue that, although his hypothesis suggests that words may be ultimately meaningless insofar as there are no real objects to which they refer, they can still be meaningful *for us within our experience.* For we can take the term 'brain', for example, to refer not to a physical object but to a certain pattern of perceptions; we can similarly construe 'vat', 'scientist', etc. These patterns of perceptions may not derive from things outside the mind, but they can still serve as the meanings of the words we use. In short, let 'scientist' refer to a scientist-in-our-experience; 'brain' to a brain-in-our-experience, etc. Thus the skeptic's hypothesis (the idealist's thesis) can be meaningfully stated without presupposing the existence of external objects. As Putnam puts it,

> 'vat' refers to vats in the image [created by the mad scientist] in vat-English . . . but certainly not to real vats. . . . Similarly, 'nutrient fluid' refers to liquid in the image in vat-English. . . . It follows that if . . . we are really brains in a vat, then what we now mean by "we are brains in a vat" is that we are brains in a vat in the image or something of that kind (if we mean anything at all).[31]

Now Kumārila actually considers the same ploy as it was developed in Indian philosophy. The Buddhist idealist can attempt to defend the coherence of his thesis by resorting to the *saṁvṛtivāda*, the theory of provisional truth. According to this theory, the categories of things mentioned in the process of bringing a disciple to enlightenment—namely, the Four Noble

Truths, the Eightfold Noble Path, enlightenment and non-enlightenment, the Buddha, the *dharma* the *saṅgha*, etc.—are all ultimately unreal. Once the student realizes the ultimate Truth that all is empty or mere consciousness, he sees that these things and their distinctions are illusory. Nevertheless, until he attains the Truth, they are real *for him*.[32] As the Buddhist opponent of the NVA puts it: "Isn't it possible that even though there is no external object, nevertheless [the distinction of *hetu*, *pakṣa*, and *sādhya* upon which proof depends] is valid insofar as it is superimposed upon the mind, the result of different notions arising from various words and memory impressions (*vāsanāśabda-bhedotthavikalpavibhāgataḥ*)?"[33]

Kumārila's response to this strategem is, ostensibly, to draw attention to the implausibility of the Yogācāra doctrine of illusion, the thesis that somehow within an originally pure, homogeneous reality, an illusory system of differences—the world—is fabricated by means of words and ideas.[34] Putnam, on the other hand, makes a logical point: the skeptic (idealist) may *say* that his words should be taken to refer only to things within consciousness. But in fact he *means* that we really might be brains in a vat! That is to say, he ultimately wants the words he uses to be able to refer to things in the physical world. Thus he is unable to escape incoherence. He wants to entertain a possibility about how the world might be in fact; but insofar as he entertains that possibility, he is also considering the possibility that his words do not refer to anything outside his own consciousness.[35]

Certainly, however, this is also the thrust of Kumārila's negative argumentation in the NVA. The Buddhist wants to claim not merely that everything *seems* to be consciousness, but that everything *really is* consciousness. He wants to make a claim about the actual nature of reality. His thesis does not appear to be intended to have merely provisional truth at all. Yet his thesis entails that no objectively true statement can be made about the world—even one that says it exists only in consciousness! Idealism must ultimately be based somehow on observations of experience, in particular, observations concerning the relations of ideas to their causes. It must hold that these observations, which serve as its evidential basis, are true. But how can they be true, if none of our ideas correspond to how things are?

Thus, indeed, it would seem that Kumārila's demonstration of the incoherence of the idealist position is successful.[36] The incoherence of the statement that the world is just consciousness cannot be dismissed as insignificant; for that statement is the very gist of idealism and is intended to be fully *true*, not just provisionally so. The idealist cannot avoid incoherence by resorting to a theory of two truths.

It would seem that this sort of refutation can be used against any form of idealism regardless of the arguments upon which it is based; for the conclusion of those arguments, insofar as they are arguments for *idealism*, will always be that reality consists only of ideas occurring in consciousness. Once again, in order for that claim be of interest it must be intended as a claim about the nature of the world. In that case, however, it will be self-refuting. If all ideas are in effect hallucinations, then the idea that all ideas are hallucinations will also be a hallucination.

Thus I believe that the negative arguments of the NVA are meant by Kumārila to apply to idealism in general and not just idealism as it is based on the Dreaming Argument. Kumārila was obviously aware that the Dreaming Argument had fallen out of fashion and that the Yogācāras had gone on to develop more sophisticated ways of proving their position. Moreover, he seems to have been aware that the Dreaming Argument as the Hindus formulated it was patently invalid by virtue of a 'deviant' middle term.[37] However, he saw Śabara's discussion of the Dreaming Argument as an opportunity to call attention to the basic *aporia* of all forms of idealism before going on to refute in his *Śūnyavādādhikaraṇa* the more viable, epistemological form of it that had been developed by the Yogācāra logicians.

Yet the NVA does not result in a purely negative conclusion. It must be seen, ultimately, not as a refutation of idealism, but as a demonstration and defense of realism. In order to see this we must now, finally, step back and view the larger frame in which the critique of idealism of the NVA is placed.

III

The *Ślokavārttika*, of which the NVA is a chapter, is of cource a commentary on Śabarasvāmin's *Mīmāṁsāsūtrabhāṣya*. In attempting to understand the NVA we must consider the passage of the *Śabarabhāṣya* upon which it is based.

In discussing *Mīmāṁsāsūtra* 1.1.4, which presents a definition of perception, Śabara offers two distinct interpretations of the *sūtra* based on different readings. One interpretation, which Śabara develops only briefly, is based on the text: *satsamprayoge puruṣasyendriyāṇāṁ buddhijanma tat pratyakṣam*. The other interpretation, which Śabara presents at length by quoting from his predecessor, the Vṛttikāra, is based on the text: *tatsamprayoge puruṣasyendriyāṇāṁ buddhijanma sat pratyakṣam*.

What does the *sūtra* mean according to this latter reading, the reading Śabara obviously prefers? It means: "True perception is the arising of a cognition when there is contact of the sense organs of a man with that"—i.e. with that which is the intended object of the cognition. In other words, perception is valid when it results from contact of the sense organs with the actual object it represents. The significance of this statement, according to the Vṛttikāra, is that we are assured that a perceptual cognition is true as long as it is the result of the interaction of the normal factors of perception: sense organ, mind, object, etc. As long as these factors are normal—as long as the sense organ is not defective, the mind alert, the object neither too small nor far away—then the perception will represent the object as it really is. In short, our faculties are so constituted as normally to give rise to valid cognitions. Thus there is always a presumption in favour of the truth of our perceptions (as well as other types of cognitions). So long as they are not contradicted by other cognitions and one discovers no defects in their causes (sense organ, mind, object, etc.), they are to be considered true. Perceptions, as it is often put, are to be held 'innocent until proven guilty'; indeed, if they are never proven guilty we may be assured that they *really are* innocent—true. This is the well-known Mīmāṁsā doctrine of *svataḥ prāmāṇya* or the 'intrinsic validity' of cognitions, applied to perceptions.[38]

Now it is at this point that the Buddhist is allowed to raise an objection: No perceptions are in fact true! We know that all cognitions, including perceptions, are without object—*nirālambana*. For they are indistinguishable from dream experiences, and the latter are illusory. This is of course the

Dreaming Argument. The beginning of Kumārila's NVA corresponds to the stating of this objection.[39]

From the above we are finally able to understand the dialectical significance of Kumārila's NVA. We now see that it is, essentially, the refutation of an objection against the Mīmāṁsā theory of perception. More specifically, it is the refutation of an objection against the realist metaphysics that theory implies. To say that perception is true when it results from the contact of a sense organ with its object is to imply that there are real objects external to consciousness with which the senses come into contact. This is the *prima facie* position at issue throughout the NVA; it is the background against which the whole discussion proceeds.[40] The Dreaming Argument attacks it; Kumārila's critique of the Dreaming Argument in turn defends it. As the *prima facie* view, the view of common sense, it stands undefeated once it is shown that the principal objection against is either meaningless or self-refuting.

Thus the NVA has ultimately a positive result: it is a defense of realism, not just a refutation of idealism. It is not just taken up with *tarka*, the *reductio ad absurdum* of the opponent's position—which, as I have said, would be inadmissible in Indian logic; rather, it defends the Vṛttikāra's positive claim of realism, that certain cognitions do correspond to the way things are in fact: they are true. Yet the Mīmāṁsaka must do more than merely appeal to common sense in upholding this position. He must give us proof. And so Kumārila in fact does present us with a positive argument for realism in the NVA. Although not extensively developed, this argument must be seen, logically, as the main argument of the NVA, to which the critique of Buddhist idealism is ultimately subordinate; for *tarka* must be seen as an auxiliary of *pramāṇa*.

The argument in question is first mentioned in the opening *ślokas* of the NVA, where Kumārila considers Śabara's answer to the Buddhist claim that 'all cognitions are without object'. Śabara suggests that there can be no doubt that a waking cognition has an object because it is 'quite distinct' or definite (*supariniścitā*), and a vivid, definite cognition certainly cannot turn out to be false. Kumārila points out that this reply, as far as it goes, is quite insufficient: some dream cognitions are just as vivid as our most vivid waking cognitions.[41] However, he goes on to say that Śabara's appeal to 'distinctness' can be construed as a valid criticism in another way, namely, one may take it as suggesting that the Buddhist argument is contradicted by perception.[42] Indeed, not just perceptions, but all true cognitions establish the presence of an external object.[43] For it will be shown in the *Śūnyavādādhikaraṇa* that a cognition *cannot possibly* apprehend itself—a thing cannot be both agent and object in the same act; therefore it must apprehend something other than itself, its object must be external to it. Thus every cognition one has implicitly contradicts the Dreaming Argument—provided of course that it is not a mistaken cognition, a dream or hallucination which itself is specifically contradicted by other cognitions. This constitutes a decisive refutation of the Dreaming Argument. For all our other cognitions have more force than it, because they do not call themselves into question as the Dreaming Argument does: "By [mentioning] the 'exceeding distinctness' (*suniścayena*) of these [cognitions] it is asserted that they are stronger than this [Dreaming Argument], since without any specific sublating cognition (*bādhakapratyayād ṛte*) they cannot be false."[44]

Somewhat later in the NVA Kumārila returns to this point. Now he suggests that the occurrence of perceptions, etc., establishes the existence of an external object, not implicitly, insofar as it can be shown that they cannot apprehend themselves, but rather directly insofar as they immediately convey an impression of the reality of their object. Kumārila asserts that no matter how the Dreaming Argument is formulated, the following counterargument can always be brought to bear against it:

> The notion that a cognition has an external object is valid; for it is an idea devoid of any contradiction, like the idea [that one has upon waking] that contradicts a dream.[45]

That is to say, every cognition contains as part of its content the idea that its object is external. As the modern phenomenologist puts it: most objects that appear to us in experience have an aspect of 'transcendence'; they appear as independent and external to the perceiver—as *real*. Now sometimes this notion of the transcendence of the object gets nullified, namely, in those cases where we later discover that the object was quite illusory—a dream, a mirage, or a magical illusion. That, in fact, is the only situation in which we are really justified in saying that a cognition is 'without object.'[46] Most of the time, however, our cognition is not sublated and the sense of the reality of the object is retained. For example, the idea one has upon waking which sublates one's dream—'I was just dreaming!'—is rarely itself overturned by another perception. And, Kumārila notes, waking experience as a whole is never refuted by an emergent higher state of consciousness, as dreaming is.[47] Hence, according to the principle of *svataḥ prāmāṇya* that cognitions are true unless revealed to be otherwise, the idea of the transcendence of the object is true. Therefore, perception, as well as the other *pramāṇas* which purport to tell us objective facts, directly establishes the existence of external objects![48]

Let us reflect on the precise meaning of this argument. The Mīmāṁsaka notes that idealism is directly contradicted by our perceptions and other cognitions: every perception, etc., tells us its object is real. To leave matters at that, however, would be to beg the issue; for the claim of the idealist is that perception cannot be trusted. The question before us, then, is how do we know that the impression of the reality of the object conveyed by perception is *true*? Kumārila answers: We know it is true by virtue of the principle of intrinsic validity, *svataḥ prāmāṇya*. According to that principle, a cognition is false only if it is overturned by another cognition. Most waking cognitions are not overturned by other cognitions, and waking consciousness is never sublated as a whole. Therefore, our waking cognitions are not false; they are true, they represent reality as it is in fact. So the impression of the actual existence of their objects which they typically involve will also be true. Therefore, objects exist. Kumārila's argument for realism in the NVA is more than simply an appeal to perception. It is, rather, an argument for the *veracity* of sense perception (and other valid modes of cognition), based on the principle of *svataḥ prāmāṇya*, and so for the veracity of the idea of the reality of external objects which perception, etc., includes.

What are we to make of this argument? As I have noted, other philosophers agree that perception posits its object *as real.* In his 'Sixth Meditation' Descartes notes that we have been given 'a very great inclination to believe that. . . ideas come from corporeal objects';[49] for we receive many ideas passively and are unaware of any faculty within ourselves that produces them. Sartre similarly analyzes transcendence as an aspect of intentionality: 'Consciousness is consciousness *of* something. This means that transcendence is the constitutive structure of consciousness; that is, consciousness is born supported by a being that is not itself. . . .'[50] But there is no consensus about the answer to the question of how, or whether, we know that this impression of the independent reality of the object is *true.* Descartes appeals to the infallibility of all clear and distinct ideas: God would be a deceiver if he had created us so as to have clear and distinct ideas which are false; and the notion that our perceptions derive from things outside our minds is a clear and distinct idea. But this reasoning, based ultimately on Descartes' proof of the existence of God, is quite precarious.

Will the Mīmāṁsā doctrine of *svataḥ prāmāṇya* serve us any better in this matter?; can it be used to insure the truth of our belief in the reality of objects, which we seem to derive immediately from our ordinary waking cognitions? We cannot answer this question adequately without entering into an evaluation of the theory of intrinsic validity, which space does not allow. Suffice it to say that its appeal lies in its proximity to common sense. *Svataḥ prāmāṇya* says, in effect, that if a cognition appears in every way true, then it is. Falsehood cannot conceal itself forever; a cognition that is really false will eventually be revealed as such. Ultimately, we must accept some of our cognitions as true without demanding positive, external corroboration; otherwise we will fall into a regress. If we cannot accept as true those of our ordinary, waking cognitions which are never called into question, then what ever can we accept as true? The theory of *svataḥ prāmāṇya* is not an indefensible epistemology. Nor, despite the way in which it is sometimes presented in the Mimāṁsā sources, does it necessarily presuppose realism.[51] (Obviously, if it did, it could not be used to ground realism.)

In summary, the negative arguments against Buddhist idealism in the NVA are to be seen as ultimately subsidiary to a positive argument for realism, even though they comprise the bulk of the text. The latter positive argument seeks to establish the validity of perception and other cognitions by appeal to the principle of *svataḥ prāmāṇya*; for perception, Kumārila alleges (in agreement with other philosophers), conveys immediately a sense of the real existence of its object. Given this proof of realism, the Dreaming Argument completely collapses; for, as we have seen, it attacks the truth of all propositions, including its own conclusion. Kumārila's argument for realism from perception, on the other hand, is not self-refuting; therefore, it clearly has more force.[52] Thus the realism of common sense remains true.

Abbreviations

MSBh	*Mīmāṁsāsūtrabhāṣya* of Śabarasvāmin, in *Materialien zur ältesten Erkenntnislehre der Karmamīmāṁsā* (Vienna: Österreichische Akademie der Wissenschaften, 1968)
NR	*Nyāyaratnākara* of Pārthasārathimiśra, in *Ślokavārttika*
NS	*Nyāyasūtra* in *Nyāyadarśanam*, ed. Taranatha Nyaya-Tarkatirtha (Delhi: Munshiram Manoharlal, 1985)
NSBh	*Nyāsūtrabhāṣya* of Vātsyāyana, in *Nyāyadarśanam*
NVA	*Nirālambanavādādhikaraṇa*, in *Ślokavārttika* of Kumārila with the Commentary *Nyāyaratnākara* of Pārthasārathi Miśra, ed. Svāmī Dvārikadāsa Śāstrī (Varanasi: Tara Publications, 1978)
NVTT	*Nyāyavārttikatātparyaṭīkā* of Vācaspatimiśra, in *Nyāyadarśanam*
ŚVA	*Śūnyavādādhikaraṇa*, in *Ślokavārttika*

NOTES

1. NVA 23.

2. But cf. Śabara's formulation: *nanu sarva eva nirālambanaḥ svapnavat pratyayaḥ? pratyayasya hi nirālambanatā svabhāva upalakṣitaḥ svapne. jāgrato 'pi stambha iti vā kuḍyam iti vā pratyaya eva bhavati. tasmāt so 'pi nirālambanaḥ* (MSBh, p. 26). Śabara appears to be construing the structure of the argument to be roughly as follows: X has the same nature as Y; therefore X has all the same properties as Y. Just as one piece of gold will melt at a certain temperature, so another piece of gold will melt at that same temperature. This, too, however, is a fallacy. It does not follow from two things having the same nature that they have all the same properties, but only that they have all the same *essential* properties. It would seem that it is not obviously an essential property of a mental state that it lacks a real object.

3. See NVA 102ab: *sādhyābhedād avācyatvād hetor nobhayasiddhatā*; 'the *hetu* is not established for both [you and me], because it is identical with what is to be proved and hence unmentionable [as a middle term].' (I have followed Jhā here. In the sequel the translations are my own.) That is to say, the reason 'because it is a cognition' can only mean 'because it is an *illusory* cognition'. In that case, we have a petitio principii. See also note 44 below.

4. As Kumārila explains at the beginning of the NVA, the Mīmāṁsaka considers Buddhist idealism to be based on two main arguments in the following way. There are two Buddhist opponents who call the inquiry into *dharma* which constitutes Mīmāṁsā (Mīmāṁsā=*dharmajijñāsā*) fundamentally into question: those who would deny the reality of an object external to consciousness, and those who would deny both the reality of an external object and consciousness itself. The former are the Yogācāra philosophers, who may be properly considered idealists; the latter are the Mādhyamikas (see, e.g. Nāgārjuna's *Vigrahavyāvartinī* 30–51), who were not really idealists, since they (or at least the Prāsaṅgika Mādhyamikas) held no philosophical views of any sort. Since the denial of an external object is common to both positions—the Mādhyamika effectively denies the reality of consciousness *because* its object is unreal, according to Kumārila—it is incumbent upon the Mīmāṁsā philosopher to show that there is an external object; in this way he will refute both types of Buddhism (see NVA 14-16).

Now there are two approaches one can take in denying the external object, that is to say, two ways of approaching idealism. One can argue that the object (*prameya*) itself is impossible, insofar as it would have to be an aggregate of atoms; for the Buddhists denied the reality of aggregates. This approach is taken, e.g., by Vasubandhu in his *Viṁśatikā*, *karikās* 11–15, and Dignāga in his *Ālambanaparīkṣā*. On the other hand, one can argue that, even if an external object is possible, cognition never in fact apprehends one, or is incapable of apprehending one. To take this approach is to deny the existence of the external object 'on the basis of [consideration of] the means of knowledge' (*pramāṇam āśritaḥ*) (see NVA 17-18b). This approach in turn is divided into two strategies. One is to attempt to show directly by an *anumāna* that cognition is *in fact* devoid of an object; this is where the Dreaming Argument comes in. The other strategy is to attempt to show that cognition, in particular, perception, is *incapable* of interacting with anything outside of consciousness (*jñānapravṛttyaśakti*; see NVA 18c-19b and ŚVA 1). Such an argument was developed in Buddhism principally by Dignāga and Dharmakīrti.

Kumārila takes up the Dreaming Argument and the epistemological idealism of the Buddhist logicians separately in his NVA and ŚVA. He considers the former to be presented in Śabara's text beginning with the words *nanu sarva eva nirālambanaḥ*, etc., while the latter is presented with the words beginning *śūnyas tu*, etc. (see MSBh, p. 28, lines 14ff.). The approach to idealism based on the denial of the possibility of the object (*prameya*) itself, meanwhile, is dismissed with two *ślokas* at the end of the ŚVA (262-63). Finally, the Madhyamaka position is declared untenable—because it depends on the denial of an external object—with ŚVA 264.

The *Śūnyavādādhikaraṇa*, therefore, despite its title, does not really concern Madhyamaka philosophy. The title is simply derived from Śabara's text. That is to say, the ŚVA is the *adhikaraṇa* that considers the argument for idealism beginning with the words *śūnyas tu*. Pārthasārathi notes, ad ŚVA 1, that confusion arises from the fact that the only plausible modificandum of the adjective *śūnyaḥ* in Śabara's *bhāṣya* is the term *pratyayaḥ*, which suggests that the Madhyamaka philosophy, which denies the reality of cognition as well as the object of cognition, is the topic. From the rest of Śabara's discussion, however, (see MSBh, pp. 28–30), it is obvious that he has in mind new Yogācāra arguments for the non-existence of an external object.

The Mīmāṁsā philosophers seem to have been influenced by Nyāya in their analysis of the relation of different Buddhist philosophies to each other. In the discussion of idealism in the *Nyāyasūtra* and its commentaries both the reality of *pramāṇa* and *prameya* are questioned by the Buddhist on the basis of the occurrence of illusory experiences (NS 4.2.31: *svapnaviṣayābhimānavad pramāṇaprameyābhimānaḥ*). After having established the reality of the external object, the *prameya*, the Naiyāyika argues that the reality of the cognition (*buddhi*) or *pramāṇa* immediately follows (NS 4.2.36: *buddheś caivaṁ nimittasadbhāvopalambhāt*). Vācaspati explicitly identifies the holder of the view that neither object *nor* cognition exists as the Mādhyamika.

5. *ayaṃ jāgradavasthopalabdhānāṁ viṣayāṇāṁ cittavyatirekiṇām asattve hetuḥ khyātiḥ svapnavad iti*, NV, p. 1077. Cf. NVTT: *pratyayatvam eva svapnodāharaṇasahitaṃ pramāṇaprameyābhimānamithyātve hetur ity arthaḥ*, loc. cit.

6. NV ad NS 4.2.33, p. 1085, lines 9ff., alludes to *Viṃśatikā* 3; p. 1086, lines 11ff. alludes to *Viṁśatikā* 7.

7. Vasubandhu explains the *hetu* in the following way in his *Vādavidhi*, as reconstructed by Frauwallner: "Der Grund ist die Mitteilung einer Eigenschaft welche mit einem solchen (zu Beweisenden) untrennbar verbunden ist'; E. Frauwallner, 'Vasubandhu's Vādavidhi,' *Wiener Zeitschrift für die Kunde Süd-und Ostasiens* 1 (1957), p. 118.

8. Neither the *Mahāyānasaṅgraha* of Asaṅga nor the *Vijñaptimātratāsiddhi*

of Hsuan-tsang elaborates the Dreaming Argument as interpreted by the Hindu philosophers. Both texts appeal mainly to Mahāyāna scripture (e.g., *Sandhinirmocanasūtra* 8.7) in support of *vijñaptimātratā*. In addition, it is noted that the object of meditation in *samādhi*, which is experienced as vividly as an object of waking experience, is certainly merely a form of consciousness (*Mahāyānasaṅgraha*, tr. E. Lamotte (Louvain: Institut orientaliste, 1973), vol. 2, pp. 95-96). Asaṅga also points to such facts as different beings having distinct ideas of the same object; our having ideas of things that are not present e.g., things of the past or future; yognis being able to manifest objects merely by thinking about them; and those in the state of *nirvikalpakajñāna* being aware of no objects at all (ibid., pp. 104-105). In general, the Yogācāra doctrine that 'all is consciousness' appears to have its roots in mystical experience.

8a. Since the writing of this it has been brought to my attention that Candrakīrti, *Prasannapadā* 1.3 (ed. P.L. Vaidya, *Buddhist Sanskrit Texts*, no. 10 (Darbhanga: Mithila Institute, 1960), p. 20, lines 8–10, considers the objection to the Madhyamaka rejection of causation, that we *experience* phenomena as originating. To this, Candrakīrti replies that "this experience is false, because it is experience, like the experience of a double moon of a person with an eye disease, etc." (*anubhava eṣa mṛṣā anubhavatvāt taimirikadvicandrādyanubhavavad iti*). Since the very status of mundane experience is in question, it cannot be appealed to in challenging the Madhyamaka argument. While this passage reminds us of the idealist argument cited by the Hindu writers, it does not amount to a serious attempt to expound or vindicate it. I am grateful to Thomas Wood for this reference.

9. Cf. Śaṅkara, *Brahmasūtrabhāṣya*, ed. Anantakrishna Śāstri (Varanasi: Krishnadas Academy, 1982), 2.2.28, p. 544. See D.H.H. Ingalls, 'Śaṅkara's Arguments Against the Buddhists', *Philosophy East and West* 3 (1954): 291–306.

10. *agrāhyatvāc ca bhedena viśeṣaṇaviśeṣyayoḥ/*
aprasiddhobhayatvaṁ vā vācyam antarasya vā//

11. *Tarkasaṅgraha*, ed. Y.V. Athalye (Poona: Bhandarkar Oriental Research Institute, 1974), sec. 56, pp. 46-47 and 305-307.

12. *vak tṛśrotroś ca yaj jñānaṁ viśeṣaṇaviśeṣyayoḥ / tannirālambanatvena svavāgbādho dvayor api //...tasmān nirūpaṇaṁ nāsti prajijñārthasya śobhanam//*

13. Cf. NVA 57: *bahirbhāvāprasiddhatvāt tenānālambanā matiḥ / kathaṁ ca sādhyate naiṣa pakṣo hi jñāyate tadā //*

14. NVA 38.

15. NVA 39. Cf. 59: *nāprasiddhe padārthe hi vākyārthaḥ sampratīyate/ tatpūrvakatvāt pakṣaś ca vākyārthaḥ sthāpayiṣyate //*

16. See NVA 107–113b. This point is construed, technically, as a fault of the example (*dṛṣṭānta*) of the Dreaming Argument. The theory had already been developed in Nyāya; cf. NS 4.2.34. See note 22. For further arguments against the major term *nirālambanatā*, see NVA 65-66.

17. NVA 44ab.

18. NVA 43.

19. NVA 44cd.

20. NVA 72-73.

21. Cf. NVA 157. If something is a proof, then it really must exist; for nothing that is real can be proved by what is unreal.

22. NVA 150–52. Cf. 119c-120b, where the criticism is formulated specifically as a fault (*doṣa*) of the *hetu* The *dṛṣṭānta* or example is criticized on different grounds, 107c-109b: it is devoid of the *sādhya* (*sādhyavaikalya*, NR ad NVA 107). That is to say, a dream is *not* an example of a state of consciousness independent of an object; for what we see in dreams are objects we have previously experienced. Similarly for other illusions (109c-114b). Vasubandhu, interestingly, appears to be responding to an objection of this sort at *Viṃśatikā* 17ab. Kumārila also discusses whether the Dreaming Argument is invalid because a negative example is not provided (121c-128b). He does not resolve this issue, noting that in cases where there is nothing that has the opposite property of the major term (*vaidharmyāsambhave*) a negative example may not be required.

23. *sarvathā sadupāyānāṁ vādamārgaḥ pravartate* / *adhikāro 'nupāyatvān na vāde śūnyavādinaḥ* // (NVA 128c-129b). Although Kumārila refers to the *śūnyavādin* in this verse, it is clear that he has in mind the Yogācāra and not the Mādhyamika; for he attributes to this philosopher the positive thesis of 'consciousness only'(144), whereas the Mādhyamika holds no such thesis.

24. NVA 129c–149 discusses the interesting question of whether the idealist may put forward a proof which he himself does not believe. Kumārila argues that both the proponent of a position and the person he is trying to persuade must accept the validity of the means of proof employed. In this connection, according to Pārthasārathimiśra, he alludes to a statement of Dignāga's: *yo vādiprativādiniścito hetuḥ sa sādhanam* (NR ad NVA 131ab).

25. *buddhyā vivecanāt tu bhāvānāṁ yāthātmyānupalabdhiḥ*..., NS 4.2.26.

26. *yadi buddhyā vivecanaṁ bhāvānāṁ na sarvabhāvānāṁ yāthātmyānupalabdhiḥ. atha sarvabhāvānāṁ yāthātmyānupalabdhir na buddhyā vivecanam;* NSBh ad 4.2.27. Cf. NSBh ad 4.2.30.

27. 'The Mīmāṁsā Theory of Self-Recognition', *Philosophy East and West* 40 (1990): 35-36. See also above, notes 4 and 16.

28. See NS 1.1.40 and 1.2.3.

29. *Metaphysics*, Gamma, 4. For a word to have meaning, it must refer to something definite. But, Aristotle alleges, if one denies the principle of non-contradiction, then one denies that things have definite natures: everything is both what it is and what it is not! Alan Code has argued that Aristotle's argument only succeeds in showing that the principle of non-contradiction is the *most certain* of all first principles, not that it is true; for any indirect proof of a thesis by *reductio ad absurdum* of its negation tacitly appeals to the principle of non-contradiction ('Aristotle's Investigation of a Basic Logical Principle: Which Science Investigates the Principle of Non-Contradiction?', *Canadian Journal of Philosophy* 16 (1986): 341–58).

30. (Cambridge: Cambridge University Press, 1981), chapter 1.

31. Putnam, pp. 14-15.

32. NVA 164. Cf. *Madhyamakakārikā* 24.

33. NVA 167: *nanv asaty api bāhye 'rthe buddhyārūḍhena siddhyati| vāsanā-śabdabhedotthavikalpavibhāgataḥ ||*. According to Pārthasārathi, the Buddhist is appealing to a statement of Dignāga's—*sarva evānumānānumeyavyavahāro buddhyāruḍhena dharmadharminyāyena na bahiḥsattām apekṣate*—which Kumārila approximately quotes in 168.

34. See NVA 169a–170d. 'How', Kumārila asks, 'could any distinction of that which does not exist arise from the imagination of words and ideas? A word or idea can hardly originate in regard to something void of reality.' And how could a variegated illusion based on words and ideas arise if the distinctions of words are also unreal? Cf. NVA 9cd: *kalpanāpi tv abhinnasya naiva nirvastuke bhavet*. Kumārila may have in mind here the first verse of the *Madhyāntavibhāgaśāstra: abhūtaparikalpo 'sti dvayaṁ tatra na vidyate*. His discussion of this issue extends into a lengthy critique of the Yogācāra theory of *vāsanā*, NVA 178–200. At the beginning of the NVA he attacks the *saṁvṛtivāda* in general terms (NVA 6-10): 'There is no truth to *saṃvṛti*, for how could it be a kind of truth? If *saṁvṛti* were true, what would it be [i.e. how would it be different from just the truth]? If it is false, then how could it be truth? That which is not, really is not, and that which really exists, exists. The false is something else. There is no notion of two kinds of truth (*satya-dvayakalpanā*).'

35. Putnam, p. 15. Putnam goes on to criticize the skeptic's proposal on the grounds that it is based on a 'magical theory of reference', pp. 17-21. See also chapter 2.

36. Or else one must resort to the more radical defense which holds the truth or falsity of idealism or skepticism to be independent of its intelligibility. This is the approach Matilal takes in his discussion of Putnam's refutation of skepticism in his recent book, *Perception* (Oxford: Clarendon Press, 1986, pp. 235–38). I think this approach is doomed, because, given the unintelligibility of idealism, even the suggestion that it might be true independent of its being able to be stated coherently must be considered unintelligible. In other words, given that idealism is incoherent, we have no idea what it means to suggest that it might still be true! It is, on the other hand, not as clear whether Kumārila's (or Putnam's) argument is effective against the Mādhyamika, who refuses to adopt any position. As Nāgārjuna says: 'I have no claim' (*Vigrahavyāvartinī* 29). The Yogācāra is indeed vulnerable precisely because he wants to hold a certain statement to be true.

37. See note 3 above.

38. See MSBh, p. 26.

39. See NVA 19c-22.

40. Kumārila, however, does conceive the issue somewhat more broadly at the beginning of the NVA. The denial of an external object amounts to the undermining of all the distinctions of the science of *dharma*, he says. If one believed that the fruits of right actions were merely happy dream experiences, one would never undertake right actions (NVA 11-13).

41. Cf., however, Matilal, *Perception*, p. 234. He suggests that the faults of *vikalpasamatā* and *vaidharmyasamatā* mentioned at NVA 28-29 are attri-

buted to the Buddhist argument. As I read those *ślokas*, they are, rather attributed by Kumārila to Śabara's response to the Buddhist argument. See Pārthasārathi's commentary.

42. NVA 30cd: *pratijñādoṣaṁ evāhuḥ kecit pratyakṣabādhanam.*

43. Cf. NS 4.2.29.

44. NVA 33: *suniścayena caiteṣāṁ bādhakapratyayād ṛte/pramāṇābhāsatā nāstīty etasmāt kathyate balam//.* Kumārila also says here that some consider Śabara's discussion as showing that the Dreaming Argument is a kind of *jāti: duṣṭatvāt pūrvapakṣasya jātyuktiḥ kaiścid āśritā* (NVA 30ab). Of course, to say that it is a *vikalpasamā jātiḥ* is to imply that it is simply a fallacy based on a deviant (*vyabhicārin*) middle term. Indeed, Śabara points out that, besides waking cognitions being generally more distinct or vivid than dream cognitions, they are also generally not overturned by other cognitions, while dream cognitions are. Thus it is not the case that all cognitions are the same: some are true, others false. The Buddhist cannot prove that a cognition lacks an object just on the grounds that it is a cognition.

45. NVA 79c-80b: *bāhyārthālambanā buddhir iti saṁyak ca dhīr iyam/ bādhakāpetabuddhitvād yathā svapnādibādhadhīḥ//.* This is, technically, the fault of the middle term called *satpratipakṣatva:* the *hetu* is one 'for which there is an existing [i.e. unrefuted] counterthesis.' A middle term is not conclusive so long as there is another argument which proves the negation of what it is supposed to prove.

46. See NVA 54-55. One calls the cognition of a double moon 'objectless,' not because there is no object at the basis of the experience at all (*nārthasaṁvittyabhāvataḥ*), but because one has ascertained that the sense organ has not actually come into contact with an object of that nature (*indriyāprāptitaḥ*). Cf. NSBh 4.2.35: *tattvajñānena ca mithyopalabdhir nivartyate, nārthaḥ.* But this implies that some cognitions will have to be true. To say that all cognitions are without object or false is to undermine the very meaning of 'false'. See NVA 88c–89b: *pratiyogini dṛṣṭe ca jāgrajjñāne mṛṣā bhavet/ svapnabuddhir asmākaṁ tava bhedo 'pi kiṅkṛtaḥ?//.* Cf. 80c8-1b: the Dreaming Argument requires that dreams be acknowledged as false. How can they be that unless there are some true experiences that contradict them? Cf., again, NSBh 4.2.34: *tatra jāgradbuddhivṛttivaśāt svapnaviṣayābhimāno mithyeti vyavasāyaḥ*; 'It is due to the status of ideas of waking that the notion of the object in the dream is considered false.'

47. NVA 89c-90b. One cannot say, e.g., that the supernatural experiences of yogins refute the waking state. For, asserts Kumārila, we do not know that anyone in this life or the next has such experiences! (NVA 93c-94b).

48. Cf. *Brahmasūtrabhāṣya* 2.2.28, p. 548: 'Why should we pay attention to the words of a man who, while conscious of an outward thing through its approximation to his senses, affirms that he is conscious of no outward thing, and that no such thing exists, any more than we listen to a man who while he is eating and experiencing the feeling of satisfaction avers that he does not eat and does not feel satisfied?' (Thibaut's translation).

49. *Meditations on First Philosophy*, trans. L. Lafleur (Indianapolis: Bobbs-Merrill, 1951), p. 75.

50. *Being and Nothingness*, trans. Hazel Barnes (New York: Washington Square, 1966), p. 23.

51. See my article, 'Svataḥ Prāmāṇya', forthcoming in *Journal of the American Oriental Society*.

52. Cf. NVA 65-66.

3

KUMĀRILA BHAṬṬA'S DENIAL OF CREATION AND DISSOLUTION OF THE WORLD

PERI SARVESWARA SHARMA

Traditionally, Kumārila Bhaṭṭa was an older contemporary of Śaṅkarācārya, the founder of the Advaita Vedānta philosophy (the philosophy of nondualism). And Maṇḍanamiśra was his disciple (for details see Mādhava's *Śaṅkaradigvijaya*). It is certain that he lived after Diṅnāga, the greatest Buddhist logician, and Bhartṛhari, the greatest grammarian.[1] He was probably a contemporary of Dharmakīrti, a Buddhist logician, whose work *Pramāṇavārttika* is very famous (for details, see my work entitled *Anthology of Kumārila Bhaṭṭa's Works* published by Motilal Banarsidass, Delhi-110 007, 1980).

Kumārila Bhaṭṭa has devoted nearly sixty verses in the Section called *Saṁbandhākṣepaparīkṣā* (an examination of objections with regard to eternality of the relation between word and its meaning) to remove the misconception common among the people spread over through the ages on the basis of the *arthavāda* passages in the Vedas (*mantra*, *brāhmaṇa* and *upaniṣads*), the *smṛtis*, the *Mahābhārata* and the *Purāṇas* and reject different theories particularly those of the Vaiśeṣikas, Naiyāyikas and Sāṁkhyas about the c r e a t i o n and d i s s o l u t i o n of the w o r l d.

We know that for the Vaiśeṣika the Veda is authoritative, but it is neither eternal nor authorless. It is the word of God and this makes it authoritative. And God is omniscient, eternal and perfect. He is the lord. He is guided by the Law of *Karma* representing the unseen power of Merits and Demerits. Unseen Merit is unintelligent and needs God as the Supervisor and Controller.

He is the efficient cause of the world and the atoms are its material cause. Atoms and Souls are co-present and co-eternal with God. He cannot create them. He simply causes motion in atoms by which they go on combining and thus the entire world is created.

Although Kaṇāda, the author of the *Vaiśeṣika Sūtras*, does not refer to God directly, the aphorism in the beginning and in the end of his work, namely, 'The authority of the Veda is due to its being His Word' (*tadvacanād āmnāyasya prāmāṇyam*: Vaiśeṣika Sūtra, I.1.3 and X.2.9) has been interpreted by the commentators in the sense that the Veda is the Word of God.

Praśastapāda, the author of the *Bhāṣya* on the *Vaiśeṣika Sūtras*, has many times used the word *Īśvara* (God) as the cause of the world and as the author of the Veda.[2] He has described also elaborately the procedure of creation and dissolution of the world (See paragraphs 57, 58 and 59, pp. 60-64, of the *Praśastapādabhāṣyam* with the Commentary called *Kiraṇāvalī* of Udayanācārya, edited by Jitendra S. Jetly and published by Oriental Institute, Baroda, 1971).

According to the Naiyāyikas also the material cause of this universe is eternal atoms of Earth, Water, Fire and Air and the efficient cause is God. Gautama, the author of the *Nyāya-sūtras*, has openly referred to God.[3] The individual souls are co-eternal with atoms. And God is coeternal with souls and atoms and external to both. Creation means the combination of atoms and destruction means dissolution of these combinations through the motion supplied to or withdrawn from the atoms by the Unseen Power working under the guidance of God. Vātsyāyana, the author of the *Bhāṣya* on the *Nyāyasūtras*, commenting on the *Nyāyasūtras* IV.1.19, 20 and 21 gives the reason why one should accept God and His Omniscience and Omnipotence. According to him, God is just like a father. He helps human beings by bringing about the fruits of their actions. He is a Super Soul with all good qualities, like *dharma*, knowledge, and *samādhi* (=eight kinds of powers, viz. *aṇimā*, *mahimā*, *garimā*, *laghimā*, *prāpti*, *prākāmya*, *īśitva*, *vaśitva*). God can be as small as an atom; as big as the Himālaya mountain; as heavy as iron; as light as cotton; He can attain anything; He can desire anything; He is the lord over all; and entire universe is under His control.[4]

According to the Sāṁkhya system of philosophy, all material effects are the modification (*pariṇāma*) of the Primordial Matter (*Prakṛti*). They pre-exist in the eternal bosom of *Prakṛti* and simply come out of it at the time of c r e a t i o n and return to it again at the time of d i s s o l u t i o n. There is neither new production nor utter destruction. Production means development or manifestation (*āvirbhāva*) and destruction means envelopment or dissolution (*tirobhāva*). Their theory is called *satkāryavāda*, the theory that a product exists in a latent state in its cause even before its production.

Prakṛti is the uncaused root-cause. It is the first principle of this Universe (*Pradhāna*); the unmanifested state of all effects (*avyakta*); the extremely subtle and imperceptible (*atisūkṣma*); a thing which is only inferred from its products (*anumeya*); and it is an unintelligent and unconscious principle (*jaḍa*). It is eternal and co-present with the Soul (*Puruṣa*).

Puruṣa is the principle of pure consciousness. He is also called Soul, Self, Spirit, Subject, Knower and Enjoyer. He is neither body nor senses nor brain nor mind (*manas*) nor ego (*ahaṅkāra*) nor intellect (*buddhi*). It is not a substance which possesses the quality of consciousness. Consciousness is its essence. It is itself pure and transcendental Consciousness

Evolution is regarded as cyclic and not linear. There is no continuous progress in one direction but alternating periods of e v o l u t i o n (*sarga*) and d i s s o l u t i o n (*pralaya*). Evolution is again said to be teleological and not mechanical or blind. Evolution takes place for serving the purpose of *Puruṣa*. *Prakṛti* and its three ingredients (i.e. *guṇas*: *sattva*, *rajas* and *tamas*), senses, motor organs, mind, ego, intellect, subtle body—all are constantly serving the end of *Puruṣa*. Both his bondage and liberation are accomplished by Intellect (*buddhi*), which is a product of *Prakṛti*. The Sāṁkhyas say, that Bondage comes through ignorance and Liberation through knowledge.[5]

The Mīmāṁsakas believe in the reality of the external world and of the individual souls. There are innumerable individual souls, as many as there are living bodies. They believe also in bodiless liberated souls and the other eternal and infinite substances. They also believe in the Law of Karma, in Unseen Power (*apūrva*), in heaven and hell, in liberation and in the ultimate authority of the Eternal and Authorless Veda. Mīmāṁsakas do not admit periodic Creation and Dissolution of the World. The world was never created and never shall it be destroyed. God is ruled out as an unnecessary hypothesis. Though individuals come and go, though the finite material products arise and perish, yet the world as such, the universe as a whole goes on for ever, uncreated and imperishable. According to the Mīmāṁsakas, there was never a time when the universe was different from what is now (*na kadācid anīdṛśam jagat*).

Supremacy and power, according to the Mīmāṁsakas, can be obtained by *dharma* only; and the source of *dharma* is the eternal Veda. Without performing the Vedic rites nobody can attain *dharma* and without excess of *dharma* even the Creator cannot differ from ordinary people. Even the existence of a Creator is, therefore, to be rejected in the same manner as an Omniscient Person.[6]

Jaimini has devoted the entire Ist *Pāda* of the Ist *Adhyāya* to defining *dharma* and proving eternality of the Veda, its ultimate authoritativeness and its authorlessness. One may refer particularly to the first five *Sūtras* and the *Bhāṣya* on them for details.

I am giving below a summary of views of Kumārila Bhaṭṭa about creation and dissolution of the world expressed by him in the Section called *Saṁbandhākṣepaparīkṣā* (an examination of objections with regard to eternality of relation between word and its meaning) of the *Ślokavārttika*:

Prajāpati (God)[7] is supposed to have created this world, but as there were no five Elements, viz. Earth, Water, Fire, Wind and Ether or Space before their creation, what could have been the condition of the universe? As for Prajāpati Himself what could be His position? Where could He stand? And of what materials could His body be composed? And at that time, when no men existed, who would know Him and explain His character to the later created persons? If it be held that He cannot be perceived by any man, then without perception or cognition of some sort by some person, how can we determine this fact of His existence? Then again, if it be held that the world was brought about by Prajāpati by a desire, since Prajāpati is held to be without a material body, how could He have any desire towards creation? Because, desire is a function of the mind and the mind cannot exist without a material body. If it is accepted that Prajāpati has a body, then it must be held to be eternal. And when His body is eternal, how could we deny the eternality of other bodies—our own, for instance? The only ground of the belief in the transient character of our own bodies consists in the fact of its being corporeal or material. And when one material body is transient, there is no reason why Prajāpati's body should be held to be eternal. For if His body is eternal, ours also must be eternal. And again, Prajāpati cannot create His own body. Thus we should have to postulate another Creator for His body and so on, which would lead to *ad infinitum*. And again, in the first place, how is it that Prajāpati should have desire to create a world which is to be stored with all sorts of troubles to living beings. People hold that all the trouble in the world is due to the vicious deeds of living beings in the previous birth. This may be quite true. But at the very beginning of creation, there being no previous birth, no such guiding principle would be available; and the blame of creating a troublous world would rest with the creating Prajāpati. And how can any creator create anything in the absence of means and instruments? Even production of a spider's net is not held to be without some sort of a material basis; as the net is spun out of the saliva, which is produced out of the body of flies etc. eaten by the spider. If it be held that Prajāpati creates the world out of compassion, we say in the absence of objects of compassion in the shape of living beings, no pity or compassion could be possible for Him. If He were urged to Creations by pure compassion, then He would create only happy beings. But in reality, it is not so. Many living beings are unhappy in this world. If it be urged that without some pain, neither the Creation nor the continuation of the World would be possible, we should say when our Creator is all-powerful and everything depends upon His mere Will, what could be impossible for Him? If He were really moved to c r e a t i o n by sheer compassion, why did He not create a World of eternal happiness? And if He were to depend upon Laws and Agencies, then this fact would deprive Him of His boasted independence and a l m i g h t i n e s s. And again, it has been said that He desired to create the w o r l d. Had He not created the w o r l d, would He have lost anything? Or in the other words, what He had gained by creating this unhappy w o r l d? For without some e n d in view, even a fool does not act. Then if He did create this World without any motive, what would be the good of His intelligence?[8] If it be held that Creator created the World for His amusement, that would go against His ever-contentedness. Of course, one has recourse to an amusement with a view to please himself. Hence, if the Creator wants amusement, He cannot be said to be eternally happy and contented. Moreover, instead of affording any amusement, the amount of work required for c r e a t i o n would be a source of infinite trouble for Him. Even if He were known in form, the fact of His being the Creator could never be known. Because, at that time, i.e. in the infancy of c r e a t i o n, what could the living beings, appearing at the beginning of c r e a t i o n, understand? Because they have appeared after Prajāpati has finished His operations, they could not understand wherefrom they have been born; nor could they know the state of the w o r l d prior to c r e a t i o n, nor the fact of Prajāpati being the Creator. Nor could the idea that they would derive from His assertion with regard to His being the Creator, be altogether trustworthy; because even though He may have not created the w o r l d, He might speak of having done so, in order to show off His great power. In the same manner, the Veda that would proceed from Him would only be doubtful, and hence could not be admitted as a sure proof of His e x i s t e n c e and His c r e a t i v e p o w e r. And as for that, i.e. the Veda which is e t e r n a l, how could it make a mention of facts and processes with reference to the c r e a t i o n of l i v i n g b e i n g s? For, if the Veda existed before the objects created, then there can be no connection between the Veda and the objects created. Therefore the passages occurring in the Veda which appear to describe the process of creation, must be interpreted as praising up something else, i.e. some injunctions of sacrifices, etc. The idea common among ordinary people that the Veda mentions of the creation as proceeding from Prajāpati is a mistaken one, caused by certain valedictory passages praising up certain injunctions (*arthavāda*).[9] Because whenever a passage is not duly considered and interpreted together with the passages that proceed and follow it, it is bound to give rise to a misconception. The use of the *Mahābhārata*, the *Purāṇas*, the *Smṛtis*, etc. too to the matter of *dharma* etc. is in the form of telling stories exemplifying and praising up certain duties and sacrifices, just like that of the Vedic passages which seem tom ention certain processes, while they only praise up certain sacrifices.[10] Therefore, the notion of the creation proceeding from Prajāpati got from the passages occurring in the *Mahābhārata*, the *Purāṇas* and the *Smṛtis* would also be a mistaken one. Because mere story-telling cannot have any use, therefore, in all these stories making up the *Purāṇas*, we must admit something that could be the object of praise or dispraise embodied in the stories; and this something may be that which is enjoined either in the Veda.

If there were any such thing as the first activity of the Veda towards Injunction (*codanā*), etc., this would mean that the Veda has had a beginning and then we could never have an idea of the fact of its not being composed by anybody but being eternal itself. The theory too, that during universal Dissolution the Veda resides in the person of Prajāpati, could at best, only be considered doubtful. As a matter of fact, Prajāpati's desire to destroy the world too would be hardly explicable. And above all such a Creator could never be known by anybody.[11] This is the summary of nearly 21 verses (i.e. 45 to 66) which were devoted by Kumārila Bhaṭṭa to remove the misconception spread over through the ages among the ordinary people about the creation and dissolution of the world on the basis of the *arthavāda* passages in the Veda and the story-tellings in the *Purāṇas* and the *Mahābhārata*. The relevant verses have been given in the Footnote.

From the verse 67 begins the rejection of the theory of the Vaiśeṣikas and Naiyāyikas about creation and dissolution of the world.

Pārthasārathi Miśra, commenting on the verse 67, summarises the views of Praśastapāda, the author of the *Bhāṣya* on the *Vaiśeṣika Sūtras*, about creation and dissolution of the world as follows:

'Vaiśeṣikas say: The process of creation and dissolution are eternal. After a hundred years of Brahmā have elapsed during the existence of the world, there arises in the mind of God (Maheśvara) a desire to destroy the world; and in obedience to this desire, there comes about a universal disconnection of atoms, and in the end all that left behind is only a number of disjointed atoms of Earth, Water, Fire, Air, Ether (Space) and Soul. During this time all *dharma* and *adharma* of individual men are kept in abeyance by Divine Will. These *dharmas* and *adharmas* lie latent in the soul of each individual. When the period of dissolution passes, the same God seeing the souls of men lying idle, without obtaining the results of their deeds, takes pity on them. And this pity gives rise to a desire on His part for creation, and directly all homogeneous atoms combined; and these combinations bring into existence all the various objects of the world. And then *dharma* and *adharma* of the men are let loose and this going forth into activity comes to effect the destiny of each individual soul, throwing some of them down into animal life while raising others to lives in nobler families. And then the same God creates the veda with a view to explain *dharma* and *adharma* to the world. Thus it is that the *Veda* comes to differ with each cycle of creation. But inasmuch as this process itself is eternal, the Veda, the creation and dissolution should all be considered eternal, and so also the Creator.' (Compare this statement of Pārthasārathi Miśra with the *Bhāṣya* of Praśastapāda, i.e. paragraphs 57, 58 and 59 of *Padārthadharmasaṁgraha.*)

Rejecting this theory of the Vaiśeṣikas, Kumārila Bhaṭṭa states: 'If, however, you assume the eternality of the Creator, and the process of creation and dissolution, then too, we could only admit of a gradual process of creation, such as we see in the case of present living beings creating the jar, etc. But according to you (=the Vaiśeṣikas), both creation and dissolution are simultaneous which we can never come across in ordinary life, where every process is distinctly gradual. Hence we cannot admit of any such simultaneous creation. And as a *pralaya* in the form of universal destruction, we find no proofs for admitting it. And no intelligent Creator could have recourse to such a suicidal process, unless it served some very important purpose of His; and since we cannot think of any such purpose, we cannot believe in a universal dissolution. And you hold that during *pralaya* the souls of men continue to exist with all their *dharma* and *adharma* laying latent, without bringing any results. This theory is not acceptable, because the souls which have the load of *dharma* and *adharma* upon them cannot continue to exist with out enjoying the fruits of their actions and the *dharma* and the *adharma* cannot lie latent without bringing about any results. Nor can the results of one action be restrained by any other action in the shape of the Creator's desire as held by you. And it is not possible for all actions to continue to remain devoid of their results. Nor is there any single action, the result of which could be the non-fruition of all other actions and which single action would thereby keep the other actions in check. If it is held—to avoid all these inconveniences—that at the time of *pralaya* all actions are destroyed; then it would be contradictory to your own theory; because according to you (i.e. the *Vaiśeṣikas*), when God desires to create again, then *dharma* and *adharma* of men come out; and it is in accordance with these that He regulates the next creation. But when all actions are destroyed at *pralaya*, they would cease to exist and there would be no means of bringing them into activity. If the desire of God be held to be such a means, then it would be a needless complication to assume that it is God's wish that manifests the destroyed actions which regulate the creation. God being omnipresent and omnipotent according to you, if His wish had anything to do with creation, there would be no need for any other agency, such as *dharma* and *adharma* of the souls. And again, God's desire too cannot be eternal; as that would lead to eternal creation and eternal dissolution. If, on the other hand, the desire be non-eternal, there must be some cause that gives rise to it in the mind of Creator. And then for the activity of this cause also, we would require another cause, and so on, *ad infinitum*. Even granting the possibility of a cause for the God's desire, if there be such a cause, that alone could suffice for the creation of the world, and there would be no need of postulating an intermediate agency, in the shape of God's desire. If it is argued that the production of the bodies of living beings is controlled by an intelligent agency in the form God's desire, because they are made up of certain constituent parts,—like a house, etc.,—then, it should be answered thus: If by 'control' it is meant only the fact of some intelligent agency being the cause of creation,—then, inasmuch as all creation could be accomplished by the actions of all living beings, which are intelligent agents, your argument would become redundant proving a fact already proved; for no one denies the fact that the diversity of the world is regulated by the actions of living beings. And you have the same redundancy even if by 'control' you mean that the creation of bodies is preceded by the desire of an intelligent agent; because the actions of living beings too are preceded by it. Thus, because it only proves that the World is affected by intelligent agencies; and as the actions of even individual living beings are such intelligent agencies, your argument does not necessarily establish the superintendence of a supramundane intelligent cause, in the shape of an omniscient God. The premises of your argument are deficient and doubtful with regard to the body of God Himself. For His body too must have had a beginning, inasmuch as it is also a body, like ours made up of constituent parts. And thus the body of God also would have to be controlled by an intelligent agent, in accordance with your argument. But you deny such control over divine body, and thereby you weaken your own argument.

If it be argued that the production of God's body too is controlled by His own intelligence, then He could do so only in a bodiless state; inasmuch as so long this controlling force has not been exerted, His body could not have been produced. And just as a soul, that has been emancipated from the world and has become bodiless, cannot exert any controlling force over anything, so too a bodiless God could not exert any control. And if in case of the jar, &c. (that you recite as an instance) you refer to the superintendence of the potter, &c., then the control of God would not apply to these and as such the instance could not prove the fact of the creation of the body being controlled by God. If, on the other hand, you mean that the making of the jar is controlled by God, then you would have the deficiency of the major term in the argument; that is to say, the fact of the jar, &c., being controlled by God is not recognised by us, and hence these could not serve as instances to prove the same with regard to the body, &c. Because the jar is found to be made by the potter, who is not a God, and who is perishable. Hence in accordance with this instance, the argument would stand thus: The body is not controlled by God, —because it is controlled by intelligence—as for instance, the jar, &c.; and thus the premise that you have brought forward to prove the creation to have been brought about by God comes to prove something quite to the contrary.

If it be held that God does not Himself carry on any operations, as the potter does towards making the jar, as all that He does is to express a desire, that is instantly obeyed by the eternal atoms of matter, which proceed to combine homogeneously and thus form the endless substances. To this we say that how could an insentient entity in shape of the atoms follow His desire?[12] Thus, Kumārila Bhaṭṭa has devoted nearly sixteen verses to refute the theory of the Vaiśeṣikas and the Naiyāyikas about creation and dissolution of the world. The relevant verses have been given in the footnote 12.

In verses 82 and 83, Kumārila Bhaṭṭa rejects the theory that *Ātman* or *Puruṣa* has transformed Himself into Ether, Air, Fire, Water, Earth, etc.[13] He states: If it be held that the Person (*Puruṣa*) is extremely pure and the world is the modification of this single Person and that the evils in the world are due to the past *adharma* of the men, then, inasmuch as this *adharma* also would be under His guidance, He might, on account of His extreme purity, remove the impurities of the world which would be left absolutely pure and be happy. Further, if you grant the fact of the creation of the world having its character regulated by *dharma*, &c.,

then it would amount to an acceptance of agencies other than that of divine will, operating towards creation of the world.[14]

The Vedānta theory that *Brahman* is the reality and the appearance of the World is due to ignorance (*avidyā*)[15] has been rejected in verses 84-86. It is as follows: Even the Vedānta theory is not tenable by itself. Because when nothing but brahman (n.) exists, what is it that causes the nescience (*avidyā*) to operate towards the creation of the world? It could not be brahman itself; as That can have nothing to do with nescience, which is a false entity and whose functioning is as unreal as a dream. If nescience were natural, then to whom would it belong? Certainly not to brahman; as That consists of Absolute Knowledge and as such could not have any connection with nescience. Then the existence of nescience apart from the brahman would bring about duality which is not acceptable to Vedāntins. Above all if nescience is natural, like brahman, it could never be set aside, and hence no liberation from it is possible. The Advaitins (Non-dualists) hold that the only means of destroying nescience is the knowledge of the brahman or ātman; but since this is not possible, and other adequate means such as meditation, etc. is not admitted; therefore, nescience, if held to be natural entity, could never be destroyed.[16]

The theory of the *Sāṁkhya* system of philosophy is also not tenable. According to this theory, *Puruṣa* does not operate towards the creation of the world, which is brought about by a disturbance in the three Attributes (*guṇas*, i.e. *Sattva*, *Rajas* and *Tamas*) of *Prakṛti* (the Primordial Matter) that function along and bring about the various objects of creation; and the agency that disturbs the equilibrium of the three Attributes (*sāmyāvasthā*) is that of the deeds (karman) of individual souls to take their births in the forthcoming creation. But in the beginning of the first, creation, no deeds of the souls are present. Then on what basis the creation will take place? Some people hold that the cause of the bondage of souls lies in their actions existing in a latent state of potentiality. But this is not correct; inasmuch as the effect is not produced from a cause which is only latent and does not function towards its production. For instance the potentiality of curd,--so long as it is only lying latent in milk and has not come out in the form of curd itself,—is not able to bring about a special substance prepared out of curd (=*dădhika*). This potentiality of the curd in the milk is the cause of the curd only which is prepared from the milk directly. And as for the special substance prepared out of curd (i.e. *dădhika*), the cause is only the curd and not the milk as it cannot be prepared directly from milk. A child cannot perform the feats of the grown up man although it has all the strength and energy of the man lying latent in it. If the effect were to be produced from the cause still in the state of latent potentiality,—then there would be bondage to the soul by the *karma* even when this *karma* will have already produced its results. Because it is held by the Sāṁkhyas that even on its destruction by fruition, *karma* continues to exist in a state of latent potentiality, even the performance of an action would be useless, as even before it has been performed, its potentiality must exist and this would bring about the results for the sake of which the action is sought to be performed. Because according to the Sāṁkhyas, everything that is done or produced in this world already exists in a latent state finally in *Prakṛti*, the Primordial Cause, and again because at the time of creation also, the attachment &c. of the soul must be continuing in their latent state, why cannot you attribute the soul's bondage directly to these? And why should you seek for its cause in the actions only?

And again, as the actions are brought by ignorance, as soon as knowledge would appear, the actions would cease to be performed. But they would still continue to exist in their latent forms according to you (i.e. the Sāṁkhyas); and inasmuch as these potentialities of actions would not be effects of ignorance, no amount of knowledge could remove them. And, according to you (i.e. the Sāṁkhyas), latent causes also bring about their effects; consequently, these latent potentialities of actions would be sure of bringing about their effects in the shape of the soul's bondage, no Deliverance (*mokṣa*) is possible. Therefore, knowledge cannot be held to be means of Deliverance. And again, as the destruction of actions by means of knowledge is not proved, so also the theory, that through the force of knowledge the action exhausts itself by producing its result in the smallest degree in order to free the knowing soul from bondage, is false. And again, because you (i.e. the Sāṁkhyas) hold that at the time of dissolution (*pralaya*), all things become dissolved into, and continue to lie latent in, in *Prakṛti* (the Primordial Matter),—to burst forth again into creation at a suitable time,—you must admit that the actions have their potentialities lying latent in the same *Prakṛti*; as according to you, nothing can be totally annihilated. And then, even at the time of dissolution of the world, there would be nothing to prevent the actions from bringing about their effects. And again, in ordinary life, we find that it is the function or active state of the mind of a person, that is the cause of his actions. But this activity of the mind does not exist at the time of dissolution. And even if such activity of the minds were possible at the time of dissolution, since at that time all minds would be mixed up in *Prakṛti*, there would be an admixture of their functions, and consequently also of actions. Therefore, the actions in a state of latent potentiality cannot be held to be the cause of bondage. If it is held that in the assertion that 'the cause of bondage is *adhikāra* (*adhikāro bandhahetuḥ*)', what is meant by the word *adhikāra* is not the potentiality of actions to be performed, but *the capability of Prakṛti to be enjoyed and that of soul to enjoy*; this view is also not tenable. Because neither *Prakṛti* nor *Puruṣa* could ever be severed from this capability; and as such, the cause of bondage continuing for ever, there could be no Liberation (*mokṣa*). Just as intelligence never leaves *Puruṣa*, so in the same manner, non-intelligence never leaves *Prakṛti*. And again, the destruction of the cause could only result in the non-production of its further effects. Consequently, even when ignorance would be destroyed by knowledge, all that we could expect would be that no more actions would be brought about. But this destruction will, in no way, be able to affect the fruition of the seeds sown by the actions of the past; for the simple reason that the fruition is not the effect of ignorance, whose destruction, therefore, could not affect the former. It is not by means of sense-perception (*pratyakṣa*) and inference (*anu-

māna), that knowledge is cognised to be the cause of Liberation (*mokṣa*). Nor does the *Veda declare that Liberation* (*mokṣa*) *results from knowledge*; such as it is held to be by the Sāṁkhyas and others (see *Sāṃkhya-kārikā* 44). The statements such as 'Self is to be known' (*ātmā vā are draṣṭavyaḥ*, see the footnote 15) have not been enjoined with a view to the attainment of Liberation (*mokṣa*). All that indicates is the fact that the knowledge of Self is a cause of activity towards certain sacrifices. For instance, the knowledge of discriminating *Puruṣa* from *Prakṛti* is of use in *Jyotiṣṭoma* and other sacrifices that lead to results beyond the physical world. Inasmuch as, unless the Soul is learnt to be discriminated from the body, how can people believe that such results as are not obtainable in the physical world could be attained by men? And unless one believes in the possibility of such results being obtained, he can never engage himself in the performance of those sacrifices of which the results are said to accrue to the performer in a superphysical world. Consequently, it is with a view to making people take to the performance of such sacrifices, that the Soul is enjoined to be distinguished from *Prakṛti*. And having this perceptible result, the said knowledge cannot be said to have any other result in the shape of Liberation (*mokṣa*). As a matter of fact, bondage consists of attachment to the body; and it is the negation of this that constitutes Liberation (*mokṣa*). Therefore, Liberation must be held to be the destruction of the present body and the non-production of any future body for the particular Soul. Bondage again is due to *karma*; so when *karma* is destroyed by fruition, the consequent bondage ceases by itself on the cessation of its instigating cause *karma*; and thus Liberation being of a negative character, would be eternal, in fact all total destructions are eternal; and Liberation too has been shown to be only the total destruction of the present body, &c. Barring its negative character, there is no other ground for the eternality of Liberation. And no negation can ever be the effect of any action. Therefore, Liberation cannot be held to be the direct effect of knowledge, because it is only *karma* that brings about the confinement of the Soul in a body. When there are no actions left to bring about their results, there is no cause left for such production of the body. Since all persons so liberated are found to be knowing the character of the Self, therefore, we must admit that such knowledge is only indirect auxiliary aid to Liberation (*mokṣa*). One desiring Liberation, therefore, would not engage in such actions as are either prohibited or are enjoined with a view to the attainment of certain material results. But he would continue to perform those actions which are enjoined as necessary and to be performed daily; and those that are enjoined as to be performed on certain specific occasions such as eclipses and the like,—in order to avoid the sin accruing from the non-performance of such actions. The effects of the necessary sacrifices are known to result only when they are desired by the agent; and as such they could not accrue to one who does not desire them. And as this aversion to results exists in one who knows one's real Self; it is in this that such knowledge comes to be of *indirect use* to the attainment of Liberation (*mokṣa*). It is not at all necessary for people who are conscious of their bodies as being the only impediment to Liberation, to have an idea of c r e a t i o n and d i s s o l u t i o n, beyond their own bodies, with regard to the whole u n i v e r s e. Therefore, the theory of c r e a t i o n and d i s s o l u t i o n must be admitted to resumble the present everyday processes of production and destruction; and any particular idea of these with regard to the p r o d u c t i o n and d e s t r u c t i o n of the whole u n i v e r s e cannot be established, for w a n t o f p r o o f.

Even the existence of a c r e a t o r is to be rejected in the same manner as an o m n i s c i e n t p e r s o n.[17]

Any such Creator cannot differ from ordinary people, except through an excess of *dharma*; nor is *dharma* possible without performances of sacrifices; and performance is not possible without an idea of sacrifices to be performed; and this idea is not possible except from the *Veda*; nor is the knowledge of the *Veda* possible without a comprehension of words, &c. Therefore, it must be admitted that all these Vedic Words, &c., existed before the Creator. And again, such a Creator may be proved to have been preceded by the *Veda*, on account of His being an intelligent being, like ourselves who are preceded by the *Veda*.[18] Thus, Kumārila Bhaṭṭa has devoted nearly 29 verses to reject the theory of the Sāṁkhyas with regard to c r e a t i o n and d i s-solution of the world and liberation from the world. The relevant verses have been given in the footnote 18.

Summary

Unquestionably, Kumārila Bhaṭṭa has used his sharp logic and unparalleled arguments to reject the theories of the Vaiśeṣikas and the Naiyāyikas who believe that God is the efficient cause of creation and dissolution of the world and the author of the Veda. He also mercilessly refutes the theory of the Sāṁkhyas about creation and dissolution of the world and liberation of soul. With the same sharp logic he tries to remove the misconceptions among the ordinary people also which crept into their minds basing the *arthavāda* passages in the *Veda*. It is very interesting for the students of Indology that a great Vedic scholar like Kumārila Bhaṭṭa rejects the existence of God and creation and dissolution of the world.

Bibliography

1. Mīmāṁsādarśanam (prathamabhāgāntargataḥ kevalas tarkapādaḥ) together with a commentary called Prabhā by Vaidyanātha Śāstry, published by J.P. Gangadhar Rao Bapurao Kale, Pune, 1953, being the Ānandāśrama Series 97.
2. Mīmāṁsādarśanam together with the Bhāṣya of Śabarasvāmin and the Tantravārttikam of Kumārila Bhaṭṭa (adhyāya I pāda 2, 3 and 4 and the adhyāya II pāda 1), Ānandāśrama Series 97, Pune, 1970.
3. Mīmāṁsādarśanam together with the Bhāṣya of Śabarasvāmin and the Tantravārttikam of Kumārila Bhaṭṭa (adhyāya II pāda 2, 3 and 4), Ānandāśrama Series 97 Pune, 1971.
4. Mīmāṁsādarśanam together with the Bhāṣya of Śabarasvāmin and the Tantravārttikam of Kumārila Bhaṭṭa (adhyāya III complete), Ānandāśrama Series 97, Pune, 1972.

5. Mīmāṁsādarśanam together with the Bhāṣya of Śabarasvāmin and the Ṭupṭīkā of Kumārila Bhaṭṭa (adhyāya IV to the end of the VII adhyāya), Ānandāśrama Series 97, Pune, 1973.
6. Mīmāṁsādarśanam together with the Bhāṣya of Śabarasvāmin and the Ṭupṭīkā of Kumārila Bhaṭṭa (adhyāya VIII to the end of the XII adhyāya), Ānandāśrama Series 97, Pune, 1974.
7. Ślokavārttikam of Kumārila Bhaṭṭa together with a commentary called Nyāyaratnākara of Pārthasārathi Miśra, edited and revised by Svāmī Dvārikādāsa Śāstrī, Tara Publications, Varanasi, 1978.
8. Ślokavārttika, translated by Ganga Nath Jha from the original Sanskrit with extracts from the commentaries 'kāśikā' of Sucarita Miśra and 'Nyāyaratnākara' of Pārthasārathi Miśra; published by Satguru Publications, Delhi-110 007, Second edition, 1983. First edition: Calcutta, 1900-1908.
9. Praśastapādabhāṣyam with the commentary Kiraṇāvalī of Udayanācārya edited by Jitendra S. Jetly; published by Oriental Institute, Baroda, 1971.
10. A Critical Survey of Indian Philosophy by Dr. Chandradhar Sharma: published by Motilal Banarsidass, Delhi, 1973.
11. Nyāyasūtra by Gautama, with the Bhāṣya of Vātsyāyana and the Vṛtti of Viśvanātha Nyāyapañcānana and Nyāyasūcīnibandha of Vācaspati Miśra (place and date are not known).
12. Nyāyavārttikam, a Gloss on Vātsyāyana's Commentary of the Nyāya-Aphorisms, by Uddyotakara: edited by Pt. Vindhyeśvarī Prasād Dvivedin; with an introduction by Prof. R.C. Pandey: published by Eastern Book Linkers, 5825, New Chandrawal, Jawahar Nagar, Delhi-110 007, 1986.
13. The Sāṁkhya Kārikā by Īśvarakṛṣṇa with a commentary by Gauḍapādācārya: edited with full notes and Hindi translation of Kārikās by Pt. Dhundhirāja Śāstrī: published by Jaya Krishna Das Haridas Gupta, the Chowkhamba

Sanskrit Series of Banares city, 1940: Being the Haridas Sanskrit Series No. 120.

14. The Ṛgveda-Saṁhitā, edited by Pt. Śrīpāda Dāmodara Sātavalekar and published by Svādhyāya Maṇḍala, Pāradī, Gujarat, IV edition.
15. Atharva Veda Saṁhitā, edited by Pt. Śrīpāda Dāmodara Sātavalekar and published by Svādhyāya Maṇḍala, Pāradī, Gujarat, IV edition.
16. Yajurvedīya-Kāṭhaka-Saṁhitā, edited by Pt. Śrīpāda Dāmodara Sātavalekar and published by Svādhyāya Maṇḍala, Pāradī, Gujarat, IV edition, 1983.
17. The Taittirīya Saṁhitā of the Black Yajurveda with the Commentary by Bhaṭṭa Bhāskara Miśra: edited by A. Mahadeva Sastri and K. Rangacharya and foreworded by R.N. Dandekar (in ten Volumes), published by Motilal Banarsidass, Delhi, Reprint: 1986. First edition: Mysore Government Oriental Library Series, 1894.
18. Vājasaneyī—Mādhyandinīya — Śuklayajurveda — Saṁhitā together with the Bhāṣyas of Uvvaṭa and Mahīdhara: published by Motilal Banarsidass, Delhi-7, 1971.
19. Taittirīya-Brāhmaṇam in four Volumes together with the Bhāṣya by Bhaṭṭa Bhāskara Miśra: published by Motilal Banarsidass, Delhi-7, 1985 (Reprint).
20. Upaniṣatsaṁgrahaḥ: published by Motilal Banarsidass, Delhi-7, 1970.
21. Vākyapadīya of Śrī Bhartṛhari: edited by Prof. K.V. Abhyankar and Āchārya V.P. Limaye, Bhandarkar Oriental Research Institute, Poona, being the University of Poona Sanskrit and Prakrit Series Volume II, Poona 1965.

NOTES

1. Kumārila Bhaṭṭa refers to the definition of *pratyakṣa* furnished by Diṅnāga, 'pratyakśam kalpanāpoḍham', in his *Ślokavārttika* on the *pratyakṣasūtra* in the following way:

"tadadhīnatvasāmye 'pi *kalpanāpoḍhaśabdanāt*/ 137a, b. (See Ślokavārttika on pratyakṣasūtra, p. 127).

Kumārila Bhaṭṭa cites the following verses from Bhartṛhari's *Vākyapadīaya* in his *Tantravārttika* (I.2, 3, 4 and II.1, pp. 239, 199, 209)

"yathāhuḥ: asty arthaḥ sarvaśabdānām iti pratyāyyalakṣaṇam/
apūrvadevatāśvargaiḥ samam āhur gavādiṣu// Vā II.119

"yad api kena cid uktam: tattvāvabodhaḥ śabdānāṃ nāsti
vyākaraṇād ṛte/ Vā I.13cd

"brāhmaṇārtho yathā nāsti kaś cid brāhmaṇakambale/
devadattādayo vākye tathaiva syur anarthakāḥ// Vā. II.14

2. praṇamya hetum *īśvaram* muniṁ kaṇādam anv ataḥ / 1ab.
*taccеśvara*codanābhivyaktād dharmād eva /2
*maheśvare*cchātmāṇusaṁyogajakarmabhyaḥ.../ 57

3. *Īśvaraḥ* kāraṇaṁ puruṣakarmāphalyadarśanāt / Nyāyasūtra, IV.1.19
na puruṣakarmābhāve phalāniṣpatteḥ / Nyāyasūtra, IV.1.20
tatkāritvād ahetuḥ / Nyāyasūtra, IV.1.21

4. puruṣakāram īśvaro 'nugṛhṇāti, phalāya puruṣasya yatamānasyeśvaraḥ phalaṃ saṁpādayatīti/ yadā na saṃpādayati tadā puruṣakarmāphalaṁ bhavatīti / guṇaviśiṣṭam ātmāntaram īśvaraḥ / adharmamithyājñānapramādahānyā dharmajñānasamādhiṣaṃpadā ca viśiṣṭam ātmāntaram īśvaraḥ / tasya ca dharmasamādhiphalam aṇimādyaṣṭaiśvaryam / yathā pitāpatyānāṁ tathā pitṛbhūta īśvaro bhūtānām / āgamāc ca draṣṭā boddhā sarvajñātā īśvara iti /" (Vātsyāyana's Bhāṣya on the Nyāyasūtra, IV.1.21) One may also consult the *Nyāyavārttika* of Uddyotakara on this *Bhāṣya*.

5. mūlaprakṛtir avikṛtir mahadāydāḥ prakṛtivikṛtayaḥ sapta /
ṣoḍaśakas tu vikāro na prakṛtir na vikṛtiḥ puruṣaḥ //Sāṃkhyakārika 3

saukṣmyāt tadanupalabdhir nābhāvāt kāryatas tadupalabdheḥ /
mahadādi tac ca kāryaṃ prakṛtivirūpaṃ sarūpaṃ ca // S.K. 8

triguṇam aviveki viṣayaḥ sāmānyaṁ acetanaṃ prasavadharmi /
vyaktaṃ tathā pradhānaṁ tadviparītas tathā ca pumān // S.K. 11

asadakaraṇād upādānagrahaṇāt sarvasaṁbhavābhāvāt /
śaktasya śakyakaraṇāt kāraṇabhāvāc ca sat kāryam // S.K. 9

tasmāt tatsaṁyogād acetanaṁ cetanavad iva liṅgam /
guṇakartṛtve ca tathā karteva bhavaty udāsīnaḥ // S.K. 20

sarvaṃ praty upabhogaṃ yasmāt sādhyati buddhiḥ /
saiva ca viśinaṣṭi punaḥ pradhānapuruṣāntaraṃ sūkṣmam // S.K. 37

dharmeṇa gamanam ūrdhvaṃ gamanam adhastād bhavaty adharmeṇa /
jñānena cāpavargo viparyayād iṣyate bandhaḥ // S.K. 44

For details see also the *kārikās* 10, 12, 13, 14, 16, 17, 18, 19, 21, 22, 36, 42, 56, 57 and 63.

6. pralaye 'pi pramāṇaṁ naḥ sarvacchedātmake na hi /
na ca prayojanaṁ tena syāt prajāpatikarmaṇā // 68, p. 466. Ś. Vā.
sarvajñavan niṣedhyā ca sraṣṭuḥ sadbhāvakalpanā/
na dharmādṛte tasya bhavel lokād viśiṣṭatā // 114, p. 477. Ś.Vā.
na cānanuṣṭhito dharmo nānuṣṭhānam ṛte mateḥ /
na ca vedād ṛte sā syād vedo na ca padādibhiḥ // 115, p. 477. Ś. Vā.

(Please refer to the Ślokavārttika of Kumārila Bhaṭṭa as given in the Bibliography No. 7.)

7. prajāpatir akāmayata prajāyeyeti / sa bhūr iti vyāharat / sa bhūmim asṛjata / sa bhuva iti vyāharat / so 'narikṣam asṛjata / sa suvar iti vyājarat / sa divam asṛjata / imān khalu vai lokān anu prajāḥ paśavaś chandāṁsi prājāyanta / (Taittirīya-Brāhmaṇam II.2.4.21, 22 and 23)

About Prajāpati and his creation, see also Taittirīya-Saṁhitā, II.1.2.7; II.2.1.1; II.4.4.12; II.4.11.34. Kāṭhaka-Saṁhitā, VI.1.7; IX.9; Kāṭhaka-Saṁhitā, IX.16; X.11; Taittirīya-Brāhmaṇaṁ, I.1.10.75; I.2.6.44. Chāndogyopaniṣat IV.17. Bṛhadāraṇyakopaniṣat, IV.5.11.

8. yadā sarvam idaṃ nāsīt kvāvasthā tatra gamyatām /
prajāpateḥ kva vā sthānaṃ kiṃrūpaṃ ca pratīyatām // 45 //
jñātā ca kas tadā tasya yo janān bodhayiṣyati /
upalabdher vinā caitat kathm adhyavasīyatām // 46 //
pravṛttiḥ katham ādyā ca jagataḥ saṃpratīyate /
śarīrāder vinā cāsya katham icchāpi sarjane // 47 //
prāṇināṁ prāyaduḥkhā ca sisṛkṣāsya na yujyate // 49 cd//
sādhanaṁ cāsya dharmādi tadā kiñcin na vidyate /
na ca nissādhanaḥ kartā kaś cit sṛjati kiñcana // 50 //
nādhāreṇa vinā sṛṣṭir ūrṇanābher apīṣyate /
prāṇināṇ bhakṣaṇāc cāpi tasya lālā pravartate // 51 //
abhāvāc cānukampyānāṁ nānukampāsya jāyate /
sṛjec ca śubham evaikam anukampāprayojitaḥ // 52 //
athāśubhād vinā sṛṣṭiḥ sthitir vā nopapadyate /
ātmādhīnābhyupāye hi bhavet kiṃ nāma duṣkaram // 53
tathā cāpekṣamāṇasya svātantryaṁ pratihanyate /
jagac cāsṛjatas tasya kiṃ nāmeṣṭaṁ na sidhyati // 54 //
prayojanam anuddiśya na mando 'pi pravartate /
evam eva pravṛttiś cec caitanyenāsya kiṃ bhavet // 55 //

9. The *arthavāda* passages are not sufficient in themselves, because they serve no independent purpose; but it is necessary that they should lead to knowledge resulting in some end; therefore, their acceptability consists in their forming parts of the Injunctory (*vidhi*) passages, through the glorification, etc. of the objects of Injunction. *Arthavāda* passages are of four kinds: (1) *Praśaṃsā* (glorification); (2) *Nindā* (depreciation); (3) *Prakṛti* (the description of doings of other persons); (4) *Purākalpa* (citing foregone examples).

For details about the *Vidhi* and the *Arthavāda*, please refer to *Pūrvā-mīmāṁsā-Sūtras* I.2.1 to I.2.45 and the *Bhāṣya* on them.

10. krīḍārthāyāṃ pravṛttau ca vihanyeta kṛtārthatā /
bahuvyāpāratāyāṃ ca kleśo bahutaro bhavet // 56 //

svarūpeṇopalabdhe 'pi sraṣṭutvaṃ nāvagamyate /
sṛṭyādyāḥ prāṇino ye ca budhyantāṃ kiṃ nu te tadā // 58 //

kuto vayam ihotpannā iti tāvan na jānate /
prāgavasthāṃ ca jagataḥ sraṣṭutvaṃ ca prajāpateḥ // 59 //

na ca tadvacanenaiṣāṃ pratipattiḥ suniścitā /
asṛṣṭvāpi hy asau brūyād ātmaiśvaryaprakāśanāt // 60 //

evaṃ vedo 'pi tatpūrvas tatsadbhāvādibodhane /
sāśaṅko na pramāṇaṃ syān nityasya vyāpṛtiḥ kutaḥ // 61 //

yadi prāg apy asau tasmād arthād āsīn na tena saḥ /
saṃbaddha iti tasyānyas tadartho 'nyaprarocanā // 62 //

stutivākyakṛtaś caiṣa janānāṃ mativibhramaḥ /
paurvāparyāparāmṛṣṭaḥ śabdo 'nyāṃ kurute matim // 63 //

upākhyānādirūpeṇa vṛttir vedavad eva naḥ /
dharmādau bhāratādīnāṃ bhrāntis tebhyo 'py ato bhavet // 64 //

11. ākhyānānupayogitvāt teṣu sarveṣu vidyate /
stutinindāśrayaḥ kaś cid vedas tacodito 'pi vā // 65 //

vedasyādipravṛttau ca nākṛtatvamatir bhavet /
pralayeṣu sthitiś cāsya sāśaṅkā syāt prajāpatau // 66 //

12. kartṛsargavināśānām athānāditvakalpanā /
saivaṃ yuktā yathedānīṃ bhūtānāṃ dṛśyate kramāt // 67//

pralaye 'pi pramāṇaṃ naḥ sarvacchedātmake na hi /
na ca prayojanaṃ tena syāt prajāpatikarmaṇā // 68 //

na ca karmavatāṃ yuktā sthitis tadbhogavarjitā /
karmāntaraniruddhaṃ hi phalaṃ na syāt kriyāntarāt // 69 //

sarveṣāṃ tu phalāpetaṃ na sthānam upapadyate /
na cāpy anupabhogo 'sau kasya cit karmaṇaḥ phalam // 70 //

aśeṣakarmanāśe vā punaḥ sṛṣṭir na yujyate /
karmaṇāṃ vāpy abhivyaktau kiṃ nimittaṃ tadā bhavet // 71 //

īśvarecchā yadīṣyeta saiva syāl lokakāraṇam /
īśvarecchāvaśitve hi niṣphalā karmakalpanā // 72 //

na cānimittayā yuktam utpattuṃ hīśvarecchayā /
yad vā tasyā nimittaṃ yad tad bhūtānāṃ bhaviṣyati // 73 //

saṃniveśaviśiṣṭānāṃ utpattiṃ yo gṛhādivat /
sādhayec cetanādhiṣṭhāṃ dehānāṃ tasya cottaram // 74 //

kasya cid dhetumātratvaṃ yady adhiṣṭhātṛteṣyate /
karmabhiḥ sarvajīvānāṃ tatsiddheḥ siddhasādhanam // 75 //

icchāpūrvakapakṣe 'pi tatpūrvatvena karmaṇām /
icchānantarasiddhis tu dṛṣṭānte 'pi na vidyate // 76 //

anekāntaś ca hetus te taccharīrādinā bhavet /
utpattimāṃś ca taddeho dehatvād asmadādivat // 77 //
atha tasyāpy adhiṣṭhānaṁ tenaivety avipakṣatā /
aśarīro hy adhiṣṭhātā nātmā muktātmavad bhavet / 78 //
kumbhakārādyadhiṣṭhānaṁ ghaṭādau yadi ceṣyate /
neśvarādhiṣṭhitatvaṁ syād asti cet sādhyahīnatā // 79 //
yathāsiddhe ca dṛṣṭānte bhaved dhetor viruddhatā /
anīśvaravināśyādikartṛmattvaṁ prasajyate // 80 //
kulāvac ca naitasya vyāpāro yadi kalpate /
acetanaḥ kathaṃ bhāvas tadicchām anurudhyate // 81 //
tasmān na paramāṇvāder ārambhaḥ syāt tadicchayā // 82ab //

13. See *Puruṣasūkta:* RV. X.90.1ff; VS. XXX.1ff; AV. XIX.6ff; From Ātman Ether etc. are produced: See Taittirīyopaniṣad II.1.

14. puruṣasya ca śuddhasya nāśuddhā vikṛtir bhavet // 82cd //
svādhīnatvāc ca dharmādes tena kleśo na yujyate /
tadvaśena pravṛttau vā vyatirekaḥ prasajyate // 83 //

15. satyaṃ jñānam anantaṃ brahma: Taittirīyopaniṣat II.1;
ātmā vā are draṣṭavyaḥ śrotavyo mantavyo nididhyāsitavyaḥ:
Bṛhadāraṇyakopaniṣat II.4;
yatra vā asya sarvam ātmaivābhūt tat kena kaṃ paśyet kena kaṃ śṛṇuyāt tat kena kam abhivadet kena kaṃ manvīta tat kena kaṃ vijānīyād yenedaṁ sarvaṁ vijānāti taṃ kena vijānīyād vijñātāram are keana vijānīyād iti / Bṛhadāraṇyakopaniṣat IV.14;
sarvaṃ khalv idaṃ brahma tajjalan iti śānta upāsīta:
Chāndogyopaniṣat XIV.1;

16. svayaṇ ca śuddharūpatvād asattvād anyavastunaḥ /
svapnādivad avidyāyāḥ pravṛttis tasya kiṁkṛtā // 84 //
anyenopaplave 'bhīṣṭe dvaitavādaḥ prasajyate /
svābhāvikīm avidyāṃ tu nocchettuṃ kaś cid arhati // 85 //
vilakṣaṇopapāte hi naśyet svābhāvikī kva cit /
na tv ekātmābhyupāyānaṃ hetur asti vilakṣaṇaḥ // 86 //

17. See the *Ślokavārttikam* under the 'codanāsūtra', verses 111ff.

18. pumāṅ akartā yeṣāṃ tu teṣām api guṇaiḥ kriyā /
katham ādau bhavet tatra karma tāvan na vidyate // 87 //
mithyājñānaṃ na tatrāsti rāgadveṣādayo 'pi vā /
manovṛttir hi sarveṣāṁ na cotpannaṁ tadā manaḥ // 88 //
karmaṇāṃ śaktyavasthānāṃ yair uktā bandhahetutā /
sā na yuktā na kāryaṃ hi śaktisthāt kāraṇāt bhavet // 89 //
dadhiśaktir na hi kṣīre dādhikārambham arthati /
dadhyārambhasya sā hetus tato 'nyā dādhikasya tu // 90 //
kāraṇāc chaktyavasthāc ca yadi kāryaṃ prajāyate /
bandhaḥ punaḥ prasajyeta phale datte 'pi karmaṇā // 91 //
śaktyavasthatvam eveṣṭaṃ vināśe 'pi hi karmaṇām /
prāk cāpi śaktisadbhāvād anuṣṭhānaṃ vṛthā bhavet // 92 //

śaktyavasthaṁ tu rāgādi kiṁ neṣṭaṃ bandhakāraṇam /
karmādattaphalatvāc cen nāvyaktim api tad vrajet // 93 //

tacchaktyapratiyogitvān na jñānaṁ mokṣakāraṇam /
karmaśaktyā na hi jñānaṁ virodham upagacchati // 94 //

yady apy ajñānajanyatvaṁ karmaṇām avagamyate /
rāgādivat tathāpy eṣāṃ na jñānena nirākriyā // 95 //

karmakṣayo hi vijñānād ity etac cāpramāṇavat /
phalasyālpasya vā dānaṁ rājaputrāparādhavat // 96 //

adyatve 'pi hi śaktisthaṁ yadi syāt karma kāraṇam /
tataḥ pradhānakāle 'pi yujyate kāraṇābhidhā // 97 //

manovṛttir idānīṁ tu hetur nāsti ca sā tadā /
manasāṁ saṃkarāc cāpi tadā syāt karmasaṁkaraḥ // 98 //

tasmān naiṣo 'dhikārākhyo bandhahetuḥ prakalpate /
yogyatve 'py adhikārākhye viprayogo na yujyate // 99 //

caitanyaṁ yogyatā puṃsaḥ prakṛtes tadanātmatā /
bhoktṛbhogyatvayos te ca na tābhyām apagacchataḥ // 100 //

utpatiau karmaṇāṁ ceṣṭaṁ ajñānaṃ kāraṇaṁ yadi /
tannāśāt syād anutpattis teṣāṃ na phalavarjanam // 101 //

jñānaṁ mokṣanimittaṁ ca gamyạte nendriyādinā /
na ca sāṁkhyādivijñānān mokṣo vedena codyate // 102 //

ātmā jñātavya ity etan mokṣārthaṁ na ca coditaṃ /
karmapravṛttihetutvaṁ ātmajñānasya lakṣyate // 103 //

vijñāte cāsya pārārthye yāpi nāma phalaśrutiḥ /
sārthavādo bhaved eva na svargādeḥ phalāntaram // 104 //

sukhopabhogarūpaś ca yadi mokṣaḥ prakalpyate /
svarga eva bhaved eṣa paryāyeṇa kṣayī ca saḥ // 105 //

na hi kāraṇavat kiṃ cid akṣayitvena gamyate /
tasmāt karmakṣayād eva hetvabhāve na mucyate // 106 //

na hy abhāvātmakaṁ muktvā mokṣanityatvakāraṇam /
na ca kriyāyāḥ kasyāś cid abhāvaḥ phalam iṣyate // 107 //

tatra jñātātmatattvānāṁ bhogāt pūrvakriyākṣaye /
uttarapracayāsattvād deho notpadyate punaḥ // 108 //

karmajanyopabhogārthaṁ śarīraṃ na pravartate /
tadabhāve na kaś cid dhi hetus tatrāvatiṣṭhate // 109 //

mokṣārthī na pravarteta tatra kāmyaniṣiddhayoḥ /
nityanaimittike kuryāt pratyavāyajihāsayā // 110 //

prārthyamānaṁ phalaṁ jñātaṁ na cānicchor bhaviṣyati /
ātmajñe caitad astīti taj jñānam upayujyate // 111 //

sargapralayavijñānaṁ samastajagadāśrayam /
svaśarīravidāṁ puṃsāṁ nadhikāyopayujyate // 112 //

tasmād adyavad evātra sargapralayakalpanā /
samastakṣayajanmabhyāṃ na sidhyaty apramāṇikā // 113 //

sarvajñavan niṣedhyā ca sraṣṭuḥ sadbhāvakalpanā /
na ca dharmād ṛte tasya bhavel lokād viśiṣṭatā // 114 //

na cānanuṣṭhito dharmo nānuṣṭhānam ṛte mateḥ /
na ca vedād ṛte sā syād vedo na ca padādibhiḥ // 115 //

tasmāt prāg api sarve 'mī sraṣṭur āsan padādayaḥ /
syāt tatpūrvakatā cāsya caitanyād asmadādivat // 116 //

4

THE CONCEPT OF TRUTH AT KUMĀRILA BHAṬṬA AND K. R. POPPER: A COMPARISON

LARS GÖHLER

This paper will be concerned with a comparison of two philosophical concepts far apart from each other in space and time. All doubts towards such a comparison are justified, they are my doubts too. Thus, one should take this as a sort of experiment which is intended to underline the necessity of future comparative historiography of Philosophy. The basis of this comparison is the assertion of an asymmetry of truth and falsity, viz. verification and falsification of cognition. According to this view the judgments 'true' and 'false' cannot be applied in the same way to cognition. This statement forms a basic idea of the philosophies of Kumārila Bhaṭṭa, India, 7th century C.E. and Karl Raimund Popper, Austria and Great Britain 20th century. To make differences as well as similarities as clear as possible I shall outline some patterns of the systems of both philosophers.

Originally, Mīmāṁsā was concerned with the exegesis of the ritual texts of the Veda. In post-Vedic period Vedic ritual had been interpreted in various ways, from total rejection to passionate apology. The defenders *par excellence* of Vedic ritual were the adherents of Mīmāṁsā. In order to remove contradictions in ritual performance, to underline the authority, absoluteness and eternality of the Veda, to refute Buddhist criticism, Mīmāṁsā developed philosophical ideas of its own. In the early texts e.g. of Jaimini, philosophical ideas are very scarce; whatever ideas there are should be taken as germs or seeds of philosophical thought. Many philosophical ideas of later importance were evolved a so-called 'commentator' (Vṛttikāra) quoted by Śabara (100-300 CE). Mīmāṁsā became a philosophy in the proper sense of the word in the works of Kumārila and Prabhākara (7th century CE).

In what follows I shall concentrate on Kumārila because his concept of truth seems to be close to that of Popper. The 'Chapter on the features of dharma' (*dharmalakṣaṇādhikaraṇa*) in his *Ślokavārttika* (ŚV on MS I.1.2) is the most important part on Kumārila's concept of truth. Having discussed the properties of ritual duty (dharma) Kumārila raises the problem of the authority of Vedic injunctions and of the authoritativeness, which also means 'truth' in general. He considers four possible answers to the problem: (1) Authoritativeness and non-authoritativeness of cognition are due to cognition itself. (2) Authoritativeness and non-authoritativeness of cognition are due to external factors, not belonging to the cognition itself. (3) Cognition derives its non-authoritativeness from itself and authoritativeness from external factors, and (4) Authoritativeness is a feature of cognition itself and non-authoritativeness is due to external factors (ŚV on MS I.1.2. 33-40). For Kumārila the first view renders itself impossible because one cannot infer authoritativeness and non-authoritativeness from the same reason. The 2nd and 3rd variants can be excluded due to the *regressus ad infinitum* involved in them (ibid. 51).—If authoritativeness and truth with it are ascertained by external factors, a further criterion is necessary to ascertain the authoritativeness of this conclusion and another criterion to ascertain this etc. (ibid. 56).

According to Kumārila only the fourth view remains: Cognition is authoritative from its origin (*utpatteḥ*) and might be *falsified* only by the cognition of the contrary (*viparyayajñāna*, ibid. 57). This is a continuation of ideas of the Vṛttikāra who deemed the 'falsity of cognition' a *contradictio in adjecto*. Thus, for Kumārila, cognition is considered to be true as long as its falsehood is proved by experience external and contradictory to the original cognition or determination of disarranged causes of cognition (*doṣajñāna*), e.g. the wrong application of the means of right cognition (ibid. 53).

Since knowledge is a result of certain causal factors, its complete falsity can never be proved. What can be proved is that cognition is wrong with reference to a certain object, but it can be true with reference to another object (ibid. 58).

It is significant that in the texts of the Mīmāṁsā the very term 'truth' (satya) seldom occurs. Instead they use the term prāmāṇya, frequently translated as 'authoritativeness', 'validity'. In most of the cases, however, the explanations of this term are very vague. In an excellent article on Indian concepts of erroneous knowledge[1] Lambert Schmidthausen makes an interesting point: Kumārila's prāmāṇya includes both the aspect of truth and the aspect of novelty of knowledge. Both is evident: a statement that is not new cannot be a cognition; according to Kumārila it must be remembrance of an object already cognized. That a cognition has to reflect an object in the sense of a relation of truth is due to the origin of the cognition in a causal process. An important meaning of prāmāṇya, which is also the very basis of the whole Mīmāṁsā, Schmidthausen did not mention. 'Authoritativeness' in Mīmāṁsā always means 'authoritative *for* something' in an elliptical sense. This 'something' is in the Mīmāṁsā definitely stated: authoritativeness does not mean only truth and novelty but 'authoritative for human action'. First of all it refers to 'ritual action'. Even Śabara has it: *dharma* means what is to be done—and *prāmāṇya* or *aprāmāṇya* say whether we have reliable (ritual) injunctions for this or not.[2] With Kumārila '*prāmāṇya*' acquires a secular (*laukika*) meaning, not only saying what is to be done in ritual but also in *loka*, in the world.

At first sight the position of the Critical Rationalism, above all that of its founder Karl Raimund Popper, seems to be incomparable with that of the Mīmāṁsā. But before going deeper into that matter I shall try to mention some facts of its history: the Critical Rationalism does not originate in such a continuous tradition as Mīmāṁsā. It tries to answer some problems that occurred in the theory of science of the so-called Vienna Circle. The exponents of the Vienna Circle on the one hand attempted to expound revolutionary results of modern science for the theory of knowledge, on the other hand they evolved a general methodology of knowledge as an analogy to the methods of knowledge in physics and mathematics. As a main purpose they tried to construct a way of cognition, free of contradiction, from perception or experience to the formation of general statements and theories, in the sense of Positivism. This might be called the 'inductive' way, which means that one can conclude from true particular statements to true general statements and theories. The Theory of knowledge built upon these basements did not only contain logical problems but was also hardly applicable in its complexity by scientists. Gerlach and Mocek describe the situation as follows: "Theoretical problems of knowledge that were delegated by the sciences to the Neopositivism came back to them, unsolved, but with a great deal of logical and/or linguistic reflections. The Neopositivism could not redeem its original credit from many scientists. In the beginning of the thirties a critical situation emerged for the theses of the 'Vienna Circle' viz. for those scholars that adhered to this tradition."[3]

In this situation, in 1934, Karl Raimund Popper published his book 'Logics of Scientific Discovery'. In this book he tried to solve the problems of the Vienna Circle without rejecting its methodological dispositions entirely. Popper characterized the problems of cognitional inductivism as unsolvable and he meant that theories are not inferable from experience but always built first. Their empirical adequacy is proved then by conclusion logically deduced from the respective theory. In that way it could be falsified but never verified because a theory always contains much more than one single or any given fact. Popper's example, often quoted, reads as follows: The observation of any number of white swans could not verify the sentence 'all swans are white'. The observation of but one black swan could falsify it. Theoretically speaking, verification and falsification are not symmetrical procedures of proving knowledge. Moreover, this means, according to Popper, that a theory can never be verified ultimately, no matter how many examples support it. But it can be justified for a certain time, as long as it is not actually falsified, but falsifiable in principle. Besides, an important reason for non-verifiability of theories, for Popper, is the imminent *regressus ad infinitum* which Kumārila also draws attention to.

Now, before I try to compare the conceptions of truth in a narrow sense and the concepts of validity and authoritativeness in a broader sense, some more words on the concepts of truth: basically, there are two types of concepts of truth: the so-called 'classical', taking truth as a relation of correspondence of an image and its object, as did Aristotle. Non-classical concepts of truth consider truth for instance to be a property of an object, but at least not the relation described above.

How do both philosophers correlate to this classification? If we speak of a falsification principle in a broader sense as a conception of truth, both philosophers might be said to move within classical patterns. A mental image, statement, theory can be falsified in comparison with its object. This relation is absolute according to Popper and relative according to Kumārila. In Popper's theory a general statement or a theory is falsified completely if a basis or perception sentence is in contradiction to it. As already mentioned, Kumārila is of the opinion that, if an image does not correlate with one object, it can correlate with other objects and, furthermore, it must correlate with another object because it originated in a causal process. As for the verification or truth of knowledge and the concept of truth in the narrow sense both authors seem to move along non-classical patterns. To Kumārila, the Veda as every statement and injunction not yet falsified is authoritative from itself and consequently true. Truth as an aspect of authoritativeness is a property that applies to the Veda absolutely and to the secular knowledge relatively, depending on the proper use of the senses and other means of knowledge, and with it on the reliability of the subject of knowledge. Consequently it is not a relation but a property of a mental image etc. in the sense of the non-classical concept of truth.

According to Popper, truth is a very vague characteristic of knowledge and it is always a relative, imperfect truth, an approximation. By the way, it seems that to Popper every theory is authoritative from itself, as it is to Kumārila, as long as it is not falsified. The difference to Kumārila is that every general knowledge that can be considered to be a science must be falsifiable. Statements and theories that, due to their logical form, withdraw from criteria of falsification, have a certain justification but no relation to empirical data and cannot be considered a science. That means 'truth' and 'false' cannot be applied to them. If we confront classical and non-classical tendencies in Popper's concept of truth in the narrow sense non-classical elements seem to predominate. Truth in the sense of a relation does not play an important role as a criterion, of theories in it.

Kumārila and Popper have in common that they conceive the asymmetry of truth and falsity in that way that they consider only falsity in a classical sense as a relation. But truth is considered by both, Kumārila even more than Popper, as a property of mental images in a non-classical way. A priori or absolute elements in a theory of knowledge are closely related to the outlined problem of truth. As already mentioned Kumārila as well as Popper try to avoid a *regressus ad infinitum* in their theory of knowledge. But to avoid this infinite regress of criteria of knowledge one has to replace them by a principle that has, so to speak, absolute significance not deserving a substantiation by other criteria. The Mīmāṁsā uses several of these absolute principles that are related together. First of all it is the Veda which is eternal, authorless and of absolute significance. By the proclamation of the absoluteness of the Veda, a corpus of texts, the Mīmāṁsā is compelled also to ascribe absolute significance to the language used in the Veda and in everyday life. Absoluteness of language, according to Mīmāṁsā, consists in an eternal, constant relation of the word and its object (*nityaḥ saṁbandhaḥ śabdasyārthena*). Self-validity of all verbal knowledge is based on this relation. As for Karl Raimund Popper, things are not that plain. No knowledge seems to have absolute validity, all knowledge is relative. But if one follows the general rule that every consistent relativism requires absolute premises then it might be worth going a bit deeper in that matter. I think that it is the falsification principle itself that withdraws any falsification and thus is of absolute significance, not referring to empirical data. According to Popper's premises it is thus non-scientific. As a deductive procedure it has been proved to be the valid method of knowledge by exclusion of the inductive procedure. This is the appearance of a philosophical problem which is more fundamental. Comparing induction with deduction Popper takes both as procedures of pure formal logics, excluding each other and necessarily excluding every inner contradiction. Thus, Popper's escape from obvious insufficiencies of inductive ways of knowledge towards deductive ones seems to be an attempt to save a general methodology of science that takes all patterns from formal logics and consequently excludes contradictions as basic elements of the object and its mental representation. The presupposed absolute, the actual a priori of Popper's philosophy seems to consist primarily in this methodology and in the second place in the principle of falsification. Perhaps this is a result of lacking self-confidence towards *philosophical* methodology evolved by classical German and Indian Philosophers. Hegel's warning to the philosophy not to borrow its method from other sciences as well as for instance Nāgārjuna's advice not to think in strict oppositions, excluding one from the other, are clearly neglected. Kumārila tries to evolve a methodology which includes both the removal of contradictions between ritual rules and the admission of oppositions within philosophical categories e.g. the difference and non-difference as in the case of the subject and object of knowledge (ŚV, *ātmavāda* 41:.. .*bhedābhedau prasaṅktavyau grāhyagrāhakayor yāthā*).

At this point it is paradox to come to the conclusion, that, in spite of progressive intentions the asymmetry of truth and falsity in the philosophies of Popper and Kumārila is a result of a more conservative attitude. This attitude tries to conserve formal logics as a methodology of sciences in the case of Popper and the importance of Vedic texts and ritual in the case of Kumārila. In both philosophies the aim is to remove contradictions, in one case within theory and between theory and empirical data and in the other case within the system of ritual rules of the Veda, though not within philosophical concepts.

As already mentioned, in Kumārila's theory truth is a subordinate aspect to authoritativeness or validity. Truth in the proper sense also plays a subordinate role in Popper's theory. He frequently refers to the concept of validity of Kant in the sense that the value of theories does not consist in their descriptive but prescriptive character.[4] This definite emphasis on validity and authoritativeness, less on truth, is probably due to the intention of both philosophers to influence social action and social values. The position of both philosophers within the respective systems of social values cannot be discussed further in this paper, but one thing seems to be obvious: owing to their intention to influence action both philosophers could not evolve an entirely sterile rationalism which excludes all values. Also in this point Popper becomes unfaithful to the Vienna Circle, that considered all valuations unscientific.

In India from the earliest times onwards truth and valuation are more closely related with each other than in Europe of the 19th and 20th century. Kumārila in that way was also continues Indian traditions. He wants to (re-)establish Vedic ritual as an exclusive social value on the hand and on the other he discusses essential problems of validity and knowledge in opposition to other systems, above all Buddhism, in both cases practical intentions lead to doubt about truth as the only characteristic of knowledge and theories.

Up to this point I tried to examine what both philosophies have in common. But one should not forget the differences between the theories. Besides similarities in the concept of truth these differences are considerable. In many respects Poppers theory of science is incomparable to Kumārila's philosophy though the latter has been looked at, by the Indians, as a theory of science and text exegesis too. The intentions, traditions and systems of concepts can also hardly be compared in all points. But it remains to be a remarkable fact that Kumārila Bhaṭṭa, in a special point, evolved philosophical ideas, 13 centuries in advance, that resemble very much that of a well-known 20th century philosopher.

Notes

1. Lambert Schmithausen: Maṇḍanamiśra's *Vibhrahmavivekaḥ*. Mit enier Studie zur Entwicklung der indischen Irrtumslehre. In Sitzungsberichte der Osterreichischen Akademie der Wissenschaften, Philosophisch-historische Klasse 247. Abhandlung 1. Vienna 1965, especially p. 193.

2. Commentary to Jaimini's Sūtra I.1.2. *Prāmāṇya* is always discussed in the Mīmāṁsā following this Sūtra on *codanā* 'injunction' and hence seems to refer primarily to injunctions and the respective actions.

3. Translated by the author from : Hans Martin Gerlach, Reinhard Mocek: Bürgerliches Philosophieren in unserer Zeit. Berlin 1982, p. 137.

4. Karl Raimund Popper: Objektive Erkenntnis. Ein evolutionürer Entwurf. Hamburg 1984, p. 24: 'Kant hatte damit recht, daβ unser Verstand der Natur die Gesetze vorschreibt. . . Es gibt ein allgemeines Bedürfnis nach einer Welt, die unseren Erwartungen entspricht. . ."

5

ESCAPING THE PARADOX OF SCRIPTURE: THE MĪMĀṀSĀ SOLUTION

SHLOMO BIDERMAN

When paradoxes take on linguistic forms, their natural jurisdiction lies within the sphere of words. More precisely, a paradox is a *relation* between two statements that are contradictory to one another. Assuming that the paradox is a genuine one, each of the two statements can be proved by a sound argument; but the two arguments cannot, in sound logic, be stated together.

A paradox can be defined as follows: 'An apparently unacceptable conclusion derived by apparently acceptable reasoning from apparently acceptable premises.'[1] To solve a paradox is to do away with it, that is, it simply vanishes. To quote R.M. Sainsbury on the vanishing of a paradox: 'Appearances have to deceive, since the acceptable cannot lead by acceptable steps to the unacceptable. So, generally, we have a choice: Either the conclusion is not really unacceptable, or else the starting point, or the reasoning, has some nonobvious flaw.'[2]

In this essay, I should like to deal with one of the central paradoxes that seems to be a natural accompaniment of the many religions that rely upon scriptures. I am referring to what may be called *the Paradox of Scriptures*, which I should like to contrast as it appears in the monotheistic religions with the way it appears in orthodox Hindu religion. I will argue that the Paradox in the monotheistic religions is a kind of 'semantic paradox' absent in Hindu religion but replaced there by a 'pragmatic paradox'.[3] As I hope to show, this pragmatic paradox is no less resistant to solution than the semantic one. However, there is a great practical difference between the two species of paradox. In the presence of a semantic paradox, it is impossible to continue to use language clearly, but under certain circumstances, it is possible to leave the pragmatic paradox as it is without reaching a logical dead end or speaking nonsense. I will argue that one of the more interesting original characteristics of the ancient Mīmāṁsā doctrine is that it makes it possible for the pragmatic paradox to remain innocuous, by opening new possibilities of understanding the role that interpretation plays in religion.

The Mīmāṁsā has suffered many contemptuous attacks both in India and the West. It has been condemned for being a sterile, or mechanistic, or dogmatic, or fundamentalistic ritualism. Fortunately, this negative attitude has been giving way to a more positive one according to which ancient Mīmāṁsā has made a genuinely interesting contribution to the philosophy of language, the philosophy of religion, and the philosophical grasp of the meaning of life. The present essay is a modest attempt to develop this relatively new, positive attitude.

Before I begin, I should like to make a general remark. The Paradox of Scriptures as I shall deal with it is based on the assumption that sacred scriptures, whether Eastern or Western, contain (among the rest) injunctions directed at human beings that require unqualified obedience. The centrality of such scriptural injunctions in religion was formulated lucidly by Plato in the *Euthyphro* (9e), where he explains the religious attitude as requiring that one must see what God wills as good simply because *He* wills it and not as good in and for itself. In other words, according to such a religious attitude, the obligatory status of the commands is totally dependent on God's status as the supreme commander. In India, the Mīmāṁsā is the major advocate of the injunctive nature of scripture, that is, the Veda. In the second verse of the *Mīmāṁsāsūtra*, the identification of *dharma*—taken to be the purpose of 'scripture'—with Vedic injunctions is explicitly made by Jaimini.[4] Thus the Mīmāṁsā was often portrayed as advocating the demand for unconditional observance of inexplicable commands, as conveying the "firmly paternal air of 'do what I say because I say so, and don't ask question' ".[5]

According to the prevailing monotheistic view, God is the source of religious commands. He is the one who has given the scriptures to the faithful. Within these scriptures, the holy writ, one finds the basic religious injunctions. God is also the essential guarantor of the validity and infallibility of the injunctions. The prime distinction between what is permitted and what is prohibited, between right and wrong, stems from the divine source of the religious injunctions or commandments.

The status of God as the absolute authority behind the religious commandments seems necessary not only from the religious viewpoint but also from that of the logic of commands. First, for any act of command to be applicable, the presence of a commander and a 'commandee' is required. In other words, each command must have both a source and a recipient. Secondly, a command has to be grounded on the authority of the commander. As Rescher correctly points out, "The source should have some entitlement or authority for giving a command to the recipient."[6] Moreover, the existence of an authoritative source of a command is essential to the attribution of the status of a command to verbal utterances. As Searle points out, the difference between 'request', on the one hand, and 'order' and 'command' on the other is that in the case of 'order' and 'command' there is a preparatory rule that the commander must be in a position of authority over the commandee.[7]

Within the monotheistic context, then, a sentence will be regarded as expressing a command only if it is ascribed to God or said on his authority. Relating the imperative nature of religious expressions to the identity of its authoritative source is tantamount to abandoning the sole grammatical criterion of the imperativeness of an expression. This is so because not every expression put in the imperative mood should be taken as a command and not every command is necessarily issued by the performance of a speech act in the imperative mood. In a military context, for example, nobody will take a recruit's expression 'Leave me alone!' when addressed to his sergeant-major, as the expression of a command, even though it has the obvious grammatical form of imperative sentence. Analogously, sentences in the indicative mood sometimes function as commands. Consider, for example, signs carrying the words 'This is a private property' meant to keep possible trespassers off the premises.

The question of the authoritativeness of scriptures and of the search for a validator leads to what can be called the *monotheistic version* of the Paradox of Scriptures. This monotheistic version can be formulated in the following two seemingly contradictory statements:

1. God is the ultimate source of scripture. Scripture is valid, sacred, and infallible because handed down by God. Scripture can be seen as stemming from God's self-nature or as given by God, that is, revealed to human beings at some historical moment. Be that as it may, God logically precedes scripture.

2. The most central way of gaining any knowledge of the religious commands is by means of the holy writ. Scripture informs the believer of the commands, of their source, and of their content. More specifically, it is scripture that grants the status of authority and infallibility to the word of God. Thus, scripture logically precedes God.

I call this paradox a semantic paradox because it manifests that the contradiction is one of meaning itself—a paradox formed by the clash between the meaning attributed to *God* and the meaning attributed to *scripture*.

Needless to say, the more orthodox Hindu tradition is hardly subject to this kind of the semantic paradox. This is for the simple reason that this kind does not accept God as the source of authority of *śruti*. The more radical among the orthodox go even further and deny the existence of God and so put before Westerners the fascinating example of an undoubtedly atheistic undoubted religion. Others among the orthodox accept some form of a transcendent or quasi-transcendent being, but to all of them, even if such a being is taken to exist, it is in no way responsible for the existence of Veda or for its authority. Veda is grasped by them as authoritative in and by itself.

As the result of this removal of God as the source of authority for scripture, the semantic paradox so prevalent in monotheistic religions plays no important role in the development of the Hindu religion. Indeed, when we turn to the writings of ancient Mīmāṁsā, we immediately find out that God had nothing whatever to do with the authority of the Veda.

Before dwelling on the Mīmāṁsā's standpoint, I should like to offer a short description of what can be called the orthodox Hindu attitude toward scripture. I shall make use of recent terminology and follow Eco's description of the triangular contrast, widely discussed in the course of a critical, secular debate, "among interpretation as research of the *intentio auctoris*, interpretation as research of the *intentio operis*, and interpretation as imposition of the *intentio lectoris*."[8]

As far as the research of the *intentio auctoris* is concerned, the orthodox Hindu standpoint is unequivocal. The sacred texts are authorless:

> Revelation is by no means God's word—because, paradoxically, if it were to derive from a divine person, its credibility would be impugned. It is held to be authorless, for if a person, human or divine, has authored it, it would be vulnerable to the defects inherent in such a person.[9]

Therefore, the very existence of God is sometimes subject to a fierce philosophical attacks even by highly religious thinkers. Because Hindus generally believe in a multitude of gods, it is easy for them to concede the existence of one god or another; but it is equally easy for an orthodox Hindu such as a Mīmāṁsaka to deny that any god is the creator of the universe or the authoritative source of *dharma*, the truth of which cannot be dependent on even a godly person, but which must be self-evident or, at least, self-sustaining. The authorlessness of the Veda makes it impossible to interpret it by reference to the presumed intentions of a godly author.

As far as the research of the *intentio operis* is concerned, one should be aware of a condition that has been somewhat neglected in spite of its importance. I should have shown signs of hesitation in calling the sacred pronouncements of the Hindus—what was heard or what has been remembered—'texts', for the same reason that I hesitate to call them 'scriptures', even though there is no other good word by which to refer to them. This is because they are *oral by nature*,[10] so that the most immediate way of grasping them is through the personal relation between the student and the teacher. What is orally taught and orally learned is ontologically prior to the written text. 'In the Indian context, it is not the inability to write that has resulted in the supremacy of the oral form of religious texts, but the conscious choice of oral transmission as the only appropriate vehicle for holy utterance.'[11] The 'scriptural' quality of sacredness is established within the relationship between persons and as part of a continuous tradition. As Coburn reports, by ancient custom, if an ageing teacher is unable to find a student worthy of inheriting the tradition he guards, he should throw the traditional sacred texts in his possession into the river as if they were no more than ashes, since, in themselves, lacking the continuity of an oral passage from teacher to disciple, they lack both authority and value; "written documents, unvivified by personal relationship, are lifeless."[12]

If so, any 'meaning' that may be found in the sacred texts is the result of its having been heard and pronounced, i.e. of its performance. The dependence of meaning on performance makes it impossible for the meaning of the Veda to be understood from its words alone. To some degree, the relation between a Vedic text and its performance is like that between a musical score and the performance of the score. I mean that the music notes alone are both ineffective and seriously incomplete unless they are properly performed, proper performance being dependent, in the usual case, on a tradition of performance. This conception leaves the source of the 'text's' authority an open matter. The source of authority is not inherent in the sacred words themselves, but rather in the relationship between these words and some trusted *ṛṣi* or sage and those who believe in the text because they believe in the sage. As for *ṛṣi*, he is the person who finds the words, perhaps quite intuitively, and reveals them to his followers. Let me quote Grant who puts this point nicely:

> . . . the teacher who knows the sacred text by heart and has devoted his or her life to studying and explicating it is the one and only reliable guarantor of the sacred truth. The power of the holy word is realized only through the human word of the seer, prophet, or spiritual master, not through a manuscript, even when the latter is also important.[13]

This is the sense in which the Vedic texts are not subject to place and time. The Veda is a-historical because it depends on the successive repetitions that preserves it. It is, therefore, clear that the *intentio operis* of the Veda should not be considered apart from the *intentia lectoris* of the believers, without whom the authority of the text could not be and cannot be maintained. The active attitude granted to the Hindu believer does not render the meaning of *dharma*, which is to be found in the Veda, subjective or dependent of the beholder's eyes. The reason for this is that the role that the guru or believer plays is *not* the role of granting *meaning* to the sacred texts; rather his role is *to confer the status of authority* upon them. The guru or believer, therefore, acts as the actual validator of the scriptures. Granting validity is not a formal procedure, nor can it be expressed in assertions and understood to be the content of these assertions. Instead, it is a performative, or, more exactly, an illocutionary speech act: the validity of scripture is established by the very act of saying, chanting, repeating, and otherwise performing them.

One of the central assumptions of monotheistic religions is that sacred texts are inexhaustibly loaded with meanings. They can refer to everything and thus are in principle open to infinity of interpretations, each of which can at most give only part of their assertions and values. In such a view, the openness of interpretation is, therefore, a matter of meanings, that is, of content. In contrast, the Hindu picture is altogether different. The openness of the text is not expressed by the multiplicity itself of legitimate interpretations, but rather by what may be called their irrelevance. This irrelevance is due to the view that the semantic aspect of the Veda is strangely insignificant. Furthermore, the intelligibility of the texts is not a prior condition to its authoritative status: "For many Hindus, the holiness of holy words is not a function of their intelligibility. On the contrary, sanctity often appears to be inversely related to comprehensibility."[14] True, the extreme view according to which the Vedic formulas are unintelligible was eventually rejected in Hindu orthodox circles, but, as Heesterman rightly adds, "the fact that such a theory could be discussed is significant."[15]

To recapitulate what I have said until now, the validity of the Veda is acquired through a dynamic process of validating rather than a static state of affairs. By this I mean that the authoritativeness of 'scripture' does not depend on the acceptance of any specific content; rather, it is guaranteed by the existence of a performative model of validation. The Indian sacred text is wholly open, precisely because the role of any particular interpretation of its contents has no special importance. Openness of the text is achieved by disregard of its semantic factor in favour of reciting it, chanting, memorizing it, or performing the ritual motions it prescribes. As Heesterman argues, the exclusive concern with technicalities and with the intricacies of recitation and chanting of scripture, has apparently left little room for productive concern with its contents.[16] As Renou sharply puts it, "meaning, in relation to the form, had only a minor importance." He concludes that "This is, over and above everything, quite Indian."[17] Performance of the texts, together with adherence to the ritualistic injunctions and prohibitions that may be found in them, constitute the texts as authoritative, infallible and absolute.

I have previously said that Hindu orthodoxy is free of the semantic paradox that appears in the monotheistic religions, but I did not mean that the Hindu position is free of paradox in general in its relation to scripture. The opposite is the case. Paradoxes often have a very stubborn ability to survive. When we encounter them, we sometimes are in a position like that of Alice when she saw the notorious Cheshire Cat in Lewis Carroll's masterpiece. In *Alice* there is a strenuous debate over the possibility of cutting off the head of the cat—a head that is not attached to any body. During the debate, the head itself turns the debate futile by simply disappearing and leaving its smile behind, but, by this remainder, making the paradox return in the form of the mocking smile. Paradoxes, as I have said, take linguistic forms; but concern with them is neither a merely linguistic matter, nor a mere intellectual diversion. Quite on the contrary, the existence of a paradox can testify to the existence of a critical problem within a tradition. Therefore, when it sometimes seems to us that we have succeeded in overcoming the paradoxical relationship between two statements, the paradox returns in a different form. So, too, in India, in which the Paradox of Scripture returns as a pragmatic paradox.

What do I mean by the phrase *pragmatic paradox*? Let me begin by giving an example, that of one of the many entertaining paradoxes of Kafka, one related even in its content to what we have been saying:

Leopards break into the temple and drink the sacrificial vessels dry; this is repeated over and over again; finally is can be calculated in advance and it becomes a part of the ceremony.[18]

As this passage shows, a paradox is possible not only in the clash between the meaning of two statements, but is possible also between, on the one hand, the meaning of a statement and, on the other, the action performed by means of this very statement. When I say something, in addition to the explicit content of what I have said, I have also performed a certain speech act—I have asserted a standpoint, assumed a hypothesis, made a request, delivered a promise, and the like. A pragmatic paradox is created when I perform a speech act the content of which contradicts the act itself—for example, 'I order not to obey any order whatever!' In the case of Kafka's paradox, the breaking of the leopards into the temple clearly means the disruption of the ritual; but, at the same time, it is in effect an act that, in the long run, preserves the ritual.

As I see it, the attitude of Hindu orthodoxy to scripture involves a pragmatic paradox, one in which there is a discrepancy between an act and its meaning. Thus we find a clear statement upholding the eternity and infallibility of the Veda and the believer is required to uncover the meanings that lie hidden in the text. However, when we pay attention to the act of uncovering of meanings, we discover that it is purely an act of granting validity. In every such procedure of the granting of validity, there must be an implicit assumption that, if not for the granting, scripture would lack all authority. What takes place here is a process that resembles that in Kafka's parable, although in an inverse direction: the act of the leopards meant to destroy the ritual in fact maintains it; the act of the believer meant to strengthen the validity of scripture, in fact weakens it. To be more technical: the locutionary content of the act of granting validity to Veda requires the authoritative status of Veda; the illocutionary force of this act of granting has the effect of weakening this status.

Does orthodox India provide any solution for this paradox? To this question a quick, decisive answer can be given from a sociological standpoint. I have already said that one of the leading characteristics of the orthodox attitude to the Veda is the minimizing of the relevance of the semantic aspect. Now I can add the argument of a number of scholars, according to which the general attitude of believers to the Veda is one of disregard. *Śruti* was completely cut off from the religious practices of daily life. In daily life, religious practices were regulated by *smṛti*. Of course, *smṛti* received its general authority from *śruti*; but this remained quite general, and *śruti* had no other function in relation to *smṛti*. So, beyond this provision of general authority, say the scholars in question, the Veda remained almost unknown. For example, Louis Renou holds that the attitude to the Veda was no more than a ceremonial raising of the hat, that is, the paying of empty respects to the Veda that immediately thereafter could be disregarded.[19] As Heesterman puts it, the high prestige of the Veda is comparable only with the high level of disregard for it.[20] Renou puts it in sharper terms: "One always believes oneself to be in the wake of the Veda, when one turns one's back on it."[21] If we accept such a sociological approach, it is clear that the pragmatic paradox vanishes of itself.

It is not my intention or within my ability to question the correctness of the sociological generalizations on which this solution is based. But it appears to me that this solution is not the only possible one. I see the position of the school of Mīmāṁsā as an attempt to propose an additional way of minimizing the pragmatic paradox. Their attempt is more intellectual and does not destroy the essential status of the Veda that it is meant to explain. In my view, the Mīmāṁsā offers this possibility of minimizing the paradox by means of its grasp of the idea of interpretation.

The Mīmāṁsā is usually represented as a school of exegesis, and, indeed, its close and constant interest in the Vedic text is exemplified in the two first sūtras of the *Mīmāṁsāsūtra*, which say that the subject-matter of Mīmāṁsā is *dharma*, and that *dharma* consists of total obedience to all the injunctions that can be found in the Veda.[22] But the view of the Mīmāṁsā as nothing more than a school of exegesis cannot do full justice to its ambitions and to the philosophical enterprise it takes on itself. When I speak of its philosophical enterprise, I am not referring only to its two central philosophers, Kumārila and Prabhākara. To my mind, it is possible to find a kind of intellectual spinal column in the *Mīmāṁsāsūtra* itself, and certainly in Śabara's commentary on this work. This spinal column is, to my mind, the emphasis put on the active central role of consciousness and on the nature of understanding.

Let me be more specific. It appears to me that the Mīmāṁsā follows a path highly reminiscent of that of contemporary hermeneutics. The Mīmāṁsā sees interpretation as actually constituting meaning, and therefore, at least in a sense, as constituting the world. I propose to characterize this attempt as one of internalization. What do I mean by 'internalization'? Something similar to what Richard Gombrich means, in a different context, when he describes the way in which the Buddha has treated the notion of *karma*: the Buddha took a concept that refers to an external, impersonal ritualistic reality and internalized it, seeing it as lying within the intrinsic sphere of mental intentions.[23] Likewise, it appears to me, the attitude of the Mīmāṁsā to language can also be seen as an emphasis on internalization. In the present article, I cannot make a full survey of all the passages in the *Mīmāṁsāsūtra* and Śabara's commentary in which this emphasis is shown. I will, however, take a single step in this direction and propose a reconstruction of a number of stages in the process of internalization. Since I am making a reconstruction, I do not mean to say that it represents the historic course taken by Mīmāṁsā; it is only a way that it might possibly have taken, as it is a way for us to attempt to understand the Mīmāṁsā.

To make clear the first stage of this hypothetical process of internalization, I should once again mention how important it was for the Mīmāṁsā to consider the Veda to be authorless. As we know, to the Mīmāṁsā, scripture is in no way connected with any agent, either divine or human; and in the Mīmāṁsā literature we find various arguments that aim at cutting the Veda off from any possible (personal) author.[24] I should like now to point out that the very authorlessness of Veda makes it essential *to seek its meaning within itself*. In other words, the meaning of the text must be taken to depend directly on its internal organization.

This is the first step in the process of internalization to which I am referring: meaning does not depend at all on external factors, whether ontological or psychological. A second stage in the process of internalization is the seeing of the entire Vedic language as reducible to a single unifying principle. The insistence on this principle can already be found in the *Mīmāṁsāsūtra* in Jaimini's conception of a grammatical sentence as a self-sufficient unit, the unifying principle of which is the uniqueness of the purpose that it serves. Jaimini adds that when the words of a given sentence are being separated, they "are found to be wanting [i.e. incapable of affecting the purpose of the sentence]."[25] But this unity of language is not characterized only by the unity of the sentences that make it up. As I said earlier, the whole Vedic language is reduced to a single principle, which is not derived from the external world and plays no regulative function within it. For example, the Mīmāṁsā refuses to see Vedic language as something that can be reduced to a means of communication.

The principle of the unity of the Vedic language is internal to it, and is, in effect, the injunctive force that—according to the Mīmāṁsā—lies behind each and everyone of the Vedic sentences. It is ordinarily assumed that the injunctive force of a sentence is something that is, so to speak, added to it because the very sentence—or one much like it—is not necessarily injunctive. The standpoint of the Mīmāṁsā, is therefore, so unusual and so radical that it must make the injunctive force of the Vedic sentence internal to the sentence itself, that is, this force becomes the essence of the sentence. Therefore, even sentences that are merely declarative, those that describe and do not prescribe, undergo at the hands of the Mīmāṁsā a transformation of meaning and are presented as by nature auxiliary to the explicitly injunctive sentences. As Jaimini points out, declarative sentences should be understood as tied to injunctive sentences, as auxiliaries of a kind to the latter, serving the role of praising the religious injunctions.[26]

We can now construe the third stage in this process of internalization. Up till now, I have spoken of the Mīmāṁsā attitude toward Vedic language. Abstractly, it would certainly have been possible for them to regard Vedic language as different in kind from ordinary language. However, for the sake, no doubt, of consistency, the whole view of the Vedic language as injunctive was applied to ordinary language as well. Accordingly, to Jaimini and Śabara, the meaning of the language of the Veda does not differ from that of ordinary language. Jaimini goes so far as to state explicitly that the two must be regarded as conveying the same meaning, since, if it were not so, religious commands would be incomprehensible and consequently useless: "The meaning must be one and the same, as such alone are injunctions of actions possible."[27] Śabara elucidates:

> The words in the Veda are the same as those in common parlance and the things expressed by them are also the same.—Why?—Because *thus alone are injunctions of actions possible*; it is possible to have an injunction of action, only when the words are the same and the things denoted by them are the same. If the two sets of words were different, then their meanings could not be understood.[28]

Up until now, I have presented three stages of the internalization of lauguage by the Mīmāṁsā. At the first stage, the Vedic language was internalized in that it was cut off from external sources and criticism. At the second stage there appeared the principle of injunction as the internal unifying principle of Vedic language. At the third stage, the injunctive essence of Vedic language was discovered to be the essence of language in general. At this third stage, language is presented, at all its levels and in all of its contexts, as an internal instrument independent of anything beyond itself. And now language is open to the fourth and final stage of internalization.

As is obvious, language has not only sense but also reference to external objects. External reality appears at first to be independent of the language that refers to it. But, at this fourth stage, the Mīmāṁsā widens the scope of internalization to the connection between language and the world. This connection is presented as an inherent capacity inherent in the human being.

When I speak of this fourth stage I am referring primarily to the well-known sūtra of the *Mīmāṁsāsūtra* in which Jaimini says that "The relation between *śabda* and its object is *autpattika*."[29] M. Monier-Williams distinguishes between several related meanings of the term *autpattika*: 'relating to origin, inborn, original, natural, inherent, eternal'[30] to which, I suppose, we may add 'innate'. In commenting on this sūtra, Śabara explains that language does not acquire its meaning by means of any implicit or explicit accord among those who use it, but that it is inborn, innate, *autpattika*. Our use of language and our ability to join a word with its meaning depend upon the inborn capacity to speak in accord with the rules of meaning and so to make of language such a useful tool for our social lives.

I have pointed out only a few of the leading characteristics of the process of internalization which characterize the Mīmāṁsā position. I believe that this process has both important implications and significant developments. Elsewhere, I have explained one of these developments, which is the internalization of the concept of *apūrva* in Kumārila's thought.[31] However, in the context of the present essay, I have pointed out internalization only in order to show that by its means it is possible to minimize the damage that can be caused to a religion by the pragmatic Paradox of Scripture. Since both the authoritative status of the Veda and the act of granting the Veda authority are considered by the Mīmāṁsā to be internal, the result is that the contradiction—between the locutionary content of the statement that the Vedas are authoritative and between the illocutionary force of the same argument—tends to fade away and perhaps to disappear. The reason is that both sides of the contradiction are absorbed within the same internality of the interpretive process that is taken to constitute meaning. If meaning is understood as always the outcome of the process of interpretation, then interpretation can indeed be seen as a world system or world-making system within which the circular connection between the act and its content has ceased to be vicious.

This process of internalization underwent very many changes in the course of the development of Indian philosophy. On the metaphysical level, we know of the process of internalization found in some of the Upaniṣads. On the epistemological level, I think that internalization accounts for the seeing of *śabda* as *pramāṇa*—a means of knowledge, a way of knowing the world that complements the internal processes of perception and inference (the Mīmāṁsā played an important role in this process of epistemological internalization). In the present essay, I have dealt only with the linguistic size of this internalization. I am well aware that the implications of this linguistic internalization do not remain confined to the linguistic sphere. I agree completely with D'sa's convincing exposition of the Mīmāṁsā as a school of thought that takes a clear stand not only on linguistic but also on metaphysical issues. The philosophy of the Mīmāṁsā deals not alone with the meaning of language, but also with the meaning of life. Let me conclude by quoting a few sentences from what D'sa considers to be 'the original Mīmāṁsā':

> As I understand it, the basic 'insight' that we have inherited from the Mīmāṁsāka-s could be formulated thus: *what is meaningful to us both as individuals and as a community cannot be ultimately explained through any space-time category*. It is something that is 'given', not created.[32]

NOTES

1. R.M. Sainsbury *Paradoxes* (Cambridge University Press, 1988), p. 1.

2. *Ibid.*

3. I am indebted to Roy W. Perrett for this term; see his 'The Rationality of Asceticism' in *Rationality in Question: On Eastern and Western Views of Rationality*, ed. by S. Biderman and B.A. Scharfstein (Leiden: E.J. Brill,1989), pp. 57–76.

4. *Mīmāṁsāsūtra* I.1.2: *'codanālakṣaṇo artho dharmaḥ'*. For a Sanskrit edition of Jaimini's *sūtras* and Śabara's commentary see: *Mīmāṁsādarśana with the Commentary of Śabara*, ed. by R.G. Bhatta (Benares, 1910).

5. Karl H. Potter, *Presuppositions of India's Philosophies* (Englewood Cliffs N.J.: Prentice-Hall, 1963), p. 250.

6. N. Rescher, *The Logic of Commands* (London, 1966), p. 16. Some philosophers deny that authority is an essential prerequisite in all cases of giving a command. See C.K. Grant, 'Imperatives and Meaning' in *The Human Agent: Royal Institute of Philosophy Lectures, Volume* 1 (London: Cambridge University Press, 1968), p. 183. As an example for a command issued without authority Grant gives the case of "a passenger who knows the route, saying to the driver who does not, 'Turn right'." It seems to me, however, that Grant's example misses its point; surely, the passenger *does* have an authority of some kind on the driver (possessing knowledge that the latter does not have).

7. John R. Searle, *Speech Acts: An Essay in the Philosophy of Language* (Cambridge: Cambridge University Press, 1969), Chapter 3.

8. See his recent book, Umberto Eco, *The Limits of Interpretation* (Bloomington: Indiana University, Press, 1990), p. 50ff.

9. Eliot Deutsch and I.A.B. van Buitenen (eds.), *A Source Book of Advaita Vedānta* (Honolulu: The University of Hawaii Press, 1971), p. 5.

10. See, for example, William A. Graham, *Beyond the Written Word: Oral Aspects of Scripture in the History of Religion* (Cambridge: Cambridge University Press, 1987). It is important to realize that the orality of the Veda cannot be explained in 'technical' terms; as Graham puts it, "...the Vedas have been orally transmitted for three millennia or more—for the majority of that time not because writing was unknown, but rather by choice, in explicit preference to writing them down." (p. 4).

11. *Op. cit.*, p. 68.

12. Thomas B. Coburn, "Scripture in India: Towards a Typology of the Word in Hindu Life", *Journal of the American Academy of Religion*, Volume 52(3), 1984, pp. 443-44.

13. Grant, *Op. cit.*, p. 68.

14. Coburn, *Op. cit.*, p. 445.

15. J.C. Heesterman, "Veda and Dharma", in W.D. O'Flaherty and J.D.M. Derrett (eds.), *The Concept of Duty in South Asia* (London: School of Oriental and African Studies, 1978), p. 81.

16. J.C. Heesterman, *Op. cit.*, p. 81. See also Staal's superb book on Hindu Ritualism: Frits Staal, *Rules Without Meaning: Ritual, Mantras and the Human Sciences* (New York: Peter Lang, 1989).

17. Louis Renou, *The Destiny of the Veda in India* (Delhi: Motilal Banarsidass, 1965), p. 25.

18. Franz Kafka, 'The Collected Aphorisms', in *Shorter Works*, Volume I, trans. Malcolm Pasley (London: Sacker & Warburg, 1973), p. 87.

19. Renou, *Op. cit.*, p. 2.

20. Heesterman, *Op. cit.*, p. 80.

21. Renou, *Op. cit.*, p. 1.

22. *Mīmāṁsāsūtra* I.1.1: "*athāto dharmajijñāsā*"; *Mīmāṁsāsūtra* I.1.2: "*codanālakṣaṇo artho dharmaḥ*".

23. Richard Gombrich, *Theravāda Buddhism* (London and New York: Routledge & Kegan Paul, 1988), pp. 66ff.

24. See for example Śabara's commentary on *Mīmāṁsāsūtra* I.1.5; *Mīmāṁsāsūtra* I.1.27–I.1.32 and Śabara's commentary. See also *Sarva Darśana Saṁgraha*, trans. E.B. Cowell and A.E. Gough (Delhi: Cosmo Publications, 1976, first published in 1900).

25. *Mīmāṁsāsūtra* II.1.46: "*Arthaikatvāt ekaṁ vākyaṁ sākāṅkṣaṁ cet vibhāge syāt.*"

26. *Mīmāṁsāsūtra* I.2.7: "*vidhinā tvekavākyatvāt stutyarthena vidhīnāṁ syuḥ.*" See also *Mīmāṁsāsūtra* I.2.8–I.2.18 and Śabara's commentary.

27. *Mīmāṁsāsūtra* I.3.30: "*prayogacodanābhāvād arthaikatvam avibhāgāt*".

28. Śabara's commentary on *Mīmāṁsāsūtra* I.1.30, quoted from *Śabara-Bhāṣya*, trans. G. Jha (Baroda: Oriental Institute, 1973), Volume 1, p. 116.

29. *Mīmāṁsāsūtra* I.1.5: '*autpattikas tu śabdasyārthena saṁbandhaḥ*'.

30. M. Monier-Williams, *A Sanskrit-English Dictionary* (Delhi: Motilal Banarsidass, 1963; First published by Oxford University Press, 1899), p. 237.

31. S. Biderman, "Dharma and the Limits of Interpretation", in *Interpretation in Religion*, ed. by S. Biderman and B.A. Scharfstein (Leiden: E.J Brill, 1992), forthcoming.

32. Francis X. D'sa, *Śabdaprāmāṇyam in Śabara and Kumārila* (Vienna: Indological Institute University of Vienna, 1980), p. 27.

6

THE THEORY OF ANUMĀNA IN THE BHĀṬṬA MĪMĀṀSĀ: NIYAMA AND THE MEANS TO DETERMINE NIYAMA

TOMOYASU TAKENAKA

Vṛttikāra gives us the following definition of anumāna, which is found in the Śābarabhāṣya[1]: *anumānaṁ jñātasaṁbandhasyaikadeśadarśanād ekadeśāntare 'saṁnikṛṣṭe 'rthe buddhiḥ*. In the Anumāna chapter of the *Ślokavārttika*, Kumārila gives the possibility of four kinds of interpretation to the compound *jñātasambandha* included in the definition. After that, he proceeds to examine the second part of the compound, viz. the word *sambandha*. This 'sambandha' means the relation between two *ekadeśas* (portions) written in the Vṛttikāra's definition. To say in other words, it means the relation between a *liṅga* (sign) and a *liṅgin* (one which has the *liṅga*). When we infer one *ekadeśa* (*liṅgin*) from another one (*liṅga*), there must be a well-known relation between the two *ekadeśas*. If not so, the result of inference (*anumiti* or inferential knowledge) would have non-validity.

Kumārila called this relationship *vyāpti* or the invariable concomitance of the *liṅga* with the *liṅgin*, and his successors gave it the name of *niyama* or *sāhityaniyama*.[2] In this paper, comparing with the opinions of other schools, I will examine and make clear the theory of *anumāna* in the Bhāṭṭa Mīmāṁsā school, especially the following two points: (i) what is the relation between the *liṅga* and the *liṅgin*?; (ii) how can we get the knowledge of *vyāpti*, that is, by what kind of means (*pramāṇa*) is this relation ascertained?

I

According to Kumārila, when there is *vyāpti* (the invariable concomitance) of the *liṅga* with the *liṅgin*, the *liṅga* is regarded as *vyāpya* (the pervaded), and therefore works as *gamaka* (one which makes known). On the other hand, because the *liṅgin* is *vyāpaka* (the pervader), it becomes *gamya*[3] (one which is made known). Using the relativity of extension of the two, he explains the fact from the viewpoint of ontology. '[Of the two, P and Q] when P, in time and space, is either the equal or less in comparison with Q, P is the *vyāpya* of Q. On the other hand, when Q is the equal or more in comparison with P, Q is the *vyāpaka* of P. Therefore, it is only after the *vyāpya* (P) have been recognized that the *vyāpaka* (Q) can be cognized. Otherwise there would be no such relation between the two as that of the pervaded and the pervader (*vyāpyavyāpakatā*, viz. *vyāpti*).'[4] From this explanation, we get an understanding that the knowledge of the *liṅga* (= *vyāpya*) necessarily leads to the one of the *liṅgin* (= *vyāpaka*). To say in other words, if we get the knowledge of Q whenever we know P, these two (P and Q) have the *vyāpti*-relation in which P is the *vyāpya* and Q is the *vyāpaka*. And it is this relation that Kumārila recognizes as the one between the *liṅga* and the *liṅgin*.

Taking into account this opinion of Kumārila, his commentators criticize other schools' theory of the relation between the *liṅga* and the *liṅgin*. For example, the *Vaiśeṣikasūtra* mentions the following four cases as the relations where one (P) is regarded as the *liṅga* of the other (Q): (1) P is conjunct (*saṁyogin*) with Q, (2) P is co-inherent in Q, (3) P is co-inherent in the same substratum (*ekārthasamavāyin*) with Q, and (4) P is repugnant (*virodhin*) to Q.[5] Dharmakīrti, one of the most important Buddhist philosophers, calls this relation between *liṅga* (*sādhana* or the thing to establish; probans) and liṅgin (*sādhya* or the thing to be established; probandum) *avinābhāva* (inseparable relation), and acknowledges that only two cases belong to it.[6] One of them is the case that *sādhana* is the result of *sādhya* (*tadutpatti* = *tatkāryatā* or causation) and the other is the case that *sādhana* is the nature of *sādhya* (*tādātmya* = *svabhāvatā* or identity). However, besides the above cases, we know many instances in which the knowledge of one thing leads necessarily to that of another. For example, whenever we see the rising up of the lunar mansion Roniṇī, we can know the one Kṛttikā will come up soon. But there is neither causality nor identity between the two lunar mansions. Moreover, when we eat some fruit in a dark room, we can infer the fruit colour from the taste, namely, the green colour from the sour taste, or the red from the sweet. In this instance also, there is neither *tadutpatti* nor *tādātmya* that brings *avinābhāva*. Explaining the above inconsistency, Dharmakīrti says, 'Because colours depend on the same whole causal apparatus (*sāmagrī*) with tastes, through inferring the nature which the cause of tastes have, we can know colours from tastes.'[7] To say minutely, at first we infer the material causes of tastes (*rasopādāna*) from tastes, and then infer colours from the material causes of colours (*rūpopādāna*) which are co-existent with the material causes of tastes in the same causal apparatus. According to the Bhāṭṭa Mīmāṁsā, this is also not good. If we can infer colours from tastes in this order, it follows that we can infer the result (viz. colours) from the cause (viz. the material cause of tastes). And this is also contradictory to both *tadutpatti* relation and *tādātmya* which Dharmakīrti acknowledges as *avinābhāva*.

As for the Bhāṭṭa, colours are not *indirectly* inferred from tastes but they are *directly* done. It is also the case with the inference of Kṛttikā from Rohiṇī.[8] Then by what relation? The Bhāṭṭa says it is by the *sāhityaniyama* relation. Pārthasārathimiśra, one of the Bhāṭṭa, defines this relation. "When one thing (P) is necessarily connected with another (Q) in some manner, even if P should be seen in any place and time, P will make us know Q, which exists in the same place and time."[9] According to Rāmānujācārya, his commentator, when, in the instance (*dṛṣṭāntadharmin*), P is known to be necessarily, directly or indirectly, connected with Q which exists in the same place and time, in some manner—in a relation of *saṁyoga* (conjunction), *samavāya* (inherence), *ekārthasamavāya* (co-inherence in the same substratum), or *kāryakāraṇabhāva* (causality)— P, being recognized in another place, makes us infer Q which exists in the same place and time, and connects with P in the same relation. Now we can understand that the relation between P and Q defined by the Bhāṭṭa indicates the larger notion than the one defined by the *Vaiśeṣikasūtra* and Dharmakīrti. Therefore, whatever relation these two may have, if the knowledge of P necessarily lead to that of Q, the relation should be known as *niyama*.

II

It is necessary that *niyama* should have been established by some means of valid knowledge (*pramāṇa*) so that we may get the right inferential knowledge, which depends on it. What *pramāṇa* then can determine *niyama*? Now let us examine this problem.

Kumārila says that *vyāpti* [of the two] is recognized through *bhūyodarśana* (a repeated cognition).[10] His expression which only means that *niyama* is induced from our experiences, is not so clear, therefore, even his commentators show different views. Pārthasārathi puts in order the views concerning *pramāṇas* of *niyama* and mentions as follows:[11]

(A) *tadutpatti* (*kāryakāraṇabhāva*) and *tatsvabhāvatā* .... Dharmakīrti's view.
(B) *mānasapratyakṣa* (mental perception).
(C) *pratyakṣa* (perception).
  (a) *prāthamikapratyakṣa* (the first perception) . . . Prabhākara's view.
  (b) *bhūyodarśanasahāyacaramapratyakṣa* (the last perception accompanied with a repeated cognition) .... Sucaritamiśra's view.
(D) *arthāpatti* (presumptive testimony) . . . Umbeka's view.
(E) *vyabhicārādarśanasahāyabhūyodarśana* (a repeated cognition accompanied with non-perception of deviation).... Pārthasārathimiśra's view.

(A) Dharmakīrti argues that *avinābhāvaniyama* is determined by *kāryakāraṇabhāva* and *svabhāva* (*-tā*) which establish non-deviation of *sādhana* from *sādhya*, but neither by non-perception [of *sādhana* in counter instances] nor by perception [of *sādhana* in similar instances].[12] Depending on this description, Pārthasārathi seems to mention Dharmakīrti's view. He denies this view in the following way:[13]

(i) If *kāryakāraṇabhāva* (= *tadutpatti*) and *svabhāva* (= *tādātmya*) established *avinābhāvaniyama*, there would not be this one between Rohiṇī and Kṛttikā. Because these two have not the above two relation, viz. *tadutpatti* (causality) and *tādātmya* (identity).

(ii) *Kāryakāraṇabhāva* is nothing but the inevitable relation of prior and posterior in time (*paurvāparyaniyama*). If this *niyama* establish *avinābhāvaniyama*, it follows that one *niyama* is the *pramāṇa* of another *niyama*. This is a logical fault of dependence on itself (*ātmāśrayadoṣa*).

(iii) We don't have any *pramāṇa* of the result (*kārya*) and the own nature (*svabhāva*). It is only co-existence (*sāhitya*) that a perception cognizes, neither the relation between a result and a cause (*tatkāryatā* or causality) nor the one depending on the nature (*tatsvabhāvatā* or identity). After seeing smoke repeatedly where there is fire and never seeing smoke where there is not, it is the relation of co-existence that there is smoke where fire is and there is not smoke where fire is not, that we come to find in this deductive way. But not *tatkāryatā*. Therefore, because *tatkāryatā* has no proof by *pramāṇa* that gives it validity, it cannot be the *pramāṇa* of *niyama*.

(iv) *Tatsvabhāvatā* also has no proof. 'This is a tree. Because of being *śiṁśapā*.' This inference is a example of the one based on *tatsvabhāvatā*. It is true that *śiṃśapā* is a tree. But *śiṁśapā*-ness and tree-ness cannot be bound together for ever. That which is the nature of one thing should be inherent to that thing alone. But tree-ness does not inhere in *śiṁśapā* alone, because there are trees other than *śiṁśapā*. Therefore, we have not any *pramāṇa* to decide if tree-ness is the nature of *śiṁśapā*. Thus having no proof, *tatsvabhāvatā* also cannot be the *pramāṇa* of *niyama*.

This is the summary of the denial which Pārthasārathimiśra gave to Dharmakīrti's view. The problem on the *pramāṇa* which gives a proof to *tatkāryatā* and *tatsvabhāvatā* had remained vague in Dharmakīrti's description and was examined minutely by later Buddhist philosophers. They presented us some new views to get rid of Dharmakīrti's vagueness. The theory of *pañcakāraṇī*, namely the five cognitions which determine causality, quoted in *Sarvadarśanasaṃgraha*, is the most famous one of them.[14]

(B) The view that *niyama* is determined by *mānasapratyakṣa* (mental perception) is not only referred to Pārthasārathimiśra's works, but also Sucaritamiśra's *Kāśikā* (Commentary on the *Ślokavārttika*) and Śālikanātha's *Prakaraṇapañcikā*. But it is not clear who argues this. We can summarize Pārtasārathi's criticism of this view as follows:[15]

(i) Because *manas* (mind) works as the inner organ (*antaḥkaraṇa* or the inner instrument of knowledge), it is not possible for this to connect external objects (*bāhyārtha*). Therefore *manas* cannot determine the *niyama* which is between external objects, namely, smoke, fire and so on.

(ii) It is the case with the *manas* accompanied with the impression (*saṁskāra*) which is made by a repeated cognition (*bhūyodarśana*). It is because the impression is the cause for only recollection (*smṛti*), and it cannot assist the *manas*.

(C) Because perception grasps only the object which exists presently and nearby, it is not suitable that it determines the *niyama*. It is only individual co-existence (*sāhitya*) in particular time and place that perception can grasp.

(a) According to the Prābhākara Mīmāṁsā school, *niyama* is apprehended by the very first observation of the two together. And a subsequent repeated cognition works only to remove extraneous conditions (*upādhi*) and confirm the *niyama* apprehended in the first perception. For them, this is the function of *bhūyodarśana*.[16] When the connection of smoke with fire is perceived, it is only smoke or fire as substance (*dravya*), but not their connection as quality (*guṇa*) that is subject to limitation in time and place. It is because the form of our knowledge is 'These two are connected' (*saṁyuktau imau*), but not 'This connection is of these two' (*ayam anayoḥ saṁyogaḥ*), and this fact means that 'this-ness' (*idantā*), which conveys proximity (*sannidhi*) in time and place, namely, 'being at present time' and 'being at near place', belongs to substances only, but not to their connection. That the connection has no limitation in time and place means that it is permanent. Therefore, once when the connection of smoke with fire without limitation in time and place has been apprehended in the first perception, thereafter knowing only the existence of smoke (*dhūmasattā*) will inevitably bring us the knowledge of its connection with fire.

Pārthasārathi's rejection of the Prābhākara view is based on the contention that connection should be subject to limitation in time. The view that only substances are limited by time and place, and their connection is not, is contradictory to our usual experience. It is usual for us to have the following knowledges: 'These two *were* connected' (*saṁyuktau etau vahnidhūmau*). 'These two *are* connected' (*saṁyujyete*), and 'These two *will be* connected (*saṁyokṣyete*)'. These expressions by three tenses indicate that it is the connection that is subject to limitation of past, present and future times. As far as the connection is limited by time, we cannot regard it as *niyama*. And each perception that apprehends several connections limited by each time cannot be considered to be the instrument which determine *niyama*.[17]

(b) Śucaritamiśra says in his *Kāśikā*, 'At the final perception accompanied with impressions which occurred from many previous perceptions, one comes to know that smoke possesses the nature of being inevitably connected with fire (*vahniniyatasvabhāvatva*).'[18] We have had many experiences of the relationship of co-existence between smoke and fire repeatedly, and these experiences are retained in the mind in the form of latent impressions. And at the final perception, these impressions remind us of the co-existential relationship which had been experienced in a repeated cognition. At this moment, the organs help to bring forth the knowledge of *vyāpti* in the form of grasping (perceiving) a smoke. Therefore, even though recollection (*smṛti*) works here, as far as the organs also work, it is doubtlessly perception. In this final perception, first a smoke is grasped in a indeterminate cognition (*nirvikalpaka*), and then the determinate cognition (*savikalpaka*) whose object is the nature of smoke that it is inevitably connected with fire, occurs. It is the *niyama* that this determinate cognition apprehends as its object.[19]

Pārthasārathi's criticism of this view can be summarized as follows:[20]

(i) Because perceptions apprehend the object existing before our eyes, they cannot apprehend *niyama* which has the relation with other times and places as own nature. *Niyama* must be what pervades every time and every place.

(ii) It is not right to say that *niyama* is the nature of smoke, therefore, it is apprehended at the very moment when smoke is observed. Even if *niyama* be the nature of smoke, it must not deviate. In other words, the *niyama* must apply to fire which exists at all the times and all the places that smoke exists. Therefore, if the *niyama* were apprehended by perception, the relation of *niyama* with past time and future time or remote places would be apprehended by the same perception. But this is unreasonable.

(iii) On the contrary, if the relation of *niyama* with other times and places is not apprehended, even when *niyama* should be apprehended by perception, inference will not work.

(D) Umbeka says in his *Ślokavārttika Tātparyaṭīkā*, 'When we observe smoke a hundred times where fire is, and recognize non-existence of smoke where fire is not, the knowledge of the *niyama* that smoke is invariably connected with fire occurs to us by presumption *(anyathānupapatti = arthāpatti)*.'[21] It is because we cannot explain this fact, which was gained by the repeated experiences, otherwise than by presuming the *niyama* that smoke is concomitant with fire.

Pārthasārathi, however, rejects this view. It is quite proper that our perceptions and experiences should be limited by time and place. Therefore, even though we should observe non-existence of smoke a hundred times where fire is not, we cannot determine non-existence of smoke at all the place where fire is not. Likewise, even if we should observe smoke many times where fire is, we cannot determine existence of smoke at all the places where fire is. So it is not valid that presumption is the right instrument (*pramāṇa*) for determining the *niyama*.[22]

(E) Lastly, let's examine Pārthasārathi's own view. He also, following Kumārila's view, admits that we know *niyama* from a repeated cognition (*bhūyodarśana*), but he says that we cannot specify the *pramāṇa* which brings it. His explanation is as follows: "We cannot mention some specific *pramāṇa* [to determine *niyama*]. But when the co-existence of *liṅga* (smoke) and *liṅgin* (fire) is repeatedly known by one of the recognized *pramāṇas*, for example, perception, inference, etc., the very *pramāṇa* accompanying with the non-apprehension of [*liṅga* in] contrary instances (*vipakṣa*), becomes to be admitted as the *pramāṇa* of *niyama*."[23] Even if a repeated cognition be admitted as the *pramāṇa* of *niyama*, it is only the co-existence limited by particular time and place that it can determine. In other words, a repeated cognition proves the co-existence of *liṅga* and *liṅgin*, namely, *liṅga-liṅgin* relationship only in a limited number of cases, not in all cases, and non-observation of contrary instances proves the relationship between the absence of *liṅgin* and the absence of *liṅga* only to the extent to which non-observation has actually gone.

Nevertheless, it is not possible to know the above two types of relationships in all cases. According to Pārthasārathi, it is not necessary to know them in all cases in order that we may infer validly, because we can validly infer the presence of fire from the observation of smoke so long as we know the two relationships in a limited number of cases, which work fully as the primary factor of inference. Therefore, he argues that we do not need the *niyama* in the form of the *vyāpti* that applies to all times and places to infer validly. He says, "The invariable co-existence (*sāhityaniyama*) of smoke with fire in all the places where smoke has been observed, and the non-observation of smoke where fire has not been observed, only these two are the cause which can give us the right inferential knowledge."[24] It is the very *sāhitya-niyama* of *liṅga* with *liṅgin* in the perceptible time and place that he calls *niyama*, which is regarded as the primary factor of inference.[25]

Now, what *pramāṇa* does determine the *niyama* which takes the form of *vyāpti* (*vyāptiniyama*)? Pārthasārathi says that this *vyāptiniyama* is known by inference (*anumāna*) [26] and shows the following syllogism:[27]

(thesis) Except [the cases already observed], whatever thing, past, future, or remote, has smoke, has fire;
(reason) Because it has fire;
(example) Like the hearth already observed.

Why did he accept two kinds of *niyama*, that is, *sāhityaniyama* and *vyāptiniyama*? Why did he give a different *pramāṇa* to each *niyama*? Commonly speaking, it is true that *vyāptiniyama* seems to be the so-called *niyama*. But it is not determined by perception, because perception can grasp only the object which exists presently and near. In order to solve this problem, he thought out that it could not be determined otherwise than by inference. If *vyāptiniyama* were determined by inference, and inference were accomplished by means of *vyāptiniyama*, there would happen the fault of mutual dependence (*anyonyāśraya*) or infinite regression (*anavasthā*). For fear that he might commit this fault, it was necessary for him to admit *sāhityaniyama* as the primary factor of inference, and regard *bhūyodarśana* as the *pramāṇa* to determine it.

NOTES

1. *Śābarabhāṣya*, (Critical ed. by E. Frauwallner, Materialien zur ältestn Erkenntnislehre der Karmamīmāṁsā, Wien, 1968 (Osterr. Akad. der Wiss., phils.-hist. Klasse, Sitzungsberichte, 259. Bd., 2 Ahb.), p. 30.18-19.

2. cf. *NR* (*Nyāyaratnākara* of Pārthasārathimiśra, Chow. S.S., No. 3, 1898), p. 385.5; *NRM* (*Nyāyaratnamālā* of Pārthasārathimiśra, Gaekwad's O.S., No. 75, 1937), p. 326.13; *ŚVK* (*ŚV-Kāśikā* of Sucaritamiśra, Triv. S.S., No. CL, 1934), p. 9.2; *ŚVT* (*ŚV-Tātparyaṭīkā* of Umbeka, Madras Univ. S.S., No. 13, 1971), p. 305.19-20.

3. cf. *ŚV* (*Ślokavārttika* of Kumārila), kk. 4-11.

4. *ŚV*, kk. 4cd-6: vyāpyasya gamakatvaṁ ca vyāpakaṁ gamyam iṣyate//4cd// yo yasya deśakālābhyāṁ samo nyūno 'pi vā bhavet/ sa vyāpyo vyāpakas tasya samo vābhyadhiko 'pi vā//5// tena vyāpye gṛhīte 'rthe vyāpakas tasya gṛhyate/ na hy anyathā bhavaty eṣā vyāpyavyāpakatā tayoḥ//6//

5. cf. *Vaiśeṣikasūtra* (of Kaṇāda, Gaekwad's O.S., No. 136, 1961), and III.i.8, IX.18: Praśasta pādapointed that this view was invalid and inadequate. cf. *Praśastapādabhāṣya* (Viz. S.S., 1895), p. 205.1-10; *NRM*, p. 325.14-16; *Nyāya-vārttika-tātparyaṭīkā* (of Vācaspati, Cal. S.S., No. 17, 1936), p. 138ff.

6. cf. *PV* (*Pramāṇavārttika* of Dharmakīrti, ed, by R. Gnoli, Ser. Ori, Roma No. 23, 1960), I,k.2, k.31; *Nyāyabindu* (of Dharmakīrti), II.22.

7. *PV*, I,k.9.

8. cf. *NR*, p. 348.2-3; *NRM*, p. 325.18-23; *ŚVK*, pp. 6.11-8.19; *ŚVT*, pp. 306.14-307.14.

9. *NRM*, p. 326.3-4 and ff.

10. *ŚV*, k.12ab: bhūyodarśanagamyā ca vyāptiḥ.

11. cf. *NRM*, p. 325.8-11.

12. *PV*, I, k.31.

13. cf. *NRM*, p. 236.17–29.

14. cf. *Sarvadarśanasaṁgraha* (of Sāyaṇa Mādhava, ed. by V.S. Abhyankar, Bhandarkar O.I, 1951), p. 17.2–6; Yuichi Kajiyama, *Tripañcakacintā*, Miccellania Indologica Kiotiensia, Nos. 5.6, Kyoto Univ. 1963.

15. cf. *NRM*, pp. 327.1–328.3; *ŚVK*, p. 14.1–15; *PP* (*Prakaraṇapañcikā* of Śālikanātha, ed. by T.R.V. Murti, Banaras H.U.D.S., No. 4, 1978), pp. 203.16–205.3.

16. cf. *PP*, pp. 204.6–205.3.

17. cf. *NRM*, p. 328.4–8 and ff.
18. *ŚVK*, pp. 16.14–15.
19. cf. *ŚVK*, pp. 16.20–17.15.
20. cf. *NRM*, pp. 330.5–331.14.
21. *ŚVT*, p. 308.10–12; cf. Karṇakagomin's *PV-Svavṛttiṭikā* (ed. with PV and Svavṛtti, by Rāhula Sāṃkṛtyāyana), p. 88.14-16.
22. cf. *NRM*, p. 333–1–4.
23. *NRM*, p. 333.10–12.
24. *NRM* p. 334.4–5.
25. cf. *NRM*, pp. 333.5–334.11; *NR*, p. 350.13–16.
26. cf. *NRM*, pp. 334.29–335.5; *NR*, p. 350.16–19.
27. *NRM*, p. 335.3-4.

7

THE 24TH CHAPTER OF THE *TATTVASAṀGRAHA*: REFUTATION OF THE MĪMĀṀSĀ DOCTRINE OF *VEDĀPAURUṢEYATVA*

J. M. VERPOORTEN

§ 1. The 24th chapter of the *Tattvasaṁgraha* (*TS*) of Śāntarakṣita (Ś) (725-83 C.E.) is called *Śrutiparīkṣā* 'Inquiry into the Revealed Word', and contains 725 *kārikās*, that is approximately one-fifth of the total amount of stanzas of the work. It goes without saying that it has been commented by the pupil of Ś, Kamalaśīla (740-95 C.E.).[1]

The *Śrutiparīkṣā* is a lengthy piece of controversy confronting

—a Buddhist who rejects the eternality of the Veda as well as of its components from the sound up to the sentence,

and

—his opponent, actually a Mīmāṁsaka of the Kumārila's persuasion, who regards upon the Veda as eternal and, therefore, entirely reliable and authoritative. It is indeed faultless and unerring because it has no origin at all—neither divine nor human. It is *apauruṣeya* (*k*. 2794 or 95) or *narākṛta* (*k*. 2085/86).[2]

The chapter is divided into unequal sections:

—*kk*. 2084-2350, the prima facie view where the *kārikās* are mostly taken over from the *Ślokavārttika* (*ŚV*) of Kumārila (7th *c*. C.E.).[3]

—*kk*. 2351-2809, the *siddhānta* or final view of Ś who seeks to prove the absence of the above qualities in the Veda.

The dialectical structure of the text, however, is such that neither of both parts is a plain account of a viewpoint, but rather an intermingling of statements and answers. So the greatest attention is required from the reader if he wants to trace at which point in the debate he is.

§2. From *k*. 2084 up to 2131, Ś lets the Mīmāṁsaka speak and expound a series of ideas significant for him. Among them, two remarks of dialectical import must be emphasized:

—the first one is made in *k*. 2096. The Mīmāṁsaka points out that the refutation of the view of the opponent (a *tārkika*, a 'logician') is tantamount to the demonstration of his own.

—the second belongs to the *P*. introducing *kk*. 2110 (=*ŚV Codanāsūtra* 93) ff.: the Buddhist is invited to join the discussion even though he disagrees with its starting point.

Out of the 47 *kārikā*s of that section, a number stem from the *ŚV*, even though they are sometimes quoted with slight modifications (see below ft. 15). These are

—*kk*. 2110-11 =*ŚV*, *Codanāsūtra* 92-3: it is not allowed to deny the validity of the Veda by reason of sheer malice (*dveṣamātra*). By lack of acquaintance with the Veda,[4] the Buddhist is disqualified to condemn it.

—*kk*. 2118-19=*ŚV*, *Śabdanityatādhikaraṇa* (*Śn*) 414-15 deal with the Recognition of the universal.[5]

—*kk*. 2121c/d-2125a/b=*ŚV*, *Śn* 418-19, 420, 416, summarize the reasons of admitting the eternality of the word.

—*k*. 2130=*ŚV*, *Śn* 422c/d-423a/b: the universality of the word does not annul the diversity of the things (f.e. the jar).[6]

§3. From *k*. 2132 onwards, a prima facie view (*pūrvapakṣa*) starts. It is made up of *kārikā*s also coming from the *ŚV*, but rearranged by Ś and ascribed by him to the Mīmāṁsaka who seeks to demonstrate that

—the various elements composing the Veda are eternal,

—the diversity-transiency therein is a false impression due to the presence of manifesting agents,

The summary of this long extract is as follows:

A. *kk*. 2131-39=*ŚV*, *Śn* 359-66: the word never perishes, cannot be destroyed. Refutation, *k*. 2742 and below § 10A.

B. *kk*. 2140-54=*ŚV*, *Sphoṭavāda* 22, 32, 34, 28, 38, 39, 40-44, 50-51: the letters are everlasting and there is no diversity in them. Refutation below, § 10B.

C. *kk*. 2155-68=*ŚV*, *Śn* 52-66 raise the problem of an all-pervading sound, of an *ākāśa* without parts etc. Refutation § 10F.

D. *kk*. 2169-72 = *ŚV*, *Śn* 42-45: the *dhvanis* ('articulations', Jhā) are the manifesters of the eternal *śabda* through the moulding (*saṁskāra* 'embellishment', Jhā) of the ether (*ākāśa*) or space (*dik*, kk. 2197-203) enclosed in the ear-cavity.[7] Refutation § 10D.

E. *kk*. 2173-81 = *ŚV*, *Śn* 119-30: the Buddhist is wrong to rule out any contact between ear and sound, when explaining the hearing process. Refutation § 10E.

F. *kk*. 2182-96 = *ŚV*, *Śn* 66-73, 76-83: the ubiquitous (*vyāpin*, k. 2184) auditory organ (*śrotra*) can be particularized by the *dhvanisaṁskṛti* so that the *śabda* is just heard by such or such man and nobody else.

G. *kk*. 2203-207 = *ŚV*, *Śn* 154-5, 183-87, 126-28, 122: the ear-cavity consists of space (*dik*); the differentiating agent allowing somebody to hear in his own way is the *dhvani*.[8] Refutation § 10F.

H. *kk*, 2210-13, 2209, 2214-24, 2225-28 = *ŚV*, *Śn* 172-76, 178-91, 197-201: albeit all-pervading, the sound is not perceived everywhere[9]; the necessary diversity is brought about by the manifesting (*vyañjaka*) *dhvani*; the *śabda* remains one (*na bhidyate*, *k*.2226), even if it comes up in a diversity of places (*deśataḥ*, *k*. 2227) or times (*kālabhedena*, ibid.).[10]

I. *kk*. 2229-32 = *ŚV*, *Śn* 217-21: the *dhvani* is bearing sound qualities; length and shortness of the *varṇa*'s (phonems) rest on the articulation.

J. *kk*. 2233-50 = *ŚV*, *Śn* 241-52, 256-63: the connection word-meaning is eternal.[11] Refutation, § 10G.

K. *kk*. 2252-55, 2256-73 = *ŚV*, *Saṁbandhākṣepaparihāra* 12-4, 21-42: there are objections undermining the theory of the eternality of word,[12] but there are counterarguments too avering this eternality versus the Buddhist doctrine of the word convention resulting in its impermanency. Refutation § 10G.

L. *kk*. 2278-301 = *ŚV*, *Śn* 278-305: the *varṇa*'s ('letters', Jhā, phonems) and their order are without beginning; that order has a usage eternality (*vyavahārāt nityatā*, *k*. 2287).[13] Refutation, § 10B.

M. *kk*. 2303-15 = *ŚV*, *Śn* 313-27: the Buddhist thesis 'Word is non-eternal' (*śabdānityatā*, *k*. 2303) must be criticized.

N. *kk.* 2316-20, 2321-31a/b = *ŚV*, *Śn* 343-48, 22-32: are also disputable the reasons adduced by the Buddhist in favour of the non-eternality of word, namely

—because it is perceptible by the sense-organs,

—because it is invariably concomitant with effort.

Consequently, the subtle or uncaused destruction is refuted and a clear pronouncement is made in favour of

O. *kk.* 2331-34 = *ŚV*, *Śn* 350c/d-53: the dual nature (*śabalākāra*) of the beings.[14] Refutation, *k.* 2750.

P. *kk.* 2335-38, 2340c/d-42, 2346, 2347-8 = *ŚV*, *Vākyādhikaraṇa*, 1, 108-10, 365-67; *Saṁbandhākṣepavāda* 2; *Codanāsūtra* 184-5 : the Buddhist negation of the eternality of the sentence must be rebutted. Refutation § 10I.

From k. 2337 onwards, the word Veda again occurs and the *kārikās* gradually cease being borrowed from Kumārila.[15]

§ 4. Now, some aspects of the concept of Vedic eternality must be stressed. *Nityatā* is conceived as

—a subjective consciousness stated in the words: 'I am uttering words that have been used be other persons' (*k.* 2290 = *ŚV*, *Śn* 293). These persons form the longstanding beginningless line of teachers and pupils.

K. 2678 may be held on as the refutation of the above opinion that is said to proceed from an illusion, viz. the recognition of the similarity (*tulyapratyavamarśa*)

—an absence of remembrance in reference to its author (*P.* on 2342).

—an absence of beginning and end (*k.* 2104).[16] This fact needs no proof because it has the nature of an absolute negation (*niṣedhamātra*, *kk.* 2430ff. and *P.*).[17] The negation of the two ends of the Veda amounts to claim its eternality (*k.* 2103). The Buddhist rejects this idea in *kk.* 2429-34.

Lastly, another way of paraphrasing the concept of eternality is to name it 'absence of personal origin', *apauruṣeyatva/tā* (*kk.* 2096, 2420, 2802 f.i.).[17a]

§ 5. Yet the eternality of the Veda is not sought for itself, but as the soundest basis of its reliability or authority. As a matter of fact, the assessment of these qualities is at the heart of the debate between Mīmāṁsaka and Buddhist.[18] In order to undermine the Vedic authority, the Buddhist claims the Veda to be a compilation (*saṁghāta*), a human production (*pauruṣeya*), like any book of stories (*kathāvat*, *kk*. 2137, 2420). It is unreliable because it does not proceed from an authoritative person (*āpta puruṣa*, *k*. 2337).[19] It has indeed an author, even if his name remains unknown (*k*. 2412).

Paradoxically, the main argument of the Mīmāṁsaka to bolster the validity of the Veda, the lack of an author, is, according to the Buddhist, the clearest proof of its deficiency (*P*. on *kk*. 2353 ff.), since the Veda has no doubt an author, and, furthermore, an author whose reliability is uncertain (see also below, § 9).

Now why is the Veda deprived of eternality? Because it presents itself in a sequential form (*vyañjanakrama*, *k*. 2420), like dramas and stories. Now in what is eternal, there is no sequence since it is unable to be manifested (*k*. 2421). Regarding eternal things—the *P*. says—there is nothing that a manifester can do (on *k*. 2494) and all the words are synchronous (*samakālatva*, *P*. on 2421, 2761-65). On the other hand, if the Veda were extant all the time, the cognitions it yields should be present for ever and arise simultaneously (*kk*. 2358-59).[20]

§ 6. The Buddhist adds further reasons in order to confirm the non-eternality and the non-validity of the Scripture.

—When the Vedic sentence is heard for the first time, it does not reveal its meaning to a man who does not know the conventions (*k*. 2373+*P*.). So it is unable to express that meaning by itself, and, accordingly, is not valid (*kk*. 2393-98).

As a matter of fact, the comprehension of the Veda is not supplied by its sentences themselves, but through the explanations of the human commentators (*kk*. 2355-56+*P*. = Jhā, p. 1104), acting as lamps (*puruṣaiḥ dīpabhūtaiḥ*, *k*. 2365, *P*. on *k*. 2772). Let us mention among them Manu and Vyāsa (*k*. 2380). Therefore, the Veda is made efficient (*prasakta*) through the help of personalities (*narāśrayāt*) and, thus, is their work (*pauruṣeya*, *k*. 2364).

—On the other hand, if the Veda is ill-explained, it ceases being the light of the man (*k*. 2374), and that is bound to be so because not a single member of the traditional line of pupils and teachers is capable of perceiving supersensuous things (*k*. 2378 : *yasmād eko 'pi tanmadhye naivātīndriyadṛṅ mataḥ*). This spiritual lineage, even beginningless, is just a line of blind persons (*andhaparaṁparā*).

—The *apauruṣeyatva* of the Veda, if there is any, could not prevent it from being unreliable and a source of illusions, since a forest-fire, though of non-personal origin, can have a blue lotus perceived as red (*k*. 2402). This is what is realized by all men of keen intellectual vision (*sūkṣmadhīdṛk*, *k*. 2410).

§7. There is also a complete opposition between the Mīmāṁsaka and the Buddhist over the way of interpreting such stock-phrases of the Mīmāṃsā[21] as

—*Svargakāmo 'gniṣṭomena yajeta* quoted in the *P*. on *kk*. 2084 and 2784.

—*Agnihotraṃ juhuyāt svargakāmaḥ* quoted in the *P*. on *kk*. 2335-37.

—*Svargakāmo yajeta* quoted in the *Śābara-bhāṣya* ad *Mīmāṁsā-sūtra* I 1 2, referred to in the *P*. on *kk*. 2345-49 and 2386.

The gist of those injunctions is embodied in the *k*. 2386, put into the mouth of the Mīmāṁsaka who is reaffirming his stand: 'The cognition that arises in regard to heaven and to such things from the Vedic sentences speaking of the Agnihotra etc. is found to be free from doubt and uncertainty'.[22]

They are also hinted at in the *P*. on *kk*. 2388-89, in order, this time, to be fought:

'The notion that the intelligent man has of Agnihotra leading to Heaven is just as uncertain as that of Agnihotra not leading to Heaven.'[23]

So the Mīmāṁsaka holds that the Vedic message is as true as a direct perception (*P*. on *kk*. 2355). It does not depend on a convention, for the latter is holding good for the words related to perceptible things and not to the ones beyond the reach of the senses (*P*. on *kk*. 2338-39).

Eventually, the view of the Buddhist comes out of his demerit (*adharmaja*), as he hates the Veda like an owl hostile to the light (*k*. 2350).

§8. But such a taunting declaration is not confined to the Mīmāṁsaka side. The validity of the *Śruti*—the Buddhist says—is emphasized on account of the false pride of the twice-borns (*dvijātīnāṁ mithyāmānavijṛmbhitam k*. 2351) As a matter of fact, there is no proof of the Vedic phrase being reliable, because in reference to the supersensuous knowledges, any assertion is acceptable (*tulyabalābala*, *k*. 2443). 'There can be no certainty regarding their existence or non-existence' (*nātīndriye yujyete sadasattāviniścayau*, *k*. 2389).

§9. The Mīmāṁsaka said that the Veda was without author because there is perception of none (*k*. 2087: *kartā tāvad adṛṣṭaḥ*). From *k*. 2412 onwards, the Buddhist undertakes to counter that argument. He declares that a lot of works were brought about by men who fell into oblivion. Likewise, the author of the Veda is not amenable to the 'non-apprehension' (*abhāva*), the means of knowledge that witnesses to the total absence of something.

On the contrary, the Veda, being expressive of clear meanings, requires an author (*k*. 2413). And precisely, the perception is said to reveal who he is, who are the creators (*kartāraḥ*) of the Veda (*k*. 2417). These are the readers (*adhyetāraḥ*, *k*. 2417)[24] or the speakers (*vaktṛ*, *k*. 2799). The Veda is—so to say—the outcome of their action. When not read, indeed, it is without any manifester (*vyañjaka*, *k*. 2417). The cognition of the Veda amounts to its interpretation by man (*vyākhyānāt puruṣāśrayāt k*. 2772) or to its remembrance. And the 'remember' is the creator (*P*. on *kk*. 2790-91: *karotiḥ-smaraṇārthaḥ kiṃ na vyākhyāyate*).

The practitioners, though, have their intelligence dulled by the constant contemplation of the Veda, and, prompted by false attachment, have failed to detect the sources of error therein (*k*. 2445: *mithyānurāgasaṁjātavedādhyayanajaḍīkṛtaiḥ mithyātvahetur ajñātaḥ*). They are misled by faith (*śraddhayā*), even in regard to things that are open to doubt (*k*. 2773).

In reference to the Veda's eternality, we may use a conclusion concerning an other question[25] and running thus: 'All this assumption by the Vedic scholar is absolutely baseless; it is not agreeable to the learned (*viduṣāṁ prītaye na*) and shines only among Vedic scholars (*śrotriya*)' (*k* 2536). How could any intelligent person (*prekṣāvant*, *P*. on *k* 2774) undertake any activity on the authority of such a scripture, 'the exact form or subject-matter of which is like dense darkness (*tamobhūta*) and for which only dull-witted persons (*manda*) can have an attachment' (*k*. 2806)?

On the contrary, the wise followers of the Buddha have recourse to their scriptures in full accordance with reason and not by hearsay (*P.* on *k.* 2773: *tatra nyāyam eva anupālayantaḥ saugatāḥ sudhiyaḥ pravartante na pravādamātreṇa*).

§ 10. Against Kumārila's claim of the eternality of each Vedic constituent (see above § 3), Ś argues that

A. *Gotva,* viz. the name *go* 'cow' envisaged as a universal and here exemplifying any word whatsoever, cannot be considered as eternal (*gotvaṁ nityam apāstam, k.* 2471) (Refutation of § 3A). It is 'through illusion that people come to treat and speak of the word cow (f. i.) as one only, regarding all as the same', whereas it applies to a variety of objects (*k.* 2614).

B. it is not possible to posit the oneness of the letters (*k.* 2482), and thus their eternality is not real. Each occurring of a letter is a separate phenomenon and not one of the successive manifestations of the same substrate (*kk.* 2483-84) (Refutation of § 3B). The letters pronounced by each man must be regarded as distinct (*k.* 2680). They are not eternal (*k.* 2734), for, only in this case, they are expressive (*sārthaka*), endowed with distinct meanings (*pravibhaktārtha*) and particular order of sequence (*viśiṣṭakrama, k.* 2781).

C. there is no eternal order of sequence for the letters and their articulations, both of which are deprived of any universal (*kk.* 2675 ff., refutation of § 3L).[26]

D. if the *śabda* is capable of being apprehended, that must happen without restriction nor instrument (*kk.* 2497-98), viz. without mainfester nor mainfestation taking place. On the other hand, the Buddhist argues that, if things are eternal as urged by the Mīmāṁsaka, they cannot be manifested,[27] for manifestation means some kind of sequential appearance, what is precluded for eternal things. Refutation of § 3D.

Accordingly, it is futile to assume tools of manifestation such as the *dhvani* 'articulation' or the *saṁs-kṛti/kāra* 'embellishment' (*kk.* 2506-08).[28] Refutation of § 3H.

E. the word-sound, appearing at sundry places, must be diverse (*k.* 2604); it is not grasped by a contact with the ear (*kk.* 2518ff.). Refutation of § 3E, H etc.

F. the auditory organ is neither part of *ākāśa* nor of *dik* (*k*. 2560). *Ākāśa*, on the other hand, is undefinable and vague (*k*. 2607). Refutation of § 3D, G.

G. an eternal connection between word and meaning is a groundless assumption (*nityaśabdārthasaṁbandhakalpanā vo nirarthakā*, *k*. 2659), and the opportunity of error (*mithyātvasaṃbhava*) is never missing (*k*. 2657). Refutation of § 3J, K, M etc.

This connection, far from being eternal, is a pure convention (*saṁketa/samaya*) between the speakers (*k*. 2620). The words, indeed, are unable, according to the Buddhist, to reflect and reach the realities. They are meant to point out the presence (in the speaker) of the desire to speak (*k*. 2618). They do not bring about the cognition of things directly, because there is no invariable concomitance between them and the external objects. On the contrary, they contain a certain amount of whim.[29] The convention constituting the relationship does not rest on the factors word and meaning only; man must also be taken into account. Therefore, terms like *yāga* or *svarga*, so significant for the Mīmāṁsaka, are created by the whim of man just as other technical terms (*vṛddhi* and so on, *k*. 2767). If the word were eternal, it could not be expressive (*k*. 2735: *nityā satī na vāg yuktā dyotakā*), because it would not have any connection with an order of sequence (*anupūrvyāyogena*) or a production in succession.

H. it is useless to define the connection (*saṁbandha*) word-meaning as an eternal potency (*śakti*) of producing the cognition of the meaning (*arthabodhajanana*, *k*. 2643). Such a view entails a great deal of difficulties and is conflicting with that of language as a convention (*kk*. 2640-51). The latter gives us the opportunity of explaining as well why a corrupt form (*gāvī* instead of *go*) is also conveying a sense (*kk*. 2667-69).

I. the sentence is not eternal either (*kk*. 2760, 2766). Refutation of § 3P. The joining of the letters in a phrase like *svargakāmo 'gniṣṭomena yajeta* is not beyond the human capacities (*P*. on *k*. 2784).

§11. Besides these reasons disproving the eternality of the Veda, there are some clues pointing out that it is a human work.

A. It speaks of wrongful sexual acts (*kk.* 2786ff.).

B. The alleged unique power of its incantations can be found elsewhere also (ibid.).

C. It cannot avoid the *kṣaṇabhaṅga* or 'Continual decay' of everything (*kk.* 2670-72, 2814-16).

D. If it is put among the non-personal productions, it cannot be true (*tataś ca apauruṣeyeṣu satyāśā tyajyatām iyam, k.* 2794). And the *P.* reads: the *apauruṣeyatva* is not a proof of truth (*apauruṣeyatvaṁ satyārthaṁ na siddhyet*). On the other hand, this *apauruṣeyatva* remains uncertain (*aniścita, k.* 2802).

E. Even if there is no desire of altering the Vedic text, this risk cannot be definitely excluded (*k.* 2674: *anyathecchāpravṛttau tu nāśaṅkā vinivartate*).

§ 12. Conclusion. The great gap between Buddhist and Mīmāṁsaka lies in their different approach to the supersensuous realities as evoked in the language. The former is inclined to deny them any existence since anything told in reference to them is uncertain (§ 8). The latter is willing to put his full trust in them because they cannot be sublated by anything (§ 7). Out of both debaters, the Buddhist, as an agnostic, would probably endorse the Wittgensteinian command: 'What we cannot speak about, we must pass over in silence".[30]

From an other point of view, the Buddhist is hampered by a conspicuous shortcoming: the absence in his ontological framework of the notion of potency, nay the denial of it. Hence he would not easily agree with Aristotle when this latter says: it is absurd to contend that a builder who does not build now is absolutely unable to build.[31] Ś is rather inclined to declare: the Veda is not a means of knowledge since it does not supply any knowledge by itself and at the very outset.[33]

At a still deeper level, such a conviction is linked with the tenet of the universal momentariness. Granted that each entity is either totally in actuality or completely destroyed, with no possible middle term,[33] every Mīmāṁsaka attempt at reconciling unity and diversity, eternality and temporality with the help of notions like potency or manifes-ter/-tation fails. So, 'When the perpetual Flux has been established, the Veda, as something eternal by itself, becomes cleary discarded' (*k.* 2803).

NOTES

1. In his *Tattvasaṁgrahapañjikā*, quoted below by the letter *P.* before the number of the *kārikā*. The *TS* and *TSP* have been published in a handy way by Dvarikadas Shastri, 2 vol., Varanasi, 1981-2, Bauddha Bharati Series 1-2, and translated by G. Jhā, 1st ed. Baroda, G.O.S. 83, 1939; reprint, 2 vol., Motilal Banarsidass, Delhi, 1986.

2. The lower figure is that of Shastri; the higher is that of Jhā. Below, the numbering of Shastri is kept and the quotations are made according the Jhā's translation which is quite satisfactory. For *apauruṣeya*, see below fn. 17a.

3. On K in general and the *ŚV* in particular, see J.M. Verpoorten, *Mīmāṁsā Literature*, pp. 22–28 (Wiesbaden, Harrassowitz, 1987, History of Indian Literature, vol. VI.5).

4. In a hostile debate like this one—the *Caraka-saṁhitā* says—it is right to consider the demerits of the opponent, e.g. his lack of proficiency, cf. E. Solomon, *Indian Dialectics*, I, p. 75 (Ahmedabad, Sheth Bholabhai... Research Ser. 70, 74, 1976-78).

5. Let us notice that *k.* 2119c is actually *Śn* 383c rather than 415c.

6. These *kārikā's* are not traced back to the *ŚV* by Jhā who starts pointing out the borrowings only from 2131 onwards. Let us add a few *ślokas* of K. occurring in the *P.* on *TS* 2084 (=*ŚV*, *Codanāsūtra* 13, 14, 191, 200), 2140 (=*ŚV*, *Śn* 422-3) etc.

7. =*ŚV*, *Śn* 150–55. Cf. K.K. Dixit, *Slokavārtika. A Study*, pp. 22ff, Ahmedabad, LS. Ser. 92, 1983; F.X. D'sa, *Śabdaprāmāṇyam in Śabara and Kumārila*, pp. 225ff., Vienna, Publ. of the De Nobili Research Library VII, 1980. The doctrine of the temporal and limited manifestation of an eternal word-sound is the means used by the Mīmāṁsaka in order to ward off the Buddhist emphasis on the immediate destruction of everything.

8. E. Abegg, *Die Lehre von der Ewigkeit des Wortes bei Kumārila*, Antidoron f.J. Wackernagel, p. 262, Göttingen 1923. For a definition of *dhvani*, see fn. 13.

9. D'sa, p. 127; Dixit, p. 23.

10. D'sa, pp. 117-18.

11. *K.* 2251 is a personal conclusion of Ś; *k.* 2305: a non-eternal word (*pratijñā*) cannot express its meaning.

12. The Buddhist view summarized in these *kk.* and enclosed in the *Pūrvapakṣa* held by the Mīmāṁsaka runs thus: the relationship word-meaning originates in a convention (*samaya*), cf. Dixit, pp. 19ff.

13. D'sa, p. 121; p. 119: a *varṇa* is nothing but *śabda* itself perceived through a particular perspective called *dhvani*. The difference in the *varṇas* is merely an indication of the observer's perspective; p. 120: *dhvani*=limited means of access to *śabda*.

14. *K.*2333c/d: *śabalākāram ekaṁ hi vastu prāk pratipāditam*. Those *pādas* are not found in the *ŚV*.

15. Further in the text, we still come across *kk.* 2776-78=*ŚV*, *Saṁbandhākṣepaparihāra* 136–39a/b and 2792=*ŚV*, *Codanāsūtra* 144. The variant

readings with both authors deserve a special study. F.e. *TS* 2124c *hyastanoccā-raṇo vāpi. . .* is a modified version of *ŚV, Śn* 416: *hyastanoccāritas.tasmāt. . .*

16. *Akṛtatvānāśabhyāṁ nityatvaṃ hi vivakṣitam. tau cābhāvātmakatvena nāpekṣete svasādhanam.*

17. Absolute (*prasajyapratiṣedha*) and relative (*paryudāsa*) negations belong to the logical devices of the Buddhist and non-Buddhist speculation. The former is pure non-existence such as that of the sky-lotus; *paryudāsa* is the fact of not-being this and consequently, of being that. On the distinction, see f.i. E. Steinkellner, *Dharmakīrtis Hetubindu*, Teil II, Anmerkungen III.98 (Österreichische Ak.d.Wiss., Phil.-hist.Kl., Sitzungsber. 252/2, Vienna 1967); F. Staal, *Universals. Studies in Indian Logic and Linguistics* (Un. of Chicago, 1988), pp. 110–25, 241, 253, 260.

17a. Derivatives from *puruṣa*, not only meaning 'human creature', but also 'personal being'.

18. The tight association of these qualities is borne out in *k.* 2431: just as the eternality (*nityatā*) of the sky-lotus is not real, in the same way, the reliability (*prāmāṇyam*) of the Veda also does not become established.

19. The word *āpta* is used in the Nyāya also for the authoritative man, M. Biardeau, *Théorie de la connaissance et philosophie de la parole dans le brahmanisme classique* (Paris-La Haye 1964), pp. 120-27. According to the *P.* on this *kārikā*, the Veda is as shown of validity as the words of a man by the roadside (*rathyāpuruṣavākyavad apramāṇaṁ vedaḥ syāt*).

20. We find here, applied to the Veda, a well-known scheme of the Buddhist thought, namely that an everlasting cause must bring about all its effects immediately and at the same time or never produce them. Such an extremist theory results from the disregard for such a notion of potency as that of the Greek philosopher Aristotle (384–322 B.C.). See below fn. 31. For the onto-logical implementing of the scheme, see L. Silburn, *Instant et Cause*, pp. 340–44 (Paris 1955); E. Steinkellner, *Dharmakīrti's Hetubindu* II, Anmerkung III.107.

21. Those phrases are not genuine quotations because they are not found verbatim in the Vedic Literature (Verpoorten, *Mīmāṁsā Literature*, fn. 83). The problem they raise is discussed by Śabara on *Mīmāṁsā-sūtras* VI 1.1–3. See thereabout J.M. Verpoorten, *Une discussion sur le ciel dans le commentaire de Śabara aux Mīmāṁsā-sūtra* (*MīmS. VI* 1-2-3), Annali dell' Istituto Orientale di Napoli, vol. 41, pp. 381–402; F.X. Clooney, *Devatādhikaraṇa: A Theological Debate in the Mīmāṁsā-Vedānta Tradition*, Journal of Indian Philosophy 16 (1988), pp. 277-88.

22. *Nanv ārekādinirmuktā svargādau jāyate matiḥ || agnihotrādivacaso niṣkampyādhyakṣabuddhivat.* Tr. Jhā II, p. 1115.

23. *Prekṣāvatām 'agnihotrād svargo na bhavati' ity ato viparītānyavākyād iva 'agnihotrāt svargo bhavati' ity ato 'pi saṁśayaḥ samāna eva.* The sentence '*agnihotrāt. . .*' which is still less Vedic than the previous ones, occurs again in *P.* on 2355, 2442.

24. The *Vedādhyāyana* or 'Memorization of the Veda' is discussed by Śabara in his paraphrase of the first *sūtra* of Jaimini (*athāto dharmajijñāsā*),

see J.M. Verpoorten, *Le premier sūtra de la Mīmāṁsā et ses commentaires,* Bulletin d'études indiennes 4 (Paris, 1986), pp. 353–66.

25. The one about the nature of the auditory organ which the Mīmāṁsaka says to be space (*dik*).

26. The Buddhist is inclined to support the notion of simultaneousness (*yaugapadya*) against that of succession (*krama*), *kk*. 2721–24; but in §10 I, *krama* is emphasized.

27. *K*. 2477. See also *kk*. 2493, 2600–04, 2610: that the articulations (*dhvani*) are the manifesters of the word-sound has been refuted (*dhvaninām vyañjakatve hi tat syāt tac ca nirākṛtam*); 2617: the idea that the word, though one, is variously manifested has been discarded.

28. According to the Mīmāṁsaka, the diversity is superimposed on the word-sound by the articulations (*dhvani*, *kk*. 2600–604), whereas the Buddhist puts it into the core of the word-sound (*kk*. 2594–98).

29. *K*. 2393: *narecchā; P*. on *k*. 2444: *icchāmātravṛttitva; k*. 2663: *narecchāmātrasaṁbhūta; k*. 2767: *icchāviracitārthaka.*

30. *Tractatus Logico-philosophicus* 7= last sentence of the book (English tr. Pears-Mac Guinness, London, 3 1978).

31. *Metaphysics*, Bk 8, 1046b 29: "There are some...who say that a thing only has potency when it functions, and that when it is not functioning, it has no potency; 1047a 11:...Thus these theories do away with both motion and generation; for that which is standing will always stand, and that which is sitting will always sit...Since, then, we cannot maintain this, obviously potentiality and actuality are different...Thus it is possible that...that which is capable of walking may not walk and that which is capable of not walking may walk..." (Transl. of the Loeb Collection). Didactical explanation of this theory in F. Copleston, *A History of Philosophy* I, pp. 310ff. (London).

We can trace the same shortcoming in the explanation of motion by Nāgārjuna, of. I.W. Mabbett, *Nāgārjuna and Zeno on motion*, Philosophy East and West 34 (1984), pp. 414ff. See also here above §10H.

32. See above §5 end and fn. 20.

33. Formulations like *k*. 2508: "Hence the cognition of that sound would either be produced at all times or it would not be produced at all" and *kk*. 2562-73: "If the word-sound did not possess the capacity to produce cognitions, then it could never be cognised by anyone anywhere. If it did possess the capacity, then it would be cognised by all men, at all times and at all places" are unsatisfactory and exemplify too radical a use of the principle of contradiction.

8

ACTIVISM IN INDIAN THOUGHT*

P. T. Raju

The often expressed opinion that Indian thought has had no activism must be false. But is it false? We can easily see that it is. There is a wrong impression in the world, which is due to several reasons, that Indian philosophy means the Vedānta, and Vedānta means Śaṅkara's Advaita; that the world is *māyā* for every Indian, who attaches no importance to the values of the world; that Indian philosophy preaches retreat from the world of action to the world of contemplation; that Indian thought is unrealistic and quietistic; and that the Indian therefore is made passive and inactive. For producing this impression, we in india are to a certain extent responsible. For instance, dozens of theses have appeared in the philosophy departments of Indian universities, but so far as my knowledge goes, not a single thesis has been produced on Indian activism. A thesis or two might have appeared on Indian ethics, not from the activistic point of view, but as imperfect Vedāntic thought; so that activism as found in its purity has not been brought to the notice of scholars and thinkers. Our chief activistic philosophy is the Mīmāṁsā; but there has been little research on this important school. Those who have taken interest in this school of thought are Sanskritists, orientalists and jurists: philosophers have taken only a passing notice of it. But the genius of Lokamanya Tilak recognized the importance of activism for the health and strength of our nation.

But should we say that this school is not important? One reason may be advanced for saying that it is not important. If all philosophy is *mokṣa-śāstra* or science of salvation, then the Mīmāṁsā is not philosophy, because it was not originally meant to be a *mokṣa-śāstra*, but a *dharma-śāstra* or science of duty or right action. It was a philosophy of *karma* or action.

*From the Address delivered at the Bhandarkar Oriental Research Institute, Poona, on the 17th September 1958, Ṛṣi Pañcamī day of the Hindu Calendar. Reprint from *Annals of the Bhandarkar Oriental Research Institute* Vol. XXXIX, Parts III-IV, pp. 186–225.

Later Mīmāṁsā writers accepted the concept of *mokṣa* and made the Mīmāṁsā subservient to the Vedānta, thereby making it an incomplete and imperfect Vedānta and so an incomplete and imperfect philosophy. The Mīmāṁsā preaches *karma*; but the fashion of treating *karma* (action) as subservient to *bhakti* (devotion) and *jñāna* (knowledge, gnosis) has grown. Thus by interpreting the Mīmāṁsā as what it was not intended to be, it was represented as incomplete, imperfect and so unimportant; and thus the very spirit behind the philosophy was lost sight of. But most of the protagonists of this school did not accept this interpretation.

Every philosophy, whether in India or outside, has claimed and is still claiming to have the final say in the matter and to possess the final truth; and it never has said and is saying that it is a handmaid to another philosophy. The question is not whether the claim is justified or justifiable, but whether it is made or not. In India, the Sāṅkhya-Yoga, the Nyāya-Vaiśeṣika, the Mīmāṁsā, and the Vedānta have advanced the claim. If any of these schools interpreted the others as stepping-stones to itself, each of the others also interpreted the others as similar stepping-stones. If we accept any of these claims, it is due to our own inclinations and convictions, but not due to the protagonists of the schools. Further, there is another feature of Indian philosophical thought, namely, corresponding to each of the four values of life, *artha* (wealth), *kāma* (enjoyment), *dharma* (duty), and *mokṣa* (salvation), we have four kinds of philosophies developed, called *arthaśāstra* (science of wealth), *kāmaśāstra* (science of enjoyment), *dharmaśāstra* (science of duty), and *mokṣaśāstra* (science of salvation). Of these four, the first two are not as well systematized into theories as the last two. Of the last two again, the first is not as well developed as the next. The reason is that the Mīmāṁsā, which devoted itself to a study of right action, was more concerned with the Vedic ritual of sacrifice than the other; and ritual does not easily lend itself to theorizing. And yet there is a vast amount of theory in the Mīmāṁsā literature.

We should note that each of these sciences or disciplines generally claims to be the ultimate philosophy and rejects the others. No one will question that the idea of salvation has developed the most elaborate systems of metaphysics; and everyone will concede that the idea of duty, though associated with, and even entangled in sacrificial ritual, has developed a philosophy. But whether the other two values, *artha* (wealth) and *kāma* (enjoyment), have philosophies at all may be doubted. It can be said that the former has a philosophy, namely, the Cārvāka. Madhusūdana Sarasvatī in his *Prasthānabheda*[1] does not mention it. But Jayarāśi in his *Tattvopaplavasiṁha* says that his philosophy is the sunrise of *artha* (wealth), meaning thereby that it is the supporting philosophy for the acquisition of wealth by all means and without any limiting principles.[2] I have not seen any such philosophical basis for *kāmaśāstra* (science of enjoyment). And I am not sure whether philosophical literature on *kāma-kalā* (should we translate the word as 'Phases of Desire' or 'Power of Desire', explaining 'Desire' as the desire of the Ātman to create?) can be made a philosophical basis for *kāmaśāstra*. However, just as there have been philosophies in the West to defend scientific values and their concepts, mathematical values and their concepts, biological values and their concepts, ethical values and their concepts, psycho-analytic values and their concepts, spiritual values and their concepts etc., there were philosophies in India for defending each of the four values and its concepts, whether the philosophies were equally well developed or not. Each philosophy was concerned with a value of life and claimed to be the philosophy of whole life. It is wrong to think that they were always mere intellectual exercises in system-building and formulating of doctrines in order each to preserve its own individuality and to refute the others. The idea that is more and more appreciated now, namely, that philosophers do nothing but create artificial problems and solve them by showing that they are artificial and fictitious, certainly does not apply to our chief classical philosophers. And I doubt whether it applies even to the contemporary philosophers[3] wholesale. It will be unfair to say that they create only artificial and fictitious problems one after another; they are interested in certain values taken by them to be unquestionable, and discover and face certain problems connected with them. The final difficulties in which each lands are not solved merely by showing that the problems are fictitious non-sense, but by showing that the value which the whole line of thought makes its basis is not the only value of life. Human life is wider and richer than any single value can cover.

The value which the Mīmāṁsā wants to defend is an indispensable value of life. Treating it as an ultimate value, this school developed its own doctrines. And it is an integral part of Indian philosophy of life.

How is it an integral part? All the orthodox schools accept the Veda as authoritative and claim to be based on it, whether they succeed in substantiating their claim or not. And whatever be the opinion of the followers of Jainism and Buddhism, both the schools originated in the Vedic atmosphere, which constituted their matrix. We can safely say that the Vedas are the origin and basis of our Indian culture. For a non-partisan student, the Vedas have four parts: Saṁhitās, Brāhmaṇas, Āraṇyakas and Upaniṣads. The Mīmāṁsā is based on the first two parts, and the Vedānta on the next two. Thus both the Mīmāṁsā and the Vedānta are equally important philosophies of life, and somehow were originally meant to constitute one philosophy. But if the Veda is one and has to give us one unitary philosophy of life, how can both the philosophies be true? Each philosophy claims that the other is subsidiary to itself, and the contrast between the two is sharp. The uncommitted student is perplexed. Attempts have been made to reconcile the conflict by saying that the Mīmāṁsā is meant for one of immature intelligence, and the Vedānta for one of mature intelligence. But this attempt is not satisfactory. First, the Mīmāṁsakas themselves do not accept it. Secondly, each school has a distinct metaphysics or theory of ultimates. And ultimates, when they conflict with each other, cannot be reconciled. In the third place, no metaphysics, whether monistic or pluralistic, can be for an immature intellect. One who can understand the intricacies of the Mīmāṁsā doctrines can understand the intricacies of the Vedānta doctrines also. If it is said that the two philosophies are meant for people with different values of life, we have said that any philosophy meant for defending any one value of life will remain incomplete as a philosophy of life, not able to explain and defend other values of life. In the fourth place, if both philosophies are true at different levels of man's maturity, then they are accepted with reference to man, whatever the level of maturity; and so the reality of man and his importance have to be accepted and asserted first and any philosophy that treats man as unreal cannot be true, for any philosophy given by a fictitious being can only be fictitious. Thus a new kind of humanism, unrecognised and unaccepted so far, has to be recognised as inherent in the philosophy of the Veda. In the fifth place, there is a final difficulty. The Vedānta, for instance, is said to be true for the higher level of maturity. But how is this higher level to be recognised? If the level is recognised to be the higher because it accepts the Vedānta, then we are arguing in a vicious circle: the Vedānta is true because it is accepted by the higher level; and the level is higher because it accepts the Vedānta. If it is said that the higher level is marked by *vairāgya* or disinterest in the values of the world, then this is what is questioned by the Mīmāṁsā; *vairāgya* is not a virtue but escapism, and life-long celibacy is not a virtue but a cover behind which one hides one's impotency. Then the only way open is to propound our philosophy independently of the consideration whether the reader's intellect is mature or immature. This both the schools claim to have done.

Thus the problem remains where it was. How can the same Veda propound two systems of metaphysics? I have not come across a satisfactory solution of this difficult cultural and philosophical problem. I can offer only a tentative solution. Both systems of metaphysics refer to man, as we have seen. We may then bring man to the centre of philosophy. We have to study him, his nature, and his relation to the environment both inwards and outwards. For man's conscious being is not exhausted by his outwardness or by his inwardness; it spreads both ways. This insight is not absent in our classical literature. The *Mahābhārata* says:

> *guhyam brahma tadidam vo bravīmi/*
> *na mānuṣāt śreṣṭhataraṁ hi kiṁcit //*

(This, I tell you, is the secret Brahman: there is nothing greater than man.) However this stanza may be interpreted, (we shall see how the Mīmāṁsakas would interpret it) at least for philosophical purposes, there is no more important concept than that of man to be used as basic and central, as is shown by the reference made to him for reconciling the truths of both the Mīmāṁsā and the Vedānta. Thus the inherent humanism of the Vedas has to be made explicit. This remains our task now, which is however beyond the purpose of the present address, which is to show that, if the truth of Veda is to be accepted, then the truth of the Mīmāṁsā also has to be accepted, whatever be the difficulties involved. To dismiss the Mīmāṁsā as meant only for the immature intellect is only a cavalier solution of the problem, which is false to the very nature of our culture. The Mīmāṁsā, therefore, has to be accepted as an integral part of Vedic philosophy and, therefore, of our culture. If not, we shall be unable to explain not only how the Veda is an integral whole, but also why and how our culture still survives. There is no life without action, and the Mīmāṁsā supplies the necessary activistic element.

II

Now, two questions will naturally arise. First, how can we accept the Mīmāṁsā with all the ritualistic elements it contains? Secondly, is the Mīmāṁsā activism? We may take up the first question first. The *Brāhmaṇas* deal with sacrificial ritual and so the Mīmāṁsā doctrines are entangled in the ritual. But our faith in most of the ritual is slowly disappearing. The sacrifices are addressed to several gods like Indra and Agni; but we now think that these are really inorganic natural forces without mind, and these fictitious gods cannot help us in obtaining results. The Mīmāṁsā treats the Veda as sacrosanct and as not composed by anyone; but we think that every statement of the Veda is not significant, and some are even unacceptable, and we cannot understand how any scripture can come into existence without being composed by someone. Similar objections were advanced by ancient rival schools also.

But the acceptance of these objections should not deter us from making a serious study of the Mīmāṁsā. Similar objections can be brought not only against other Indian schools, but also against philosophies outside India. Every religion has its sacred scriptures, and every school has its basic texts. For the reason that we cannot accept the dogma of Virgin Birth, we do not reject the teachings of Christ. Even Plato indulged in mythology; but for that reason we do not discard the whole of Plato's philosophy. Judaism is not less ritualistic than the Brahmanical religion of the Mīmāṁsā; and yet we do not say that the ten commandments are valueless; on the contrary, we appreciate the high ethicalism of the Jews. We may discard the ritual; but we should appreciate the philosophy underlying the ritual. We have to treat the rituals as examples of ethical acts. All philosophies developed in circumstances when man had a particular outlook. But when he tried to theorize, he formulated doctrines of universal applicability. In his doctrines also, he may be mistaken. Subsequent generations have the right to sift the true from the false, purify the doctrines, and develop them. But what is true and important also should not be rejected. The Mīmāṁsā represents one important aspect of India's philosophical thought, and that is activism.

III

Now, we may ask whether the Mīmāṁsā is really activism.

Ethical activism: The Mīmāṁsā is not an activism of the Bergsonian type. The idea of evolution, as understood after Darwin, was foreign to the minds of the thinkers of the time. The Mīmāṁsakas say that the world had no beginning in time and will have no end; and so the question of the evolution of the world does not arise for them. Even to the other thinkers, evolution as only a speculative idea may be said to be present; but evolution as producing the *ātman* was not present, which, if at all, can be traced only to the Cārvākas. Again, the Mīmāṁsakas do not derive the categories of substance, quality etc., from that of activity, as for instance, Bergson and the modern process philosophies would. Such derivation can be found among some Nairuktas. Yet, the Mīmāṁsā would regard the category of activity (*karma*) as primary for any explanation of the universe. Substance, quality etc. are accepted. The reality of a world independent of mind is accepted. It is independent of even activity; for all activity presupposes a pre-existent material on which it is imposed. But what is presupposed by this ethical activism is that the material world allows itself to be moulded according to ethical law by action; and further, that without action the conditions of existence cannot be changed. Kant and later Huxley were worried about the indifference of nature to moral law. Nature works according to its own fixed laws; but morality works according to ideals, postulates freedom of man to do or not to do what is required of him, and also assumes that this law of freedom in man and the laws of determinism in nature can somehow be reconciled. But we cannot understand how, and hence the worry of Kant and Huxley. But the Mīmāṁsakas do not feel the keenness of the conflict between freedom and determinism or morality and nature. They have for them the support of the Veda, the validity of which they do not doubt. If the Vedas say that ethical law governs the universe, they mean that the determinism of nature adjusts itself to the freedom of man. We moderns may not be confident of the conformity of freedom and determinism, and may call it the faith of the Mīmāṁsakas based on their trust in the Vedas. But we have to recognise that they have this faith and believe in the conformity.

Thus the Mīmāṁsā activism is not evolutionism. It is ethical activism. The world processes conform to the moral and the immoral, prescribed and prohibited activities of man by producing corresponding results. The freedom of man to do the prescribed or prohibited action is accepted; but once the act is done, the causal relation between the act and the result is fixed, and there is no freedom here. The act guides the processes of the world, which has its own laws. The Mīmāṁsā is activism so far as it asserts that the processes of the world are guided by ethical action: the controller of the world is ethical action.

God not necessary: Jaimini and his early followers do not think that for controlling the processes of the world God is necessary. Action itself as prescribed by the Veda is enough. If God is the creator of man and the world, then he should be responsible for all the imperfections of his creatures. So an omnipotent, omniscient, and benevolent God could not have created this world; or if there is a creator of the world, he cannot have these perfections. In fact, no creator is necessary, because the world is not created but is eternal. All that man wants is that the forms of his environment must be conducive to his happiness; and he can bring about the required forms through action.

Therefore, instead of accepting a hypothetical entity like God, about whose existence we can never be sure, it is better to accept that *karma* (action) itself as prescribed by the Vedas controls the world processes. *Karma* can control the world process, because it produces results according to its own good and evil nature. Thus *Karma* is made to occupy the place of God in the Mīmāṁsā. That is why we read

yam śaivāḥ samupāsate śiva iti brahmeti vedāntinaḥ/
bauddhāḥ buddha iti pramāṇasacivāḥ karteti naiyāyikāḥ//
arhannityatha jainaśāsanaratāḥ karmeti mīmāṁsakāḥ/
so'yam vai vidadhātu vāñchitaphalaṁ trailokyanātho hariḥ//

(May Hari, the Lord of the three worlds, confer the desired result: He who is worshipped by the Śaivas as Śiva, by the Vedāntins as the Brahman, by the Buddhists aided by logic as Buddha, by the Naiyāyikas as the agent of world-creation, by those who are versed in Jaina law, as the Arhat, and by the Mīmāṁsakas as *karma.*)

The Mīmāṁsakas do not accept God. But a unitary controller is necessary in order to see that the *karmas* of the different *ātmans* do not come into conflict. Hence there must be unitary *karma*, that is, *karma* must be one controlling the different processes of the world, obtaining stimulus at the same time from the different *karmas* of the different *ātmans*. Then the different *karmas* must be different forms of the same unitary *karma*. This is practically implied in the philosophy of the Mīmāṁsā.

atra jagatītalavartinī ekaiva karmavyaktiḥ. abhivyaktimātram tu bhidyate. athavā māstu vyaktibhedaḥ. śabdāntarādipramāṇaiśca āgneyādijātaya eva bhidyante.[4]

(In the whole world there is only one individual *karma*; its manifestations are different. Let there be no different individuals, that is, individual *karmas*; the universal forms of *karma* like *āgneya* etc., are different, because of different Vedic statements.) Thus in the Mīmāṁsā, the unitary *karma* is substituted for the unitary Divine Power.

Karma (action) then becomes the Divine Principle. God (Īśvara) is not accepted for two main reasons. First, the Vedas are not composed by anyone; they are eternal. They are not written symbols, but uttered words. Between the word and its meaning, the relation also is eternal. So, God is not necessary for composing the Vedas.[5] Secondly, he is not necessary for creating the world. For the world is never created and will never be destroyed; it goes on for ever. So no creator is necessary.[6] There is a relation between the two arguments. If the world is eternal, then ethical law also must be eternal; if the former is uncreated, then the latter also must be uncreated. And as it is contained in the Vedas, then the Vedas also could not have come into being at any time by being composed by someone. These two doctrines are known to every student of the Mīmāṁsā. They are held by this school, because it wants to give absolute primacy to ethical action, but not to a Being who is above ethical action and in whom ethical law has its source.

Injunctive sentences primary in the Veda: The primacy of ethical activity is supported by another doctrine for interpreting the Veda. According to the Mīmāṁsā, as it is to the other orthodox schools, the whole Veda is authoritative. But to the Vedāntins, the Āraṇyakas and the Upaniṣads are more important than the Saṁhitās and the Brāhmaṇas, because the former deal with *mokṣa* (salvation), which, according to them, is the highest value (*puruṣārtha*). But to the Mīmāṁsakas, *dharma* (duty, right action) is more important than salvation; and so they regard the first two parts of the Veda as more important than the other two. In fact, they classify the Veda into two parts only, *mantra* (which is another name for Saṁhitā) and Brāhmaṇa. They would include the Āraṇyakas and the Upaniṣads in the Brāhmaṇas.[7] The *mantras* are statements for recalling the things concerned at the time of performing an act. The Brāhmaṇas are statements enjoining action. All else is subsidiary to the Brāhmaṇas. Thus the primary sentences of the Veda are those enjoining action.

But Madhusūdana Sarasvatī, who is a Vedāntin, divides the Veda into three classes: *vidhi* (injunction), *arthavāda* (praise and blame), and what is different from both. The third comprises Vedāntic statements which are not injunctions.[8] The reason for this division is that, if the Upaniṣads are treated as part of the Brāhmaṇas, and the Brāhmaṇas as enjoining action, then the importance of the Upaniṣads, which do not enjoin action, is lost.

Then the importance of the Vedānta as preaching *mokṣa* (salvation) is also lost.

To obtain salvation is not a duty (dharma): Though Madhusūdana Sarasvatī does not regard the Upaniṣads as enjoining action and as consisting of *vidhis* (injunctions), there are other Vedāntins who regard them as injunctions. The author of *Prakaṭārtha* held the view that the statement, 'The *ātman* has to be realised', is a *vidhi* (injunction) or duty.[9] But Vācaspati maintains that it is no *vidhi* at all.[10]

The author of *Arthasaṁgraha*[11] divides the Veda into five kinds: *vidhi* (injunction), *mantra* (hymn), *nāmadheya* (names of sacrifices), *niṣedha* (prohibition), and *arthavāda* (commendatory and condemnatory passages). Of the five, again, *vidhi* is primary. Thus this division also does not give a separate place for passages on salvation.

In fact, it is the Mīmāṁsā tradition that only the injunctive passages of the Veda are primary, and the rest are subsidiary to them. Kumārila, who is the most popular exponent of the Mīmāṁsā says:

tasmād vedapramāṇārtham ātmā atra pratipādyate |
yadyapi prakṛtaṁ vākyaṁ vyākhyāyetārthavādataḥ ||[12]

(Hence for establishing the authority of the Veda, *ātman* is here propounded. But the present sentence has to be explained as commendatory.) The sentence here referred to is that the *ātman* is not the agent, but is beyond all activity. The doctrine of the *ātman* as propounded by the Veda is meant only for action (*kratvartha*); knowledge of the *ātman* is useful for action producing other-worldly fruit; and the other-worldly fruit can be enjoyed only if the *ātman* is eternal and can have other-worldly life.[13] And when man realises that there is such an *ātman*, he will perform actions producing other-worldly fruit.

ātmā jñātavya ityetat mokṣārthaṁ na ca coditam|
karmapravṛttihetutvam ātmajñānasya lakṣyate||[14]

(The exhortation '*Ātman* has to be known', is not given for the sake of *mokṣa*; knowledge of the *ātman* is meant for induction into *karma*.)

We can appreciate why realisation of the *ātman* is not regarded as a *vidhi* or duty by the Mīmāṁsakas and even by some Vedāntins. We do not say that one who does not care for salvation but, observing all the ethical laws, enjoys the values of the world, is an unethical person. We may call him irreligious, atheistic, but not immoral. The Mīmāṁsā was concerned with what it conceived to be right ethics, and was not interested in salvation. Nay, it even goes farther and says that even enquiry into the nature of the Brahman for the sake of salvation is unnecessary and unimportant, thereby questioning the value of the *Brahmasūtras* themselves, which begin with the aphorism, 'Now, the enquiry into the Brahman':

> *ahaṁdhiyā ātmanaḥ siddheḥ tasyaiva brahmabhāvataḥ /*
> *tajjñānāt muktyabhāvācca jijñāsā nāvakalpyate //*[15]

(*Ātman* is established by the cognition of the 'I'; it is the same as the Brahman. There is no salvation from the cognition of the 'I'. So enquiry into the nature of the Brahman is without any purpose.) Thus the whole of the Veda, according to the Mīmāṁsā, is meant for ethical action, not for salvation.

The ātman is primarily the agent of action and enjoyment (*kartā* and *bhoktā*): The main contention of the Mīmāṁsā is that the *ātman* is the agent of action and is the enjoyer of its fruit. Its nature is not that of a mere onlooker, but of the participator and agent. For this reason the *ātman* is equated to the *ahaṁ* or *ahaṁkāra*[16] (ego, I). On this point, the Mīmāṁsakas generally differ from the Vedāntins, who contend that the *ātman* transcends the ego. According to Kumārila, the *ātman* is the *āśraya* (locus) of *apūrva* (the potential state into which all actions enter):

> *ātmaiva cāśrayastasya kriyāpyatraiva ca sthitā /*
> *ātmavāde sthitam hyetat kartṛtvam sarvakarmasu //*[17]

(*Ātmā* is the locus of *apūrva*; action also resides in it. This is implied in the *ātman* doctrine, that the *ātman* is the agent of all actions.) That is, the agent of action is not the *ahaṁkāra* or ego as distinct from the *ātman*, but as the *ātman* itself.

But Prabhākara seems to have conceded that the *ātman* is not the agent of action.[18] Both Kumārila and Prabhākara accept that the *ātman* is all-pervasive, and what is all-pervasive cannot move and cannot act. But Kumārila says that the *ātman*, though all-pervasive, acts through its body:

> *sākṣāt yadyapi sambandho nātmano yajñasādhanaiḥ |*
> *tadāpi lakṣaṇāvṛttyā śarīradvārako bhavet ||*[19]

(Though there is no direct relation of the *ātman* with the instruments of sacrifice, yet the relation exists through the body, which can be explained by *lakṣaṇā*.) But the concession made by Prabhākara to the Vedāntins has to be treated as a provisional one and is not consistent with the spirit of the Mīmāṁsā. He does not concede that the *ātman* is not the enjoyer (*bhoktā*).[20] It has to enjoy the fruit of its actions: this has to be accepted.[21] But none can enjoy the fruit of the actions of others; and so it has to be accepted that every *ātman* has to enjoy the fruit of its own actions, which means that it is the agent of its own actions. Being an agent and being the enjoyer refer to the same subject.[22] That the *ātman* is the enjoyer is the basic idea, because enjoyment belongs to the inward[23] *ātman* but activity belongs to the *ātman* through the body. However, activity also has to be attributed to the *ātman*, because enjoyment and activity belong to the same agent. Moreover, even enjoyment is an act,[24] and so the *ātman* becomes an agent even then. Then why have the Vedāntins and the Purāṇas declared that the *ātman* is not the agent (*kartā*) of any action? Because it is all-pervasive and does not move.[25] Yet, action has to be attributed to it, because, it moves the body into action through effort (*prayatna*). And when the Upaniṣads declare, 'Not this, not that' (*neti, neti*), they mean that the 'I' cannot be grasped through any other cognition.[26] That there is no cognition at all after death has to be explained as only commendatory (*arthavāda*), but not as there being no cognition of the enjoyment of the fruit of actions. The Upaniṣadic exhortation that the *ātman* has to be realised is meant for *dharma* (right action) only; for one who has realised the *ātman* in its purity can understand the nature of *dharma* better than one who has not, and can become an authority (*pramāṇa*) for good conduct[27] (*sadācāra*).

Thus for both Prabhākara and Kumārila, the foremost exponents of the Mīmāṁsā, the *ātman* is in truth both the agent of actions and the enjoyer of their fruit.[28]

Action becomes the property of the ātman: Not only is the *ātman* the agent of action, but also action once performed becomes its property and gets imputed to it. For instance, we say that a person's conduct is the outcome of his character, and also that the character is his attribute. But we think also that the performance of a particular kind of action produces a particular attitude, which later on becomes a sort of attribute, and so a factor in the character of the person. This means that not only character determines conduct but also conduct determines character. As we shall see presently, the term 'attribute' has to be understood with a difference in the context of the Mīmāṁsā; for character, the Mīmāṁsā would say, is an attribute of the will, and is not an inactive quality like the colour of an object, but a force that determines activity.

The occasion for the problem was the difficulty realised by the Mīmāṁsakas that a sacrifice performed for obtaining heaven did not produce the result immediately but after death. In such cases, the continuity between cause (sacrifice) and effect (heaven) is lost. But there can be no causation without the continuity of cause and effect. Kumārila, therefore, says that the act performed by the agent assumes the form of *apūrva* (extraordinary state), and resides in the *ātman*. It cannot reside in the deity to whom the sacrifice is addressed, because it has to produce the result for the agent, not for the deity. It cannot reside in the sacrifice, because it is finished and is over. Therefore, it must reside in the *ātman* of the agent, which is to enjoy the fruit. If the action is good, the *apūrva* will be favourable: if bad, it will be unfavourable.

On this point, there seems to be a minor difference between Kumārila and Prabhākara. The latter maintains that the Vedic injunction commands one to produce *apūrva* itself by performing certain action, and the injunction to perform the action is not the primary one. But Kumārila maintains that the main injunction is about the action, which in its turn produces *apūrva*.[29] The reason for Prabhākara's view seems to be that the Vedas tell us what cannot be known otherwise, and the reality of *apūrva* cannot be known otherwise than through the Vedas; but when once *apūrva* is accepted, the injunction to perform a particular act tells us only what is partly unknown, because we do not know which act produces which *apūrva*. The reason for Kumārila's view seems to be that the Vedas ordain actions, because they produce some good results. However, this difference seems to us to be of scholastic interest; for both accept *apūrva*, though Prabhākara's view seems to be more conservative and orthodox. In fact, Śabara, whom both interpret, tells us that *apūrva* is the potential form of the power of action, which will after some time produce the result. It may at first be in the action itself; but when the action is once finished, it has to pass on to the agent. This seems to be in Kumārila's mind. But when it passes on to the agent, it becomes his property. We may, therefore, agree at least for our present purpose, that what both Kumārila and Prabhākara say comes to the same thing.[30]

The view that finally the act accrues to the agent and becomes his property is similar to, but not the same, as the view that positive law has its source in the individuals constituting society and is really their attribute. It is said that the criminal is punished, because the crime has become his attribute and he is called a criminal because of the attribute. It is not an attribute like the colour of a rose, but an imputed attribute or an ethical attribute.[31] It is a new tendency or force of his will.

In the case of the Mīmāṁsā, as there is no one above the *ātman* to punish or reward it, the spiritual world of the Mīmāṁsā is a sort of self-constituted democracy of the *ātmans*, each performing certain actions and readily accepting the rewards and punishments resulting from them—the act by accruing to the *ātman* entitles it to its own rewards and punishments. Hegel and the Hegelians say that the criminal's freedom is violated if he is not punished; and their view is apparently strange. But as a free individual of a particular society, the criminal has freely chosen its laws; and so it is his freedom that necessitates the punishment. Similarly, the Mīmāṁsā *ātman* freely chooses the results of its own actions; and the action necessarily produces the fruit for the enjoyment of the *ātman*; and this does not violate the freedom of the *ātman*, which voluntarily invites the fruit of its actions.

The Right and the Good: The conflict between the Right and the Good, which we come across in Western ethics, is found in the Mīmāṁsā also. In Western ethics the conflict can be traced to the Jewish and the Greek conceptions of 'what ought to be done' by man. The Jews believed implicitly in the commands given by God through Moses, and never allowed any to raise questions about their validity. They maintained that the commands were good because they were given by God, but not that God gave the commandments because they were good. The Greek mind would not accept such an idea, and always asked for reasons. It would rather say that any commandment, including even that of God, was right, because it was good.

A similar controversy is found between Kumārila and Prabhākara, the former maintaining the doctrine of the Good and the latter that of the Right. Indeed, both of them believed in the injunctions of the Veda as implicitly as the Jews in the commandments of God: to that extent both were followers of the Right. Both accept that, of the sentences of the Veda, those which are injunctive are primary. But in answering the question: Is the injunction a command to act (*kriyā* or *karma*) or is it a command to produce *apūrva* (merit, force of actions)?, they differ. Prabhākara says, that the definition of *dharma* given by Jaimini has to be interpreted as enjoining the production of a result (*kārya*),[32] not as enjoining a particular act (*kriyā*). But Kumārila says that the injunction is for the act (*kriyā*). Kumārila is, therefore, called *kriyāvādī* and Prabhākara *kāryavādī*. So far, Kumārila may be taken to be on the side of the Right and Prabhākara to be on the side of the Good. But Kumārila introduces another idea, namely, the purpose of action. The injunction is indeed for action; but the action is right not merely because it is due to a command of the Veda, but also because it is directed towards the production of the Good (*prayojanavat*). That is why his followers later defined *dharma* as

vedapratipādyaḥ prayojanavadartho dharmaḥ.[33]

(*Dharma* is that object which is beneficial and which is propounded by the Veda.) This definition omits the word injunction (*codanā*) and the reference to action, and retains reference only to the Good and the Veda. For it is emphasized by the followers of Kumārila that no one acts without a purpose:

prayojanamanuddiśya mando'pi na pravartate.

(Without a purpose even the stupid does not act.) But Prabhākara and his followers remain consistently conservative in demanding implicit obedience to the injunctions of the Veda without asking questions about purpose, and finally come out as the advocates of the Right. The result (*kārya*), which is *apūrva*, has to be produced; but we are not to ask whether the *apūrva*, which the Veda asks us to produce, will bring about favourable or unfavourable fruit.

Now, in ordinary language, an action is right with reference to the purpose, and the purpose, which is the result attained by the action, is the good. An action is called good also, but with reference to the good aimed at; and it is called evil with reference to the evil aimed at. But by itself, it is neither good nor right. But Kumārila's contention is that, if it is performed in obedience to the Vedic commands, it becomes right. But by introducing purpose, he turns the right into the good. But from man's point of view, the act is good, not because it produces something beneficial to man, because man does not know how the act produces the fruit and he is completely ignorant how it produces the other-worldly fruit, but because it is a Vedic injunction. In such cases, we call the act right, but not good. Just as Kant said that the rational will itself is the good, Prabhākara would say that the Vedic injunction itself is the good. Obviously Prabhākara is concerned with the Right, and Kumārila with the Good also, not merely with the Right, in the precise sense of these terms. We can appreciate Prabhākara's position. Ultimately, all the Vedic injunctions command man to accumulate *dharma* or *apūrva*. But the injunction cannot be of the form, 'Produce *apūrva*', as man does not know how to produce it, but of the form, 'Act in such and such a way'. The direct meaning of the injunction is therefore action (*kriyā*), not the result or purpose of action. But according to Prabhākara, the intention of the Vedic command ultimately is that 'man ought to aim at *dharma*, which he does not understand, which is known only to the Veda, and which is the result (*kārya*) of the act'. Man of course can understand the act. But Kumārila would say that, if man wanted the result, he should perform the act; while Prabhākara would say that man ought to want the result and so should perform the act. In this controversy much scholastics is indulged in, so that many of us may miss the philosophical importance. But we see that Prabhākara's position is more in line with the doctrine of the Right, fixing even the purpose of action for us, and that it is pressing the activism of the Mīmāṁsā into service of the Right. However, both Kumārila and Prabhākara are more or less on the side of the Right.

Activistic interpretation of meaning: Consistently with the activistic interpretation of duty, Prabhākara propounds an activistic interpretation of meaning also. According to him, the child first learns the meaning of the word 'cow', not by looking at the object when the word is uttered, but by associating the word with action[34] as in 'Bring the cow' or 'Milk the cow'. If the doctrine that the injunctive sentences and their meanings are primary in the Veda is accepted, then the doctrine that in ordinary speech also the meanings of the words are first learnt when associated with verbs enjoining action is considered to be a necessary corollary. Kumārila and the Vedāntins do not accept the view. They say that when an elder points to the object cow and tells the child, 'This is a cow', the child learns the meaning of the word.

One may think that the difference between the two views seems to be too scholastic and academical to be important. But as Russell says often, very important theories are based on what may appear to be simple truisms and unimportant distinctions. Dewey says that the test of any philosophy is its theory of education. Taking these two views with reference to the theory of child education, we may say that Prabhākara would support the theory that teaching should be done through action and practice, and the others that it should be done through imparting knowledge. If life is activity and is meant for activity (*karma*), then the importance of an activistic theory of knowledge cannot be over-estimated. In the context of educational theory then, we see the importance of the difference. Our present aim is not to be partisans in the controversy, but only to show that the Mīmāṁsā contains well-pronounced activism.

The doctrine of Prabhākara is called *anvitābhidhānavāda* or that a sentence consists of words meaningfully connected with a verb, and the doctrine of Kumārila is called *abhihitānvayavāda* or that a sentence is a meaningful connection of uttered words with independently obtained meanings. The difference is that, according to Prabhākara, the noun must have already been connected with a verb before it is uttered in order to form a meaningful sentence, and that, according to Kumārila, the noun and verb are uttered with separate meanings and then connected to form a sentence.

Nouns derived from verbs: Another important doctrine connected with the above is that all nouns are derived from verbs. Yāska says that according to Śākaṭāyana and the Nairuktas, all nouns without exception are derived from verbs.[35] But one Nairukta by name Gārgya and some grammarians do not accept this view, but say that some nouns are not derived from verbs.[36] Yāska, being the author of *Nirukta*, accepts the former view and answers the objections of the latter.

The Nairukta view is interesting, being an extreme form of activism and process philosophy. *Nirukta* is the earliest lexicon, which is at the same time the first work on semantics. Durgācārya, the commentator on *Nirukta*, says that grammar deals with the nature of the words, but *Nirukta* deals with the relation between words and meanings and is therefore more important.[37] Unlike the Mīmāṁsā, it is not a treatise on *Dharma* but on the meaning of the words used in the Veda; and so it treats the Mantra (Saṁhitā) as the primary part of the Veda.[38] Yet, the Nairuktas also, as belonging to the Brahmanical religion, regard action as primary, and maintain that activity is the essential truth of the world and every other aspect is a form which activity assumes. This idea is like Bergson's. Then, if language is to give a true picture of the world, it has not only to treat the verb as primary, but also has to treat all nouns as derivations of verbs. In every sentence, the noun and the verb are primary, and the rest secondary;[39] of these two again, the verb is primary and the noun secondary.[40] In the meaning of a sentence, nouns, adjectives, prepositions etc., appear as modifications of the verb. In other words, the phenomenal world, is adverbial.

In this connection, Durgācārya expounds an extremely interesting doctrine,[41] which he calls the secret of the Brāhmaṇas.[42] The truth of the world is Becoming, Activity (*bhāva*). It has two aspects, the causal aspect (*kāraṇarūpa*) and effect aspect (*kārya-rūpa*).[43] The causal aspect is pure Becoming; it is the same as the *Ātman*. It exists as pure Becoming (*bhavanamātra*) during the dissolution of the world when all the manifold of forms disappears. We might note that this is opposed to the Vedāntic view, according to which the *Ātman* in its essence is pure Being or Existence (*sat, sattā*), not Becoming (*bhāva, bhavana*). Substance, quality, the various mundane forms of activity (*karma*) etc., which are expressed in language as nouns, adjectives, verbs etc., are only transformations (*vikāras*) of the original Becoming. It is wrong to say that this original Becoming is the Prakṛti or Puruṣa of the Sāṅkhya. It is not even the atoms of the Vaiśeṣikas, which are only forms of Becoming; it is also not the Śūnya of the Buddhists. The pure Becoming as the *Ātman* is eternal.[44]

The forms of the effect aspect of Becoming, as explained by Vārṣāyaṇi and accepted by Yāska and Durgācārya, are six: birth, existence (being), modification, growth, decline (decay) and death (destruction). These six states are given for convenience;[45] there are many others, but they are further transformations of these six states of Becoming. What we have to note here is that existsnce (*sat, sattā, sattva*) is only a form, modification of Becoming. It is not pure existence that becomes something, but that Becoming passes through existence as one of its states or transformations. Names or nouns stand for existence and verbs stand for Becoming.[46] And because Becoming is the original truth of the world and is its essence, verbs are the primary parts of the sentence in which both nouns and verbs occur.[47] Thus even existence is a form of Becoming, act; it is an act that is directed towards the subject itself, and the verb is called intransitive.[48]

We can see that this philosophy comes into direct conflict with Śaṅkara's Advaita. According to it,

asti bhāti priyaṁ rūpam nāma cetyaṁśapañcakam |
ādyaṁ trayaṁ brahmarūpaṁ jagadrūpaṁ tato dvayam ||

(Every known object has five aspects: existence, known-ness, affective aspect or *priyam*, form and name; of these the first three are forms of the Brahman, the other two belong to the mundane world.) But according to the Nairuktas, activity, which is the essential form of Becoming and which is expressed by the verb in sentences, will be the form of the Brahman, and the others will belong to the mundane world.

Thus this is an important activistic philosophy of India. If the world is *saṁsāra* or an eternal flow of forms, then it can be explained only if its origin also is a pure process. The Mīmāṁsakas do not seem to have adopted this philosophy wholesale. But we can see that the Mīmāṁsā is closer to this thorough-going activism than any other orthodox school. Prabhākara's doctrine that the child cannot understand the meaning of a noun unless it has already been associated with action seems to be influenced by the Nairuktas. Again, though the Nairuktas treat the Mantra as the primary part of the Veda, Durgācārya says that this activism is the essential teaching of the Brāhmaṇas, which are treated as the primary part of the Veda by the Mīmāṁsā. So for both, true philosophy is that of the Brāhmaṇas, which lay primary emphasis on activity and *dharma*. Though unlike the Nairuktas, the Mīmāṁsakas do not say that the *Ātman* is pure activity (Becoming), the latter also treat activity in the form of *dharma* as the controller of the universe. It is difficult to find a more thorough-going activism than that of the Nairuktas, who wanted to turn it into a systematic semantics of activism. But unfortunately, this school has not produced much independent literature, entering into controversy with the other schools like the Mīmāṁsā; and so it has not been well known. The difference between the Mīmāṁsā and *Nirukta* comes to this: If we define will as self in action, then the Nairuktas will say that the self is the same as the will and the Mīmāṁsakas will say that the self possesses the will. In any case, the Nairukta philosophy goes to show that the first two parts of the Veda are essentially activistic.

Outlook of the early Aryans: The activism of the Mīmāṁsā, which is based on the earlier parts of the Veda, shows that the outlook of the early Aryans was one of eternal hope, eternal activity and self-reliance. Man considered himself to be the only master of his destiny. He did not rely upon a Supreme Being for his future, but on himself alone. He thought only of building up his *apūrva* or *adṛṣṭa*, which is mistakenly translated as Fate, because it is the result of his own actions. He felt that without action there was no life, no future, no knowledge even. And he was not tired of action, and did not think of retreating from action. Life and the world were an eternal process. Man was to build up his *apūrva*, and after enjoying and exhausting it, he was to build it up again and again enjoy it. The Mīmāṁsā was opposed to *saṁnyāsa* (renunciation) and even to a life-long celibacy (*brahmacarya*). Such was the origin of the doctrine of *karma*, which, ironically enough, later became the doctrine of Fate and resignation, and led to the doctrine of freedom from action and *saṁsāra*.

Exalted humanism: We have referred to the view of the *Mahābhārata* that the secret of the Brahman is that there is nothing greater than man. This statement for the Mīmāṁsā does not mean merely that man is the highest of all creatures, but literally that there is nothing higher than man either in this world or the next. We referred above to the stanza,

ahaṁdhiyā ātmanaḥ siddheḥ tasyaiva brahmabhāvataḥ etc.,

that is, the *ātman* is the same as the 'I' and that is the same as the Brahman. That the *ātman* and the Brahman are the same is accepted by the Mīmāṁsakas[49] also, but only for exalting man and not to make him an insignificant creature. Yet the 'I' is not the same as the body or the senses or the mind. The Mīmāṁsakas refer to Manu also, who says that the *ātman* is all the deities (devatās), the lord of everything, pervades everything, and like a wheel turns through birth, growth and decay.[50] Yet this circle of *saṁsāra* is not an object of fear and misery, but something to be enjoyed through ethical action. For

parāñci khāni vyatṛṇat svayambhūḥ|
tasmāt parāṅ paśyati nāntarātman||

kaścit dhīraḥ pratyagātmānamaikṣat|
āvṛtya cakṣuramṛtatvam icchan||

(Prajāpati created the senses as outward-looking; so man perceives the outward objects. But some great man desiring immortality, sees the inward *ātman* by turning back the eye.) This stanza of the *Kaṭha Upaniṣad* is interpreted by the Mīmāṁsakas as exalting man, not as merely exhorting him to realise the *ātman* within. If man consists of the senses and the *ātman* also, it is as necessary to realise the *ātman* as it is to use the senses: but one who realises the *ātman* should not give up using the senses. The difference between man and inorganic matter is that the latter has no senses, and cannot know the *ātman*; but man can. So in order to be a full man, one has not only to use the senses properly, but also realise the *ātman*.

This exalted conception of man is often more prominent in the Prabhākara branch of Mīmāṁsā than in the Kumārila branch. If man is really the Brahman working through the senses, then no cognition of his can be mistaken. That is why there is no false knowledge or error according to Prabhākara. For him what we call illusory knowledge is absence of knowledge. It is *agraha* or *akhyāti*, that is, absence of cognition. If there were cognition, it could not have been mistaken; for how can any cognition of the Brahman be mistaken? And has not it been declared, therefore, that all cognitions are true (*svataḥprāmāṇya*)? So when a rope is said to be mistaken for a snake, there is non-cognition of the difference between the rope and the snake.

Man is the Brahman acting—not in the dramatic sense—in this world. Hence, if man does not use the senses, he will not be different from insentient matter.[51] Thus the stanza quoted from the *Kaṭha Upaniṣad* is given a new turn in meaning: it is made to condemn a person who does not use the senses, mind and reason (*buddhi*), but is content only with the realisation of the *ātman* or the Brahman. Man is really a combination of the *ātman*, reason (*buddhi*), mind (*manas*), senses and the organs of action. He is, therefore, more than the *ātman* alone.[52] He is more than any of the other creatures including the deities, which do not possess one or more of these factors. That is why the *Mahābhārata* says that there is nothing greater than man. But this greatness has conferred on him the power also to misuse his greatness. Hence he has to be told what is *dharma* and what is *adharma*, the distinction between right and wrong. The Veda, the Mīmāṁsā, and the *dharmaśāstras* (ethical codes) teach us *dharma*, and *dharma* is right action. They are more important than any other system of philosophy. And man is great because he alone can perform *dharma*.

Deities inferior to man: The deities cannot perform *dharma*, because they have no body. Śabara says that man alone can perform sacrifices, not even the sages and the deities.[53] The reasons given appear scholastic: the deities cannot perform sacrifices, because sacrifices have to be addressed to deities, who cannot address them to themselves; and sages cannot perform sacrifices, because the sages cannot have *gotras* (names of founders of families) as they are themselves such founders. However, leaving out the sages,[54] who might have performed sacrifices during their own time, we can appreciate why deities cannot perform sacrifices.

But there is a subtle reason for giving a lower place to deities than to man, though man is asked to address the sacrifices to deities. As some scholars think, the idea of deities might have originated out of some kind of animatism or religion of nature, and within that religion itself the deities as spirits might have been distinguished from their bodies, which were the natural material forms. But still later when ethical law residing in the soul of man was conceived to be the controller of the universe, and therefore *karma* was considered to be that controller, the deities were made subservient to *karma* and its law. But if the law and the *karma* reside in the *ātman*, then the deities become less important than the *karma* performed.

We have already referred to a difficulty which the Mīmāṁsakas felt, namely, the *apūrva* which results from *karma* cannot reside in the deity to whom the sacrifice is addressed, but only in the *ātman* of the agent. It cannot reside in the objects used in sacrifice, because they are material objects and many of them are destroyed during and after the sacrifices. It cannot exist in the deity, because many people may address many sacrifices to the same deity, and it will be difficult to apportion the results to the different agents. Besides, some of the results are produced in the next cycle,[55] but the life of the deities is limited to one cycle. Again, it is not the deity which enjoys the fruit of action, but the agent of action. So the potential form of an act must reside in the *ātman* of the agent himself, and it is eternal.

Thus, in any sacrifice the act of sacrifice is primary and the deity, like the objects used in sacrifice, is secondary[56] (*gauṇa*). Further, in the controversy whether the deities have shape (*vigraha*) as we find in idols, some of the Mīmāṁsakas maintain that they do not have even shape.[57] They say

> *śabdātmakā eva devatā śabdabodhyā vā manaḥkalpitarūpā vā devatāḥ svīkāryāḥ.*[58]

(The deities are of the nature of words only; they have to be accepted as cognised through words or as created or projected by our mind.) This is an important advance made by the Mīmāṁsa from the religion of deities (polytheism) controlling natural forces. It is still accepted that the sacrifices have to be addressed to the deities, and that as such they are important. But they have now become mere names and mental creations of the sacrificer, and their independent reality is practically annulled. Has not Manu declared that the *ātman* itself is all the deities? Ethical activity has become supreme, and the agent of activity has become more important than gods. The sacrifice and therefore action has to be performed in order to produce *apūrva*, a kind of new transcendent will that accrues to the *ātman* of the agent and produces the results automatically. If the result is obtained from the act itself, why should one beg the gods for[59] it? The deities can at the most prevent obstacles to the successful completion of the act.[60] Thus the religion of animatism and animism, in which man begged gods for favours, is turned into a religion of ethical activism and self-reliance by the Mimāṁsā. Man and his ethical activity are primary; the universe has to be explained in their terms and is controlled by them. The deities are not merely inferior to man; they have become the creations of his mind.

Heaven only a state of happiness or pleasant existence: If the deities are only mental creations and names, then the so-called heaven is the name of a state of happiness, which is the result of action. The popular notions of heaven as ruled by Indra and inhabited by beautiful damsels etc., does not belong to the philosophical Mīmāṁsā. It is a state in which the *ātman* experiences only happiness (*sukha*) without any admixture of misery (*duḥkha*). It is the result of *karma* (action). As it is produced by *apūrva*, and as everything that is produced has an end, heaven also has an end. After experiencing heaven, man has to come back to the earth, and has again to accumulate *apūrva* through fresh action in order to enjoy heaven again. This is the ideal of life according to the Mīmāṁsā, an ideal of eternal activity.

Mokṣa or salvation: Though Jaimini was not concerned with *mokṣa* or liberation from the world of action, Kumārila and Prabhākara accept its possibility. Both recommend it to those who are wearied of active life and have lost attachment to the values of the world. But its nature is neither pleasure nor pain, but the absence of both.[61] It is not of the nature of pleasure (*sukha*) for

> *sukhopabhogarūpaśca yadi mokṣaḥ prakalpyate /*
> *svarga eva bhavedeṣa paryāyeṇa kṣayī bhavet //*[62]

(If *mokṣa* is of the form of enjoyment of pleasure, then it is the same as *svarga* or heaven, and so comes to an end.) But *mokṣa* is said to be eteral and so cannot be the same as pleasure. *Mokṣa* is, therefore, negative in form and nature. It is yet one of the values of life (*puruṣārthas*).[63] For though it is a negative state, people strive for it, as this world contains great misery also like birth, disease, death, and fruits of evil actions.

At this point Prabhākara supports the view of the Vedāntins that I-ness and Mine-ness (*ahaṁkāra* and *mamakāra*) do not belong to the *ātman* but are super-imposed on[64] it; but he adds that the distinction is not meant for those who are engaged in active life (*karmasaṅgins*). Unlike some of the other Mīmāṁsakas, he does not accept that the *ātman* is the same as the 'I'. If it is asked why did not Śabara elaborate this difference, he says that Dvaipāyana advised him not to distinguish between the *ātman* and the 'I' for the sake of those in active life; Śabara himself was aware of the distinction.[65]

Then how is man to obtain *mokṣa*? He is fo accumulate neither *dharma* nor *adharma* and should end or cut off both.[66] This is possible only when the fruits of both are exhausted. Then man should not perform prohibited actions and actions with self-interest (*niṣiddha* and *kāmya karmas*), but only the prescribed daily and occasional duties (*nitya* and *naimittika karmas*). The fruit of these prescribed duties does not accrue to him, for no reward can go to a person who refuses to receive it.[67]

Thus the philosophy of the Mīmāṁsā, which at first laid all the emphasis on action or *dharma*, gradually gave place to *mokṣa* (salvation) and developed the doctrine of what is called *karma-yoga* or *niṣkāmakarmayoga* in the *Bhagavadgītā*. It may be that the growing popularity of the idea of *mokṣa* obliged the later Mīmāṁsakas to give a place to it in their philosophy; or it may be that the distinction originally drawn between *kratvartha* (for sacrifice) and *puruṣārtha* (for man) actions in the Mīmāṁsā gradually took the form of the distinction between *niṣkāma-karma* and *kāmyakarma* (action without desire for fruit and action with the desire), for *puruṣārtha* can be interpreted as *kāmyakarma*, even though *mokṣa* is called *puruṣārtha*, for even *mokṣa* can be an object of desire. Even in the *Bhagavadgītā* we read

yajñārthāt karmaṇo'nyatra loko'yaṁ karmabandhanaḥ.[68]

(Man is bound by all actions except those meant for sacrifice.) The Mīmāṁsā writers often refer to the *Bhagavadgītā*, which is earlier than Kumārila and Prabhākara. But the Gītā idea itself might have originated in the original Mīmāṁsā distinction. There was a time when the Mīmāṁsā was called atheistic (*nāstika*), by which was meant that it was unspiritual. Kumārila says in the beginning of his work:

prāyeṇaiva hi mīmāṁsā loke lokāyatīkṛtā |
tasmāt āstikapade kartum ayaṁ yatnaḥ kṛto mayā ||

(The Mīmāṁsā has almost been rendered unspiritual in the world; and to bring it into the path of the spiritual this attempt is being made by me.) And all that he does is: establishing the reality of the *ātman* or spirit as against the Buddhists, and accepting *mokṣa* as one of the values of life. This is done by Prabhākara also. Though *dharma* is still stressed and action is still commended, we can see a little weakening of the stress on action in the admission of *mokṣa*. Yet God and his Grace have not assumed importance as, for instance, in the work of Laugākṣi Bhāskara, who ends his work[69] by referring to God and exhorting man to offer himself and his actions to God alone. Man, for Kumārila and Prabhākara, is still the agent of his actions, whether he desires *mokṣa* or *svarga* (salvation or heaven), and has to rely on himself alone.

Dharma in the Mīmāṁsā and Buddhism: The difference between the Mīmāṁsā and Buddhist conceptions of *dharma* is not only of historical but also of philosophical interest and importance. Their conceptions are at the opposite poles of each other, and so the significance of each can be grasped by contrast with the other. The Mīmāṁsā conception is activistic and the Buddhist quietistic. Kumārila says that *dharma* is *karma* itself; for Prabhākara, it is *kārya*: in either case, *dharma* is directly connected with *karma* (action). But the Buddhists finally answered that it is *nirvāṇa* (unagitated), *śūnya* (void), *vijñāna* (pure consciousness) and *anirvacanīya* (inexplicable). The Mīmāṁsakas wanted to explain Vedic Dharma, which they called Ārya Dharma. The Buddhist also wanted to explain Ārya Dharma, though they did not like Vedic Dharma. Both claimed to be expounders of Ārya Dharma, and both had to explain, therefore, *dharma*.

In between the Mīmāṁsā and Buddhism comes the Vaiśeṣika philosophy, which also claims to explain *dharma*. But what the Vaiśeṣika system means by *dharma* is different. It is merit. This is obtained by listening and cogitating over the Vaiśeṣika categories, and this listening and cogitating is an injunction[70] of the Veda, which is composed by God (Īśvara). Inthis system we have God,[71] who indirectly through the Veda gives the command to listen and think over the categories. Thus listening etc., constitute *dharma*, not by themselves, but by producing *dharma* (merit). Thus what produces *dharma* is also called *dharma*.

The very first aphorism of Kaṇāda, like that of Jaimini, professes to explain *dharma*. But this is not merely *pravṛtti* (action) as in Jaimini, but also *nivṛtti*[72] (withdrawal from action). Further, the Mīmāṁsā would not regard the attainment of *mokṣa* as an injunction at all; but the Vaiśeṣika would.[73] It is also interesting to note that Praśastapāda, the commentator of the

Vaiśeṣikasūtras, calls his commentary *Padārtha-dharma-saṁgraha* and Aniruddha, the Buddhist, calls his work *Abhidharmārtha-saṁgraha*; Vasubandhu calls his work *Abhidharmakośa* and there is the major Buddhist work, *Abhidharma-piṭaka*. All these show that by this time the word *dharma* was used not only in the Mīmāṁsaka sense, but also in the sense of *nivṛtti* and that of everything that was knowable and thinkable. Already the word had acquired the meaning of category. But the word is not so extensively used in the new meaning by the Vaiśeṣikas as by the Buddhists.

Most of us know Yamakami Sogen's observation[74] that the word *dharma* in Buddhism is a blank cheque which can be filled by everyone as he likes. It means thing, quality, activity, ethics, religion, law, norm and Ultimate Reality. It also means categories or what the Naiyāyikas call *padārthas*[75] (meanings of words). In no other philosophy is the word more extensively used in order to mean everything in the world than in Buddhism. It is difficult to say what exactly was the reason to do it. We may make a guess.

Radhakrishnan says: "In the Pūrva Mīmāṁsā the emphasis is on the ethical side. The ultimate reality of the world is looked upon as the constant principle of karma. God is righteousness or dharma."[76] Regarding Buddhism also, he says: "Early Buddhism had an implicit trust in an eternal right that dwells in the constitution of things. The structure of the universe is ethical. It is *dharmabhūta*."[77] One may conclude from these statements that the Mīmāṁsā and Buddhism offer the same philosophy of life. But as one can easily see, they are poles apart. Then why do they claim to be philosophies of *dharma*? We should imagine that by the time Buddhism became philosophical or even by the time of Buddha, the word *dharma* as a philosophical and religious term was on the lips of every Indian. The followers of the Brahmanic religion were contending that *dharma* meant *karma*, and without *karma* nothing could be achieved. But we have noticed that the word *dharma* means for the Vaiśeṣikas not only *pravṛtti* or action but also *nivṛtti* or withdrawal from action. Nay, they go even further and say that what are called *padārthas* are themselves *dharmas*.[78] Naturally the Buddhists take up the thread, and ask themselves what should be the ultimate nature of *dharma*, if substance, attribute, nature (*svabhāva*), form, action, law are all called *dharma*. Their answer is that it is transcendental and not something to be produced, but only to be realised as eternally existent, whereas the Mīmāṁsakas and the Vaiśeṣikas hold that it is something to be done or achieved. Thus we get the peculiar significance of the Mīmāṁsaka conception when it is contrasted particularly with the Buddhist. For the former the true nature of *dharma* is action; but for the latter it is an unagitated and indescribable state. The Vedānta accepted the Buddhist interpretation, and apparently remained at the opposite pole of the Mīmāṁsā.

IV

So far I have presented what is known to many, but for several reasons what has been ignored and neglected, namely, that Indian thought does not lack the necessary element of activism, without which our culture could not have survived. But this activism is on the whole ethical activism, not a pure process philosophy, which can be found in the minor philosophy of the Nairuktas. Right action is the controller of the universe; it is not the universe. Ethical activity postulates an objective field that is independent of man and his mind: this realism is present in the Mīmāṁsā. Ethics postulates freedom and autonomy of man, who is not to be a puppet dragged on to the stage and out of it by wires pulled by an invisible hand; it requires the conformity of a deterministic world to free action; and it requires man's responsibility for everything he does: all these requirements are met by the Mīmāṁsā.

And on the whole, the Mīmāṁsā is a philosophy of the Right rather than of the Good. Ethical law is not an inductive generalization on the basis of the Good, but a command of the Veda implicitly to be obeyed. In a sense, we may say, it is *a priori*,[79] because it is not *a posteriori*. The Mīmāṁsā, unlike Kant, does not attribute the source to the human will, but to the Veda; yet we may call it *a priori*, because the Good is to conform to it, but not *vice versa*. In this respect, it is akin to the Jewish conception, which treats the law as a command of God. Yet it is not theological, because the Mīmāṁsā refuses to accept God in this connection. By acting according to the Right, man becomes righteous; and righteousness, as a power or force (*śakti*), becomes his property, in the sense in which Kant[80] understood the word property in the legal sense. Property is what enables a man to enjoy, it is not an attribute but power or force, not an adjective but an act that is not yet actualized. Though the Mīmāṁsā speaks of *dharma*, it is really concerned with what originally in the Veda is called *Ṛta*, the Right, and the Right is what binds the universe into a unity, and therefore the universe conforms to the forms of the Right. The Right, it is thought, is known to the Veda[81] alone, which is eternal and eternally contains the secret of the universe that is important for man and his life; and that secret is right action.

Before concluding this paper, I should like to point to one implication of the doctrine of the Mīmāṁsā, which is very important for a philosophy of law also. It is often thought that, so far as jurisprudence goes, it is not the philosophy of the Mīmāṁsā that is important, but only its rules of interpretation and application of laws. This, I think, cannot be the complete truth. Even the rules of interpretation and application must have been based on philosophy and must have a theory behind them. The complete truth has not been brought out decause the jurists are generally not very much interested in philosophy and philosophers have not recognised the importance of the Mīmāṁsā. The *dharmaśāstras*, with which the jurists are mainly concerned, are not philosophical works in the sense in which we usually understand them, and are generally studied without reference to Mīmāṁsā philosophy. But the philosophy of the *dharmaśāstras* cannot be understood without knowing the philosophy of the Mīmāṁsā. First, the Mīmāṁsā, the *dharmasūtras* and the *dharmaśāstras* all deal with *dharma*. Secondly, all claim to be *karmayogaśāstras*, and Manu explicitly says that his work is on *karmayoga* (way of action). In the third place, the *dharmaśāstras* are extensions of the concept of *dharma* to fields not covered by the Mīmāṁsā. The Mīmāṁsā deals with actions producing mainly other-worldly results; but the *dharmaśāstras* particularly have to deal with actions producing this-worldly results also like punishments for crimes, legalizations of social practices, and enforcement of law in general. But the concept of *dharma* underlying all is the same. The philosophy of Hindu jurisprudence, therefore, is the philosophy of *dharma* as expounded by the Mīmāṁsā, which all the writers of the *dharmaśāstras* accept.

There are many philosophical questions concerning law. The mutual relation between law, action, and man is one such question. The origin of law is another. We have to ask ourselves whether we can find answers to such questions in the Mīmāṁsā philosophy, apart from whatever semi-philosophical and mythological answers have been given by the *dharmaśāstras*. So far, there has perhaps been no discussion of this topic in a philosophically systematic manner. In the *dharmaśāstras* we find that the authors derive their laws from the Vedas, the *Smṛtis*, and customs of groups living at the time. This is the general practice of the law-givers, though they add that one may follow, in cases not covered by the above three, great men and one's own desires. To group all the five is not a philosophical derivation. A metaphysical derivation of law can be found, if at all, only in the Mīmāṁsā. For a satisfactory exposition a deeper study of concept of *dharma* in all its aspects is wanted. But we may try to get a clue.

Dharma, according to the Mīmāṁsā, is either action (according to Kumārila) or *kārya* (result of action, according to Prabhākara). In either case, it is not the law. The law is the command of the Veda. So the source of law is the Veda. But when it is asked why the Veda gives a particular cammand, Kumārila at least answers that it is for the Good of man. Yet the good is not a *siddha* (ready-made, accomplished) as it is for Buddhism, but *sādhya* (to be accomplished). The source of law is, therefore, something that issues commands, which we may interpret as the Will of the universe; and in the words of the Mīmāṁsā, which gives the highest importance to *śabda* (word) and verbal knowledge, we may say that the Veda is the embodiment of the Universal Will in words.

This interpretation is supported by their conception of *apūrva*. *Apūrva* is the latent form, potency, which *karma* (action) becomes before producing the results. And it resides in the *ātman* of the agent of action, neither in gods nor in objects used in action. Now, what is its nature? The Vaiśeṣikas say that it is nothing but *adṛṣṭa* in the form of *dharma* (merit) and *adharma* (demerit), and these two are qualities, attributes, *guṇas* of the *ātman*. That is, by performing an act, the *ātman* obtains a new quality in the form of *dharma* or *adharma*. But the Mīmāṁsakas do not accept this view.[82] They say that *apūrva* is not a *guṇa* of the *ātman*, but its potency. It is described as

> *apūrvam yāgānantaravyāpāraḥ kiṁvā yāgajanyā kācit śaktiḥ kartṛsamavāyinī.*[83]

(*Apūrva* is a mediating activity after the sacrifice. Or rather it is a force produced by the sacrifice and residing in the agent.) The Mīmāṁsakas, consistently with their activism, are opposed to reducing force to inactive quality like colour. *Apūrva* is a new force accruing to the *ātman* and transforms itself into the result. But the force or power or energy of the *ātman* is what we can safely interpret as will. But this will can be produced only through action, not by imagination or contemplation. It is not what we call a mere wish. The Vedic command is a command to generate a will, of whose work the agent may or may not be conscious; it is a will that works and produces effects, whether the agent is or is not conscious of its processes. It works spontaneously according to the law of Right that controls the universe. We know from our own experience that in habitual actions our wills work automatically without our deliberation.

Ethical command or law is, therefore, a unit of the will, just as a proposition or judgment is a unit of thought or cognition. Thus action, *dharma* and *adharma* are not accepted by the Mīmāṁsā as attributes of man, but as forces, potencies or energies. Now, can we apply this conception to cases of positive law? The Vedic command to man may be interpreted, as Prabhākara would do, to produce a will in himself as commanded. If the *dharmaśāstras* as legal codes are to be interpreted in conformity with the Mīmāṁsā conception of *dharma*, then positive law also will be a command to produce a will in conformity with the social[84] will as recorded in tne *dharmaśāstras*. A will thus produced will transform itself into desirable social acceptance of man and the resulting advantages. A criminal produces the opposite kind of will which transforms itself into undesirable social reception and the resulting disadvantages. The phrase 'the will transforming itself' may sound strange. But what the Mīmāṁsā would mean is that the criminal wills his own punishment, and the law-abider wills his own social acceptance. The Mīmāṁsā would not accept that the criminal is punished by society because he obtains a new attribute or quality called 'evil' or 'criminal', but because he produces a will, a potency, that produces its own punishment. Such would be an activistic philosophy of law. And this philosophy is well-worth being worked out, as it has been the implicit basis of our law. I am here giving only a clue to what seems to be a very important basic doctrine of legal philosophy.

In fact the Mīmāṁsā philosophy of ethics and law does not easily fit into any of the well-known Western schools of law. In a way, it is what Holland calls both ethics and nomology.[85] It is ethics, because, external legislation of its law is not possible and it is nomology because conformity of action to laws is demanded. But in a way it is neither; it is not ethics, because there is no explicit demand for conformity of human character to a type, and there is very little discussion of character which is a quality of man's will and all the stress is on action; and it is not nomology because there is no external legislation for all the acts it enjoins. It is actually a combination of both; and the *dharmaśāstras* also are such combinations. Yet there is a system of thought, ethical and legal, implicit in the Mīmāṁsā and the *dharmaśāstras* taken together. And a new line of philosophical activity is needed to bring it out.

It is not my aim to discuss and present the philosophy of the Mīmāṁsā and its sub-schools and their internal differences. My main aim is to present the activistic tendencies in our thought and culture, and contradict the opinion that India has had no activism, that all its philosophies are only *mokṣaśāstras*, that there has been no ethical philosophy, that the conception of the Right as distinct from that of the Good is absent from Indian thought and that Indian thought has to be interpreted as contemplative quietism. Till recently I myself followed this line of thinking. The more we think, read, talk and write about contemplation and the less about action, the more we tend to think that action is unimportant in this world and wishes can produce results. Now that we have attained independence and are ourselves responsible for our future, it is time to read, talk, think and write about action at least as much as about contemplation. We should see that the golden ages in the history of India followed revolts of activism against quietism; and disasters followed when some quietistic philosophy of life gained ascendance. We may draw a lesson from our own history. In this context at least it is necessary to think or re-think what our classical activists thought, which is found right in the Vedic philosophies. This paper is not a plea for the revival of sacrificial ritual but for a revival of activistic thought in order to have a balanced view of life.

NOTES

1. Printed at the end of *Sarvadarśanasaṁgraha* (Anandasrama Press, Poona, 192?).

2. *Tattvopaplavasiṁha*, p. 125 (Gaekwad Oriental Series, Baroda). Jayarāśi calls his book *mahārthodaya*, and says that, as all the doctrines of the ethical and spiritual philosophies are refuted, all kinds of activity are justified. Without any scruple, one can do what one likes in order to obtain wealth.

3. Cp. the philosophies of idealists, realists, analysts, logical positivists, existentialists, humanists etc. Each school wants to stress the importance of a particular aspect of experience and value, which the others want to explain away. But a healthy and complete culture needs all; even eclecticism is less unhealthy than one-sidedness so far as life and culture go, and is generally a sign of approaching synthesis.

4. *Mīmāṁsākośa*, p. 1399, by Kevalananda Sarasvati (Prājña Pāṭhaśālā Maṇḍala, Wai, District N. Satara, 1954). Quoted from *Bhaṭṭadīpikā* of Khaṇḍadeva. According to *Ṛjuvimalā* also *karma* is *nityānumeyam*. *Op. Cit.*

5. *Śāstradīpikā* of Pārthasārathi Miśra, pp. 465 foll. (Chowkhamba Sanskrit Series, Banaras, 1913).

6. *Ibid.*, p. 310.

7. Kṛṣṇa Yajvan's *Mīmāṁsā Paribhāṣā*, p. 2 (edited and translated by Madhavananda, Ramakrishna Mission, Sarada Pith, Belur, 1948).

8. *Prasthānabheda*, pp. 2-3.

9. Appaya Dīkṣita's *Siddhāntaleśasaṁgraha*, pp. 8 foll. (Chowkhamba Sanskrit Series, Banaras, 1916).

10. *Ibid.*, p. 32.

11. P. 31. (Oriental Book Agency, Poona, 1932).

12. Quoted by Rāmakṛṣṇa in his Commentary on *Śāstradīpikā*, p. 340.

13. *Ibid.*, p. 373.

14. *Ibid.*, p. 374.

15. Quoted by *Sarvadarśanasaṁgraha*, p. 147. This stanza is attributed to *Ācārya*', perhaps Upavarṣa.

16. *Śāstradīpikā*, p. 350. Prabhākara seems to think that the *ātman* is not directly (*sākṣāt*) known through the cognition of the 'I', but only through *śabda* (word) (*Bṛhatī*, p. 175). For the present we may ignore this difference.

17. Quoted in the *Mīmāṁsākośa*, p. 888. See also pp. 894 and 900.
18. *Ibid.*, pp. 895-96.
19. Quoted by Rāmakṛṣṇa in his Commentary on *Śāstradīpikā*, p. 338.
20. *Mīmāṁsākośa*, p. 904. Also *Bṛhatī*, p. 173.
21. *Op. cit.*
22. *Mīmāṁsākośa*, p. 907. *sarvatra hi kartṛbhoktṛśabdayoḥ sāmānyādhikaraṇyam dṛśyate.*
23. *Ibid.*, p. 905. *pratyagātmani bhogadarśanāt.* See also *Bṛhatī*, p. 174.
24. *Mīmāṁsākośa*, p. 904. *yo bhoktāramabhyupagacchati abhyupagacchati asau bhuktirūpāṁ kriyām.*
25. *Ibid.*, p. 908.
26. *Ibid.*, p. 906. See also *Bṛhatī*, pp. 168 and 181. (The *Bṛhatī* referred to all along belongs to the Chowkhamba Sanskrit Series, Banaras, 1932).
27. *etena vaidikānantadharmadhīsaṁskṛtātmanām /*
ātmatuṣṭeḥ pramāṇatvaṁ prasiddhaṁ dharmaśuddhaye. //
Mīmāṁsākośa, p. 896.
28. *Bṛhatī*, pp. 163 and 173.
29. *Mānameyarahasyaślokavārtikam*, p. 201 (by L. Srinivasacharya, Government Press, Mysore, 1925).
30. G.N. Jha: *Pūrvamīmāṁsā*, p. 260. (Banaras Hindu University, Banaras, 1942).
31. The Vaiśeṣikas accept that *dharma* and *adharma* are qualities of the *ātman* and so its attributes. But the Mīmāṁsakas reject this view. Cp. also the view of Leon Petrazycki that morality is imperative and law is attributive-imperative. (*Law and Morality*, p. xxiv, tr. by N.S. Timasheff, Harvard Univeristy Press, 1955). We have to note that the Mīmāṁsā is the source of both morality and jurisprudence in India.
32. *Bṛhatī*, p. 16. *kārye arthe vedasya prāmāṇyam.*
33. Laugākṣi Bhāskara: *Arthasaṁgrahaḥ*, p. 7.
34. Bhavadeva: *Tautātitamatatilaka*, pp. 5 foll. (Government Sanskrit Library, Banaras, 1939).
35. *Nirukta*, p. 56 (Sri Venkateswar Press, Bombay, 1947).
36. *Op. cit.*
37. *Ibid.*, p. 3.
38. *Ibid.*, p. 3. *brāhmaṇam api ca vidhyarthavādarūpam aśeṣamantrārthaśeṣabhūtameva.* The Mīmāṁsakas also say that in *pāṭha* (study), Mantra is primary. Āpadeva: *Mīmāṁsā-nyāyaprakāśa*, pp. 92-3 (Chowkhamba Sanskrit Series Banaras, 1949).
39. *Nirukta*, p. 8
40. *Ibid.*, 10.
41. *Ibid.*, pp. 21-2.
42. *Ibid.*, p. 22. *saṁsūcito vedarahasyo brāhmaṇaiḥ.*
43. *Op. cit.*, *dvividho bhāvaḥ kāraṇarūpaḥ kāryarūpaśca.*
44. *Ibid.*, p. 22. *bhavaterātmabhāvena idaṁ jagannityam.*
45. *Ibid.*, 23.
46. *Ibid.*, p. 9. *bhavapradhānam ākhyātaṁ sattvapradhānāni nāmāni.*

47. *Ibid.*, p. 13. *tadyatra ubhe bhāvapradhāne bhavataḥ.*

48. The root for 'exist' is $\sqrt{}$*as*, from which the English word 'is' is derived; and the root for 'become' is $\sqrt{}$*bhū*, from which the English word 'be' is derived. In these philosophies the two words retain their different meanings. But in literary Sanskrit, as in English, the two words are used indifferently. But the distinction is very important for the Nairuktas, who advocate a philosophy of absolutist activism, equating pure activity with the *Ātman* itself.

49. *Śāstradīpikā*, p. 351.

50. *Sāṁskṛtika Vyākhyāna Pañcikā*, p. 92. (Manavasrama, Durgapura, Jaipur, 1958). This work constituted five lectures given by Moti Lal Sarma, a leading contemporary Mīmāṁsaka, before the President of India. It is in Hindi and Sanskrit.

51. *Sāṁskṛtika Vyākhyāna Pañcikā*, p. 96.

52. *Ibid.*, p. 90.

53. G.N. Jha: *Pūrvamīmāṁsā*, pp. 306-7.

54. *Op. cit.*, See Pārthasārathi Miśra's opinion.

55. *Mīmāṁsākośa*, p. 2126.

56. *Ibid.*, 2123.

57. *Ibid.*, 2122.

58. *Op. cit.*

59. *Ibid.*, 2122.

60. *Op. cit.*

61. *tasmāt sukhaduḥkhasamastavaiśeṣikaguṇocchedo mokṣaḥ—Śāstradīpikā*, p. 372.

62. Quoted from *Ślokavārtika* by the commentary on *Śāstradīpikā*. p. 361.

63. *Ibid.*, p. 369.

64. *Bṛhatī*, p. 187.

65. *Op. cit.*

66. *Śāstradīpikā*, p. 372.

67. *Ibid.*, p. 361.

68. III.9.

69. *Arthasaṁgraha.*

70. *Vaiśeṣikadarśana* with Praśastapāda's commentary, p. 20. (Chowkhamba Sanskrit Series, Banaras, 1934).

71. *Ibid.*, p. 6.

72. *Vaiśeṣikadarśana* with Śaṅkara Miśra's commentary, p. 4 (Chowkhamba Sanskrit Series, Banaras, 1923) *sa ca dharmo nivṛttilakṣaṇo vakṣyate.*

73. *Op. cit.*, *yadi tu nididhyāsanādiyogasādhyo dharmaḥ adṛṣṭameva tadā vidhirūpaḥ.*

74. *Systems of Buddhistic Thought*, pp. 213-4 (Calcutta University Press, 1912).

75. *Abhidharmakośa* p. 2 (Kasi Vidyapitha, Banaras) *avabodhopayoginaḥ padārthāḥ dharmāḥ.*

76. *Indian Philosophy*, Vol. II, p. 427 (George Allen & Unwin Ltd., London, 1927).

77. *An Idealist View of Life*, p. 71 (George Allen & Unwin Ltd., London, 1947).

78. *Vaiśeṣikadarśana*, Dhundiraja's Gloss, p. 5. *yadyapi dharmāḥ na ṣaṭpadārthātiriktāḥ kiṁtu anyonyāpekṣayā ta eva dharmāḥ dharmiṇaśca bhavanti.* (Chowkhamba Sanskrit Series, Banaras, 1932).

79. Cp. the Kantian and Neo-Kantian view of law. *A Text-Book of Jurisprudence*, p. 93. By G.W. Paton (Oxford, 1955).

80. *Ibid.*, p. 438.

81. I should like to warn the reader that all along I have been giving the views of the Mīmāṁsā, not mine.

82. *Bṛhatī*, pp. 26-7.

83. Quoted from *Jaiminīya Nyāyamālā* by *Mīmāṁsākośa*, p. 514.

84. This conception of law is very important for character understood as the form of will. Otherwise, positive law may be interpreted as the limit of man's freedom in the sense of license, a limit practically of wilful and selfish behaviour, which is often the case in actual practice. Law should be meant ultimately to produce character in the individual, useful and approved by society at least, not merely to put a limit on his freedom of action. This is done when the individual is asked by law to develop the required kind of will; and as such law may rightly be interpreted.

85. *Elements of Jurisprudence*, p. 27 (Progressive Publishers, Calcutta, 13th edition).

9

PROBLEM OF CATEGORICAL IMPERATIVE IN THE PHILOSOPHY OF PRABHĀKARA SCHOOL: A BRIEF NOTE

HAJIME NAKAMURA

It was a remarkable contribution that the late Professor Th. Stcherbatsky located a problem of categorical imperative in the philosophy of Prabhākara and the *Nyāyakaṇikā*, a commentary by Vācaspatimiśra (9th century C.E.) on Maṇḍanamiśra's *Vidhiviveka*. As Stcherbatsky's article[1] is not easily accessible, I shall first cite his sentences from the German original, and, passage by passage, I shall insert my own translation from German into English. Scrutinizing and examining of these passages in collation with the original texts will be up to later scholars.

> "Zu einer Zeit, als die erkenntnistheoretischen Fragen in den Vordergrund traten, haben sich die Philosophen auf beiden Seiten über die Frage den Kopf zerbrechen müssen, woher denn die Allgemeingültigkeit der religiösen Gebote oder die des Sittengesetzes stammte, zumal die empirischen Erkenntnisquellen keine genügende Bürgschaft dafür bieten. Auf beiden Seiten ist dann eine Lehre von einem allgemeingültigen Gesetz entwickelt worden, dessen Forderung von jeglicher Rücksicht auf die nur empirisch bestimmbaren Zwecke oder Folgen einer Handlungsweise unabhängig gilt, was somit ein kategorischer Imperativ ist."

(English Translation by H.N.)

> "In a period when epistemological problems came to the fore, philosophers on both sides had to rack their brains about the problem: from where the general validity of religious commands (precepts) or moral laws originates, especially for the reason that empirical epistemological sources provide no suffi-

cient security (qualification) for it. On both sides a doctrine of a generally valid law developed, whose claim (demand) is independent of any regard for the empirically determinable (ascertainable) aims or the effects of a way of behaviour. This amounts therefore to categorical imperative."[2]

The problem of categorical imperative has been very important in modern Western philosophy, such as in the case of Immanuel Kant. In the Mīmāṁsā school also this idea played an important role. The Bhāṭṭas took the empirical standpoint, whereas the school of Prabhākara maintained the idea of categorical imperative.

"Nach der herrschenden Schule der *Bhāṭṭas* enthält das Gebot eine Offenbarung über geeignete Mittel, den ersehnten Endzweck des Lebens zu erreichen (samīhitopāyatāvidhi). Die gewöhnlichen empirischen Erkenntnisquellen (mānāntara) geben Aufklärung nur über Gegenwärtiges oder Tatsächliches, aber die ewige Offenbarung der heiligen Schrift weist auf die Endziele des Lebens durch ihre Gebote. Dagegen meint die Schule *Prabhākara's* daβ die Gebote unmittelbar. an und für sich, bindend sind. Sie unterscheidet zwischen dem empirischen Inhalte der vorgeschriebenen Handlung (kriyākartavyatā) und dem Gebote oder der Verpflichtung schlechterdings (apūrvakartavyatā = niyoga). Die vorgeschriebene Opferhandlung (karman), die entsprechende zum Opfer berechtigte Person (adhikārin), die Einzelheiten der Ausführung (itikartavyatā), die angestrebte Frucht (phalam) sind zwar unentbehrlich, damit ein Gebot in Wirklichkeit realisiert werde, aber sie sind nur nebensächliche Einzelheiten, die in einem Dienstverhältnis zum eigentlichen Gebote stehen. Das reine Gebot, die reine Form des kategorischen Imperativs ist der Herr, die vorgeschriebane Handlung und ihr Resultat die Diener."

(English Translation)

"According to the ruling, predominent school of the Bhāṭṭas a revelation contains the command (precept) on the means suitable for attaining the desired final aim of life (samīhitopāyatāvidhi). The ordinary empirical sources of cognition (mānāntara) make clear only those things that are present or factual, but the eternal (perennial) revelation of the Holy Scriptures point to the final aims of life through their commands (precepts). On the contrary the school of Prabhākara maintains the opinion that the commands (precepts) are diectly (immediately) in themselves restrictive. They make distinction between the empirical contents of the prescribed action (kriyākartavyatā) and the command or obligation of duty as such (apūrvakartavyatā = niyoga). The prescribed sacrificial action of offering as such (apūrvakartavyatā = niyoga), the respective qualified person for the sacrificial offering *(adhikārin)*[3] the details of rituals (itikartavyatā),[4] the aimed-at effect (phalam) are indispensable so that the command is realised in actuality. But they are only accessory, subsidiary elements that stand in a servile situation in relation to the primary command. The genuine command, the genuine form of categorical imperative is the lord, the prescribed action and its effect are the servants."

The passage of Maṇḍanamiśra's *Viahiviveka* and the passage of Vācaspatimiśra's *Nyāyakaṇikā*, in which the problem of categorical imperative is discussed, is on p. 48, 1.7ff. of the *Pandit* edition. This corresponds to Gr. Mahaprabhu Lal Goswami's edition (Varanasi: Tara Publications, 1978), p. 35, 1.7f.

In the following I shall cite Stcherbatsky's German translation for three reasons: (1) his translation is not easily accessible now, (2) his German style is clear, and useful for comparative philosophy, and (3) I am not well versed in Mīmāṁsā dogmatics, so I cannot render with confidence a translation which might be better than Stcherbatsky's.

Übersetzung der Einleitung der niyogaparīkṣā.[5]

Maṇḍanamiśra p. 48.7 fübrt die Theorie Prabhākaras mit folgenden Worten ein:

„Ein Gebot ist ein durch den Imperativ ausgedrückter Sinn, der nicht durch andere (empirische) Erkenntnismittel zu erfassen ist, er beruht ausschlieβlich auf dem Worte (der Offenbarung), er wird auch innerlich von jedem gefühlt, in der Form „es ist meine Pflicht!“ Er ist (zeitlos, weil) von den drei Zeiten unberührt“ . . . .

(English Translation)

Translation of the Introduction to the Niyogaparīkṣā[5] Maṇḍanamiśra p. 48.7 introduces the theory of Prabhākara with the following words:

"A command (injunction) is a meaning (sense) which is expressed by imperative and which is not comprehended through other (empirical) means of cognition. It is based solely on Word (of Revelation). It is also felt internally in the form: "It is my duty!" It is (valid at all times, for) it is untouched by three time-periods" . . . .

Vācaspatimiśra fügt hinzu (49.17):

„Das ist die Bedeutung des Imperativs. In dieser Bedeutung ist der Imperativ kategorisch (anapekṣa), und in dieser Form steht seine (unbedingte) Geltung fest."

Der Bhāṭṭa-Mīmāṁsaka fragt nach einem Beweise, daß das Wort wirklich so etwas wie das reine Sollen ausdrücken kann. Von Seiten Prabhākaras wird geantwortet:

(52.1) Diese Bedeutung (saṃbandha) wird erfaßt, wenn wir imgewöhnlichen Leben das Schicken und dergleichen (Befehle) verstehen, denn sie bildet die Grundlage desjenigen (Sinnes), der in dem (Befehlen) enthalten ist.

Vācaspatimiśra erklärt:

(52.7) Folgendes ist da gemeint. Daß die Imperative usw. das Sollen ausdrücken, wird zunächst aus den Worten des Lehrers verstanden, wenn er z. B. sagt: „Kind, schaffe Holz herbei." Denn tatsächlich bemerkt ein Beobachter, der den (Vorgang) verstehen will, daß der Schüler, unmittelbar nachdem er diese Worte des Lehrers gehört hat, sich auf den Weg macht, um Holz herbei zu schaffen. (52.10) Dabei konstatiert er folgendes: „Diese Handlung ist eine bewußte, weil er aus freiem Willen hingegangen ist, wie ich es auch tun würde, und was ich, bei dieser Gelegenheit, im Sinne haben würde, das gerade muß er auch gehabt haben, denn zwischen uns besteht kein Unterschied. (52.12.) Ich aber handle in (solchen Fällen) nicht weil ich etwa mir dieser Tätigkeit im allgemeinen bewußt bin, nicht weil ich mir bloß die Folge davon vorstelle, und nicht weil ich die Mittel der Ausführung kenne, sondern weil ich mir meiner Pflicht bewuβt bin. Denn am Ende handelt auch das neugeborene Kind (nicht anders). Es unternimmt das Saugen der mütterlichen Brust nicht früher, als es (einfach) dazu durch sein Bewuβtsein angetrieben wird (ohne an die Folgen zu denken). (52.15) Auch kann man nicht behaupten, daβ es kein anderes Sollen gibt, als nur das Streben nach dem eigenen Wohl, denn beides sind heterogene Begriffe. Man kann unmöglich (behaupten), daβ es keine andere Aufgabe für (unsere) Tätigkeit, für das menschliche Bestreben gibt, als nur seine Wünsche zu verwirklichen. (52.18) Es ist (wahr, daβ) die Arbeit (an und für sich) beschwerlich ist, darum haben einige gedacht, daβ die Pflicht (, sie trotzdem in Angriff zu nehmen,) immer mit einer Frucht verbunden sein muβ; denn wenn es sich nur um Angenehmes handelt, wird die Aufgabe (unmittelbar) verstanden, ohne daβ man dabei an die Erreichung einer (entfernten) Frucht denken muβ. Darum sind meine bewuβten Handlungen durch die Idee des Sollens hervorgerufen, welche nicht gleichbedeutend ist mit dem Erreichen eines (erwünschten) Zieles. So hat auch der Schüler deshalb gehandelt, weil er sich dieser (seiner Pflicht) bewuβt war.“ Zu solchem Schluβ (muβ der Beobachter) kommen. (53.2) Da dieses Bewuβtsein unmittelbar nach den Worten des Lehrers entsteht, so ist es jedenfalls durch die Worte desselben hervorgerufen. Auf diese Weise nimmt er eine Fähigkeit der Worte an, das Sollen auszudrücken. (53.3) Nachdem es festgestellt ist, daβ diese Pflicht durchwegs durch die Worte ausgedrückt wird, so soll man die im sechsten Kapitel der Mīmāṁsāsūtra's dargelegte Methode befolgend die Sätze wie „der den Himmel Anstrebendo soll das Agnihotra-Opfer vollziehen“, so interpretieren, daβ da die ausgesprochene Pflicht durch ein Subjekt der Pflicht zu ergänzen ist, was durch die Worte „der den Himmel Anstrebende“ angedeutet wird. Das steht fest. (53.6) Derjenige, der sich seiner Pflicht bewuβt wird, ist Subjekt der Pflicht. Es ist einer, der den Himmel anstrebt, und dieses Streben zum Himmel, den er erreichen will, ist sein Attribut. Er ist an solch eine Pflicht gebunden, welche ihn allein zum erwünschten Ziele führen wird.

(53.8) (Bhāṭṭa) Jede Handlung, nachdem sie vollzogen ist, hört auf. Sie kann unmöglich eine Wirkung zu einer anderen entfernten Zeit haben, darum ist die Verbindung der auszuführenden Handlung mit dem Subjekt der Pflicht nicht möglich.

(Prabhākara:) Nein! Die Pflichterfüllung, die andauert, kann mit diesem Subjekt in Verbindung bleiben. Die Imperative drücken aber ein Sollen aus, das über die vorgeschriebene Handlung hinaus etwas anderes ist, etwas, was auf anderem Wege nicht erkannt werden kann. Und weil sie mit Bezug auf andere (empirische) Erkenntnismittel transzendent ist, wird sie transzendente Pflicht genannt. Weil aber sie als ein Sollen erkannt wird, welches den Menschen innerlich bindet, wird sie Pflicht genannt. (53.13) Obschon die (transzendente Pflicht) unmittelbar nach der vollzogenen Handlung erfüllt ist, tritt die Realisierung der Existenz im Himmel nicht sofort ein, weil das von mitwirkenden Ursachen des Raumes und der Zeit abhängt. (56.15.) Daβ die Erzeugung der Frucht, als untergeordneter Umstand, dabei in Erscheinung kommt, ändert nichts an der Tatsache, daβ der Satzsinn beim Imperativ die (reine) Pflicht ausdrückt. Die Pflicht ist wie ein Herr sie ist von der Wirkung nur insofern abhängig, als sie sich dasjenige Subjekt, das dazu paβt, nimmt. Just wie ein Herr den Diener Garbhadāsa nur so weit beeinfluβt, als es ihm selber nutzt, so ist es auch hier, (die Pflicht ist Hauptsache, die Folge Nebensache). (53.18) Auch darf man nicht meinen, daβ diese Bedeutung des Imperativs nur in der heiligen Schrift gilt. Auch im gewöhnlichen Leben, wenn man die Imperative analog den Sätzen der Schrift analysiert, laufen sie am Ende auf Pflichterfüllung hinaus. (53.19) (Bhāṭṭa.) Im Leben haben die Imperative die verschiedensten Bedeutungen (Schicken, Bitten, Unterweisen), ist das (im Veda) nicht der Fall?

(53.20) (Prabhākara.) Nein! Wir sagen ja, daβ das Kind handelt, weil der Lehrer es befohlen hat, d. h. das Kind ist sich seiner Pflicht bewuβt. Ein vernünftiges Wesen kann überhaupt nicht anders handeln.

(53.22) Und weil dem so ist, weil das Schicken und ähnliche Befehle des praktischen Lebens verstanden werden, und weil eine Tätigkeit ohne die Idee des Sollens nicht vor sich gehen kann, so wird die darin enthaltene (Pflichtvorstellung) als

Grundbedeutung erfaßt, weil auch die Imperative der heiligen Schrift, wenn man alles Nebensächliche hinwegdenkt,) auf dieselbe (reine Pflicht) hinauslaufen (53.23).

[English Translation]
Vācaspatimiśra adds (49.17):

"That is the meaning of Imperative. In this sense this imperative is categorical (anapekṣa), and in this form its (unconditioned) validity stands firmly."

The Bhāṭṭa-Mīmāṁsaka poses a question about the proof that word can actually express something like the genuine "Ought to" (Sollen). From the side of Prabhākara it is replied:

(52.1) This meaning (saṃbandha) is comprehended when we understand injunctions and so on in conventional worldly life, for it constitutes the foundation of the sense which is implied in the order (injunction).

Vācaspati explains:

(52.7) here the following is meant. The fact that Imperative and so on expresses "Ought to" (Sollen) is first understood from words of the teacher when he says, for example, "Oh boy! bring here firewood!" For actually an observer notices that the disciple, immediately after he has heard these words of the teacher, goes on the way to bring firewood.

(52.10) On this occasion he confirms the following: "This action is one to be done deliberately, because he went there out of free will, in whichever way I may have done, and whatever I may have meant on this occasion, he also must have had, for between us there exists no distinction.

(52.12) However, in such cases I act, not because I was conscious of this activity in general, not because I imagine only the effect of it, not because I know the means of performance, but because I am conscious of my duty. For, at the end, the newly born child matters (not otherwise). This child does not start sucking up the breast of the mother earlier than it is simply driven to the act through his consciousness (without thinking of the effects, i.e. the fruit of this action).

(52.15) Also, one cannot assert that there exists no other

"Ought to" (Sollen) than the endeavour toward one's own welfare (benefit), for both are heterogeneous concepts.[7] It is impossible to assert that there exists no other task for our activity, for human endeavour, than only to realize one's own desires. (52.18) It is true that work itself is painstaking, therefore, some people have thought that duty (although it may have been started) must be always connected with an effect (fruit); for if only something pleasant matters, the task will be immediately understood, without that one must think of the attainment of a remote effect. Therefore, my conscious actions are evoked through the idea of "Ought to" (Sollen). "This idea is not of the same significance as the attainment of a (longed-for) aim. The disciple has also acted for the reason that he was conscious of this duty of his"—The observer must come to such a conclusion.

(53.2) As this consciousness originates directly according to the words of the teacher, so it is evoked in any case through the words of the teacher. In this way he assumes the capacity of the words to express "Ought to" (Sollen).

(53.3) After he has confirmed that this duty is expressed ordinarily through Words, one should interpret, following the method laid down in the sixth chapter of the *Mīmāṁsāsūtra*, such sentences as "The person who desires to be born in Heaven, should practise the Agnihotra-sacrifice", in such a way as the expressed duty is to be supplemented with a subject of the duty by the words "the person who desires". This is implied through the words: "the person who desires to be born in Heaven". This is confirmed.

(53.6) The person who becomes conscious of his duty is the subject of duty. The person who wants to be born in Heaven is one, and the endeavour for Heaven which he will attain is his attribute. He is bound to such a duty. This duty alone will take him to the longed-for aim.

(53.8) (Bhāṭṭa)[8] Any action disappears after it has been done. It is impossible for an act to wield influence on a different, remote time. Therefore, the connection of an act to be performed with the subject of the duty is not possible.

(Prabhākara) No! The fulfilment of duty which continues

can remain in connection with this subject. But the imperative expresses an "Ought to" (Sollen), which is something different throughout the prescribed act, something that cannot be cognized in another, different way. And because the prescribed act is transcendent with regard to the other (empirical) means of cognition, it is called 'transcendent duty'. But the act is cognized as an "Ought to" (Sollen), which binds men internally, is named 'duty'.

(53.13) Although the (transcendent duty) is fulfilled directly after the completion of the act, the realization of the existence in Heaven is not brought about immediately, because this depends on co-working causes of space and time.

(56.15) That the producing of effects as subordinate circumstance comes to appearance, does not change anything in the fact that the sense of a sentence in case of Imperative expresses genuine duty. Duty is just like a lord. It is dependent on effect only insofar as it takes subject which is suitable for it. A lord influences the servant Garbhadāsa only in so far as it is useful for himself. Here also in the same way. (Duty is the main thing; effect or fruit is an accidental thing.)

(53.18) Also one should not think that the meaning of Imperative is valid only in holy scriptures. Also, in conventional, worldly life, if one analyses Imperatives like the sentences of the Scripture, these Imperatives transgress fulfilment of duty at the end.

(53.19) (Bhāṭṭa) In life Imperatives have various, different meanings (to conform, to request, to advise). Is it not the case (in the Veda)?

(53.20) (Prabhākara) No! We say, indeed, that the child acts because the teacher has ordered, i.e. the child himself is conscious of his duty. An intelligent being cannot act otherwise. And, things being so, because making suitable and similar orders of practical life are understood, and because an activity cannot get along without the idea of "Ought to" (Sollen), the conception of duty, implied therein as the fundamental meaning, is comprehended, also because Imperatives of Holy Scripture is aimed at the same (genuine duty), if one neglects[9] all minor, accidental things. (53.23)

So for is Stcherbatsky's translation.

Maṇḍanamiśra says: *liṅādīnām artho vidhir iti.*[10]

Vācaspatimiśra in this connection explains:

evaṃvidhārthatve ca codanāyā anapekṣatāyā prāmāṇyavidhir iti.[11]

So, the Indian equivalent to the Western idea of categorical imperative would be *anapekṣo vidhiḥ* or *anapekṣā codanā*, although we cannot find this expression in the original texts. It is 'pratyātmavedanīya'[12], i.e. it should be intuitionally known.

The term *niyoga*, which can mean injunction, order, command, mandate, was highly controversial among the Mīmāṁsakas. According to the Prabhākara school order is not an integral factor in the action, so it cannot as a rule be an object of injunction. In some cases the action is enjoined by another injunctive sentence.[13] The exertion produces in the agent a result (*kārya*) to which also the name of *Niyoga* is given by Prabhākara on the ground that it is this which acts as an incentive to the agent to put forth exertion towards the performance of the action denoted by the verb of the injunctive clause. The *Niyoga*, however, is unable to produce its result, unless aided by something which Śālikanātha styles fate.[14]

The meaning of the term is not clear to us. We need still further investigation.

Anyhow, in this case injunction does not depend on other means of knowledge (*pramāṇāntara*), but it depends upon Scriptures (*śabdamātrālambana*). It may be called categorical, but it still depends on some authority. Can we regard such an attitude as something of universal significance?

Regardless of scriptures the *Bhagavadgītā* teaches categorical imperative in a more direct and straightforward way.

To Arjuna who was shrinking from killing his own kinsmen, Kṛṣṇa makes an appeal to a sense of duty.

svadharmam api cā' vekṣya
na vikampitum arhasi
dharmyād dhi yuddhāc chreyo 'nyat
kṣatriyasya na vidyate

"Further, having regard for thine own duty, thou shouldst not falter, there exists no greater good for a Kṣatriya than a battle enjoined by duty."[15] (*Bhagavadgītā*, II, 31)

Here the idea of *svadharma* is set forth as the basis for one's action. Radhakrishnan explains the purport of this stanza as follows:

atha cet tvam imaṁ dharmyaṁ
saṁgrāmaṁ na kariṣyasi
tataḥ svadharmaṁ kīrtiṁ ca
hitvā pāpam avāpsyasi (ibid. II, 33)

But if thou does not this lawful battle, then thou wilt fail thy duty and glory and will incur sin.

One should make action without concern for the results.

karmaṇy evā 'dhikāras te
mā phaleṣu kadācana
mā karmaphalahetur bhūr
mā te saṅgo 'stv akarmaṇi (II, 47)

"To action alone hast thou a right and never at all to its fruits; let not the fruits of action be thy motive; neither let there be in thee any attachment to inaction."

yogasthaḥ kuru karmāṇi
saṅgaṁ tyaktvā dhanaṁjaya
siddhyasiddhyoḥ samo bhūtvā
samatvaṁ yoga ucyate (II, 48)

"Fixed in yoga, do thy work, O Winner of wealth (Arjuna), abandoning attachment, with an even mind in success and failure, for evenness of mind is called yoga."

So far, the purport of the sayings is similar to the opinion of Prabhākara.

Then, what should be the ultimate basis for one's action? The *Gītā* teaches:

śrutivipratipannā te
yadā sthāsyati niścalā
samādhāv acalā buddhis
tadā yogam avāpsyasi (II, 53)

"When thy intelligence, which is bewildered by the Vedic texts, shall stand unshaken and stable in spirit (*samādhi*), then shalt thou attain to insight (*yoga*)."

Here the ultimate basis for injunction is not the Veda, but the Inner Self. The authority of Vedic Scripture is cast away, which makes quite a difference from the case of Prabhākara. Scriptures are nothing but entanglements. One should seek for something which is deeper.

In Buddhist philosophy the ideal of categorical imperative was set forth, not in the form of *niyoga* as in the case of the Prabhākara school, but in the spirit of *maitrī* or *karuṇā*.

The term *maitrī* is derived from the word *mitra*, which means 'friend'. "A bodhisattva who is not concerned with his own good"[16] is highly extolled.

The spirit of the true friend is to do acts without any expectation of good results or benefit. This ideal is embodied in the person of the 'unsolicited friend' (*anadhīṣṭa-kalyāṇamitra*).[17] The meaning is as follows: friends render help to him who is suffering, when he solicits them to help. But true friends willingly render help to him in case of his adversity, even if he does not solicit them to help him.

Guṇabhadra's Chinese translation uses the same term,[18] saying "(a devout Buddhist) becomes for all sentient beings spontaneously friendly, compassionate, giver of solace, merciful, and is called 'world mother of the Dharma'."[19]

The ideal of categorical imperative among Buddhists was also set forth by the teaching of 'purification of three circles'.

trimaṇḍala-pariśuddhi,[20] *ḥkhor gsum yoṅs-su dag-pa.*

It means usually the purity of three things in donation, viz. the giver, the receiver, and the gift, based upon the idea of 'non-substantiality' (*śūnyatā*). One should practise donation categorically without the expectation of reward. If any egoistic inclination is crept in on the part of the giver, his act is not pure, but defiled.

Was it possible that Prabhākara was influenced by Buddhists in the formation of the idea of categorical imperative? Stcherbatsky's opinion is in the affirmative. He says:[21]

"Nun hat sich offenbar Prabhākara in vielen Fragen durch die buddhistische Lehre beeinflussen lassen, infolgedessen er den Versuch gemacht hat, die buddhistische Logik den Zwecken der Mīmāṁsakas anzupassen. Namentlich seine Analyse des negativen Urteils (anupalabdhi) und auch die Unterscheidung eines primären und sekuṇdären Bewuβtseins,) die Theorie über die Unfehlbarkeit des primären (sarvaṃ jñānaṃ pramāṇam) bewegen sich durchaus in den von Dignāga und Dharmakīrti gebrochenen Bahnen. Der Beschuldigung, ein verkappter Buddhist zu sein, die sich die Vertreter der verschiedensten Schulen damals recht oft an den Kopf geworfen haben, ist auch Prabhākara nicht entgangen. Darauf weist folgender Vers hin, der sich unter den Pandits erhalten hat:

asti vijñāto loke 'smin bauddha-bandhuḥ Prabhākaraḥ."

(English Translation)

"Now it is clear that Prabhākara was influenced by Buddhist teachings on many problems (topics). Accordingly he made the attempt to adapt (apply) Buddhist logic to the aims of the Mīmāṁsakas. Especially his analysis of negative judgment (Anupalabdhi)[22] and also the distinction between primary and secondary consciousnesses,[23] the theory of infallibility of primary consciousness (sarvaṃ jñānaṃ pramāṇam) are to be located thoroughly in the lines started by Dignāga and Dharmakīrti. The blame of being a crypto-Buddhist was often rightly directed onto the head of representatives of various schools, and even Prabhākara cannot escape from this blame. The following verse that has been preserved among Pandits shows the fact:

asti vijñāto loke 'smin Bauddha-bandhaḥ Prabhākaraḥ."

However, I am rather doubtful on this point. The influence by Buddhism on Prabhākara seems to be limited to logical and epistemological aspects alone. In ethical and social repects Prabhākara seems to have been a staunch Brahmanist.

The ideal similar to the Buddhist ideal of *trimaṇḍala-pari-śuddhi* was set forth by the Jains also. Donation (*dāna*) by lay believers to homeless ascetics was encouraged. Jainism taught dravya-śuddhaṃ dayakaśuddhaṃ pratigāhaka-śuddhaṃ trividhaṃ trikaraṇa-śuddhaṃ dānam.[24]

In spite of such similarities which underlie among various thinkers of ancient India, I think we need not necessarily suppose the fact of cultural or ideological interchange among them. The esteem of the attitude to do good without the expectation of favourable results is based originally on human nature. This tendency brought about its various representations with different accentuation in different contexts.

Notes

1. Th. Stcherbatsky: Uber die Nyāyakaṇikā des Vācaspatimiśra und die indische Lehre vom kategorischen Imperativ. *Beitrage zur Literaturwissenchft und Geistesgeschichte Indiens. Festgabe Hermann Jacobi zum 75. Geburtstag*, herausgegeben von Willibald Kirfel, Bonn, Kommissionsverlag Fritz Klopp, 1926, S. 369–80.

2. Op. cit., S. 372.

3. *adhikarin*, qualified person (to perform a rite and receive its fruit). (F. Edgerton: *The Mīmāṁsā Nyāya Prakāśa*, New Haven: Yale University Press, 1929, p. 278).

4. *itikartavyatā*, manner (of performance = kathaṃbhāva). F. Edgerton: op. cit. p. 287. Cf. *itikāryatā*, any proper or necessary duty, obligation (Apte: *Sanskrit English Dictionary*, s.v.).

5. Stcherbatsky cites from Vidhiviveka, reprint from the Pandit, Benares 1907.

6. *saṃbandha* means 'connection', relationship between a word and its meaning. It is not expressed by words etymologically interpreted.

7. On parasparaparihāralakṣaṇavirodha, cf. Nyāyabindu, Bibl. Buddh. VII, p. 69.

8. Through the words *na ca* the question raised by the opponent is cited allusively in most cases, and then the opinion of the opponent is rejected. [according to Stcherbatsky]

9. Tadupagraham (=tadupādhim) a podya.

10. *Vidhiviveka*, Mahaprabhu's edition, p. 35, 11.8-9.

11. *Nyāyakaṇikā*, Mahaprabhu's edition, p. 36, 11.12-13.

12. *Vidhiviveka*, op. cit., p. 35, 1.8.

13. Ganganatha Jha: *The Prabhakara School of Purva Mimamsa* (Reprint Delhi: Motilal Banarsidass, 1978), p. 302.

14. A.B. Keith: *The Karma-Mīmāṁsā* (Reprint New Delhi: Oriental Books Corporation, 1978), p. 75.

15. I have cited the English translation from S. Radhakrishnan: *The Bhagavadgītā* (New York: Harper and Brothers), pp. 112ff.; 122ff.

16. *Bodhicaryāvatāra*, I,31.

17. *Gaṇḍavyūha*, ed. by D.T. Suzuki and Hokei Idzumi, Kyoto, 1934, p. 5. Its Chinese translation runs: *pu-ch'ing-yōu*. This Chinese translation is mentioned in the Tang version. (*Taishō Tripiṭaka*, vol. 10, p. 103a)

Kumārajīva's Chinese translation of the *Vimalakīrtinirdeśasūtra*, chuan 1 (*Taishō Tripiṭaka*, vol. 14, p. 537a).

The Wei version of the Larger Sukhāvatīvyūha Sūtra (*Taishō Tripiṭaka*, vol. 12, p. 266b.

Cf. Prince Shōtoku's Commentary on *Vimalakīrtinirdeśa-sūtra* (*Taishō Tripiṭka*, vol. 56, p. 21c.)

Prince Shōtoku's Commentary on *Śrīmālāsiṃhanāda-sūtra* (*Taishō Tripiṭaka*, vol. 56, p. 6c).

18. Guṇabhadra's Chinese translation of the *Śrīmālādevīsiṃhanāda-sūtra* (*Taishō*, vol. 12, p. 218b).

19. Alex Wayman: *The Lion's Roar of Queen Śrīmālā*, Columbia University Press, 1974, p. 72. The Tibetan version simply says: *sems can thams cad kyi gshi rten du gyur pa*. (Tsukinowa Kenryū's edition, Kyoto, 1940, p. 44).

20. *The Ratnagotravibhāga Mahāyānottaratantraśāstra*, edited by E.H. Johnston and T. Chowdhury (Patna:The Bihar Research Society, 1950), p. 6, 1.5. Cf. Jikidō Takasaki: *A Study on the Ratnagotravibhāga* (Roma: Istituto Italiano per il Medio ed Estremo Oriente, 1966), p. 151; 383. Cf. Ratnamati's Chinese translation (*Taishō Tripiṭaka*, vol. 31, p. 822a);

Ta-ch'êng-pên—shêng-hsin-ti-kuan-ching (*Dai-jo-hon-jō*-kwan-gho, chuan 1; 7).

21. Op. cit., 5.371.

22. Cf. Prakaraṇapañcikā, Benares 1903, p. 123ff. (Chowkhamba).

23. Ibid., p. 54ff.

24. *Vivāgasuya* II, 1 (*Suttāgame*, I. 1283–84). teṇaṃ davva-suddheṇaṃ dāyaga-suddheṇaṃ paḍigāhaya-suddheṇaṃ tiviheṇaṃ tikaraṇa-suddheṇaṃ aṇagare paḍilābhie.

'The monk was given the gift (which was) pure in three ways and in respect of the three modes of action, pure with regard to the substance, the donor and the taker.'

(Nalini Balbir: The 'micro-genre' of *dāna*-stories in Jaina Literature: Problems of Interrelation and diffusion, *Indologica Taurinensia*, vol. XI 1983, pp. 148).

In *Viyāhapannatti* XV (*Suttāgame* I, 711) we find the same sentence, with the only difference that the final aṇagare paḍilābhie is changed to dāṇeṇaṃ mae paḍilābhie.

SECTION TWO

Language
Meaning
Grammar

10

AUTPATTIKA: THE 'ORIGINARY' SIGNIFIER-SIGNIFIED RELATION IN MĪMĀṀSĀ AND DECONSTRUCTIVE SEMIOLOGY

PURUSHOTTAMA BILIMORIA

Preamble

The Mīmāṁsā view of language holds a particular fascination for me, and I come to it not as a linguist, a philologist or even as an indologist, but rather as a philosopher for whom a large number of conceptual problems remain unresolved. Hence I look to cross-traditional reflections as a means of advancing the debate on a given issue. Here I shall confine myself to an aspect of Pārthasārathi Miśra's responses to the issues in language that stemmed directly from the Mīmāṁsā position on the inviolable authority of *Śruti.** I am less interested, for the purposes of the present discussion, in the religious discourse within which their concerns about *Śruti* or Vedas would seem to be grounded at the most obvious level. I have no argument with people who seek to reframe the Mīmāṁsā speculations in the context of a ritualistic world view, and structurally identify various aspects of their pronoucements on the great metaphysical questions of the day with the underlying Brāhmaṇical preoccupations with power, purity, social control and perpetuation of its declining or threatened hegemony. In a way, crossing to another tradition, Plato, Aristotle, the Thomists, down through Maimonides, Hegel, Heidegger among others, were no less embroiled in the political and ideological issues of their times, and their judgments (intended or otherwise) might have even privileged the ruling elite, but this did not necessarily handicap them from being able to make certain significant advances on the philosophical or intellectual front. Indeed, one might say, this kind of dialectics works in rather mysterious ways! That particular problematic, then, will not be my concern. And it is generally overlooked that despite the intense ritualistic foreground of the traditional Mīmāṁsakas, with Kumārila a shift occurs from the ritualistic to the speculative, epistemological and grammatical, and this is achieved with some degree of dialectical acumen.[1] Except for Prabhākara this dialectical turn is rigorously sustained by later Mīmāṁsakas.

Introduction

One of the great challenges that faced the Mīmāṁsakas in their defence of the authority of the Vedas was to show how *Śruti* or more technically *śabda* as a *pramāṇa*, in their conception, escaped the limitations and fallibilism of the other *pramāṇas*, such as perception, and so on. Since fallibilism, in their view, is associated with, perhaps even endemic to, the human faculties, whether it be in the area of morality or in the quest for higher understanding, a source entirely outside and independent of all human agency and intervention, the Mīmāṁsakas felt, should surely help obviate or by-pass such pitfalls. In various traditional cosmologies where the human race is in some sense or other seen as a subject of a 'fallen' state, there is invariably recourse made, either through myth or some other conduit, to the extra-human, to the gods, a God, the divine, the transcendent, the supersensible Forms or whatever, in the hope of a redemptive turn or return. For some historical reason, as is well-known, the Mīmāṁsakas had rejected belief in a transcendent being, and accorded an insignificant ontological status to the gods, or to any beings conceived in any way to be superior to humans.[2] However, again for various historical reasons, they did not shirk the erstwhile Brāhmaṇical faith in the scriptural texts, especially the Brāhmaṇas; indeed, an assertion of the superiority of the scriptures over all other *auctoritates* was a corollary to the defence of orthodoxy (*āstikatva*). The problem that faced, especially the later Mīmaṁsakas, was to demonstrate not so much how the texts of scriptures originated, but how they are devoid of or independent of any human intervention, for that itself might bolster the argument that the scriptures are incorrigible and incontrovertible. But surely, it is axiomatic that all texts, whether spoken or written, are rooted in conventions established by the respective language communities for their generation and comprehension. Or, as the

American philosopher David Lewis has argued, a population uses language by virtue of certain conventions prevailing in that population?[3] Why should the texts of scriptures escape this fundamental formative fact? Unless, of course, we suppose that God revealed the *Word* to man as in Genesis 2, or spoke the first word to a woman as in Eden; but the Mīmāṁsā would not accede to such a view of 'revelation'.[4] What, therefore, would be the convincing conditions for the scriptural texts if they are not at all to be dependent on such a framework of conventions (*saṁketa*)?

Three issues are generally taken in the effort to establish *Śruti's* non-human dependency (*anapekṣatva*). These pertain to the following:

(*i*) the relation between word and meaning: *śabdārthasambandhaḥ*;

(*ii*) relation between sentence and its signification: *vākyavākyārthasaṁyoga*;

(*iii*) *dṛśyādarśanabādhitam* or nonperception of an author where such is capable of being perceived (*yogyānupalabdhi*), hence *apauruṣeyatva*.

In this paper I intend merely to focus on the first issue and discuss how the problematic concerning the relation of word and meaning has been dealt with by the Mīmāṁsakas. (Issues ii and iii have been treated elsewhere.[5] This issue is discussed under the famous *autpattika* thesis.[6]) Here I intend also to compare the Mīmāṁsaka view with the semiological insights from de Saussure's work and their extension in the writings of the contemporary French philosopher, Jacques Derrida. And I shall be more concerned in my analysis with its implications for *laukika* expressions than in respect of *vaidika* expressions, i.e. for a theory of natural language within a more or less naturalistic framework —tendentious and controversial as this move might seem, given that, as we are often reminded, the Mīmāṁsakas had *Saṁskṛta* in mind, and not, say for instance, Chinese or Swahili, if they were at all aware of such other languages! Still, the Mīmāṁsakas were not alone in suggesting the possibility of linguistic entities and their logical relations existing independently of the utterances of any individual: Plato with his theory of forms is a good, albeit early and influential, (Western) example of this leaning.[7]

Autpattika

Jaimini's *autpattika sūtra* (I.i.5) reads: *autpattikas tu śabdasyā'rthena sambandhas tasya jñānam upadeśo 'vyatirekaś cā 'rthe 'nupalabdhe, tat pramāṇaṃ bādarāyaṇasya anapekṣatvāt.*[8]

'But the relation (*sambandha*) of word (*śabda*) with its meaning (*artha*) is originary (*autpattika*); instruction is the (means of) knowledge of that (*dharma*, etc), and it is faultless in regard to thing(s) beyond sense-perception, it is authoritative, (because) for Bādarāyaṇa (too), it is independent (of the empirical means).'

What is important for us here is the first line: *autpattikaḥ śabdasyā'rthena sambandhaḥ*. What does this mean? The standard practice has been to render *autpattikaḥ* as 'eternal', largely because that is the sense Śabara seems to have given it when he commented: *autpattikaḥ—iti nityaṃ brūmaḥ*. But, *autpattikaḥ* is constructed from *utpattiḥ+(dhak)='origin'*, which could mean 'originating or arising instantaneously, inseparably, or without interruption'. Hence Jaimini's use of the term *autpattikaḥ* in the above may be read as 'the relation between word and meaning is originary', in the sense that the presentment of the word and its meaning is simultaneous, so that there is no moment in which they are separable one from the other. In other words, the word and its meaning arise (upon hearing) as *if* psychically or episodically co-present or coeval. Such is the 'founding binary combination' (to borrow an expression from Derrida). I think it is often forgotten that Jaimini is actually referring to the actual instance in linguistic practice in describing this relation and that it is not an abstraction about the temporally primordial source of the word, as if rooted in some historical or cosmological act of origination (*origine*) (not in this sūtra anyway).

In fact, even in Śabara, despite his use of the term *nitya*, this reading is quite clear, for consider what Śabara goes on to say in expanding on what he means by *utpatti*: it is *bhāva* (presence) *that is spoken metaphorically as utpattiḥ* ('origin').[9] The relation between word and meaning is inseparable (*aviyuktaḥ*) by virtue of their (coeval) presence; the relation is not (constituted) after both are arisen.' In other words, their 'origin' rests in their arising together in unison or in mutual presence. The relation is *sui generis*, natural and with a sense of permanency about it.

If we take 'origin' [*Ursprung*] as Heidegger defined it: 'that from which and by which something is what it is as it is'—origin is thus a source which is also a condition which makes a thing what it is.[10] Heidegger illustrated the different senses of origination in the context of art, in asking the question 'what is the origin of the work of art?', and suggested three possibilities: the artist as the origin of work of art; the work as the origin of the artist, and art as the origin of both artist and work. And he drew a circle linking all three, to highlight the hermeneutical circle which forms the horizon of all discursive expressions. Heidegger, therefore, presses the point that our quest should not be for an original language, nor discursive primordiality but for an ontologico-existential immediacy, i.e. for the roots and basic *a priori* structure which make discourse or speaking possible, and in which signification is ultimately embedded.[11] We should keep this metaphysical problematic in the foreground here.

Now, *nitya* does indeed have the more general connotation of 'eternity', 'outside time', 'beginningless'.[12] But here the term '*nitya*', as Madelaine Biardeau[13] rightly points out, 'does not connote eternity nor does it even specifically refer to permanence'; rather it has the sense of an 'internal exigency' (*svābhāvika*), a description that recurs in later Mīmāṁsakas. And for this there is no dependency on any kind of extrinsic appropriation, such as a qualification of existence in terms of time or its exclusion, or substance by quality, or the sender. It essentially defines a relational structure (hence *sambandhena*) that belongs to the very nature of *śabda* and *artha*. The emphatic stress is on the constancy of the relation: '*śabda* is never outside of or apart from the *autpattika* relation.'[14] In this sense it is "originary", which I believe is better nuanced in the French *originaire* and *originel* (native, primordially prefigured), than in the English 'original' (first, novel, originating). Thus, I find it more instructive to render *autpattika* as 'preeminently given' or 'prefigured' in the sense of the inseparability of one from the other, read within a synchronic-structural matrix more than in some presumed diachronic time-frame (with or without a beginning). In this sense, then, Śabara characterises the relation as '*apauruṣeyaḥ* [*śabdasyārthena sambandhaḥ*]'[15], and all the Mīmāṁsakas after him followed in using *autpattika*, *apauruṣeya* and *nitya* as synonyms.[16]

Within the Indian tradition, the Mīmāṁsakas were not the first to come up with such a thesis that postulates a differential yet inseparable interplay between word and meaning. Patañjali in his *Yogasūtra* admits that one cannot deny that in ordinary human discourse the presence of one (the word) brings about the other (meaning or the conceptual image).[17] Ultimately, of course, Patañjali wants to argue that the relation of words and meanings and their referents are established by convention (*saṁketa*), and that in the practice of meditation the false notion of any identity between them is shattered, revealing what one might say is the inherent *difference* of the *śabda*, *vikalpa* and *artha*. Similarly, the Grammarian held the view that the relation between the name and the nameable, as between knowledge and the knowable, is *anādiyogyatā* (a beginningless capacity)[18], although the manifestation of this relation is made co-eval with the origin of the world (which is denied by the Mīmāṁsā). Bhāmaha's definition of *kāvya* also echoes something of this unity, in that for him the 'expression and meaning are combined' (*śabdārthau sahitau kāvyam*).[19]

Returning again to the Mīmāṁsakas, Śabara outlines the function of this relation in its linguistic manifestation, in responding to the question why it is that upon uttering the word 'razor' the speaker does not have his mouth slit open? Because he says the relation is to be charactertised as that of *pratyāyaka* and *pratyāyya*, i.e. (as I would like to render them) signifier and signified respectively; Śabara further describes their function in speech in terms of the *name* (*saṁjñā*) and the *named* (*saṁjñin*),[20] which in broad terms is the *vācya/vācaka* or meaning/expression relation. We may note in passing that 'difference' is already at work in this formulation: the naming of the object or reference is deferred, a distinction is made within the word (*śabda* as a unit of speech) between the signifier and the signified (which I indicate by placing a bar between *vācya/vācaka*), and since there is *ākāṅkṣā* or expectancy between them they are binary. I might just mention in passing that the Bhāṭṭa view broadly of cognition is that there is no *saṁjñā* or apprehension of the cognition—it simply discloses its *artha*. Likewise with *śabda*, the *saṁjñā* does not last long, rather it vanishes as soon as the *saṁjñin* is revealed: this is its aesthetic potency (*śakti*).

Pārthasārathi Miśra, picking up on this general view, similarly observes that in ordinary speech there is a relation between word and meaning which is of the nature of *pratyāyya* and *pratyāyaka*, and that it is by virtue of this intrinsic relation that the word comes to have this significative or denotative character (*pratyāyakatva*); and so the word conveys its meaning (in other uses as well) independently of other relations, such as of sense-organ contact or that involved in inference.[21] He also rejects that this is a cause-effect relation or one dependent on the mind,[22] in making the point that it is an extra-psychic relation. The signification is called *abhidhāna* and the relation is defined as *saṁjñā-saṁjñin*, which may be comparable to *nominans-nomen*.[23] (Although Śabara restricts its use in human naming.) Interestingly enough he considers but rejects the suggestion that the relation might be one of *saṁyoga*, mere conjunction, or even *tādātmya*, identity, for he wants to avoid the possibility of there being, on the one hand, any artificiality about this relation, and, on the other hand, an absolute identity; both are qualified by *pratyāyakatva*, in that it holds the signifier and signified together, yet severs them once the signified has surfaced, until its next occurrence; in other words, in the very functioning of the *pratyāyakatva* (signifying) the difference between the signifier and the signified is stamped, otherwise the signifier would be self-reflexive, and it would hang loose as a bit of animated 'sound'; hence there is here a unity but also a differential and deferral function embedded in this relation.

The point I want to underscore at this juncture is that insofar as *autpattika* marks the difference, indeed the *différance*, of *śabda* and *artha* as also their integral association, as a notion it exudes a profound psychological insight into the linguistic process; but the Mīmāṁsakas, as I just hinted, go a step further and move this phenomenological insight into the domain of pure linguistics (by which I do not mean any metalinguistic discourse, but rather textuality *par exellence*). This is to be understood in terms of their broader theory of language. Before, however, moving to this more complicated thesis, I want right now to sketch some parallels I see here with the semiological insight, particularly those of de Sausurre in his germinal text, *The Course of General Linguistics*, and laterly of Derrida.

Semiological Model

In very general terms, de Saussure's semiological thesis postulates that in any system of signs there is an integral union of the signifier (*signifiant*) and the signified (*signifié*). The signifer is the psychological trace or impression of a sound, which is a *phoné* or phoneme (the sound-image), and the signified is an idea or concept (the meaning); the linguistic sign for Saussure is a two-fold entity, a Janus-faced thing, both sides or faces of which are absolutely necessary for it to function as a sign, as with any set of binary pairs: to invoke one is to invoke the other.[24] The linguistic sign unites or is a binary, not a thing or object and a name, but a concept and a sound-image, as the signified and the signifier respectively. The two elements are intimately united, and each recalls the other, or creates a tension of mutual expectancy. This theory of signification comports a sense (an idea acting as signified) and a 'voice' (acting as the signifier). This indissoluble union of the two primordial ('originary') components is the only essential thing in language, according to this model, which has been represented variously as:

S $\dfrac{\text{Sr}}{\text{Sd}}$ ——————(signification)—————— 'tree'

Sr/Sd signifier ⇆ signified (⇆ binary)

$S_3 \leftarrow S_2 \leftarrow S_1 \leftarrow \dfrac{\text{Sr}}{\text{Sd}}$

Figure I

What is important to note for our purposes is the fundamental unity of the signifier and the signified, albeit in a relation of mutual tension, and this is what makes it possible for the signifier, by becoming transparent, to allow the meaning to present itself; referring to nothing other than its presence. Saussure, it seems, wants to say that there is something of a *natural* bond between the *order* of signified *in general* and the order of phonic signifiers *in general*, as though the need to express meaning through sound was built into mankind's very mode of being. However, in respect of the more specific or particularised expressions, Saussure was emphatic that in any given language the relation between the signifier and the signified is entirely *arbitrary*. That is to say, in speech the bond is constituted by conventions accepted by the language-community, and the signs are artificially produced. Furthermore, the signs in themselves do not have signification, linguistic value, but only achieve this in interrelation with other signs or a chain of signifiers in a system, i.e. in language. Nevertheless, Saussure does mean to say that there is no "motivation" on the part of the individual to form such a bond or even to change it; although he attempts to ground the process in an extended but complex social matrix, dispersed in the history of the speech-community, and is also suggestive of its indefiniteness. In other words, there is something of a "fixity" about the signifier-signified relation, certainly in terms of *la langue* but as well in *la parole*; yet, paradoxically, there is no real 'origin' of it other than the conditions which make it possible, which is language itself. But how can language be prior to the constituents that are supposed to make up language?

Saussurean semiological model has been taken up and developed in different ways by post-structuralists. There has, though, been a tendency to understand the signifier and signified in radically non-psychological terms, i.e. not simply related to the senses, such as hearing, but in purely material or entitive terms. For example, Jacques Lacan takes the signifier as pure materiality, a sound, a written trace that can be a vehicle to its meaning part and that generates multiple effects through its contextualisation or its 'play', as much outside language as in language. He further claims that signifiers do not actually exist, for all signifieds are simply substituted or displaced signifiers. Hence Lacan takes the differentiation of signifier and signified to its extreme. This analysis opens up the possibility of an endless *link* chain of signs acting as the instrument of communication (whether this be in dreams, within the unconscious, or in speech).

Jacques Derrida, the contemporary French philosopher who has gained some notoriety among philosophers and considerable devotion among literary critics, also takes the Saussurean model as his starting point. Derrida argues for the primacy or comprehensiveness of writing, of the *word*, over all else, including language.[25] All meaning is traced back to signs; or more precisely, meaning is located within the system of differences between signs rather than simply in the relationships between signs and objects, events or context (i.e. referents), to which they refer as linguistic items. The emphasis on the differential mark that exists between one sign and another relativised to the differentation of the signifier-signified relation is extended far beyond that envisaged by Saussure. Put simply, Derrida focuses on the separation, the difference, the indissoluble disunity, the opposition between signifier and signified as well as the mark that distinguishes one sign from other signs. (Derrida does not, however, want to suggest that elements which are different from each other cannot combine or 'bind together' [like ghee with flour], only that there can never be identity or complete presence of one in the other.) To press this point about the absence of identity (or the presence of difference, he coins the neologism *différance* (from *différer*, to differ and to defer, or, grossly put, difference in space and time, in any relationship), which has the dual sense of differentiating and deferral, and is often indicated by a "/" (bar). The fixing of the relation which Saussure had located in a social matrix Derrida places it or rather traces it within textuality (understood in the broadest possible sense as discourse). He decenters the subject as author and makes the *text* the context that accomplishes this inter-play of signs, their split or dissembling and their endless dissemination. Derrida even goes as far as to suggest that there is no life to signs outside of the text: '*il n'y a pas de hort-texte*'.[25] Derrida makes the 'interval' that marks the distinction between signifier and signified as the most significant part of the Saussurean insight. And he is of the view that there is no ultimate concept—the 'transcendental signified', *sacra archē*, *logos*, much searched for in metaphysics—independent of language that accounts for the 'origin' of the relationship and broadly of the relationship of language, or text, to consciousness, presence, history and so on.[26] Although he does concede that, "even if the inherited opposition between signifier and signified can be shown to be programmed by the metaphysical desire for the transcendental, other-worldly meaning (that is often derived from the theological model of the presence of God), this does not mean that the opposition. . .can simply be abandoned as an historical delusion".[27] Derrida explicitly states, "That this opposition or difference cannot be radical and absolute does not prevent it from functioning, and even from being indispensable within certain limits—very wide limits. For example, no translation would be possible without it."[28] What Derrida seems concerned about is the way and extent to which the signifier in its phonetic image (*phoné*) is privileged as a mode of expression over the written (*graphé*); which is not to say that for Derrida speech is opposed to writing (*l'ecriture*) for speech is forever writing.[29] These latter more technical concerns, which inform the bulk of Derrida's writings on language, we shall not dwell on here.

Yet, in Derrida's work on Husserl's *Origin of Geometry* there is the same fascination for the relation between eternal objects of geometry as the Mīmāṁsakas had for the relation between words and meaning (the objects of language).[30] However, the deconstructive turn hinges in the final analysis just on the recognition of the utter 'conventional nature of language'.

Again on the question of origin, the classics had identified the signified as the originating factor of the signifier (voice), e.g. God the Father begets the Son, the Son in turn reflects the Father, and a chain of signifiers is set up *and* disseminated infinitely. But, as we said, Derrida rejects the possibility of an ultimate ground, transcendental or metaphysical, as the originating factor of the signified and the 'founding binary combination'; rather, he believes, and tries to show through a series of complicated arguments, that there are really only signs which form an indefinite link chain *in reverso modo*. There is for him no *logocentre* which originates the sign; indeed, the absolute identification of language and ontology is resisted here with the device of *différance* and a trenchant critique of the metaphysical desire. Saussure's suggestion about the arbitrariness of the relation is exploited by Derrida to its logical limit in that he questions

Saussure's insistence on the natural bond between the two general 'orders' of sound and meaning (we referred to earlier). Derrida contends that, not only the binary combination, but the sum total of the phonic signifiers, that is each and every one of them, is arbitrary.[31] And further, Derrida wants to say that 'every signified is also in the position of a signifier, [hence] the distinction between signified and signifier becomes problematical at its root'.[32]

Thus there is nothing natural about the 'order' or totality if there isn't naturalness for each signifier. Of course, Derrida wants to guard against any possibility of the ontologisation of this 'order', and to have it removed from its context of origination, which is psyche (voice) itself, transformed into the exteriority of the text or the graphic sign. Hence, while in conventional representation we have the signified being mirrored in the signifier, with Derrida, it is the signified which mirrors the signifier, and by a doubling back effect (*dédoublement*) the signifier becomes a signified, changes itself, and attaches itself to another signifier; this process could repeat itself setting up a chain link of signifiers, of which none has any independent or 'natural' signified attached to it. The *n*th signifer would have to transgress a whole series of signifiers to return to the 'original' signified, which however itself might have been simply another signifier, and so on *ad infinitum*! The so-called signs can only be pure signifiers, through and through. An infinite number of signs come into play.[33] This dissemination of the signifier, then, also marks the endless dissemination of the sign: which is akin to the idea of *anādivyavahāratvam*.[34]

Again, as we said, although Derrida dismisses any radical and absolute grounds for the inherited difference or opposition between signifier and signified, he does not think that, therefore, it has no function or relevance; in fact, the relation might even be indispensible within certain limits. The fixed locus is abandoned for the function. One might retort that Derrida has made his *différance* the originating principle, the source of it all. No. Because '[T]o say that *différance* is originary is simultaneously to erase the myth of a present origin. Which is why 'originary' must be understood as having been *crossed out*, without which *différance* would be derived from an original plenitude. It is non-origin which is originary'.[35] 'The absence of the transcendental signified extends the domain and the play of signification infinitely.'[36]

Now it is my contention that the *autpattika* principle could be read in similar terms, as being *originary without having an origin*, or as Śabara says, the term 'origin' is simply a metaphor here: for what? we might say, for a presence which no sooner that it arises 'crosses out itself', for another presence and so on. As Derrida would put it: 'If one erases the radical difference between signifier and signified, it is the word "signifier" itself which must be abandoned as a metaphysical concept'.[37] What Derrida intends is to simply expell the signifier by substituting it with the signified, or with concept (*submitting* the sign to thought, which is the classic way). The sign remains deeply paradoxical, poised in opposition, and this says Derrida is true for all sentences, and most especially the sentences of metaphysics.[38]

I have laboured on this deconstructive thesis simply for the purpose of highlighting the conceded possibility that the quest for the origin of the signifier (and the signified, regardless of how their relation is conceptualised) can recede infinitely backwards 'effacing itself in its own production'. Indeed, this idea of an infinitely transmissible tradition is Derrida's cherished project.

Less dramatically, suppose we take the expression (*vidhi*) 'One who desires *svarga* should perform sacrifice'. Without concerning ourselves at this stage with questions of syntax, we notice here a string of signs, which breaks up into the signifiers, basically, as the *liṅ+dhātu*, *svargaśabda*, *kāraka* (which is neutral in the instrumental) etc, and the signifieds as the twofold *bhāvanā* or impulse (efficiency), namely, 'performative action' and 'the *phala* (*svarga*, etc)'. But the *phala* is not actually observed or is not forthcoming in the sacrifice, for it is deferred or postoned; which means that the two *bhāvanās* in turn become signifiers portending a third signified: namely the *apūrva* (an 'unprecedented' efficiency), this is the 'transcendental signified' (*adṛṣṭārtha*, literally, 'unseen effect or entity').

However, the *apūrva* is 'transcendental' only in a provisional and operational sense, for its significance is not so much in its being *adṛṣṭatva* (as Verpoorten rightly points out)[39] as in being a mysterious result 'which has nothing before it' or being without a preceding instance, i.e. in its novelty and prior unknownness, and so also in its near-empirical givenness for it retains the phenomenality of the *almost certain phala* (result), and further it will erase itself the moment the *phala* has matured (*siddha*) later. Hence, once again, *phala* functions as the signifier for the deferred but now-imminent signified, namely, *svarga*, and which too, like the *devatās*, has no ultimate or absolute ontological status in Mīmāṁsā, being possibly a signifier for an inner state of happiness in another birth, or something to be consummated, and so its self-identity is eroded. And, of course, *apūrva* can be annulled (*bādha*) by a wrong step in the sacrifice. What is interesting is that the *apūrva* has no sign for it in the expression itself, and so it cannot achieve reference to itself self-reflexively, as happens when I say 'I'; yet the 'hidden' (*avyakta*), unmanifest and 'not yet visible', does achieve signification, though at the upper split level, i.e. as the pure signified. But how can this split occur if *autpattikatva* is to be taken literally, i.e. as prefiguring an inseparable relation? We have to say that this occurs through displacing another signifier, or by metonymy, or because the *vācaka* as a syntagm is the signifier in this instance (of performative utterance). And in all this the subject as *auctor* need hardly be relevant.

This inter-looping or inter-playing of the binary pairs is, I believe, a significant indicator of the differential already impressed in the *autpattika sambandha*, or rather this itself marks another binary held in tension beneath the *śabda-artha* pair, namely, that of difference and naturalness. And this is most important from the point of view of a critique of metaphysics, for by this very recognition the Mīmāṁsakas check the tendency of any self-identification of signifier-signified, as occurs, say, in the Bhartṛhari's *Śabdabrahman* or in the dissolution of all expressions into the Brahman of Advaita, or a Being that might unite the opposites, overcome the tension, or a *parousia*, as Mahādeva or *Īśvara*, that governs their presence (*ousia* as presence/essence/existence, substance or subject), which is absent. (This would be true even if we admit that Mīmāṁsās hold word as *varṇas*, syllables or phomenes, to be universal and *nitya* (even *kūṭastha nitya*), and meaning or *artha* as somehow *nitya* also, but note that it is never *varṇasphoṭa* (meaning-saturated syllables); the *sphoṭa*-like function emerges with *pada* (putative word), which as *śabda* (sonic whole) and *artha* (sense) are united, yet remain forever in tension—this position, for all its ambiguity and paradoxicality, is most marked in Kumārila Bhaṭṭa.[40] (And if we return to *artha* the magical sense, incantational and potency of the *mantras*, then we move it away from concept, the intelligible in spoken language, we then have a system of signs—rhythms, silences, gestures, noises—which is not exhausted by logical speech or rational discourse.) But I am straying here. This process is best represented with the help of the following diagram:

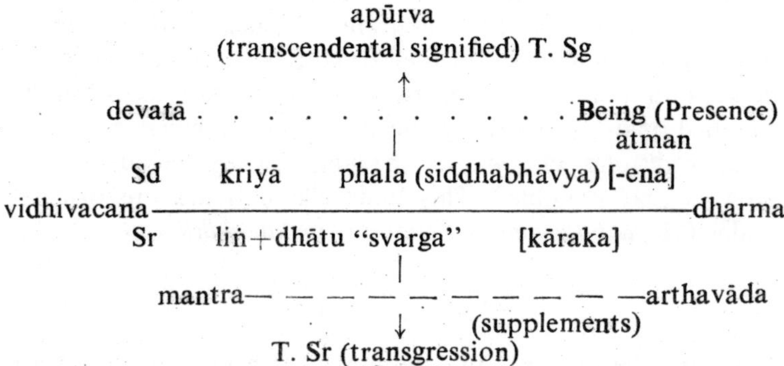

Figure II

I will conclude with remarks on some semantical consequences and difficulties this thesis presents. The *autpattikatva* thesis as presented in the Mīmāṁsā appears, in some ways, to be counter-intuitive. One could object that a long process of historical repetition of the pairing of word and meaning in any medium gives the appearance that no personal agency or traditional convention was responsible for fixing the relation. Further, we can only have access to a finite number of words in any given language at any given time and from looking at these we cannot pronounce that *autpattikatva* is true for all words. Also, there are words that have no meaning, and some words have more than one meaning, and many words have the same meaning. We do also observe that, as with names, new words are created with new meanings attached to them. And, as Frits Staal once remarked, if anything is eternal it would be the lexicon!

Pārthasārathi considers some of these objections (as indeed

had Śabara), but the one he chooses to address in rejecting all of them is the questionable assumption that word expresses meaning. His short answer is: it is a fact that immediately upon hearing a word its meaning arises in one who knows the language even if the word is used by an ignoramus.[41] But we also observe that sometimes when words are first heard they convey no meaning. Again, his answer is that this is because certain attendant conditions are not fulfilled, such as absence of impediments in the medium, and so on, or because one has not learnt it from another. This does imply that the meanings of words have to be learnt, from another who learns it from another and so on (the requirement called *vṛddhavyavahāra*). But this does not entail for the Mīmāṁsakas that anyone of the persons in the process of transmission actually fixes signifier-signified relation. More significantly, he says, when a sentence is uttered, one who knows the language apprehends its sense. How is that possible? This and related issues are discussed under *Vākyādhikaraṇa* or *Vedapratyāyakatvādhikaraṇa* (7).[42]

Abbreviations

MS *Mīmāṁsāsūtras* of Jaimini. *Mīmāṁsādarśanam with Śābarabhāṣyam.* (edited by Jīvāndanda Vidyāsāgar Bhaṭṭācāryya.) Adhyāya I—VIII. Calcutta: Sārasudhānidhi Press. 1883. (Also, *Mīmāṁsādarśanam* with *Śābarabhāṣyam*. Anandasrama Sanskrit Series, no 97. Poona, 1973-84.)

NMV *Jaiminīyanyāyamālāvistara* (ed. Jīvānanda Vidyāsāgar Bhaṭṭācāryya). Saraswatī Press, Calcutta, 1883.

NRM *Nyāyaratnamālā* of Pārthasārathi Miśra. Gaekward Oriental Series, no 75, Baroda 1937.

SB *Śābarabhāṣya* of Śābarasvāmi (in *Mīmāṁsādarśanam*).

SD *Śāstradīpikā* of Pārthasārathi Miśra (edited by Rāmamiśraśāstrī) Kāshi 1881 [So 1949]. (Also, *Śāstradīpikā* with commentary *Prabhā* by Vaidyanātha Śāstrī [edited by P. N. Paṭṭābhirāmaśāstri] Sri Lalbahadur Kendriya Sanskrit Vidyapitha, New Delhi, 1978).

SV *Ślokavārttika* of Kumārila Bhaṭṭa with commentary *Nyāyaratnākara* of Pārthasārathi Miśra (edited by Svāmī Dvārikādāsaśāstrī), Tara Publications, Varanasi, 1978.

NOTES

*Pārthasārathi Miśra's *Śāstradīpikā*, *Nyāyaratnamālā* and *Nyāyaratnākara* are the main sources. I am grateful to Professor K. T. Pandurangi of Bangalore for his guidance in this enquiry.

1. Jean-Marie Verpoorten, *A History of Indian Literature—Mīmāṁsā Literature*. Otto Harrassowitz, Wiesbaden. 1987, p. 31.

2. See Puruṣottama Billimoria 'Hindu Doubts About God: Towards a Mīmāṁsā Deconstruction'. *International Philosophical Quarterly* (Fordham, NY), December 1990, 30 (4) pp. 481–99.

3. See *Australasian Journal of Philosophy*, March 1990, p. 161, and John Searle, *Speech Acts*. Cambridge University Press, 1969, pp. 43ff.

4. See Puruṣottama Billimoria, 'On the Idea of Authorless Revelation (*Apaūruṣeya*).' In: R.W. Perrett (ed.) *Indian Philosophy of Religion*. Kluwer Academic Publishers, Dordrecht, 1989, pp. 143–66.

On other possible interpretation of the concept of 'revelation' see, Stewart R. Sutherland, 'The Concept of Revelation', in *Religion, Reason and the Self Essays in Honour of Hywel D Lewis*, edited by Stewart R. Sutherland, T.A. Roberts. Cardiff: University of Wales Press, 1989, pp. 35–46.

5. Paper entitled 'Pārthasārathi Miśra on Sentence Formation and the infinite regress argument', presented at the XIIIth World Sanskrit Conference, University of Vienna, September 1991; Proceedings of.

6. See *Śāstradīpikā* (=SD) on I.i.5 p. 28 discussing absence of *puruṣānupraveśaḥ* or three kinds of human contact with word, p. 131 Vedāpauruṣeya; 87 end p. 67 [D. Venkataramiah, GOS, no. LXXXIX. p. 123, 230].

7. T.R.V. Murti, however, went ā bit too far in his following remark:"The eternality of words as propounded by the schools of Mīmāṁsā and Grammar is the Indian counterpart of the[Platonic] doctrine of Ideas". Krishna Sivaraman rightly cautions us against taking the resemblance to the Platonic *Ideas* to be anything more than an aesthetic resemblance. K. Sivaraman, 'The Word as a Category of Revelation', in H. Coward and K. Sivaraman (es.) *Revelation in Indian Thought*. A. Festschrift in honour of T.R.V. Murti, Dharma Publishing, California, 1977. (pp. 45-64), pp. 59-60, n. 9.

On general comparison on Indian theories of meaning and linguistic understanding to Western theories, see Puruṣottama Billimoria, *Śabda-Pramāṇa: Word and Knowledge A Doctrine in Mīmāṁsā-Nyāya Philosophy, towards a framework for Śruti-prāmāṇya*. Foreword by Professor J. N. Mohanty. Kluwer/Reidel Publishing Company, Dordrecht. 1988.

8. Mīmāṁsādarśanam (MS), p. 161.

9. *utpattirhi bhāva ucyate lakṣaṇayā aviyuktaḥ śabdārthyor bhāvaḥ sambandhaḥ* [*sambandhena*], *notpannayoḥ paścāt sambandhaḥ*. (SB, 1883 edn. p. 8).

10. M. Heidegger, 'The Origins of the Work of Art', in *Poetry, Language, Thought*, (Trans Hofstadter), NY: Harper & Row, 1975, p. 17, pp. 132ff.

11. *Being and Time* (trans. John Macquarie) NY: Harper & Row, 1962, p. 209; *On the Way to Language* (trans. Peter Hertz), NY: Harper, 1982, 124ff.

12. From Billimoria, '*Apauruṣeya*' (note 4 *supra*), p. 159.

13. Mdme Biardeau, *Théorie de la Connaissance et Philosophie de la Parole dans le brahmanisme classique*. Paris: Mouton. 1964, pp. 156-57. See also Frits Staal, 'Sanskrit Philosophy of Language'. In Thomas A. Sebeok (ed.) Current Trends in Linguistics, Vol. 5. The Hague; Mouton.

14. Othmar Gachter, *Hermeneutics and Language in Pūrvamīmāṁsā: A Study in Śābara Bhāṣya*. Delhi: Motilal Banarsidass, 1983, p. 44.

15. SB, p. 13.

16. SD p. 28#3; *padapadārthasambandhasya nityatvamatrautpattika-śabdenoktaṁ vākyārthasya ca padārthamūlatvam* . . . and sentence meaning is contingent on word-meaning;at p. 67 87 Pārthasārathi refers to *autpattikatva*; and *nityatva* of *sambandha* again in opening #88, p. 67-8.

17. Patañjali in *Yogasūtra* (42).

18. See Gopinath Kavirāja, *Aspects of Indian Thought*, University of Burdwan, 1984, pp. 14–17.

19. *Kāvyālaṁkāra* I.16 see A.K. Warder, *The Science of Criticism in India*, (Adyar, 1978) p. 31.

20. SB (op cit). p. 14; cf. *yat śabde vijñāte'rtho vijñāyate.*

21. *pratyāyyapratyāyakatvalakṣaṇo'satyeva sambandhāntare svabhāvata*, #89, SD p. 68.

22. Both being *vijñānas* according to Vijñānavāda, #88 SD p. 68.

23. See Rovert Magliola, *Derrida on the Mend*. Purdue Press, 1984, p. 13.

24. Ferdinand de Saussure, *Cours de linguistic générale*; trans. Wade Buskin as *Course in General Linguistics*, Glasgow: Collins/Fontana, 1974; especially 'The Linguistic Sign', reprinted in Robert E. Innes (ed.) *Semiotics: An Introductory Anthology*, Bloomington: Indian University Press, 1985. pp. 28-46.

25. *Of Grammatology*. trans. by Gayatri Spivak-Chakraborti. John Hopkins University Press, Baltimore 1972, 1976, pp. 8-9.

26. *Ibid.*, pp. 10-11.

27. Alan Bass, Translator's Introduction to: Jacques Derrida, *Writing and Difference*. (p. xv) The University of Chicago Press, 1978. See also p. 12, (note 35 below).

28. Derrida, *Positions*, trans., Alan Bass. 1981, p. 31; Ibid., p. xv.

29. Ibid., p. 30; also, *Speech and Phenomena*, trans. D.B. Allison. Evanston: Northwestern UP, 1973. *La Dissémination* (Paris: Minuit, 1972).

30. See Introduction to *Writing and Difference*, p. xi–xii.

31. *OG* p. 44.

32. *Positions*, pp. 19-20.

33. 'Structure, Sign and Play' in *Writing and Difference*, p. xv,

34. *anantavākya'rthasādhāraṇatvāt* (*SD* p. 125f). Useful discussion in John Taber, 'The Theory of the Sentence in Pūrva Mīmāṁsā and Western Philosophy'. *Journal of Indian Philosophy*. December 1989. Vol. 17, no. 4, pp. 407–30, p. 409, p. 417.

35. 'Structure, Sign and Play', *Writing and Difference*, p. 303.

36. *Ibid.*, p. 280 or *passim*.

37. *Ibid.*, p. 281.

38. *Ibid.*, Derrida insists that what applies to signs applies also to the whole history of metaphysics, which he says, like the history of the West, is the history of metaphors and metonymies. "Its matrix,. .is the determination of Being as *presence* in all senses of this word. It could be shown that all names related to fundamentals, to principles, or to the centrer have always designated an invariable presence—*eidos*, archē, *telos*, *energeia*, *ousia* (*essence existence*, *substance*, *subject*), *alētheia*, transcendentality, consciousness, God, man, and so forth", p. 280. With the concept of the *sign* generalised to all the concepts and all the sentences of metaphysics, Derrida hopes to shake the roots of the metaphysics of presence. The whole Platonist thrust is etased in the process.

39. Op. cit., pp. 20. Although the *apūrva* may be established via *arthāpatti*, the point is that a deferred signified is being pointed to in the rite, as an incentive or a final cause for Kumārila, and a product or result of exertion (*kārya*) for Prabhākara (p. 34).

40. *Ślokavārttika* (16=*sphoṭavāda*#69), stressing the significative capacity of something more than *varṇas*, which serve collectively as vehicle for the release of the *artha*.

41. SD see under *autpattika adhikaraṇa*, and p. 125 (under *Vedapratyāyakatvādhikaraṇa*).

42. See notes 5 (and 4, 6) above.

11

MIMĀṀSĀ VIEWS ON SENTENCE-MEANING: SOME PROBLEMS

K. KUNJUNNI RAJA

Mīmāṁsā is also known as *Vākyaśāstra*, 'the science of sentences'. It was this school that started a detailed study of sentences and developed elaborate canons of interpretation. This study was mainly based on individual words and the word meanings and consequently the relation between words and the sentence constituted by them and between word meanings and sentence meaning remained the central problem for this school. The *Mīmāṁsā* school first enunciated and the other schools of thought later accepted with minor modifications the three factors of *ākāṅkṣā* (mutual expectancy), *yogyatā* (consistency) and *saṁnidhi* (contiguity) among the word meanings in a sentence as constituting the bases for the unity of the sentence. The important role played by *tātparya* or the general purport as understood from contextual factors was also stressed by this school.

According to the Mīmāṁsakas the primary meaning of a word is the universal (*ākṛti*) which is the essential quality common to the particular instances of the class. Both Jaimini and Śabarasvāmin use the term *ākṛti* to refer to the universal; but Kumārila Bhaṭṭa makes it clear that the term is used in the sense of *jāti* or universal.

jātimevākṛtiṁ prāhurvyaktirākriyate yayā (*Ślokavārttika*, Ākṛti section, verse 3). Patañjali, the grammarian, has also used the term *ākṛti* in this sense in his *Mahābhāṣya*. Later writers in the field of Mīmāṁsā use the term *jāti* itself.

Mīmāṁsakas assume that the relation between a word and its meaning is *autpattika* or permanent (literally, from the beginning of the word itself, since a word is a word only when it has a meaning). The unit of language is taken as *varṇa* or phoneme, which is permanent, and word is a collection of phonemes in a particular order of sequence. The primary meaning of a word is something permanent and cannot be the particular instances of the class. It was, however, admitted that in a sentence it is the particular (*vyakti*) that enters into syntactic relationship.

Regarding the question as to how the particular is cognized from the universal there are different views, even among Mīmāṁsakas. According to the Prabhākara school the particular is cognized from the universal through *abhidhā* or the primary significatory function of the word itself, because of the invariable connection between the two and since the same cognition can comprehend both the universal and the particular.

jāter vyaktisamānasaṁvitsaṁvedyatayā
(*Vedāntaparibhāṣā*, p. 70 Adyar Library edition)

Though *Śakti* itself gives both the universal and the particular, the former is *jñātā satī*, known through the understanding of the relation between the word and its meaning, while the latter is *svarūpasatī*, the meaning *per se* (as itself existent).

yadvā gavādipadānām vyaktau śaktiḥ
svarūpasatī, na tu jñātā (*Vedāntaparibhāṣā*, p. 158)

To explain this Prābhākaras distinguish between real *śakti* giving the meaning of the universal and *kubja śakti* (a smaller or dwarfish *śakti*) to explain the denotation of the particular:

(1) *anvitābhidhānavādimate śaktyā, abhihitānvayavādimate ca lakṣaṇayā vācyārthabhūtasaṁsargasya vṛttijñāpyatvāt, ādyapakṣe kubjaśaktyaṅgīkārāt, dvitīyapakṣe lakṣaṇāyāḥ jñātāyā eva padārthaniṣṭhāyāḥ vṛttitvāṅgīkāraḥ*
(*Advaitasiddhi*, pp. 655-6)

(2) *kubjavādinas tu gavādipadānām gotve gavi ca śaktiḥ; paraṁtu jātau śaktirjñātā satyupayujyate, vyaktau kubjā satyupayujyate* (*Prabhāṭīkā* on *Kārikāvali*, p. 570)

(3) *jātiśakter jñātatvaṁ ca śābdabodhajanakasmṛtinirūpitaśaktijñānaniṣṭhakāraṇatānirūpitaviṣayatā-sambandhāvacchinna-*

śaktiniṣṭhāvacchedakatāyāṁ jātiviṣayakatvāvacchinnatvam eva. tādṛśāvacchedakatāyāṁ vyaktiviṣayakatvānavacchinnatvam eva śakter vyaktyaṁśe kubjatvam. tādṛśaśaktigrahasya gopadanirūpitagotvaviṣayatāśaktimati gaurityākāraḥ etādṛśaśaktijñāne gotvaviṣayakatvena śakter viṣayatvāt gotvāṁśe śakter jñātatvaṁ goviṣayakatvena śakter aviṣayatvāt tadaṁśe kubjatvam (Ibid).

According to the Bhāṭṭa Mīmāṁsakas who follow the *Abhihitānvaya* theory of sentence meaning, the primary meaning of a word is only the universal. The particular is got from the universal by resorting to *lakṣaṇā* because of the discrepancy of the literal meaning in the context. *Nyāyaratnamālā* puts it clearly:

tasmāj jātyabhidhāyitvāt śabdas tām eva bodhayet/
sā tu śabdena vijñātā paścād vyaktim prabodhayet//
(*Vākyārthanirṇaya*, v. 42)

In a sentence every word conveys its primary meaning which is the universal; isolated word meanings in the form of universals cannot convey a connected unitary meaning; but we know that the utterance of a sentence is for the purpose of conveying a connected meaning. This is the *mukhyārthabādha* or discrepancy which prompts the resorting to *lakṣaṇā*. Kumārila Bhaṭṭa says in the *Ślokavārttika*:

jāter astitvanāstitve nahi kaścid vivakṣati/
nityatvāl lakṣyamāṇāyā vyakteste hi viśeṣaṇe//
(*Ākṛti* Section, p. 932)

"Nobody wants to speak about the existence or non-existence of the universal which is eternal; these two (existence and non-existence) apply to the particulars which are got through *lakṣaṇā*." The Bhāṭṭas are definite that the apprehension of the particular from the universal is through *lakṣaṇā*.

There has been some confusion among the Naiyāyikas from the time of Gaṅgeśopādhyāya down to the modern times regarding this theory of *lakṣaṇā* explaining the comprehension of the particulars from the universal. Gaṅgeśa ascribes this theory of *lakṣaṇā* to Maṇḍanamiśra. The verse from "*Ślokavārttika, jāter astitvanāstitve . . .*" quoted above (*Ākṛti* section, p. 932), is quoted by Gaṅgeśa and ascribed to Maṇḍana (*Tattvacintāmaṇi, Śaktivāda*, p. 87). This mistake is continued in later works like Jagadīśa's *Śabdaśaktiprakāśikā* (p. 587). In a paper presented to the International Congress of Orientalists at Delhi in 1961 I had pointed out that the verse quoted by Gaṅgeśa as from Maṇḍana is actually a quotation from the *Ślokavārttika* of Kumārila, who is earlier than Maṇḍana.

Gaṅgeśa seems to have considered that according to Kumārilabhaṭṭa, the particular is obtained from the universal through *ākṣepa* or implication as distinct from Maṇḍana's view of *lakṣaṇā*. But there is no difference between *lakṣaṇā* and *ākṣepa*. Pārthasārathimiśra uses the term *ākṣepa* also to explain this:

vyaktipratītirasmākaṁ jātir eva tu śabdataḥ/
prathamāvagatā paścād vyaktiṁ yāṁ kāṁcid ākṣipet//

Ākṣepa involves *arthāpatti*; even for *lakṣaṇā*, *arthāpatti* is the basis.

When I presented my paper at the International Congress of Orientalists at Delhi, I thought that I was the first to point out this discrepancy. But later I found that other earlier writers have also noted it. Thus in the *Nyāyadīpa* commentary on *Tarkatāṇḍava*:

yady api maṇau bhāṭṭamate tu vyaktistvākṣepalabhyetyuktvā, ākṣepapakṣa eva doṣān uktvā "jāter astitvanāstitve..." iti maṇḍanaślokaṁ sammatitvenoktvā maṇḍanamatatvenopanyasya khaṇḍitavān. tathāpi maṇḍanasya bhaṭṭaśiṣyatvāt bhāṭṭāstu lakṣyetyāhur ityuktam. ākṛtyadhikaraṇavārttikamate vyaktilakṣaṇāpakṣasya sphuṭatvācca. Vol. II, p. 230, Mysore Uni. edn.

The Bhāṭṭa Mīmāṁsakas who advocate the theory of *Abhihitānvayavāda* of verbal comprehension of a sentence resort to *lakṣaṇā* for conveying the syntactic relation among the word meanings. The *Śabarabhāṣya* statement seems to be more in favour of this theory than that of Prabhākara.

padāni svaṁ svam artham abhidhāya nivṛttavyāpārāṇi; athedānīm padārthāḥ avagatāḥ santaḥ vākyārthaṁ gamayanti.

(The words in a sentence convey their individual meanings and stop with that; then the word meanings convey the syntactically connected sentence meaning.) All the authorities on Bhāṭṭa Mīmāṁsā have stated that it is through *lakṣaṇā* that the sentence meaning is comprehended.

1. *vākyārtho lakṣyamāṇo hi sarvatraiveti naḥ sthitiḥ.* (Kumārilabhaṭṭa quoted in *Tattvabindu*, p. 153)

2. *padasvarūpābhihitaiḥ padārthaiḥ saṁlakṣyate'sāviti siddham etat.* (Pārthasārathimiśra, *Nyāyaratnamālā*, p. 125)

See also, *Mānameyarahasyaślokavārttika*, by Lakshmipuram Srinivasacharya (Mysore, 1925), p. 85.

śaktir jātau, vyaktilābho lakṣaṇādhīna iṣyate
iti maṇḍana-siddhāntaḥ gadādharasudhīritaḥ
"jāter astitvanāstitve . . . vyaktes te hi viśeṣaṇe"
iti padyam śaktivāde mānatvena hyanūditam.
vākyādhikaraṇe ślokavārttike'pi ca dṛśyate.

3. *padābhihitaiḥ padārthaiḥ lakṣaṇayā vākyārthaḥ pratipādyate.* (*Śāstradīpikā*, p. 154)

4. *labhyate ca samabhivyāhārānyathānupapatyā padānām anvitārthaparāṇāṁ svārthābhidheyārtharūpasamavetānvitāvasthāpratyāyanaṁ lakṣaṇayā* (*Tattvabindu*, p. 131)

5. *padārthā eva vākyārthaṃ lakṣayanti* (Cidānanda, *Nītitattvāvirbhāva* TSS ed., p. 232)

6. *vayam tu padārthāḥ lakṣaṇayaiva vākyārtham bodhayantīti brūmaḥ.* (*Mānameyodaya*, p. 94)

Thus it seems that Bhāṭṭa Mīmāṁsakas have to resort to *lakṣaṇā* to get the meaning of the particulars from the universals which are the primary meanings of the words; they have also to resort to *lakṣaṇā* to explain how the *saṁsarga* or syntactic relation among the word meanings is conveyed. Now the problem is whether we should assume two *lakṣaṇās* to explain these two functions or whether the same *lakṣaṇā* can produce the two results. This problem has not been raised seriously by earlier writers; nobody speaks of two *lakṣaṇās*. It is simpler to assume that the same *lakṣaṇā* can produce the two effects—universal to particular, and the addition of the syntactic relationship. Nārāyaṇa Bhaṭṭa's statement in the *Mānameyodaya* seems to support this view.

vayaṁ tu padārthāḥ lakṣaṇayaiva vākyārtham bodhayantīti brūmaḥ. vācyārthānupapattyā hi lakṣaṇā bhavati. atra ca padaiḥ smāryamāṇā gavādipadārthāḥ yady anyonyānvayaṁ vinā sāmānyarūpā evāvatiṣṭheran tarhi padānāṁ vyutpattisamayāvadhṛtam ekaviśiṣṭārthabodhatātparyaṁ virudhyeta iti sāmānyarūpasya vācyasyānupapatteḥ anyonyānvayarūpe viśeṣa eva padārthāḥ paryavasyanti.

"But we say that the sense of the words conveys the meaning of the sentence only by secondary implication. Indeed secondary implication comes in through the non-intelligibility of the expressed meaning. And here senses like 'cow' etc., recollected by the words, if they should remain in their generic form without mutual syntactical relation, then there would be contradiction of the purport of the words to indicate unitary qualified object as determined at the time of learning. And so since the generic form signified is unintelligible, the meaning of words leads up to the particulars consisting in mutual syntactical relation." (Adyar ed., p. 96.)

The incompatibility in the context (*tātparyānupapatti*) is the lack of a unified, connected sentence meaning. This can be removed only by resorting to both the operations—*jāti* to *vyakti*, and the addition of syntactic relationship(*anvaya*). The process of *lakṣaṇā* can be completed only by removing the contextual incompatibility, and this can be done only by effecting both the operations. Hence it is proper that both the operations are to be considered as being effected by the same *lakṣaṇā vyāpāra*.

There has been some confusion regarding the process of understanding the sentence meaning according to the Bhāṭṭa School of Mīmāṁsā advocating *Abhihitānvaya* theory. Jayanta Bhaṭṭa, the Naiyāyika who was a contemporary of Ānandavardhana in the second half of the ninth century suggested that *Tātparyaśakti* may be assumed as responsible for getting the sentence meaning according to the *Abhihitānvaya* theory. He was the first scholar to bring forward the theory about *tātparyaśakti*: Ānandavardhana does not speak about it; it was Abhinavagupta and later literary critics who referred to it with favour. The Bhāṭṭa Mīmāṁsā view regarding *lakṣaṇā* as responsible for conveying the *saṁsarga* or syntactic relationship among the word meanings is not acceptable to the Naiyāyikas since they do not recognize *lakṣaṇā* for the sentence, but only for words. Jayanta advocates a modified form of *Abhihitānvaya*, substituting the *tātparyaśakti* for the Bhāṭṭa's *lakṣaṇā*:

abhidhātrī matā śaktiḥ padānāṁ svārthaniṣṭhatā/
teṣāṁ tātparyaśaktis tu saṁsargāvagamāvadhi//

(*Nyāyamañjarī*, p. 371f)

This *tātparyaśakti* is the same as the *saṁsargamaryādā* accepted by the later Navyanyāya school.

Since *Abhihitānvaya* theory is generally associated with the Bhāṭṭa Mīmāṁsakas, some later Ālaṁkārikas wrongly stated that the *tātparyaśakti* is the view of the Bhāṭṭas:

1. Jhalkikar, commentary on *Kāvyaprakāśa*; *abhihitānvayavādinām iti . . . bhāṭṭamīmāṁsakānām ity arthaḥ*.

2. K.C. Pandey (*Comparative Aesthetics*, I, p. 217). "The followers of the Nyāya school and the Bhāṭṭa Mimāṁsakas maintain the additional power of the word, namely, *tātparyaśakti*."

3. P.V. Kane (*Sāhityadarpaṇa*, Notes p. 86): "This view is held by that school of the Pūrvamīmāṁsā which is called *Abhihitānvayavāda*."

I had pointed out this mistake in my book (*Indian Theories of Meaning*, pp. 213ff); but this confusion is found in the writing of authoritative scholars now and then even now.[1]

The Bhāṭṭa Mīmāṁsāka view of *Abhihitānvaya* is found in its earliest form in the theory of Vājapyāyana referred to by Kātyāyana in his *Vārttika* to Pāṇini's *Aṣṭādhyāyī*. Vājapyāyana held

1. Cf. B.K. Matilal, *The Word and the World* (Oxford University Press, 1990), p. 168. "In fact Abhinavagupta talks about threewell-recognised 'powers' or 'functions' of words, instead of two (*abhidhā* 'denotative' that gives the lexical meanings and *lakṣaṇā* 'indicative' that gives the metaphorical sense). In this he seems to follow that Bhaṭṭa view of *Abhihitānavaya* (syntactic connection after designation). On this view, besides 'denotative' and 'indicative' there is another power called *tātparyaśakti* by virtue of which the isolated word meanings given by *abhidhā* together generate a connected whole, the sentence meaning."

that the meaning of a word is the universal (*jāti*) and that the meaning of a sentence is the *saṁsarga* or the mutual association of the word meanings.

ākṛtyabhidhānād vaikaṁ vibhaktau vājapyāyanaḥ
(*Vārttika* on Pāṇini, 1.2.64)

See also Helārāja on *Vākyapadīya* III, 1.2.

jātivādino vājapyāyanasya tu mate saṁsargo vākyārthaḥ

As far as the Prābhākara school of Mīmāṁsā is concerned the same *abhidhā* function of words can convey the literal lexical meaning of the words (both *jāti* and *vyakti*)[1] as well as the syntactic relationship.

1. In the Śābdabodha the *Śakti* which is not directly involved to get the particulars is called *kubja śakti*. See *Mānameyarahasyaślokavārttika*, p. 86.

12

KUMARILA'S THEORY OF WORD MEANING IN RELATION TO THE *SPHOPTA* THEORY OF *BHARTRHARI*

HAROLD COWARD

Kumārila of the *Mīmāṁsā* school and Bhartṛhari of the Grammarian school share many points of agreement with regard to word meaning. Over against schools such as the *Cārvāka, Jaina, Nyāya* and *Buddhists*, that see the relationship between word and meaning as human-made or conventional, Kumārila and Bhartṛhari agree that the relationship between the word (*śabda*) and its meaning (*artha*) is inborn, eternal and therefore not subject to creation by any person including even God.[1] The *Mīmāṁsā* doctrine that the word and its meaning are in an eternal relationship has evoked much controversy. How, for example, can the word be held to be eternally unchanging when it is not *always* present in our consciousness; when it seems to cease and grow silent and to require human effort for its production again; and when we hear the same word uttered in varying forms of dialect, accent, or loudness? *Mīmāṁsā* replies to such questions by saying that what is brought about by human effort is only the making present or manifestation of the already existing word.[2] When the sound of the spoken word is no longer heard, this is not due to any destruction of the word itself; rather, it is a case of non-perception of the word that remains eternally present. When we think of the great variety of accents, dialects, etc., that exist, it is evident that only on the assumption of an eternally existing and unchanging word could communication between individuals take place. Consequently *Mīmāṁsā* concludes that all this reasoning supports the Vedic texts which speak of the word as eternal.[3]

The place where the *Mīmāṁsā* and the Grammarians part

company is over the question as to how this eternal word meaning makes itself known. According to Kumārila it is the eternal meanings related to each letter-sound that, when added together, convey the whole word-meaning. Bhartṛhari, the Grammarian, disagrees and maintains that the letter sounds uttered evoke a pre-existing meaning-whole (that he calls a *sphoṭa*). For Kumārila the logic is that the meaning-whole is the sum of the parts (the letter-sounds), whereas, for Bhartṛhari, the logic is that the meaning whole (the *sphoṭa*) exists prior to the sum of the parts and indeed makes their summation into a whole possible. The debate between Kumārila and Bhartṛhari as to how words reveal their meaning is clearly summarized in the *Sphoṭasiddhi* of Maṇḍana Miśra.[4] In the *Sphoṭasiddhi* Maṇḍana Miśra, following the argument offered by Bhartṛhari in his *Vākyapadīya*, attempts to show that the existence of an inner meaning-whole or *sphoṭa* as distinct from its letter-sounds can be demonstrated in terms of logical necessity and consistency. Maṇḍana applies his logical analysis not only to the *Sphoṭa* theory but also to the alternative hypothesis put forward by Kumārila. As Gaurinath Sastri observes, Kumārila was the most formidable critic of the *Sphoṭa* theory—later writers have offered no new criticisms but only repeated Kumārila's arguments.[5]

Kumārila, arguing against Bhartṛhari, maintains that the word or *śabda*, whether it be the sentence or the individual word, is nothing more than a collection of word-sounds or spoken letters, and it is with this collection alone that the word-meaning is associated. When such a collection is brought to the mind of the hearer by the sounds uttered by the speaker, the hearer understands the meaning from the sounds alone. No mystical entity, such as *sphoṭa*, need be postulated at all.[6] According to Bhartṛhari, however, "the essence of the *Sphoṭa* doctrine is the idea that the word, mainly in the form of the sentence and secondarily in the form of the individual word and the phoneme (the articulated letter sound), is an entity over and above the sounds and not a mere collection of them and that it is this entity which is the bearer of the meaning."[7] This is the argument in its most general form. Since this argument goes on at great length, in true scholastic form, I have simply summarized the chief points as follows:

OUTLINE OF CHIEF POINTS IN THE ARGUMENT

Kumārila (*Mimāṁsā*)	Maṇḍana (*Sphoṭa*)
1. *Śabda* refers to phoneme as uttered.	*Śabda* refers to *sphoṭa* or indivisible word-whole which is a felt-fact in common experience.
2. Phonemes cause the understanding of meaning when grouped together in the form of words (*pada*).	Because of their ubiquitous and eternal nature, phonemes (as defined by *Mimāṁsakas*) can only exist singly and cannot possibly co-exist as *pada* so as to convey meaning. This inability of the phonemes to convey meanings points to the *sphoṭa* as the revealer of meaning.
3. Various suggestions as to how the phonemes could be grouped together so as to convey meaning:	Difficulties vitiating each suggestion:
(a) *e.g., seed.* Just as a seed will produce a new effect (sprout) when helped by other factors, so also the phonemes when combined with a group of helping factors (such as being uttered by the same person in a particular sequence) will result in the conveying of meaning.	How can being uttered by the same person in a particular sequence make the discrete phonemes c-o-w into a word when each letter vanishes completely before the subsequent one is uttered?
(b) *via saṃskāras.* Phonemes leave memory traces so that the traces of the earlier phonemes together with the utterance of the last phoneme conveys the meaning.	*Saṃskāras*, like their original individual phonemes, have only discrete existences vanishing completely before subsequent ones come into existence —therefore no possibility for grouping into a word or conveying meaning exists.

Kumārila (*Mimāṁsā*)	Maṇḍana (*Sphoṭa*)
(c) *via apūrva*. Phonemes leave impressions different from the ones which cause remembrance, and are like *apurva* in a sacrifice, where the unified result is different in nature from the individual causes (parts of the sacrifice). When spoken by a single person in a determinate order, the *apūrva* of the phonemes inheres in the self so that when the last phoneme is uttered the *śabda* is understood and its meaning conveyed.	Analogy from the *apūrva* of religious merit (which is based on an inference from scripture so as to validate the moral law) to the *saṃskāras* of phonemes rendering them capable of conveying meaning is unjustifiable. Rather it is the case that the ordinary memory traces of the phonemes reveal the already existing inherent *sphoṭa* which provides awareness of the whole and determines the order of the phonemes.
4. In the above view 3 (c) only one new thing (i.e. the special *apūrva*-like power) need be postulated, whereas Maṇḍana postulates two or three new things—a special *saṃskāra* and a *sphoṭa* (and a special power of that *sphoṭa*—conveying of meaning).	Only new thing postulated is *sphoṭa* itself and even that need not be postulated since it is directly perceptible. *Saṃskāra* referred to is the common memory trace which has the same object as that of the uttered phoneme (i.e. the *sphoṭa*). The unified *sphoṭa* was the original cause of the phoneme and is the end-object of both it and its *saṃskāra*. Thus no special or illogical power, such as *apūrva* is postulated.

Although Maṇḍana in presenting this debate clearly favours the Grammarian position, a dispassionate reading of the analysis suggests a draw rather than a victory for one side or the other. Neither Kumārila nor Bhartṛhari solve the question of how words convey meaning on purely logical grounds. Both take recourse to non-logical argument. For Kumārila it is the postulation of *apūrva*, based on the revelation of the Veda, that is found to be necessary for words to convey meaning. For Bhartṛhari it is the postulation of the *sphoṭa*, based on the intuitive experience of the speaker and hearer, that is found to be necessary for words to convey meaning. Both Kumārila and Bhartṛhari ground themselves upon the Vedas and argue that their respective schools provide the true understanding and prescription for life offered by the Vedic revelation.[8]

NOTES

1. See the *Śabara Bhāṣya* in Ganganatha Jha, *Pūrva-Mīmāṁsā in Its Sources* (Varanasi: Banaras Hindu University, 2nd Edition, 1964), p. 98.
2. See Kumārila's *Bhāṣya* on the *Mīmāṁsā Sūtras* of Jaimini, *sūtra* 12.
3. See the *Mīmāṁsā Sūtras* of Jaimini and *Bhāṣya* of Śabara, *sūtra* 23.
4. *Sphoṭasiddhi* of Maṇḍana Miśra, trans. by K.A.S. Iyer (Poona: Deccan College, 1966).
5. Gaurinath Sastri, *The Philosophy of Word and Meaning* (Calcutta: Sanskrit College, 1959), p. 103.
6. *Ślokavārtika of* Kumārilabhāṭṭa, trans. by Ganganatha Jha (Calcutta: Asiatic Society of Bengal, 1909), *sūtra* v, section 12, pp. 261–68. Śaṅkara offers essentially the same argument against the *Sphoṭa* Theory (see Śaṅkara's *Bhāṣya* on the *Brahma Sūtras* 1.3.28).
7. K.A. Subramania Iyer, 'Introduction' to *Sphoṭasiddhi*, *op. cit.*, p. 3.
8. Gopinath Kaviraj points out that the *Mīmāṁsā* denial of the possibility of direct mystical intuition, such as would be required for the perception of *sphoṭa*, differentiates them from all other schools of the Brahmanical tradition. The *Mīmāṁsā* denies the possibility of omniscience of any kind whether it be the *samādhi* of Patañjali's *Yoga Sūtras* or the *sphoṭa* of Bhartṛhari. Kaviraj suggests the reason behind this denial is the *Mīmāṁsā* conception of *śabda* as eternal, impersonal, self-revealed and the source of all knowledge. With this high conception of *śabda*, not only would it be superfluous to posit a personal omniscient being, but such knowing via personal mystical experience rather than by *śabda* would open the door to doubting *śabda* since personality is a limitation that inevitably results in the relativity of consciousness, and the impossibility of omniscience and eternality. Not only that, but the firm foundation for following the ethical teadhings and ritual requirements of the *Veda* would be put in question. See Gopinath Kaviraj, "The Doctrine of *Pratibhā* in India Philosophy, *Annals of the Bhandarkar Oriental Research Institute*, 1924, pp. 120-21. This same article is reprinted in Gopinath Kaviraj *Aspects of Indian Thought* (Burdwan: University of Burdwan, 1966).

is found to be necessary for words to convey meaning. For Bhartṛhari it is the revelation of the sphoṭa that is the intuitive apprehension of the speaker and hearer, that is found to be [illegible]. [illegible] Both [illegible] and Bhartṛhari ground their theories upon the Vedic assumption that [illegible] provide [illegible] and the [illegible] by the Vedic [illegible].

Notes

1. [illegible] Vārāṇasī: [illegible] University, 2nd Edition, 1963, p. 88.
2. [illegible] p. 12.
3. [illegible] p. 28.
4. [illegible] Dacca [illegible].
5. [illegible] College, 1959, p. 101.
6. [illegible] of Kumārila [illegible] essentially the same argument against the sphoṭa [illegible] in the Brāhma Sūtra [illegible].
7. [illegible]
8. [illegible] Kumārila [illegible] Vedas would [illegible] The Doctrine of [illegible] Indian [illegible] University of Burdwan, 1966.

13

CREDO, QUIA OCCIDENTALE: A NOTE ON SANSKRIT *VARṆA* AND ITS MISINTERPRETATION IN LITERATURE ON MĪMĀṂSĀ AND VYĀKARAṆA

ALBRECHT WEZLER

1. The first time J.-M. Verpoorten comes to speak about the *sphoṭavāda* in his booklet on 'Mīmāṃsā Literature',[1] he gives the following explanation:[2] "an argument with the grammarians about the *sphoṭa*.[3] According to the realist viewpoint of the *M*", i.e. the Mīmāṃsā, "a word is nothing more than the phonemes making it up. The text is as follows:

> As a matter of fact also, such a word as *go* ('cow') is never actually preceived apart from the letters *ga* and the rest... From this it is clear that the word *gauḥ*, beginning with the letter *ga-* and ending with the *ḥ* is only the letters themselves, and hence there is no thing as 'word' (*pada*) apart from these letters."

And he adds the reference "tr. Jhā, 1973-74²:20", i.e. p. 20 of Ganganatha Jha's translation of the Śābara-Bhāṣya[4] [= ŚBh]. Quite evidently, however, "phoneme" and "letter" are entirely different concepts; for, whichever definition of "phoneme" one prefers, or approves of,[5] this much is clear: What is referred to are sounds of speech or language whereas "letter" is defined[6] as "symbol, usually written or printed, representing a speech sound and constituting a unit of an alphabet"; and it need hardly be emphasized that one has to clearly distinguish between a symbol and that what it represents.

I do not, of course, want to intimate that Verpoorten himself failed to recognize them as different; but the change from the term he himself uses to that found in Jha's translation is too abrupt not to call for some kind of explanation[7] (for which one looks however in vain). In any case the question arises, which of the two expressions is the correct one here, since Verpoorten evidently has in mind the same passage of the ŚBh as that partially quoted by him from Jha's translation, so that there cannot be the least doubt that it is not two different words in Sanskrit which are referred to by Verpoorten's "phoneme" and Jha's "letter" respectively.

Now, the original reads thus:[8] *na ca pratyakṣo gakārādibhyo 'nyo gośabda iti / (bhedadarśanābhāvād abhedadarśanāc ca / gakārādīni hi pratyakṣāṇi /) tasmād gaur iti gakārādivisarjanīyāntaṃ padam akṣarāṇy eva / ato na tebhyo vyatiriktam anyat padaṃ nāmeti /*. Thus it turns out that Jha uses "letter" to render Skt. *gakāra*, etc., and equally Skt. *akṣara* and that Verpoorten's "phoneme" also covers both words. Both scholars can certainly not be criticized for not having chosen two different English words to render the two Sanskrit expressions; for the passage just quoted is evidence enough to show that *akṣara* refers exactly to what is stated in the same sentence as making up the *pada* '*gauḥ*', viz. *gakāra*, etc.: quite clearly the denotatum of *gakāra* etc., is what is said here to be an "*akṣara*",[9] and therefore any translator is indeed free to use the some equivalent for both (although he should not also feel relieved from the obligation to check whether there is not perhaps nevertheless a semantic difference between the two Sanskrit expressions; for to have the same referent does not imply having exactly the same meaning).

The wider context of the passage renders further assistance in that the discussion—which culminates in the subsequent assertion *tasmād akṣarāṇy eva padam*[10]—begins thus:[11] *atha gaur ity atra kaḥ śabdaḥ / gakāraukāra*[12]*-visarjanīyā iti bhagavān upavarṣaḥ / śrotragrahaṇa hy arthe loke śabdaśabdaḥ prasiddhaḥ / te ca śrotragrahaṇāḥ /*. For there is no denying the fact that the entity referred to by *gakārādi* as well as *gakārādivisarjanīyānta* in the passage quoted previously and fully described here by the dvandva compound *gakāraukāravisarjanīyā(ḥ)*, is expressedly stated to be something which can be "grasped", i.e. cognized, perceived, "by the ear / the sense of hearing", and evidently what is meant is: by it only. There cannot hence be the least doubt that Jha's "letter", with which he of course operates in his translation of this passage, too,[13] is completely inappropriate and that Frauwallner's translation of it[14] is by far better inasmuch as it reads thus: "(Reply:) What is the word when one utters 'cow' (*gauḥ*)—(The sounds) *g*, *au*, *ḥ*, says the venerable Upavarṣa. For in everyday life the word 'word' refers to an object grasped by the sense of hearing. And the (sounds) are grasped by the sense of hearing."[15]

Since they are stated, and by way of argument at that, to be *śrotragrahaṇa*, what is meant by *gakāra*, etc. cannot by any means be "letters" representing (speech) sounds, but indeed only something which belongs to the—epistemological—category of sound, i.e. a "sensation perceived by the sense of hearing".[16] And since further *gakāraukāravisarjanīyāḥ* is undeniably—not the spelling of the word *gauḥ*, but—the enumeration of the sounds or phonemes of which this word consists, the rendering "sounds" ("Laute") of Frauwallner is indeed fully justified. In fact this statement of mine, too, is nothing but a truism, and one so easily recognizable as such, that one would naturally shrink from making such a remark were there not paṇḍitammanyas like F.X. d'Sa[17] who, even more than 20 years after the publication of Frauwallner's important study, quite unnecessarily misses the mark by replacing "Laute" ("sounds") by "syllables"; and his reference to G.V. Devasthali is of no help to him.[18] Has it really to be restated that *gauḥ* is a monosyllabic word that is made up of the sounds/phonemes *g*, *au* and *ḥ* and that *akṣara*, in the previous passage, is therefore also used in the second of the three meanings given e.g. by Renou in his 'Terminologie grammaticale du Sanskrit'[19] s.v., viz. "syllable'; 'phoneme" . . . plus spec. voyelle"? And d'Sa could also not refer to Jha as a witness because the latter's rendering of *gakāra* by "(the letter) *ga*" is demonstrably wrong, or at least[20] misleading: For *gakāra* is the name (*ākhyā*) of the consonant *g* and not of the syllable *ga*! This is clear not only from the corresponding usage of Vedic texts, as has been pointed out by me already on an earlier occasion,[21] but also from the corresponding rules of Prātiśākhyas.[22]

The continuation of the passage quoted last from the ŚBh is no less noteworthy;[23] for in it the expression *varṇa* is used, viz.

in the sentence:[24] *pūrvajanitasaṃskārasahito 'ntyo varṇaḥ pratyāyaka ity adoṣaḥ*, and this sentence forms, to be sure, an argument of the Mīmāṃsaka engaged in a discussion with the Sphoṭavādin. Because of the context in which it is found, the argument cannot but refer to the stock example, mentioned at the very outset, viz. the word (form) *gauḥ*; and it is clearly its phonemes[25] which are meant here by the term *varṇa*. And this term is—one is tempted to add: of course—also rendered by "letter" in Jha's translation.[26]

In view of these specimens from his translation of the ŚBh it is no wonder that similar observations can be made in his translation of the Tantravārttika too. Suffice it to draw attention to the verses

sarvavarṇasamūho 'pi na saṃskāryaḥ kathaṃcana/
na tasyārthaprayuktatvam asti hy anabhidhānataḥ//
atha tricaturā varṇāḥ saṃskriyante pade pade/[27]

which are rendered thus by Jha:[28] "Nor is it possible for a collection of all the letters of the alphabet to undergo any process of purification; because any such collection not having any meaning, it cannot be used to any useful end. And if groups of three or four letters in each individual word be held to be purified. . . ." And again there cannot be any doubt that Jha almost grotesquely distorts the original; for what has most aptly been stated by Sten Konow though with regard to the term *samāmnāya*—and as the final member of the compound *akṣarasamāmnāya* of the Śikṣās[29] at that—, viz. that it "indicates a traditional enumeration handed down verbally from teacher to pupil, and not a written list", this statement of Konow's, no doubt, holds equally good for Kumārila's *sarvavarṇasamūha*, too.

Finally Jha's translation of the Ślokavārttika[30] is quite expectedly also not an exception; and it is rather difficult to understand how e.g. a verse like the tenth of the Sphoṭavāda Section

alpīyasāpi yatnena śabdam uccaritaṃ matiḥ/
yadi vā naiva gṛhṇāti varṇaṃ vā sakalaṃ sphuṭam//

could ever be rendered by "even when the letter is uttered with the least effort, it is either clearly recognised as a full letter, or it is not recognised at all"[31]—a statement which is only intelligible if "letter" is interpreted to mean "sound (represented by a letter)".

However, Jha is not the only black sheep; he either set a precedent or at least enjoys the company of other scholars, e.g. R.N. Sharma, a Vyākaraṇa-Mīmāṃsā-Śāstrī, who in his booklet on the 'Mīmāṃsā Theory of Meaning',[32] reports Vātsyāyana, the author of the Nyāyabhāṣya, to state that the process through which "one can acquire the knowledge of the sentence meaning" "is like this – each letter (*varṇa*) in a sentence is heard after it is uttered, then the letters heard, be it one or many, are joined together in the form of a word and then it comes to be understood as a word. . .". And the reference is to the NBh on NS 3.2.58, as it is also quoted by Sharma:[33] *vākyastheṣu khalu varṇeṣūccaratsu prativarṇaṃ tāvac chravaṇaṃ bhavati/śrutaṃ varṇam ekam anekaṃ vā padabhāvena pratisandhatte/pratisandhāya padaṃ vyavasyati/* . . .

On the other hand, Jha is evidently not the first one to dish up such nonsensical an equivalent; he has at least one predecessor in M.L. Sandal who in 1923 translated MS 1.1.16 *varṇāntaram avikārah* by "the change of letters is not a modification".[34] But it is quite possible, nay even highly probable that he also does not lead this 'dancing procession'; yet for reasons which I shall explain a little later,[35] I don't think that it is necessary to hunt down and identify the first parent, so to say.

2. What has to be noted next is that similar observations can be made in the realm of secondary literature on another important Śāstra of Ancient and Mediaeval India, viz. grammar (*vyākaraṇa*). In this case, too, I do not, of course, intend to achieve completeness—and to finally wear out my readers' patience—, but shall confine myself to a few selected, but significant examples.

In K.V. Abhyankar's 'Dictionary of Sanskrit Grammar'[36] what one reads s.v. *varṇa* is "phonemic unit; a letter", and the latter alleged equivalent regularly is met with again in the explanations of compounds having *varṇa* as prior member like *varṇagrahaṇa*, *varṇapāṭha*, *varṇarāśi* ("the collection of letters as mentioned in works on grammar and Prātiśākhyas"), *varṇavikāra*, etc.

This is echoed, as it were, by K.C. Shastri[37] who explains the term *varṇa*, as attested in Brāhmaṇa texts, by adding in brackets "letter"; not to forget P.B. Junnarkar whose 'Introduction to Pāṇini'[38] contains among others an appendix on "*it* letters" and on "*savarṇa* letters", and who accordingly renders Pāṇ. 1.1.9 *tulyāsyaprayatnaṃ savarṇam* by "letters which have a like place of utterance and which, in pronouncing, require a like internal effort, are treated as 'savarṇa' ", yet not without adding a reference to Section 3 of Chapter I of his work dealing with "the Sanskrit alphabet" that consists "of (the following) letters . . ." ![39]

Returning to K.V. Abhyankar it has to be noted in addition that he knows also a very special kind of letters, viz. "mute letters".[40] Thus s.v. *anubandha*, in his Dictionary, he speaks of "*anubandha* letters" and "*it* letter(s)", and states that "the term *anubandha* was chosen for mute significatory letters by ancient grammarians . . .". Therefore he is only consistent in explaining *pratyāhāras* like e.g. *ṅit* by "affixes with the mute letter *ṅ* . . ." or *kit* by "marked with the mute letter *k*."

Quite evidently it would be a waste of time were one to enter into a discussion with Abhyankar, e.g. ask him what he wants to say by this term, as a letter by its very nature is something entirely mute, etc.; because nobody familiar with the history of research on Indian grammar will fail to perceive immediately that Abhyankar simply fell a prey, directly or indirectly, to O. Böhtlingk's—admittedly also rather unfortunate—designation "stummer Laut" ("mute sound") for Pāṇini's technical term *it*, but that he made it even worse by replacing "sound" by "letter".[41]

The definitions of what has to be regarded, in the *upadeśa*,[42] as an *it*, viz. the sūtras 1.3.2 sqq., leave no room for doubts that anything else than—particular—sounds are referred to, viz. certain sounds of those mentioned in the so-called Śiva-Sūtras, although no term like *akṣara* or *varṇa* is actually used by Pāṇini here.

3. However, the word *varṇa* is not by any means unknown to Pāṇini, but in the meaning "Laut" ("sound") it occurs according to Böhtlingk[43] only as final member of compounds; and these are *avarṇa* (6.1.182; 6.2.90 and 6.3.112), *yīvarṇa* (7.4.53) and the—better known—*savarṇa* (defined in the sūtra quoted just now, viz. 1.1.9, and used in several instances in the Aṣṭādhyāyī).

Avarṇa is clearly a bahuvrīhi in 6.1.182 and 6.2.90, and it cannot be doubted that what is referred to are the sounds *a* and *ā*, at the end of a nominal stem, and not the corresponding letters. Even if in the times of Pāṇini script was known in India,[44] and even if he used it himself, what he dealt with is quite evidently language as something that is spoken or recited, and not as something that may be represented in writing. Significantly "form" (*rūpa*) is to him nothing but the phonetic form (of a word) (1.1.68). Similarly *avarṇa* in 6.3.112, though a tatpuruṣa in this case, refers to the sounds *a* and *ā* of the verbal roots *sah* and *vah* (and the changes they undergo in the process of the formation of certain word forms) which are mentioned in the sūtra itself.

And finally, the expression *yīvarṇa* of 7.4.53—although the length of *ī* has not yet been convincingly explained if I am not mistaken[45]—, equally a tatpuruṣa,[46] cannot but refer to the initial sounds of certain affixes, viz. the sounds *y*, *i* and *ī*.

In contradistinction to what is referred to, which is always clear, these compounds pose by themselves a twofold problem:

(a) What is the reason for Pāṇini's using e.g. *avarṇa* alongside with *a* (cf. e.g. 3.1.80 or 7.2.104), since both of them denote the short and the long vowel (and in certain cases or at least theoretically the pluta vowel, too)?
(b) And what is the exact meaning of the final member °*varṇa*?

The answer to the first question is rather easy as regards sūtras 6.1.182 and 6.2.90: *a* as the name of the vowels *a* and *ā* could not possibly be used as a bahuvrīhi compound! A similar explanation is not, of course, possible in the case of *yīvarṇayoḥ* of 7.4.53 and of *avarṇasya* of 6.3.112. But, as for the latter, it is, I think, sufficient to try out the other alternative, viz. to form a genitive sg. of *a*, which could not but be *asya*, in order to realize that Pāṇini obviously wanted to avoid ambiguity.[47] Could not similar deliberations have led him also to the use of the expression *yīvarṇayoḥ* in 7.4.53 as the alternative *y-yor* could not be said to be sufficiently clear and easy to pronounce (in contradistinction to *yvoḥ* in 6.4.77)?

Regarding the second question, the translation given e.g. by S.M. Katre,[48] "phoneme class /a/", etc. contains the clue to solving the semantic problem. For, what I want to argue is that e.g. *a-varṇa* literally means "class of *a*" or, if it is a bahuvrīhi, "something the class of which is *a*", and that what is meant by it is "class of [the] *a*[-sound]", inasmuch as *a* is by its very nature a sound. Although originally the concept "sound" itself was hence not denoted directly by the term, a semantic development of *varṇa*, abstracted from such compounds, from "class [of a particular sound]" to "class of sound" and further "sound (in view of forming a class)" and, finally, "sound", or "vowel",[49] in general, is not only possible, but highly plausible.

I can not also warm myself at all to the explanations of *varṇa* which start from the assumption that the term has the meaning "colour" in this case, too. Thus, K.C. Chatterji,[50] e.g., contends that " 'varṇa' primarily means 'colour', then it came to mean 'sound, letter of the alphabet', probably because the letters when written were covered with a coating of colour". This is mere guesswork, and one at that which is based on extremely improbable, nay practically untenable presuppositions. Chatterji himself also quotes from an article of Baṭakrishna Ghosh's[51] who holds the following view: "The meaning of the word *varṇa* should have been developed first in the Brāhmaṇas of the Sāmaveda in which we constantly come across locutions like *rathantaravarṇā ṛc*, 'verse which gets the *colour* of Rathantara Sāman in chant'. In these passages the word *varṇa* is visibly changing its meaning from 'colour' to 'sound' of melody. Thus gradually the 'sound of melody' became 'sound in general'." This is also far from being convincing, first of all, because it cannot by any means be taken for granted that °*varṇa* in these cases is used in its meaning "colour"; the interpretation "a verse from the Ṛgveda the class of which (in terms of melodies of the Sāmaveda) is the rathantara">'which belongs to the group of rathantaras" is at least equally possible.

The impression which one cannot fail to gather with regard to Ghosh's thesis, viz. that he was unconsciously led by English idioms like "tone colour", becomes even stronger in the case of W.S. Allen.[52] For he starts from the—problematic—observation that "*varṇa* primarily denoted not a sound-unit but a more comprehensive sound-quality . . . : as Patañjali expresses it, it is a generic term comprehending a whole 'family of sounds' (*varṇakula*). This function of the term is consistent with its meaning in other contexts, namely 'colour'—a band of the vocalic spectrum". The fact that "colour" can in English, and its German equivalent "Farbe", too, be used metaphorically to denote particular qualities of a sound, its timbre, etc., or that in English it is possible to speak of a "vocalic spectrum", is of no, or at least very little, significance for the problem at issue unless it could be shown that a similar metaphorical use is attested to in Sanskrit also; and, to be sure, the evidence should be of a more convincing nature than that pointed out by Ghosh.

But is this requirement not fulfilled by the passage quoted by Chatterji[53] from the Nāradī Śikṣā?[54] Not really, because it is not "different colours of different melodies", as Chatterji would have it, which are mentioned here, but each of the seven musical tones is assigned a particular colour of the (optical) spectrum (except for the *niṣāda* which is said to "have all colours"). Although I fail to understand what is meant by this correlation, I feel nevertheless entitled to emphasize that this is clearly different from speaking of the "colour" of a tone, i.e. from using this word metaphorically. And this latter observation leads to the final remark that it is, in terms of semantic development, a long way even from "colour of a tone" to "class of x [sound]/sound unit", the primary meaning of the grammatical term.

Besides, against Allen it has to be remonstrated that a 'family' (*kula*) is not a quality, but "a group of people of common ancestry" or "living under one roof", etc.[55]; Patañjali's *varṇakula*, as may be noted in passing, shows that the prior member did not any longer denote the "class of a (particular) sound" in his times, so that it was necessary, at least for the sake of clarity, to add another word in order to express this idea; but in a way *varṇakula* can be regarded as confirming the interpretation of *varṇa* as "class", viz. insofar as *kula* may have been meant to fill the gap that was created by the semantic development of *varṇa*, i.e. denoting the concept "class" or "group".

There is hence every reason to assume that the grammatical term *varṇa* is derived from the social one denoting something like a "class"[56] and not the common word meaning "colour".[57] How this latter meaning is related to that of "colour" is not only still an open question, but it has also been pointed out by Bodewitz,[58] and I think on good grounds, that "the meaning of the term *varṇa* 'colour' is not as certain as . . . most scholars assume".

Further, the adoption of this term by grammarians or phoneticians does not appear particularly strange once it is taken into consideration that most people, in these early days, did not most probably think, in connection with *varṇa*, of a (particular) group of all the Aryans, but rather of the much smaller group of Brāhmins, Kṣatriyas, etc., living in their own and the neighbouring villages.

In a similar way Pāṇini's term *savarṇa* can more plausibly be explained, viz. by assuming that he has also taken it from the object language, but had now, of course, to define the very special meaning in which he wants to use it. He mentions[59] the Sanskrit word *varṇa* twice, viz. in 5.2.132 and 6.3.85, and in both cases there is every likelihood that what he has in view is *varṇa*, "class"; the latter sūtra is directly relevant in that it is meant to teach among others the compound *savarṇa*=*samāno varṇo yasya/ yayoḥ/ yeṣām*, i.e. the word which, in my view, was but adopted by Pāṇini and adapted to his needs, and most probably in its meaning "of one and the same class (in terms of the distinction between Brāhmaṇas, Kṣatriyas, etc.)", "having a common class", which became "of one and the same class (in terms of the phonetic distinction of sounds)."[60]

I may add here that °*kāra* used to form names[61] of sounds, vowels or consonants, or even syllables and rarely words, is still quite often explained to originally mean "making". The correct explanation has already been given by Debrunner[62] who states that it is derived from *kṛ* "to produce (a sound)", and he rightly refers to expressions like *vaṣaṭkāra* occurring already in Vedic Saṃhitās.[63] The literal translation of e.g. *pakāra* would therefore be "that which is uttered *p*". My predecessor Ludwig Alsdorf[64] used to say that °*kriyā* of *satyakriyā* (P. *saccakiriyā*) also means "uttering", but he was unfortunately not permitted by destiny to expound his view, and to justify it in writing, although it appears to be clearly preferable to the usual one. In any case I am convinced that it has to be admitted that the meaning "to utter, to use", listed already in the Larger Petrograd Dictionary,[65] whatever the explanation in terms of the semantic development of the root *kṛ*, is much more common than has been recognized so far; further highly probable examples are among others the idiom *iti kṛtvā*,[66] and the term *ahaṃkāra* which, I think, should be understood to literally mean "uttering of 'I', saying 'I' ".

However Allen, to return to him again for a moment, deserves attention first of all because he is, in all seriousness, of the opinion that "a happier rendering" of *varṇa* than 'sound-unit' is 'letter'—letters after all come very near to being unselfconscious phonemes." This has already justly been refuted by Thieme[67] with whom I fully agree when he states that "one could not choose a more unfortunate point of departure than Priscian's doctrine of *nomen, figura* and *potestas* of the *littera*", as it is done by Allen at the very outset of the chapter on "Terminology", i.e. when he says[68] that "a particular problem is presented by the word *varṇa* which can be most conveniently discussed by reference to the terminology of the Latin doctrine of letters". I for one had a profound sense of unease when I first read this sentence; the cases where such references to the ancient Greeks and Romans have, to say it mildly and politely, obstructed the view of Indologists, and other Orientalists, are simply too numerous not to arouse suspicion; and in the case of Allen the suspicion proves to be justified, too, in that his remark "and one which would fit into the Latin terminological tradition", added to "a happier rendering", i.e. found in the sentence quoted just now, clearly shows that the Latin terminology is to him much more than a "convenient" means of clarification, viz. a standard of measurement which he practically forces upon the Indian material.

In view of this methodically highly unsatisfactory procedure one cannot but emphatically subscribe to Thieme's remark:[69] "After all the most fundamental difference between the Indian and the classical teachings on language is that the Classical τέχνη γραμματική is founded, not only as regards the name but also by its very nature, on letters; as against this, the Indian teaching is entirely founded on the spoken word, and this is a matter on which Allen too is in no doubt at all". Unfortunately, however, Allen does not give this fact its due and this on his part contributes to obfuscate the Indian tradition which is in this regard not only absolutely clear by itself, but evidently also surpasses its European counterpart in a remarkable manner.

4. In fact not only the Mīmāṃsā and Vyākaraṇa literature, but actually the whole of classical Indian tradition is evidence of what Thieme says, viz. that reflection on language was based as a matter of course on the fact that language is first of all something that is spoken, or recited, and that after the introduction of writing Indian authors not only clearly distinguished between spoken and written language, but did not also allow any system of writing to obtrude on their grammatical, linguistic or philosophical discussions.[70]

And this is precisely the reason why the incorrect translations of *varṇa* and similar terms by Indian scholars like Jha, Abhyankar etc. cannot simply be put aside, or I should rather say: ignored, for this is the usual and ultimately only adequate reaction to the nonsense in which not a few Indian publications abound. In the present case the situation is entirely different: precisely because the Indian tradition itself is unequivocal to so large an extent one cannot avoid addressing the question why, in the name of heaven, Jha and the others broke away from it.

The answer is practically already implied in Thieme's remark quoted above: It cannot but be due to the influence of the European tradition which is not only predominantly script oriented, but has also time and again, even in the philosophical disciplines, committed the sin of carelessly confusing language and script, or at least of not being sufficiently aware of the difference between the two. In Europe there are "alphabets" in India "*varṇamālās*", in Europe words are spelt, i.e. their letters named in order, in India the sounds are named of which words consist. As pointed out by Thieme, the very name "grammar" is in itself evidence of the fact that in Europe since of old attention has been focused on the written language, and even a scholar of the stature of Jacob Grimm, one of the two German brothers who were the first to take a scholarly approach to the compilation of folk stories, was not entirely immune against the use of "letter" where he should have said "sound".[71]

That Europe is the source of the almost incredible misinterpretation of terms like *varṇa* in Indian secondary literature is obvious to such a degree that I don't deem it methodically necessary to prove in individual cases the dependence of an Indian author A from his European model X. In terms of the logic of proof it is sufficient to adduce just a few examples of European Indologists of the 19th and early 20th century who render e.g. *varṇa* by "letter". The first whom I should like to mention is H.H. Wilson who gives in his dictionary[72] among others the equivalent "a letter of the alphabet". Th. Benfey follows in his track, but adds "syllable",[73] and H.T. Colebrooke's 'Miscellaneous Essays'[74] it is stated: "and the same *Sanscrit* word, varṇa, also signifying a literal character, letters are accordingly employed . . .". In their translation of the Sarvadarśanasaṃgraha[75] Cowell and Gough render e.g. *sa evāyaṃ gakāraḥ* by "we recognize the letter *g* . . . as the same we have heard before", or the argument *nanv aśarīrasya parameśvarasya tālvādisthānābhāvena varṇoccāraṇāsaṃbhavāt kathaṃ tatpraṇītatvaṃ vedasya syād iti cet* by "but [asks the Mīmāṃsaka] how can the Veda have been uttered by the incorporeal Parameśvara who has no palate or other organs of speech, and therefore cannot have pronounced the letters?" Another work to be mentioned in this connection, and a very probable candidate as regards the triggering off of this wrong usage in India, is Max Müller's two-volume "Lectures on the Science of Language"[76]: The first pages of "Lecture III" are devoted to the "classification of letters"—e.g. by Greek grammarians and in the Prātiśākhyas—, and it seems that the author sticks to this expression, instead of the correct one "sound", throughout this chapter which culminates, as it were, in the remark that "letters are formed in different places by active and passive organs. . .".

And it should be noted that P. Deussen, too, when dealing with the Mīmāṃsā of Jaimini within his 'Allgemeine Geschichte der Philosophie'[77] uses first the word "sound" ("Ton") in summarizing the doctrine of the *śabdanityatva*, but at the end states: "As the letters of the word so its meaning is eternal". That is to say, there is no dearth of examples in Indological works written in other languages than English although it is, of course, the English language authors who have in the first place to be regarded as the 'culprits'. To add but one more German example: The famous Franz Bopp divides, not the sounds of the Sanskrit language, but its letters ("Buchstaben") into two groups, "dull ones" ("dumpfe", i.e. voiceless) and "voiced" ("tönende"), viz. in his 'Kritische Grammatik der Sanskrita-

Sprache in kürzerer Fassung' which was published in Berlin in 1834 (for the first time). Wilhelm von Humboldt speaks, in a letter of 27th April 1820, of "dem in der Flexion hinzukommenden Buchstaben" ("the letter which is added in inflexion")[78] although in the same paragraph he also uses the correct terms "consonant" and "vowel". A considerably earlier forrunner of v. Humboldt, Bopp etc. was J. Ch. Gottsched who does not at all seem to have distinguished between the expressions "Buchstabe" ("letter") and "Laut" ("sound").[79]

5. The next question that has to be answered is why Indian scholars not only accept, but even imitate a mistake committed by European Indologists, in spite of the fact that because of their own tradition they could and should know better. Here, too, I think there is basically one answer only which is also so evident that it immediately suggests itself and saves us the trouble to enter into a lengthy discussion of the various reasons that cause people to do something against their better judgement. The answer, of course, is that alluded to already by the Latin title of my article,[80] viz. a principal and widerspread overestimation of Western culture, the almost blind belief that something simply for the reason of being European cannot but be superior to the corresponding element of Indian culture.

It is the concept of "inferiority complex"[81] that forces itself upon one's mind here; and I should like to emphasize that I am indeed of the opinion that it is legitimate to apply such concepts of psychology, though they are primarily meant to explain the behaviour or mental states or diseases, etc., of an individual, to a group of people or a nation, too;[82] but not because I want to talk in favour of those who deal with society or culture like with an organism, i.e. who profess a kind of biologism; I rather start from the assumption that a number, even a considerable number, of individuals of a society can develop basically the same or similar feelings and ideas in a particular situation or, at least, share them in the sense of readily taking them over once they have been developed and expressed by one of them. Nevertheless it should be noted that the term "inferiority complex" has often been abused in that it is ignored that it refers to a system of partly or wholly unconscious desires, feelings and ideas, and not to a conscious feeling of inferiority.

But there are many reasons which support the assumption that the Indian reactions to the experience of inadequacy vis-à-vis European culture are not entirely rational so that I propose to stick to the term albeit with certain reservations, i.e. I shall use it within inverted commas only.

This 'inferiority complex' is so clearly tangible and multifarious that one cannot avoid perceiving that the encounter with European culture ultimately had a traumatic effect on India,[83] left her deeply wounded, and, no doubt, first of all because of the historical conditions under which this encounter took place: The deep-seated sense of inferiority is not the least important, in fact one of the fundamental legacies of the Colonial period. The overestimation of Western culture is not, of course, its only result, but an aspect which in my view deserves particular attention. Psychologically speaking it is a form of compensation, and it need hardly be added that many a feature of intellectual life even in present day India, e.g. the belief that modern Western physics, mathematics, nuclear technology etc. have been anticipated in the Veda, bears ample evidence to the fact that the term overcompensation seems more than justified. But it is easy, to say the least, to point one's finger at and to deride such spectacular 'proturberances' of the Indian mind, shimmering in various poisonous colours which remind one of outbursts of insanity; they should rather be viewed as indicating the remarkable persistence and dangerous gravity of the trauma which is not by any means entirely overcome even today. A real cause of concern, however, is the response which such in fact crack-brained ideas have in India, i.e. that they are by and large not taken as what they are in reality, viz. symptoms of a disease.

I have deliberately chosen a rather inconspicuous symptom in the present essay because I wished to emphasize that the 'disease' has extraordinarily many ways of expressing itself some of which are of a distinctly subtle nature. But my general aim has not, to be sure, been to denounce Indian culture, but, on the contrary, to contribute to its recovery out of respect, and love for it. What is absolutely necessary towards this end is, I am convinced, an unbiased but also entirely unsentimental analysis of the state of the 'patient', especially of the various forms of compensation of the 'inferiority complex'; but it is essential and imperative that this kind of cultural studies is carried out not only by non-Indians, but that Indian scholars and intellectuals also join them.

Returning finally to *varṇa*, my modest 'message' is this: It is the Europeans who can learn, or could and should have learnt,[84] from the Indian grammarians and linguists, and not the other way round: There has not been and is no need at all for the Indians to listen to the Europeans' advice as regards distinguishing between language as a primarily spoken means of communication, on the one hand, and systems of writing meant to represent them, on the other. They do know—e.g., to quote from the Sphoṭasiddhi,[85] one of the works of the famous namesake of the colleague to honour whom this contribution has been written—: *loke ca śrotrendriyavijñeyamātrānupātinī śabdaśabdapravṛttiḥ/ ataḥ śravaṇagrahaṇataiva śabdalakṣaṇaṃ nyāyyam/varṇā eva cedaṃ śabdalakṣaṇam anupatanti/*. However this is not, of course, by any means the only achievement of Indian culture of which it representatives may be genuinely proud. But such pride, if it is not to have again a ridiculous effect, can only grow out of passionate love combined with a keen mind.

Notes

1. A History of Indian Literature ed. by J. Gonda, Vol. VI, Fasc. 5, Wiesbaden 1987.
2. P. 18.
3. Verpoorten refers here to §35 of his work, i.e. p. 26f.
4. GOS 66, 70 and 73, originally published Baroda 1933, 1934 and 1936 and reprinted 1973-74.
5. To give but a few examples of such definitions: "a minimum unit of distinctive sound feature; the smallest units which make a difference in meaning" (Bloomfield, Language); "a distinctive sound, a minimum same of vocal feature" (Bloomfield, Def.) "a family of sounds consisting of an important sound of the language, (i.e. the most frequently used member of that family) together with other selected sounds which take its place in particular sound-sequences" (Jones).
6. The quotation is from the 1986 edition of "The New Penguin English Dictionary".
7. On p. 26, e.g., Verpoorten quotes from Jha's translation of the Ślokavārttika, but adds: "with slight modifications"; what he has done is in fact to replace "letters" by "phonemes"!
8. In the ĀSS edition I 48, 7ff. and in the BI edition I 14.11ff.

9. Cf. ŚBh I 54.9f (ĀSS)=I 13.9f. (BI):
yady evam arthapratyayo nopapadyate / katham / ekaikākṣaravijñāne 'rtho nopalabhyate / na cākṣaravyatirikto 'nyaḥ kaścid asti samudāyo nāma yato 'rthapratipattiḥ syāt / yadā gakāro na tadaukāravisarjanīyau yadaukāravisarjanīyau na tadā gakāraḥ / ato gakārādivyatirikto 'nyo gośabdo 'sti yato 'rthapratipattiḥ / antarhite śabde smaraṇād arthapratipattiś cen na/

10. I 48.12 (ĀSS)= I 14.16 (BI). Jha translates this (o.c., p. 20) thus: "From all this we conclude that the letters themselves are the word".

11. I 45.6ff. (ĀSS)=I 13.7ff. (BI).

12. *gakārokāra°* of the ĀSS edition is, of course, a printing error.

13. See o.c., p. 19.

14. Materialien zur ältesten Erkenntnislehre der Karmamīmāṃsā, Wien 1968, p. 39.

15. The German original reads thus:"(Erwiderung:) Was ist, wenn man "Kuh (*gauḥ*)" sagt, dabei das Wort?—(Die Laute) g, au, h (sic!); so sagt der ehrwürdige Upavarṣa. Denn im täglichen Leben gilt das Wort "Wort" für einen durch das Gehör erfaβten Gegenstand. Und die (Laute) werden durch das Gehör erfaβt."

16. See note 6 above.

17. Śabdaprāmāṇyam in Śabara und Kumārila. Towards a Study of the Mīmāṃsā of Language, Vienna 1980; cf. p. 78f.

18. Mīmāṃsā. The Vākyaśāstra of Ancient India, Bombay (1950), p. 18ff.

19. Paris (1957).

20. The reservation seems justified since it is after all possible that Jha, inadvertently, uses the name of the sounds of the *varṇamālā* as it is usually uttered, or recited, viz. "*ka, kha, ga, gha, ṅa*" etc.

21. Viz. in my review of H. Scharfe, Pāṇini's Metalanguage, Philadelphia 1971, published in: Kratylos 18 (1975), p. 22–32.

22. E.g. TP 1.21 *akāro vyañjanānām;* cf. also 1.16-17.

23. The reference is to note 9 above.

24. I 46.1f. (ĀSS)=I 13.15f. (BI).

25. I use this term although I, of course, agree with Allen (o.c. [note 52] p. 15) that "no phonemic theory is implied" by Sanskrit *varṇa,* except for the fact that the essential aspects of being semantically diacritical has been observed by Indian grammarians also.

26. O.c., p. 19.

27. II 208.2–4 (ĀSS).

28. P. 296 of the translation originally published (as no. 161 of the BI). Calcutta 1903–24 and reprinted 1983 in Delhi (Sri Garib Das Oriental Series 9 and 10).

29. Cf. his article "The Authorship of the Śivasūtras" in: Acta Orientalia XIX (1943), p. 291–328, viz. p. 296.

30. Originally published (as no. 146 of the BI) Calcutta 1900–1908 and reprinted 1983 in Delhi (Sri Garib Das Oriental Series 8).—The original is found on p. 512f. of the edition of the ChSS.

31. P. 263.

32. Delhi 1988 (Sri Garib Das Oriental Series 75), p. 8.

33. O.c., fn. 4 on p. 21.

34. Mīmāṃsā Sūtras of Jaimini (Sacred Books of the Hindus XXVII and XXVIII), Allahabad 1923–1925, repr. Delhi 1980, vol. I, p. 5.

35. Viz. in § 4.

36. (GOS 134), Baroda 1961.

37. Bengal's Contribution to Sanskrit Grammar in the Pāṇiniyan and Cāndra Systems, Part 1: General Introduction, Calcutta, 1972, p. 27.

38. Book I, Baroda 1977, p. 109 (and p. 1).

39. Non-sense to the second power, so to say, is the use of the term "alphabet" with reference to an individual *akṣara*, and one example (out of many one could quote) is found in D.N. Thakur's contribution "Tantric Language: A Bird's Eye View" to the book entitled "Philosophy and Language. A Collection of Papers" (A Publication of the Dept. of Philosophy; Bihar University), ed. by R. Chaudhury, Delhi 1984, pp. 24-38.

40. The 'muteness' Abhyankar has in mind is, of course, different from that referred to e.g. by J. Grimm when he (o.c. [cf. note 69], chapter XV) speaks of "the mute ones", i.e. voiceless consonants, a usage going back to the Latin term *mutae*.

41. E. Windisch's "indikatorischer Buchstabe" ("indicatory letter") is clearly an improvement upon Böhtlingk's proposal, but also not entirely satisfactory (Geschichte der Sanskrit-Philologie und Indischen Altertumskunde, Strassburg 1917, p. 55f.)

42. On this expression see the summary of G. Cardona's paper in "Summaries of Papers", First International Sanskrit Conference, Delhi 1972, vol. p. 23–25 and: Pāṇini, A Survey of Research, The Hague–Paris 1976, 163f.— The explanation of *upadeśa* by *ādyoccāraṇam* in the Siddhāntakaumudī on Pāṇ. I.3.2 is anticipated, as it were, by Śabara who in his Bhāṣya on MS 1.1.5 states: *upadeśa iti viśiṣṭasya śabdasyoccāraṇam*. Especially in the Indian context it is no wonder at all that "instruction" is associated with "pronouncing" a word, or series of words, for it is exactly this what is done since of old by a teacher.

43. The reference is to the index called "Pāṇini's Wortschatz" in his Pāṇini's Grammatik, Leipzig 1887, repr. Hildesheim 1964.

44. For most convincing arguments showing that this has not been the case, see O. von Hinüber's recent monograph: Der Beginn der Schrift und frühe Schriftlichkeit in Indien, (Akad. d. Wissenschaften u.d. Literatur, Mainz, 1989, Nr, 11), Stuttgart 1990.

45. For the problem clearly stated already by Böhtlingk (o.c. p. 423) cannot be regarded as solved by S.M. Katre who (Aṣṭādhyāyī of Pāṇini, Delhi–Varanasi–Patna–Bangalore–Madras 1989, p. 957) writes by way of explanation *y—i=i—varṇay-or*, i.e. contends (cf. p. XI for the meaning of underlining) that the first *i* only serves for pronounciation (i.e. is *uccāraṇārtha* only), a view justly refuted by Böhtlingk.

46. As there are more than just two affixes which are referred to in 7.4.53 the dual of *yīvarṇayor* cannot be otherwise accounted for.

47. This confirms Nāgojībhaṭṭa's conviction that paribhāṣā CXXII (*ardhamātralāghavena putrotsavaṃ manyante vaiyākaraṇāḥ*) has in fact not been observed by Pāṇini.

48. Viz. o.c. (note 45), p. 702 (etc.). Thieme speaks of "sound types" in a recent article of his (JAOS 105.3 (1983), p. 564.

49. Allen states (o.c. [note 52] p. 14) that "*varṇa* primarily denoted. . .(in fact always a vowel-quality)", but adds in footnote 9 the remark: "A solitary exception is provided by Pāṇ. 7.4.53(*yī-varṇayor*. . .)". However, the problem of the long *ī* apart, the compound is not such that one has to draw the conclusion that Pāṇini uses *varṇa* as final member of a name of the consonant *y*, too. It is hence highly probable that ° *varṇa* is used with (short) vowels only. Yet the final decision depends on the solution of the problem posed by the long *ī*. Should we perhaps read *yevarṇayor* (*ya—ivarṇayor*) or assume in spite of Böhtlingk's reluctance, that the attested reading is an ungrammatical formation containing a loc. sg. *yi* which is caused by the fact that °*varṇa* cannot be combined with the name of a consonant? It should, however, be noted that Böhtlingk himself later, viz. in the index entitled "Erklärung der grammatischen Elemente" on p. 177 s.v. *yīvarṇa*, remarked: "Jetzt kann hinzugefügt werden, daß sich wohl *ti* für *t* findet, aber, was in's Gewicht fällt, vor einem Consonanten" ("It can now be added that we do indeed find *ti* for *t*, but—and this is what matters—before a consonant"). But he does not seem to have realized that in analogy to *ti*, used as a name of *t* in 3.4.107 and 7.2.104, *yi* would indeed also be possible in a compound *yivarṇa*—where too it is followed by a consonant, so that *yīvarṇayor* of 7.4.53 could be explained as a dvandva formed of *yivarṇa+ivarṇa*; in this case Allen would, of course, be right.

50. Technical Terms and Technique of Sanskrit Grammar, Calcutta 1964, p. 279.

51. The reference is to his contribution to the B.C. Law Commemoration Volume, I, Calcutta 1945, p. 338.

52. Phonetics in Ancient India, London—New York–Toronto 1953, p. 14ff.

53. O.c. (cf. note 48 above), p. 280.

54. *padmapattraprabhaḥ ṣaḍja*
ṛṣabhaḥ śukapiñjaraḥ |
kanakābhas tu gāndhāro
madhyamaḥ kundasaprabhaḥ ||
pañcamas tu bhavet kṛṣṇaḥ
pītakaṃ dhaivataṃ viduḥ |
niṣādaḥ sarvavarṇaḥ syād
ity etāḥ svaravarṇatāḥ || 8.1–2,

according to Chatterji, but 4.1.2 in my edition (BSS 44, 1892).

55. See note 6 above.

56. I use this term within inverted commas only so to say.

57. Attested to e.g. in Pāṇ. 2.1.69.

58. Cf. his review of H. Brinkhaus, Die altindischen Mischkasten, Wies-

baden 1978 in: WZKS 26 (1982), p. 216. What Bodewitz has in view are, of course, the earliest occurrences of *varṇa*, i.e. in Vedic texts.

59. Not "uses", as V.S. Agrawala (India as known to Pāṇini, Varanasi 1963², p. 77) wrongly says.

60. The equivalent "genus" ("Gattung") which Thieme (see note 67 below) proposes—besides "colour" ("Farbe")—should better be reserved for Pāṇini's *jāti* with which I shall deal elsewhere. Cf. also Patañjali's Vyākaraṇa-Mahābhāṣya. Paspaśāhnika. . . by S.D. Joshi and J.A.F. Roodbergm, Poona 1986, p. 786 n. 783.

61. Cf. vārtt. 3 on Pāṇ. 3.3.108 (II 154.20) which implies that *kāra* is added to "a *varṇa*" to form its name (*ākhyā* or *nirdeśa*). Cf. S.D. Laddyu's article "An Interpolation in Kātyāyana's Vārttikapāṭha", ABORI LXX (1989), 312–316.—Cf., on the other hand, Pāṇ. 6.3.70.

62. See J. Wackernagel, Altindische Grammatik Bd. II, 2: Die Nominalsuffixe von A. Debrunner, Göttingen 1954, § 376 (p. 542).—In passing it may be pointed out that Debrunner calls *akāra* etc. "Buchstabennamen" ("names of letters").

63. As pointed out also by Chatterji, o.c. (cf. note 50), p. 280.

64. On him see now: Ludwig Alsdorf and Indian Studies, ed. by K. Bruhn, M. Duckwitz and A. Wezler, Delhi 1990.

65. S.v. *kar*, meaning no. 9.

66. The use of *kṛ* elliptically for *manasi kṛ* is apparently not attested.

67. Viz. in his review of Allen's study (cf. note 52 above) in: ZDMG 107 (1957), p. 664–666=Kleine Schriften ed. by G. Buddruss, Wiesbaden 1971, pp. 719-721. The German original is: "...kann man m.E. gar keinen unglücklicheren Ausgangspunkt wählen als die Lehre Priscians von *nomen*, *figura* und *potestas* der *litterae*".

68. O.c. (cf. note 52 above), p. 13.

69. L.c. (cf. note 67).p. 665f.(=720f): "Das ist ja gerade der tiefgreifendste Unterschied zwischen der indischen und der antiken Sprachlehre, daß die antik τέχνη γραμματιχή nicht nur dem Namen nach, sondern in ihrem Wesen auf dem Schriftbild, die indische dagegen gänzlich auf dem gesprochenen Wort aufbaut, worüber sich auch Allen nicht im Irrtum befindet."

70. With the possible exception of Tantrism which cannot however simply be subsumed under "Indian philosophy". Cf. the article of B. Kölver's published in StII 16 17, pp. 101ff. which confirms what I am saying here in that he shows that in India quite in contradistinction to Europe the name of a sound could secondarily be used also to denote the *mātṛkā* graphically representing it.

71. See his Geschichte der deutschen Sprache, Leipzig 1880⁴, e.g. p. 5 and 291; cf. also his Dentsche Grammatik, Gütersloh 1882² p. 4 and passim. My thanks are due to my friend Prof. Dr. G. Buddruss for drawing my attention to J. Grimm.

72. A Dictionary Sanskrit and English, Calcutta 1819.

73. Sanskrit English Dictionary . . , London 1866.

74. Viz. Vol. I, Madras 1982², p. 431.

75. London 1904[4], p. 189.

76. New edition, London 1885.—Cf. also his Rig-Veda-Pratisakhya. Das älteste Lehrbuch der vedischen Phonetik ..., Leipzig 1869, e.g. pp. X and CCLX.

77. Vol. I, 3, Leipzig 1908, p. 395. The German original reads thus: "Wie die Buchstaben des Wortes, so ist auch seine Bedeutung ewig".

78. Cf. S. Lefmann, Franz Bopp, sein Leben und seine Wissenschaft. Nachtrag, Berlin 1897, p. 10.

79. Cf. his "Vollständigere und neuerläuterte Deutsche Sprachkunst", Leipzig 1776.

80. Which is, of course, a pun on the famous *credo, quia absurdum*, wrongly attributed to St. Augustine.

81. Developed by A. Adler, not by S. Freud.

82. In German speaking countries it is, among others, the name of Mario Erdheim that comes to one's mind in this connection; cf. e.g. the articles written by him between 1980 and 1987 and published under the title "Die Psychoanalyse und das Unbewußte in der Kultur", Frankfurt 1988. However, what can be called 'psychological anthropology' is in itself a very complex and heterogeneous phenomenon, even as regards its methodological foundations.

83. Admittedly, this is a generalisation: It will clearly be necessary in pursuing this topic in future research to differentiate between various socially etc. defined groups of the population and their respective reaction to the encounter with the West.

84. And one of those who have learnt is clearly A. Padoux e.g. that "a mantra is sound (*śabda*) or word (*vāc*), it is never, at least, in its nature, written" (quoted from his contribution to Mantra ed. by H.P. Alper, New York, 1989, p. 297).

85. Viz. on Kārikā 2ab.

14

KUMĀRILA BHAṬṬA ON THE PRAYOJANA OF VYĀKARANA

P. SRI RAMACHANDRUDU

In the Vyākaraṇādhikaraṇa, Jaimini discusses, in six *Sūtras*, (1.3.24-29) whether all the words which convey the same meaning, like *Go*, *Goṇi*, *Gopotalikā* etc., should be accepted as correct (*sādhu*) words or some of them should be declared as *Apabhraṃśas* and so discarded as incorrect. After a brief discussion it is maintained by Jaimini and Śabara that only such words as are coming to us through the *Abhiyuktas* (those who are well acquainted with the rules and their examples) should be taken as *sādhu* as they are preserved in the same form from times immemorial and others as incorrect being produced by the defective pronunciation of the speakers of different times. From a close examination of the *Sūtras* and the *Bhāṣya* thereon it is not clear if they had the grammar of Pāṇini or any grammar at all in their mind while saying that whichever is declared as *sādhu* by the *Abhiyuktas* should be taken as correct (1.3.27) because the *Prātiśākhyas* and *Kośakāras* (lexicographers) and others also help us in finding the *sādhu śabdas*. But Kumārila understands the word *Abhiyukta* in the sense of grammarian only. Thus he appears to be responsible to name this *Adhikaraṇa* '*Vyākaraṇādhikaraṇa*' while it is perhaps known only as '*Sādhupadaprayuktyadhikaraṇa*' (as noted at the end of the *Bhāṣya* under the *Sūtra* '*Ekadeśatvācca*. . .' 1.3.29).

While ultimately agreeing that only such words as have the sanction of the grammarians are correct Kumārila does not agree with the views of Patañjali who lists several *Prayojanas* of grammar. In the very long *Pūrvapakṣa* Kumārila maintains that none of those which are listed by Patañjali can be accepted as the

Prayojanas of *Vyākaraṇa*, all of them being achieved through other means.

According to *Patañjali Vyākaraṇa* has five *Prayojanas—Rakṣā* (preservation of the Vedas), *Ūha* (substituting a proper word for an existing word), *Āgama* (Vedic authority), *Laghu* (easy method) and *Asandeha* (absence or removal of doubt).[1] Kumārila examines all these *Pryojanas* which are considered to be the important ones, one by one and declares that none of them can be the *Prayojana* of *Vyākaraṇa*.

1. The contention that it is not possible to preserve Veda without knowing from *Vyākaraṇa* where to drop or add a letter or to make a slight change (*Vikāra*) in it is not correct because a student gets guidance in these matters from his teachers, fellow-pupils and others, well-versed in the Vedas and is never found consulting a grammarian or being guided by him.

2. The help of *Vyākaraṇa* is not needed even for *Ūha* because *Ūha* involves not only substituting a word for another in a *Mantra*; it involves the knowledge of many other particulars regarding the *Prakṛtiyāga* and *Vikṛtiyāga* which can be known only through other *Śāstras* like Mīmāṁsā, *Kalpa* etc. It is unlikely that a man who has to depend on other *Śāstras* for so much of information would not get a correct word for substitution from the same.

3. It is not correct to say that *Āgama* is the *Prayojana* of *Vyākaraṇa* because *Āgama* being the source (*Mūla*) of all the *Karmas* it cannot be the *Prayojana* of anything else.[2] If it is understood in the sense of *Prayojaka* as is evident from the sentence quoted '*Brāhmaṇena niṣkāraṇo dharmaḥ ṣaḍaṅgo vedo'dhyeyaḥ*' etc., this need not be interpreted as referring to the so-called six *Vedāṅgas* including *Vyākaraṇa*. It is referring only to the six *Aṅgas* like *Śruti*, *Liṅga* etc., which are useful in determining *Vedārtha*. There is only one well-known statement '*Svādhyāyo-'dhyetavyaḥ*' which enjoins *Vedādhyayana*. The above sentence '*Brāhmaṇena*' etc., can be interpreted as saying '*Vedārtha* should be contemplated upon with the help of *Śruti* etc.', by splitting the words as '*Vedaḥ dhyeyaḥ*' but not as '*Vedaḥ adhyeyaḥ*'. Moreover, there are many passages in the Vedas explaining the etymology of words (*Taddadhno dadhitvam* etc.) and many *Prātiśākhyas* which exclusively deal with Vedic words

and passages. They are the real *Vyākaraṇas* which are useful for the interpretation and preservation of Vedic texts, but not the *Vyakaraṇas* of writers like *Pāṇini* which only deal with words but not with sentences etc., and that too of limited number (so far as the Vedic words are concerned).

4. To say that there is *Lāghava* because one can know the language easily with the help of *Vyākaraṇa* is far away from truth for such a highly complicated procedure like the *Dhātupāṭha, Gaṇapāṭha, Uṇādisūtras* with various technical terms and long discussions is introduced to explain only those words which are already known in the world (*Lokaprasiddha*) and nothing new is added.[3] To call this '*Lāghava*' is a misnomer.[4]

5. The claim that *Vyākaraṇa* helps in clearing the doubts is untenable because it is mainly concerned with the formation of words but not with the meanings of either the words or the sentences for which one has to depend on the usage of the learned (*Vṛddhavyavahāra*) and on the *Śāstras* like Nirukta, Kalpasūtra etc. Moreover some of the etymological explanations found in *Vyākaraṇa* are not satisfactory; for example the word '*Go*' is formed according to *Vyākaraṇa* by adding the suffix '*Ḍo*' to the root "*Gam*". In such case '*Go*' should denote any one who goes but not the bull or cow only. Some of the derivations like those of words *Kāleya* and *Vāmadevya* etc., are against the explanations given in the Veda.[5] There are hundreds of doubts which can be cleared only by *Kalpasūtras*, *Arthavādas* and the traditional commentaries (*Vyākhyātṛ paramparā*) but not by *Vyākaraṇa*. If it is contended that all such things are left by *Vyākaraṇa* because they are dealt with in *Śāstras* like *Mīmāṁsā*, then the words like *Sthūlapṛṣatī* etc., for understanding the meaning of which *Vyākaraṇa* is said to be needed are commented upon in works like *Kalpasūtras* etc. Your statement suggesting that one should not find fault with *Vyākaraṇa* but should go to the commentaries to get his doubt cleared can be applied in the case of Veda also. Thus your statement '*Vyākhyānato viśeṣapratipattirna hi sandehādalakṣaṇam*' may be modified '*Vyākhyānato viśeṣapratipattirna hi sandehādavedaḥ*'.[6]

After listing the above five *Prayojanas* Patañjali quotes fourteen sentences (from Vedas and Smṛtis) which, as he contends, are indicative of the importance and *Prayojana* of the *Vyā*-

karaṇa.[7] Taken as they are as the *Ānuṣaṅgikaprayojanas* (incidental purposes), even by Patañjali, Kumārila remarks at the outset 'after the so-called main *Prayojanas* are refuted to depend upon the incidental ones is to hang on the *Kuśa-blade* for support'.[8]

1. The Mantra '*Te'surāḥ . . . Mlecchco ha vā yadapaśabdaḥ*'[9] etc., is quoted by Patañjali to prove that it is not possible to know which is *Apaśabda* without the help of *Vyākaraṇa* but Kumārila maintains that '*Na mlecchita vai nāpabhāṣita vai*' only means 'don't distort and spoil the words in the Veda'; therefore it does not indicate the need to study the *Vyākaraṇa.*[10]

2. Regarding the Mantra '*Duṣṭaḥ śabdaḥ*' etc., Kumārila remarks that nobody disputes about the importance of the correct pronunciation of the letters and the accent of a *Mantra* which can be known through the teacher only as was already explained; but my only objection is that you (Patañjali) have replaced the word '*Mantra*' by '*Śabda*' in the well-known *Mantra* quoted by *Śikṣākāra* because the *Mantra* as quoted by *Śikṣūkāra* is '*Mantro hīnaḥ*' etc., but not '*Duṣṭaḥ śabdaḥ*' etc., as cited by you.[11]

3. The next *Mantra* '*Yadadhītam*'[12] etc., which is quoted by Patañjali says that no study of the Veda without understanding the meaning would shine just as the fuel without fire, does not imply the importance of *Vyākaraṇa*, for *Vedārtha* can be known only with the help of *Kalpasūtra*, *Nirukta* and *Mīmāṁsā* but not of *Vyākaraṇa* which deals with only the word.

4. Quoting the *Mantra* '*Yastu prayuṅkte*'[13] etc., Patañjali states that a man of good knowledge of *Vyākaraṇa* can use correct words, come out victorious even in the next world and that a man who uses incorrect words incurs *Pāpa*. But Kumārila maintains that even this Mantra refers only to the correct use of the Vedic words. The word '*Vāgyogavit*' in this Mantra means 'a man who is able to understand with the help of the *Brāhmaṇas* which is the intended meaning of a word and which is its *Gauṇārtha* and how the Mantras convey different meanings in different contexts'. For this one can get help only from works like *Kalpa* and *Mīmāṁsā* etc., but not from *Vyākaraṇa*. The phrase '*Duṣyati cāpaśabdaiḥ*' in the above Mantra refers only to the wrong use of *Mantras* at the time of teaching and learning

the Veda and the performance of sacrifices etc., because there are statements in Veda which say 'the *Yajña* gets spoiled by an incorrect use of the *Mantras*.'[14]

5. Quoting a verse from *Dharmaśāstra* ('*Avidvāṃsaḥ*'[15] etc.) which says that those men who do not know where to use *Pluta* while receiving a salutation form the young people should be treated like women, *Patañjali* maintains that only with the help of *Vyākaraṇa* one would know about the use of the *Pluta* in *Pratyabhivādana*. But Kumārila says that what is *Pluta* is well-known and where to use it can be known from the *Smṛtis* and so there is nothing new to be learnt from *Vyākaraṇa*.

6. According to the statement of the *Yājñikas* the *Prayājas* should be used making necessary changes in the case-endings (*Vibhaktis*) and so one should study *Vyākaraṇa* to know what *Vibhakti* is, says Patañjali. But Kumārila maintains that one may know the *Vibhaktis* from the passages in the *Brāhmaṇas* where the six *Vibhaktis* are clearly explained.[16]

7. The passage ('*yo vā*'[17]) which says that only he can become a good *Yajamāna* who can identify each word, accent, and the letter in a sentence refers only to a person who studies Veda carefully in a systematic manner but not to a grammarian as is claimed by Patañjali; says Kumārila.[18]

8. The following *Ṛk* 'Catvāri vāk parimitā'[19] etc., is interpreted by Patañjali in a way suitable to maintain the importance of *Vyākaraṇa*. According to him it means 'There are four types of words: *Nāma*, *Ākayāta*, *Upasarga* and *Nipāta*. They can be understood only by scholars (in *Vyākaraṇa*). The first three are concealed in a cavity; the fourth can be spoken by the ordinary people.' Kumārila does not accept this interpretation. By 'Four types of words' if you take those words, *Praṇava* and the three *Mahāvyāhṛtis* which are mentioned in *Nirukta* while explaining the meaning of this *Mantra* they do not come under the purview of *Vyākaraṇa*. (In Nirukta while explaining the meaning of this Mantra six different views regarding the four types of Padas are mentioned including the one referred to above.[20]) If 'By four types of words' the *Nāma* etc., are meant as they are well-known in the *Loka* one need not seek the help of *Vyākaraṇa*. Moreover it is not correct to say that only the fourth one is spoken by the men because the other three also are spoken by

them. It is to be noted that the commentators of *Mahābhāṣya* tried to avoid this criticism by saying that each one of the *Nāma* etc., have four *Aṃśas* (stages), *Parā*, *Paśyanti* etc., so that it may be said that ordinary men know only *Vaikhārī*. But the passage in Mahābhāṣya does not allow such interpretation. After rejecting the interpretation of Patañjali Kumārila twists the passage in his own way and explains it as follows. '*Catvāri padāni*' means the four *Pramāṇas—Pratykṣa*, *Anumāna*, *Upamāna* and *Arthāpatti*. Thus the meaning of the Mantra is 'Men do not talk about those which are known through the three *Pramāṇas*, *Anumāna* etc., based on other factors like the *Pratikavidhi*, etc., because they are already known, through them. They talk about only those which are known through *Pratyakṣa*.' This is a far-fetched explanation. The one which is given by the commentators on *Bhāṣya* appears to be more plausible though their claim that only the *Vaiyākaraṇas* would be able to know the first three *Aṃśas* (Parā etc.,) may not be acceptable to all.

9. Patañjali quotes another Mantra '*Catvāri śṛṅgā*'[21] etc., and explains it in such a way that it refers to subjects connected with *Vyākaraṇa* and thus claims that *Vyākaraṇa* is extolled by *Sruti*. 'The great god (*Mahān devaḥ*), i.e. the word which is a *Vṛṣabha* (bull) because it showers all the desired objects has four horns, the four types of the *Padas*, *Nāma*, *Ākhyāta*, *Upasarga* and *Nipāta*, three feet, the three tenses, two heads, *Nityaśabda* and *Kāryaśabda* and is found in three places, in the chest, throat and the head.' One should learn *Vyākaraṇa* so that he may become identical with *Mahādeva*, he concludes.

Kumārila does not accept this interpretation. According to him this *Mantra* is intended to praise the *Yāga* in order to create *Utsāha* in the hearts of the performers. While *Śabara* interprets this *Mantra* as referring to *Yāga* Kumārila interprets it as referring to *Āditya*[22] and *Nirukta* has a different interpretation.[23] After citing his own explanation Kumārila remarks if the interpretation of the *Vaiyākaraṇas* is to be accepted just on account of the identity of the numbers without any reference to the context, other *Sāstrakāras* like *Vaiśeṣikas* also may interpret it to suit their own theories.

10-11. Patañjali quotes the *Mantra* '*Uta tvaḥ*'[24] and '*Saktu-*

miva'[25] etc., which according to him indicate the importance of *Vyākaraṇa.* The first *Mantra* says 'One may try to see the *Vāk* but he cannot see her. Another may listen to her, but he cannot listen. She reveals her own person (secrets) to another like a wife wearing beautiful garments who reveals her body to her husband.' The second *Mantra* says, 'Those highly intelligent people who purify tne speech by the intellect, like the barley-flour by a sieve and use it can know about the learning of one another, because on their speech resides the auspicious *Lakṣmī* of knowledge.'

While Patañjali explains the above two Mantras as referring to *Vyākaraṇa* which alone can help a man to understand the real meanings of the Veda and to purify his speech Kumārila maintains that these Mantras refer to the perfect knowledge of a man which he acquires with the help of the *Loka* (usage in day-to-day life), *Nirukta, Kalpasūtra* and *Mīmāṁsā* but not to *Vyākaraṇa.*

12. On the strength of the statement '*Āhitāgniḥ*'[26] etc., Patañjali says that an Āhitāgni (one who has installed the sacred fires) has to perform *Sārasvateṣṭi* as a *Prāyaścitta* if he uses a wrong word (*Apaśabda*) and so one should be well acquainted with *Vyākaraṇa.* But according to Kumārila the above sentence does not in any way refer to the use of an ungrammatical word but only to a wrong use of Vedic words because almost every *Āhitāgni* is found, in his day-to-day life, using words which are not correct according to the grammar and is never found fault with.[27]

13. Quoting another statement which lays down certain rules regarding the naming of the new-born baby[28] Patañjali says that one can know about the *Kṛt* and *Taddhita* only with the help of *Vyākaraṇa.* But according to Kumārila the names like *Kṛt* and *Taddhita* are borrowed in *Vyākaraṇa* from earlier works and such technical names like *Ghoṣa* etc., are known from the *Prātiśākhyas* and so any *Śrotriya* would be in a position to select a correct name without the help of *Vyākaraṇa.*[29]

14. In the *Ṛk* '*Sudevo asi*'[30] etc., even if the words '*Sapta sindhavaḥ*' are taken in the sense of seven *Vibhaktis* as is claimed by Patañjali there is nothing specially to be known through *Vyākaraṇa* because though the name '*Vibhakti*' is given by

Vyākaraṇa (and it is also possible that an existing name only is borrowed in *Vyākaraṇa*) the forms of the *Vibhaktis* are known through *Loka* and *Veda*. If the above words refer to the seven rivers or seven *Ṛtviks* etc., there is no use of *Vyākaraṇa* at all because they are to be known with the help of the *Aitihāsikas* and *Yājñikas*, maintains Kumārila.[31]

Before examining the views of Patañjali regarding the *Prayojanas* of *Vyākaraṇa* Kumārila makes a few observations some of which are sarcastic about *Vyākaraṇa* in general and also about the views expressed by Patañjali:

'*Ekaḥ śabda*'[32] etc., which says 'even a single word correctly used according to *Śāstra* leads one to *Svarga*' refers only to the Vedic work which is acquired correctly through *Adhyayana* but not the word found correct according to *Vyākaraṇa* as is contended by Patañjali.

While Kātyāyana states that one achieves *Dharma* by using the correct words after ascertaining their correctness from *Vyākaraṇa*, Patañjali says that *Dharma* can be acquired by merely knowing the correctness even without using the words. But *Kumārila* feels that it is not proper to say that mere knowledge results in acquiring *Dharma*. It should be taken as an *Arthavāda* like the statement '*Yo'śvamedhena yajate ya u cainamevaṃ veda*'.[33] If mere theoretical knowledge of *Aśvamedha* were to give desired result who would undertake the trouble of performing *Aśvamedha*?

Kumārila ridicules the three *Munis*, Pāṇini, Kātyāyana and Patañjali for having used words which are not correct even according to the rules laid down by themselves and exclaims 'one is at a loss to understand how a horse-rider would forget about the horse he is riding on'.[34]

At the beginning of his *Bhāṣya* Patañjali states that both the types of *Śabdas*, *Laukika* and *Vaidika* are going to be discussed and he gives words like '*Gauḥ*', '*Aśvaḥ*' etc., as examples of *Laukika śabdas* and '*Śaṃ no devīḥ*' etc., for the *Vaidika śabdas*. But Kumārila finds fault with these examples because he says all these words are common in both *Loka* and *Veda* and he feels such words as are used only in Loka should have been given as examples of *Laukika padas* and words like *Agṛbhṇan* etc., of Vaidika[35] *padas*.[36]

There are a few more points raised by Kumārila under *Pūrvapakṣa*:

1. While writing such a difficult work on *Vyākaraṇa* Pāṇini should have mentioned at the beginning, its *Prayojanas* which he did not do.[37]

2. The Vyākaraṇa which has a beginning cannot be the *Aṅga* of the Veda which is *Apauruṣeya* and so has neither beginning nor the end.[38]

Jayantabhaṭṭa repeats almost all the arguments against *Vyākaraṇa* in *Nyāyamañjarī*[39] and adds a few more points criticising the treatment of subjects like *Kārakas* by Pāṇini. He quotes a Sūtra of *Bṛhaspati* which says that *Vyākaraṇa* is an incurable disease which continues to trouble the man till his death.[40]

Jayantabhaṭṭa feels that *Vyākaraṇa* would be studied only by a haunted person or a person, afraid of the punishment from the king or by one who is cursed by his parents.[41]

In the *Siddhānta* which follows the very long *Pūrvapakṣa*, Kumārila maintains that Vyākaraṇa should be accepted as an authority in determining which is the correct word (*sādhu śabda*) and which is incorrect. He also supports *Vyākaraṇa* on the following grounds:

(a) Only such *Śabdas* as are correct according to *Vyākaraṇa* should be used in *Yajña* and they only would help in producing[42] *Apūrva*.

(b) By '*Vyākaraṇa*' one need not understand only the *Vyākaraṇa* by Pāṇini. There is *Pravāhānāditā* in *Vyākaraṇa* also (because one grammarian writes his grammar following the earlier grammars) and therefore it can be accepted as the *Aṅga* of the eternal Veda.[43]

(c) One should not find fault with Pāṇini for not having indicated the *Prayojana* of Vyākaraṇa because he is justified in being silent on this point which is well-known in the *Dharmaśāstras* which extol *Satya* as means to *Svarga* and *Yāga*. *Satya* is of two types, *Arthasatya* (talking about a thing as it exists) and *Śabdasatya* (using the correct word): the use of *Śuddhaśabdas* comes under *Śabdasatya* and so its *Prayojana* need not be mentioned separately.

The outcome of the Adhikaraṇa is summarised by Khaṇḍadeva in *Bhāṭṭadīpikā*: Two *Nyāyas* (rules), he states, follow from this Adhikaraṇa, viz. *Sādhūneva Prayuñjīta nāsādhūn* and *Gavādaya eva sādhavaḥ na gāvyādayaḥ*—'Only those words which are correct according to *Vyākaraṇa* should be used' and 'the words like '*Go*' only are correct but not *Gāvī* etc.'.[44] At the end of this *Adhikaraṇa* he makes it clear that these *Niyamas* are to be followed only while performing *Yajñas*.[45]

Though accepting the authority of *Vyākaraṇa* in deciding the correctness or otherwise of words Kumārilabhaṭṭa appears to be not in favour of approving the *Prayojanas* of *Vyākaraṇa* as listed by Patañjali because he does not try to meet all the objections raised under *Pūrvapakṣa* and so as per the well-known saying 'The views of the opponents, if not contradicted would be deemed as accepted' ('*Paramatam apratiṣiddhaṃ anumatam bhavati*') Kumārila must be in agreement with the so-called *Pūrvapakṣin* on those points.

The whole criticism of Patañjali's views regarding the *Prayojanas* of *Vyākaraṇa* appears to be based on the assumption that he is arrogating all these *Prayojanas*—*Rakṣā*, *Ūha*, *Lāghava* (Kumārila accepts indirectly that there is Lāghava in Vyākaraṇa[46]) and Asandeha etc.—exclusively to *Vyākaraṇa*. Once a *Śāstra* is declared as an *Aṅga* of the Veda it has to fulfil all these functions in its own way and so what is meant by Patañjali is to show that *Vyākaraṇa* also, as a *Vedāṅga*, does some of these functions like *Rakṣā* etc., while other *Aṅgas* also may be doing the same or similar functions according to their nature. As Kumārila himself has accepted that the use of the *sādhu-śabdas* is *Kratvartha* and so is helpful in producing *Apūrva* in *Yajñas* Patañjali's interpretations of the fourteen verses in favour of *Vyākaraṇa* can be accepted though in some cases he appears to be reading his own mind in them. We have seen how Kumārila also twists the *Mantra* (*Catvāri vākpārimitā* etc.) to suit his purpose. That is why Khaṇḍadeva in his *Mīmāṁsākaustubha* discusses some of the *Mantras* quoted by Patañjali, and explains how the use of the *sādhu-padas* is the source of *Dharma* and remarks that some of the *Prayojanas* like *Rakṣā* also should not be denied.[47] He also makes it clear that the theories of the *Vaiyākaraṇas* which are against the *Śruti* and the *Nyāya* (like the

Sphoṭa-vāda) need not be accepted. Jayantabhaṭṭa also supports the *Prayojanas* as shown by Patañjali and remarks that there is nothing wrong if the commentators show the *Prayojanas*, some of them being important and others incidental.[48]

NOTES

1. 'रक्षोहागमलघ्वसन्देहाः प्रयोजनम्' (Mahābhaṣya (MB) Paspaśāhnikam.) According to Sāyaṇācārya this is the statement of Vārtikakāra (*Ṛgveda-bhāṣyabhūmikā*, p. 26). This appears to be correct because Patañjali after explaining the prayojanas with suitable examples states that Ācārya has mentioned these Prayojanas—'तेभ्य एवं विप्रतियन्नबुद्धिभ्योऽध्येतृभ्य आचार्यः इदं शास्त्रमन्वाचष्टे इमानि प्रयोजनान्यध्येयं व्याकरणम् इति।' (MB p. 40) Nāgeśa's attempt to explain the word 'Ācārya' as referring to Patañjali himself appears to be unnecessary.

2. It is perhaps, in view of this objection that Kaiyaṭa explains the meaning of the word 'Prayojana' as connected with 'Āgama' as the 'Prayojaka', i.e. that which makes one act. (MB., p. 40)

3. 'अत्यन्तविषम...आक्षेपसिद्धान्तविचारैः क्लेशेनान्तं गत्वा यथावस्थितानुवादमात्रमेव क्रियते।' (Tantravārtika [TV] Part II p. 199).

4. 'तेनात्यन्तगुरुः सन्नयमुपायस्तुत्यर्थमेव लघुरित्युपचरितः।'

(TV p. 199)

5. TV p. 200.
6. TV p. 201.

7. 'इमानि च भूयः शब्दानुशासनस्य प्रयोजनानि—'तेऽसुराः'...'सुदेवो असि वरुण' इति।' (MB Paspaśāhnika)

8. 'अर्थवत्त्वं न चेज्जातं मुख्यैर्यस्य प्रयोजनैः।
तस्यानुषङ्गिकेष्वाशा कुशकाशावलम्बिनी॥' (T.V p. 202)

9. 'तेऽसुरा हेलयो हेलय इति कुर्वन्तः पराबभूवुः, तस्माद् ब्राह्मणेन न म्लेच्छित वै नापभाषित वै। म्लेच्छो ह वा एष यदपशब्दः।' (MB p. 21)

10. 'तस्माद् ब्राह्मणेन...इति तत् संप्रदायगतवैदिकशब्दविनाशप्रतिषेधार्थमेव।'

(TV P 189)

11. 'दुष्टः शब्द इत्यत्रापि बहुजनप्रसिद्धशिक्षाकारपठितमन्त्रपदोद्धारेण शब्दपदं प्रक्षिपता स्वपक्षानुरागो दर्शितः।' (TV p. 202)

12. यदधीतमविज्ञातं निगदेनैव शब्द्यते।
अनग्नाविव शुष्कैधो न तज्ज्वलति कर्हिचित्॥' (MB p. 24)

13. 'यस्तु प्रयुङ्क्ते कुशलो विशेषे शब्दान् यथावद्व्यवहारकाले ।
सोऽनन्तमाप्नोति जयं परत्र वाग्योगविद् दुष्यति चापशब्दैः ।' (M.B. p. 24)

14. ''यद्दृक्तो यज्ञ आर्तिमियात् ।' (TV p. 203)

15. 'अविद्वांसः प्रत्यभिवादे नाम्नो ये न प्लुतिं विदुः ।
कामं तेषु तु विप्रोष्य स्त्रीष्विवायमहं वदेत् ।' (MB p. 28)

16. ब्राह्मणे च षडह विभक्तयः अग्निर्वृत्राणि जघ्नत्, अग्निं वो वृत्रहन्तमम्, अग्निनाग्निः समिध्यते इत्येवमादिविभक्तविभक्तिप्रयोगदर्शनात्।. . .''
(TV p. 203)

17. 'यो वा इमाः पदशः स्वरशोऽक्षरशः वाचं विदधाति स आर्त्विजीनो भवति ।'
(MB p. 30)

18. TV p. 204.

19. 'चत्वारि वाक्परिमिता पदानि तानिविदुर्ब्राह्मणा ये मनीषिणः ।
गुहा त्रीणि निहिता नेङ्गयन्ति तुरीयं वाचो मनुष्या वदन्ति ॥'
(MB p. 32)

20. Nirukta, p. 527.

21. 'चत्वारि शृङ्गा त्रयो अस्य पादा द्वे शीर्षे सप्त हस्तासो अस्य ।
त्रिधा बद्धो वृषभो रोरवीति महो देवो मर्त्यां आविवेश ।'
(MB p. 30

22. जैमिनिसूत्र । 1.2.38.

23. Nirukta, p. 527.

24. 'उत त्वः पश्यन्न ददर्श वाचमुत त्वः शृण्वन्न शृणोत्येनाम् ।
उतो त्वस्मै तन्वं विसस्रे जायेव पत्य उशती सुवासाः ॥'
(MB p. 34)

25. 'सक्तुमिव तितउना पुनन्तो यत्र धीरा मनसा वाचमक्रत ।
अत्रासखायः सख्यानि जानते भद्रैषां लक्ष्मीर्निहिताधिवाचि ।'
(MB p. 35)

26. 'आहिताग्निरपशब्दं प्रयुज्य प्रायश्चित्तीयां सारस्वतीमिष्टिं निर्वपेत् ।'
(MB p. 37)

27. TV p. 190.

28. 'दशम्युत्तरकालं पुत्रस्य जातस्य नाम विदध्यात् घोषवदाद्यन्तरन्तस्थम-वृद्धं त्रिपुरुषानूकमनरिप्रतिष्ठितम् । तद्धि प्रतिष्ठिततमं भवति द्व्यक्षरं चतुरक्षरं वा नाम कृतं कुर्यान्न तद्धितम् ।' (MB p. 37)

29. TV p. 205.

30. 'सुदेवो असि वरुण यस्य ते सप्त सिन्धवः ।
अनुक्षरन्ति काकुदं सूर्म्यं सुषिरामिव ॥' (MB p. 38)

31. TV p. 205.

32. 'एकः शब्दः सम्यग् ज्ञातः शास्त्रान्वितः सुप्रयुक्तः स्वर्गे लोके च कामधुग् भवति ।' (MB 6.1.84)

33. According to Sāyaṇācārya if a person who performs Aśvamedha gets rid of Brahmahatyādoṣa, a man who knows the theory would be free from the sin of contemplated Brahmahatyā. (Ṛgveda-bhāṣya, Part I. p. 14)

34. TV p. 188 and pp. 226-27.

35. 'सूत्रवार्तिकभाष्येषु दृश्यतेऽचापशब्दनम् ।
अश्वारूढाः कथं चाश्वान् विस्मरेयुः सचेतनाः ॥' (TV p. 192)

36. TV p. 193.

37. TV p. 187.

38. TV p. 188.

39. *Nyāyamañjarī* Part I. pp. 374–92.

40. 'तथा च बृहस्पतिः—'प्रतिपदमशक्यत्वात् लक्षणस्याप्यव्यवस्थितत्वात्तत्रापि स्खलितदर्शनात् अनवस्थाप्रसंगाच्च मरणान्तो व्याधिर्व्याकरणम् इत्यौशनसाः' इति ।" (*Nyāyamañjarī* Part. I p. 384)

41. 'दुष्टग्रहगृहीतो वा भीतो वा राजदण्डतः ।
पितृभ्यामभिशप्तो वा कुर्याद् व्याकरणे रतिम् ।'
(*Nyāyamañjarī* Part I, p. 384)

42. TV p. 226.

43. TV p. 219.

44. *Bhaṭṭadīpikā*, p. 62.

45. अयं च निषेधः प्रकरणात् ज्योतिष्टोमाङ्गम्; यज्ञमात्रेऽपि च निषेधः, "याज्ञे कर्मणि नियमोऽन्यत्रानियमः" इति महाभाष्यानुसारात् ।"
(भाट्टदीपिका, p. 66)

46. TV p. 216.

47. 'अतश्चोक्तविधधर्माधर्मोपयोगिसाध्वसाधुज्ञानमेव व्याकरणप्रयोजनमिति सिद्धम् । रक्षोहाद्यपि च यथासंभवं सिध्यन्न निराकर्तुमुचितम् ।'
(मीमांसा कौस्तुभम् p. 134, 1.3.27)

48. 'व्याख्यातारस्तु मुख्यानुषङ्गिकभेदभिन्नप्रयोजनप्रपञ्चं प्रयोजनातिशयव्युत्पादनद्वारकश्रोतृजनोत्साहपरितोषसिद्धये दर्शितवन्त इति न कश्चिदुपालभ्यः। ।'
(*Nyāyamañjarī* Part I, p. 391)

15

मीमांसाशास्त्रे आख्यातार्थः

पेरी सूर्यनारायण शास्त्री

मीमांसाशास्त्रे आख्यातार्थो मतभेदप्रदर्शनपूर्वकं प्रस्तूयते।

तत्र (१) प्रभाकरगुरवः (२) मण्डनमिश्राः (३) पार्थसारथिः (४) खण्डदेव इत्येते आख्यातार्थविषये विप्रवदन्ते।

(१) प्रभाकरगुरवः

ते हि कार्याभिधायिलिङादीनामेव कार्यविशेषणीभूतकृतिरूपा भावना वाच्या। तदतिरिक्ताख्यातस्य न भावना वाच्या। प्रकृत्यर्थफलेनाक्षेपेण, संसर्गमर्यादया वा तत्प्रतीतिसंभवात्। फलमात्रं धात्वर्थः। आख्यातार्थस्तु कालः संख्या चेति प्रतिपन्नाः। उक्तञ्च प्रभाकरशिष्येण शालिकनाथेन प्रकरणपञ्चिकायाम् "येऽपि सर्वाख्यातानामेव भावनाभिधानमाहुस्तेषामपि मतमस्मभ्यं न रोचते। न हि कार्यानभिधायिषु भावनाभिधाने प्रमाणमस्तीति। यस्तु देवदत्त ओदनं पचतीत्यादौ वृद्धव्यवहार एव प्रकृत्यार्थातिरिक्ते प्रयत्ने प्रयोगादाख्यातानां तदर्थकतामाह, स एवं शिक्षयितव्यः—वत्स! किं न वेत्सि अनन्यलभ्यः शब्दार्थ इति। प्रकृत्यर्थाक्षेपेणापि यत्नप्रतीत्युपपत्तेर्न शक्यते तद्वाचितामाश्रयितुमिति। ननु प्राभाकरा अपि भावनावाचकतां कथमाख्यातप्रत्ययस्येच्छन्ति, उच्यते। न सर्वाख्यातानां भावनावाचकत्वमभ्युपेमः, किन्तु कार्याभिधायिनो लिङादयः कार्यस्थान्यानभिधानात् कृत्यभिधायिन इष्यन्त" इति च।

शास्त्रदीपिकायां वाजपेयाधिकरणे पार्थसारथिमिश्रैरपि प्राभाकरमतमेवमुपन्यस्तम्—"ये तु कार्याभिधायिनामेव भावनाभिधेयत्वं, न सर्वाख्यातानामाहुस्तेषां काष्ठैः पचतीत्यादौ भावनाभावाद्धात्वर्थे नैव कारकाणां संबन्धात्क्रियारूपत्वं धात्वर्थस्याभ्युपगन्तव्यम्। अतश्च स्वरूपेणैव धात्वर्थः कारकसम्बन्धमर्हतीति विनैवाऽऽवृत्त्या यज्यभिहितेनैव रूपेण साध्यसाधनाभ्यां संबध्यत इत्यधिकरणमिदमनुपपन्नं स्यात् इति। 'तेषां मते कार्याभिधायि लिङादीनामेव कार्यविशेषणीभूतकृतिरूपभावनावाचित्वम्। लङादिप्रत्ययानां तु भावनावाचित्वं नास्ति। तेषां

कार्याभिधायित्वाभावात् । किन्तु संख्यामात्रवाचित्वम्" इति तद्व्याख्याने मयूखमालिकायां सोमनाथः ।

शब्दशक्तिप्रकाशिकायामाख्यातप्रकरणे जगदीशतर्कालङ्कारा अपि प्राभाकरमतमेवोपन्यास्तन् । "ननु कृत्यादिकं नाख्यातार्थः । किन्तु कालः संख्या च, तयोः प्रकारान्तरालभ्यत्वात् । चैत्रः पचति, रथो गच्छतीत्यादौ धात्वर्थपाकगत्यादेः कृतिमत्त्वाश्रयत्वसम्बन्धेन चैत्रादौ प्रकारत्वादिति प्राभाकराः" इति ।

अयमत्र गुरुमतसारांशः—यजेत, दध्यात्, जुहुयादित्यादौ कार्याभिधायिलिङादीनामेव कार्यविशेषणीभूतकृतिरूपा भावना वाच्या । पचति, पपाच इत्यादि लिङतिरिक्ताख्यातस्थले धातोः प्रत्ययस्य वा कृतिवाचकत्वं नास्ति । कालः संख्या चाख्यातार्थः । विक्लित्तिसंयोगादिरूपं फलं धातुवाच्यम् । तस्य च स्वप्रयोजककृतिमत्त्वसम्बन्धेन चैत्रादौ प्रथमान्तार्थेऽन्वयः । रथो गच्छतीत्यादावचेतनस्थले तु धात्वर्थस्य आश्रयतासम्बन्धेन रथादावन्वय इति ।

गुरुमते दोषाः—वस्तुतस्तु प्राभाकरमतमयुक्तम् । फलमात्रस्य धात्वर्थत्वे (भावनाया अवाच्यत्वे) चैत्रस्तण्डुलं पचतीत्यादौ तण्डुलादेः कर्मत्वस्य निर्वचनायोगात् । न च फलस्य धातुवाच्यत्वेन फलाश्रयत्वं कर्मत्वमिति तद्वक्तुं शक्यमिति वाच्यम् । घटो भवति इत्यादावपि भूधात्वर्थसत्तारूपफलाश्रयत्वेन घटादेः कर्मत्वापत्तेः । न च व्यापाराश्रयत्वेन घटस्य कर्तृत्वात् तत्संज्ञया कर्मत्वस्य बाधान्न दोष इति वाच्यम् । प्राभाकरमते कर्तृत्वस्यापि दुर्वचत्वात् । कृत्याश्रयत्वरूपकर्तृत्वस्य अचेतने घटादावसम्भवात् । व्यापाराश्रयत्वं कर्तृत्वमित्यपि न युक्तम् । फलानुकूलव्यापारस्य सर्वकारकनिष्ठत्वेन चैत्रस्तण्डुलं काष्ठैः स्थाल्यां पचतीत्यादौ यौगपद्येन सर्वेषामपि कर्तृत्वापत्तेः । कारकचक्रप्रयोक्तृत्वं कर्तृत्वमिति स्वीकारेऽपि अचेतने दोषतादवस्थ्यमेव । काष्ठानि पचन्ति, स्थाली पचतीत्यादावचेतने असम्भव एव । अतो गुरुमतमयुक्तम् ।

(२) **मण्डनमिश्रमतावतारः**—गुरुमतप्रसक्तदोषवारणाय श्रीमद्भिः मण्डनमिश्रैरेवमुपन्यस्तम्—फलमात्रं धात्वर्थः । सर्वेषामप्याख्यातानां व्यापारवाचित्वम् । तथा चाख्यातार्थ व्यापाराश्रयत्वेन घटो भवति इत्यादौ घटादेः कर्तृत्वं सिद्ध्यति । तत्संज्ञयाः कर्मत्वस्य बाधात् घटो भवतीत्यादौ घटादेर्न कर्मत्वम् । आख्यातार्थव्यापारव्यधिकरणफलाश्रयत्वं कर्मत्वं निर्वाच्यम् । व्यापारस्य धातुवाच्यत्वन्तु न युक्तम् । व्यापारस्य प्राधान्यानापत्तेः । अस्मन्मते तु प्रत्ययार्थःप्रधानमिति स्मृत्या व्यापारस्य प्राधान्यं सेत्स्यति । किञ्च 'तदागमे हि तद्दृश्यते' [४/१/१५/] इति पश्वेकत्वाधिकरणसूत्रमप्यस्माकमनुकूलम् । स च सूत्रैकदेशोऽन्वयव्यतिरेकप्रदर्शनपरः । पचतीत्यादावाख्यातश्रवणे व्यापारः प्रतीयते । पाक इत्यादौ तदश्रवणे स न प्रतीयते । अतः फलं धात्वर्थः, व्यापारः प्रत्ययार्थ इति सम्यगेव ।

मिश्रमते दोषाः—फलमात्रस्य धात्वर्थत्वे फलस्यैव वर्तमानत्वमादाय लटः साधुत्वलाभेन फलोत्पत्तेः प्राक् व्यापारसत्ताकाले पचतीत्यनापत्तिः । फलस्य भावित्वेन पक्ष्यतीत्यापत्तिः। व्यापारविगमे फलसत्तादशायां पचतीत्यापत्तिः, पपाचेत्यनापत्तिश्च । किञ्च ग्रामस्य संयोगाश्रयत्वेन 'गमनवान् ग्राम' इति प्रयोगापत्तिः । गमनजन्यसंयोगाश्रयो ग्राम इत्यनापत्तिश्च । अतो मिश्रमतमपि न सम्यक् ।

(३) **पार्थसारथिमतावतारः**—पार्थसारथिना एवमुपन्यस्तम् । गुरुमतं, मिश्रमतञ्चायुक्तमेव । अतः विक्लित्तिसंयोगादिरूपं फलं तदनुकूलः फूत्कारपादचलनादिरूपव्यापारश्च धातुवाच्यम् । तादृशव्यापारानुकूलः आन्तरचेष्टारूपः यत्न आख्यातार्थः । स च यत्नः व्यापारत्वेन रूपेण वाच्यः । न तु यत्नत्वरूपेण । पचतीत्यत्र पाकं करोतीति व्यापारसामान्यार्थककरोतिना आख्यातविवरणात् । न हि करोतेर्यत्नार्थकत्वं सम्भवति । यततेरिव करोतेरपि यत्नार्थकत्वे अकर्मकत्वापत्तेः । अन्यथा चैत्रेण घटः क्रियते, चैत्रेण कर्तव्यो घटः चैत्रेण घटः कृतः, चैत्रेण घटः सुकर इत्यादौ कर्मणि ल–, कृत्य–, क्त–, खलर्थानामप्रवृत्त्यापत्तिः । अतः फलव्यापारौ धात्वर्थः, तदनुकूलो व्यापारो व्यापारत्वेनाख्यातार्थ इति स्वीकारे न कश्चिद्दोषः ।

(४) **खण्डदेवमतावतारः**—खण्डदेवस्त्वेवमभिप्रैति—करोतेर्यत्नार्थकत्वमेव; न व्यापारसामान्यार्थकत्वम् । तथा हि—कश्चिन्मनुष्यः वातरोगेण स्पन्दते । तटस्थः पृच्छति कथं त्वं स्पन्दं करोषीति । रोगी कथयति नाहं स्पन्दं करोमि; किन्तु रोगेण मम शरीरं स्पन्दत इति । कृञो व्यापारसामान्यार्थकत्वे व्यापारसामान्यस्य तत्रापि सत्त्वेन नाहं स्पन्दं करोमीति निषेधो न घटते । अतः यत्नार्थक एव करोतिः । तेन विवरणात् आख्यातस्य यत्नार्थकत्वमेव । न चैवं यततेरिव करोतेरप्यकर्मकत्वापत्तिरितिवाच्यम् । कर्माकाङ्क्षधातुत्वं सकर्मत्वमिति निर्वचनेनादोषात् । तथा हि–आकाङ्क्षा हि शब्दविशेषधर्मः । तेन करोतियतत्योः यत्नार्थकत्वेऽपि करोतेः किमिति कर्माकाङ्क्षा दर्शनात् सकर्मकत्वम्, यततेस्तदभावादकर्मकत्वञ्च सेत्स्यति । यथा—समानार्थकत्वेऽपि घटः कर्मत्वमित्युक्ते न आनयेत्याकाङ्क्षत्वम् । घटमित्युक्ते तत्साकाङ्क्षत्वम् । यथा वा एकस्यैव ग्रथधातोश्चैत्रनिष्ठव्यापारवाचित्वरूपधर्मपुरस्कारेण कर्मसाकाङ्क्षत्वात् सकर्मकत्वम् । पुष्पनिष्ठव्यापारवाचित्वेन कर्मानाकाङ्क्षत्वात् अकर्मकत्वञ्च । तद्वत्प्रकृतेऽपि ।

किञ्च पचतीत्युक्ते भावनायाः प्रतीयमानत्वात् तद्भानकारणजिज्ञासायां धातोरन्यत्रव्यापृतत्वात् पारिशेष्यात् आख्यातवाच्यत्वमेव भावनाया इत्यध्यवसीयते । अतः फलव्यापारौ धात्वर्थः । तदनुकूला कृतिरूपा भावना आख्यातार्थं इति निश्चिनुमः । इति खण्डदेवमतमेव सिद्धान्तेऽवशिष्यते ।

SECTION THREE

Hermeneutical Essays

16

मीमांसाभिमतस्तर्कस्सर्वो वेदसमुद्भवः

पट्टाभिराम शास्त्री

भगवता जैमिनिमहर्षिणा वेदवाक्यार्थनिर्णयाय मीमांसाशास्त्रं प्रवर्तितम् । तत्र वाक्यार्थनिर्णयाय सहस्राधिकन्यायाः प्रदर्शिताः । एभिरेव न्यायैः वेदवाक्यार्थो निर्णेतव्यः । अत इदं वाक्यशास्त्रमिति, न्यायनिबन्धनशास्त्रमिति अध्वरेषु सम्बद्धानां वाक्यानां विचाराय गृहीतत्वादध्वरमीमांसाशास्त्रमिति च नामानि व्यवहाराय तत्र तत्र ग्रन्थकारैर्गृहीतानि । निरुपपदमीमांसाशास्त्रस्य 'पूर्वतन्त्रम्' इति च व्यवहारः । केवलं मीमांसेत्युक्ते पूर्वमीमांसाया एव ग्रहणम् । एवमत्रानुमातुं शक्यते—यज्जैमिनिबादरायणौ चर्चागोष्ठ्यां मिथस्संलप्य 'अहं सर्वा उपनिषदो विवृणोमि' इति बादरायणः, 'त्वं मन्त्रब्राह्मणात्मकं वेदभागं विवृणु' इति महर्षि बादरायणेन नियुक्तो जैमिनिरिति उत्तरतन्त्रं पूर्वतन्त्रञ्च प्रवर्तयामासतुः । पूर्वतन्त्रे बादरायणस्य उत्तरतन्त्रे च जैमिनेः नामोपलम्भेन ज्ञायते यदुभावपि वेदवाक्यचर्चावसरे स्वस्वाभिमतं विषयभेदं नामग्राहं निर्दिशतः । एतेनेदं निश्चेतव्यं भवति—सूत्रात्मना शास्त्रप्रणयनात्पूर्वमपि उभयविधवेदवाक्यार्थविचारश्चर्चागोष्ठ्यामासीदिति । उभावपि स्वस्वसूत्रेषु अन्येषामपि महर्षीणां नामानि गृह्णीतः । तेन चर्चायां ये निर्णीता अभवन् विषयाः ते पश्चात्सूत्ररूपेणोपनिबद्धा इत्येष्टव्यं भवति । चिरन्तनभारतस्येदं स्वरूपम् यत्, लोकाः कयापि विद्यया विहीना नासन्, स्वस्वपरम्परागतविद्याया अर्जने सर्वोऽपि जागरूकोऽभवत् । 'स्वाध्यायोऽध्येतव्यः' इति विधौ 'स्व' पदमिममेवार्थमवबोधयति । स्वकुलपरम्परागतां विद्यामधीत्यैव विद्यान्तराध्ययने स्वस्याधिकार इति प्राचां सिद्धान्तः । एवमेव प्राचामाचरणमपि । प्राचामाचारेषु विद्यमानान् पदार्थानवेक्ष्यैव स्मर्तारः स्वस्वग्रन्थेषु तानुपनिबध्नन्ति । स्मर्तृभिरुपनिबद्धान् पदार्थान् वीक्ष्य तदनन्तरं तानाचरन्तिस्म लोका इति साधनं दुश्शंकम् । न खलु शिशोरुत्पत्तेः पूर्वं नामकरणसंस्कारः क्रियते । उत्पत्त्यनन्तरं नाम धार्यते व्यवहाराय । तद्वत् वृद्धेषु परम्परया समागतानाचारान् वीक्ष्य ते शब्दैरुपनिबद्धाः स्मर्तृभिः उत्तरवर्तिनोऽवबोधनाय । अर्थं बुध्वैव खलु शब्दरचना भवति । अतो मनुयाज्ञवल्क्यपराशरप्रभृतयस्समाजपरिष्कर्तारो मनीषिणः वृद्धा-

चारतः परिप्राप्तान् विषयान् अवगत्य ग्रन्थरूपेण सन्दृब्धवन्तः इत्येव मार्गस्सुगमः।

इममेव पन्थानमवलम्ब्य महर्षिजैमिनिरपि पूर्वजानां महर्षीणां चर्चागोष्ठीषु आचरणेषु व्यवहारेषु चानिदम्प्रथमताकात्कालात्परिप्राप्तां मीमांसामनुभूय प्राक्तनैर्निर्धारितान् सङ्गृह्य मीमांसां सूत्ररूपेण जग्रन्थ। अत्र विषयभेदेन द्वादशाध्यायाः, तेषु तृतीय-षष्ठ-दशमाध्यायान् विहाय प्रत्यध्यायं चत्वारः चत्वारः पादाः, तृतीयषष्ठदशमेषु त्रिष्वध्यायेष्वष्टौ पादाः, प्रतिपादं विषयभेदेनानेकान्यधिकरणानि, प्रत्यधिकरणं चर्चायै विषयवाक्यं लौकिकं वैदिकं वोदाहृत्य तत्र संशयपूर्वोत्तरपक्षान् सूत्रैः प्रदर्श्य न्यायानुपदिशति। इमे न्यायाः चर्चया निर्द्धारिताः, न तु वादविवादेन। चर्चायां ये समवेता भवन्ति ते एकं प्रमाणं निश्रित्य प्रवर्तन्ते। वादविवादे तु विभिन्न प्रमाणावलम्बिनस्समवेता भवन्ति । मीमांसायां यावन्त्यधिकरणानि तानि सर्वाणि चर्चात्मकान्येव। पूर्वपक्षी भवतु सिद्धान्ती वा वेदं प्रमाणमङ्गीकृत्यैव स्वस्वपक्षं तर्कैरुपपादयेदिति द्वयोःसमयो निश्चितो भवति। तत्र यस्तर्कैः स्वपक्षं पूर्वपक्षी वा सिद्धान्ती वोपस्थापयति ते तर्काः वेदसमुद्भवा वेदाविरोधिनो भवेयुः। जैमिनिरेवं प्रत्यधिकरणं चर्चारूपेणैव न्यायान्निर्धारयति । 'अधिकरण' शब्दो लोके न्यायालये प्रसिद्धः 'अधिकरणं गच्छाव' इति वादिप्रतिवादिनोर्व्यवहारात्। अत्राप्यधिकरणं न्यायालयवाच्येव। जैमिनिना सहस्रं न्यायालयाः कल्पिताः। लोकन्यायालये वादिप्रतिवादिनोः प्रवेशः, मीमांसाधिकरणे पूर्वपक्षिसिद्धान्तिनोः प्रवेशः। लोके वादी प्रतिवादी च विभिन्नप्रमाणावलम्बिनो भवतः। मीमांसाधिकरणे तु पूर्वोत्तरपक्षावलम्बिनौ तुल्यप्रमाणावलम्बिनौ इति भेदः।

तत्रैकमुदाहरणं पश्यामः—विविधफलप्राप्तये वेदः काम्यानि कर्माणि विदधाति। तेषु 'चित्रया यजेत पशुकामः' इति विहितमेकं कर्म। पशुफलप्राप्तये आहिताग्निर्यजमानः यागीयद्रव्याणि सङ्गृह्य निश्चिते काले सङ्कल्पपूर्वकं अन्वाधानादिकं कृत्वा कर्म कर्तुमारभते । आरम्भानन्तरं कश्चन वदान्यः स्वेच्छया यजमानाय दोग्ध्रीः धेनूः ददाति । अथवा कर्मणो मध्ये यजमानस्य फलेच्छा वीता। अस्यामवस्थायां प्रारब्धं कर्म न समापनीयम् उत समापनीयम् इति विचारविषयः । तत्र न समापनीयमिति पूर्वपक्षी, समापनीयमिति सिद्धान्ती।

तत्र पूर्वपक्षिणस्तर्कः—'यजेत पशुकामः' इति वाक्यं पशुफलावाप्तये उपायं बोधयति। उपायश्चोपेयावाप्तये। उपेयश्चावाप्तः। 'यजेत पशुकामः' इति वाक्यस्योपायबोधनमेव शास्त्रार्थः, न त्वारब्धं कर्म समापनीयमित्यर्थः। आरब्धं कर्मापरिसमाप्य मध्ये तस्य त्यागे सति शिष्टविगर्हा भवेत्—अयं केवलं प्राक्रमिकः आरम्भशूर इति। अतः प्रारब्धस्य कर्मणस्समापनमपि वाक्यस्यार्थं इति सिद्धान्तिना

पृष्टः पूर्वपक्षी शिष्टविगर्हणं दोषाधायकमित्यभ्युपेत्यैवोत्तरं ब्रूयात् यच्च वेदानुमोदितं स्यात्। एवमत्र पूर्वपक्षी उत्तरं वदेत्—यदि नाम 'प्रारब्धं कर्म समापनीयम्' इति शिष्टानां प्रत्यक्षं स्मरणं स्यात्तदा तत्स्मरणं मिथ्यासङ्कल्पजनितदोषनिर्हरणायेति नेतुं शक्यते। वस्तुतस्तु तादृशं स्मरणं नोपलभ्यते। काम्यकर्मविधायकशास्त्रं फललाभाय कर्म विदधाति। तदनुसारेण कर्म समारब्धम्। अपर्यवसिते कर्मणि फलं लब्धम्। शास्त्रार्थः पर्यवसितः। प्रक्रान्तस्य कर्मणः समाप्तिः कर्तव्येति नेदं शास्त्रमुपदिशति। ननु काम्यविधिस्थले कर्मानुष्ठाय फलकामना निमित्तं भवति। निमित्ते सति नैमित्तिकमनुष्ठेयमिति न्यायः। कर्ममध्ये लब्धेऽपि निमित्तप्रयुक्तं कर्मानुष्ठेयमेव। यथा 'यस्याहिताग्नेरग्निः गृहान् दहेत् सोऽग्नये क्षामवतेऽष्टाकपालं निर्वपेत्' इति विहिता नैमित्तिकेष्टिः विनष्टेऽपि निमित्तेऽनुष्ठीयते, तद्वत् कामनायां नष्टायामपि तत्प्रयुक्तं कर्मानुष्ठेयमेव। अतः प्रक्रान्तं कर्म समापनीयम् इति चेत्—न; 'यजेत पशुकामः' इति विधिगतं 'पशुकाम' पदं स्वर्गकामाधिकरणन्यायेन फलपरम् न कामनापरम्। विधिः फलमपेक्षते, अपेक्षितं फलं समर्पयितुं पशुकामपदं प्रवृत्तम्। भावनायास्साध्याकाङ्क्षायां फलमेव पूरणीयम् फलस्य च पूरकत्वं पशुकामपदस्येष्टव्यम्, न निमित्तस्य। सर्वोऽपि फलं कामयते न निमित्तम्। अतः फलार्थिनः कर्मविधानात् प्रक्रान्ते कर्मणि लब्धफलस्य वीतरागस्य वा न कर्मसमापननियमः इति पूर्वपक्षिणस्तर्कः। अत्र कस्यापि वेदवाक्यस्य विरोधो वा मीमांसान्यायविरोधो वा न प्रतीयते।

सिद्धान्तिनस्तर्कमवलोकयामः। स तु वदति—प्रक्रान्तं कर्म समापनीयमेवेति। यद्यपि 'आरब्धं कर्म समापनीयम्' इति शिष्टानां प्रत्यक्षं वचनं नास्ति, तथापि शिष्टविगर्हणं नावदस्त्येव। विगर्हणं व्यवहाररूपम्। वृद्धव्यवहारश्च 'पील्वधिकरणन्यायेन' प्रमाणम्। तदिदं पूर्वपक्षिणापि स्वीकर्तव्यम्। यतो ह्यस्मिन् शास्त्रे चर्चावसरे पूर्वोत्तरपक्षिभ्यां कश्चन नियमोऽङ्गीकृतः—चर्चार्थमधिकरणे स्वीकृतविषयस्य तदधिकरणात्पूर्वमुत्तरं वा यो न्यायो निर्धारितः स उभाभ्यामङ्गीकर्तव्यः इति। कोऽपि वक्तुं न शक्नोति—तं न्यायमहं न स्वीकरोमीति। अनेन न्यायेनेदमत्र निर्गलति—यदितः पूर्वं प्रथमाध्याये आचाराधिकरणे शिष्टाचारः प्रमाणमिति व्यवस्थापितम्। आचारः क्रियारूपः शब्दव्यवहाररूपश्च। तस्य च प्रामाण्यं स्मृतिश्रुती कल्पयित्वा। तदनुसारेण 'अयं यज्ञविभ्रष्टः' 'अयं प्राक्रमिकः' 'अयमारम्भशूरः' इत्यादीनां वृद्धव्यवहाराणां स्मृतिं श्रुतिञ्च कल्पयित्वा प्रामाण्यं तावदङ्गीकर्तव्यं पूर्वपक्षिणा। स्मृतेः श्रुतेर्वा कल्पिताकारः—'प्रारब्धं कर्म समापनीयम्' इत्यानुपूर्वीघटितो भवति। एवं कल्पनेऽयमत्र तर्कः—'नित्याग्निहोत्री अयम्' इत्यस्ति व्यवहारः। अग्निहोत्रञ्च 'सायमुपक्रमः प्रातरपवर्गः' इति न्यायेन सायमारभ्य

प्रातरपवर्गः—समाप्तिरिति अनुष्ठेयम् । तत्र केवलं सायमग्निहोत्रं कृतम्, तावता सोऽग्निहोत्री न भवति । प्रातर्मात्रं तदनुष्ठितं तावता स न भवत्यग्निहोत्री । अग्निहोत्रानुष्ठानमात्रेण सोऽग्निहोत्री न परिगण्यते, किन्तु सायमारभ्य प्रातरनुष्ठिते एवाग्निहोत्री परिगण्यते । तथैवोपक्रम-प्रभृत्यपवर्गपर्यन्तं चित्राष्टिरनुष्ठेयेति सिध्यति । आरभ्य मध्ये तस्मिन् कर्मणि परित्यक्ते चित्रेष्टिरनुष्ठितेति 'चित्रया यजेत पशुकामः' इति विधिः न स्वीकुर्यात् । यथा हि लोके शतहस्तपरिमितस्यास्य कूपस्य लङ्घनं यः करोति तस्मै शतं रूप्यकाणि दीयन्ते इति समये कृते कश्चनाशीतितमे पदे निपत्योत्थाय अशीतिपदानि मयोल्लङ्घितानि, अशीति रूप्यकाणि देहीति यदि पृच्छेत् न कोऽपि दद्यात् । समग्रे खलु विधिः प्रवर्तते, नावयवे । पशुफलकामनया चित्रेष्टौ प्रवृत्तिर्यजमानस्य या जाता, तस्याः प्रवृत्तेः प्रवर्तको विधिः, फलं न प्रवर्तकम्, फलञ्च प्रयोजकं भवितुमर्हति । प्रवर्तकस्तु विधिरेव । विधिं दृष्ट्वैव फललाभाय तदुपायभूते कर्मणि प्रवर्तते । यद्ययं विधिर्ना-भविष्यत् तदा कथं उपेयभूतफलकामनावान् उपायभूतं कर्माकरिष्यत्? अतो विधिः प्रवर्तकः फलञ्च प्रयोजकमिति न्यायोऽङ्गीकार्यः ।

निमित्तनैमित्तिकस्थले क्षामवतीष्ट्यादौ विधिं विना केवलं निमित्तं प्रायश्चि-त्तेष्टौ प्रवर्तकं न भवेत् । अस्मिन्निमित्ते सतीदं प्रायश्चित्तमिति विधिद्वाराऽव-गते सत्येव निमित्तं प्रयोजकं भवेत् । फलं यथा उद्देश्यं भवति तथैव निमित्तमपि । उद्देश्यश्च विधेयान्वयि भवति । विधेयश्च विधिद्वाराऽवगन्तव्यः । विधिश्चाज्ञातज्ञा-पनाय प्रवर्तते । उद्देश्यश्च ज्ञातमेव ज्ञापयति । विधिमुपजीव्यैव फलकामना-यास्स्वरूपसिद्धिः । सा च कामना कथमुपजीव्यं विधिमुपरुन्ध्यात्? न खलूप-जीव्यविरोधो न्याय्यः । अतः फलेच्छायां वीतायाम् कर्ममध्ये प्राप्ते वा फले प्रक्रान्तं कर्म समापनीयमित्येव 'यजेत पशुकामः 'इत्यस्यार्थः ।

अत्र तुषोपवापन्यायोऽप्यानुकूल्यमावहति । विषयनिरूपणात्पूर्वं केचन पदार्थाः प्रत्येतव्याः । दर्शपूर्णमासयोः यदाग्नेयादिवाक्येनाग्नेययागो विहितः, स चाग्नि-देवताकः पुरोडाशद्रव्यकः । पुरोडाशश्च तण्डुलानां यवानां वा पिष्टेन निर्मीयते । पिष्टञ्च प्रकृतिद्रव्यमपेक्षते । तच्च 'व्रीहिभिर्यजेत' 'यवैर्वा यजेत' इति विहितम् । तत्र व्रीहीन् यवान्वाऽवहत्य तुषेभ्यस्तण्डुलान् पृथक्कृत्य तण्डुलान् पिष्ट्वा, पिष्टञ्च भर्जयित्वा मदन्तीजलेन संयुत्य कूर्माकारेण पिण्डं कृत्वा 'कपालेषु श्रपयति' इति विध्यनुसारेण कपालेषु श्रपणं–पाकः कर्तव्यः । तप्ताः कपाला भवेयुः, तदुपरि पुरोडाशं निक्षिप्य तदुपरि अङ्गारानध्यूह्य यथा विदग्धो न भवति तथा पाक-स्सम्पादनीयः । अत्र तण्डुलानां पेषणात्पूर्वं अवहननान्तरं 'शूर्पेण विविनक्ति' इति विधिना तण्डुलेभ्यः तुषेषु पृथक्कृतेष्वपि तण्डुलेषु केचन संलग्नतुषा भवेयुः । ते तुषास्तेभ्यः पृथक्कर्तव्याः तत्पृथक्करणं शूर्पेण न भवतीति तदर्थं विधि प्रवृत्तः—

'पुरोडाशकपालेन तुषानुपवपति' इति । उपवापः—पृथक्करणम् । संलग्नतुषाणां पृथक्करणं लोकत एव प्राप्तम् । केन साधनेन पृथक्करणं इत्येवाकाङ्क्षा भवति । लोके तत् हस्तेन सम्पाद्यते । अत्र च 'पुरोडाशकपालेन' इति कपालस्साधनं विधिर्विधत्ते । कपालोपादाने विधिरेव प्रवर्तकः ।

अत्र कपालं प्रति तुषोपवापः प्रयोजको भवति न वेति विचारः । यथा 'यजेत स्वर्गकामः' इत्यत्र साध्यस्य स्वर्गस्य यागप्रयोजकता वर्तते तथा तुषोपवापे साध्यता वर्तत इति साध्यस्तुषोपवापः तृतीयान्तकपालपदमेवोपात्तस्य साधनस्य प्रयोजकं भवति इति पूर्वपक्षिणस्तर्कः । सिद्धान्तिनस्तु—केवलस्य कपालस्य नात्र साधनता किन्तु पुरोडाशकपालस्य—पुरोडाशश्रपणप्रयुक्तस्य कपालस्य साधनता । अन्यप्रयुक्तत्वात्कपालस्य तुषोपवापो न प्रयोजकः । यद्यपि कपालनिष्ठसाधनतानिरूपितसाध्यता तुषोपवापे विद्यते, अस्ति च तुषोपवापं प्रत्यङ्गता कपालस्य, तथापि यो योऽङ्गी स सर्वः प्रयोजक इति न व्याप्तिः । किन्तु यो यः प्रयोजकः सोऽङ्ग्येव भवति । यदि साध्यं फलं प्रवर्तकं स्यात् तदा नित्येषु नैमित्तिकेषु च कर्मसु फलाभावेन प्रवर्तकाभावात् कस्यापि प्रवृत्तिरेव न स्यात् । न च विश्वजिन्न्यायेन तत्र फलं परिकल्प्य तस्य प्रवर्तकत्वं साध्यतामिति वाच्यम्, नित्यनैमित्तिकविधीनां निर्विषयत्वापत्तेः । अतः साध्यं फलं प्रयोजकमेव न प्रवर्तकम् इति तर्कः ।

काले प्रक्रान्तस्य कर्मणो मध्ये एव कर्मजन्ये फले लब्धेऽपि प्रक्रान्तं कर्म समापनीयमित्यत्र न्यायः प्रदर्शितः । अकाले नियतसमयात्पूर्वमेव प्रक्रान्तस्य कर्मणः का व्यवस्थेति चिन्तयामः—दर्शेष्टिरमावास्यायामारभ्य तदुत्तरदिने प्रतिपदि समापनीया । एवं पौर्णमास्यामारभ्य तदुत्तरप्रतिपदि पौर्णमासेष्टिस्समापनीयेति कर्मद्वयमिदं द्विदिनसाध्यम् । प्रथमदिनेऽमावास्यायां प्रत्यूष एवोत्थायाहिताग्निः स्नानसन्ध्यादिके निर्वर्त्य दर्शेष्ट्यर्थं सङ्कल्प्यान्वाधानं कृत्वा हविर्निर्वापाख्यमङ्गमाचरेत् दर्शेष्टौ त्रयः प्रधानयागाः—आग्नेयः अग्निदेवताकः पुरोडाशद्रव्यक एको यागः, इन्द्रदेवताकपयोद्रव्यकः द्वितीयः तथा इन्द्रदेवताको दधिद्रव्यकस्तृतीयः । कश्चिदाहिताग्निः चतुर्दश्यामेवामावास्याभ्रान्त्या सङ्कल्पपुरस्सरं क्रतुमारभ्य हविर्निर्वापमाचरितवान् । तदैव पुरस्तादुदितां चन्द्रकलां पश्यति । अद्य चतुर्दशी अमावास्येति मे भ्रमो जात इत्यवगच्छति । तत्रेदमाम्नायते—'यस्य हविर्निरुप्तं पुरस्ताच्चन्द्रमा अभ्युदियात् त्रेधा तण्डुलान् विभजेत्, ये मध्यमाः (अर्थान्न्यूनखण्डिताः) तानग्नये दात्रे पुरोडाशमष्टाकपालं कुर्यात्, ये स्थविष्टाः (अखण्डिताः) तानिन्द्राय प्रदात्रे दधन् (सप्तम्यन्तम्) चरुम्, येऽणिष्ठास्तान् विष्णवे शिपिविष्ठाय शृते (पयसि) चरुम् 'इति । 'विभजेत्' इत्यन्तं विभागविधायकम् 'ये मध्यामाः' इत्यादि त्रीणि विभागप्रकारपराणि वाक्यानि मिलित्वैकं वाक्यं

अकाले प्रक्रान्तत्वात्प्रायश्चित्तविधायकम्। प्रायश्चित्तस्य निमित्तं अकाले दर्शारम्भः। अकाले प्रक्रान्तं कर्म भ्रमनिवृत्त्यनन्तरमाहिताग्निना त्यक्तुं न शक्यते। यदि त्यजेत्तदा स प्रायश्चित्ती भवेत्। निमित्तसत्वात् नैमित्तिकं समापनीयमेव पूर्ववत्।

अत्रान्यो विचारः—किमिदं प्रायश्चित्तरूपेण विहितं प्रकृतदर्शाख्यकर्मणो भिन्नम्? उत दर्शकर्मैव एवंरूपेणानुष्ठातव्यमिति। अर्थात् निमित्ते सति विहितं नैमित्तिकं कर्मान्तरम्? उत प्रक्रान्तकर्मणस्सकाशात् द्रव्यदेवतापनयपूर्वकं द्रव्य-देवतान्तरसम्बद्धं प्रक्रान्तमेव दर्शतन्त्रम्। तत्र पूर्वपक्षी वदति—नैमित्तिकं कर्मा-न्तरमेव कर्तव्यम्, न दर्शतन्त्रम्। यजमानेनाकाले दर्शयागः प्रारब्धः, स च दोषः। दोषे निमित्ते दोषनिर्हरणाय प्रायश्चित्तमनुष्ठीयते। निमित्ते सति नैमित्तिकानुष्ठानं इति न्यायः। यदि दर्शतन्त्रमेवानुष्ठीयते तदा नित्यानुष्ठानमेव सम्पद्येत न नैमित्तिकानुष्ठानम्। नैमित्तिककर्मणोऽननुष्ठाने दोषनिर्हरणं न भवेत्। तस्मान्नै-मित्तिकं कर्मान्तरमेवेदम्।

सिद्धान्तिनोऽयं तर्कः—यथा प्रक्रान्तं काम्यं कर्म समापनीयमेवेति प्राङ्निरू-पितम् तथैव नित्यं कर्म प्रक्रान्तं समापनीयमेव। अत्र दर्शयागचिकीर्षया सङ्कल्प-पूर्वकं दर्शदेवतायै हविषो निर्वापः कृतः। अकाले कर्म समारब्धमित्यवगच्छति यजमानः। तदा किमिदं कर्म समापनीयम् उत नेति सन्देहो ऽजायत। तन्निवृत्त्यर्थं प्रवृत्तमिदं वाक्यम्—'यस्य हवि' रिति। अत्र 'विभजेत्' इत्यन्तं वाक्यं निरुप्तस्य हविषो विभागं विदधाति। तदुत्तरं 'ये मध्यमाः' इत्यादीनि त्रीणि वाक्यानि विभागप्रकारं गुणसम्बन्धञ्च बोधयन्ति। तथाहि—अत्र 'तण्डुलान्' इति पदं दर्शेऽनुष्ठीयमानानां यागानामुपलक्षकम्। त्रेधेतिपदमनुवादकम्। तण्डुलपदस्य याग-लक्षकत्वे तात्पर्यग्राहकम्। अत्र हविर्निर्वापो व्रीहीणामेव भवति, न तण्डुलानाम्। व्रीह्यवस्थायामेव 'अग्नये जुष्टं निर्वपामि' इति विधानात्। विभागश्च पृथक्करणम्। पृथक्करणमत्र न कायिकव्यापारो विवक्षितः, किन्तु चिकीर्षितानि दार्शिककर्माणि त्रीणि मनसा पृथक्कृत्य तत्रत्यद्रव्यदेवता अपनीय द्रव्यान्तराणां देवतान्तराणाञ्च संयोजनरूपप्रकार एव 'ये माध्यमाः' इत्यादिवाक्यैरवबोध्यते। एवंप्रकारेणा-वबुध्य प्रक्रान्तं कर्म समापनीयम्, न कर्मान्तरत्वे नाचरणीयम् इत्येव सन्दर्भस्याशयः। कर्मान्तरत्वाश्रयणे प्रक्रान्तस्य कर्मणोऽसमापनं दोषः। येन दोषेण यत् कर्म विगुणमजायत तस्य कर्मणस्तद्दोषनिवृत्तिपूर्वकं सगुणं विधातुं प्रायश्चित्तमनुष्ठीयत इति न्यायः। प्रायो नाम दोषः-पापम् तेन कर्मणो वैगुण्ये प्राप्ते तत्प्रतिसन्धानाय प्रायश्चित्तानुष्ठानम्। तच्च प्रकृतसम्बद्धमेव भवति। अकाले प्रक्रान्तो दर्शयागो-ऽकालप्रक्रान्तदोषेण दूषितः। तन्निवारणाय क्रियमाणं प्रायश्चित्तं तत्सम्बन्धि भवति। प्रायश्चित्तरूपेण विहितस्य कर्मणो निमित्तं अकाले प्रक्रमः। निमित्तं प्रयोजकमेव भवति निमित्तोद्देश्ययोर्भेदाभावात्। यथा फलं प्रयोजकमेव भवति,

न प्रवर्तकम्, तथा निमित्तमपि। अत्र प्रवर्तकस्तु नित्यकर्मणो विधायको विधिरेव। एवं सति कर्मान्तरत्वमस्यानुपपन्नं भवेत्। कर्मान्तरत्वे भवन्ति शब्दान्तरादीनि प्रमाणानि। विना प्रमाणेन कर्मान्तरत्वाश्रयणं न्यायविरुद्धम्। अतो नेदं कर्मान्तरमिति।

प्रयाजशेषाभिधारणन्यायः

दर्शपूर्णमासयोः पञ्च प्रयाजयागा अनुष्ठीयन्ते। आज्यद्रव्यका इमे यागाः। आज्यं किञ्चित् जुह्वामवशेष्य यागाः कर्तव्याः। अवशिष्टं यदाज्यं तस्योपयोगायेदं वाक्यमाम्नायते—'प्रयाजशेषेण हवींष्यभिघारयति' इति। अत्र सन्देहः—किमिदमभिघारणं हविषां संस्कारकम्? उतावशिष्टद्रव्यसंस्कारकम्? इति। पूर्वपक्षिणस्तर्कः—'प्रयाजशेषेण' इति तृतीयया 'हवींषि' इति द्वितीयया च हविषां प्राधान्यम्, तृतीयया च शेषस्याप्राधान्यं बोध्यत इति तावत्स्पष्टं प्रतीयते। अतः प्रयाजशेषस्याङ्गत्वम् हविषश्चाङ्गित्वमित्यङ्गाङ्गिभावो निश्चीयते। अङ्गन्तु प्रधानस्य कृते भवति। तस्माद्धविषां संस्कारार्थं शेषाभिघारणमिति।

सिद्धान्तिनस्तर्कस्तु—तृतीयया द्वितीयया च गुणप्रधानभावः प्रतीयत इति सुसत्यम्, किन्तु हवींषीति द्रव्यापेक्षया क्रियमाणाभिधारणक्रियाया गुणत्वं भवेत्—अभिधारणेन हविस्संस्कुर्यादिति। कार्यं हविः, तत्संस्कारोऽभिधारणमित्यभिधारणस्य गुणकर्मत्वमापतेत्। तेन च निष्प्रयोजनत्वमभिधारणस्य भवेत्। जुहां द्विरवत्तस्य हविषो होमावसरे जुहां हविर्लेपस्सम्पृक्तो यथा न भवेत् तदर्थमभिधारणं प्रयोजनवद्भवतीति वक्तुं न शक्यते, यतो हि हविर्होमात्पूर्वम् 'सकृदुपस्तृणाति द्विर्हविषोऽवद्यति, सकृदभिधारयति' इत्युपस्तरणाभिधारणयोर्विहितत्वेन लेपसंसर्गशङ्काया अनुदयात्। किञ्च हविस्संस्कारार्थत्वं यद्यभिधारणस्य स्वीक्रियेत तर्हि प्राजापत्यपशुषु जुहूपात्रान्तरं कल्पनीयं भवेत्। तस्मात्सक्तुन्यायेन विभक्तिविपरिणाममाश्रित्य प्रयाजशेषं हविष्षु क्षारयेत्—अभिधारयेदिति वाक्यार्थो वर्णनीयः। तथा सति जुहूरिक्तीकरणरूपं दृष्टं फलं लभ्येत। अन्यथाऽदृष्टार्थमभिधारणमापद्येत, अवशिष्टस्य प्रयाजशेषस्य प्रतिपत्तित्वं सम्पादितं भवेत् यदि प्रधानकर्मत्वमाश्रीयेत इति।

एवमादीन् न्यायान् अप्पयदीक्षितखण्डदेवपार्थसारथिमिश्रभवदेवप्रभृतयो ग्रन्थकृतः स्वीयग्रन्थेषु सञ्चारयन्तो मीमांसाग्रन्थान् प्राणैषुः।

वेदवाक्यार्थनिर्णयाय प्रवृत्ता न्याया अन्यत्रापि स्मृत्यादिवाक्येषु सञ्चारमर्हन्ति। एतदर्थं पृथग् ग्रन्थ एव निर्मातुं शक्यते। तथापि दिङ्मात्रं प्रदर्शयितुमिच्छामि। स्मृत्यधिकरणे मन्वादिभिः प्रणीतानां स्मृतीनां श्रुतिमूलकत्वेन प्रामाण्यं व्यवस्थापितम्। प्रत्यक्षा श्रुतिर्यदि विद्यते तदा तन्मूलत्वेन, यदि च नास्ति,

प्रत्यक्षश्रुत्यविरुद्धा च स्मृतिः तस्या अनुमितश्रुतिमूलकत्वेन प्रामाण्यमिति च व्यवस्था। एवं होलाकाद्याचाराणामपि कल्पितश्रुतिमूलत्वेन प्रामाण्यं होलाकाधिकरणे व्यवस्थापितम्। होलाकाधिकरणे प्राच्यप्रतीच्योदीच्यदाक्षिणात्येषु विभिन्ना आचाराः—प्राच्या होलिकोत्सवमाचरन्ति, प्रतीच्या उद्‌वृषभयज्ञमाचरन्ति इत्येवमाचारेषु विभेदो दृश्यते। अत्र किं अनुमीयमाना श्रुतिः प्राच्यादिपदघटिता भवेत्? 'उत होलाका कर्तव्या' 'उद्‌वृषभयज्ञः कर्तव्यः' इति साधारणी। यदि प्रथमः पक्षः तदा प्राच्यानामेव होलाकोत्सवः प्रमाणं नेतरेषाम् प्रतीच्यानामेवोद्‌वृषभयज्ञः प्रमाणम् नेतरेषाम् इति स्यात्। यदि च द्वितीयः पक्षः तदा सर्वेषां तत्तदाचारेषु तुल्यं प्रामाण्यं सिद्धं भवेत्। तत्र केनापि प्रकारेण प्राच्यादयः शब्दा निर्वक्तुमशक्या इति हेतोः अनुमीयमानायां श्रुतौ तानि पदानि निवेशं नार्हन्तीति 'होलाका कर्तव्या' 'उद्‌वृषभयज्ञः कर्तव्य' इत्येवं साधारणी श्रुतिरेवोचितेति न्यायः प्रदर्शितः। प्राचीप्रतीच्यादयो दिग्वाचकाश्शब्दाः केवलं व्यवहाराय कल्पिताः। यद्येवं नाङ्गीक्रियेत तदा भारतदेशो विखण्डितस्स्यात्, इमे प्राच्या इमे उदीच्याः शिष्टा विरुद्धमाचरन्ति इत्येवं द्वेषबुद्धिस्समुदियात्। तेन च कलहः प्रादुर्भवेत्। सर्वत्र विद्यमानाः शिष्टा एकरूपत्वं न प्राप्नुयुः। अतो हेतोराचाराणां प्रामाण्यं सार्वत्रिकमेकरूपं भवत्विति होलाकाधिकरणन्यायस्य तात्पर्यमेष्टव्यम् इति स्थितिः। दायविभागे पिता स्वेच्छया पुत्राणां दायविभागं करोति तत्र 'जीवन्विभागे तु पिता गृह्णीतांशद्वयं स्वयम्' 'द्व्यंशं ज्येष्ठो हरेत्' इत्यादिस्मृतीनां मूलश्रुतिकल्पनावसरे होलाकाधिकरणन्यायेन साधारणी श्रुतिः 'अंशद्वयं गृह्णीयात्' इत्येव कल्पनीयेति पूर्वपक्षिणोक्ते सिद्धान्ती वदेत् प्राच्यादिपदानां निर्वचनमशक्यमिति हेतोः तत्र साधारणश्रुतिकल्पनमुपपन्नम्, प्रकृते तु पितामहादिपरम्परासमागतधनापेक्षया स्वस्वार्जितधनस्यापि सत्त्वात्, स्मृतिषु च पितृपदस्य ज्येष्ठपदस्य च प्रयोगात्, तयोः पदयोर्निर्वचनसम्भवेन अर्जकपदघटितैव श्रुतिः कल्पनीयेति।

उद्योगपतयो वणिजः नटनर्तकाः शिल्पज्ञाः कृषीवला भारवाहकादयस्सम्भूय द्रव्यलाभप्राप्तये किञ्चिदेकं महत्कार्यमारब्धवन्तः। तत्र यद्द्रव्यमवाप्तं तद्विभागे कलहे समुत्पन्ने तच्छमनायाधिकरणं गच्छन्ति। अधिकरणे व्यवहाराणां द्रष्टा राजा प्राड्विवाको वा प्राप्तं धनं केन प्रकारेण विभज्य दद्यात् इति विषये महर्षिजैमिनिः दशमतृतीये 'समं स्यादश्रुतित्वात्' इत्यधिकरणे स्वयमनुशास्ति एवं विभज्य दातव्यमिति—ज्योतिष्टोमे सन्ति षोडशर्त्विजः गणचतुष्टयेन विभक्ताः—अध्वर्युगणः, ब्रह्मगणः, होतृगणः, उद्‌गातृगणः। एकैकस्मिन् गणे चत्वार ऋत्विजः। तत्र मुख्याः, अर्धिनः तृतीयिनः, पादिन इति विभागः। मुख्या यावदवाप्नुवन्ति चत्वारः, तदर्द्धं अर्धिनः, मुख्यतृतीयांशं तृतीयिनः, मुख्यचतुर्थांशं पादिनः अवाप्नु-

पुरिति विभागः। मुख्यस्य द्वादश गावः इति चेत् तदर्धं षट्, तृतीयश्चांशः चत्वारः. पादश्च त्रयम् इति पञ्चविंशतिः, एवं चतुर्भ्यो गणेभ्यो विभागे क्रियमाणे शतं गावो भवन्ति। तस्य तस्य ऋत्विजः परिश्रमं योग्यताविशेषञ्च वीक्ष्य दक्षिणा-विभागः कल्पितः। अयमेव न्यायः लाभरूपेण प्राप्तस्य (बोनस् इत्युच्येत) तस्य विभागः। अस्मिन्नधिकरणे पूर्वपक्षी समविभागमभिप्रैति, सिद्धान्ती च कार्यं परिश्रमं योग्यताञ्च पर्यवेक्ष्य विभागे वैषम्यमनुजानाति।

एवमादयो न्याया दार्शनिकैः शास्त्रज्ञैः स्वीयग्रन्थेषु विचारविषयपरिपुष्टौ उपनिबध्यन्ते। लौकिकेष्वपि विषयनिर्द्धारणाय इमे न्याया अतिदेशमर्हन्ति। विशेषतश्च धर्मनिबन्धग्रन्थेषु उच्चावचा इमे न्याया ग्रन्थकृद्भिरालिख्यन्ते येन च स्मृतिवाक्येषु परिदृश्यमाना विरोधाः परिहृता भवन्ति। यथा हि महाकवीनां हृदयं काव्यशास्त्रविद्भिस्सहृदयैरुद्घाटितं भवति तथैव स्मृतिकृतां हृदयं मीमांसानय-विद्भिर्निबन्धकारैरुद्घाटितं भवति। काव्यनाटकेष्वलङ्कारग्रन्थेषु च मीमांसा-न्यायान् सञ्चारयन्तो दार्शनिकाः श्रीमदप्पयदीक्षितेन्द्रप्रभृतयस्सहृदया अनेके। किं बहुना! वेदमनपेक्ष्य प्रवृत्तानि यानि दर्शनानि तान्यपि मीमांसाभिमतैस्तर्कैः समीचीने पथि नेतुं शक्यन्ते। सर्वमिदमालोच्यैव भट्टपादाः प्राहुः—

'मीमांसाख्या तु विद्येयं बहुविद्यान्तराश्रिता' इति।

इदमपि तेऽभिदधति—'मीमांसा तु लोकादेव प्रत्यक्षानुमानादिभिरविच्छिन्न-सम्प्रदायपण्डितव्यवहारैः प्रवृत्ता। न हि कश्चिदपि प्रथममेतावन्तं युक्तिकला-पमुपसंहर्तुं क्षमः' (तंत्रवार्तिक, पृ. १६७, पूना संस्करणं) इति। एतेन 'मीमांसाभिमतस्तर्कस्सर्वो वेदसमुद्भवः' इत्युक्तिः समर्थिता भवति।

17

अपच्छेदन्यायसंचारमार्गः

एन० एस० रामानुजताताचार्यः

पूर्वमीमांसायां षष्ठाध्याये पञ्चमपादे अपच्छेदपेटिकायां पञ्चषेष्वधिकरणेषु अपच्छेदन्यायः शिक्षितः। तत्संचारविषये दार्शनिकेषु मतभेदाः दृश्यन्ते। तद्विमर्शार्थमयं लघुनिबन्धः प्रस्तूयते।

ज्योतिष्टोमे प्रातस्सवने बहिष्पवमानस्तोत्रार्थं हविर्धानात् बहिष्पवमानदेशं गच्छतां परस्परमन्वारम्भः श्रुतः 'अध्वर्युं प्रस्तोता संतनुयात् प्रस्तोतारमुद्गाता उद्गातारं प्रतिहर्ता प्रतिहर्तारं ब्रह्मा ब्रह्माणं यजमानः यजमानं प्रशास्ता' इति। अन्वारम्भो नाम स्वस्य पुरतो गच्छतः पृष्ठभागकच्छग्रहणम्। संतनुयात्-इत्यस्य कच्छं गृह्णीयात् इत्यर्थः। एवमन्वारभ्य पिपीलिकावत् पङ्क्त्याकारेण गच्छतां मध्ये कच्छग्रहणरूपस्यान्वारम्भस्य विच्छेदे प्रायश्चित्तं श्रूयते—'यदि प्रस्तोतापच्छिन्द्यात् ब्रह्मणे वरं दद्यात्, यदि प्रतिहर्ता सर्ववेदसं दद्यात्, यद्युद्गातापच्छिन्द्यात् अदक्षिणं तं यज्ञमिष्ट्वा तेन पुनर्यजेत, तत्र तद्दद्यात् यत् पूर्वस्मिन् दास्यन् स्यात्' इति।

तत्रैकैकापच्छेदे तत्तन्निमित्तकं प्रायश्चित्तं कर्तव्यमित्यविवादम्। यत्र चोभाभ्यामृत्विग्भ्यां युगपद्विच्छेदः तत्र नैमित्तिकानुष्ठानस्य शक्यत्वे सति न कस्यचिन्नैमित्तिकस्य बाधः। यत्र तु विरोधः यया उद्गातृप्रतिहर्त्रोर्युगपदपच्छेदे, तत्र युगपदेव नैमित्तिकप्रायश्चित्तविधायकवाक्यद्वयप्रवृत्तेः नैमित्तिकयोः सर्वस्वदानादक्षिणाकत्वयोर्युगपदनुष्ठातुमशक्यत्वात् अनुष्ठाने विरोध इति तयोर्विकल्प इति सिद्धान्तितम्—'तत्र विप्रतिषेधाद्विकल्पः स्यात्' (पू.मी.सू. ६.५.४८) इति।

ततः यदोद्गातृप्रतिहर्त्रोः क्रमेणापच्छेदः कच्छग्रहणविच्छेदः तत्र किं पूर्वोत्पन्ननिमित्तकं प्रायश्चित्तं कर्तव्यम् उतोत्तरनिमित्तकम् इति संशये, पूर्वनिमित्तमसंजातविरोधं निर्विघ्नमवगम्यते। तद्विरुद्धत्वादुत्तरमवगन्तुमशक्यम्। अतः पूर्वस्य बलीयस्त्वम् यदि तु उपक्रमपर्यालोचनयैवोपसंहारस्यात्मलाभस्थले एव पूर्वस्य प्राबल्यम्। अत्र तु पूर्वमनपेक्ष्यैवोत्तरस्यात्मलाभ इति न पूर्वस्य प्राबल्यमिति

वैषम्यमित्यालोच्यते, तदा युगपदपच्छेद इव क्रमेणापच्छेदेऽपि विकल्पोऽस्तु इति पूर्वपक्षे प्राप्ते सिद्धान्तितम्—

"पौर्वापर्ये पूर्वदौर्बल्यं प्रकृतिवत्" (पू.मी.सू. ६.५.५४) इति। नात्र पूर्वेणोत्तरस्य ज्ञानस्योत्पत्तिः शक्यते निरोद्धुम्। प्रत्यक्षेण वाक्येन उत्तरस्य ज्ञानमवश्यमुत्पाद्यत एव। तच्चोपजायमानं स्वविरुद्धं पूर्वज्ञानं बाधमानमेवोत्पद्यते। तेनोत्पन्नमपि पूर्वप्रायश्चित्तज्ञानं मिथ्या—अप्रमा भवति, बाधितत्वात्। उत्तरस्य तु न किंचित् बाधकमस्ति। न हि पूर्वविज्ञानमुत्तरबाधेनोत्पद्यते, तस्यामवस्थायामुत्तरस्यानुपजातत्वात्। जाते तूत्तरविज्ञाने जायमानेन तेन बाधितं पूर्वविज्ञानमसत्कल्पं नोत्तरं बाधितुं क्षमते। तस्मात् पूर्वस्य दौर्बल्यम्, परस्य प्राबल्यम्। सूत्रे प्रकृतिवदित्यस्य यथा प्राकृतस्य कुशादेः वैकृतशराद्यपेक्षया दौर्बल्यं तद्वदित्यर्थः।

अथास्य न्यायस्य संचारप्रकारः समीक्ष्यते। जिज्ञासासूत्रे भामत्यां (निर्णयसागर संस्करण पृ० १०) कर्तृत्वादिविशिष्टात्मविषयकप्रत्यक्षस्य श्रौतस्याकर्त्रात्माद्वैतविषयकज्ञानस्य च विरोधे पूर्वोत्पन्नस्य प्रत्यक्षस्य प्राबल्यमाशङ्क्य पूर्वस्याप्युत्तरापेक्षितस्यैव प्राबल्यम्, न त्वनपेक्षितस्य पूर्वस्य। पूर्वस्यानपेक्षितत्वे उत्तरस्यैव प्राबल्यम्। तेन पूर्वस्य बाध इत्युक्तम्—

'ज्येष्ठत्वं चानपेक्षितस्य बाध्यत्वे हेतुः न बाधकत्वे। रजतज्ञानस्य ज्यायसः (पूर्वोत्पन्नस्य) कनीयसा बाधदर्शनात्। तदनपबाधने तदपबाधात्मनस्तस्य उत्पत्तेरनुपपत्तेः। दर्शितं च तात्त्विकप्रमाणभावस्यानपेक्षितत्वम्। तथा च पारमर्षं सूत्रम्—'पौर्वापर्ये पूर्वदौर्बल्यं प्रकृतिवत्' इति। तथा—

> पूर्वात्परबलीयस्त्वं तत्र नाम प्रतीयताम्।
> अन्योन्यनिरपेक्षाणां यत्र जन्म धियां भवेत्।।

इति। अनेन पूर्वमुपजीव्य यत्रोत्तरशास्त्रं प्रवर्तते तत्र पूर्वं प्रबलम्। यत्र तु पूर्वमनुपजीव्य उत्तरं प्रवर्तते तत्रोत्तरस्य प्राबल्यमिति सिध्यति।

'पूर्वात् परबलीयस्त्वम्' इति वार्तिककारैरपच्छेदन्यायस्थलं निष्कर्षद्भिः अन्यत्रोपक्रमाधिकरणप्रवृत्तिर्दर्शिता। अनेन च यदपेक्षया यस्य प्राबल्यं वर्णनीयम्, तन्निरपेक्षं तत्र बोधोत्पत्तिरपेक्षिता। प्रतिहर्त्रपच्छेदनिमित्तकप्रायश्चित्तशास्त्रं हि उद्गात्रपच्छेदनिमित्तकप्रायश्चित्तशास्त्रनिरपेक्षमेव बोधं जनयति। तस्मात् योऽपच्छेदः परः तन्निमित्तकं प्रायश्चित्तं प्रबलमिति। अत्र अन्योन्यनिरपेक्षाणामित्यनेन एकैकप्राबल्यविषयेऽपि उभयगतं निरपेक्षत्वं प्रयोजकत्वेन नोच्यते। किं तु तन्निरपेक्षं बोधकत्वात् इदमपि कदाचित् प्रबलम्, एतन्निरपेक्षं बोधकत्वात् तदपि कदाचित् प्रबलमित्येव। उपक्रमाधिकरणन्यायश्च तत्र, यत्र सापेक्षं

बोधजनकत्वम्। यथा 'अग्नेर्ऋग्वेदः, वायोर्यजुर्वेदः, आदित्यात् सामवेदः' इत्युपक्रमस्यार्थवादानां, 'उच्चैर्ऋचा क्रियते, उपांशु यजुषा, उच्चैः साम्ना' इत्यनन्तरविधीनां च। न हि तत्तन्नैमित्तिकशास्त्रवत् अर्थवादविध्योरन्योन्यनिरपेक्षं प्रवृत्तिरस्ति। तथा च उपसंहारस्यः विधिरपि उपक्रमस्यार्थवादनिरपेक्षमबोधकत्वात् प्रथमप्रतीतार्थवादिकार्थाविरोधाय लाक्षणिकार्थपरतयैव प्रामाण्यं लभते।

न्यायामृते संचारप्रकारः

द्वैतवेदान्तिभिः व्यासतीर्थैः न्यायामृते (कुम्भकोणम् संस्करणे पृ० २१५) एवमुपपादितम्—यत्तूक्तं वाचस्पतिना पूर्वस्य प्रत्यक्षस्य परेणागमेन अपच्छेदन्यायेन बाध इति। तन्न। न ह्यस्माभिः पूर्वत्वमात्रेण प्रत्यक्षस्य बाधकतोक्ता किं तूपजीव्यत्वेन। न चापच्छेदे पूर्वमुपजीव्यम्। प्रतिहर्त्रपच्छेदं पूर्वमनुपजीव्यैव परस्योद्गात्रपच्छेदस्योदयात्। किं च प्रतिहर्तुद्गात्रोः क्रमेणापच्छेदे प्रतिहर्त्रपच्छेदनिमित्तकसर्वस्वदानस्य परेणोद्गात्रपच्छेदनिमित्तकेन अदाक्षिण्येन बाधेऽपि नात्यन्तबाधः। प्रयोगान्तरे—प्रतिहर्तृमात्रापच्छेदे द्वयोरपि युगपदपच्छेदे क्रमेणापच्छेदेऽपि प्रतिहर्त्रपच्छेदस्य पश्चात्त्वेऽपि 'यदि प्रतिहर्तापच्छिन्द्यात् तर्हि सर्ववेदसं दद्यादिति शास्त्रस्य प्रामाण्यसंभवात्। उक्तं हि टुप्टीकायां (आनंदाश्रम संस्करणे पृ० १४७९) 'तस्य प्रयोगान्तरे निक्षेपः क्रियते' इति। तथा चोपजीव्योपजीवकभावरहितपौर्वापर्यस्थल एवापच्छेदन्यायः प्रवर्तते। प्रकृते च प्रत्यक्षागमयोः पौर्वापर्ये सति उपजीव्योपजीवकभावस्याप्यङ्गीकारात् अपच्छेदन्यायो न प्रवर्तते। अतो नाद्वैतश्रुत्या द्वैतप्रत्यक्षस्य बाधः। एवमेव सगुणनिर्गुणश्रुत्योर्विषयेऽपि अपच्छेदन्यायाप्रवृत्त्या न निर्गुणश्रुत्या सगुणश्रुतेर्बाधः इति।

वस्तुतस्तु भामतीकारैरपि पूर्वं परस्यानपेक्षितं चेदेव परेण बाध्यमित्युक्तम्। परेणोपजीव्यस्य पूर्वस्य न बाध्यत्वमुक्तम्। अतोऽपच्छेदन्यायस्वरूपं न तैरन्यथाकृतम्। भेदग्राहिप्रत्यक्षं ब्रह्मप्रतिपादकशास्त्रस्योपजीव्यमिति द्वैतिनः। नोपजीव्यमित्यद्वैतिनः इत्येतावान् भेदः। उपजीव्यत्वे अपच्छेदन्यायः न प्रवर्तते। अनुपजीव्यत्वे प्रवर्तत इति तत्त्वम्।

सिद्धान्तलेशसंग्रहे (सिकन्दराबाद संस्करणे पृ० २३५) अप्पयदीक्षितैः—अपच्छेदन्यायेन श्रुतेः प्रत्यक्षापेक्षया प्राबल्यवत् उपक्रमाधिकरणन्यायेम प्रत्यक्षस्यापि श्रुत्यपेक्षया प्राबल्यावगमात् तयोः बाध्यबाधकभावे विनिगमनाविरह इत्याशङ्क्य, यत्रैकवाक्यता प्रतीयते तत्रैकस्मिन्नेवार्थे पर्यवसानेन भाव्यम्। अर्थभेदे सति प्रतीतायाः एकवाक्यतायाः भङ्गप्रसङ्गात्। अतस्तत्र असंजातविरोधेन उपक्रमेण योऽर्थो निश्चतः तद्विरुद्धमुपसंहारगतं पदजातं संजातविरोधित्वात् यथाश्रुतार्थबोधने उपक्रमेण सहैकवाक्यताया अनुपपत्त्या एकवाक्यतानिर्वाहाय उपक्रमाविरोध्यर्थ-

बोधकमिति निश्चीयते। यथा 'प्रजापतिर्वरुणायाश्वमनयत्' इत्युपक्रमवाक्येन दातुरिष्टौ बुद्धावारोपितायां तद्विरुद्धार्थं 'यावतोऽश्वान् प्रतिगृह्णीयात् तावतो वारुणान् चतुष्कपालान् निर्वपेत्' इत्युपसंहारपदजातं प्रतिगृह्णीयादित्यस्य णिजर्थमन्तर्भाव्य प्रतिग्राहयेत् (दद्यात्) इत्यर्थपरतया उपक्रमानुगुणमेवार्थं प्रतिपादयति । यत्र तु परस्परमेकवाक्यता न प्रतीयते तत्र पूर्ववृत्तमविगणय्य लब्धस्वरूपं विरुद्धार्थकं वाक्यं स्वार्थं बोधयत्येवेति न तत्र पूर्ववृत्तस्य प्राबल्यम्। एवं चाद्वैतागमस्य प्रत्यक्षेणैकवाक्यत्वशङ्काविरहात् पूर्ववृत्तमविगणय्य स्वार्थबोधकत्वमव्याहतम् । अतस्तत्र नोपक्रमन्यायः प्रवर्तते । अपि तु—

पूर्वं परमजातत्वादबाधित्वैव जायते ।
परस्यानन्यथोत्पादात् नाद्याबाधेन संभवः ।।

इति तन्त्रवार्तिकोक्तरीत्या अपच्छेदन्यायस्यैव प्रवृत्तिः । अत एव लोकेऽपि प्रथमप्रवृत्तं शुक्तिरूप्यप्रत्यक्षम् आप्तोपदेशेनबाध्यते इति प्रत्यपादि ।

वस्तुतस्तु—सम्यङ्मीमांसने सति असंजातविरोधित्वतदभावयोः प्रमाणान्तरसमावेशस्थलेऽपि सुवचत्वेन उपक्रमाधिकरणन्यायस्य शब्दमात्रविषयकत्वाभावात् एकवाक्यताविरहेऽपि पूर्वप्रवृत्तस्य परापेक्षितत्वे उपक्रमन्यायः प्रवर्तते। पूर्वस्य परापेक्षितत्वाभावे अपच्छेदन्यायः प्रवर्तत इत्येव युक्तम् । पूर्वमीमांसायामुपक्रमाधिकरणे एकवाक्यतास्थलमुदाहृतमित्येतावता तत्रैव स न्यायः प्रवर्तत इति कथनं नोचितम् । अत एव 'सदेव सोम्येदमग्र आसीत्' इति पुरोवादवाक्यस्य 'सर्वाणि ह वा इमानि भूतान्याकाशादेव समुत्पद्यन्ते' इत्यनुवादवाक्यस्य च एकवाक्यत्वाभावेऽपि अनुवादस्य पुरोवादसापेक्षत्वात् पुरोवादसंजातचेतनकारणत्वप्रतीत्यविरोधेन आकाशशब्दः योगव्युत्पत्त्या चेतनब्रह्मबोधक इति निर्णीतं शारीरकमीमांसायाम् ।

श्रुतप्रकाशिकानिर्णयः (टी. वीरराघवाचार्य संस्करणे पृ० १६५)

श्रीभाष्यव्याख्यायां श्रुतप्रकाशिकायामुपक्रमन्यायापच्छेदन्याययोः विषयविवेचनमेवं कृतम्—

सगुणं ब्रह्म, निर्गुणं ब्रह्म इति प्रतिपादिकयोः सगुणनिर्गुणश्रुत्योर्विरोधे अपच्छेदन्यायेन परस्य बलीयस्त्वात् परया निर्गुणश्रुत्या सगुणश्रुतेर्बाधात् ब्रह्म निर्गुणमिति सिद्धान्तो नोपपद्यते। यत्र पौर्वापर्यं विरोधश्चेत्युभयं न नियतं तत्रैवापच्छेदन्यायः । तदुक्तम्—

पौर्वापर्यं विरोधश्च (पूर्वाप्रामाण्यमेव च ।)
नियमान्नास्ति यत्रासौ अपच्छेदनयो भवेत् ।।

इति । तथा हि—उद्‌गातृप्रतिहर्त्रोरुभयोरपच्छेदनियमो नास्ति । तत्रापि उभयोः क्रमेणैवापच्छेद इत्यपि नास्ति नियमः । तन्नियमे सति हि सर्वस्वदक्षिणाकत्वादक्षिणाकत्वयोर्विरोधनियमो भवेत् । एवमुद्‌गातृप्रतिहर्त्रोरुभयोरपच्छेदे तस्य क्रमभावित्वे च उद्‌गात्रपच्छेदः पूर्वभावी, प्रतिहर्त्रपच्छेदः पश्चाद्भावी इति वा विपर्ययेणेति वा पौर्वापर्यनियमोऽपि नास्ति । अतः अपच्छेदन्यायस्य अनुष्ठानावधिको विरोधो विषयः, न तु स्वरूपतो विरोधः । सगुणनिर्गुणवाक्यविरोधस्तु स्वरूपप्रयुक्ततया नियतः, न त्वनियतः । एवं सगुणनिर्गुणवाक्ययोः पौर्वापर्यं च नियतम्, विधिनिषेधरूपत्वात् । अतः सगुणनिर्गुणवाक्ययोः विरोधाभ्युपगमेऽपि तस्य नियतत्वात् विधिनिषेधरूपतया तयोः पौर्वापर्यस्य नियतत्वाच्च अनियतविरोधविषयकः अनियतपौर्वापर्यविषयकश्चापच्छेदन्यायो न प्रवर्तते अपि तु नियतविरोध-नियतपौर्वापर्यविषयकः विरोधाधिकरणन्याय एव प्रवर्तते। विरोधाधिकरणविषये हि पौर्वापर्यनियमो विरोधनियमश्च विद्यते । तथा हि—

'औदुम्बरीं स्पृष्ट्वोद्‌गायेत्' इति श्रुतिः । 'औदुम्बरी सर्वा वेष्टयितव्या' इति स्मृतिः । तत्र श्रुतिः प्रथमत एव प्रमां जनयति, निरपेक्षप्रमाणत्वात् । स्मृतिस्तु स्वमूलभूतश्रुत्यनुमानसापेक्षतया विलम्बितप्रवृत्तिका । अतस्तत्र पौर्वापर्यं नियतम् । औदुम्बरीस्पर्शतद्वेष्टनयोर्विरोधश्च नियतः । अतस्तत्र प्रथमप्रवृत्तया श्रुत्या पश्चात्प्रवर्तमाना स्मृतिर्बाध्यते । एवं सगुणश्रुतिः प्रतियोगिसमर्पकतया पूर्वा । तत्सापेक्षा निर्गुणश्रुतिः परा इत्युभयोः पौर्वापर्यं नियतम् । सगुणत्वनिर्गुणत्वयोर्विरोधश्च नियत इति विरोधाधिकरणन्यायेन सगुणश्रुत्या निर्गुणश्रुतिर्बाध्यते । किं च नियतविरोध-पौर्वापर्यस्थले उपक्रमाधिकरणप्रवृत्त्या पूर्वस्य प्राबल्यम्, परस्य दौर्बल्यम् ।

एतावता एतत् सिद्धं यत् यत्र परशास्त्रं पूर्वशास्त्रसापेक्षं न भवति, यत्र च पूर्वपरयोः विरोधपौर्वापर्ये न नियते तत्रापच्छेदन्यायेन परस्य बलीयस्त्वम्, पूर्वस्य दौर्बल्यम् । यत्र तु परं पूर्वसापेक्षम्, यत्र च पूर्वपरयोः विरोधपौर्वापर्ये नियते तत्र विरोधाधिकरणस्य उपक्रमाधिकरणस्य प्रवृत्त्या पूर्वस्य प्राबल्यम्, परस्य दौर्बल्यमिति ।

ननु प्रथमप्रवृत्तं विलम्बितप्रवृत्तस्योत्पत्तिं प्रतिबध्नाति चेत् नेदं रजतमितिधियं प्रथमप्रवृत्ता इदं रजतमिति भ्रमात्मकधीः प्रतिबध्नातु इति चेत्-न । सत्तया ज्ञापकस्य ज्ञायमानतया ज्ञापकस्य चात्यन्तवैषम्यात् । सत्तया ज्ञापकं हि प्रमाणं पूर्वापरपरामर्शनिरपेक्षं ज्ञानं जनयति । तत्र पश्चादुत्पद्यमानं ज्ञानं 'पूर्वबाधेन नोत्पत्तिरुत्तरस्य हि सिध्यति' इति न्यायात् पूर्वं बाधित्वैवोदेति । ज्ञायमानतया ज्ञापकं तु योग्यतापरामर्शादिसापेक्षतया प्रमितिं जनयति । तत्र परामर्शदशायां पूर्वप्रमाणेन विरुद्धप्रमितिश्चेत् सोत्तरप्रमितिं प्रतिबध्नातीति वैषम्यमिति ।

एवं तर्हि नेदं रजतमिति ज्ञानस्य प्रतियोगिज्ञानविधया इदं रजतमिति ज्ञानसापेक्षतया तेन प्रतिबन्धात् नेदं रजतमिति ज्ञानस्यानुदयप्रसङ्ग इति चेत्-न। शुक्तिरियमिति शुक्तित्वविषया ह्युत्तरप्रमितिः। सा न रजतज्ञानसापेक्षा। शुक्तित्वे ज्ञाते सति तज्ज्ञानफलभूतः नेदं रजतमिति व्यवहारः नञुल्लिखितत्वात् प्रतियोगि-ज्ञानसापेक्षः प्रवर्तते। तत्सापेक्षत्वं च शब्दस्वभावाधीनमिति सर्वं चतुरश्रम्।

18

THE PRINCIPLE OF UPASAṀHĀRA AND THE DEVELOPMENT OF VEDĀNTA AS AN UTTARA MĪMĀṀSĀ

FRANCIS X CLOONEY, S.J.

Introduction

We know that the Vedānta[1] is both a continuation of the Mīmāṁsā and a new departure, possessed of views incompatible with the Mīmāṁsā. As a *mīmāṁsā*, it continues to insist on the primacy of textual knowledge and the central importance of an approved, orthodox pathway to correct, textual knowledge; as *uttara*, it insists that new texts—the *Upaniṣads*—lie at the heart of orthodoxy, and that these texts envision meditation as a 'post-ritual practice" which leads to a definitively 'post-ritual knowledge'.

The *Uttara Mīmāṁsā Sūtras* 1.1.1-4, as elaborated in Śaṁkara's *Bhāṣya* and the commentaries thereon,[2] are our most familiar classical locus for an understanding of how (Advaita) Vedānta follows upon and diverges from Mīmāṁsā. Because the specific purpose of the *catuḥsūtrī* is to introduce, define and justify the Vedānta project as legitimately new, it tends toward generalization, philosophical grounding, and an apologetic, even polemical, differentiation of the Vedānta from the Mīmāṁsā. Indeed, if the student's familiarity with the *Uttara Mīmāṁsā Sūtras* is limited to the *catuḥsūtrī*, she or he may be left with the impression that the Mīmāṁsā and Vedānta are more different than alike, and that their differences are due largely to theoretical and philosophical arguments.

In the following pages I wish to present the continuity and difference of the Mīmāṁsā and Vedānta from a less general, less philosophical and less apologetic angle, by examining the articulation of a properly Vedāntic mode of exegesis in *Uttara Mīmāṁsā Sūtra* 3.3. Although my analysis will in part confirm the familiar conclusions about Vedānta, the exegetical version of the matter presented in 3.3[3] will enable us to grasp more skilfully the 'grammar' of this continuity and difference—i.e., the series of smaller, exegetical decisions out of which the Vedānta is fashioned as a true Uttara Mīmāṁsā. My intention is to show, in a preliminary fashion, that we discover in 3.3 an exegetical enactment of that distinctive task of the *Uttara Mīmāṁsā* which is elsewhere philosophically articulated: the negotiation of a balance between a never-superseded *knowledge of the Upaniṣads* and a cumulative, intelligible *discourse about Brahman* which legitimately guides and forms the reading of the Upaniṣads. I will argue too that the principle of *upasaṁhāra*, though not without precedents in Mīmāṁsā, is an important principle of exegesis which distinguishes the Uttara Mīmāṁsā as a school of exegesis with its own problematic;[4] if we understand the why and how of *upasaṁhāra*, we understand the practice of the Uttara Mīmāṁsā, even before further explorations of key theories such as *advaita, upādānatva* and *nirguṇatva*.

I will comment on the following sections of 3.3: 3.3.1-4, which applies to the Upaniṣads an important Mīmāṁsā rule enunciated in *Pūrva Mīmāṁsā Sūtras* 2.4.8.33: i.e., the *sarvaśākhāpratyayanyāya*, the rule that (most) differences which accrue from *śākhā* ('Vedic school') to *śākhā* in the descriptions of rites do not differentiate rites which are in the most important respects identical; 3.3.5, in which we find a properly Vedānta understanding and practice of *upasaṁhāra* as an intelligent, skilled 'borrowing' among Upaniṣadic texts; 3.3.16-17 as an example of *upasaṁhāra*; 3.3.11-13 and 58 as illustrative of the Vedānta's effort to establish parameters within which the coherence of knowledge and exegesis could be maintained.

The appeal to Pūrva Mīmāṁsā Sūtras 2.4.8-33 *in* 3.3.1-4

In order to show that the admitted plurality of texts handed down in various *śākhās* ('Vedic schools') can be analyzed and combined in ways that cut across the established *śākhā* boundaries, in 3.3.1 Bādarāyaṇa's argument in favour of combination includes an appeal to a well-known Mīmāṁsā *adhikaraṇa*: "[A complete meditation/text] can be composed from all the Vedānta texts—'for it is not distinguished by injunction [*codanā*], etc.'" (*sarvavedāntapratyayaṃ codanādyaviśeṣāt*).

Codanādyaviśeṣāt refers us to *Pūrva Mīmāṁsā Sūtras* 2.4.8-33, a long *adhikaraṇa* in which the continuity of ritual description across *śākhā* boundaries is defended. Key to the Mīmāṁsā *adhikaraṇa* is the following sūtra, the one recalled by Bādarāyaṇa:

> 9 [A rite referred to in more than one *śākhā*] is one, for it is not distinguished [from *śākhā* to *śākhā*] by connection, form, injunction or name. [*ekaṁ vā saṁyogarūpacodanākhyāviśeṣāt.*]

This siddhānta sūtra presents the basic argument (to be defended in detail in *Pūrva Mīmāṁsā Sūtras* 2.4.10-33) as to why difference of *śākhā* does not indicate difference of rites too. Small differences do not matter, since there is continuity across *śākhā*-boundaries in four areas that count: the *saṁyoga* (connection with the rite's promised result [*phala*,])[5] *rūpa* (the form of the rite, its named deity and offering material), *codanā* (the injunction or injunctive force instigating the performance) and *ākhyā* (the name of the rite—'*agnihotra*' etc.). Thus, the Mīmāṁsā discussion of *karma-bhedābheda* in *Pūrva Mīmāṁsā Sūtras* 2.2-4 concludes with a case in which the claim of *bheda* is rejected.

This Mīmāṁsā principle is introduced by the Vedānta in support of the view that the information contained in different Upaniṣadic texts can be selectively combined for the sake of more complete meditations. Comparable meditations—i.e. those which are legitimately similar in name, content or form—can be determined to be the 'same' everywhere, and so combinable, even if they are not identical in every detail.

In lieu of describing the long and detailed commentarial discussion of the applicability of the text and its pertinence to Vedānta,[6] I will cite only the basic correlation discerned by Śaṁkara:[7]

> When it says, 'Let him make an oblation', it is the same human effort that is being enjoined regarding the same *agnihotra*, whatever the differences among the *śākhās* [in

> which the injunction is heard]. So too, there is a similar injunctive force [*codanā*] in this text [which is found in the Upaniṣads of both] the Vājasaneyins and Chandogas: 'Who know what is the oldest and the best.' [*Bṛhadāraṇyaka* 6.1.1; *Chāndogya* 5.1.1]
>
> Nor is the connection [*saṁyoga*] with the motivation [i.e. the result] differentiated, since [in both] it says, 'He becomes the oldest and the best.' [*Bṛhadāraṇyaka* 6.1.1; *Chāndogya*; 5.1.1]
>
> So too, there is the same form [*rūpa*] for the act of knowledge in each text, namely 'being made of *prāṇa*,' as specified by the qualifications of being oldest and best, etc. Just as the offering material and the deity are the form of a sacrifice, so too the object of knowledge [*vijñeya*] is the form of the act of knowledge [*vijñāna*], since it is informed by that [object].
>
> The name [*samākhyā*] too is the same, 'the meditation on the *prāṇas*'. Therefore acts of knowledge are to be [more completely] composed from all [by drawing on] all the Vedānta texts.

This application of the Mīmāṁsā *nyāya* to the Upaniṣads helps shape the linguistic and epistemological practice of the Vedānta as a school of thought committed to exegesis. Both schools insist on the mediation of knowledge by text; indeed, this mediation is a distinguishing mark of the two schools. It motivates their effort to regularize texts and reconcile observable differences from *śākhā* to *śākhā*. Just as the Mīmāṁsā bases the performance of ritual in the reconstituted Vedic discourse about ritual, the Vedānta bases the performance of meditation in its own reconstituted version of Upaniṣadic knowledge. Text and practice—ritual performance, meditation—remain strongly connected in both systems; texts are generative of a kind of action otherwise either impossible or fruitless.

In both schools, the *sarvaśākhāpratyaya-nyāya* permits the active correlation of information from hitherto dispersed texts, for the sake of more complete and efficient practice. Like the Mīmāṁsā, the Vedānta in effect argues for a 'post-*śākhā*/post-traditional' commitment to the sacred text, a reverence which, though real, claims for itself the power to evaluate and dispose of smaller and larger textual differences. This measured and moderate commitment to the Mīmāṁsā way of doing things is a very important contribution to our understanding of the Vedānta as a school of thought which always thinks *from* texts, even when it constructs meanings not literally *in* the texts.[8]

Mīmāṁsā and Vedānta are also parallel in the way they structure the knowing and the known. According to the Mīmāṁsā understanding of ritual, the named deity (*devatā*) and material (*dravya*) constitute the (visible and operative) form of any given sacrifice.[9] In Vedāntic meditation, (*Saguṇa*) *Brahman* constitutes meditation's (visible and operative) form. We have already seen how Śaṁkara puts it at 3.3.1: "Just as the offering material and the deity are the form of a sacrifice, so too the object of knowledge is the form of the act of knowledge, since it is informed by that [object]." At 3.3.58 he says (in the voice of *pūrvapakṣin*) "the object of knowledge [*vedya*] is the form of the act of knowledge [*vidyā*] just as the offering material and the deity are the form of a sacrifice." Prior to the performance, or comprehension, of any particular action or content, the practices of ritual and meditation are *informed* respectively by *dravya-devatā* and *Brahman*; though different implications may later be drawn, *Brahman* is 'placed' in a way that replicates Mīmāṁsā's placement of sacrifice's component parts.

But the analogy between Mīmāṁsā and Vedānta as to the basis, nature and form of knowledge is not exact, since they decide differently about how to build on the shared presuppositions. For the Mīmāṁsakas, performance is constituted entirely out of textual knowledge. There is no recognized referent, outside the texts,[10] which is allowed to compete with the texts in determining how rituals are to be understood and performed, since the primary candidates for an enduring extra-textual position are denied that role. The materials offered are merely *śeṣa* (*Pūrva Mīmāṁsā Sūtras* 3.1.3), deities are denied a central, determinative role (*Pūrva Mīmāṁsā Sūtras* 9.1.4-10) and, though in a more complex fashion, the sacrificer is denied centrality in (at least) the early Mīmāṁsā.[11]

Nor, finally, can *artha* be said to have an established referential role in Mīmāṁsā. The Mīmāsaṁkas do take *artha* very seriously, as the referent of words (*śabdārtha*), the purpose of actions (*kriyārtha*), and the motivating human goal (*puruṣārtha*). *Artha*'s rich multivalence enables the Mīmāṁsaka to reinterpret texts, revise actions and rethink the role of performers, continually balancing the one against the other; it is extra-textual in the sense that it is not reducible to meaning, just as it is 'extra-ritual' and 'extra-teleological'. However, *artha* remains intentionally, permanently unformalized; it is not formally constituted as extra-textual, nor objectified as a referent about which things can be *said*. It is always there—in the *act* of meaning, performing, intending.[12]

Although the Advaitins deny any commonsense image of *Brahman* as the (merely) objectively knowable, they insist that knowledge tends toward *Brahman* as an 'extra-textual' reality which is not the construct of texts and which can, in theory at least, be known apart from texts. The meditator can progress in a fruitful dialectic which moves him back and forth between the text and the (increasingly familiar) object of text and knowledge, *Brahman*. The *Nirguṇa/Saguṇa* distinction and the concomitant literary complications notwithstanding, salvific Upaniṣadic knowledge does have an object about which something can be said, in a manner that is always provisional but which nevertheless contributes to a gradually more adequate comprehension, knowledge.[13]

The Advaitins thus operate within a 'three-cornered' matrix: (1) *the performance of meditation*, which is dependent on (2) *the Upaniṣads*, but which also looks toward (3) *Brahman as the object of meditation*. Over the generations of commentary, their use of the Upaniṣads in meditation and then in more theoretical expositions of the Vedānta is continually adjusted by their increasing knowledge of *Brahman*. Indeed, the Vedānta as a system of thought and practice is defined by this task of keeping in tension the act of meditation, the texts, and the single significant object of all the meditations and texts; it is in the balancing of the three that the *Advaita* 'theory of revelation' is practised: *Brahman is* revealed, *in* the text.

There is then an asymmetry between the Vedānta and Mīmāṁsā systems; Vedānta affords a definiteness of reference to *Brahman*, and therefore also a role in the interpretation of texts, which are not paralleled in Mīmāṁsā's reflection on ritual. This asymmetry is key to the development of Vedānta as an Uttara Mīmāṁsā.

Upasaṁhāra as a Vedānta tool in 3.3.5

3.3.1-4 authorizes the Vedāntins to draw appropriately on other Upaniṣads in order to complement any particular meditation mentioned in one Upaniṣad, because the differences among Upaniṣads are insufficient to exclude this borrowing. The rest of the *pāda* uses this authorization to identify or disallow a series of combined meditations about *Brahman* which draw on different texts while yet respecting the integrity of each.

3.3.5—*upasaṁhāro 'rthābhedāt vidhiśeṣavat samāne ca*[14]—and Śaṁkara's brief *Bhāṣya* comment on it present us with the rule which will be operative in the rest of 3.3: because the object (*artha*) of all meditations is the same, the characteristics (*guṇa*) mentioned in any particular meditation are possibly applicable in other, comparable meditations.[15] Acts of meditation which are legitimately comparable can be determined to be 'about the same thing'—e.g., about *Brahman* qualified in the same way—and so can be legitimately combined. This legitimate, selective borrowing is the practice of *upasaṁhāra*.

To explain the ritual reference in the sūtra—*vidhiśeṣavat*—Śaṁkara offers a ritual analogy:

> "Just as is the case with the auxiliary part of injunctions" [*vidhiśeṣavat*]: for just as the characteristics of the *agnihotra*, etc., from the auxiliary parts of injunctions, are combined "since the object is not different [from text to text]" [*arthābhedāt*]—for there is just one *agnihotra*, etc. everywhere—so too here [there are single meditations partially described in various Upaniṣads].

This principle too follows from *Pūrva Mīmāṁsā Sūtra* 2.4.8-33, which conclude that because the *agnihotra* is a single rite that is mentioned in different *śākhās*, there can be (in Śabara's words) *śākhāntarīyāṇām* [*vidhīnām*] *upasaṁhāraḥ*.[16] Just as we are entitled to draw on a variety of texts in our effort to construct a full practical assessment of the *agnihotra*, meditations can be similarly amplified.

This version of the principle of *upasaṁhāra* is not greatly developed in the Mimāṁsā.[17] In *Pūrva Mīmāṁsā Sūtras* 2.4.8-33, it is simply determined that the *agnihotra* is to be fully elaborated in a process that draws on multiple *śākhās*; but since, in theory at least, this is a clear even if complex task, the principle does not require as much refinement by the Mīmāṁsakas as do *atideśa* and *tantra*, for instance.[18]

The most important Mīmāṁsā discussion of this form of *upasaṁhāra* occurs in the first two *adhikaraṇas* of the *Pūrva Mīmāṁsā Sūtras* 6.3, 1-7, 8-10. In the first (1-7) it is determined that in certain conditions *naimittika* rites may be performed without the full complement of their supporting, *guṇa* activities, if the performer is unable to perform all of these. For the obligation to perform takes precedence over the ideal of completeness, and so the task of the *upasaṁhāra* of those *guṇa* rites from all possible texts may be left unfinished. In the second (8-10) the siddhāntin denies an extension of the same permission to *kāmya* rites: since these are not obligatory, there is no valid reason for performing them incompletely, and so *sarvaguṇa-upasaṁhāra* is required. We shall see in a moment the Vedānta use of these *adhikaraṇas*. Here I wish to note simply that this version of *upasaṁhāra* is not directly an exegetical rule; it refers primarily to the practice of ritual performance.

The Vedāntins highlight *upasaṁhāra* in the course of their characteristic back and forth interpretive movement between a reorganization of Upaniṣadic knowledge based on the Mīmāṁsā functional systematization of the Veda, and one based in part on the fact that *Brahman* is the known object of that knowledge, its referent. They argue from the grammatical sense of texts *and* from their reference, and so highlight *upasaṁhāra* as one of their key, *Uttara* Mīmāṁsā principles.

In any given meditation, then, a meditator's knowledge can be composed in the way that a performer's knowledge of the *agnihotra* is. The potential of this particular ritual analogy is explored by the commentators largely through their rejection of alternative Mīmāṁsā strategies for the collation of texts. I will consider just two of these alternatives, *prakṛtivikṛtitva* and *upakāratva* in order to clarify the shift that occurs. The first entails the conception that rites can be related as simpler and more complex versions of one another, and the second that ritual 'accessories' (*guṇa*) are 'helps' in the enactment of rituals. Let us consider them in turn.

The *prakṛti-vikṛti* model of rituals, employed and analyzed in great detail in the 7th-12th *adhyāyas* of the *Pūrva Mīmāṁsā Sūtras*, has several important explanatory advantages. First, it affords us an economical and concise version of the relation of rituals to one another, and so too of the texts about these rituals; the diversity of detail and plurality of texts is arranged manageably by a delineation of the connections between ritual and text. Yet, the differences among rites are not undervalued. Second, a precise reason is found for the fact that some but not all of the necessary details in a ectypal (*vaikṛta*) rite are mentioned: some details are noted in order to exclude other details that would apply automatically—*codakena*—from the archetype. Hence, what is mentioned is purposely introduced, and it can be purposely combined with what potentially accrues from the archetype.

Upakāratva—compatible with the *prakṛti-vikṛti* model and not necessarily an alternative to it—is presented by Vācaspati from two slightly different angles. First, it entails the simple notion that the Veda always supplies us with sufficient *upakāra*: if only a few ritual details are mentioned, it is because they are sufficient for the performance of the rite. So too, if only a few characteristics of *brahman* appear in a text, it is because they are sufficient for an efficacious performance of the meditation. If this were not true, the reasoning goes, scripture would have provided more details; our faith in scripture tells us that there is no reason for borrowing from other texts, *upasaṁhāra*.

A second angle focuses on the analogy with the *naimittika* class of rites mentioned above: meditations are like *naimittika* rites, and mentioned *guṇas* are like supporting ritual activities, since they support the main action of meditation. Even if one could perform an ampler meditation by borrowing details from other Upaniṣads, one does not need to, since what is at hand is sufficient. The advantage here include a respect for what is actually said in the text, and the realization that one does not need to supplement it from elsewhere.

Whatever the advantages, however, the commentators reject both models in their exposition of *upasaṁhāra*. The *prakṛti-vikṛti* model is simply discarded by Śaṁkara as a matter of fact: "there is no *prakṛti-vikṛti* relationship among *guṇas*." Vācaspati disallows the relevance of Mīmāṁsā examples based on the model, arguing that each meditation is a single and underived practice, and so that calculations from archetype to ectype are irrelevant. Or, to put it the other way: the Vedānta understanding of the Upaniṣads as expressive of *Brahman* does not require the construction of a *prakṛti-vikṛti* version of how Upaniṣads work.

Upakāratva is disposed of by a denial that meditations are *naimittika*. Meditation, says Amalānanda, is comparable not to *naimittika* rites but to *kāmya* rites, since one is not obliged to meditation; therefore, according to *Pūrva Mīmāṁsā Sūtras* 6.3.8-10, meditations require full implementation of potential details if they are to be performed fruitfully. They must be done as completely as possible, or not at all.

Underlying this rejection of the *naimittika* model and the accompanying notion of limited, sufficient *upakāra* is an important shift in the use of *upasaṁhāra*. The ritual calculation of the requirement of *guṇa* actions by *naimittika* and *kāmya* rites is transposed first into a calculation of how acts of meditation need, or do not need, their *guṇas*, those qualifications of *Brahman* which contribute to the performance of meditation. But it is then transposed into a calculation of how *guṇas*, as attributes, belong to their bearer, their *guṇi*. Govindānanda states this more metaphysical perspective in the *Bhāṣyaratnaprabhā* on 3.3.5, where he notes an inference which underlies *upasaṁhāra*:

> Since *guṇas* are invariably connected to that which possesses them [i.e. *guṇi*] a meditation [*vidyā*] set in one *śākhā* has the *guṇas* which are mentioned regarding that [meditation] in other *śākhās*, since [the *guṇi*] is undivided; by the inference '[this meditation] is like that meditation,' one establishes the practice of *upasaṁhāra* in cases where there is [really only] one meditation.[19]

The Vedānta employment of *upasaṁhāra* includes an incompletely effected shift from a ritual to a metaphysical model, from *guṇas* as contributory components of meditation performance to *guṇas* as qualities of the referent of meditation. Although meditation remains a kind of performance, the core of it is ultimately found to lie in the desire to know, which is satisfied not by a certain, predictable amount of effort or adequate construction, but by the attainment of what it seeks to know. Hence, one cannot resist the tendency to collate texts, to learn from two together more than one can learn from one alone—no matter what might be considered performatively adequate. It is in this gradually shifting sense of the motivation of *upasaṁhāra*, I suggest, that we glimpse the emergence of Vedānta as an *Uttara Mīmāṁsā.*[20]

The Tensions of Upasaṁhāra in 3.3

The remainder of 3.3 is devoted to the task of balancing exegesis with a gradually acquired 'post-textual' knowledge which changes how exegesis is done; it is an extended series of exercises in *upasaṁhāra*, the negotiation of the 'space' between what is said in any particular text and what is already/otherwise known about *Brahman* from other texts and from meditation experience. In lieu of a (much needed) full analysis of the whole of 3.3, I will illustrate the principle of *upasaṁhāra* by just one example, 3.3.16-17, and then by attention to the predictable limits of *upasaṁhāra* as illustrated in two *adhikaraṇas*: 3.3.11-13, where the enduring nature of *Brahman* is recognized as a factor in interpretation, and 3.3.58, where the integrity of texts is insisted on.

(a) *Upasaṁhāra in* 3.3.16-17

The second version of 3.3.16-17[21] aligns a pair of *Chāndogya* and *Bṛhadāraṇyaka* texts and asks whether they can be composed as a single meditation. Śaṁkara identifies the texts as these: one from the fourth *adhyāya* of the *Bṛhadāraṇyaka Upaniṣad*, extending from 4.3.7 ('what is the self? Among the *prāṇas*, it is the one made of knowledge, the light in the heart, the person") to 4.4.25 ("that great, unborn self, is undecaying, immortal, undying, fearless, *Brahman*") and the other from the sixth *adhyāya* of the *Chāndogya Upaniṣad*, from 6.2.1 ("In the beginning all this was but existence, one only, without a second") to 6.8.7ff., the repeated declaration, 'it is the self, you are that.'

The *pūrvapakṣin* argues that these texts cannot be used together since the *Bṛhadāraṇyaka* text from its start is clearly about the Self, whereas the *Chāndogya* text does not mention the Self until 6.8.7. The *siddhāntin* holds that they can be used together, even though it is true that there are almost no verbal cues which explicitly link the themes of the two texts. He argues as follows: *Chāndogya* 6.2.1, on the primordial unity, presupposes 6.1.1—"That by [knowledge of] which the unheard becomes heard, the unthought becomes thought, the unknown becomes known." Neither text, he says, will be true—plausible, convincing—unless its topic is the eternal Self, *Brahman,* which alone could fit the claims that are made. Anything less than this Self would be inadequate. The concluding 'it is the self, you are that' (6.8.7) merely validates the initial claim, since those who properly understand "you are that" realize that it is the same Self which was implied from the start of the section. Therefore, the *Bṛhadāraṇyaka* and *Chāndogya* texts can be used together; by *upasaṁhāra* one can selectively combine their contents, to construct a fuller meditation.

Although the argument is carefully, even cautiously, presented as based entirely on a reading of the two texts, it nevertheless relies on a mature understanding of what they are about, an understanding which reaches beyond their literal expression. The *siddhānta* requires of the reader an understanding of what is implied by the discussion of the originative source of the world, and by the claim that there is a single knowledge by which all is known; it asks too that one be able to use this acquired understanding to recognize in texts what is not literally said in them—here, to conclude that all of *Chāndogya* 6 is about *Brahman* the Self, even those parts of it in which the Self is not mentioned, and that it therefore has the same object as the *Bṛhadāraṇyaka* text. The *siddhāntin* performs *upasaṁhāra* (as the act of combination); on the basis of a fuller understanding of the two texts, he re-uses them together, in a way that reaches beyond the original intention of either.

(b) *The boundaries of upasaṁhāra in* 3.3.11-13 *and* 3.3.58

In 3.3.11-13 it is proposed that our knowledge of the nature of *Brahman*—i.e., what is entailed by our basic understanding of what we are doing when we meaningfully use the word "*brah-*

man'—requires us to recognize certain *guṇas* as inherent in *Brahman*. The sense of *Brahman* which the Vedāntin develops from tradition, familiarity with scripture, and meditation practice authorizes him to decide that certain terms—true (*sat*), conscious (*cit*,) blissful (*ānanda*,) etc.—pertain to the essence of *Brahman* and are implied every time the word '*brahman*' is used, while other terms—e.g., 'its head is joy' (*priyaśiras*,) 'uniting all that is pleasant' (*saṁyadvāma*,) etc.—characterize *Brahman* only in one or another meditation, and so are applicable only in those places.[22]

This legitimation of the attribution of certain essential qualifications to *Brahman* authorizes the Vedāntin to construct a context of intelligibility for any given Upaniṣadic text, to perform *upasaṁhāra* with an awareness of what he knows must be everywhere true of *Brahman*, introducing key qualifications from wherever they are found. The meditator must be someone familiar with the various Upaniṣads, someone who has learned to read each text intelligently, in the context of other texts. One has to be able to know what *Brahman* is like, so as to be able to distinguish an inherent characteristic of *Brahman* from what is useful only as part of one particular meditation. While skills in discerning reading are essential to Mīmāṁsā too, Vedānta's insistence that *Brahman* is an extra-textual referent and not merely the fiction of each particular text makes it all the more important that the Vedāntin be able to make a wider set of choices which subordinate the text to the emerging, acquired 'relationship' of meditator and *Brahman*.[23]

According to the *Advaita*, 3.3.58 serves to reject the collapse of all meditations into one, and the brief *adhikaraṇa* thus counterbalances 3.3.11-13 by defending the integrity of the plurality of Upaniṣadic texts. The idea that all meditations are reducible to one can be interpreted as having a narrower or broader import. First, it can be simply a revival of a charge countered in *Pūrva Mīmāṁsā Sūtras* 2.4.11, where the *siddhāntin* limits the significance of name (*nāma*) by arguing that if name were determinative of identity, then all the rites in the *Kāṭhaka* or *Kālāpaka* text would have to be treated as one rite. This 'nominalism' is clearly impractical and unacceptable, and it is rejected as such. Analogously, one might entertain the idea that all the meditations in the *Chāndogya* are one meditation because they are all '*Chāndogya*', and the Vedāntin must reject this possibility.[24]

The broader version of the position can be posed as follows: if *Brahman* is the single referent of all meditations, then a universal act of *upasaṁhāra* is warranted, by which *all guṇas* are composed into a single, comprehensive meditation. One would then be in effect replacing the Upaniṣads with a post-Upaniṣadic 'manual' which would say more concisely and comprehensively what the texts had previously said partially and repetitively.

Śaṁkara rejects the possible reduction/confusion of texts—in either version—by an appeal to *Pūrva Mīmāṁsā Sūtras* 2.2.1. There, at the beginning of the discussion of *karma-bhedābheda* (which concludes in *Pūrva Mīmāṁsā Sūtras* 2.4 with the *sarva-śākhāpratyayanyāya* considered above,) certain verbal differences in root—*yajati, dadāti, juhoti*—are judged able to distinguish kinds of rites, even if all can be said to share in 'action', 'surrender,' 'human effort', etc. Verbal differences need to be respected. Analogously, Śaṁkara says, meditations are distinguished by the root meanings of the 'knowledge-verbs' contained in them—*veda, upāsīta, sa kratuṁ kurvīta*, etc.—even if all meditations involve the 'same' mental effort and ultimately have the same object.[25] Or, to put it another way: if we need to admit that the unity of *Brahman* as the object of meditation can never be replicated in the plurality of hings said about it, we need also to remember that this inadequate plurality has an important practical function and so needs to be preserved.

In either the narrower or broader interpretation, the *adhikaraṇa* serves to ward off the "philosopher's" tendency to dispense altogether with the distinction of texts and so to collapse all pertinent Upaniṣadic passages into a uniform, generalized and abstractly available knowledge of *Brahman* which is available apart from meditation. The Mīmāṁsā *nyāya* enunciated in *Pūrva Mīmāṁsā Sūtras* 2.2.1 is well-used, to defend the Upaniṣads from decomposition in the face of their extra-textual referent *Brahman*. Though the object of knowledge is simply one, one ought not to seek to reduce language to the same simplicity; for the unity of the known is available by the practice of "working through' the plurality of the Upaniṣads.

The Vedāntins thus conclude 3.3 (though several *adhikaraṇas* remain) by balancing the *pāda*'s primary interest in defending the unity of reference underlying the Upaniṣads and the consequent right to make connections and combinations across the boundaries of texts with a preservation of the distinctiveness of texts. The *Advaita* tradition declines to argue that the texts themselves are reducible to perfect identity.

Conclusion: Mīmāṁsā and the Contempory Relevance of Vedānta

In the preceding pages I have traced the contours of a key example of the practical, exegetical way in which Vedāntins remained Mīmāṁsakas while following through on the implications of their own understanding of texts and of *Brahman* as an extra-textual reserent. I have argued that the general features of Vedānta's self-definition and self-presentation are made available to us in 3.3 in a documented and detailed textual practice which shows us how the Uttara Mīmāṁsā actually 'worked'; for the practice of *upasaṁhāra* replicates in exegesis the major tensions that are presented more theoretically, philosophically and even polemically elsewhere in the *Uttara Mīmāṁsā Sūtras*.

It may seem then that our understanding of Vedānta as Uttara Mīmāṁsā remains much the same as before: the Vedāntins partly diverge from their Mīmāṁsā heritage, because their inquiry has a different kind of object, *Brahman*, and because it concludes in a different kind of knowledge. How precisely they reach this position, and how they use Mīmāṁsā thinking to get there, may appear to be of interest only to the philologist or historian; the general conclusions about the Upaniṣads, *Brahman* and knowledge, which continue to deserve the attention of a wide audience, may seem much more readily accessible in the *catuḥsūtrī*.

I wish to conclude by suggesting three reasons which justify the effort, merely exemplified here, to retrieve in detail the foundations of Vedānta in Mīmāṁsā exegesis. First, by taking exegetical thinking very seriously, we observe in practice a Vedānta position which we generally encounter as a theory: Vedānta invests heavily in the authority of scripture, and maintains *śrutipramāṇa* no matter how large its claims about *Brahman* become. By our examination of 3.3, we have been able to illustrate how the claim for an extra-textual truth is argued/performed most carefully *within* the boundaries of the Upaniṣadic texts and not apart from them. The 'transgression' of the literal word and the practice of *upasaṁhāra* occur only within the realm of a maintained commitment to the text and a right reading of it. 3.3 makes no sense at all unless even the Advaitin wants to locate his claims in texts and according to the Mīmāṁsā heritage; we are not going to make sense of Vedānta if we pay little attention to the details of its exegesis.[26]

Second, the exegetical accomplishment of the Vedānta position is not inferior to its philosophical rendering, and its deserves comparable attention; exegesis is the basis on which Vedānta theory is built, and the existence of exegetically-inclined commentaries should remind us that the Vedāntins were never entirely finished with exegesis. Although we need to refrain from reading the *Uttara Mīmaṁsā Sūtras* as a drama which proceeds to a climax—as if it is only the third and fourth *adhyāyas* that show us what the Vedāntins are *really* interested in—we need also to refrain from reading the *catuḥsūtrī* as an adequate summary and replacement for all that follows. Indeed, as a remedy to our custom of focusing on the beginning of the *Uttara Mīmaṁsā Sūtras* only, it may help us to read backwards—e.g., to reread 1.1.1-4 *after* a thorough study of 3.3.1-5, or to rethink the practice of *samanvaya* which is accomplished in the first *adhyāya* *after* studying in detail *upasaṁhāra* in the third.[27]

For those of us concerned about the status of the study of Vedānta today, there is a third reason: today we find among scholars of all disciplines a renewed and lively interest in textuality and in the strategies by which texts signify and have meanings. This exploration of textuality calls into question the habitual and often hasty effort to move from texts into the minds of their authors, or from spatially-temporally dispersed verbal communication in speech and writing to ideal philosophical systematizations. Though not entirely dismissed, the recovery of textuality 'puts philosophy in its place.'[28]

Therefore, a revitalization of the Vedānta's position as a premier intellectual influence in the global context will be greatly aided by a retrieval of its textuality, its status as Uttara Mīmāṁsā. Instead of dwelling on the search for philosophical parallels between Vedānta and philosophical or mystical systems elsewhere in the world, we would do well to explain for a wider audience how the Vedānta is indeed a Mīmāṁsā, a profoundly textual thinking. Ironically, then, renewed attention to Mīmāṁsā may prove to be the most solid foundation for Vedānta's position in the larger academic and theological discourse over the next few generations; an understanding of *upasaṁhāra* may help us to reappropriate the truth of *Advaita*.[29]

NOTES

1. Vedānta in any of its schools, but especially the earlier ones. My remarks here are limited to the Advaita Vedānta tradition.

2. The following remarks are based on my reading of a variety of commentaries, including: *Bhāṣya* (Śaṁkara), *Bhāmatī* (*Vācaspati*), *Vedānta-kalpataru* (Amalānanda,) *Kalpataruparimala* (Appaya Dīkṣita,) *Brahma-vidyābharaṇa* (Advaitānanda), and *Śārīrakanyāyasaṁgraha* (Prakāśātman). Limitations of space have made it impossible to cite all pertinent commentarial remarks. Throughout, all references to commentaries are by *sūtra*, and are available in any published edition of these texts.

3. Henceforth I will make reference to the *Uttara Mīmāṁsā Sūtras* simply by indicating the *adhyāya*, *pāda* and *sūtra*; thus, 3.3.1, etc.

4. Along with *samanvaya*, the project of *Uttara Mīmāṁsā Sūtra* 1.1-4. On *upasaṁhāra* and *samanvaya*, see my essay, 'Binding the Text: Vedānta as Philosophy and Commentary', in Jeffrey Timm, editor, *Texts in Context: Traditional Hermeneutics in South Asia* (Albany: State University of New York, 1991, Pages 47-68).

5. Thus Śabara; but it is possible also to understand *saṁyoga* more generally as indicating a connection with—place in—a comparable text.

6. The detailed positions put forth in Śabara's *Bhāṣya* on 2.4.8–33 are introduced and debated in the Vedānta commentaries; Vācaspati and his successors elaborate the Mīmāṁsā discussions at great length.

7. Throughout, all translations are my own, although regarding Śaṁkara I have profitably consulted the two standard translations: George Thibaut, *The Vedānta Sūtras of Bādarāyaṇa with the Commentary by Śaṁkara* ([Reprinted from the Sacred Books of the East 34, 38], New York: Dover Publications, 1962) and Swami Gambhirananda, *Brahma-Sūtra Bhāṣya* (Calcutta: Advaita Ashrama, 1983).

8. It is within the frame of this commitment to a Mīmāṁsā) method of interpretation that we ought to assess the Śaṁkara school's insistence, enunciated in response to a preliminary *pūrvapakṣa* at the beginning of 3.3.1, that it is *Saguṇa Brahman* (or the *prāṇa*, etc.) which is discussed in 3.3, and not *Nirguṇa Brahman*, which by definition does not require *guṇas* or the practice of *upasaṁhāra*. The *Advaita* distinction of *nirguṇa* and *saguṇa*, as either a simple textual strategy or a theoretical position about 'the real', is always

to be located within a framework defined by the *Advaita* practice of exegesis. The advaita *practice* of *saguṇa* exegesis defines the realm of upaniṣadic knowledge within which the *nirguṇa* is identified, discussed and finally preferred; we must understand the relationships among the *saguṇa*, the texts and their apparent referents, if we are to feel the full force of the preference for the *nirguṇa* and consequent abandonment of the *saguṇa*.

9. Cf. *PMS* 4.2.2.7: *yajaticodanā dravyadevatākriyāṁ samudāye kṛtārthatvāt*.

10. The rituals themselves, of course, exist outside the texts about them, but this extra-textual existence is always temporary, dependent on a repeated enactment of the texts.

11. See my *Thinking Ritually: Rediscovering the Pūrva Mīmāṁsā of Jaimini*, De Nobili Research Series 17 (Vienna: Indological Institute of the University of Vienna, 1990) chapter 5.

12. It would be interesting to construct an analogy between the Mīmāṁsā *artha* and the Vedānta *Brahman*, thinking of both as present but never—adequately expressed 'enablers' and 'instigators' of meaning and purpose; this analogy would help us to avoid overly substantialist versions of *Brahman*.

13. On the objective nature of *Brahman*, see for instance the beginning of the *Bhāṣya* comment on 3.3.1: "For it is not possible to propose that there is a plurality of *Brahman* just as there is a plurality of rites. For *Brahman* is one and has one form, and it is not possible that acts of knowledge which are plural in form should apply to what is only one in form." Śaṁkara accepts this principle, but by appealing to the *nirguṇa/saguṇa* distinction avoids having to accept the corollary, that the *pāda* is fruitless.

14. "There should be a combination [of appropriate qualifications from various texts], regarding what is their common [object/referent,] since the object/referent [*artha*] is not different [from text to text]; just as is the case with the auxiliary part of injunctions."

15. I.e. the claim is not that any text in any Upaniṣad can be combined with any other, but that certain combinations are plausible due to similarities in vocabulary, conclusion, structure, etc.

16. *Pūrva Mīmāṁsā Sūtras* 2.4.33.

17. A (possibly) related version of *upasaṁhāra* is introduced at *PMS* 3.1.26-27, as a calculation of how more general and more specific rules relate; Āpadeva succinctly defines this kind of *upasaṁhāra*: '*Upasaṁhāra* is a restriction to the [more] specific of what is [more] generally applicable." (*upasaṁhāro nāma sāmānyaprāptasya viśeṣe nyamanam;* paragraph 111 in F. Edgerton's edition of the *Mīmāṁsā Nyāya Prakāśa* [New Haven: Yale University Press, 1929]). Although the Vedāntins apparently do not explain *upasaṁhāra* according to the model, it would be interesting to speculate on the correlation between *upasaṁhāra* as 'combination' and *upasaṁhāra* as 'specification.' In a third usage, *upasaṁhāra*, the 'conclusion of a text'. (balanced with *upakrama*,) is employed in Vedānta and elsewhere in determining the correct meaning of texts.

18. Unless, of course, one conceives of the 3rd–6th *adhyāyas* as devoted to the project of identifying the rules for proper *upasaṁhāra*.

19. The same point is made also by Prakāśātman in the *Śārīrakanyāya-saṁgraha* on 3.3.5.

20. My reference in this paragraph to the 'desire to know' takes us beyond what any of the commentators say in 3.3.5, but I believe it is implied by their positions.

2.. Amalānanda explains that the first explanation of the *adhikaraṇa* may appear out of place in 3.3—its identification of the right topic of a text more appropriate to 1.1–4 and the practice of *samanvaya*—and so this second explanation is introduced to preserve the coherence of the *pāda* as focused on *upasaṁhāra*.

22. Vācaspati distinguishes qualifications which belong to the object in itself, the *vāstava*, from those which humans posit regarding it provisionally, the *vidheya*.

23. Again, the Mīmāṁsā clearly tried to thwart this emergence by its insistence on the *guṇatva* of *devatā* and *puruṣa*.

24. Śaṁkara does not explicitly limit the issue to the status of the multiple meditations within one *śākhā*, but since all the examples of texts he adduces are from the *Chāndogya*, it is not impossible that this is what he has in mind.

25. Vācaspati is again our source for an ampler reflection on the productive, generative role of language; according to him, the various meditation texts constitute various acts of knowledge about *Brahman*, and do not merely offer us information about it. Unlike in the case of rituals, wherein the rite is enjoined and then *guṇas*, meditations are esentially characterized by the *guṇas* they express.

26. There are exceptions, but most of this careful exegesis continues to be done in Sanskrit. See for instance K. Balasubrahmanya Sastri's recent "Jaiminīya-nyāyānām anyatra sañcāra-yogyatā," *Journal of Oriental Research* (Madras) Vols. 47–54 (1989), 169–81. In English, P.M. Modi's *A Critique of the Brahmasūtra* III. 2.11–IV (2 vols., Bhavnagar, Baroda: Mahodaya Press, 1956) remains by far the best example.

28. Modi has argued forcefully for the priority of the third *adhyāya:* see Vol. 2, pp. 187–217.

28. A helpful introduction to the (post)modern return to textuality is Christopher Norris' *Contest of Faculties: Philosophy and Theory After Deconstruction* (London: Methuen, 1985).

29. On the possibilities for a 'post-modern retrieval' of Vedānta through attention to Mīmāṁsā, see my "Why the Veda has No Author: some contributions of the Early Mīmāṁsā to Religious and Ritual Studies", *Journal of the American Academy of Religion* 55 (1988) 659–84, and "Vedānta, Theology, and Modernity: Theology's New Conversation with the World's Religions," *Theological Studies* 51 (1990) 268–85.

19

ON THE THREE-FOLD CLASSIFICATION OF THE ARTHAVĀDA

KUNIO HARIKAI

It is well known to scholars of Mīmāṁsā that the *Mīmāṁsā-nyāyaprakāśa* of Āpadeva (*ca.* 16 C. C.E.), which is supposed to be a much enlarged version of *Arthasaṁgraha* of Laugākṣi Bhāskara,[1] contains just a poor reference to the classification of *arthavādas*. Āpadeva divides *arthavādas* into just two, *vidhiśeṣa* and *niṣedhaśeṣa*, i.e. (the *arthavāda* which is) subsidiary to injunction and (the *arthavāda* which is) subsidiary to prohibition. On the other hand, Bhāskara gives in the *arthavāda* section of his *Arthasaṁgraha* a three-fold classification of *arthavādas* which includes *vidhiśeṣa* and *niṣedhaśeṣa*. It seems rather strange that the topic of the classification of *arthavādas* in the *Mīmāṁsānyāya-prakāśa* is much shorter than that of *Arthasaṁgraha*, though we do find other topics in the *Mīmāṁsānyāyaprakāśa* that give more detailed arguments than the *Arthasaṁgraha*. Is this just an accident or does it have any reasonable ground?

The present author wishes to propose in this paper that Āpadeva, the author of the *Mīmāṁsānyāyaprakāśa*, must have set aside the three-fold classification of *arthavādas* of the *Artha-saṁgraha* intentionally and that the reason Āpadeva did so was that he considered it to be an unacceptable theory in the Mīmāṁsā school.

The three-fold classification of *arthavādas*, as is well-known, runs thus:

virodhe guṇavādaḥ syād anuvādo 'vadhārite/
bhūtārthavādas taddhānād arthavādas tridhā mataḥ//

'In (case of) contradiction, (*arthavāda*) would state a quality;

in (case of) ascertainment (it would be) a repetition; on account of the absence (*hānam*) of (both of) those (viz. contradiction and ascertainment it would) state the real state of affairs (*bhūtārthaḥ*) . . . (thus) an explanatory passage (is) regarded to be three-fold.'[2]

According to this verse the first category of *arthavāda* is *guṇa-vāda*, which, according to this translation, would state a quality in (case of) contradiction. In the autocommentary of Laugākṣi Bhāskara on this verse, he explicates *virodhe guṇavādaḥ syāt* as *pramāṇāntaravirodhe saty arthavādo guṇavādaḥ*, i.e. 'when there is a contradiction with another means of proof an explanatory passage states a quality.'[2]

Then Bhāskara gives an illustration of *guṇavāda* as follows *yathā ādityo yūpaḥ ityādi. yūpa-ādityābhedasya pratyakṣabādhi-tatvād ādityavad ujjvalatvarūpaguṇo 'nena lakṣaṇayā pratipādyate.*

'As the sacrificial post (is) the sun' and the like. On account of the non-difference or identity with the sun being contradicted in the sacrificial post, this (explanatory passage) conveys by impli-cation the quality of the form of brilliance like (that of) the sun.'[2]

This translation would not be accurate, for *pratyakṣa*, the first member of the compound word *pratyakṣabādhitatvād*, is not translated. So the correct meaning of the first portion of the above sentence would be 'On account of the non-difference or identity of the sacrificial post with the sun being annuled by sense perception, . . .' At any rate we understand with the help of the commentary of Laugākṣi Bhāskara the meaning of the passage *virodhe guṇavādaḥ syāt* in the verse of the three-fold classification being *pramāṇāntaravirodhe saty arthavādaḥ guṇavādaḥ* and here *pramāṇāntara* would mean some proofs other than verbal authority, the word of the *Veda* itself.

It might be said that, in the general meaning of the term, *arthavāda* is a statement or explanation (*vāda*) of the meaning (*artha*) of a formula prayer (*mantra*) or injunction (*vidhi*) in a *Brāhmaṇa* text. But in the Mīmāṁsā system the function of *arthavāda* is stated thus: '*vidhinā tv ekavākyatvāt stutyarthena vidhīnāṁ syuḥ* (JS. 1.2.7)', i.e. they (*arthavādas*) might be (useful) as praise for injunctions, because of their syntactical oneness with injunctions. This description applies to the *arthavāda* which follows a positive injunction. On the other hand, the function of the *arthavāda* correlating to the negative injunction, i.e. a prohibition (*pratiṣedha* or *niṣedha*), is stated to be *nindā*, i.e. the censure, in that it censures the matter prohibited by the prohibitive injunctions. Thus, from its function, *arthavāda* would be classified into two kinds, viz. *stuti* and *nindā*. But from the historical viewpoint, this two-fold classification of *arthavādas* does not exist independently, but is included in the so-called four-fold classification. Besides *stuti* and *nindā*, the two other categories of the four-fold classification are *parakṛti* and *purākalpa*. *Parakṛti* and *purākalpa* are translated, respectively, as 'a passage descriptive of any act done by an individual' and 'a passage descriptive of any act done by a large number of individuals[3]'. Jaimini states, '*parakṛtipurākalpaṁ ca manuṣyadharmaḥ syād arthāya hy anukīrtanam* (JS 6.7.26)'.

The origin of this four-fold classification seems very old, as we find it in the *Paribhāṣā sūtra* of the *Āpastambaśrautasūtra*, namely *sūtra* 24.1.33 which runs thus: *brāhmaṇaśeṣo 'rthavādo nindā praśaṁsā parakṛtiḥ purākalpaś ca.*[4] It goes without saying that the *praśaṁsā* in this *sūtra* corresponds to *stuti* in the two-fold classification.

We think that there exists a problem at least with regard to *guṇavāda*, one division of *arthavāda* in the three-fold classification. The term *guṇavāda* itself in the three-fold classification might be adopted from *Mīmāṁsāsūtra* 1.2.10 '*guṇavādas tu*'. But in the *Śābarabhāṣya* and its subcommentaries, e.g. *Tantravārttika* of Kumārila Bhaṭṭa and *Bṛhatī* of Prabhākara Miśra, we do not find any reference to its ground as '*virodhe sati*' or '*pramāṇāntaravirodhe sati*' 'when there is a contradiction with another means of proof *guṇavāda* establishes'. We think that the three-fold classification was not originally derived from the Mīmāṁsā school, but from the Vedānta school or some heterodoxical Mimāṁsakas. The materials below would show how this supposition is a reasonable one. We would like to start from describing how Śabarasvāmin and some other authorities of Mīmāṁsā school understood *guṇavāda*.

As stated above, according to Jaimini, the authority (*prāmāṇya*) of *arthavāda* consists in its syntactical unity (*ekavākyatā*) with the injunctive sentence (*vidhi*). Needless to say, this syntactical unity between *vidhi* and *arthavāda* presupposes the sameness of the 'object to be prescribed (*vidheya*) by the *vidhi*, and 'the object to be eulogized or praised by the *arthavāda* (*stutya*).' Under JS 1.2.7 Śabarasvāmin adduces an example from *Taittirīya Saṁhitā* 2.1.1.1 of such syntactical unity of *vidhi* and *arthavāda*.

vāyavyaṁ śvetam ālabheta bhūtikāmaḥ (*vidhi*),

'One who desires prosperity should sacrifice a white (goat) to the god of wind (*Vāyu*)'. (*vidhi*)

vāyur vai kṣepiṣṭhā devatā, vāyum eva svena bhāgadheyenopadhāvati sa evainaṁ bhūtiṁ gamayati (*arthavāda*),

'Verily the god of wind is the swiftest deity. He (the god *Vāyu*) verily leads one who approaches *Vāyu* with his property to prosperity' (*arthavāda*).

In these two sentences the *vidheya* and *stutya* are the same *vāyavyapaśu-ālambhana* 'the sacrifice of a white goat for the god *Vāyu*, the god of wind', although the *arthavāda* directly eulogizes the god *Vāyu*

There are, however, some cases in the *Brāhmaṇa* where the *vidheya* and *stutya* seem to have different referents. As it is a rule that words comprising *vidhi* sentences must be understood literally, a word or some words in the *arthavāda* passages cannot but be understood in such a case in a metaphorical sense so that *vidhi* and *arthavāda* might have syntactical unity. Jaimini explains such a case by the *Mīmāṁsāsūtra* 1.2.10 '*guṇavādas tu*' 'But it is a *guṇavāda*.' On this *sūtra* Śabarasvāmin starts a discussion on the *guṇavāda* theory.

The illustration Śabara adduces on this *sūtra* is as follows:

vetasaśākhayā-avakābhiś cāgniṁ vikarṣati (*vidhi*, TS. 5.4.4.3)

'He (should) sweep on the fire altar with the twig of *vetasa* and *avakā* plant[5]'. (*vidhi*)

āpo vai śāntāḥ (*arthavāda*, TS 5.4.4.3)

'Verily water is tranquil'. (*arthavāda*)

In this illustration, the *vidhi* sentence enjoins the *vikarṣaṇa*, sweeping, on the *agnicayana* altar with twigs of *vetasa* and *avakā* plant[8]. The *arthavāda* passage, however, praises water to which *vidhi* sentence is not referring, so that there stands a discrepancy in this case between *vidheya* (*vikarṣaṇa*) and *stutya* (water). According to Śabarasvāmin, however, this is just a seeming discrepancy and should be reconciled by putting the following interpretation on water which the *arthavāda* praises. Through praising water the *arthavāda* eulogizes the origin (*abhijana*) of *vetasaśākhā* and *avakā* plant with which *vikarṣaṇa* is enjoined to be done by the *vidhi*, and in a secondary sense the *arthavāda*, through praising water, eulogizes the *vetasaśākhā* and *avakā* themselves. Thus 'water' is interpreted as a metaphorical word (*gauṇa*). When any word in an *arthavāda* sentence is interpreted metaphorically, the *arthavāda* is called *guṇavāda*. Through putting such an interpretation on the *arthavāda* passage, the *arthavāda* would have syntactical unity with the *vidhi*. And thus the *arthavāda* passage, in which lies some discrepancy with the injunctive sentence, becomes authorized as a *śruti*. In other word, the authority (*prāmāṇya*) of *arthavāda* becomes thus established.

In another chapter (JS 1.4. *Adhikaraṇa* 12-17, *sūtra* 23 *tatsiddhiḥ jātiḥ sārūpyāt praśaṁsā bhūmā liṅgasamavāyāt.*) Jaimini gives full accounts on the *gauṇa* theory. This is because, according to Kumārila, Jaimini did not afford any theoretical explanation of the *gauṇa* theory in the *Arthavāda Adhikaraṇa* (i.e. JS 1.2 Adhikaraṇa).[9]

Here we would not have any necessity to enter full details of discussions under those items on the *gauṇa* theory that the *sūtra* 1.4.23 mentions. It will be enough to specify that there occurs the *arthavāda* '*ādityo yūpaḥ*' under the first item of the *sūtra* 1.4.23, the illustration of a *guṇavāda* in the *Arthasaṁgraha*. And it must be significant to indicate that Jaimini affords in this *sūtra* six grounds under which the word comprising *arthavāda* may be interpreted as *gauṇa*, while the three-fold classification gives just one condition for *guṇavāda*, i.e. *virodhe* 'when there is a contradiction'. This fact might indicate that Jaimini does not consider it appropriate for *guṇavāda* to be subject to just one such principle as '*pramāṇāntaravirodhe sati*'.

We do not find the three-fold classification of *arthavāda* in the *Mīmāṁsāsūtra*, *Śābarabhāṣya*, *Tantravārttika* and *Bṛhatī* which are the most essential texts of the Mīmāṁsā school. On the other hand, we find in some texts belonging to the Vedānta school either a variant version of the three-fold classification or the three-fold classification itself. First of all in the *Śāṅkarabhāṣya* on the *Brahmasūtra* 1.3.33, we find sentences which run thus:

tad yatra so 'vāntaravākyārthaḥ pramāṇāntaragocaro bhavati, tatra tadanuvādārthavādaḥ pravartate. yatra pramāṇāntaravirud-dhas tatra guṇavādaḥ. yatra tu tad ubhayaṁ nāsti tatra . . . vidya-mānavāda āśrayaṇīyaḥ,[7] 'Thus when the meaning of the subsidiary sentence (becomes) the object of the other means of proof, the *arthavāda* engages in its explanation (*anuvāda*). When there is a contradiction with other means of proof, (the subsidiary sentence) is the *guṇavāda*. But when there exists neither of them, the *vidyamānavāda*, an account of something existing, is to be relied on'.

The difference between Śaṅkara's explanation and the three-fold classification consists just in the item *vidyamānavāda*, which substantially corresponds to the *bhūtārthavāda* in the three-fold classification. The difference is in name only. The explication by Śaṅkara on the *guṇavāda* is also substantially the same as that of the three-fold classification, i.e. '*pramāṇāntaravirodhe sati guṇa-vādaḥ*' in the *Arthasaṅgraha*.

Ānandagiri (*ca.* 13 C.), a commentator on the *Brahmasūtra-śāṅkarabhāṣya*, introduces in his *Ṭīkā* the verse of the three-fold classification, when he comments on the above *Bhāṣya*. If this verse in the *Ṭīkā* of Ānandagiri is not an interpolation in later years, the verse, a fixed form explicating the three-fold classification of *arthavādas* naturally existed before Ānandagiri. Noteworthy is the fact that Śaṅkara, the most outstanding figure of the Vedānta school, explains *arthavāda* by way of the three-fold classification and further Ānadagiri in his *Ṭīkā* and Madhusūdana Sarasvatī in his *Prasthānabheda*, both belonging to the Vedānta school, quote the verse of the three-fold classification.

In two philosophical treatises, we find refutations to the *guṇa-vāda* theory which the three-fold classification formulates. The first illustration is the *Bṛhatī* of Prabhākara Miśra (*ca.* C.E. 7C.), the founder of the Prābhākara school of Mīmāṁsā. In his *Bṛhatī* on JS 1.1.5, Prabhākara discusses the *guṇavāda* theory. He shows a *pūrvapakṣa* in interpreting a sentence of a *Brāhmaṇa* passage '*sa eṣa yajñāyudhī yajamāno 'ñjasā svargaṁ lokaṁ yāti*', i.e. this very sacrificer equipped with sacrificial tools goes straight on to the heavenly world' as follows:

(The meaning of) some Vedic sentences is contradictory to the experienced fact. (A *brāhmaṇa* passage) after laying down the accumulation of sacrificial vessels declares *sa eṣa yajñāyudhī yajamāno 'ñjasā svargaṁ lokaṁ yāti.*[8] (The word *yajamāna* in this sentence) points to the visible corpse (of the *yajamāna*). But it does not go to the heaven, for it is perceptively burnt (in the fire of cremation). And '*eṣa . . . yāti*' (*this* man *goes* to the heaven) is not an injunctive passage. Such (sentences as) contradictory to the means of proof are not authoritative. (Question) Then, why is this sentence contradictory to the means of proof? (Answer) This sentence is an *arthavāda*. Concerning *arthavāda* sentences all (sentences) contradictory to the means of proof have been explained as *guṇavāda.*[9]

Prabhākara, denying the above *pūrvapakṣa*, demonstrates his own *siddhānta* view as follows: When the *arthavāda* is interpreted as *guṇavāda*, the above statement is (to be) rejected, for (the condition of) the *guṇavāda* maintained above does not appear in this case. The *guṇavāda* originates by means of the knowledge which is established by other means of proof (*pramāṇāntara-pratipattibalena*). Here the knowledge established by other means of proof consists just in the corpse. We do not perceive any other thing except corpse . . .[10]

Although in the *pūrvapakṣa* view Prabhākara does not use the same expression regarding the condition of *guṇavāda* as '*virodhe guṇavādaḥ*' of the three-fold classification, it would be reasonable to assume that Prabhākara is writing above sentences keeping the same *guṇavāda* theory as that of the three-fold classification in his mind. And it may be understood that Prabhākara holds '*pramāṇāntara-pratipatti*' as the ground of *guṇavāda* in opposition to '*pramāṇāntaravirodha*', the theory of the *pūrvapakṣa* view, which is identical with the *guṇavāda* theory in the three-fold classification.

The other scholar who was opposed to the *guṇavāda* theory

of the three-fold classification was Maṇḍana Miśra (*ca.* C.E. 7-8 C.). In the Tarkakāṇḍa of his *Brahmasiddhi*, Maṇḍana propounds the ground of *guṇavāda* as follows: (Question) How does *guṇavāda* hold good in the *Veda*? (Answer) When there is no room for the accomplishment of the authoritative meaning through the directly expressed meaning of the *Veda*, we shall obtain the authoritative meaning even through the secondary operation of words (of the *Veda*), because we observe actions (motivated through such a secondary operation of words). But when words (of the *Veda*) obtain its (authoritative) meaning by themselves, they do not turn away from the inconsistency with other means of proof.'[11]

In the above passage Maṇḍana says that the ground for occasioning *guṇavāda* is '*yatra śrautair arthaiḥ pramāṇārthaniṣpatter asaṁbhavaḥ*' (when there is no room for the accomplishment of the authoritative meaning through the directly expressed meaning of the *Veda*), not '*pramāṇāntaravirodhe*'. Although it appears that Maṇḍana did not directly deny the *guṇavāda* theory of the three-fold classification, it would be natural for us to think that he was opposed to the theory, for he is referring to the compound word '*pramāṇāntaravirodha*' which is another expression in the *guṇavāda* theory of the three-fold classification. In order to corroborate this conjecture it might be useful to have recourse to a commentary on the *Brahmasiddhi*.

Śaṅkhapāṇi (*ca.* C.E. ?),[12] a commentator on the *Brahmasiddhi* of Maṇḍana Miśra, understands the above sentences of *Brahmasiddhi* to be a refutation to the same *guṇavāda* theory as that of the three-fold classification. Śaṅkhapāṇi exemplifies two cases of *arthavāda* to be distinguished in interpreting as *guṇavāda*. The first is the same example given by Śabarasvāmin on *Mīmāṁsāsūtra* 1.2.10, i.e. *vetasaśākhayā 'vakābhiś cāgniṁ vikarṣati* (*vidhi*), *āpo vai śāntāḥ* (*arthavāda*). Śaṅkhapāṇi comments regarding this example that *vidhi* and *stuti* do not syntactically connect with each other and do not establish proper meaning of the sentences, and that even if there is no contradiction with another means of proof (*pramāṇāntaravirodha*) in this case, through eulogizing the origin (*abhijana*: water) of *vetasa* and *avakā*, the originated (*abhijāta*: *vetasa* and *avakā*) comes to be praised by the passage of the *arthavāda*. And thus we come to understand that in this case the object of a praise expressed by the *arthavāda* is *vetasaśākhā* and *avakā*.

Śaṅkhapāṇi continues explaining Maṇḍana's intention as follows: In the *Veda* the cause of the metaphorical sense (*gauṇatvahetu*) is not that there is 'a contradiction with other means of proof (*pramāṇāntaravirodha*)' but rather the 'inapplicability to the establishment of authoritative meaning (*pramāṇārthāniṣpatti*)' when comprehended in terms of the direct meaning (of words). Śaṅkhapāṇi introduces a question from a *pūrvapakṣa*: In the case of the *arthavāda* '*ādityo yūpaḥ*' etc. the *gauṇatva* is (understood) from *pramāṇāntaravirodha*, because the sacrificial post being the sun is contradictory (of itself), (which fact is understood) through the non-perception by other means of proof (i.e. the eye). Śaṅkhapāṇi answers to this *pūrvapakṣa* as follows: In this case also the *pramāṇāntaravirodha* is not the ground of the *gauṇatā* but just the *pramāṇārthāniṣpatti* 'the incompletion of the authoritative meaning' is the ground thereof. Because in the case of '*vetasaśākhā*' etc. it (*pramāṇārthāniṣpatti*) is functioning and not subject to exceptions. The cause '*pramāṇārthāniṣpatti*' belongs to (the *arthavāda*) '*ādityo yūpaḥ*', in that it does not have any relation with the meaning of the sentence which (enjoins) the binding of cattle (to the sacrificial post). (The principle) '*pramāṇāntaravirodha*', as the ground of *guṇavāda*, however, is subject to exception (*vyabhicāri*), for in the case of *vetasaśākhā* etc., we have recourse to *gauṇatā* even if it (*pramāṇāntaravirodha*) is not there. It is the right ground that is not subject to exceptions. Therefore the principle '*pramāṇārthāniṣpatti*' is established as the sound ground of *gauṇatā* in the case of (the *arthavāda* to the effect that) the sacrificial post (is the sun)[13].

Thus we understand through the explication by Śaṅkhapāṇi, which would be wholly acceptable for Mīmāṁsakas, that Maṇḍana Miśra denied '*pramāṇāntara-virodha*' as the ground of *guṇavāda*, and established '*pramāṇārthāniṣpatti*' as the reasonable ground in interpreting an *arthavāda* as *guṇavāda*.

The authoritative character of the three-fold classification is thus questionable for Mīmāṁsakas, as we have seen, in view of the theory on the *guṇavāda*.

On *bhūtārthavāda*, one category in the three-fold classification,

Śaṅkarabhaṭṭa (*ca.* C.E. 16 C.), in his *Mīmāṁsābālaprakāśa*, observes as follows, which is worth noticing: The follower of Upaniṣads (i.e. a Vedāntin) exemplifies with regard to (the phrase in the verse of the three-fold classification) '*bhūtārthavādas tad-dhānāt*' following *arthavāda* which makes clear the benevolence of a deity bestowing (on another living being) a fruit of satisfaction to eat through separating his body by himself, e.g. *prajāpatir ātmano vapām udakkhidat* (TS 2.1.1.4) 'Prajāpati cut out his own omentum' etc. But it is not a proper illustration of the *bhūtārthavāda*, because in the ninth (chapter) Jaimini denies the five (items) consisting of separating etc. We shall maintain this opinion on the occasion of the discussion on the meaning of the ninth (chapter). Therefore even if there is no contradiction (with other means of proof) in these cases, we might regard it as a *guṇavāda*.[14]

Thus Śaṅkarabhaṭṭa, accepting the authority of the three-fold classification, makes exception to the theory on the *guṇavāda*. Another point noticeable in the reference by Śaṅkarabhaṭṭa is the fact that he is referring to an anonymous Vedāntin, *not a Mīmāṁsaka*, who adduces examples of the *bhūtārthavāda*.

As we pointed out before, we do not find in the most authoritative texts of the Mīmāṁsā school the three-fold classification of *arthavāda*, one category of which is the *guṇavāda* whose ground is proposed to be *pramāṇāntaravirodhe sati*, although we can trace back in these texts some references to a two or four-fold classification. On the other hand we find the three-fold classification in the Vedānta texts alone not in Mīmāṁsā texts except in the *Arthasaṁgraha* of Laugākṣi Bhāskara. Thus we may safely conclude that the three-fold classification of *arthavāda* has a close relation with the Vedānta school. It seems plausible superficially in the case of the *arthavāda* '*ādityo yūpaḥ*' that the *guṇavāda* comes into existence as there is a contradiction with other means of proof. But as stated above, the *guṇavāda* also comes into being in the relation of *vidheya* (to be enjoined by *vidhi*) and *stutya* (to be praised by *arthavāda*), where there might be no contradiction with other means of proof, as in the case of the *arthavāda* '*āpo vai śāntāḥ*'. As we have shown above, Śaṅkhapāṇi explicated this fact in detail. And it is evident that the theory of *guṇavāda* in the three-fold classification is not to be accepted as authoritative for Mīmāṁsakas.

There remain, however, some problems concerning the three-fold classification. For instance, we cannot so far indicate the source of the verse which formulates it. And it is dubious whether the classification was established in Śaṅkara's time or not. And although we cannot so far find in the works of Kumārila any reference to the *guṇavāda* theory of the three-fold classification, there may be a possibility of finding some references by Kumārila in his works including dispersed fragments of his *Bṛhaṭṭīkā*, since, as we have indicated above, we could trace refutations of the *guṇavāda* theory of the three-fold classification in the works of Prabhākara and Maṇḍana, whose dates are considered not so remote from Kumārila.

Thus we might safely maintain that the reason for the lack of the three-fold classification in the *arthavāda* section of the *Mīmāṁsānyāyaprakāśa* is that its author Āpadeva removed it critically from the *Arthasaṁgraha*, although he enlarged the most of the other parts of the text.

Notes

1. Cf. F. Edgerton, *The Mīmāṁsā Nyāya Prakāśa*, New Haven 1929, p. 22-23; L. Renou, *L'Inde Classique*, Tome 2, section 1375.

2. A.B. Gajendragadkar and R.D. Karmarkar, *The Arthasaṁgraha of Laugākṣi Bhāskara*, Bombay 1934, p. 68.

3. M.L. Sandal, *The Mīmāṁsā Sūtra of Jaimini*, Allahabad 1923–1925, p. 397.

4. Cf. *Nyāyasūtra* 2.1.65: *stutir nindā parakṛtiḥ purākalpa ity arthavādaḥ*. Jayantabhaṭṭa also refers only to this four-fold classification of *arthavādas* in his *Nyāyamañjarī*.

5. Cf. F. Staal, *AGNI, the Vedic Ritual of the Fire Altar*, Delhi 1986, Vol. 2, p. 583.

6. *Tantravārttika* on JS.1.4.23: *arthavādaprasaṅgāt tadupakāriguṇavāda-vidhitallakṣaṇaṁ tatra noktam idānīm abhidhīyate.*

7. *Brahmasūtraśāṅkarabhāṣya*, Nirṇayasāgara Press ed. pp. 342–346.

8. Cf. *Śatapatha Brāhmaṇa* 12.5.2.8. As it is well-known, the *ātmavāda*

in the Mīmāṁsā schools starts from the interpretation of this *arthavāda* sentence.

9. *Bṛhatī*, Chowkhamba S.S. ed., p. 100, *ll*.4–10: *dṛṣṭaviruddhaṁ ca kiñcid vaidikaṁ vacanam. pātracayanaṁ vidhāyā "ha sa eṣa yajñāyudhī yajamāno 'ñjasā svargaṁ lokaṁ yātīti pratyakṣaṁ śarīraṁ vyapadiśati. na ca tat svargaṁ yātīti. pratyakṣaṁ hi tad dahyate. na ca—eṣa yātīti vidhiśabdaḥ. evaṁjātīyakaṁ ca pramāṇaviruddham apramāṇam. kathaṁ punar idaṃ pramāṇaviruddham? arthavādo'yam, arthavādeṣu ca sarve pramāṇavirodhā guṇavādena vyākhyātāḥ.*

10. *Bṛhatī*, p. 101, *ll*.4–9 *sthita evārthavādānāṁ guṇavādena vyākhyāne idaṁ vacanam ākṣipyate—atra hi tad uktā guṇavādataiva na saṃbhavati. guṇavādā hi pramāṇāntarapratipattibalenopajāyante. atra ca pramāṇāntarapratipattiḥ śarīra eva. na śarīravyatiriktaṁ kiñcid upalabhāmahe. tac caiṣa iti vyapadiṣṭam, yātīty anena viruddham, dahyamānatvāc ca śarīrasya. tasmād vidhito 'rthavādataś cāyathārthatā 'vasīyate.*

11. *Brahmasiddhi*, ed. by S. Kuppuswami Sastri, p. 42, *ll*.4–7: *kathaṁ tarhi vede guṇavādaḥ? yatra śrautair arthaiḥ pramāṇārthaniṣpatter asaṁbhavaḥ, tatra dvitīyasyā 'pi vṛtteḥ śabdānāṁ pravṛttidarśanāt tayā pramāṇaviṣayalābhaḥ; yatra tu śabdāḥ svarasena labhante viṣayaṁ tatra na pramāṇāntaravirodhād apāvartante.* Cf. M. Biardeau, La Philosophie de Maṇḍana Miśra, (Publications de l'Ecole Française d'Extrême—Orient, Vol. LXXVI), Paris 1969, p. 196; see also the Review by A.W. Thrasher, Indo-Iranian Journal, 1978, p. 275.

12. Cf. Kuppuswami Sastri's Introduction to his edition of the *Brahmasiddhi*, p. lxxv.

13. *Brahmasiddhivyākhyā*, p. 119, *l*. 4–p. 120, *l*. 10: *nanu pramāṇāntaravirodhe 'pi cen mukhyam arthaṁ śabdo na jahāti, kathaṁ tarhi* āpo vai śāntāḥ *ityādiṣu guṇavādaḥ? na hy atra pramāṇāntaravirodhād anyad guṇavāde nibandhanam asti; tad etad āśaṅkayati—katham iti. yad vākyaṁ yāvat pramāṇaṁ tasya tāvato yatra śrautair abhidheyabhūtair mukhyair arthair anyonyam anvayād artho vākyārthībhūto viṣayo niṣpadyate, tatra dvitīyasyāpi vṛtter loke śabdānāṁ vṛttidarśanāt tayā śabdasya pramāṇasya viṣayalābha āśrīyate. yathā* vetasaśākhayā 'vakābhiś cāgniṁ vikarṣati-*iti vetasaśākhāvake vidhīyete;* āpo vai śāntāḥ *iti cāpaḥ stūyante. tatra vidhistutyor bhinnaviṣayatvena parasparam ananvayād vākyārthāsiddhau, asaty api pramāṇāntaravirodhe śrutām apāṁ stutim ullaṅghyābhijanastutyā abhijātaḥ stuto bhavatīti vetasaśākhāvakāstutiparatvam evāśrīyate. etad uktaṁ bhavati—na vede pramāṇāntaravirodho gauṇatvahetuḥ, kiṁ tu mukhyārthatve pramāṇaviṣayasiddhāv anupapattiḥ...nanu* ādityo yūpaḥ *ityādau pramāṇāntaravirodhād eva gauṇatvam; virudhyate hi pramāṇāntareṇa-anupalabdhyā yūpasya-ādityatā, na hi tatrāpi pramāṇāntaravirodho gauṇatāyāṁ hetuḥ, api tu pramāṇārthāniṣpattir eva. sā hi vetasaśākhādau dṛṣṭaśaktir avyabhicāriṇī ca. yūpasyādityatāyāḥ paśuniyojanavākyārtho 'nanvayāt pramāṇārthāniṣpattir asty eva. vyabhicārī tu pramāṇāntaravirodhaḥ, vetasaśākhādau asaty api tasmin gauṇatāśrayaṇāt. avyabhicāri ca kāraṇam ucitam. tasmād yūpādāv api pramāṇārthāniṣpattir eva gauṇatānimittam iti sthitam.*

14. *Mīmāṁsābālaprakāśa*, (quoted in the *Mīmāṁsākośa*, p. 635): *bhūtārthavādas taddhānād ity atra aupaniṣadā udāharanti, devatāvigrahabhojana-tṛptiprasādaphaladātṛtva-pratipādakān arthavādān* prajāpatir ātmano vapām udakkhidad āhutir eva hutādo devān prīṇāti tṛpta evainam indraḥ prajayā paśubhis tarpayaty *ityādīn. tad ayuktam. navame vigrahādipañcakanirāsāt. tad etan navamārthaprapañce vakṣyāmaḥ. tasmād atra virodhābhāve 'pi guṇavādāṅgīkārāt.*

20

श्रीभास्कररायदीक्षितानां वेदतन्त्रयोः समन्वयदृष्टिः

प्रो० बटुकनाथशास्त्री खिस्ते

दशम्यां ख्रीस्तशताब्द्यामविर्भूतानां महामाहेश्वराणामाचार्याभिनवगुप्तपादानां आगमप्राधान्यमनुरुध्यैव प्रवर्तमाना व्याख्यासरणिः समवलोक्यते। यद्यपि यत्र तत्र विषयसंवादकृते तैरपि वैदिकसंहितादिमन्त्राणां विधीनाञ्च तुलनात्मकमालोचनमुपन्यासि तथाऽपि विचारप्रवाहः सर्वोऽप्यागमैकप्रधान इति न सन्देहः। श्रीभास्कररायदीक्षिताः सप्तदश्यां शताब्द्यां प्रादुरासन्। तेषाञ्च मते वेदमूलकमेव तंत्रप्रामाण्यम्। वेदानामुपबृंहणान्येव तन्त्राणीति यथावसरं वचनानि सङ्गमयद्भिस्तैरुपपाद्यते।

वस्तुत उभावप्येतौ आचार्यौ श्रद्धेयवचनौ करतलामलकीकृतनिगमागमसिद्धान्तौ तयोर्व्याख्याभेदेऽपि वस्तुनि विचार्यमाणे न भेद इति सूक्ष्मदृशां परामर्शः। श्रीभास्कररायदीक्षितैर्वामकेश्वरतन्त्रान्तर्गतनित्याषोडशिकार्णवव्याख्यायां सेतुबन्धनामिकायां प्रथमविश्रामे सोपानारोहणन्यायेन पुरुषस्य बाल्यात् प्रभृतिक्रीडनादारभ्य ब्रह्मविद्याभ्यासपर्यन्तः क्रमो निरूपितः। ब्रह्मविद्याभ्यासपरिणामभूमिरेव श्रीविद्योपासनमिति तैर्निरणायि। तन्मते निगमागमयोरेकशास्त्रत्वात् ये नियमा वेदवाक्यविचारे प्रयुज्यन्ते, त एव तन्त्रवाक्यविचारेऽपि मीमांसाशास्त्रन्यायाः संचारणीया इति प्रतिपादितम्। सेतुबन्धप्रारम्भे तदीयं वाक्यमिदम्—श्रीमहात्रिपुरसुन्दर्याश्च गौणीं भक्तिं सेतिकर्तव्यताकां निरूपयितुमैदंपर्येण सुन्दरीतापिनीपञ्चकम् भावनोपनिषत् कौलोपनिषद्गुह्योपनिषन्महोपनिषच्चेत्यादयो वेदशिरोभागाः प्रवृत्ताः। वेदे च पूर्वकाण्डस्य शेषभूततयाऽऽश्वलायनादिकल्पसूत्राणां मन्वादिस्मृतीनां च प्रवृत्तिवत्, उपनिषत्काण्डशेषत्वेन परशुरामादिकल्पसूत्राणां यामलादितन्त्राणां च प्रवृत्तिः। पुराणानां तु काण्डद्वयं प्रत्यपि शेषत्वेन प्रवृत्तिः। ततश्च स्मृतितन्त्रपुराणानां वेदमूलकत्वेनैव प्रामाण्यम्। ये च प्रत्यक्षश्रुतिविरुद्धास्तत्तदेकदेशास्तेषां विरोधाधिकरणन्यायेन यावन्मूलश्रुतिदर्शनमननुष्ठानलक्षणमप्रामाण्यम्। यानि तु सर्वांशेनाऽपि वेदविरुद्धान्येव कानिचिन्तन्त्राणि पाशुपतविशेषपाञ्चरात्रविशेषादीनि, तानि नेदृशीं भूमिकामधिरूढस्य, अपि तु

श्रौतस्मार्तकर्माधिकारिण एव केनचित्पापेन ततश्च्युतौ, तेष्वधिकारः।

अत एव—पाञ्चरात्रं भागवतं तथा वैखानसाभिधम्।
वेदभ्रष्टान् समुद्दिश्य कमलापतिरुक्तवान्॥

इत्यादिना कतिपयानामेव परिगणनमुपपद्यते।

तेन—श्रुतिभ्रष्टः श्रुतिप्रोक्तप्रायश्चित्ते भयं गतः।
क्रमेण श्रुतिसिद्ध्यर्थं मनुष्यस्तन्त्रमाश्रयेत्॥

इत्यत्र तन्त्रसामान्यपदं तन्त्रविशेषपरम्। 'पत्युरसामञ्जस्यात्' (शाङ्करभाष्ये) इत्यधिकरणमपि तादृश तन्त्रपरमेव।

यानि तु रामकृष्णनृसिंहरुद्रपरशिवसुन्दर्याद्युपासनाबोधकान्यगस्त्यादितंत्राणि तन्मूलभूतानां रामतापिन्याद्युपनिषदां प्रत्यक्षत्वादेव तेषां नाऽप्रामाण्यशङ्काकलङ्कावकाशः।

एतावता उपन्यासेन आचार्याणां तन्त्रप्रामाण्यदृष्टिः स्फुटीभवति। एतदुत्तरं दशश्लोकी (मातृकास्तुतिः) व्याख्यारूपेण वक्ष्यमाणः सर्वोऽपि सिद्धान्तः सूत्रात्मकतया तैः स्फुटीकृतः।

आचार्याणां ग्रन्थव्याख्यासमये तन्त्रग्रंथानां विविधाष्टीका अपि प्रत्यासन्ना आसन्, तेषामपि टीकाकाराणां यथोचितमानुकूल्यं प्रातिकूल्यञ्च सप्रमाणं विविच्य सिद्धान्तपक्षः पर्यवस्थापितस्तैः।

एवं तेषां दृष्टिमुपपाद्य वेदतन्त्रयोरेकवाक्यताविचारविषये विकीर्णाः केचन व्याख्यानप्रसङ्गाःप्रदर्श्यन्ते—

नित्याषोडशिकार्णवस्य प्रथमविश्रामे चतुःषष्टितन्त्रपरिगणनावसरे चरमा पङ्क्तिः—

एवमेतानि शास्त्राणि तथाऽन्यान्यपि कोटिशः।
भवतोक्तानि मे देव सर्वज्ञानमयानि च॥

इमां स्फुटीकुर्वन्त आचार्या आहुः—
एवमिति अन्यूनानतिरिक्तानि। एतानि महामायादिविशुद्धेश्वरान्तानि चतुःषष्टितंत्राणि। शास्त्राणि वेदरूपाणि, तन्त्राणामुपनिषच्छेषत्वात्। शासनाच्छास्त्रमिति हि व्युत्पत्तिः। शासनं तु प्रवर्तनानिवर्तनाऽन्यतररूपा शब्दभावनाऽपरपर्याया भगवत्याज्ञैव। तदुक्तम्—

प्रवृत्तिर्वा निवृत्तिर्वा नित्येन कृतकेन वा।
पुंसां येनोपदिश्येत तच्छास्त्रमभिधीयते॥

इति। तेन वेद एव मुख्यतया शास्त्रपदवाच्यः। तथा च व्यासपादानां प्रयोगः—
'शास्त्रयोनित्वात्।' 'शास्त्रदृष्ट्या तूपदेशो वामदेववदि'त्यादिः। शब्दशास्त्रञ्छन्द-

शास्त्रादीनां तु तदङ्गत्वात्, मानवस्मृत्यादीनां तदर्थानुवादकत्वात्, तद्व्याख्यानानामनार्षाणामपि तदुपयोगित्वात्, शास्त्रपदेन व्यवहार इति स्थितिः। तन्त्राणां तु साक्षादेव वेदवत् भगवत्याज्ञारूपत्वाच्छास्त्रत्वे न कोऽपि विवादः। अत एव तन्त्रप्रामाण्येऽपि न विप्रतिपत्तिः, वैदिकत्वादेव। भगवान् परशुरामोऽप्याह—'पञ्चाऽऽम्नायान् परमार्थसाररूपान् प्रणिनाय' इति। एवं स्थिते यत्सौन्दर्यलहरीव्याख्याने केनचित् प्रलपितमिमानि तन्त्राण्यवैदिकानीत्यादि तत्प्रतारकभ्रान्ताऽन्यतरजल्पितत्वादुपेक्ष्यम्।

यत्तु कौलधर्मनिन्दादिकं तन्त्रान्तरे स्मर्यते, तन्नहि निन्दान्यायेन तत्तत्तन्त्रस्तुतिमात्रपरम्।

कथमन्यथा—पशुशास्त्राणि सर्वाणि मयैव कथितानि हि।
मूर्त्यन्तरं तु सम्प्राप्य मोहनाय दुरात्मनाम्॥
महापापवशान्नृणां तेषु वाञ्छाऽभिजायते।
तेषांहि सद्गतिर्नास्ति कल्पकोटिशतैरपि॥

इत्यादीनि कौलप्रकरणस्थानि परःशतं वचनानि संङ्गच्छेरन्?

वस्तुतस्तु कौलोपास्तेश्चरमभूमिकारूपतया तदधिकारिदौर्लभ्यादधिकारमज्ञात्वा तत्र प्रवर्तन्ते च तद्विरुद्धाचारावश्यंभावात्तेषां निन्दा। अधिकारसद्भावेऽपि वाऽतिरहस्ये प्रवृत्तिर्मा भूदित्येतदर्थमपि निन्दावाक्यमित्युपपद्यते। तदप्युक्तं कुलार्णव एव—

कुलमार्गरतो देवि न मया निन्दितः क्वचित्।
आचाररहिता येऽत्र निन्दितास्ते न चेतरे॥

अन्यत्राऽपि—कुलधर्ममिमं ज्ञात्वा मुच्येयुः सर्वमानवाः।
इति मत्वा कुलेशानि मया लोके विगर्हितम्॥

इति। तस्मात्—पुराकृततपोदानयज्ञतीर्थजपव्रतैः।
शुद्धचित्तस्य शान्तस्य धर्मिणो गुरुसेविनः
अतिगुप्तस्य भक्तस्य कौलज्ञानं प्रकाशते॥

इति वचनात् कुलतन्त्राऽप्रामाण्यवचनं गौरीकान्तलक्ष्मणादेरतादृशत्वं ध्वनयति।

तथा हि शिववचनम्—

कुलधर्मं हि मोहेन योऽन्यधर्मेण दुर्मतिः।
सकृत् साधारणं ब्रूयात् सोऽन्त्यजो नान्त्यजोऽन्त्यजः॥

इति शास्त्रनिरूपणप्रसङ्गात् कुलधर्मनिरूपणपराणि तन्त्राण्यपि भगवदाज्ञारू-

त्वात् वेदैकरूपाण्येवेति तेषामाशयः प्रकटीभवति। किञ्च आचार्यचरणैर्ललितासहस्रनामसु 'निजाज्ञारूपनिगमा' इति नामव्याख्यानाऽवसरे विशिष्य प्रतिपादितम्। यथा—

निजां स्वीयामाज्ञां वेदविद्भिः शब्दभावनात्वेन व्यवहृतां रूपयन्ति साध्यसाधनेतिकर्तव्यतारूपां ... शिष्टामर्थभावनाऽर्थवादादिभिः कुर्वन्ति, तादृशा निगमाः कर्मकाण्डात्मका वेदा यस्यास्तथा। अत एव 'तद्भूतानां क्रियार्थेन सामाम्नाय' इति जैमिनिः।

कौर्मेऽपि—ममैवाज्ञा पराशक्तिर्वेदसंज्ञा पुरातनी।
ऋग्यजुः सामरूपेण सर्गादौ सम्प्रवर्तते॥

इति। अथवा सन्ति वेदानुयायीनि शैवतंत्राणि कामिकादीन्यष्टाविंशतिः। वेदविरुद्धानि कापालभैरवादीनि च। तेषु वैदिकानि निगमपदवाच्यानि परमेश्वरस्य मुखादुद्भूतत्वादाज्ञारूपाणि, न पुनर्नाभ्यधोभागादुत्पन्नानि वेदविरुद्धानीत्यर्थः। इत्थमेव देवीभागवतस्कन्दपुराणयोर्वचनानि।

तान्त्रिकोपास्तेर्वेदप्रतिपाद्यताविषये संशयालूनां समाधानायैव त्रिपुरामहोपनिषदः प्रारम्भे तत्परिचयप्रदानाय श्लोकोऽयमुपन्यस्तः—

श्रीसांख्यायनकल्पसूत्रविधिभिः कर्माणि ये कुर्वते।
येषां शाकल एव मन्त्रनिचयः कौषीतकं ब्राह्मणम्॥
तैरारण्यकमध्यमन्त्रविततिर्या पठ्यते बह्वृचैः।
ऋग्भिः षोडशभिर्महोपनिषदं व्याचक्ष्महे तां वयम्॥

इतोऽग्रे सविस्तरं भूमिकारूपेण श्रीविद्योपास्तेर्वेदप्रतिपाद्यत्वमुपवर्णितम्।

श्रीभास्कररायमते वैदिकमन्त्राणामेव यथोचितमुपबृंहकाणि तन्त्रवाक्यानि। उपक्रमे च तैरुच्यते—उपासनाशास्त्रे तु देवताप्राधान्यवाद एव न कर्मणः प्राधान्यम्। क्रियाप्राधान्याभावादेव देवतारूपसिद्धवस्तुबोधका वेदान्ताः (उपनिषदः) इति वाचोयुक्तिः। देवतायाश्च त्रीणि रूपाणि स्थूलं सूक्ष्मं परञ्चेति। तत्राऽऽद्य तत्तद्ध्यानश्लोकोक्तं, द्वितीयं तत्तन्मूलमन्त्रात्मकं, तृतीयन्तु उपासनात्मकम्। देवतारूपत्रैविध्यादुपास्तिरपि त्रिविधा बहिर्याग-जप-अन्तर्यागभेदात्। तदिदं सपरिकरं ऋग्वेदपुरुषो महोपनिषद्रूपेणोपदिशति—

तिस्रः पुरस्त्रिपथा विश्वचर्षणी अत्राकथा अक्षराः सन्निविष्टा।
अधिष्ठायैनामजरा पुराणी महत्तरा महिमा देवतानाम्॥

इति प्रथमा ऋक्। अस्यैव मन्त्रस्योपबृंहणं **नित्याहृदये** परब्रह्म प्रकृत्य—प्रसृतं विश्वलहरीस्थानं मातृत्रयात्मकम्। वैन्दवं चक्रम् इत्यादि। तादृशमोक्षावच्छिन्नं ब्रह्म प्रकृत्य कालिकापुराणेऽपि—

त्रिकोणमण्डलं चास्या भूपुरञ्च त्रिरेखकम् ।
मन्त्रोऽपित्र्यक्षरः प्रोक्तस्तथा रूपत्रयं पुनः ।।
त्रिविधा कुण्डली शक्तिस्त्रिदेवानाञ्च सृष्टये ।
सर्वं त्रयं त्रयं यस्मात्तस्मात्तु त्रिपुरा मता ।।

एवमस्या उपनिषदो व्याख्याने प्रायेण सर्वत्र वेदतन्त्रयोः सम्बन्धः सूच्यते ।

अस्या एवोपनिषदः सप्तमी ऋक् सविशेषं मीमांसापद्धत्या तैर्व्याख्याता । ऋक् इयम्—

इमां विज्ञाय सुधया मदन्ति ।
परिस्रुता तर्पयन्तः स्वपीठम् ।।
नाकस्य पृष्ठे महतो वसन्ति ।
परं धाम त्रैपुरञ्चाऽऽविशन्ति ।।

अत्रमीमांसाशास्त्रीयं रेवत्यधिकरणसिद्धान्तमनुसृत्य व्याख्यातमाचार्यैः । यथा—श्रीविद्यादीक्षितो द्रव्यवता स्वपीठार्चनेन निर्विकल्पकवृत्तिद्वारा सर्वान् कामान् भावयेत् । इति भावनाविशिष्टभावनान्तरविधिः पर्यवस्यति । स च मीमांसादृष्टः प्रकारः—'एतस्यैव रेवतीषु वारवन्तीयमग्निष्टोमसाम कृत्वा ब्रह्मवर्चसकामो यजेत' इति वाक्ये प्रकृताग्निष्टुद्यागानुवादेनैतद्वाक्योपात्तगुणानां विधाने वाक्यभेदापत्तेः क्त्वाप्रत्ययोपात्तभावनोपसर्जनकं भावनान्तरं विधीयते इति **रेवत्यधिकरणन्यायः** । एवं स्थलान्तरेऽपि उपबृंहणं सूच्यते । यथा—'अजरा पुराणी' इत्यादिभिर्ब्रह्मलिङ्गैरिह पुल्लिङ्गैर्वक्ष्यमाणकामकलाध्यानगतस्त्रीलिङ्गैश्च परदेवतायास्त्रिविधं ध्यानं विहितं भवति । तथा चोपबृंहितं कुलार्णवे—

पुंरूपं वा स्मरेद्देवि स्त्रीरूपं वा विचिन्तयेत् ।
अथवा निष्कलं ध्यायेत्सच्चिदानन्दलक्षणम् ।।

इत्यादि ।

श्रीललितासहस्रनामव्याख्याने सौभाग्यभास्करनामधेये बहुषु स्थलेषु नामव्याख्याप्रसङ्गेन वेदतन्त्रयोः सहयोगित्वं सुस्पष्टमुपपाद्यते दीक्षितेन्द्रैः । तत्र स्थालीपुलाकन्यायेन कानिचिदुदाहरणानि प्रस्तूयन्ते—

विज्ञानघनरूपिणी

विज्ञानं चैतन्यमेव घनं सान्द्रं तदेकरसं रूपमस्याः । 'विज्ञानघन एवैतेभ्यो-भूतेभ्यः समुत्थाय' इति श्रुतौ विज्ञानघनपदस्य चिदेकरसपरत्वेन व्याख्यानदर्शनात् । अथवा विज्ञानशब्दो जीवपरः । 'यो विज्ञाने तिष्ठन् विज्ञानमन्तरो यमयति' इत्यादि अन्तर्यामिब्राह्मणे तथा व्याख्यानात् । तैर्घनं समष्ट्यात्मकं रूपमस्याः । जीवसमष्ट्यभिमानिहिरण्यगर्भात्मिकेत्यर्थः । 'एतस्माज्जीवघनात्' इति श्रुतौ

जीवघनपदस्य तथा व्याख्यानात्। **विश्वरूपा** इति नाम व्याख्याने तु **महता विस्तरेण** नानाविधाः शास्त्रीया अर्थाः प्रतिपादिताः। तेषु किञ्चित्क्रमदर्शनतुल्यं विषयमवलम्ब्य व्याख्यानं दर्शनीयमाभाति। तच्च यथा 'अथवा विश्वरूपमिति नपुंसकम्' तस्य च 'मिथ्या जगदधिष्ठाना' इतिवत् स्त्रीलिङ्गता। तच्च कृष्णपक्ष-पञ्चमीदिवसवाचकम्। तथा च श्रूयते—'प्रस्तुतं विष्टुतं संस्तुतं कल्याणं विश्व-रूपम्। शुक्रममृतं तेजस्वि तेजः समिद्धम्। अरुणं भानुमन्मरीचिमदभिपत्तपस्वत्। सुता सुन्वती प्रसूता सूयमानाभिषूयमाणा। पीति प्रपा संपा तृप्ति स्मर्पन्ती। कान्ता काम्या कामजाती युष्मती कामदुधा। प्रस्तुतं विष्टुतं सुता सुन्वतीति' एतौ अनु-वाकौ अपरपक्षस्य अहोरात्राणां नामधेयानि इति।

तेन तद्रूपेत्यर्थः। एवं रात्रिविशेषस्य दिवसविशेषस्य चोपलक्षणरीत्या श्लेषलिप्सया चैकैकस्योपादानेऽपि सर्वरात्रिरूपा सर्वदिवसरूपा चेत्यर्थः पर्य-वस्यति। अत एव ईदृशज्ञाने फलविशेषः श्रूयते—

'स यो हवा एता मधुकृतश्च मधुवृषांश्च वेद कुर्वन्ति हास्यैता अग्नौ मधु नास्येष्टापूर्तं धयन्ति। अथ यो न वेद न हास्यैता अग्नौ मधु कुर्वन्ति धयन्त्यस्येष्टा-पूर्तम्'। अयमत्र भावः—

अत्र मधुकृच्छब्दो रात्रिपरः। मधुवृषशब्दश्च दिवसपरः। या एताः पूर्वपक्षा-ऽपरपक्षयो रात्रयस्ता मधुकृतो यान्यहानि ते मधुवृषा इति वाक्यशेषात्। मधु कुर्वन्ति वर्षन्ति चेत्यवयवशक्तेश्च। एता यो वेद तस्यैता दिवससहिता रात्रयः अग्नौ बैन्दवस्थानात् ब्रह्मरन्ध्रात् मधु कुर्वन्ति स्रावयन्ति। अस्येष्टापूर्तं कर्मजातं न धयन्ति पीत्वा न लोपयन्ति। व्यतिरेके तु अनिष्टमाह अथ य इत्यादिना।

कुण्डल्युत्थापनेन मधुस्रावेण डाकिन्यादिमण्डलाऽऽप्लावनरूपान्तरकर्मणि सत्येव बाह्यानि यज्ञादिकर्माणि सफलानि भवन्ति। तदभावे तु यस्मिन् काले कर्माणि क्रियन्ते स काल एव तेषां कर्मणां कालमृत्युरूपो भवतीति फलितार्थः। **तदिदमुपबृंहितं चन्द्रज्ञानतन्त्रे**—

अन्तरग्नौ मधुस्रावं कुर्वतां शिशिरात्मनाम्
इष्टापूर्तादिकर्माणि फलन्ति किल कालतः॥

अन्तःस्रावविहीनानां सदा संतप्तचेतसाम्
कर्माणि क्रियमाणानि कालो ग्रसति तत्क्षणात्॥

कालकर्षिणिकैवान्तः करोति मधु वर्षति।
इति यो वेद तस्य स्याद् ब्रह्मरन्ध्रात् सुधास्रुतिः॥

वैदेही जनयामास सरघा कालकर्षिणी
अहोरात्रैरिमां विद्यां दशपञ्चभिरक्षरैः॥

अयञ्च विषयः श्रुतौ 'जनको वैदेहोऽहोरात्रैः समाजगाम' इत्यादौ 'इयं वाव सरघा तस्या अग्निरेव सारधं मधु' इति अतिरहस्ये त्वन उपदिष्ट आगमशास्त्रीयं निगूढमभिप्रायं व्याचष्टे। आचार्यचरणैरेवमेव स्थले स्थले श्रुतितन्त्रयोः सामञ्जस्यमुपपाद्य विदुषामुद्बोधनाय पन्थाः प्रदर्शितः।

उपरितनेन व्याख्यानेन आगमिकदर्शनेषु क्रमदर्शनस्याऽपि वेदसंवलितत्वमुपपाद्यते। यतो हि तत्र **'कालसङ्कर्षिणी'** एव परमोपास्या।

सन्ध्या इतिपदव्याख्यानं यथा—

आदित्यावच्छिन्नचैतन्यस्य स्वस्य च अभेदभावनं सन्ध्यापदार्थः। सम्यग्ध्यायन्त्यस्यामिति व्युत्पत्तेः। तदुक्तं महाभारते—

सन्ध्येति सूर्यगं ब्रह्म संध्यानादविभागतः।
ब्रह्माद्यैः सकलैर्भूतैस्तदंशैः सच्चिदात्मनः॥

तस्य दासोऽहमस्मीति सोऽहमस्मीति या मतिः।
भवेदुपासकस्येति ह्येवं वेदविदो विदुः॥

इति। तदभेदादियमपि सन्ध्या। तथा च व्यासः—

न भिन्नां प्रतिपद्येत गायत्रीं ब्रह्मणा सह।
साऽहमस्मीत्युपासीत विधिना येनकेनचित्॥

भारद्वाजस्मृतावपि—

ब्रह्माद्याकारभेदेन या भिन्नाकर्मसाक्षणी।
भास्वतीश्वरशक्तिः सा सन्ध्येत्यभिहिता बुधैः॥

त्रिपुरामहिमास्तवेऽपि—

गायत्री सशिरास्तुरीयसहिता सन्ध्यामयीत्यागमैराख्याता—इत्यादिदुर्वाससो वचनम्।

एवमाचार्यचरणानां व्याख्यानपद्धतिरतीव चमत्कारिणी वेदतन्त्रयोरैक्यमवगमयन्ती प्राचीनशिष्टाचारमुपोद्बलयन्ती च सर्वथा विद्वद्वरैरनुसन्धेया। अत्र तु संक्षेपादेव तत्परिचयः प्रदर्शितः।

21

अश्वमेधस्य आधिदैविकं स्वरूपम्

युधिष्ठिरो मीमांसकः

वैदिकवाङ्मये नित्यनैमित्तिककाम्यभेदेन बहूनां यागानां विधानमुपलभ्यते। एतेषामैतिहासिकं याज्ञिकं च पक्षमाश्रित्य बहवो विषया अस्माभिः "श्रौतयज्ञ-मीमांसा"[1] इत्याख्ये निबन्धे विवृताः। तत्रैव वैदिकवाङ्मये प्रसङ्गाद् यज्ञानां विषये य आधिदैविकपक्षनिर्देशकाः संकेता उपलभ्यन्ते तान् सूक्ष्मेक्षिकया विचार्य "आदौ यज्ञानां प्रयोजनं सततप्रवृत्तसृष्टियज्ञानामेव केषाञ्चिद् अंशानां व्याख्यानम्, यद्वा परोक्षरूपेण सृष्टौ घटमानानां घटनानां नाटकधर्मेण प्रत्यक्षं निदर्शनमेव आसीत्" इत्यपि संक्षेपेण प्रकटीकृतम्[2]। इह वैदिकवाङ्मयेऽतिविशिष्टं स्थानं भजमानस्य "अश्वमेध" महाक्रतोराधिदैविकं स्वरूपं संक्षेपेण प्रस्तूयते। अन्ते चास्य महाक्रतो राष्ट्रियं स्वरूपमपि निदर्शयिष्यते।

अश्वमेधयागस्य द्वौ भागौ—अश्वमेधयागस्य द्वौ भागौ स्तः। तत्र प्रथमे भागे यज्ञीयमश्वमधिकृत्य कानिचित् कार्याणि विधीयन्ते, अपरभागे यागसम्बन्धीनि कार्याणि निरूप्यन्ते।

अश्वमेधीयाश्वसम्बन्धीनि कार्याणि—अश्वमेधस्याधिदैविकस्वरूपस्य निरूपणात् प्राग् अश्वमधिकृत्य यानि कार्याणि याज्ञिका विदधते, तेषां केचन प्रमुखा अंशा आपस्तम्बीयं कात्यायनीयं च श्रौतसूत्रमनुसृत्य संक्षेपेणोपस्थाप्यन्ते। यत एतेषामाश्रयेण अश्वमेधस्याधिदैविकस्वरूपनिदर्शने सौकर्यं संपत्स्यते।

अश्वमेधस्याधिकारिणः—आपस्तम्बे श्रौतसूत्रे (२०।१।१)[3] "**राजा सार्वभौमोऽश्वमेधेन यजेत, अप्यसार्वभौमः**" इत्युक्तम्। कात्यायनश्रौतसूत्रे (२०।१।१) तु "**राज्ञोऽश्वमेधः सर्वकामस्य**" इत्युपलभ्यते। इत्थम् अश्वमेधस्य त्रयोऽधिकारिण उक्ताः। तत्र "सार्वभौमो राजा" अस्याधिकारीति प्रथमः कल्पः, "असार्वभौमो राजा" इति द्वितीयः कल्पः, "सर्वकामो राजा" इति तृतीयः कल्पः।

यः पूर्वमेव सार्वभौमत्वं भजते, तेन राज्ञा किमर्थमयं क्रतुराहर्तव्य इति नोक्तम्। या त्वश्वमेधस्य प्रक्रिया वैदिकवाङ्मये समुपलभ्यते तया त्वस्य क्रतोः प्रयोजनं सार्वभौमत्वसम्पादनमेव प्रतीयते। अतः पूर्वतः सम्पन्नेन सार्वभौमेन

राज्ञा किमर्थमय क्रतुराहर्तव्य इत्युदेति प्रश्नः। वय तु पश्यामः सार्वभौमेन राज्ञा काले कालेऽस्य क्रतोराहरणेन "कश्चिन्माण्डलिको राजाऽस्मत्प्रतियोगी तु न संवृत्तः" इत्यन्वेक्षणमेव प्रयोजनम्। यद्वा याज्ञिकमतानुसारं रात्रिसत्रन्यायेन[4] "**एतेन ब्रह्महत्यामतरन्त्सर्वं पाप्मानं तरति, तरति ब्रह्महत्यां योऽश्वमेधेन यजते य उ चैनं वेद**"[5] (तै० सं० ५।३।१२) इत्यर्थवादरूपेणोक्तं फलं कल्पनीयम्।

असार्वभौमस्य राज्ञोऽस्य क्रतोराहरणे सार्वभौमत्वप्राप्तिरेव मुख्यं फलम्। अतः समर्थेनैव राज्ञाऽस्य क्रतोराहरणे प्रवर्तितव्यं न दुर्बलेन, अन्यथा स स्वराज्यादपि भ्रश्येत। अत एवोक्तम्—**परा वा एष सिच्यते योऽबलोऽश्वमेधेन यजते**[6] (तै० ब्रा० ३।८।९।४) इति।

सर्वकामस्य राज्ञोऽस्य क्रतोराहरणे सर्वकामानामवाप्तिरेव फलम् इति सूत्रवचनाद् विज्ञायते। यत्तु विद्याधरशर्मणाऽस्य सूत्रस्य वृत्तौ "**अत्र च सर्वकाम-शब्देन मुमुक्षुरभिधीयते (श० १३।४।१।१)। मोक्षप्राप्तौ च सर्वकामावाप्तेः सम्भवादिति कर्काचार्याः**" इत्युक्तं, तदापाततो रमणीयमेव। न हि शतपथे १३।४।१।१ इत्येवं निर्दिष्टे स्थाने सर्वकामशब्दस्य मुमुक्षुरर्थ उपलभ्यते। अपि च, वैदिक-वाङ्मयेऽयं "सर्वकाम" शब्दो बहुत्र श्रूयते। यथा—**स्वर्गकामो दर्शपूर्णमासौ। एककामः सर्वकामो वा** (आप० श्रौत ३।१४।८,९)। न ह्येतादृक्स्थलेषु कश्चिदपि व्याख्याता सर्वकामशब्दस्य "मुमुक्षुः" इत्यर्थं व्याचख्यौ। वस्तुतस्तु प्रकृते सर्वकाम-शब्दे यः सर्वशब्दः स स्वाधिकारसम्बन्धिनि सर्वत्वे प्रयुक्तः। अतः "**पूर्णाहुत्या सर्वान् कामानवाप्नोति**" इत्यत्र यथा **सर्वत्वमाधिकारिकम्** (मी० ११।२।१६) एवं '**राज्ञोऽश्वमेधः सर्वकामस्य**' इत्यत्रापि द्रष्टव्यः। अर्थाद् अश्वमेधेन यो यः कामः सम्पाद-यितुं शक्यते, स सर्वोऽपि सम्पाद्यते। अश्वमेधेन राज्ञा सार्वभौमत्वरूपः कामः सम्पाद्यते। अतस्तमेवार्थं सर्वकामशब्दो ब्रवीति, न तु निरपेक्षसर्वकामत्वम्।

अश्वमेधस्य कालः—अश्वमेधक्रतुः प्रायेणैकसंवत्सरसाध्यः। यद्यप्ययं क्षत्रिय-यागः, क्षत्रियस्य च ग्रीष्मर्तुः कालः, तथाप्ययं वसन्ततौ फाल्गुनमासस्य शुक्ल-पक्षस्य अष्टम्यां नवम्यां वा आरभ्यते। तदुक्तं शतपथे—**तद्वै वसन्त एवारभेत। वसन्तो वै ब्राह्मणस्यर्तुर्य उ वै कश्चन यजते ब्राह्मणीभूयेवैव यजते**[7]······**सा या सौ फाल्गुनी पौर्णमासी भवति, तस्यै पुरस्तात् षडहे वा सप्ताहे वर्त्विज उपस-मायन्ति**······(१३।४।१।३-४)।

अश्वलक्षणानि—योऽयमश्वोऽश्वमेधायाह्रियते तस्य पूर्वोऽर्धभागः कृष्णः, पश्चाद्भागः शुक्लः, ललाटे च शकटाकारं लक्ष्म अपेक्ष्यते (द्र०—शत० १३।४। २।४)।

अश्वरशनायाः प्रमाणम्—अश्वमेधीयस्याश्वस्य दर्भमयी (क्वचिन्मुञ्जमयी) रशना द्वादशारत्निप्रमाणा त्रयोदशारत्निप्रमाणा वा भवति [अरत्निप्रमाणं तु

द्वाविंशत्यङ्गुल्यात्मकम्, क्वचित् चतुर्विंशत्यङ्गुलिप्रमाणमपि स्वीक्रियते।] तां रशनां घृतेनाञ्जयन्ति।

राज्ञः पत्न्यः—राज्ञश्चतस्रः पत्न्यः (=महिषी=प्रथमपरिणीता कृताभिषेका, वावाता=वल्लभा, परिवृक्ता=अवल्लभा, पालागली=दूतपुत्री) आभरणादि-भिरलङ्कृताः सानुचर्यः शतेन शतेन (=४००) यजमानस्य समीपमुपतिष्ठन्ति (कात्या० श्रौत० २०।१।१२) (आपस्तम्बश्रौतसूत्रे पालागल्या निर्देशो नास्ति। तेन महिषी वावाता परिवृक्ता तिस्र एव सानुचर्योः राजानमुपयान्ति)।

राज्ञो ब्रह्मचर्यपूर्वकं शयनम्—राजा वावातायाः (=वल्लभायाः) पत्न्या उर्वन्तरे शिरः कृत्वा ब्रह्मचर्यं पालयन् संवत्सरं यावद् रात्रौ शेते (कात्या० श्रौत० २०।१।१७)।

अश्वस्य निर्णेजनम् चतुरक्षशुनो मारणं च—यज्ञीयमश्वं तेन सह चतुरक्षं श्वानं च तडागादि महाजले प्रवेश्य, यत्र शुनः पादा भूमिं न स्पृशन्ति, तत्र सैध्रकेण मुसलेन श्वानं हत्वा अश्वपादानामधस्तात् प्रास्येत्। तं चाश्वं चतसृषु दिक्ष्व-वस्थिता महर्त्विजो निर्णेनिजति प्रोक्षयन्ति। चतुरक्षस्य शुनोऽभावाद् यस्य शुनोऽक्ष्णोरुपरि द्वे लक्ष्मणी भवतः, स इहाभिप्रेतः।

अश्वस्योत्सर्जनं रक्षिणां चानुगमनम्—यज्ञीयोऽश्वः संवत्सरं यावत् स्वच्छन्दः परिभ्रमणार्थम् ईशान्यां दिशि उत्सृज्यते। संवत्सरात् प्राक् न तं परावर्तयन्ति। अश्वस्य रक्षार्थं शस्त्रास्त्रकवचधारिणः शतं राजपुत्राः, शतं क्षत्रियपुत्राः खड्ग-धारिणः, शतं सूतग्रामण्या पुत्रा इषुवर्षिणः, शतं क्षात्रसंगृहीतॄणां पुत्रा वंशादिदण्डधारिण (=१००×४=४००) अनुयान्ति (शत० १३।४।२।५; कात्या० श्रौत० २०।२।१०) ते च वडवाभ्यः स्नानार्हाच्चोदकाद् अश्वं वारयितु-मादिश्यन्ते। (कात्या० श्रौत० २०।२।१२-१३)। ते रक्षकाः संवत्सरं यावद् अश्वं भ्रामयित्वा प्रत्यानयन्ति। अस्मिन्नन्तराले यदि कश्चिद् राजा स्वराज्ये भ्रमन्तम् अश्वमवरुणद्धि, तर्हि रक्षकास्तं युद्धे पराजित्य स्वानुचरं विधायाग्रे प्रयान्ति। इत्थमश्वमेधस्याश्वो यस्य यस्य राज्ञो राज्ये परिभ्रमति ते सर्वेऽश्वमेधक्रतुमाहरतो राज्ञः शासनमुररीकृत्य यज्ञकाले उपहारानादायोपतिष्ठन्ति।

यज्ञीयकार्याणि

अश्वस्योत्सर्जनानन्तरं यावत् स न प्रत्यावर्तते तावद् राजा अनेका इष्टीर्यज्ञान् च करोति। अश्वस्य प्रत्यावर्तनेऽस्य महाक्रतोः प्रमुखं यज्ञकर्म प्रारभते।

अस्मिन् क्रतौ द्वादश दीक्षाः, द्वादश चोपसदो भवन्ति। तदनन्तरं तिस्रः सुत्या (सोमयागाः) भवन्ति। तत्र प्रथमा सुत्या अग्निष्टोमसंस्थाका भवति, द्वितीया

उक्थ्यसंस्थाका, तृतीया च अतिरात्रसंस्थाका। तदनन्तरम् अवभृथस्नानम् 'उद-वसानीयेष्टिं च कृत्वा कर्मैतत् समापयन्ति।

द्वितीयसुत्यादिवसे विशिष्टं कर्म—अस्मिन्नहनि प्रत्यागतम् अश्वं रज्जुभिः सर्वतो वेष्टयन्ति। रज्जूनां पर्यन्तभागे विभिन्नदेवताकान् पशून् बध्नन्ति (कात्या० श्रौत०, भूमिका पृष्ठ १६, विद्याधरीया टीका)। सप्तविंशत्युत्तरं शतत्रयं ग्राम्याः पशवः, द्वाविंशतिरेकादशिनी पशवः, षष्ट्युत्तरं द्विशतम् आरण्याः पशवः। आहत्य नवोत्तराणि षट्शतानि (६०९) पशवो भवन्ति (द्र०—उव्वट महीधर भाष्य, यजुः २४।४६)। आरण्याः पशवः पर्यग्निकरणानन्तरम् उत्सृज्यन्ते (कात्या० श्रौत० २०।६।९)। शिष्टा ग्राम्याः पशव आलभ्यन्ते।

अश्वमेधीयाश्वस्यालम्भः, तदनुकृत्यं च—अश्वमेधीयस्य अश्वस्यालम्भ-नानन्तरं महिषी (=राज्ञा सह कृताभिषेका पत्नी) मृतस्याश्वस्य समीपं शेते। अधीवासेनाश्वमहीष्यौ प्रच्छाद्येते। महिषी अश्वस्य शिश्नं स्वोपस्थे कुरुते। तस्मिन्नेव काले अध्वर्युकुमार्यौ, ब्रह्ममहिष्यौ, उद्गातृवावाते, होतृपरिवृक्ते, प्रतीहारपालागल्यौ द्वाभ्यां द्वाभ्यामृग्भ्यां परस्परम् अश्लीलं सम्वादं कुर्वन्ति। अनन्तरं ब्रह्मोद्यं भवति।

अश्वमेधस्य आधिदैविकं स्वरुपम्—सम्प्रत्यश्वमेधक्रतोराधिदैविकपक्षं पुर-स्कृत्य विचार्यते। अश्वमेधीयाश्वं तदधिकारिणं चाधिकृत्य ये प्रमुखा अंशाःपुरस्तान्नि-र्दशिताः, तैरेतद् विस्पष्टं भवति यदिदं आश्वमेधिकं कर्म आधिदैविकस्य कस्यचित् सृष्टियज्ञस्य प्रातिनिध्यं करोति। इदमेव स्पष्टीकर्तुं वयं पुरस्तान् निर्दिष्टान् विषयान् यथाक्रमं व्याख्यातुं प्रयतामहे।

सार्वभौमो राजा—अश्वमेधस्य ये त्रयोऽधिकारिणःपुरस्तादुक्तास्तेषु "**सार्वभौमो राजाऽश्वमेधेन यजेत**" इत्येव मुख्यः पक्ष इति याज्ञिका मीमांसकाश्च मन्वते।

इदमत्रावधेयम्—यद्यपि लौकिकेऽश्वमेधे यजमानरूपः सार्वभौमो राजा, अश्वश्च भिन्नौ भवतः। तथाप्यश्वस्य राज्ञस्तेजसः प्रतीकत्वाद् उभौ परस्परं सम्बद्धौ स्तः। अतएव राजा न स्वयम् अन्यान् राज्ञः स्वाधीनान् कर्त्तुं प्रयाति, अपि तु स्वस्थाने स्वतेजसः प्रतीकरूपकमश्वं विमुञ्चति। येऽश्वमेधीयमश्वं स्वराज्ये चरन्तं न निरुन्धन्ति तेऽश्वमेधकर्तुः शासनमुररीकुर्वन्तीति सूचयन्ति। यः कश्चित् स्वाभिमानी राजाऽन्यस्य वशीभावं न सहते, स यज्ञीयमश्वमवरुणद्धि युद्धाय च सन्नद्धो भवति। अनुचारिणोऽश्वरक्षका तेन सह युद्ध्वा तं पराजित्य वशं नयन्ति।

आधिदैविकपक्षेऽस्मदीये सौरमण्डले सार्वभौमो राजा सूर्यः। अयं स्वतेजसा सर्वानपि ग्रहोपग्रहान् अभिभवति। अयं हि स्वाभीशुभिः सर्वान् ग्रहोपग्रहान् स्वस्वमर्यादायां (=स्वस्वकक्षायां) प्रवर्तयति, न कश्चित् स्वमर्यादामतिक्रामति। याज्ञिकानां मते ऋग्वेदस्य प्रथममण्डलस्य १६२-६३ तमे सूक्ते अश्वमेधविषयके

स्तः। परन्त्वनयोः सूक्तयोः क्वचिदश्वशब्देन, क्वचिच्च तत्पर्यायवाचिना सूर्यस्य स्तुतिरुपलभ्यते। अतएव क्वचित् ततः प्रसृतानां रश्मीनामपि वर्णनमुपलभ्यते। अनयोराश्वमेधिकसूक्तयोर्विषयेऽग्रे विचारः करिष्यते।

अश्वलक्षणानि—अश्वमेधीयाश्वस्य यानि लक्षणानि पुरस्तान्निरूपितानि, तान्याधिदैविकपक्षे सूर्योदयात् प्राक् प्रत्यहं लक्ष्यन्ते। तथाहि—सूर्योदयात् सार्धचतुर्घटीपूर्वं (द्विघण्टापूर्वं) रात्रेरन्तिमे भागे तमो भवति, किन्तु तस्मिन् काले पूर्वस्यां दिशि दिवि उन्नतप्रदेशे उषसः शकटाकारः प्रकाश उपलभ्यते। अयमेवाश्वस्योन्नतप्रदेशे ललाटे शकटाकारं लक्ष्म विज्ञेयम्। यद् उषःकालेऽस्मदीये भूभागे तमो भवति तदेवाश्वस्य पूर्वभागस्य कार्ष्ण्यम्, यत्तु अस्मत्प्रदेशात् पूर्वस्यां दिशि सूर्योदयात् प्रकाशः संवृत्तः, स एव तस्य पश्चिमाभिमुखमुपसर्पतोऽश्वस्यापरभागस्य शौक्ल्यं विज्ञेयम्। अग्रे अग्रे उषः प्रयाति तदनु च सूर्यस्य प्रकाशः प्रचलति। अनयैव गत्या आधिदैविकस्याश्वस्य प्रत्यहं त्रीणि रूपाणि सर्वदेशीयैरुपलभ्यन्ते।

अश्वरशनाया द्वे प्रमाणे—यत्पुरस्ताद् अश्वमेधीयाश्वस्य रशनाया द्वादशारत्निप्रमाणं त्रयोदशारत्निप्रमाणं चोक्तम्, तेऽप्यश्वमेधस्याधिदैविकं पक्षमेव पोषयतः। तथाहि—अस्मद्देशे द्वौ संवत्सरौ प्रवर्तेते। तत्रैकश्चान्द्रः, अपरः सौरः। सौरवर्षात् चान्द्रवर्षे प्रायेण दशदिवसा न्यूना भवन्ति। अत आर्यास्तृतीये वर्षे चान्द्रमेकं मासमधिकं परिगणय्य उभयोर्वत्सरयोः सामञ्जस्यं विदधति।[10] ऋग्वेद उपजायमानस्य त्रयोदशस्य मासस्य निर्देशः साक्षादुपलभ्यते।[11] यागादीनि सर्वाण्यपि शुभकार्याणि आर्याश्चान्द्रवत्सरानुसारमेव कुर्वन्ति, न सौरवत्सरानुसारम्। द्वयोश्चान्द्रवत्सरयोर्द्वादश द्वादश मासा भवन्ति, तृतीये च वत्सरे त्रयोदश। अतएवाश्वमेधीयाश्वस्य रशनाया अपि द्वे प्रमाणे निर्दिष्टे। ब्राह्मणे त्रयोदशारत्निप्रमाणस्य प्रशंसोपलभ्यते। तथाहि—

तदाहुः—द्वादशारत्नी रशना कार्या ३ त्रयोदशारत्नी ३ रिति। ऋषभो वा एष ऋतूनां यत्संवत्सरस्तस्य त्रयोदशो मासो विष्टपः। वृषभ एष यज्ञानां यदश्वमेधो यथा वा ऋषभस्य विष्टपमेवमेतस्य विष्टपं त्रयोदशारत्निं रशनामुपदध्यात्।[3] शत० १३।१।२।२॥ **विष्टपं ककुदित्यर्थः।**

अस्मिन् स्तुत्यर्थवादे रशनाप्रमाणयोः प्रत्यक्षं वत्सरस्य द्वादशत्रयोदशमासैः सह सम्बन्धः परिकीर्तितः।

सूत्रकारास्तु द्वादशारत्निप्रमाणस्य त्रयोदशारत्निप्रमाणस्य च सामान्यरूपेण विकल्पमुररीकुर्वन्ति। वयं तु मन्यामहे यजमानो यस्मिन् चान्द्रवर्षेऽश्वमेधं कर्तुं प्रारभते, तस्मिन् वर्षे यदि द्वादशमासाः स्युस्तर्हि द्वादशारत्निप्रमाणा रशना कार्या। एवं यस्मिन् वर्षे त्रयोदशमासाः स्युस्तस्मिन् त्रयोदशारत्निप्रमाणा रशना कार्या। इत्येवं व्यवस्थितविकल्पो ज्ञेयः।[13] एतादृक्प्रमाणया रशनया बद्ध आधिदैविकोऽश्वो

संवत्सरं यावद् भ्रमति।[14] यदुच्यते **"अश्वरशनां घृतेनाञ्जन्ति।"** घृतंनाम दीपकस्य तेजस्विनः पदार्थस्य उपलक्षकः (**घृ क्षरणदीप्त्योः**)। सूर्यस्येयं रशना प्रकाशेन दीप्ता तेजस्विनी च भवति।

राज्ञश्चतस्रः पत्न्यः—सार्वभौमस्य राज्ञः सूर्यस्य चतस्रः पत्न्यश्चतस्रो दिशः। पूर्वा दिक् महिषी नाम्नी प्रधाना पत्नी। अनया सहैव उदीयमानस्य सूर्यस्याभिषेको भवति। अर्थात् पूर्वस्यां दिश्येव सूर्यम् उद्यन्तं जनाः पश्यन्ति। पश्चिमा दिक् वल्लभा नाम्नी पत्नी। अस्यामेव दिशि सूर्यो निम्रोचति (=विश्राम्यति)। अत एवाश्वमेधे राज्ञो वल्लभाया ऊर्वोरन्तराले शिरो निधाय शयनमुक्तम्। अस्मिन् काले यद् ब्रह्मचर्यमुक्तम्, तस्य द्वे कारणे। प्रथमं यज्ञे दीक्षितस्य यावद् यज्ञो न समाप्नोति तावद् ब्रह्मचर्यव्रतस्य विधानम्, अपरम् आधिदैविकपक्षे अस्माकं दृष्टौ यदा सूर्यो वल्लभायां पश्चिमस्यां दिशि निम्रोचति तदा ततः परस्मिन् देशे सूर्यः प्रकाशमानो भवति, अतोऽस्मद्दृष्ट्या वल्लभायां पश्चिमस्यां दिशि सूर्यस्य निम्रोचने सत्यपि न तया सह तस्य वास्तविकः सम्बन्धो भवति। इत्थमेव अवल्लभादूतपुल्यौ उत्तरदक्षिणे दिशौ स्तः। आभ्यां सह सूर्यस्योत्तरायणे दक्षिणायने चैव संयोगो भवति, न सर्वदा।

इदं चतसृणां राज्ञः पत्नीनां याज्ञिकपक्षमनुरुध्याधिदैविकं स्वरूपं निर्दर्शितम्।

इदमत्रावधेयम्—यथा चैव याज्ञिकः पक्षस्तथा अश्वमेधकर्तॄ राज्ञो न्यूनातिन्यूनं चतस्रः पत्न्योऽवश्यमपेक्षन्ते। परन्तु भारते वर्षे दाशरथिरामसदृशा एकपत्नीव्रतिनोऽनेके राजानो बभूवुः, यैर्बहुकृत्वोऽश्वमेधक्रतुराहृत इति रामायण-महाभारतादिभ्यो ग्रन्थेभ्यो विज्ञायते। चतसृणां पत्नीनामभावे कथमेतैरश्वमेधः सम्पादितः स्यादिति?

वस्तुतस्त्वाधिदैविकस्याश्वस्य (सूर्यस्य) एकैव पत्नी, याऽस्माकं जनयित्री[15] आधारभूता च पृथिवी वर्तते। अतएवैकस्मिन् वैवाहिके मन्त्र आधिदैविकं पतिपत्नीभावमनुवर्णयन् वरः पत्नीं ब्रवीति—**द्यौरहं पृथिवी त्वम्। ताविह सं भवाव प्रजामा जनयावहै।**[16] (अथर्व० १४।२।७१)। वैदिकवाङ्मयेऽन्यत्रापि द्यावापृथिव्योः पतिपत्नीरूपेण निर्देश उपलभ्यते। यतः पृथिव्या एव पत्नीभावः, तस्माद् आस्माकीने सौरमण्डले ये ग्रहोपग्रहाः सन्ति तेष्वेकमात्रमस्यामेव जैविकीसृष्टिर्वर्तते, नान्येषु ग्रहोपग्रहेषु। एतद्विज्ञायैवास्मत्पूर्वजैर्वैज्ञानिकैरस्यैव ग्रहस्य स्त्रीलिङ्गमभिधानं कृतम्, अन्येषां ग्रहोपग्रहेभ्यः पुंल्लिङ्गाभिधानं प्रत्तम्। यतोऽस्यामेव पृथिव्यां चराचररूपिणी जैविकीसृष्टिरुत्पद्यतेऽत अस्याः "भवन्त्यस्यां प्राणिन इति भूमिः" इत्यन्वर्थं नाम। अस्यां जैविकीसृष्टेरुत्पादने सूर्य एव स्वतेजसा बीजावपनमिव प्रधानां भूमिकां निर्वर्तयति। अतएव यदा बहुदिवसपर्यन्तं सूर्यस्य तेजो मेघैराच्छादितं भवति तदौषधिवनस्पतयो म्लायन्ते।

अश्वस्य ईशान्यां दिश्युत्सर्जनम्—अश्वमेधीयोऽश्वः संवत्सरं यावत् परिभ्रमणाय ईशान्यां दिश्युत्सृज्यते। यद्यप्याधिदैविकोऽश्वः सूर्यो यस्मिन् कालेऽश्वमेधीयं कर्मारभ्यते तदा स विषुवद्रेखातो दक्षिणभाग उदेति, परन्तु तस्योत्तरायणकालत्वात् सूर्यो यत उत्तराभिमुखो भवति, अतः स ईशान्यां (उत्तरपूर्वदिगन्तरालायां) दिश्युत्सृज्यते।

अश्वस्यैकवर्षपर्यन्तं भ्रमतो मध्येऽप्रत्यावर्तनम्—एकवर्षं यावत् परिभ्रमणायाश्वमेधीयोऽश्वो न मध्ये प्रत्यावर्त्यते। इदमपि कर्म अश्वस्याधिदैविकमेव पक्षं पुष्णाति। अत एवोक्तम्—

तमेतऽउभये देवमनुष्याः संविदाना अप्रत्यावर्तयन्तः संवत्सरं रक्षन्ति। तद् यं न प्रत्यावर्तयन्ति एष[17] वा एष य एष तपति क उ ह्येतमर्हति प्रत्यावर्तयितुम्। शत० १३।४।२।१६॥

एतेन ब्राह्मणवादेन अश्वमेधीयाश्वस्य प्रत्यक्षम् आधिदैविकं स्वरूपं निरूप्यते। यथा हि सूर्यस्य परितो भ्रमतो न हि संवत्सरात् प्राक् प्रत्यावर्तनं भवति। संवत्सरान्त एव सूर्यस्तं स्थानं प्रत्यावर्तते, यतस्तेन परिभ्रमणं प्रारब्धमासीत्। अतएव यज्ञीयमश्वमपि संवत्सरान्त एव प्रत्यावर्तयन्ति।

चतुःशतमश्वस्य रक्षकाः—अश्वस्य रक्षार्थं मार्गं उपस्थितां बाधां च दूरीकर्तुं विविधशस्त्रास्त्रधारिणश्चतुश्शतसंख्याकाः पुरुषा नियुज्यन्ते। एतद्विधानमपि यज्ञीयाश्वस्याधिदैविकं स्वरूपं पुष्णाति। ऋग्वेदे सूर्यस्य सहस्रविधा रश्मय उक्ताः—**युक्ता ह्यस्य हरयश्शतादश** (६।४७।१८)। एषां सहस्रविधानां रश्मीनां त्रयो भेदा वायुपुराणे (५३।१६-२३), ब्रह्माण्डपुराणे (पूर्वभाग २४।२६-३०), मत्स्यपुराणे (१२८।१८-२२) च निर्दिष्टाः सन्ति। तेषु **चित्रमूर्तिनामानः** शतचतुष्टयं रश्मयो वर्षयन्ति।[18] यज्ञीयाश्वस्य विचरणे शत्रोः प्रतिरोधं दूरीकर्तुं शतचतुष्टयं विविधशस्त्रास्त्रधारिणः सैनिका अनुयान्ति। सृष्टियज्ञेऽपि वर्षर्तौ सूर्यस्य रश्मीनां प्रकाशस्य वा प्रचरणे मेघा अवरोधका भवन्ति। तान् विच्छिद्य वर्षकाः चित्रमूर्तिनामानो रश्मयोऽपि शतचतुष्टयमिता एव सन्ति। मेघानां विच्छेदे प्रवर्षिते च अवरोधाभावात् सूर्यस्य रश्मयः प्रकाशो वा यथेच्छं भूमिं प्राप्नोति। ऋग्वेदस्य **आणिं न रथ्यममृताधि तस्थुः** (१।३५।६) इति मन्त्रे सृष्टिसर्जका रश्मयोऽमृता अपराजिता उक्ताः।[19]

अश्वस्य सर्वाङ्गाणां रज्जुभिर्बन्धनम्—प्रत्यागतेऽश्वमेधीयेऽश्वे आश्वमेधिकं प्रधानं कर्म प्रारभते। द्वितीये सुत्यादिवसेऽश्वस्य सर्वाङ्गान् रज्जुभिर्वेष्टयन्ति। तथा तत्तत्स्थानेषु रज्जूनां प्रान्तभागेषु केचन पशवो बध्यन्त इत्युक्तं प्राक्। इदमपि कर्म सृष्टियज्ञान्तर्गतमश्वमेधमेव संकेतयति। सूर्यमण्डलस्य परितो; सूर्यरश्मयः प्रसृता भवन्ति। ते रश्मिभिरेव कृत्स्नं सूर्यमण्डलं बद्धम् अर्थाद् आच्छादितं

वर्तते । रज्जुशब्दो रश्मिपर्यायः । तथा चोक्तं वेङ्कटमाधवेन—**रज्जुः सर्गो रश्मिपाशौ रशनाभीशुरेव च । दामाभिभानिधा**..... ।[20] सूर्यरश्मिषु नद्धा एव सर्वे ग्रहोपग्रहाः स्वस्वकक्षासु परिभ्रमन्ति ।

एवमस्माभिर्विस्पष्टीकृतमेतद् यद् द्रव्यमयरूपस्य अश्वमेधस्य सम्बन्धः सृष्टियज्ञस्याश्वमेधेन सह वर्तते । एतेन साकं लौकिकस्याश्वमेधस्य एकं राष्ट्रियरूपमप्यस्ति । तस्य व्याख्यानमुपरिष्टात् करिष्यते ।

ऋग्वेदीये अश्वमेधविषयके सूक्ते—ऋग्वेदस्य प्रथममण्डलस्य १६२, १६३ तमे सूक्ते अश्वमेधे विनियुक्ते स्तः । सम्प्रति तयोः सह १६४ तमं सूक्तं सम्मेल्य त्रयाणां सूक्तानां विषयेऽतिसंक्षेपेण लिख्यते—

त्रिषष्ट्युत्तरशततमस्य (१६३) सूक्तस्य[21] प्रथममन्त्रे अश्वस्योत्पत्तिः समुद्रात् पुरीषाच्चोक्ता, द्वितीयमन्त्रे यमेन प्रदत्तस्य त्रितेन युक्तस्य अश्वस्योपरि इन्द्रः प्रथममध्यतिष्ठत्, गन्धर्वोऽस्य रशनामगृह्णात्, वसवः सूराद् अश्वमतक्षन् इति निर्दिश्यते । चतुर्थे मन्त्रे अश्वस्य दिवि अप्सु समुद्रे च त्रीणि बन्धनान्युक्तानि । षष्ठे मन्त्रे पतङ्गः (=गतिशीलोऽश्वः) द्युलोके गच्छन्निर्दिष्टः । **दशमस्य ईर्मान्तासः** मन्त्रस्य व्याख्या निरुक्तकारेण सूर्यरश्मिपरा व्यधायि (द्र०—निरुक्त ४।१३) । एकादशे मन्त्रे अश्वस्य जर्भुराणि देदीप्यमानानि शृङ्गाणि अरण्ये विचरन्तीत्युक्तम् । लौकिकस्याश्वस्य शृङ्गाण्येव न भवन्ति, पुनः कथं तेषां देदीप्यमानानाम् अरण्ये विचरणं सम्भवति? सूर्यस्य तु देदीप्यमानानि गतिमन्ति शृङ्गाणि तस्य रश्मयः । एतैः सङ्केतैर्विस्पष्टं भवति यद् अश्वमेधे क्रतौ विनियुक्ते त्रिषष्ट्युत्तरशततमे सूक्ते उक्तोऽश्वः सूर्य एव, न लौकिकः पशुः ।

चतुष्षष्ट्युत्तरशततमस्य सूक्तस्यारम्भ[22] **अस्य वामस्य पलितस्य** इत्येवं भवति । आदौ निर्दिष्टम् **अस्य** इति सर्वनामपदम् । सर्वनामानि च पूर्वनिर्दिष्टस्य स्मारकाणि उत वा अभिधायकानि भवन्ति । अनया दृष्ट्या पूर्वपठितयोः १६२, १६३ तमयोः सूक्तयोर्यस्याश्वस्य वर्णनमभूत् तमेव **अस्यपदेन** स्मारयित्वा तद्विषये विशेष उच्यते । अस्मिन् **अस्यवामीये** सूक्ते सूर्यस्य तद्रश्मीनां च वर्णनमुपलभ्यते । इदं च वर्णनं एतावत् स्पष्टं वर्तते, यदस्मिन् प्रकरणे सूर्यस्य तद्रश्मीनां च वर्णनम् अतिरिच्य नान्यस्य कस्यचित् वर्णनं स्वीकर्तुं शक्यते । निरुक्तकारो यास्कोऽप्यस्य सूक्तस्यानेकेषां मन्त्राणां सूर्यपरामेव व्याख्यां निरुक्ते कृतवान् ।

सम्प्रति द्वाषष्ट्युत्तरशततमस्य (१६२) सूक्तस्य समस्यावशिष्यते । यद्यप्यस्मिन् सूक्तेऽनेके मन्त्राः पदसमूहाश्चैतादृशाः सन्ति, ये आपाततो अश्वमेधीयाश्वस्यालम्भसम्बन्धिनः प्रतीयन्ते । तथाप्युत्तरयोः सूक्तयोः प्रकाशे एतत्सूक्तस्य मन्त्राणां विशिष्टां च पदानाम् आधिदैविकोऽर्थ एव कर्तुं न्याय्यः । अपि चास्य सूक्तस्य एकविंशा ऋक् एतादृशा पठ्यते, यस्यामश्वमेधीयाश्वस्य मरणं प्रत्यक्षं

प्रतिषिध्यते। तथाहि—**न वा उ एतन्म्रियसे न रिष्यसि देवाँ इदेषि पथिभिः सुगेभिः।** यद्युच्येत अस्यामृचि अश्वस्य यन्मरणप्रतिषेध उक्तः, स तस्य स्वर्गप्राप्तिमपेक्ष्योक्तः। यदि यज्ञे हिंसितोऽश्वः स्वर्गमेतीत्युच्यते, तर्हि चार्वाकाणां **'पशुश्चेन्निहतो स्वर्गं ज्योतिष्टोमे गमिष्यति। स्वपिता यजमानेन कथं तत्र न हिंस्यते'** इति वचनस्य किमुत्तरं स्यात्? वस्तुतस्तु अस्मिन्नपि सूक्ते सूर्यरूपस्यैवाश्वस्य वर्णनं विद्यते। स एव हि न कदाचिन्म्रियते हिंस्यते वा। स अस्तंगतोऽपि न स्वरूपं जहाति न च रिष्यति। अपरस्मिन् दिने स नियतसमये पुनरुदेति। अयमेवाभिप्रायः प्रकारान्तरेण ब्राह्मणग्रन्थेषु प्रकटीकृतः। तथाहि—

स वा एष न कदाचनास्तमेति नोदेति .... **स वा एष न कदाचन निम्लोचति** (ऐ० ब्रा० १४।६) इति।

स वा एष न कदाचनास्तमयति नोदयति .... **स वा एष न कदाचनास्तमयति नोदयति। स ह वै कदाचन न निम्रोचति** (गो० ब्रा० २।४।१०) इति।

यस्त्वत्राश्वस्याङ्गानां पचनस्य गन्ध उपलभ्यते तदप्यापाततो रमणीयमिव। काण्वबृहदारण्यकोपनिषद आरम्भे अश्वाङ्गानामाधिदैविकी व्याख्या इत्थमुपलभ्यते—

उषा वा अश्वस्य मेध्यस्य शिरः॥ सूर्यश्चक्षुर्वातः प्राणो व्यात्तमग्निर्वैश्वानरः संवत्सर आत्माश्वस्य मेध्यस्य॥ द्यौः पृष्ठमन्तरिक्षमुदरं पृथिवी पाजस्यम्। दिशः पार्श्वे अवान्तरदिशः पर्शव ऋतवोऽङ्गानि मासाश्चार्धमासाश्च पर्वाण्यहोरात्राणि प्रतिष्ठा नक्षत्राण्यस्थीनि नभो मांसानि। ऊवध्यं सिकताः सिन्धवो गुदा यकृच्च क्लोमानश्च पर्वता ओषधयश्च वनस्पतयश्च लोमानि उद्यन् पूर्वार्धो निम्लोचञ्जघनार्धो तद्विजृम्भते यद्विद्योतते यद्विधूनुते तत्स्तनयति यन्मेहति तद्वर्षति वागेवास्य वाक्।

इत्थमश्वमेधीयाश्वस्य प्रत्यङ्गमाधिदैविकीव्याख्यां सत्यां को नाम विपश्चिद् ऋग्वेदस्य प्रथममण्डलस्य द्वाषष्टयुत्तरशततमे सूक्तेऽश्वस्यालम्भनं तस्याङ्गानां निकर्तनं पचनं च व्याख्यातुमर्हति, ऋते विनियोगमोहनिमज्जितेभ्यो याज्ञिकेभ्यः।

अश्वस्य संज्ञपनम्, तदुत्तरकृत्यम्—प्रत्यागतेऽश्वे मुख्यं यज्ञीयं कर्म प्रवर्तते। तत्र द्वितीये सुत्याहनि अश्वस्य संज्ञपनम्, अश्वमहिष्योः संगमः, ऋत्विजां राजपत्नीनां च परस्परम् अश्लीलभाषणं भवति इत्युक्तं पुरस्तात्।

अत्र प्रथमम् अश्वस्य संज्ञपनविषयमधिकृत्योच्यते। अन्यकर्मणोर्विषये अश्वमेधस्य राष्ट्रियस्वरूपनिदर्शनकाले वक्ष्यते।

अश्वमेधशब्दस्यार्थः—अश्वमेधशब्दे षष्ठीतत्पुरुषः समासः—अश्वस्य मेधः = अश्वमेधः। अयं **समासस्य** (अष्टाध्यायी ६।१।२२३) इत्यनेनौत्सर्गिकेण समास-

स्वरविधायकसूत्रेणान्तोदात्त । पूर्वपदे योऽश्वशब्दस्तस्याधिदैविकं स्वरूपं पुरस्तान्निदर्शितम् । इदानीं मेधशब्दार्थे विचारः क्रियते ।

मेधशब्दस्यार्थः—मेधशब्दे **मेधृ संगमे च** इत्यस्माद् धातोः भावेऽकर्तरि च कारके संज्ञायां घञ् प्रत्ययो भवति । **मेधृ संगमे च** इति धातुसूत्रे वर्तमानेन "च" शब्देन **मिदृ मेदृ मेधाहिंसनयोः** इति पूर्वसूत्रस्थौ "मेधाहिंसनयोः" अर्थौ समुच्चीयेते । तेन मेधशब्दस्य मेधाजननम्, हिंसनम्, संगमनं चेति त्रयोऽर्था लभ्यन्ते । मया कस्यचिद् व्याकरणान्तरस्य धातुपाठे **गतिहिंसनयोः** पाठो दृष्ट आसीद् इति स्मरामि । तथा सति मेधशब्दस्य गत्यर्थोऽपि ज्ञेयः ।

मेधशब्दान्ताः केचन शब्दाः—लौकिके वैदिके च वाङ्मये बहवो मेधान्ताः शब्दाः प्रसिद्धाः । तेषु केचिन्मेधशब्दार्थस्य विचाराय प्रस्तूयन्ते । तद्यथा—गृहमेध-पितृमेध-नरमेध-अश्वमेध-पुरुषमेध-सर्वमेध-गोमेध-अजमेध-अविमेध-इत्यादीनि ।

एषु गृहमेध-पितृमेध-शब्दावीदृशौ स्तः, ययोर्न कश्चिन्मेधशब्दं हिंसार्थकं मनुते । गृहमेधशब्दो **"गृहैर्गृहिणीभि[23]र्दारै[24]र्मेधन्ते संगच्छन्ते यत्र"** इत्येवं गृहस्थाश्रमं ब्रूते । कोशकारैरप्ययमर्थो गृहमेधस्य संगृह्यते । इत्थमेव 'गृहमेधिन्' शब्दो गृहस्थाश्रमिणं ब्रूते । यथा—**"प्रजायै गृहमेधिनाम्"** इति (रघुवंश १।७)। "गृहमेधिन्" इत्यत्र "गृहमेध" शब्दात् **"अत इनिठनौ"** (अष्टाध्यायी ५।२।११५) इति मत्वर्थं 'इनि' प्रत्ययः । अस्त्येका **गृहमेधीया** इष्टिः । इयं चातुर्मास्यस्य साकमेधाख्ये तृतीये पर्वणि सायमिज्यते । तदुक्तम्—**"मरुद्भ्यो गृहमेधिभ्यः सायं चरुः पयसि"** (कात्या० श्रौत ५।६।६। एवमन्येष्वपि श्रौतसूत्रेषु) । अत्र पयसि चरुर्हविरुक्तः । पितृमेधशब्दस्तु मृतस्यान्त्येष्टिं ब्रूते । अत्र पितृशब्दो मृतस्योपलक्षकः । तदुक्तं मनुना—

गुरोः प्रेतस्य शिष्यस्तु पितृमेधं समाचरन् ।
प्रेतहारैः समं तत्र दशरात्रेण शुध्यति ॥ (५।६५)

अस्मिन्नेवार्थे 'पितृमेध' शब्दो आश्वलायनगृह्यपरिशिष्टे तृतीयाध्याये श्रूयते—**अथ पितृमेधः संस्थिते ।** कात्यायनश्रौतसूत्रे तु मृतस्य पितुः स्मृतौ संवत्सरादूर्ध्वं पितृमेधाख्यं कर्म विहितम्—**पितृमेधः संवत्सरात् स्मृतौ** (२१।३।१) । इदम् अन्त्येष्टिकर्मणो भिन्नः पितृमेधः । अत्रापि मेधशब्दो यज्ञार्थक एव ।

नरमेधः—नायं क्वचित् साक्षादनेन नाम्नोपदिष्टोऽस्माभिरुपलब्धः । अत्र मेधशब्दो यज्ञवाच्येव । तेन नरमेधो नृयज्ञस्य पर्यायः । नृयज्ञः पञ्चमहायज्ञेषूत्तमः (अन्तिमः) । **नृयज्ञोऽतिथिपूजनम्** इत्याह मनुः (३।७०)। तेन नरमेधोऽतिथियज्ञः ।

गोमेध-अजमेध-अविमेधाः—यद्यप्येतन्नामकाः क्रतवो न क्वचिदस्माभिरुपलब्धाः, तथापि पश्वालम्भवादिन एतान् उदाहरन्ति । अत एतेषां विषये यद् वक्तुं

शक्यते तदस्माभिः "श्रौतयज्ञमीमांसायाम्" (पृष्ठ ८३-८६) विस्पष्टमुक्तम्। अत एतेषां विषये नेह प्रपञ्च्यते।

पुरुषमेधः—अस्य क्रतोर्यादृशी प्रक्रिया शतपथे श्रौतसूत्रेषु च दृश्यते, तदनुसारं पुरुषमेधे ये विविधप्रकारकाश्चतुरशीत्युत्तरशतसंख्याकाः पुरुषा आनीयन्ते, ते सर्वे पर्यग्निकरणानन्तरम् उत्सृज्यन्ते न त्वालभ्यन्ते। कर्मणः समाप्तिं **ब्रह्मणे स्वाहा, क्षत्राय स्वाहा** इत्येवमाज्येन हुत्वा क्रियते। अतः पुरुषमेधे मेधशब्दः संगमनार्थक एव, न हिंसनार्थक इति विस्पष्टम्। अस्मिन् विषयेऽस्माभिः श्रौतयज्ञ-मीमांसायाम् (पृष्ठ ७१-७६) विस्तरेण विवेचितम्।

सर्वमेधः—सर्वमेधे तु केषाञ्चित् पशूनामालम्भनं भवति (द्र०—कात्या० श्रौत० २१।२।३, तदीया कर्काचार्यकृता व्याख्या)।

अश्वमेधस्याश्वं क आलब्धुं समर्थः—पुरस्ताद् यज्ञीयाश्वस्य संवत्सरात् प्राक् प्रत्यावर्तननिषेधे या शातपथी श्रुतिरुद्धृता सा इत्थं वर्तते—

तमेत उभये देवमनुष्याः संविदाना अप्रत्यावर्तयन्तः संवत्सरं रक्षन्ति। तद् यं न प्रत्यावर्तयन्त्येष[२५] वा एष य एष तपति। क उ ह्येतमर्हति प्रत्यावर्तयितुम्। यद्ध्येनं प्रत्यावर्तयेयुः परागेवेदं सर्वं स्यात्। शत० १३।४।२।१६।

अत्र भगवता याज्ञवल्क्येनाश्वमेधीयाश्वस्यापरावर्तने यत् कारणमुक्तम्—**एष वा एष य एष तपति** अर्थाद् योऽयं यज्ञीयोऽश्वः स आधिदैविको य एष तपति सूर्यस्तत्प्रतिनिधिभूतः। सूर्यं कश्चित् संवत्सरात् प्राक् प्रत्यावर्तयितुमसमर्थः, तस्मात् तत्प्रतिनिधिभूतो यज्ञीयोऽश्वोऽपि संवत्सरात् प्राक् न परावर्त्यते।

इत्थमश्वमेधीयोऽश्वो यस्य प्रतिनिधिभूतः, तमेतं तपन्तं सूर्यं काऽपि दैवीशक्तिः सहस्रचतुर्युगेभ्यो योऽस्य स्थितिकालः, ततः प्रागालब्धुं हिंसितुं प्रध्वंसयितुमर्हति, तर्हि तस्य प्रतिनिधिभूतं यज्ञीयाश्वमपि न कश्चिद् यज्ञे तस्यायुषः (जीवनकालात्) प्रागालब्धुं प्राणैर्वियोजितुमर्हति। सत्येवं यज्ञीयाश्वस्यालम्भनं यद् यज्ञे कुर्वन्ति, तत्सर्वथा युक्तिविरुद्धम्।

अपि च अश्वस्यालम्भनं कृते याज्ञिका एकामृचं पठन्ति—

न वा उ एतन्म्रियसे न रिष्यसि देवाँ इदेषि पथिभिः सुगेभिः।
हरी ते युञ्जा पृषती अभूतामुपास्थाद् वाजी धुरि रासभस्य॥

—ऋग्वेद १।१६२।२१

माध्यन्दिनसंहितायामप्यश्वस्यालम्भनानन्तरमेको मन्त्रः पठ्यते। तस्य पूर्वार्धस्तु पूर्वोक्तया ऋचा समानः, उत्तरार्धस्त्वेवम्—

यत्रासते सुकृतो यत्र ते ययुस्तत्र त्वा देवः सविता दधातु॥

—यजु० २३।१६

उभयोः समाने पूर्वार्धे अश्वस्य मरणं हिंसनं च प्रत्यक्षं प्रतिषिध्यते। अत्र इदमप्यवधेयम्—ऋग्वेद इयमृक् तस्मिन् सूक्ते वर्तते, यस्मिन् अश्वालम्भनस्य कश्चिद् गन्धोऽस्तीति वक्तुं शक्यते। (एतस्मिन् विषये पूर्वं यदुक्तं (पृष्ठ ३२९) तद् द्रष्टव्यम्)।

यज्ञेषु पशूनां हिंसनम्—यस्मिन् काले आधिदैविकस्य विज्ञानस्य परिरक्षायै, यद्वाऽऽधिदैविके यज्ञे याः परोक्षा विविधा घटना घटन्ति, ताः प्रत्यक्षं निदर्शयितुं नाटकधर्मेण यज्ञानां प्रकल्पनाः पूर्वैर्भिऋर्षिभिः कृताः। तस्मिन् काले यज्ञेषु पशूनां हिंसनं न भवति स्म। तदुक्तं चरकसंहितायां भगवता वैशम्पायनेन[26]—**आदिकाले खलु यज्ञेषु पशवः समालभनीया बभूवुः, नालम्भाय प्रक्रियन्ते स्म** (चिकित्सास्थान १९।४) इति।

अस्मिन् चरकसंहितावाक्ये **समालभनीयाः आलम्भाय** इति द्वे पदे अप्यत्यन्ते महत्त्वपूर्णे। एतस्मादिदं विज्ञायते यत् पुराकाले **लभ लम्भ** इति द्वौ स्वतन्त्रौ धातू आस्ताम्। 'आलभ' इति तु प्राप्तिस्पर्शयोरर्थयोः प्रयुज्यते स्म, 'आलम्भ' इति तु हिंसार्थे। उत्तरकाले 'आलम्भ' इत्यस्य क्रियापदानां लोपे अवशिष्टानां केषाञ्चित् पदानामुत्तरकालिकैर्वैयाकरणैः 'आलभ' इत्यत्र नुमागमं विधाय यथाकथंचित् साधुत्वं प्रदर्शितम्।[27] महाभारते पुराणेषु चोपरिचरस्य वसो राज्ञो यदाख्यानमुपलभते तेनापि हस्तामलकवत् प्रत्यक्षं सिद्ध्यति यत् पुराकाले यज्ञेषु पशूनां वधो न भवति स्म। तदानींतना ऋषयश्च यज्ञेषु पशूनां हिंसनं नोररीकुर्वन्ति स्म। इदमप्येकमाश्चर्यकरम्, यद् यज्ञेषु हिंसायाः प्रवर्तने सत्यपि अद्ययावत् पशुयज्ञो "**पशुबन्ध**" नाम्ना स्मर्यते, न "**पशुवध**" नाम्ना। अस्येदमेव कारणं यत् पुरा सर्वेषु पशुयागेषु पशूनां यूपे बन्धने सति पर्यग्निकरणानन्तरं त उत्सृज्यन्ते स्म, यथा आरण्यका पशवः, पुरुषमेधे च पुरुषा उत्सृज्यन्ते। इदमप्यतिमहत्त्वाधायि तथ्यम्, यत् सर्वविधानां पशुयागानां विधायकवाक्येषु **आलभते आलभेत** वा इत्येव क्रिया श्रूयते न **आलम्भते आलम्भेत** वा। (आलम्भक्रियायाः पूर्वं स्वतन्त्रः प्रयोगो भवति स्म, तस्य लोपस्तु बहूत्तरकालं बभूव।)

उपरि ये द्वित्रा विषया नामग्रहरूपेण अर्थादतिसंक्षेपेण उक्तास्तेऽस्माभिः श्रौतयज्ञमीमांसायां विस्तरेण विवृताः। अत उत्तरं अश्वमेधक्रतो राष्ट्रियं स्वरूपं विवरिष्यते। तन्मध्य एव च मृताश्वमहिष्योः संगमस्य, ऋत्विजां राज्ञः पत्नीनाम् अश्लीलसंवादस्य च विषये वक्ष्यते।

अश्वमेधस्य राष्ट्रियं स्वरूपम्—अश्वमेधक्रतोराधिदैविकं स्वरूपं पुरस्तादुपवर्णितम्। सम्प्रति तस्य राष्ट्रियं स्वरूपं चिन्त्यते।

अश्वमेधेन राष्ट्रस्य सम्बन्धः—अश्वमेधेन असार्वभौमोऽमाण्डलिको राजा "सार्वभौमः"=सम्राट् सम्पद्यते अर्थाद् महद् राष्ट्रं लभते। **"कार्ये कारणशब्दः"**

इति न्यायेन यथा आयुषो निमित्तं घृतम् "**आयुर्वै घृतम्**" इत्युच्यते, तथैव राष्ट्रप्राप्तौ निमित्तभूतोऽश्वमेधो ब्राह्मणग्रन्थेषु बहुत्र **राष्ट्रं वा अश्वमेधः** इत्युच्यते। अयं राष्ट्राश्वमेधयोः सम्बन्धः "असार्वभौमो राजा अश्वमेधेन यजेत" इति वचनाद् यद्वा "सर्वकामो वा राजा अश्वमेधेन यजेत" इति वचनादवगम्यते। यदा अश्वमेधेन सामान्यो राजा सार्वभौमत्वं सम्राट्त्वं वा लभते, तदा तस्य सर्व एव कामाः पूर्तिं लभन्ते।

शतपथादिब्राह्मणग्रंथानां मुख्यं प्रयोजनं यज्ञीयप्रक्रियाया व्याख्यानं वर्तते। तथाप्यश्वमेधप्रकरणे शतपथादिब्राह्मणप्रवक्तृभिरश्वमेधप्रक्रियाव्याख्यानेन सह तस्य राष्ट्रियं पक्षमपि पदे पदे प्रकटीकृतम्। राष्ट्रस्य रक्षा तदैव भवति यदा सर्वेऽपि तन्निवासिनो मनुष्या तद्रक्षणव्यापारे संलग्नाः स्युः। अयमर्थो यज्ञीयाश्वस्य रक्षणे राजपुत्राणां, सामान्यक्षत्रियपुत्राणां, सूतपुत्राणां, दूतादिकर्मणि नियुक्तानां पुत्राणां च नियोजनाल्लभ्यते। यद्वा चत्वारोऽपि वर्णा यदा राष्ट्ररक्षणे प्रवृत्ता भवन्ति, तदैव राष्ट्रं रक्षितुं शक्यते। अत एव यदा राष्ट्रस्योपरि कस्यचिन्महाबलवतोऽभियानं प्रवर्त्तेत, तदा ब्राह्मणैरपि शस्त्राण्यादेयानीति मनुराह। द्विसहस्रवर्षात् प्राग् यदा यूनानवासिनां बाहीकप्रदेशे (पञ्चनदप्रान्ते) बलवदाक्रमणमभूत्, तदा[२८] मालवमण्डलस्थानां कठशाखीयानां ब्राह्मणानां प्रत्याक्रमणेन यवनाः पराजयं प्राप्य स्वदेशं प्रतीयुरितीतिहासे प्रसिद्धम्।

अतोऽश्वमेधस्य मुख्यं प्रयोजनं सृष्टियज्ञस्यैकदेशभूतस्याश्वस्य सूर्यस्य वार्षिकी उत्तरायणदक्षिणायनरूपा च या गतिः, तस्य रज्जुभिरभीशुभी रश्मिभिर्ग्रहोपग्रहाणां मर्यादायां रक्षणरूपं च यद्विज्ञानं तस्य व्याख्यानं वर्तते। द्वितीयं च दृष्टप्रयोजनं सार्वभौमत्वप्राप्त्या सह राष्ट्रस्योपलब्धिः, तद्रक्षणं चास्ति।

अश्वमेधक्रतौ यत् स्वराज्यस्य चतसृभ्यो दिग्भ्यो जलाहरणं तत्स्वराज्यस्य चतसृषु दिक्षु या सीमा तस्या निदर्शनं प्रयोजनम्। यच्च स्वराज्ये वर्तमानानां ग्राम्याणां, आरण्यानां, जलचराणां, वायव्यानां पशुपक्षीणां समाहरणं, तत् स्वराष्ट्रस्य जङ्गमसम्पत्तेर्निदर्शनम्, यद्वा स्वप्रजानां नानाविधपशुपक्षीणां दर्शनेन ज्ञानपरिवर्धनं मनोरञ्जनं प्रयोजनं ज्ञेयम्। यथा सम्प्रति बृहन्नगरेषु "चिड़ियाघर" इति नाम्ना प्रसिद्धस्थाने विविधपशुपक्षीणां समवायेनानेकेषां तत्तत्प्राणिविषयकं ज्ञानं वर्धते बालानां सामान्यजनानां च मनोरञ्जनं भवति।

पूर्वमश्वमेधप्रक्रियानिदर्शनेऽश्वस्यालम्भनानन्तरम् अश्वमहिष्योः संगमः, ऋत्विग्राजपत्नीनां चाश्लीलभाषणं निर्दशितम्। एतत्सर्वं कृत्यं श्रौतसूत्रेषु वर्तते। कात्यायनश्रौतसूत्रे तु सर्वाधिकाः शुक्लयजुषः (२३।१९-३१) त्रयोदशमन्त्रा अत्र विनियोजिताः।

उक्तमन्त्राणां राष्ट्रपरं व्याख्यानम्—शतपथब्राह्मणे शुक्लयजुषः २३।१९-३१

संख्याकानां त्रयोदशमन्त्राणां द्वयोः स्थानयोर्व्याख्यानमुपलभ्यते (१३।२।८।४ इत्यत आरभ्य १३।२।३।६ पर्यन्तम्, तथा १३।५।२।१।८ पर्यन्तम्)। अनयोः प्रथमे स्थाने **गणानांत्वे**त्यादीनां त्रयोदशमन्त्राणां राष्ट्रपरा व्याख्योपलभ्यते। अपरत्र श्रौतसूत्रे यथा विनियोगो दृश्यते, तत्पराऽश्लीला व्याख्या वरिर्वात।

अत्र या द्वितीया श्रौतसूत्रानुसारिणी व्याख्या, तद्विषये बहवः प्रश्ना उद्भवन्ति। तद्यथा—

१—नहि समग्रे शतपथेऽन्यत्र क्वचिद् एकस्मिन्नेव प्रकरणे कस्यचित् कयोश्चित् केषांचिद् वा मन्त्राणां द्विविधं व्याख्यानमुपलभ्यते।

२—द्वितीयं व्याख्यानं तु यत्रोपलभ्यते तस्य ब्राह्मणस्यारम्भे **एते उक्त्वा यदध्रिगोः परिशिष्टं भवति** इति वाक्यमुपलभ्यते। कृत्स्नेऽपि शतपथे कस्मिन्नपि कर्मणि नैतादृशं परिशिष्टं दृश्यते। अपि च 'परिशिष्ट' शब्दः प्रायेण ग्रन्थेऽनुक्तानां विषयाणां ग्रन्थसमाप्त्यनन्तरं यत्र प्रतिपादनं भवति तस्मिन्नर्थे प्रयुज्यते, यद्वा तादृशा विषया ग्रन्थान्तरेषु व्याख्यायन्ते। यथा कात्यायनश्रौतसूत्रेऽनुक्ता विषया अष्टादशसु कात्यायनपरिशिष्टेषु संगृह्यन्ते। ग्रन्थमध्ये तु न क्वचिदपि समायोजनं भवति। इदमप्यत्रावधेयम्—इदमध्रिगोः परिशिष्टं नाश्वमेधस्य कर्मणः समाप्त्यनन्तरम्, अपित्वश्वमेधकर्मणो मध्य एव दृश्यते। यदि **गणानांत्वे**त्यादीनां त्रयोदशमन्त्राणां द्वितीयं व्याख्यानं राष्ट्रपरस्य प्रथमव्याख्यानस्यानन्तरमेवाभविष्यत्तदा शतपथकारस्योक्तानां त्रयोदशमन्त्राणां व्याख्यान्तरमप्यभिप्रेतम् इति वक्तुं शक्यमभविष्यत्। परन्तु द्वितीयं व्याख्यानं त्वश्वमेधकर्मणः समाप्तेः किञ्चिदेव पूर्वमुपलभ्यते। त्रयोदशमन्त्राणां व्याख्यानस्यानन्तरं ब्रह्मोद्यं वपाहोमो राज्ञां गाथा इत्येतान्येव कर्माण्युक्तानि।

३—"**अध्रिगोः परिशिष्टं भवति**" इति प्रकरणे ऋत्विजां राजपत्नीनां चाश्लीलभाषणानन्तरमश्लीलभाषणेन दूषितं मुखं सुरभिमत् कर्तुं सुरभिमत्या ऋचो जप उच्यते—**अथेतरे सुरभीमतीमृचमन्ततोऽन्वाहुः दधिक्राव्णो अकारिषमिति। अप वा एतेभ्य आयुर्देवताः क्रामन्ति। ये यज्ञेऽपूतां वाचं वदन्ति वाचमेवैतत् पुनते देवयज्यायै देवातानामपक्रमाय।** शत० १३।५।२।६-१०। [तै० ब्रा० (३।६।७।४) अपि शब्दभेदेनायमेवार्थ उक्तः।]

इदं याज्ञिकानां कर्म तथाभूतमेव, यथा लोके कश्चित् पूर्वं मलं भक्षयित्वा पूतिगन्धि मुखं सुरभिगन्धि कर्तुं सुगन्धि पायसमश्नीयात्। विपश्चितस्तु का वार्ता, कश्चिन्मूर्खतमोऽप्येवंविधं कर्म नाभिनन्दितुमर्हति।

एतैः कारणैर्विज्ञायते यदध्रिगोः परिशिष्टं न शतपथस्य मूलभागः, अपितु कालान्तरे श्रौतसूत्रोक्तकर्मणां श्रुतिमूलत्वं निदर्शनाय प्रक्षिप्तम्।

४—तैत्तिरीयब्राह्मणे यच्छतपथस्य प्रतिपक्षीभूतं वर्तते, तस्मिन्नपि त्रयोदशा-

न्तर्गता केचन मन्त्राः (यावन्तः तैत्तिरीयशाखायां पठ्यन्ते) तथैव राष्ट्रपरा व्याख्यायन्ते यथा शतपथस्य प्रथमस्थाने व्याख्यायन्ते। इदमप्यत्रावधेयम्—तैत्तिरीयब्राह्मणे आपस्तम्बसूत्रोक्ता अश्वमहिष्योः संगमनरूपा ऋत्विजां राजपत्नीनां चाश्लीलभाषणरूपा चान्या व्याख्योपलभ्यते। केवलं राष्ट्रपक्षीयमेवैतेषां मन्त्राणां व्याख्यानं दृष्टिपथं याति (तै० ब्रा० ३।९।६।४; ३।५।७।१-४)। तैत्तिरीयब्राह्मणस्य व्याख्याता सायणाचार्यस्तु सूत्रकारमतमनुरुद्ध्य ब्राह्मणोक्तं राष्ट्रपक्षीयं व्याख्यानमपि बलाद् अन्यथा व्याचख्यौ (भट्टभास्करीया तै० ब्रा० व्याख्या सम्प्रति नास्मत्सकाशे विद्यते)।

तैत्तिरीये ब्राह्मणे मन्त्राणां राष्ट्रपक्षीयस्यैव व्याख्यानस्योपलब्ध्याऽपि वक्तुं शक्यते यत् शतपथे अध्रिगोः परिशिष्टे यन्मन्त्राणामश्लीलं व्याख्यानं तस्य प्रक्षिप्तत्वं द्योतयति।

५—यजुषः **"उत्सक्थ्या अवगुदं धेहि"** (२३।२१) इति मन्त्रेण महिषीसंगमे यजमानोऽश्वम् अभिमन्त्रयते—"हे अश्व! अस्या महिष्या अवगुदं या योनिः तस्यां स्वलिङ्गं संचारय।" मानुषस्त्रीणां योनिप्रदेशो गुदप्रदेशादूर्ध्वं भवति न तु नीचैः। पशुस्त्रीणां गुदेन्द्रिय ऊर्ध्वं भवति, योनिप्रदेशस्तु नीचैः। अतोऽश्वमहिष्योः संगमे उक्तमन्त्रेण यजमानस्याश्वस्याभिमन्त्रणं **दृष्टविरोधादप्रमाणम्।**

६—**"यकासकौ"** (यजुः २३।२२) इति मन्त्रे **'गभे' 'पसे'** इत्येते पदे स्तः। अश्लीलभाषणपक्षे मन्त्रव्याख्यातारोऽनयोः पदयोराद्यन्तविपर्ययनियमेन स्त्रीयोनिवाचिनि **"भगे"** पुंप्रजननवाचिनि **"सपे"** रूपं परिवर्तयन्ति। शतपथब्राह्मणे (१३।२।९।६) तु राष्ट्रपरे व्याख्याने यथामन्त्रमेव पदे व्याख्याते।

इत्थमुक्त मन्त्राणाम् अश्लीलव्याख्यानं दृष्टविरोधाद् यथामन्त्रं पदयोः शतपथे व्याख्यानदर्शनाच्च दूषितं ज्ञेयम्।

अश्वमेधस्य राष्ट्रपरकव्याख्यानस्य पुनरुद्धारकः—परःसहस्रवर्षेभ्यः कल्पसूत्रोक्तं विनियोगमनुरुद्ध्य मन्त्रव्याख्यातारो याज्ञिका शुक्लयजुषः २३।१९-३१ संख्याकानां मन्त्राणाम् अश्वमहिषीसंगनरूपम् ऋत्विजां राजपत्नीनां चाश्लीलभाषणपरं मन्त्रार्थं व्याचक्षते स्म।

प्रथमं तावदिदं चिन्तनीयं यन्मन्त्रार्थानुसारं कर्मसु विनियोगो भवति, उत वा विनियोगानुसारं मन्त्राणां व्याख्यानम्। अस्मिन् विषये शास्त्रकाराणामेष निश्चयो यन्मन्त्रार्थानुसारमेव कर्मसु मन्त्रा विनियोक्तव्याः। तथा चोक्तम्—

१—**एतद्वै यज्ञस्य समृद्धं यद् रूपसमृद्धं यत्कर्म क्रियमाणमृग् यजुर्वाभिवदति** (गो० ब्रा० २।२।६)। 'यजुर्वा' इति पदरहितमिदं वाक्यमैतरेयब्राह्मणे बहुत्र (१,४,१३,१६,१७) उपलभ्यते। एतद्वचनानुसारं मन्त्रार्थानुकूलेनैव विनियोगेन भाव्यमित्येषोऽभिप्रायः स्पष्ट एव।

२—भगवान् जैमिनिरपि **तच्चोदकेषु मन्त्राख्या** (मी० २।२।३२) सूत्रेण अभिधानस्य चोदकेष्वेव मन्त्रसंज्ञां विदधन् मन्त्रार्थानुकूलं विनियोगो भवतीत्यर्थं ब्रवीति।

सत्येवं ये विनियोगा मन्त्रार्थं नानुसरन्ति तेऽप्रामाणिका एव।[29] तस्मान्मन्त्रार्थानुसारेण विनियोगेन भाव्यम्। यत्तु विनियोगानुसारं मन्त्रार्थवचनं तद् **अश्वस्य पुरस्ताद् रथयोजनवद् हास्यास्पदम्।**

अतएव दयानन्दसरस्वतीस्वामिना 'ऋग्वेदादिभाष्यभूमिका' ग्रन्थे 'भाष्यकरणशङ्कासमाधानविषये' कात्यायनश्रौतसूत्रानुसारं **गणानां त्वा** इत्यादीनां (यजुः २३।१९-३१) त्रयोदशमन्त्राणां महीधरकृतम् अश्वमहिषीसंवादादिरूपमश्लीलं व्याख्यानं निराकृत्य शतपथब्राह्मणानुसारमेषां मन्त्राणां राष्ट्रपरं व्याख्यानं व्यधायि। **राष्ट्रं वा अश्वमेधः** (शत० १३।१।६।३) इत्यादिभिर्वचनैः **"राज्ञो न्यायधर्मपूर्वकं प्रजापालनमश्वमेधः"** इत्युक्तम् (द्र०—सत्यार्थप्रकाश, समु० ११)।

एतेनेदं शक्यते वक्तुं यद् दयानन्दसरस्वतीस्वामिना शतपथब्राह्मणानुसारमश्वमेधस्य राष्ट्रपरिपालनरूपो योऽभिप्राय आसीत् तस्य पुनरुद्धारः कृतः। विनियोगानुसारं या मन्त्रव्याख्यानपरम्परा आसीत् तां निराकृत्य मन्त्रार्थानुसारस्य विनियोगस्य युक्तता प्रत्यपादि। तदुक्तं दयानन्दसरस्वतीस्वामिना—

अत्र वेदभाष्ये कर्मकाण्डस्य वर्णनं शब्दार्थतः करिष्यते। परन्त्वेतैर्वेदमन्त्रैः कर्मकाण्डविनियोजितैर्यत्र यत्राग्निहोत्राद्यश्वमेधान्ते यद्यत् कर्त्तव्यं तत्तदत्र विस्तरतो न वर्णयिष्यते। कुतः? **कर्मकाण्डानुष्ठानस्यैतरेयशतपथब्राह्मणपूर्वमीमांसाश्रौतसूत्रादिषु यथार्थं विनियोजितत्वात्। ... तस्माद्युक्तिसिद्धो वेदादिप्रमाणानुकूलो मन्त्रार्थानुसृतस्तदुक्तोऽपि विनियोगो ग्रहीतुं योग्योऽस्ति।** (ऋग्वेदादिभाष्यभूमिका, प्रतिज्ञाविषयारम्भे)

वेदानां विषये यानपि दोषान् पाश्चात्याः पौरस्त्याश्च विद्वांस उद्भावयन्ति, तस्य प्रधानं कारणं कल्पसूत्रोक्तविनियोगानुसारं वेदव्याख्यानमेव विद्यते। अत एव दयानन्दसरस्वतीस्वामिना **"युक्तिप्रमाणसिद्धः, वेदादिप्रमाणानुकूलः, मन्त्रार्थानुसृतः"** इति त्रयो गुणा विनियोगस्य प्रतिपादिताः।[30] एतैर्गुणैरन्वितो विनियोग एव प्रमाणार्हः। एतद्गुणरहिता विनियोगा न केवलं प्रमाणानर्हाः, अपि तु विनियोगशब्दः प्रयोगानर्हः।

इत्थम् अश्वमेधस्य क्रतोराधिदैविकस्वरूपं यथाप्रमाणं यथामति यथाशक्ति विवृतम्। अत्र केवलं चतुरक्षस्य शुनो मारणम् अधस्ताच्चाश्वस्य जले प्रवाहणरूपं यत्कर्म क्रियते, तस्याधिदैविकस्वरूपमिह नोल्लिखितम्। यतस्तस्य किमाधिदैविकस्वरूपमिति मयाऽद्य यावन्न विज्ञातम्। प्रमाणरहिता तु या कल्पना क्रियते सा नासत्यभाषणादतिरिच्यत इति मम मतम्।

शतपथादिब्राह्मणग्रन्थेषु **राष्ट्रं वाऽश्वमेधः** इति वचनाद् अश्वमेधीयमन्त्राणां राष्ट्रपरस्य व्याख्यानस्य च दर्शनाद् अश्वमेधस्य राष्ट्रपरं स्वरूपमपि विद्यते। दयानन्दसरस्वतीस्वामिनाऽयमेव पक्षोऽश्वमेधस्योररीकृतः।

याज्ञिकेषु य आत्मयाजिनस्तेषाम् अश्वमेधस्य अध्यात्मस्वरूपमपि विद्यते, तन्नेह विवृत्यते। अश्वमेधस्य एकदेशमाश्रित्य केचन लौकिकाः पक्षा अपि विवरितुं शक्याः। इत्थमयम् अश्वमेधनामा महाक्रतुः विविधै रूपैः समन्वितो वर्तते। यज्ञीय-पक्षस्तु तस्यैकदेशभूत एव। इत्यलमतिविस्तरेण।

टिप्पण्यः

१. इयं 'श्रौतयज्ञमीमांसा' हिन्दीभाषानुवादेन सहिता 'रामलाल कपूर ट्रस्ट, बहालगढ़ (सोनीपत, हरियाणा) [पिन १३१०२१]' इति स्थानादुपलभ्यते।

२. 'सोमयागे वृष्टिविज्ञानम्' 'सुपर्णचितेस्त्रिभिः प्रयोगैः कल्पादौ आदित्यस्य विभिन्नस्थितीनां निरूपणम्' इति द्वौ लेखौ 'वैदिक-सिद्धान्त-मीमांसा' संज्ञकस्य ग्रन्थस्य द्वितीयभागे द्रष्टव्यौ।

३. उभयोः श्रौतसूत्रयोराकरस्थाननिर्देशं समानं दृष्ट्वा नात्र भ्रमितव्यम्।

४. रात्रिसत्रन्यायो मीमांसायाश्चतुर्थाध्याये तृतीयपादेऽष्टमाधिकरणे (सूत्र १७-१८-१९) द्रष्टव्यः।

५. शबरस्वामिना मीमांसाभाष्ये (१।२।४) "तरति मृत्युं तरति ब्रह्महत्यां योऽश्वमेधेन यजते य उ चैनं वेद" इत्येवं पाठ उद्ध्रियते।

६. एवं सति यो राजा तस्करान् अश्वहारिणो जेतुं [असमर्थः] बलहीनोऽश्व-मेधेन यष्टुमारभत एष राजा परासिच्यते स्वराष्ट्रादपि भ्रश्यत इत्यर्थः। द्र० सायणभाष्यम्।

७. तुलना कार्या—"अपि राजन्यं वैश्यं वा ब्राह्मण इत्येव ब्रूयात्। ब्राह्मणो हि जायते यो यज्ञाज्जायते।" शत० ३।२।१।४०। यथा दीक्षानन्तरं ब्राह्मणं यजमानं 'दीक्षितोऽयं ब्राह्मणः' इत्युच्चैराश्राव्यते, तथैव राजन्यवैश्ययोर्दीक्षा-नन्तरं 'दीक्षितोऽयं ब्राह्मणः' इत्येव आश्रावयेत्।

८. सैध्रको महासारो वृक्षविशेष इति सायणः। तै० ब्रा० भाष्य ३।८।४।१॥

९. आपस्तम्बे श्रौतसूत्रे तु अश्वरक्षिण इत्थं निर्दिष्टाः—"शतं कवचिनो रक्षन्ति। अपर्यावर्तयन्तोऽश्वमनुचरन्ति। चतुःशता इत्येकेषाम्। शतं तल्प्या राजपुत्राः सन्नद्धाः सन्नद्धसारथिनः, शतमुग्रा अराजानः सन्नद्धाः सन्नद्धसारथिनः, शतं वैश्या विपथिनः, शतं शूद्रा वरूथिनः। तेऽस्य गोप्तारो भवन्ति।" आप० श्रौत २०।४।१०-१४॥

१०. कुरानमतानुयायिनश्चान्द्रसौरवर्षयोः सामञ्जस्यं न विदधति। अतस्ते-षाम् ईदादिपर्वाणि प्रतिवर्षं दशदिनानि पुरस्तादुपसर्पन्ति। सत्येवं षट्त्रिंशत्सु वर्षेषु तेषां सप्तत्रिंशद् वर्षाणि भवन्ति।

११. वेद मासो धृतव्रतो द्वादश प्रजावतः। वेदा य उपजायते। ऋ० १।२५।८॥

१२. इत्थमेव किञ्चिद् भेदेन तैत्तिरीयब्राह्मणे (३।८।३।३)ऽपि पठ्यते।

१३. अयं व्यवस्थितविकल्पः पाणिनीये तन्त्रे बहुत्राश्रीयते।

१४. आधिदैविकोऽश्वः सूर्यो न पृथिव्यादीनां परितो भ्रमति। तथापि 'यादृगेव ददृशे तादृगुच्यते' (ऋ० ५।४४।६) इति वैदिकन्यायेन सूर्यस्योदयं तस्यास्ताचलं च गमनं जना उपलभन्ते। अत एव सूर्यो ग्रहोपग्रहान् प्रति भ्रमतीति वादः प्रवर्तते।

१५. माता भूमिः पुत्रोऽहं पृथिव्याः। अथर्व० १२।१।१२॥

१६. अथर्ववेदस्य चतुर्दशे काण्डे पठिते द्वे सूक्ते विवाहकर्मणि विनियुक्ते स्तः। उक्तो मन्त्रः किञ्चित् पाठभेदेन पारस्करगृह्यसूत्रे-(१।६।३)ऽपि विवाहकर्मणि विनियुक्त उपलभ्यते।

१७. अत्र 'एष' शब्दः पूर्ववृत्तमश्वं ब्रवीति। एष (अश्वो) वा एष य एष तपति।

१८. तस्य रश्मिसहस्रं तु वर्षशीतोष्णनिस्रवम्। तासां चतुःशता नाड्यो वर्षन्ते चित्रमूर्त्तयः॥ वायुपुराण ५३।१६; मत्स्यपुराण १२८।१९, ब्रह्माण्डपुराण पूर्वभाग २४।२६॥

१९. उत्तरस्मिन् मन्त्रे, यदा गभीरवेपा असुरो वृत्रो महामेघो सूर्यमाच्छादयति, सूर्यो दृष्टिपथं नायाति, तदा मनुष्याः पृच्छन्ति—**क्वेदानीं सूर्यः कश्चिकेत कतमां द्यां रश्मिरस्या ततान** (ऋ० १।३५।७)।

२०. नामानुक्रमणी, पंक्ति ८५-८६ द्रष्टव्य—वैदिकनिघण्टुसंग्रह, पृष्ठ-१००। सम्पादक—पं० धर्मवीरो विद्यावारिधिः। प्राप्तिस्थानम्—रामलाल कपूर ट्रस्ट, बहालगढ़ (सोनीपत, हरियाणा) पिन १३१०२१।

२१. एतत्सूक्तस्थाः सर्वेऽपि मन्त्राः शुक्लयजुषि २९।१२-२४ पर्यन्तमुपलभ्यन्ते।

२२. एतत्सूक्तथाः सर्वेऽपि मन्त्राः शुक्लयजुषि २५।२४-४५ अपि पठ्यन्ते।

२३. द्र०—"न गृहं गृहमित्याहुर्गृहिणी गृहमुच्यते" इति सुभाषितम्।

२४. दारशब्दः पुंल्लिङ्गो नित्यबहुवचनान्त इति वचनं तु प्रायिकम्। एकवचनेऽप्यस्य प्रयोगो दृश्यते। यथा—'श्रोत्रियस्य दारेण नोपहसते।' बृह० उप० ६।४।१२॥ 'आचार्यदारे'। आप० धर्म० १।२।७॥ 'दारे'। तन्त्राख्यायिका, पृष्ठ ६७, श्लोक १५८॥ एवं 'सिकता-अप्सरस्' शब्दयोरपि बहुवचनान्तत्वं प्रायिकम्। द्र०—वैदिक-सिद्धान्त-मीमांसा, भाग २॥

२५. अस्यायमभिप्रायः—एषोऽश्वो वा एष य एष तपति......।

२६. 'चरक इति वैशम्पायनस्याख्या' काशिका ४।३।१०४॥ अत्र 'दुष्कृताय

चरकाचार्यम्' इति मदीयो लेखो द्रष्टव्यः। वैदिकसिद्धान्तमीमांसा, भाग १, पृष्ठ १७६-१६१।

२७. उभयोः 'लभ लम्भ' इति पृथग् धात्वोः शब्दानाम् एकस्माद् लभ धातोः सम्बन्धे कृते भ्रमोऽयमुत्पन्नो यद् आलभ इत्यस्य हिंसाऽप्यर्थो वर्तते। अयं भ्रम एव कालान्तरे यज्ञे पशूनां वधे मुख्यं कारणं समपद्यत।

२८. इदं मालवमण्डलं पञ्चनदस्थं ज्ञेयम्।

२६. एतद्विषये श्रौतयज्ञमीमांसायां 'काल्पनिका विनियोगाः' इति प्रकरणं (पृष्ठ ३८-४०) द्रष्टव्यम्।

३०. एषां सप्रमाणं सोदाहरणं च व्याख्या श्रौतयज्ञमीमांसायां ३३-३४ पृष्ठयोर्द्रष्टव्या।

22

MĀDHAVA ON MĪMĀṂSĀ

*With special reference to his Sarvadarśanasaṁgraha**

HARUO KURATA

The Sarvadarśanasaṁgraha[1] (*SDS*) by Mādhava is regarded as a good and authoritative introductory work to the different systems of Indian Philosophy.[2] At the beginning of the work, it is said:

"Having thoroughly searched the texts of former teachers, very hard to be crossed, the fortunate Sāyaṇa-Mādhava the lord has expounded them for the delight of the good. Let the virtuous listen with a mind from which all envy has been put far away; who does not find delight in a garland strung of various flowers?[3]

Mādhava reviews the theories of all the philosophical schools, and *SDS* is likened to a garland strung of various flowers.

The following is an attempt to throw further light on the viewpoint of Mādhava as a Mīmāṁsaka impartial to both views of Kumārila and Prabhākara.[4]

Mādhava flourished towards the middle of the fourteenth century.[5] According to the introductory remarks of the *Parāśara-mādhavīya*, Mādhava was a brahmin of *Bhāradvājagotra*, of *Baudhāyanasūtra* and a student of *Yajuḥśākhā*, that Māyaṇa was his father and Śrīmatī, his mother and that he had two brothers, Sāyaṇa and Bhoganātha.[6]

Mādhava was both an able administrator and profound scholar, or a civil as well as spiritual advisor of Bukkarāya and Harihara, sovereigns of Vijayanagara on the Godāvarī, as his father Māyaṇa had been of their father and predecessor Śaṅgama, who reigned over the whole peninsula of India.[7]

1. *Jaiminīyanyāyamālā*

Mādhava is credited with the authorship of many works. In

the field of the Mīmāṁsā, he wrote the *Jaiminīyanyāyamālā* (*JNM*), in verse, attended with his own commentary, named *Vistara* (*JNMV*) in prose. It follows the order of Jaimini's *Mīmāṁsāsūtra* (*JS*), not by way of paraphrase, but as a summary.[8]

In the preface of *JNM*, he says that he will begin to explain the *śrautadharma* for *dvijas*, after completing the explanation of the *smārta dharma* treated in the *Parāśarasmṛti* for all the varṇāśramas.[9] So *JNM* appears to have been the next performance undertaken after the completion of his commentary on Parāśara's Institutes of Law; and it suitably enough preceded the great commentaries on the whole of the Vedas, as will be cleared later. Anyway, we can easily point out that *JNM* and the *Parāśaramādhavīya* were composed by the same author, Mādhava.

He says in one of the introductory verses that of the fact that Pārthasārathimiśra's *Śāstradīpikā* (*ŚD*) has not in all *adhikaraṇas* given the *pūrvapakṣa* and the *siddhānta* views in verse, he proposes to do that uniformly in *JNM*.[10]

He sometimes explains separately the doctrine of Kumārila and of Prabhākara, under each head; but more commonly confined to that of Kumārila alone.[11]

2. Chapter XII of the *Sarvadarśanasaṁgraha* (*SDS XII*)

SDS consists of sixteen chapters, which deal with different philosophical systems one by one, culminating in the Advaita philosophy in the last sixteenth chapter.[12]

Mādhava reviews the theories of all the philosophical systems, referring to their fundamental texts or popular books current in his day, without a partial idea.

The philosophical system of the Mīmāṁsakas is dealt with in the twelfth chapter, named Jaimini-darśana (=*SDS XII*), the contents of which are—

(A) Introductory remarks (11.1∼3)

(B) Contents of the *Mīmāṁsāsūtra* (11.4∼17)

(C) Significance of the *Mīmāṁsā* (11.18∼127)

(D) *apauruṣeyatva* of the Veda (11.128∼216)

(E) *svataḥprāmāṇyavāda* (11.217~285)

(F) *abhihitānvayavāda* and *anvitābhidhānavāda* (11.286—291).

The number in parentheses show the lines in the Chapter of Jaimini-darśana in the *Sarvadarśanasaṁgraha of Sāyaṇa-Mādhava*, ed. with an original commentary in Sanskrit by Mahamahopadhyaya Vasudev Shastri Abhyankar (Poona: 1924).

3. *JNMV* and *SDS XII*[13]

A comparison of *SDS XII* with *JNMV* will make it clear that the first half of *SDS XII*, which gives the contents of *JS*[13] and the significance of the study of Mīmāṁsā, has a close relation with the latter half of the introductory part (*Granthāvataraṇikā*) and the first *adhikaraṇa* (*Jijñāsādhikaraṇa*) of *JNMV*.

The comparison of those two texts will be shown as follows:

(1) Phrases in italics show the coincidence of the phrases of *SDS XII* with those of *JNMV*, with transposition of words only.

(2) Phrases in bold italics show the correspondence of two texts.

(3) Phrases in roman show the correspondence in the meaning of two texts.

(4) The parts in brackets ([ ]) have no correspondence to each other.

(The following comparative lists are borrowed with slight changes from the paper written in Japanese by me in collaboration with Prof. S. Mayeda.)

[A]

SDS XII	JNMV (Granthāvataraṇikā)
l. 4	p. 5, *ll.* 3-10
[sā hi mīmāṁsā] ***dvādaśalakṣaṇī***.	[śāstrasyā'dhyāyānāṁ cā'sādhāraṇaṁ viṣayaṁ darśayati. . . (stanzas 11-12), lakṣaṇāny adhyāyāḥ. dvādaśānāṁ lakṣaṇānāṁ samāhāro] ***dvādaśalakṣaṇī***. [tādṛśasya dvādaśalakṣaṇopetasya śāstrasya dharmo viṣayaḥ. pra-

	māṇādayaḥ prasaṅgāntā dvādaśapadārthāḥ kramād dvādaśānām adhyāyānāṃ viṣayāḥ].
ll. 4-5 [tatra] *prathame'dhyāye vidhyarthavādamantrasmṛti**nāmadhey*** [ārthakasya śabdarāśeḥ] ***prāmāṇyam.***	p. 5, *ll.* 10-11 *prathame'dhyāye* [vidhyarthavādādirūpaṁ] ***pramāṇaṁ*** [nirūpitam]. p. 5, *ll.* 26-28 [prathame pāde]—*vidhi* [rūpaṁ mānam īritam. dvitīye] *arthavāda* [rūpam. arthavādo] *mantrasyā* ['py upalakṣakaḥ. tṛtīye] *smṛti* [rūpam. smṛtir ācāram apy upalakṣayati. caturthe udbhiccitrādi] *nāma*-[rūpam].
ll. 5-6 *dvitīye upodghātakarmabhedapramāṇāpavāda**prayogabheda*** [rūpo'rthaḥ].	p. 5, *l.* 11 *dvitīye* — [yāgadānādikarmabhedaḥ]. p. 6, *ll.* 3-6 [dvitīyādhyāyasya prathame pāde—ākhyātam evā'pūrvabodhakam, apūrvasadasadbhāvaścetyādikaḥ karmabhedacintopayukta] *upodghāto* varṇitaḥ. dvitīye—dhātubhedapunaruktyādibhiḥ] *karmabhedaḥ*. [tṛtīye—rathantarādīnāṁ karmabheda] *prāmāṇyāpavādaḥ*. [caturthe—nityakāmyayoḥ] ***prayogayor bhedaḥ.***
ll. 6-8 *tṛtīye śrutiliṅgavākyādivirodhapratipattikarmānārabhyādhītabahupradhānopakārakaprayājādiyājamāna**cintanam.***	p. 5, *ll.* 11-12 *tṛtīye*— [prayājādīnāṁ darśapūrṇamāsādyarthatvena taccheṣatvam.

p. 6, *ll.* 9-13
tṛtīyādhyāyasya prathame pāde —śeṣatvabodhakānāṁ śrutiliṅgādīnāṁ madhye] *śrutir* ***vicāritā.***
[dvitīye]—*liṅgam.*
[tṛtīye]—vākya[prakaraṇā]*di.*
[caturthe—nivītopavītādiṣv arthavādatvavidhitvādinirṇayahetuḥ śrutyādeḥ paraspara]*virodha* [sadasadbhāvaś ca].
[pañcame]—*pratipattikarmāṇi.*
[ṣaṣṭhe]—*anārabhyādhītāni.*
[saptame]—*bahupradhānopakāraprayājādīni.*
[aṣṭame]—*yājamānāni.*

ll. 8-9
*caturthe pradhānaprayojakatvāpradhānaprayojakatva**juhūparṇatādi**pha**larājasūyagatajaghanyāṅgākṣadyūtādicintā.*

p. 5, *ll.* 12-13
caturthe—[godohanasya puruṣārthatvaprayuktyā'nuṣṭhānam, na tu kratvarthatvaprayuktyety evamādayaḥ.
p. 6, *ll.* 16-19
caturthādhyāyasya prathame pāde—pradhānabhūtāmikṣā dadhyānayanasya prayojiketyādi] *pradhānaprayoktṛtvaṁ* [vicāritam].
[dvitīye tu—apradhānaṁ vatsāpākaraṇaṁ śākhācchede prayojakam ityādy] *apradhānaprayoktṛtvam.*
[tṛtīye]—***juhūparṇamayītvāder*** [apāpaślokaśravaṇādi] ***phala***-[bhāvābhāvacintā].
[caturthe]—*rājasūyagatajaghanyāṅgākṣadyūtādicintā.*

ll. 9-10
*pañcame śrutyādikramatadviśeṣavṛddhy**avardhanaprābalyada**-*

p. 5, *l.* 13
pañcame—[kramaniyatividheyatvādayaḥ.

urbalya [cintā].

p. 6, *l*. 22-p. 7, *l*. 2
pañcamādhyāyasya prathame pāde]—*śruty* [arthapāṭh] *ādibhiḥ kramo* [nirūpitaḥ].

[dvitīye—vājapeyagateṣu saptadaśasu paśuṣv ekaikadharmasamāpanam ityādi]***kramaviśeṣaḥ.***

[tṛtīye—pañcaprayājādīnām āvartanenaikādaśyam ityādi]-*vṛddhiḥ*, [adābhyagrahacitriṇyor anāvṛttir ityādi] ***vṛddhyabhāvaś*** [ca.

caturthe—kramaniyāmakānāṁ śrutyarthapāṭhādīnāṁ] *prabala*-***durbalabhāvaḥ***.

ll. 10-11
*ṣaṣṭhe' dhikāritaddharma**dravya**-**pratinidhy**a**rtha**lopanaprāyaścittasatradeya**vahni**vicāraḥ*.

p. 5, *ll*. 13-14
ṣaṣṭhe—[kartur adhikāro, nāndhāder ityādayaḥ.

p. 7, *ll*. 5-15
ṣaṣṭhādhyāyasya prathame pāde—karmādhikāraḥ kartur asti, andhāder nāsti, striyā asti, sa ca patyā sahety evamādinā] *dhikārī* [nirūpitaḥ.

dvitīye—satrādhikāriṇāṁ pratyekaṁ kṛtsnaṁ phalam, darśapūrṇamāsayoḥ kartraikyaniyamaḥ, kāmyaṁ karma samāpanīyam ity evamādayo] ***'dhikāri**-**dharmā*** [uktāḥ.

tṛtīye]—***dravyasya pratinidhir*** [asti, devādīnām agnyādīnām adhikāriṇaś ca sa nāstītyādinirūpaṇam.

caturthe]—***padārthalopanaṁ*** [vicāritam. avattanāśe saty ājyena yajeta, iḍājyasya nāśe sati śeṣān na grāhyam ityādikam.

pañcame—kālāparādhena candrodaye saty abhyudayeṣṭiḥ] *prāyaścittam*, [jyotiṣṭomasyaikādayo dīkṣāḥ, dvādaśāhasya dvādaśa dīkṣāḥ, ityādi nirūpitam.

ṣaṣṭhe—sattrādhikāriṇas tulyakalpā eva] *sattraṁ* [viprasyaivety evamādikaṁ cintitam.

saptame—pitrādikaṁ na deyam, mahābhūmir na deyety evamādir] *deya*[vicāraḥ.

aṣṭame—laukikāgnāv upanayanahomaḥ sthapatīṣṭis tathaivety evamādy] ***agnivicāraḥ*** [kṛtaḥ].

ll. 11-12
saptame pratyakṣavacanātideśa-śeṣanāmaliṅgātideśa [vicāraḥ].

p. 5, *ll.* 14-15

saptame—["samānam itarac chyenene" tyādipratyakṣavacanena, agnihotrādināmnānumitavacanena ca sāmānyato'tideśaḥ.

p. 7, *ll.* 18-21

saptamādhyāyasya prathame pāde—"samānam itarac chyenene" tyādi] *pratyakṣavacanātideśaḥ*.

[dvitīye—rathantaraśabdena gānamātrābhidhāyinā gānasyaivātideśyatvam ity etādṛśaḥ pūrvoktātideśasya] *śeṣo* [vicāritaḥ.
tṛtīye—agnihotra] *nāmnā* ['tideśaḥ.
caturthe—nirvāpauṣadhadravyādi] *liṅgātideśaḥ*.

ll. 12-13

*aṣṭame spaṣṭāspaṣṭa**prabalaliṅgātideśāpavāda*** [vicāraḥ].

p. 5, *ll.* 15-17

aṣṭame—["sauryaṁ caruṁ nirvapet" ity atra nirvāpaḥ, taddhitena devatānirdeśaḥ, ekadevatātvam, auṣadhadravyakatvam iti liṅgenā "gneyapuroḍāśetikartavyataiva, nānyasyety evamādir viśeṣato'tideśaḥ.

p. 7, *l.* 24-p. 8, *l.* 2

aṣṭamādhyāyasya prathame pāde] *spaṣṭena* [liṅgenā'tideśaviśeṣaḥ. tad yathā—sauryacarāv atideśakāni nirvāpaḥ, taddhitena devatānirdeśaḥ, ekadevatātvaṁ, auṣadhadravyakatvam ityādīni spaṣṭāny āgneyaliṅgāni. dvitīye tu]—*aspaṣṭair* [liṅgair atideśaḥ. tad yathā—vājine havissāmānyena liṅgena payovidhyanto'tidiśyate. tatra liṅgam aspaṣṭam, śīghraṁ tadbuddhyanutpādanāt.

tṛtīye]—***prabalena liṅgenā'tideśaḥ.*** [tad yathā—ābhicārikeṣṭāv āgnāvaiṣṇavasārasvatabārhastyeṣu haviḥṣu tritvena liṅgena yathākramam āgneyādividhyante prāpte dvidaivatyatvena liṅgena prathama āgnāvaiṣṇave tṛtīyasyā'gnīṣomīyasya vidhyanto'tidiṣṭaḥ. prabalañ ca dvidaivatyatvam. śabdoccāraṇamātreṇa sahasā pratibhāsāt. kramas tu vilambitapratītyā durbalaḥ.

caturthe—darvīhomeṣv atideśo] *'podyate.*

ll. 13-14 *navama ūhavicārārambhasāmohamantrohatatprasaṅgāgatavicāraḥ.*	p. 5, *ll.* 17-19 *navame* [prakṛtau "agnaye juṣṭaṃ nirvapāmī" ti paṭhite mantre vikṛtau sauryacarāv agnipadaparityāgena sūryapadaprakṣepeṇa "sūryāya juṣṭaṁ nirvapāmī" ty evamādyūhaḥ. p. 8, *ll.* 5-9 navamādhyāyasya prathame pāde upodghātapūrvakam ūhavicāraprārambhaḥ. tatra prayājādayo dharmā apūrvaprayuktāḥ avaghātamantrādiṣv avivakṣitaṁ vrīhyagnyādisvarūpam, sādhanaviśeṣatvamātraṁ vivakṣitam ityādir upodghātaḥ. savitraśvipūṣaśabdānāṁ vikṛtiṣu nā'sty ūhaḥ. agniśabdasyā' sty ūha ityādika]*ūhavicārārambhaḥ.* [dvitīye—saparikaras] *sāmohaḥ.* [tṛtīye]—*mantrohaḥ.* [caturthe]—***mantrohaprasaṅgāpatito*** *vicāraḥ.*
ll. 14-15 *daśame* ***bādhahetudvāralopavistārabādhakāraṇakāryaikatvas-amuccayagrahādisāmaprakīrṇanañarthavicāraḥ.***	p. 5, *ll.* 19-20 *daśame*—[kṛṣṇaleṣu codakaprāptasyā'vaghātasya vituṣīkaraṇāsambhavena lopa ity evamādir bādhaḥ. p. 8, *ll.* 12-24 daśamādhyāyasya prathame pāde] ***bādhaheturvdvāralopo***[nirūpitaḥ. tad yathā—"svayaṁ kṛtā vedir bhavatī" ty atra vediniṣpādanarūpasya dvārasya lopena niṣpādakānām uddhan-

anādīnāṁ bādhaḥ. kṛṣṇaleṣu vituṣīkaraṇarūpasya dvārasya lopenāvaghātasya bādhaḥ.

dvitīye—saṁkṣepeṇoktasya dvāralopasya bahubhir udāharaṇair] *vistāraḥ*.

[tṛtīye]—***bādhakāraṇaṁ kārya-ikatvam***. [tad yathā—prakṛtau gavāśvādidakṣiṇāyā ṛtvikparikrayaḥ kāryam. tathā vikṛtirūpe bhūnāmny ekāhe dhenurūpāyā dakṣiṇāyās tad eva kāryam. tato dhenvā gavāśvādidakṣiṇā vikṛtau codakaprāptā bādhyate. caturthe—nakṣatreṣṭivihitā upahomāś codakaprāptair nāriṣṭhahomais saha samuccīyanta ityādis] *samuccayaḥ*.

[pañcame—ṣoḍaśigrahaḥ prakṛtigāmī. sa cā "grayaṇapātrād eva grahītavya ityādir bādhaprasaṅgāgato] *grahādi*[vicāraḥ. ṣaṣṭhe—"ekaṁ sāma tṛce geyam" ityādir bādhaprasaṅgāgatas] *sāma*[vicāraḥ.

[saptame—paśvaṅge pratyaṅgaṁ havirbhedaḥ, na kṛtsnaḥ paśur havirbhedaḥ. gṛhamedhīyam apūrvaṁ karmetyādir bādhaprasaṅgāgataḥ] *prakīrṇa*[vicāraḥ.

aṣṭame—"nānuyājeṣv" iti paryudāsaḥ, "na some" ity arthavādaḥ, "nātirātre" iti pratiṣedha ityādir bādhopayukto] *nañarthavicāraḥ*.

ll. 15-16
*ekādaśe**tantropodghāta**tantrāvāpa**tantraprapañcanāvāpaprapañcana*** [cintanāni].

p. 5, *ll.* 20-21
ekādaśe—[bahūnām āgneyādīnāṁ pradhānānāṁ sakṛdanuṣṭhitena prayājādyaṅgenopakāra iti tantram.

p. 8, *l.* 27-p. 9, *l.* 2
ekādaśādhyāyasya prathame pāde]—***tantrasyopodghāto*** [varṇitaḥ.

dvitīye]—*tantrāvāpau* [saṁkṣepeṇoktau.

tṛtīye]—***tantram*** [udāharaṇabāhulyena] ***prapañcitam.***

[caturthe—tathaivā]"***vāpaḥ prapañcitaḥ.***

l. 17
dvādaśe prasaṅgatantri [nirṇaya] *samuccayavi**kalpavicāraḥ***.

p. 5, *ll.* 21-22
dvādaśe [pradhānasya paśor upakārāyā'nuṣṭhitena prayājādyaṅgena paśvaṅgapuroḍāśe'py upakāra ityādiprasaṅgaḥ.

p. 9, *ll.* 5-12
dvādaśādhyāyasya prathame pāde—paśudharmāṇāṁ paśupuroḍāśe] *prasaṅgaḥ*, [saumikaveder uttarakālīnakarmasu] *prasaṅga* [ityādivicāraḥ.

dvitīye—savanīyapaśos] ***tantritvam***, [na tu savanīyapuroḍāśānām. vikṛtis tantriṇī, na prakṛtiḥ, anvārambhaṇīyā vikṛtiṣv api syāt. na tu prakṛtāv evetyādivicāraḥ.

tṛtīye—tvagvāsasos] *samuccayaḥ.* [āghāragatānām ṛjutvasantatatvādīnāṁ samuccaya ityādikaṁ prādhānyena, yavavrīhyor vikalpa ityādikaṁ samu-

ccayāpavādatvenety ubhayaṁ cintitam.
caturthe ca—aindrābārhaspatyayājyānuvākyāyugalayor] *vikalpa* [ityādikaṁ prādhānyena, yājyānuvākyayos samuccaya ityādikaṁ vikalpāpavādatvenety ubhayaṁ] ***cintitam.***

[B]

SDS XII	JNMV (Jijñāsādhikaraṇa)
ll. 27-29 *artha**vabodhārtham** **adhyayanavidhir** iti vadan vādī praṣṭavyaḥ . . . kim atyantam aprāptam adhyayanaṁ vidhīyate kiṁ vā pākṣikam avaghātavan niyamyata iti.*	p. 12, *ll.* 5-6 [tatra] *artha**jñānāyā'dhyayanasya vidhir** iti vadan vādī praṣṭavyaḥ—kim atyantam aprāptam adhyayanaṁ vidhīyate? kiṁ vā pakṣe 'prāptam avaghātavan niyamyate? iti.*
ll. 29-31 *na*[tāvad]*ādyaḥ. vivādapadaṁ vedādhyayanam arthā**vabodha**hetur adhyayanatvād bhāratādhyayanavad ity anumānena vidhyan**apekṣatayā** prāptatvāt.*	*ll.* 6-8 *nā''dyaḥ. **vimataṁ** vedādhyayanam artha**jñāna**hetuḥ, adhyayanatvāt, bhāratādhyayanavat, ity anumānenai* [va] *vidhi**nirapekṣeṇa** prāptatvāt.*
ll. 31-35 *astu tarhi dvitīyo yathā **nakhavidalanādinā** taṇḍulaniṣpattisaṁbhavāt **pākṣiko'** vaghāto 'vaśyaṁ kartavya iti vidhinā niyamyate tathā likhitapāṭhenā'rthajñānasaṁbhavāt **pākṣikam** adhyayanaṁ vidhinā niyamyata iti cet . . . nai* [tac caturasram. dṛṣṭāntadārṣṭāntikayor] ***vaidharmyasambhavāt.***	*ll.* 8-11 *tarhy astu dvitīyaḥ* [pakṣaḥ, avaghātavan niyamavidhitvasaṁbhavāt]. *yathā **nakhair avaghātena vā** taṇḍulaniṣpattisaṁbhavāt **pakṣe'prāpto** 'vaghāto vidhinā'vaśyaṁ kartavya iti niyamyate, tathā likhitapāṭhena* [gurupūrvakādhyayanena vā] *'rthajñānasaṁbhavāt **pakṣe'prāptam** adhyayanaṁ vidhinā niyamyata iti cet—na, **vaiṣamyāt.***

ll. 35-37 *avaghātaniṣpannair eva taṇḍulaiḥ* [piṣṭapuroḍāśādikaraṇe] *'vāntarāpūrva**dvārā** darśapūrṇamāsau paramāpūrvam **utpādayato** nāparat**hā**. ato'pūrvam avaghātasya niyamahetuḥ.*	*ll.* 11-13 *avaghātaniṣpannair eva taṇḍulair avāntarāpūrva**dvāreṇa** darśapūrṇamāsau paramāpūrvaṁ **janayataḥ**, nā**nyathā**. ato* [darśapūrṇamāsā]*pūrvam avaghātasya niyamahetuḥ.*
ll. 37-39 ***prakṛte** likhitapāṭhajanyenā* [dhyayanajanyena] *v**ārthāvabodhena** kratvanuṣṭhānasiddher adhyayanasya niyamahetur nāsty* [eva]. ***tasmād** arth**āvabodha**hetuvicārāśāstrasya vaidhatvaṁ **nāsti*** [ti].	*ll.* 13-15 ***atra tu*** likhitapāṭhajanyenaivā*rtha**jñānena** kratvanuṣṭhānasiddher adhyayanasya niyamahetur nāsti. **ato*** [dvividhavidhyasaṁbhavād] *arthajñānahetuvicāraśāstrā*[rambha]*sya vaidhatvaṁ nā'sti.*
ll. 40-44 *tarhi śrūyamāṇasya vidheḥ kā gatir iti cet. . . svarga**phalako**'kṣaragrahaṇamātra**vidhir** iti **bhavān parituṣyatu**. viśvajinnyāyenā**śrutasyāpi svargasya kalpayituṁ śakyatvāt.*** [yathā] *sa svargaḥ sarvān praty aviśiṣṭatvād iti viśvajity **aśrutam apy** adhikāriṇaṁ **sampādayatā** tadviśeṣaṇaṁ **svargaḥ phalaṁ** yuktyā **niraṇāyi**, tadvad adhyayane'py astu.*	*ll.* 15-18 *tarhi śrūyamāṇasya vidheḥ kā gatir iti cet, svargāyā'kṣaragrahaṇamātraṁ **vidheyam** iti **vadāmaḥ**. **aśruto'pi svargo** viśvajinnyāyena **kalpanīyaḥ**, "sa svargaḥ* [syāt] *sarvān praty aviśiṣṭatvāt" iti* [sūtreṇa] ***viśvajity aśrūyamāṇam** apy adhikāriṇaṁ **sampādayituṁ** tadviśeṣaṇaṁ **svargaphalaṁ** yuktyā **sthāpitam**, tadvad adhyayane 'py astu.*
ll. 45-47 ***tad** uktam . . .* *vināpi vidhinā **dṛṣṭa**lābhān na hi tadarthatā| kalpyas tu vidhisāmarthyāt svargo viśvajidādivat||* [iti]	*ll.* 18-20 ***etad*** [evā'bhipretyo]*ktam—* *vinā 'pi vidhinā **jñāna**lābhān na hi tadarthatā | kalpyas tu vidhisāmarthyāt svargo viśvajidādivat ||*
ll. 48-51 *evaṁ ca sati vedam adhītya snā-*	p. 13, *ll.* 1-3 *evaṁ ca sati 'vedam adhītya*

yād iti ***smṛtir anugṛhītā bhavati. atra hi*** *vedādhyayanasamāvartanayor* ***avyavadhānaṁ avagamyate. tāvake mate*** *tv adhīte'pi vede dharmavicārāya gurukule* ***vāstavyam.*** *tathā saty* ***avyavadhānam*** *bādhyeta.*	*snāyāt' iti* ***śāstram anugṛhyate. asmiṁś ca śāstre*** *vedādhyayanasamāvartanayor* ***nairantaryaṁ pratīyate. tvatpakṣe*** *tu— adhīte'pi vede dharmavicārāya gurukula* [evā]'***dhivāsaḥ kartavyaḥ.*** *tathā sati* ***tannairantaryaṁ*** *bādhyeta.*
ll. 51-53 *tasmād vicāraśāstrasya vaidhatvābhāvāt pāṭhamātreṇa svargasiddheḥ samāvartanaśāstrāc ca dharmavicāraśāstram* ***anārambhaṇīyam*** *iti* ***pūrvapakṣasaṁkṣepaḥ.***	*ll.* 3-5 *tasmād vicāraśāstrasya vaidhatvābhāvāt pāṭhamātreṇa svarg*[ādi] *siddheḥ, samāvartanaśāstrāc ca dharmavicāraśāstraṁ* ***nā" rambhaṇīyam*** *iti* ***pūrvaḥ pakṣaḥ.***
ll. 54-55 siddhāntas tv anyataḥ prāptatvād aprāptavidhitvaṁ māstu. ***niyamavidhitva*** [pakṣas] ***tu*** [vajrahastenāpi] ***nāpahastayituṁ pāryate.***	*ll.* 6-7 atrocyate—yad uktaṁ lokasiddhatvān nāprāptavidhir iti, tat tathaivāstu. ***niyamavidhitvaṁ tu na vārayituṁ śakyam.***
ll. 55-66 [tathāhi, "svādhyāyo'dhyetavyaḥ" iti tavyapratyayaḥ preraṇāparaparyāyāṁ puruṣapravṛttirūpārthabhāvanābhāvyām abhidhābhāvanāṁ pratyāyayati. sā hy arthabhāvanā bhāvyam ākāṅkṣati. na tāvat samānapadopāttam adhyayanaṁ bhāvyatvena pariramate. adhyayanaśabdārthasya svādhīnoccāraṇakṣamatvasya vāṅmanasavyāpārasya kleśārthakasya bhāvyatvāsaṁbhavāt. tasmāt sāmarthyaprāpto'vabodho bhāvya-	

tvenāvatiṣṭhate. arthī samartho vidvān adhikriyata iti nyāyena darśapūrṇamāsādividhayaḥ svaviṣayāvabodham apekṣamānāḥ svārthabodhe svādhyāyaṁ viniyuñjate. adhyayanavidhiś ca likhitapāṭhādivyāvṛttyādhyayanasaṁskṛtatvaṁ svādhyāyasyāvagamayati].

ll. 66-69	*ll.* 7-9
[tathā ca] *yathā darśapūrṇamās* [ādi] *janyaṁ paramāpūrvam avaghāt**ādi**janyasyāvāntarāpūrvasya kalpakaṁ* ***tathā samasta**kratujanyam apūrvajātaṁ kratujñānasādhanādhyayananiyama**janyam apūrvaṁ kalpayiṣyati.***	*yathā darśapūrṇamāsajanyaṁ paramāpūrvam avaghāta**niyama**janyasyā'vāntarāpūrvasya kalpakam,* ***evam atrā'py aśeṣa**kratujanyam apūrvajātaṁ kratujñānasādhanādhyayananiyama**janyasyā'pūrvasya kalpakaṁ bhaviṣyati.***
ll. 69-71	*ll.* 9-11
*niyamādṛṣṭāniṣ**ṭau vidhiśravaṇavaiphalyam āpadyeta.** na ca viśvajinnyāyena* ***phalakalpanāvakalpyate. arthāvabodhe dṛṣṭe phale sati phalāntarakalpanāyā ayogāt.***	*niyamādṛṣṭā**naṅgīkāre*** [ca] ***śrūyamāṇo vidhir anarthakaḥ syāt.*** *na ca viśvajinnyāyena* ***svargārthatvaṁ yuktam, dṛṣṭaphale'rthajñāne sambhavaty adṛṣṭasya kalpayitum aśakyatvāt.***
ll. 71-73	*ll.* 11-13
tad *uktam . . .* *labhyamāne phale dṛṣṭe nādṛṣṭa**phalakalpanā**/ vidhes tu niyamārthatvān nānarthakyaṁ bhaviṣyati // iti.*	***ata*** [evo]*ktam—* *labhyamāne phale dṛṣṭe nā'dṛṣṭa**parikalpanā**/ vidhes tu niyamārthavān nā" narthakyaṁ' bhaviṣyati // iti.*
ll. 74-76	*ll.* 14-15
nanu ***vedamātrādhyāyino'rthabodhānudaye'pi sāṅgavedādhyāyinaḥ*** *puruṣasyārthāv**abodha**-*	*nanv* ***evam*** *api* [śrutavyākaraṇādy] ***aṅgasyā'dhītavedasya*** *puruṣasyā'rtha**jñāna**saṃbhavād vicā-*

saṃbhavād vicāraśāstrasya ***vaiphalyam*** *iti cet . . .* ***tad asamañjasam****. bodhamātrasaṁbhave'pi nirṇayasya vicārādhīnatvāt.*

raśāstrasya ***vaiyarthyam*** *iti cet —**na,** **jñā**namātrasambhave'pi nirṇayasya vicārādhīnatvāt.*

ll. 76-80
[tad yathā] . . . "*aktāḥ śarkarā upadadhāti*" *ity atra ghṛtenaiva na tailādinety ayaṁ nirṇayo vyākaraṇena nigamena niruktena vā na* ***labhyate****. vicāraśāstreṇa tu* "*tejo vai ghṛtam*" *iti vākyaśeṣa****vaśād arthanirṇayo labhyate. tasmād vicāra*** [śāstrasya] ***vaidhatvaṁ*** [siddham].

ll. 16-18
'*aktāḥ śarkarā upadadhātī'ty atra ghṛtenai'va, na tailādinety ayaṁ nirṇayo vyākaraṇena niruktena nigamena vā na* ***sidhyati****. vicāraśāstraṁ tu 'tejo vai ghṛtam' iti vākyaśe****ṣād arthaṁ nirṇeṣyati. ato vicāro vaidhaḥ.***

ll. 80-84
[na ca] "*vedam adhītya snāyād*" *iti śāstraṁ* [gurukulanivṛttiparaṁ vyavadhānapratibandhakaṁ bādhyete'ti mantavyam. "snātvā bhuṅkta" itivat] *pūrvāparībhāvasamānakartṛkatva****mātra****pratipattyādhyayanasamāvartanayor nairantaryapratipatteḥ. tasmād vidhi****sāmarthyād*** *e****vādhikaraṇasahasrātmakaṁ pūrvamīmāṁsāśāstram*** *ārambhaṇīyam.*

ll. 18—p. 14, *l.* 2
'*vedam adhītya snāyād' iti śāstraṁ* tv adhyayanasamāvartanayoḥ *pūrvāparībhāvasamānakartṛkatvam* evā" caṣṭe, na tv ānantaryam, *tasmād vidhi****vaśād*** *eva* ***vicāraśāstram*** *ārambhaṇīyam* [iti siddhāntaḥ].

ll. 85-86
[idaṁ cādhikaraṇaṁ śāstreṇopodghātatvena saṁbadhyate. tad āha . . .
cintāṁ prakṛtasiddhyartham upodghātaṁ pracakṣate / iti.]

ll. 87-92
idam evādhikaraṇaṁ *gurumatam* anusṛtyopanyasyate. "*aṣṭavarṣaṁ brāhmaṇam upanayīta tam adhyāpayīta*" *ity* [atrā] dhyāpanaṁ niyogaviṣayaḥ pratibhāsate. [niyogaś ca niyojyam apekṣate]. kaś cātra niyojya iti cet . . . ācāryakakāma eva. "*saṁmānana*" *ity* [ādinā] *pāṇinyanuśāsanen*ācāryake gamyamāne nayater dhātor ātmanepadasya vidhānāt. *upanayane yo niyojyaḥ sa evādhyāpane'pi. tayor ekaprayojanatvāt.*

ll. 93-96
[ata evoktam manunā muninā
upanīya tu yaḥ śiṣyaṁ vedam adhyāpayed dvijaḥ /
sāṅgaṁ ca sarahasyaṁ ca tam ācāryaṁ pracakṣate // iti.]

ll. 97-98
tataś cā*cāryakartṛkam adhyāpanaṁ māṇavakakartṛkenā'dhyayanena vinā na sidhyatīty adhyāpanavidhiprayuktyaivādhyayanānuṣṭhānaṁ setsyati.*

ll. 98-101
[prayojyavyāpāram antareṇa prayojakavyāpārasyā'nirvāhāt. tarhy "adhyetavyaḥ" ity asya vidhitvaṁ na sidhyatīti cet . . . mā saitsīt kā no hāniḥ.]

ll. 3-14
asminn evā'dhikaraṇe *gurumatam* āha—(stanzas 33-35) '*aṣṭavarṣaṁ brāhmaṇam upanayīta, tam adhyāpayīte'ty adhyāpanaṁ* vihitam. na cā'tra niyojyābhāvaḥ, ācāryatvakāmino niyojyatvāt. 'upanayīte'ty anenā''cāryakaraṇe "*sammānano* [tsañjanācāryakaraṇajñānabhṛtivigaṇanavyayeṣu niyaḥ]" *iti pāṇinisūtreṇa* vihitenā''tmanepadena niyojyaviśeṣaṇam ācāryatvaṁ pratīyate. *upanayane yo niyojyaḥ sa evā' dhyāpane'pi. tayor ekaprayojanatvāt.*

ll. 14-15
evaṁ saty *ācāryakartṛkam adhyāpanaṁ māṇavakakartṛkeṇā 'dhyayanena vinā na sidhyatīty adhyāpanavidhiprayuktyaivā'dhyayanānuṣṭhānasiddher.*

ll. 101-103

pṛthag ***adhyayanavidher abhyupagame prayojanābhāvāt. vidhivākyasya nityānuvādatvenāpy upapatteḥ. tasmād*** *adhyayanavidhim upajīvya pūrvam upanyastau pūrvottarapakṣau* ***prakārāntareṇa pradarśanīyau.***

ll. 15-17

na *pṛthag* ***adhyayane vidhir abhyupagantavyaḥ.*** [śrūyamāṇaṁ] ***vidhivākyaṁ nityānuvādatvenā'py upapadyate. tato*** *'dhyayanavidhim upajīvya pūrvam upanyastau pūrvottarapakṣāv* ***anyathā varṇanīyau.***

ll. 104-110

[vicāraśāstram avaidhatvenānārabdhavyam iti pūrvapakṣo vaidhatvenārabdhavyam iti rāddhāntaḥ.] *tatra* ***vaidhatvaṁ vadatā vaditavyaṁ*** *kim* ***adhyāpanavidhir*** *māṇavakasyārthāvabodham* ***api prayuṅkte*** *kiṁ vā pāṭhamātram. nādyaḥ.* ***vināpy arthāvabodhenā****dhyāpanasiddheḥ* [na dvitīyaḥ.] *pāṭhamātre vicārasyaviṣaya-* [prayojanayor] ***asaṁbhavāt.*** *āpātataḥ* ***pratibhātaḥ*** *saṁdigdho'rtho* [vicāraśāstrasya] *viṣayo* [bhavati]. *tathā sati yatrārthāv****agatir*** *eva nāsti tatra saṁdehasya kā kathā.*

ll. 17-22

[viṣayasaṁśayayos tu nā'sti vipratipattiḥ. vicāraśāstraṁ viṣayaḥ. avaidhaṁ, vaidhaṁ veti saṁśayaḥ.] *tatra* ***vaidhatvavādī praṣṭavyaḥ****—vidheyam* [ācāryakartṛkam] ***adhyāpanaṁ*** *kiṁ māṇavakasyā'rthajñānam* ***api prayuñjīta*** *kiṁ vā pāṭhamātram. nā''dyaḥ,* ***antareṇā****'py* ***arthajñānam*** *adhyāpanasiddheḥ. pāṭhamātre* [tu] *vicārasya viṣayo* ***na bhavati.*** *āpātataḥ* ***pratītaḥ*** *saṁdigdho'rtho viṣayaḥ. tathā sati yatrārtha****pratītir*** *eva nāsti, tatra saṁdehasya kā kathā.*

ll. 110-114

vicāraphalasya nirṇayasya pratyāśā dūrata eva. [tathā ca yad asaṁdigdham aprayojanaṁ na ca tat prekṣāvatpratipitsāgocaraḥ. yathā "samanaskendriyasaṁnikṛṣṭaḥ spaṣṭālokamadhyam adhyāsīno ghaṭaḥ" iti nyāyena] *viṣaya****prayojanayor asaṁbhavena*** *vicāraśāstram* ***anārabhyam*** *iti pūrvaḥ pakṣaḥ.*

ll. 22-23

nirṇayo vicārasya phalam. so'pi viṣayavad dūrāpetaḥ. [ato] *viṣayaprayojanā****bhāvād*** *vicāraśāstraṁ* ***nā''rambhaṇīyam*** *iti pūrvaḥ pakṣaḥ.*

ll. 115-117
adhy* ¦*pànāvidhinārthāvabodho mā prāyoji*.** *tathāpi sāṅgavedādhyāyino* ***gṛhītapadapàdārthasaṁgàtikàsya puruṣasya pauruṣeyeṣv *iva* ***prabāndheṣv āmnāye'*** *py arthāvabodhaḥ prāpnoty eva.*

ll. 24-26
[atrocyate] –***mā nāmā'dhyāpanenā'rthāvabodhaḥ pràyujyātām.*** *tathā'pi sāṅgavedādhyāyino* ***nigamānirukt̄avyākàraṇàir vyutpānnàsyà pāuruṣeyāgranthe̦ṣv*** *iva* ***vede'py*** *arthāvabodhaḥ* [svata] *eva prāpnoti.*

ll. 117-122
nanu yathā "viṣaṁ bhuṅkṣvā" ity atra pratīyamāno'py artho na ***vivākṣyàte.*** [māsya gṛhe bhukthā iti bhojanapratiṣedhasya mātṛvākyatātparyaviṣayatvāt,] *tathā****mnā****yārthasyāvivakṣāyāṁ viṣayādyabhāva* [doṣaḥ prācīnaḥ] prāduḥṣyād *iti cet* . . . maivaṁ vocaḥ, dṛṣṭāntadārṣṭāntikayor vaiṣamyasaṁbhavāt. *viṣabhojanavākyasyāptapraṇītatvena mukhyārtha* [parigrahe] ***bādhaḥ syād*** *iti* vivakṣā nāśrīyate.

l. 26—p. 15, *l.* 2
nanu yathā 'viṣaṁ bhuṅkṣve' ity atra pratīyamāno'py artho na ***vivākṣitaḥ,*** *tathā* ***vedārthasyā*** ['py] *avivakṣāyāṁ viṣayādyabhāvas* tadavastha *iti cet*—na, vivakṣāyā apanoditum aśakyatvāt. *viṣabhojanavākyasyā''ptapraṇītatvena* ***bādho mā bhūd iti*** *mukhyārthas* ***tàtrà parityaktàḥ.***

ll. 123-127
[apauruṣeye] *tu vede* [pratīyamāno]' ***rthāḥ*** *kuto na* ***vivakṣyate.*** *vivakṣite ca vedārthe yatra* [yatra] *puruṣasya saṁdehaḥ sa sarvo'pi vicāraśāstrasya viṣayo* [bhaviṣyati]. *tannirṇayaś ca prayojanam.* ***tasmād*** *adhyāpanavidhiprayuktenādhyayanen*-***āvāgāmyamānasyā****rhasya* ***vicārārhātvād*** *vicāraśāstrasya* ***vàidhatvenà*** [vicāraśāstram ārambhaṇīyam iti rāddhāntasaṁgrahaḥ].

ll. 2-4
vede tu—kuto na ***vivakṣitārthātvam.*** *vivakṣite ca vedārthe yatra puruṣasya saṁdehaḥ sa sarvo'pi vicāraśāstrasya viṣayaḥ. tannirṇayaś ca prayojanam.* ***tāto****'dhyāpanavidhiprayuktenā'dhyayanena* ***budhyamānasyā'****rthasya* ***vicāryatvād*** *vicāraśāstrasya* ***vàidhatvàṁ siddham.***

(A) would be investigated hereunder at first.

In *SDS XII*, Mādhava does not explain each *pāda*, but only refers to the contents of *pādas* in course of describing each *adhyāya*. On the contrary in the *Granthāvataraṇikā* of *JNMV*, he explains each *adhyāya* at first, then the contents of the *pādas* in detail.[14]

In *SDS*, Mādhava explains the contents of each *pāda* with the most important one word, which is seen in *JNMV*. So it will be easier to understand the meaning of those parts of *SDS XII* reading them together with *JNMV* than reading only the text of *SDS*.

With respect to (B), *SDS XII* and *JNMV* have closer connection. Though there can be seen slight changes of words, they coincide each other in almost all phrases, and both of *SDS XII* and *JNMV* quote the two same verses from *ŚD*.

The significance of starting the study of the Mīmāṁsā is considered very much important by Mīmāṁsaka philosophers, Śabarasvāmin, Kumārila, Pārthasārathimiśra and others. It has been the subject of the study under the title of *śāstrārambha*, *śāstramukha* or *jijñāsādhikaraṇa*, and it is reviewed first in *SDS XII*.[15]

According to *ŚD*, *Śāstras* have the four anubandhas; *viṣaya*, *prayojana*, *sambandha* and *adhikārin*.[16] Pārthasārathi says the *viṣaya* is *dharma*, and the *prayojana* is *dharmajñāna*.[17] *Dharmajijñāsā*, which is nothing but the Mīmāṁsā, called '*dharmavicāraśāstra*' by Mādhava,[18] should be started just after completing the Vedic study.

The formation of *adhikaraṇa* of *dharmajijñāsā* by Kumārila is different from that by Prabhākara.[19] According to *SDS XII*, *viṣayavākya* of the *adhikaraṇa* is '*svādhyāyo'dhyetavyaḥ*' (*adhyayanavidhi*) in the school of Kumārila. But the followers of Prabhākara say the *viṣayavākya* is '*aṣṭavarṣaṃ brāhmaṇam upanayīta tam adhyāpayīta*' (*adhyāpanavidhi*).[20]

The next subject in *SDS XII* is the theory that the Vedas are *apauruṣeya*, or not composed by any man, not even by God. (11.128∼216).[21]

That the Veda is only one valid means of attaining the knowledge on *dharma* is the fundamental position of the Mīmāṁsakas. According to them, the Mīmāṁsā is nothing but *dharma*-

vicāraśāstra, and *dharma* is known only by *codanā*, Vedic command.[22] The theory of *apauruṣeyatva* of the Veda is shown to give the authority to the theory of *svataḥprāmāṇya* (intrinsic validity) of the Vedas to know *dharma*.[23] Mādhava reviews the argument with the Naiyāyikas, who think, Parameśvara is the author of the Vedas. The main text of the Naiyāyikas quoted by Mādhava is the *Nyāyakusumāñjali* of Udayana,[24] as in the Akṣapāda-darśana in *SDS*, but it is not quoted in *JNMV*.

In the course of explaining *vedāpauruṣeyatva*, Mādhava reviews the theory of *śabdanityatva* of the Mīmāṁsakas.[25] He calls the Mīmāṁsakas '*śabdadravyatvavādins*', and he quotes some passages from the *Nyāyabhūṣaṇa* (properly speaking *Nyāyasāra*) of Bhāsarvajña[26] and the *Mānamanohara* of Vāgīśvara.[27] Mādhava does not quote the works of the philosophers of the Prabhākara school while he quotes some verses in the *Ślokavārttika* (*ŚV*) of Kumārila.

After the review of *vedāpauruṣeyatva*, Mādhava explains the *svataḥprāmāṇyavāda*. (11.217~285).

In the theory of knowledge of the Mīmāṁsakas, one of the most important idea is *svataḥprāmāṇya*. According to Mādhava, Mīmāṁsakas developed the theory of *svataḥprāmāṇyavāda* in order to clarify the intrinsic validity of the Veda, through which they gain the knowledge on *dharma*.[28] Schools referred to as *pūrvapakṣins* are Sāṁkhyas, Naiyāyikas and Bauddhas.[29] When Mādhava introduces the *siddhānta* view, he quotes some verses from *ŚV*, but not from the works of Prabākara, though he calls the Mimāṁsakas '*Vedavādins*', which is the name shared by even the philosophers of the Vedānta school.

The last subject in *SDS XII* is the comparison of *abhihitānvayavāda* and *anvitābhidhānavāda*. (11.286~291)[30]

Abhihitānvayavāda is the theory of sentence construction of Kumārila,[31] and *anvitābhidhānavāda* is that of Prabhākara.[32] In *SDS XII* Mādhava reviews the two theories with an impartial attitude. In *JNMV*, neither of the two views was referred.

Judging by the above-mentioned points, we may well say Mādhava stands for the position of Kumārila, but he reviews the theories of Kumārila and Prabhākara impartially.

By the way, *adhikaraṇa* is to be deemed to fall into five parts; these Mādhava reckons, in his *SDS*,[33] *viṣaya* (the subject of investigation), *saṁśaya* (the doubt), *pūrvapakṣa* (the first or prima facie view), *siddhānta* (the answer or demonstrated conclusion) and *saṁgati* (the relevance of the topic), but the last head is, in *JNMV*,[34] reckoned as the third, while *uttarapakṣa* (the answer), and *nirṇaya* (conclusion) are regarded as the fourth and the fifth members.

4. *JNMV and Sāyaṇa's Commentaries on the Vedas*

In the introduction to his Bhāṣya on the *Taittirīyasaṁhitā* (*TS*),[35] Sāyaṇa tells that when King Bukka directed Mādhavācārya to write Veda-bhāṣya, Mādhavācārya told the King that his (Mādhava's) younger brother Sāyaṇārya who was well-versed in all the Vedas should be appointed as a Vedic commentator; and that accordingly King Bukka instructed Sāyaṇa to write Veda-bhāṣya.

However, Mādhava's name does not figure in the introduction to the commentaries on the *Atharvaveda* (*AV*),[36] the *Sāmaveda*, and the *Kāṇva-Saṁhitā* and the names of only Sāyaṇa and his patron king are mentioned.[37] In the *Taittirīyasaṁhitābhāṣya* (*TSBh*), *JNMV* is cited very often. For example, commenting passages in *TS* I.i.1, Sāyaṇa cites the following explanation by Mādhava without mentioning the name of *JNMV*—

tatra vidheḥ prāmāṇyaṃ prathamādhyāye prathamapāde pratipāditam
. . ."abodhako bodhako vā na tāvad bodhako vidhiḥ/
śakter alaukike dharme grahaṇam durghaṭaṁ yataḥ //
samabhivyāhṛte dharme śaktigrahaṇasaṁbhavāt/
bodhakasya vidher mātvam anapekṣatayā sthitam" iti.
dharmo nāmānuṣṭhānajanyāpūrvaṃ taddhetur yāgo vā. tasyālaukikatvena gavādyarthavad vṛddhavyavahāraviṣayatvāt saṁgatigrahaṇaṃ nāsti. (The rest is omitted)[38]

When Sāyaṇa cites from *JNMV*, it is the way that he refers only to the numbers of *adhyāya* and *pāda*, as shown above.

In the introduction to his *Ṛgveda-Bhāṣya*, Sāyaṇa himself has made it clear that first of all he wrote his Bhāṣya on *TS*, because it is of prime importance for the performance of various sacrifices. Another reason for composing his first commentary on *TS* might have been that Sāyaṇa was a follower of the *Baudhāyana* School of this Veda.[39]

As the main aim of Sāyaṇa's commentary on *TS* is to explain the sacrificial procedure, he takes great pains to present all possible details of the ritualistic aspect of the mantras and cites copious quotations from the Brāhmaṇas and the Śrautasūtras, especially from the *Taittirīyabrāhmaṇa*, the *Baudhāyanaśrautasūtra*, and the *Āpastambaśrautasūtra*. Besides, he derives help from the Mīmāṁsā and Pāṇini also in support of his explanations as claimed by him in the introduction to his Bhāṣya. Sāyaṇa utilises the Mīmāṁsā principles of interpretation very often when he comments on passages of the *Ṛgveda*.[40]

Sāyaṇa, in his introduction to his Bhāṣya on the *Sāmaveda*, says, he wrote his Bhāṣya on the *Sāmaveda*, after composing the commentary on *TS*, and the *Ṛgveda*, because mantras of the *Sāmaveda* are dependent on those of the *Ṛgveda*.[41]

Sāyaṇa's commentary on *AV* is the last among his Veda-bhāṣyas. In the introduction to his bhāṣya it is said that he wrote the commentary on *AV*, at the instance of King Harihara. He discusses various important topics such as *trayī vidyā* and *AV*, *svādhyāya*, *dharma* and many terms following the line of argumentation adopted by the Mīmāṁsakas. Sāyaṇa discusses the meaning and the role of *adhyayanavidhi*. He says that as the seen result i.e. *arthāvabodha*, is possible, the unseen result should not be supposed as reward, citing a verse from *ŚD*[42]

labhyamāne phale dṛṣṭe nādṛṣṭaphalakalpanā/
vidhes tu niyamārthatvān nānarthakyaṁ bhaviṣyati// iti.
"When an empirical reward exists, to suppose *adṛṣṭa* (which yields *svarga*) as reward is not right; further since the injunction is one of *niyama* it is not rendered purposeless."

Prābhākaras however holding the view that *adhyayana* is undertaken as the result of the injunction pertinent to the attainment of preceptorship discuss whether *adhyayana* subserves only the purpose of securing preceptorship or of acquiring a knowledge of the meaning of the Veda and come to the conclusion that the latter is the aim of *adhyayana* since it is more immediate. And they insist that from the *smṛti* 'that twice-born man (*dvija*) who having initiated the pupil teaches him the Veda along with the Kalpasūtras and its hidden import is called preceptor', a corresponding mandatory *śruti* relating to preceptorship may be inferred, viz.,—'Having initiated, secure preceptorship by teaching.' Here *adhyāpana* (teaching the Veda) is the means by which preceptorship is attained and *upanayana*, because of the participle termination (*ktvā*-suffix in *upanīya*), is auxiliary to it. Denying the view of the Prābhākaras, Sāyaṇa insists that it cannot be maintained on the authority of the scriptures that either preceptorship or the knowledge of the meaning follows as a consequence from *adhyayana* which is productive of *niyoga* because a single *vidhi* cannot serve two purposes.[43] Judging from this standpoint of Sāyaṇa, it is clear that he is a follower of Kumārila, while Mādhava, as an author of *SDS* and *JNMV*, seems to review both views of Kumārila and Prabhākara with efforts of treating them impartially.

5. *Conclusion*

As Mādhava says, in the introductory verse of *SDS*, that let the virtuous listen with a mind from which all envy has been far banished, he reviews Prabhākara's philosophy without abusing it, in *JNM* as well as in *SDS XII*. On the contrary in the commentaries on the Vedas, especially in *AVBh*, the standpoint of the author is the same as that of followers of Kumārila, and he denied the views of Prabhākara. So it is clear that the author of *JNM* and *SDS* is different from the one who wrote commentaries on the Vedas. According to the introductory verse of *TSBh* mentioned above, the former is Mādhava and the latter is Sāyaṇa, his younger brother. Some scholars say Mādhava, an author of *SDS*, is a son of Sāyaṇa, because in the introductory verse of *SDS*, the author is called Sāyaṇa-Mādhava.[44] If it becomes true, Sāyaṇa's son, Mādhava, may be said to have adopted the viewpoint of Mādhava, his uncle, not that of his father.

NOTES

*This article develops in much greater detail some of the themes already sketched in my "Mādhava as a Mīmāṁsaka" *Tōhō* (*The East*) 7, Tokyo, 1991.

1. *Sarva-darśana-saṁgraha of Sāyaṇa-Mādhava*, edited with an original commentary in Sanskrit by Mahamahopadhyaya Vasudev Shastri Abhyankar. Government Oriental (Hindu) Series 1, Poona: Bhandarkar Oriental Research Institute, 1924.

2. Cf. H. Nakamura: "Some Notes on the Sarvadarśanasaṁgraha", *Beitrage zur Gescichte Indiens. Festschrift für E. Frauwallner, WZKS*, 1968/1969. pp. 241–51.

3. Cf. E.B. Cowell and A.E. Gough, *The Sarva-darśana-saṁgraha*, or Review of the different systems of Hindu Philosophy. The Chowkhamba Sanskrit·Studies Vol. X. Varanasi: Chowkhamba Sanskrit Series Office, 1961 (Reprint).

4. Cf. S. Mayeda and H. Kurata: *Indo Saijigakuha no Shomondai* (= Problems of Ritualistic Philosophy in India: A Study of Mādhava's Sarvadaśanasaṁgraha, Chapter XII, [1]: *Annual of Oriental and Religious Studies*. Tokyo: Suzuki Research Foundation, 1975/1976, pp. 77–100. [2]: *Bukkyo-gaku (Journal of Buddhist Studies)*, Vol. 4 (Tokyo 1977), pp. (1) =(85). In this article, they translated *SDS XII* into Japanese, compared it with *JNMV* and made a word index to *SDS XII*.

5. Mādhava's time has been fixed by scholars to be C.E. 1297–1386, and this is in agreement with the tradition that he lived for 90 years. Cf. Rao Bahadur R. Narasimhachar: "Madhavacharya and his younger brothers", *The Indian Antiquary*, Vol. XLV (1916), pp. 1–6, 17–24; V.A. Ramaswami Sastri: Introduction to the *Tattvabindu by Vācaspatimiśra*, Annamalai University Sanskrit Series No. 3 (1936), pp 80–84.

6. Śrīmatī jananī yasya sukīrtiḥ Māyaṇaḥ pitā /
Sāyaṇo Bhoganāthaś ca manobuddhisahodarau //
yasya Baudhāyanaṃ sūtraṃ Śākhā yasya ca Yājuṣī /
Bhāradvājakulaṁ yasya sarvajñaḥ sa hi Mādhavaḥ //
(*Parāśaramādhavīya*)

7. Cf. H.V. Sreenivasa Murthy: *A History of Karnataka*, New Delhi 1977, pp. 166–250.

8. *Jaiminīyanyāyamālāvistara* (Śrīmādhavapraṇītā savistarā Jaiminīyanyāyamālā. Kashi Sanskrit Series 126. Vārāṇasī: The Chowkhamba Sanskrit Series office, 1937).

9. *JNMV*, p. 3: sarvavarṇāśramānugrahāya purāṇasāraparāśarasmṛtivyākhyānādinā smārto dharmaḥ pūrvaṁ vyākhyātaḥ. idānīṁ dvijānāṁviśeṣānugrahāya śrautadharmavyākhyāyai pravṛttaḥ.

10. *JNMV*, p. 4: yady api śāstradīpikādau kvacit kvacit saṁgrahaśloko 'sti tathāpi na sarvatra vidyate. yatrāsti, tatrāpi viṣayasaṁśayayor asaṁgrahān ślokapāṭhamātreṇādhikaraṇam upanyasituṁ śakyate.

11. *JNM*, p. 18. tad evam adhikaraṇatraye vyutpādanāya bhāṭṭaprābhākaramatabheda upanyastaḥ. atha prāyeṇa bhāṭṭamatam evopanyasyate.

12. Cf. H. Nakamura, *op. cit.*, p. 241.

13. For a detailed discussion about the relation between *JNMV* and *SDS XII*, see S. Mayeda and H. Kurata, *op. cit.*, pp. 80–91.

14. Cf. *The Mīmāṁsāsūtras of Jaimini with the Bhāṣya by Śabarasvāmin and the commentaries, Prabhā, Tantravārttika and Tupṭīkā*. Ānandāśrama Sanskrit Series 97. Poona: Ānandāśrama Mudraṇālaya, 1929.

JS consists of twelve chapters:

In the first chapter is discussed pramāṇa (inquiry into the nature of the valid means of knowledge), namely the authoritativeness of those collections of words which are severally meant by the terms, vidhi (injunction), arthavāda (explanatory passage), mantra (hymn), smṛti (tradition), and nāmadheya (name).

In the second we find the discussion on bheda (whether a particular karma is the same or different from another), in particular certain subsidiary discussions, as e.g. on apūrva, relative to the difference of various rites (karmabheda), refutation of erroneously alleged proofs (pramāṇavāda), and difference of performance (prayogabheda), as in obligatory and voluntary offerings.

In the third are considered śeṣa (which karma is pradhāna and which is aṅga), and the means to know it: Śruti (revelation), liṅga (sign or sense of a passage), vākya (context), &c., and their respective weight, when in apparent opposition to one another; then the ceremonies called Pratipattikarmāṇi, anārabhyādhīta (things mentioned by the way), things accessory to several main objects, as prayājas, &c., and the duties of the sacrificer.

In the fourth is discussed on prayukti (which is prayojya and which prayojaka), the chief subject is the influence of the principal and subordinate rites on other rites, the fruit produced by juhū when made of the Butea frondosa, &c., and the diceplaying, &c., which forms part of the Rājasūya-sacrifice.

In the fifth, krama (the order in which the karma has to be done) is the subject, the relative order of different parts of a sacrifice, as the seventeen animals at the Vājapeya, the multiplication and non-multiplication of rites, and the respective force of the words of the śruti, the order of mention, &c., as determining the order of performance.

In the sixth, which deals with adhikāra (person's qualification for karma), we read of adhikārin (the persons qualified to offer sacrifices), their obligations, the substitutes for prescribed materials, supplies for lost or injured offerings, expiatory rites, the Satra-offerings, things proper to be given, and the different sacrificial fines.

In the seventh is treated sāmānyato 'tideśa (the mode of transference in general) of the ceremonies of one sacrifice to another by direct command in the Vedic text, others as inferred by 'name' or 'sign'.

In the eighth, we find viśeṣato'tideśa (special transfer), transference by virtue of the clearly expressed or obscurely expressed 'sign' or by the predominant 'sign', and cases also where no transference takes place.

In the ninth, the discussion begins with ūha (adaptation effected when transferring from prakṛti to vikṛti) of hymns when quoted in a new connection, the adaptation of sāmans and mantras, and collateral questions connected therewith.

In the tenth, the subject is bādha (cancellation), the occasions are discussed where the non-performance of the primary rite involves the 'preclusion' and non-performance of the dependent rites, and occasions when rites are precluded, because other rites produce their special results, also Graha-offerings, certain sāmans, and various other things, as well as different kinds of negation.

In the eleventh we find the incidental mention and subsequently the fuller discussion of tantra (performance of a single auxiliary karma to serve the needs of several main kármas), where several acts are combined into one, and āvāpa (the performing an act more than once).

In the twelfth, there is the discussion on prasaṅga (performance of an auxiliary to serve another auxiliary), when the rite is performed with one chief purpose, but with an incidental further reference on tantra, samuccaya (cumulation of concurrent rites) and vikalpa (option).

15. Cf. H. Kurata: Mīmāṁsāgakuha ni okeru dharma-kan no kichou (= The Mīmāṁsaka Conception of Dharma), *Saṁbhāṣā*, vol. 7. Nagoya: Association of Indian and Buddhist studies, 1986, pp. 13–23; G. Jha: *Pūrva-Mīmāṁsā in its Sources*, (Benares: Benares Hindu University, 1944), pp. 147–51; Introduction to the *Nyāyaratnamālā* (*NRM*), edited by K.S. Rāmaswāmi Śāstri, (Baroda: Oriental Institute, 1937), pp. xxxii-xxxv.

16. *Śāstradīpikā of Pārthasārathimiśra* ed. by Laxman Shastri Dravid. Chowkhamba Sanskrit Series 43. Benares: Chowkhamba Sanskrit Series Office, 1916 (ŚD), pp. 6–8; *Ślokavārttika by Kumārila Bhaṭṭa*, with the commentary Nyāyaratnākara of Pārthasārathi Miśra. Chowkhamba Sanskrit Series 3, 1898 (*ŚV*), *pratijñāsūtra*, vv. 11–25.

17. Pārthasārathi says that the relation between the Mīmāṁsā and dharma is sādhyasādhanatva. According to the Yuktisnehaprapūraṇī, viṣaya is divided into two, dharma and dharmajñāna, the relation between the Mīmāṁsā and dharma is jñāpyajñāpakabhāva, while the relation between the Mīmāṁsā and dharmajñāna is janyajanakabhāva. Cf. note 14.

18. *SDSXII*, 1.25: dharmaśāstra; 1.50: dharmavicāra; 1.52: dharmavicāraśāstra. Prābhākaras insist that dharma is nothing but Vedārtha. Cf. *Ṛjuvimalā* (Chowkhamba Sanskrit Series 391), p. 16: dharmaśabdaś ca vedārthamātraparaḥ. Therefore for the Prābhākaras dharmavicāra is equal to the inquiry into the meaning of the Vedas.

19. S. Mayeda and H. Kurata: *Problems of Ritualistic Philosophy* [2], pp. (4)—(15).

20. *Prakaraṇapañcikā of Śālikanāthamiśra*, ed. by A. Subrahmanya Shastri. Banaras: Banaras Hindu University, 1961 (PP), p. 12: kaḥ punar ācāryakaraṇavidhiḥ. upanīya tu. . .iti smaraṇānumitaḥ śiṣyam upanīya vedādhyāpanenācāryakaṁ bhāvayed ity evaṁrūpaḥ; *NRM*, p. 23: kaś cāsav adhyāpanavidhir yat prayuktam adhyayanam. yady ucyate upanīya tu . . iti smṛty-anumitam upanīyādhyāpanenācāryakaṁ bhāvayed ity evaṁrūpaṁ vacanam iti tad ayuktam; *AVBh*, p. 10: nanūktam—upanīya tu yaḥ śiṣyam ity anayā smṛtyā upanīyāpanācāryakaṁ bhāvayed ity evaṁrūpa ācāryakaraṇavidhir anumīyata iti, tan na. Cf. S. Mayeda and H. Kurata, *op. cit.*, p. (34).

21. S. Mayeda and H. Kurata, *op. cit.*, pp. (15)-(23).

22. *JS* I.1.2: codanālakṣaṇo 'rtho dharmaḥ. Śabara ad *JS* I.i.2: kriyāyāḥ pravartakaṁ vacanam. Cf. H. Kurata, *op. cit.*, pp. 16–18.

23. Cf. notes 27-28; S. Mayeda and H. Kurata, *op. cit.*, pp. (23)–(29).

24. *The Nyāyakusumāñjali of Śrī Udayanācārya with four Commentaries*. Kashi Sanskrit Series 30. Varanasi: The Chowkhamba Sanskrit Series

Office, 1957. The *Nyāyakusumāñjali* is cited at least eight times in *SDSXII*. See *SDSXII*, p. 106, I.1.; p. 107, 1.5; p. 211, 1.1; p. 220, 1.3; p. 228, 1.1; p. 229, 1.1; p. 230, 1.1; p. 230, 1.2–p. 233, 1.3; p. 234, 1.2.

25. Cf. Śabara ad *JS* I.i.6–23; *ŚV*, śabdanityatādhikaraṇa. For a detailed discussion on this view, see E. Frauwallner, "Mīmāṁsāsūtra, I.1.6–23, "*WZKSO*, V (1961), pp. 113–23.

26. *SDSXII*, p. 212: yo hi nityatve sarvadopalabdhyanupalabdhiprasaṅgo Nyāyabhūṣaṇakāroktaḥ..The *Nyāyabhūṣaṇa* is Bhāsarvajña's own commentary on his *Nyāyasāra*. We find out the passage in the *Nyāyasāra* itself, but not in the *Nyāyabhūṣaṇa*. See *Nyāyabhūṣaṇa of Bhāsarvajña*, ed. by Swami Yogindrananda. Vārāṇasī: Ṣaḍdarśana Prathiṣṭhāna, 1968. Cf. S. Mayeda and H. Kurata, *op. cit.*, p. 62.

27. As Mādhava cited, Vāgīśvara says, in his *Mānamanohara*, "sound is non-eternal from the fact of its being a special quality belonging to an organ of sense, just as colour is to the eye." (anityaḥ śabdaḥ, indiriyaviśeṣaguṇatvāt, cakṣurgatarūpavat.) See *Śrīmadācāryavādivāgīśvarapraṇītaḥ Mānamanoharaḥ*, Ṣaḍdarśanaprakāśanagranthamālāyā No. 2, (Vārāṇasī, 1973), p. 110. According to the traditional view of the Nyāya-Vaiśeṣika, śabda is ākāśaguṇa, but followers of Kumārila stand for the theory that śabda is dravya. Cf. A.B. Keith: *The Karmamīmāṁsā* (London: Oxford University Press, 1921), p. 53. In the school of the Mīmāṁsā, śabda is devided into two. One is varṇātmaka and the other is dhvanyātmaka. According to the followers of Kumārila, varṇātmaka śabda is dravya and eternal, dhvanyātmaka śabda is vāyuguṇa and non-eternal, while the followers of Prabhākara tell that both of them are ākāśaguṇa and eternal. Cf. *Mānameyodaya*, ed. with an English Translation by C. Kunhanraja. Adyar: Theosophical Publishing House, 1933, chapter of dravya 130.

28. *SDSXII*, 1.216ff.: vedasyāpauruṣeyatayā nirastasamastaśaṅkākalaṅkāṅkuratvena svataḥsiddhaṁ dharme prāmāṇyam iti susthitam. Cf. *AVBh*, p. 18.

29. *SDSXII*, I.218ff.: pramāṇatvāpramāṇatve svataḥ sāṁkhyāḥ samāśritāḥ / naiyāyikās te parataḥ saugatāś caramaṁ svataḥ / prathamaṁ parataḥ prāhuḥ prāmāṇyaṁ vedavādinaḥ / pramāṇatvaṁ svataḥ prāhuḥ parataś cāpramāṇatām // Cf. *AVBh*, p. 13: tatra bahudhā vivadante vādinaḥ, prāmāṇyam aprāmāṇyaṁ cobhayaṁ svata iti sāṁkhyāḥ. ubhayaṁ parata iti tārkikāḥ. prāmāṇyaṁ svataḥ aprāmāṇyaṁ parata iti mīmāṁsakāḥ. aprāmāṇyaṁ svataḥ prāmāṇyaṁ parata iti saugatāḥ.

30. Cf. S. Mayeda and H. Kurata, *op. cit.*, pp. (29)–(30). K. Kunjunni Raja: *Indian Theories of Meaning*, (Madras: The Adyar Library and Research Centre, 1969, 2nd ed.), pp. 189–227.

31. According to the abhihitānvaya theory of verbal comprehension, the meaning of a sentence is a concatenation of the individual items expressed by the words. The individual words have in themselves meanings which can be comprehended separately. In other words, the words convey only the individual word-meanings and their mutual relation is conveyed by the word-meanings, not by the words. Cf. K. Kunjunni Raja, *op. cit.*, pp. 203–13.

32. According to the anvitābhidhāna theory, words do not convey a meaning except in the context of a sentence; each word has a definite meaning, but it is also clear that the purpose of the word is to serve as part of a sentence. Both the individual word-meanings and their mutual relation are conveyed by the words themselves. Cf. K. Kunjunni Raja, *op. cit.*, pp. 193–203.

33. *SDSXII*, I.18ff.: adhikaraṇaṁ ca pañcāvayavam ācakṣate parīkṣakāḥ. te ca pañcāvayavā viṣayasaṁśayapūrvapakṣasiddhāntasaṁgatirūpāḥ.

34. *JNMV*, p. 4: ekaikasyādhikaraṇasya viṣayaḥ, saṁdehaḥ, saṅgatiḥ, pūrvapakṣaḥ, siddhāntaś ceti pañcāvayavāḥ. As a rule, he first gives the saṁśaya in particular Vedic passage, the main pūrvapakṣa and last the siddhānta of each adhikaraṇa, in one, two or more verses. Cf. note 10; P.V. Kane;*History of Dharmaśāstra*, Government Oriental Series—Class B, No. 6 Poona: Bhandarkar Oriental Research Institute, 1930–962, Vol. V-2, p. 1182, note 1925; Max Muller: *The Six Systems of Indian Philosophy* (Varanasi: Chowkhamba Sanskrit Series Office, 1903. (Reprint), pp. 204–06; P. Deussen; *Allgemeine Geschichte der Philosophie* I.3, S.293-94.

35. *TSBh*, p. 2: tat kaṭākṣeṇa tadrūpaṁ dadhad bukkamahīpatiḥ / anvaśān mādhavācāryaṁ vedārthasya prakāśane // sa prāha nṛpatiṁ rājan sāyaṇāryo mamānujaḥ / sarvaṁ vetty eṣa vedānāṁ vyākhyātṛtve niyujyatām // ity ukto mādhavāryeṇa vīrabukkamahīpatiḥ / anvaśāt sāyaṇācāryaṁ vedārthasya prakāśane //

36. *AVBh*, p. 3: vijayī hariharabhūpaḥ samudvahan sakalabhūbhāram / ṣoḍaśamahānti dānānyaniśaṁ sarvasya tuṣṭaye kurvan // tanmūlabhūtam ālocya vedam ātharvaṇābhidham / ādiśat sāyaṇācāryaṁ tadarthasya prakāśane //.

37. Cf. Ram Gopal: *The History and Principles of Vedic Interpretation*, (New Delhi: Concept Publishing Company, 1983), pp. 109–17.

38. *TSBh*, p. 23.

39. Cf. Ram Gopal, *op. cit.*, p. 110.

40. Cf. Ram Gopal, *op. cit.*, p. 113.

41. Cf. Ram Gopal, *op. cit.*, p. 115.

42. *ŚD*, p. 14. Cf. S. Mayeda and H. Kurata, *op. cit.*, pp. (10)–(11). This verse is cited in the *AVBh*, p. 10, too.

43. Cf. S. Mayeda and H. Kurata, *op. cit.*, pp. (12)–(15).

44. Rao Bahadur R. Narasimhachar, *op. cit.*, pp. 17–24; V. A. Ramaswami Sastri, *op. cit.*, p. 84. Cf. M. Kripacharyulu: *Sayana and Madhavavidyaranya*; A Study of their lives and letters, Guntur 1986 which the present writer could not get and consult while he wrote this article.

23

BHARTṚHARI AND MĪMĀṀSĀ*

JOHANNES BRONKHORST

1.1. Both Bhartṛhari and Śabara pay a good deal of attention to the subject of *ūha* 'modification, adjustment'. Bhartṛhari discusses it in the first Āhnika of his commentary on the Mahābhāṣya (CE I.5.1-7.15; AL 5.18-8.17; Sw 6.17-9.27; Ms 2b9-3c1), while parts of Adhyāya 9 of Śabara's Bhāṣya deal with it. Two cases in particular are treated by both the authors and allow of a detailed comparison.

The first case is most easily introduced with the help of Śabara's Bhāṣya on Pūrva Mīmāṁsā Sūtra 9.3.10:

> *asti paśur agnīṣomīyaḥ, yo dīkṣito yad agnīṣomīyaṁ paśum ālabhata iti / tatra pāśaikatvābhidhāyī mantraḥ, aditiḥ pāśaṃ pramumoktv etam iti / tathā pāśabahutvābhidhāyī, aditiḥ pāśān pramumoktv etān iti / ... / asti dvipaśur vikṛtiḥ / maitraṁ śvetam ālabheta, vāruṇaṁ kṛṣṇam apāṁ cauṣadhīnāṁ ca saṁdhāvannakāma iti / tatra codakena pāśābhidhāyinau mantrau prāptau / tayoḥ saṁśayaḥ / kiṁ bahuvacanānto'vikāreṇa pravartate, ekavacanāntasya nivṛttiḥ, uta bahuvacanānto nivartate, ekavacanānta ūhitavyaḥ, utobhayor api pravṛttir abhidhānavipratipattiś ca, utaikavacanānta ūhitavyo bahuvacanānto 'pi na nivarteta / kiṁ prāptam /*

"There is the Agniṣṭomīya animal [sacrifice] laid down in the text *yo dīkṣito yad agnīṣomīyaṁ paśum ālabhate* ('When one, being initiated, sacrifices the animal dedicated to Agni-Soma'). In connection with this there is a mantra, speaking of the

* This article was written with the financial assistance of the Netherlands Organization for Scientific Research (N.W.O.). Reprint from "Studien zur Indologie und Iranistik", vol. 15, pp. 101-117, Reinbek 1989.

singleness of the noose (*pāśa*): *aditiḥ pāśaṁ pramumoktv etam* ('May Aditi loosen this noose'); also [there is another mantra] speaking of the plurality of the noose: *aditiḥ pāśān pramumoktv etān. ...*

[Then again,] there is a modificatory sacrifice (*vikṛti*) [of the Agnīṣomīya] at which two animals [are killed], laid down in the text *maitraṁ śvetam ālabheta, vāruṇaṁ kṛṣṇam* etc. ('The white [goat] should be sacrificed to Mitra and the black [goat] to Varuṇa') In accordance with the General Law, both the mantras that mention a noose come to be regarded as to be used at this [sacrifice of two animals].

In regard to [the use of] these two [mantras at this last sacrifice of two goats, there arise] the following questions: (a) Is [the word] in the plural form to be used in its unmodified form and that in the singular form to be excluded? Or (b) should the plural form be excluded and the singular form be modified [into a dual form]? Or (c) should both [the plural and the singular forms] be used, there being a diversity of expression (i.e. option) [regarding the one to be actually used in any particular case]? Or (d) should the singular form be modified, the plural form also [in its modified form (?)] not being excluded?" (tr. Gaṅgānātha Jhā, vol. III p. 1561; modified)

The problem here raised is subsequently discussed in the Bhāṣya. Four solutions are proposed, the fourth one of which is finally accepted. For our present purposes it is however interesting to study the first solution, which is not accepted by Śabara. It reads (on PMS 9.3.10):

anyāyas tv avikāreṇa / anyāyanigado bahuvacanānto'vikāreṇa pravartate / ekavacanānto nivartitum arhati / kutaḥ / nāsyaikasmin pāśe pravartamānasya dṛṣṭaḥ pratighātaḥ / yathaivaikasmin pāśe pravartate, tathā dvayor api pravartitum arhati / nāsāv ekasya vācakaḥ, na dvayoḥ / evam ārṣaś codako'anugṛhīto bhaviṣyati / itarathā hi ūhyamāne yathāprakṛti mantro na kṛtaḥ syāt / na dvayoḥ pāśayoḥ, ekasmiṁś ca pāśe kaścid viśeṣo'sti/ tasmād avikāreṇa bahuvacanāntaḥ prayujyate, ekavacanāntasya nivṛttir iti /

" 'That which is incompatible [should be used] in its unmodified form'; [i.e.] the plural form, which is incompatible [with the primary sacrifice at which there is only one animal], is used [at the sacrifice of two animals] in its unmodified form, and the singular form should be excluded. Why so? [Because] we find no obstacle to its being used in the case of there being [only one animal and] one noose; [so that] just as it is used in the case of [one animal and] one noose, so should it be used also in the case of there being [two animals] and two [nooses; especially as the plural form] is expressive of neither one nor two. In thus [using the plural form in its unmodified form,] the scriptural injunction of the General Law becomes honoured; while in the other case, if [the words] were modified, then the mantra would not be used in the form in which it is used at the primary sacrifice. Nor is there any difference between one noose and two nooses [so far as the applicability of the plural form is concerned]. From all this it follows that the plural form is used in its unmodified form and the singular form is excluded." (tr. Gaṅgānātha Jhā, p. 1562; modified)

As said before, Śabara does not accept this position. He comes to the conclusion, under sūtra 9.3.13, that both the plural form and the singular form must be modified into a dual form. But this rejected position is rather close to the one adopted by Bhartṛhari, where he says in his commentary on the Mahābhāṣya (AL 6.8-12; Sw 7.9-13; Ms 2c7-10; CE I 5.14-17):

tathaikasminneva prakṛtipāśe pāśān iti bahuvacanāntaṁ śrūyate / aditiḥ pāśān pramumoktv iti / tatrāpi vikṛtāv ūho nāsti / vājasaneyināṁ tv ekavacanāntaḥ paṭhyate aditiḥ pāśam iti / teṣām ūhaḥ prāpnoti / . . . athavā pāśeṣu noha ity anena tu naigamavibhāṣā / bahuvacane sati yatheṣṭaṁ prayogo bhavati /

The Ms is very corrupt, but this reconstruction seems to be essentially correct. I translate:

". . . The plural *pāśān* is heard in *aditiḥ pāśān pramumoktu* even though there is but one single noose (*pāśa*) in the primary sacrifice. Here . . . there is no modification in the modificatory sacrifice. But among the Vājasaneyins [the mantra] is read in the singular, *aditiḥ pāśam* . . . For them modification applies. . . .

Or the statement that there is no modification in the case of nooses (pl.!) expresses a Vedic option: where there is a plural number [of *pāśa*] one uses [the word] as one wishes (i.e. either in the plural or adjusted to the situation)".

Bhartṛhari here represents the point of view of a particular Vedic school different from the Vājasaneyins. His Vedic school had laid down the rule that no modification takes place in the case of the word *pāśa* used in the plural, and Bhartṛhari interprets this rule in two ways. Interestingly, the line *aditiḥ pāśaṁ pramumoktv etam* does not occur in the scriptures of the Vājasaneyins, but in TS 3.1.4.4. Bhartṛhari's mistake (what else could it be?) allows us to conclude that he was not a Taittirīya either. The presence of *aditiḥ pāśān pramumoktv etān* in MS 1.2.15, KS 30.8 suggests that Bhartṛhari belonged to one of these two Vedic schools. Other evidence (see Rau, 1980; Bronkhorst, 1981; 1987) supports the view that he was a Maitrāyaṇīya.

The conclusion must be that Bhartṛhari's description of *ūha*, or rather of the absence of *ūha*, in *aditiḥ pāśān pramumoktu* does not represent the position of any group of Mīmāṁsakas, but rather the position of the Maitrāyaṇīya branch of the Yajurveda. The Mīmāṁsakas on the other hand, or at any rate Śabara, did not confine their attention to one Vedic school. Only thus could they be confronted with the situation in which both the mantras *aditiḥ pāśān pramumoktv etān* and *aditiḥ pāśaṃ pramumoktv etam* apply. The question that remains is how the similarity between the point of view accepted by Bhartṛhari and the one rejected by Śabara is to be explained.

This question gains interest in view of the fact that Śabara too may have been a Maitrāyaṇīya. It is true that the Taittirīya texts are more often quoted in his Bhāṣya, but Garge (1952:19f) has shown that Śabara's Bhāṣya nonetheless shows a clear preference for Maitrāyaṇīya readings wherever possible. Garge's data are perhaps most easily understood by assuming that Śabara, a Maitrāyaṇīya, continued and codified the Mīmāṁsaka tradition which by itself had no particular predilection for Maitrāyaṇīya texts.

1.2. Both Bhartṛhari (AL 7.10-8.8; Sw 8.16-9.17; Ms 3a2-b6; CE I 6.11-7.7) and Śabara (on Pūrva Mīmāṁsā Sūtra 9.3.22 and 9.3.27-4.27) deal in detail with the *adhrigu* mantra, a passage that occurs in but slightly differing form in a number of texts.[1] Nothing in Bhartṛhari's discussion shows any influence from Śabara. Indeed it appears that the two authors disagree on how to deal with the part *ṣaḍviṁśatir asya vaṅkrayas* 'it has twenty-six ribs'. Śabara winds up a long discussion on this matter by stating (on sūtra 9.4.16) that the total number of ribs must be mentioned where two or more animals are involved, not a repetition of the numeral 'twenty-six' (*iyattā vaṅkrīṇāṁ prakṛtau vaktavyā / ihāpi sā codakena pradiśyate / tena nābhyāsaḥ / sa hi paśunimittakaḥ / tasmāt samasya vacanaṁ vaṅkrīṇāṁ kartavyam iti /*). Bhartṛhari makes an enigmatic remark after citing the sentence that precedes *ṣaḍviṁśatir*. This remark—*tathāvyayam anekasmin paśau dvir abhyasyate*—can be interpreted with the help of MŚS 5.2.9.5 *yāny avyayāny anekāni tāni dvir abhyasyante . . . ṣaḍviṁśatiḥ ṣaḍviṁśatiḥ*. It thus comes to mean: "Then, in case there is more than one animal, the indeclinable [that follows, viz. *ṣaḍviṁśatiḥ*] is repeated".

Unlike Śabara, parts of Bhartṛhari's treatment of *ūha* show the influence of the Mānava Śrauta Sūtra. We saw how MŚS 5.2.9.5 was needed to understand one of Bhartṛhari's remarks. At two other occasions he makes a direct reference to 'the section on modification' (*ūhaprakaraṇa*) of the Mānava Śrauta Sūtra. Once (AL 7.5-6; Sw 8.11-12; Ms 2d10-11; CE I 6.6-8) he says:

> *aghasad aghastām aghasannagrabhīṣur akṣannity ūhaprakaraṇe paṭhyate*
>
> "In the section on modification the forms *aghasat, aghastām, aghasan, agrabhīṣuḥ* and *akṣan* are read".

This must refer to MŚS 5.2.9.6:

> *haviṣi praiṣe sūktavāke ca adat adatām adan, ghasat ghastāṁ*

ghasan, aghasat aghastām aghasan, karat karatāṁ karan, aghrabhīt aghrabhīṣṭām agrabhīṣuḥ, akṣan/

Then again (AL 7.20-21; Sw 9.3-4; Ms 3a8-9; CE I 6.21-22):

tatrohaprakaraṇa evaiṣaṁ mātā pitā bhrātā sanābhisaṁsargi-śabdā ity evamādīny anūhyānīty paṭhyate/

" . . . in the same section on modification it is read that of the [words mentioned earlier] the words indicative of siblings and kin *mātā, pitā, bhrātā* and the like should not be modified".

This reflects MŚS 5.2.9.7:

mātā pitā bhrātā sagarbhyo ('nu) sakhā sayūthyo nābhirūpam āsaṁsargi śabdāś cakṣuḥ śrotraṁ vāṅ manas tvaṅ medo havir barhiḥ śyenaṁ vakṣa ity anūhyam/

" 'His mother, his father, his brother from the same womb, his friend in the herd'; the form of *nābhi* joined with (the ending) *ā*; the words 'eye, ear, voice, mind, skin, fat, oblation (?), sacrificial grass, eagle-shaped breast', all these are not to be modified." (tr. Van Gelder, p. 174)

Not all of Bhartṛhari's examples regarding *ūha* can be traced to the Mānava Śrauta Sūtra, nor to any other Śrauta Sūtra. Of particular interest is the stanza which introduces his discussion of *ūha* in the *adhrigu* mantra, and which has not been traced in any earlier work (AL 7.10-11; Sw 8.16-17; Ms 3a2-3; CE I 6.11-12):

aṅgāni jñātināmā [ny upamā] cendriyāṇi ca/
etāni nohaṁ gacchanti adhrigau viṣamaṁ hi tat //

"Limbs of the body, names of relatives, comparison and organs of sense, these do not undergo modification; for it (?) is irregular in the case of *adhrigu*".

This stanza, which governs Bhartṛhari's ensuing discussion, must be assumed to have belonged to the ritualistic tradition of some

Vedic school, probably the Maitrāyaṇīyas.[2] Bhartṛhari based his discussion of *ūha* not on some preexisting works of Mīmāṁsā but on ritual works which had no, or little, connection with Mīmāṁsā.

This situation allows us to understand how Śabara could describe and reject an opinion (on *aditiḥ pāśān pramumoktu* etc., see section 1.1 above) which is so close to Bhartṛhari's. The Mīmāṁsakas, who took a broader view of the sacrificial rites than those adhering to the traditions of particular Vedic schools, would nonetheless borrow ideas from individual Vedic schools, either to accept or to reject them. All we have to assume is that Śabara was acquainted with at least some of these ritual books.

It seems that the works which Bhartṛhari used did not survive him for long. The above stanza (*aṅgāni* . . .) is quoted by Kumārila in his Tantra-vārttika on Pūrva Mīmāṁsā Sūtra 1.3.24 (p. 197) and ascribed to a *ṭīkākāra* who is also credited (p. 209) with the authorship of the stanza that we know as Vākyapadīya 2.14 (Swaminathan, 1963: 69), i.e., apparently to Bhartṛhari. That is to say, Bhartṛhari is here quoted as an authority on *ūha* in his own right.[3]

1.3. Another instance where Bhartṛhari gives evidence of drawing upon a tradition quite independent of the Mīmāṁsakas occurs on P. 1.1.5 and consists of an illustration with the help of the Śunaskarṇastama sacrifice (AL 118.3; Sw 137.26-138.1; Ms 39a 7-8; CE IV 6.11-12):

> *śunaskarṇastomayajñavad etat syāt, yathā pradhānasya maraṇenārthina iṣṭiṁ pravartayanti*/
>
> "This is like the Śunaskarṇastoma sacrifice: desirous of the main thing by means of death, they cause the sacrifice to proceed".

The Śunaskarṇa Agniṣṭoma sacrifice is discussed in Śabara's Bhāṣya om PMS 10.2.57-61. This sacrifice is enjoined by the injunction "Desiring one's own death one should perform this sacrifice, if he wishes that he should reach the Heavenly Region without any disease" (*maraṇakāmo hy etena yajeta, yaḥ kāmayetānāmayaḥ svargaṁ lokam iyām iti*; tr. Gaṅgānātha Jhā, p.

1721). The question raised under PMS 10.2.57-58 is whether or not the sacrifice should be continued after the sacrificer has taken his life by throwing himself into the fire. The answer is that the sacrifice must be completed. A number of reasons is given for this, none of them even resembling Bhartṛhari's. This is true to the extent that Pārthasārathi Miśra in his Śāstradīpikā on PMS 10.2.57-58 (adhikaraṇa 23, vol. II, p. 334f.) quotes Bhartṛhari as authority when accepting that point of view (cf. Swaminathan, 1961:315-16):

> *svarga evātra maraṇenārthinaḥ phalaṃ na maraṇam / maraṇa-kāma ity aṅgīkṛtamaraṇa ity arthaḥ/ tena yo hy evaṁ jñātvā svargaṁ prāpnavānīti kāmayate, tasyāyaṁ kratuḥ / tathā ca haribhir uktaṁ 'pradhānasya maraṇenārthina ijyāṃ pravarta-yanti'iti /*

> "Heaven is here the fruit he wishes [to attain] by means of death, not death [itself]. The words 'desiring [one's own] death' (*maraṇakāma*) mean 'accepting [one's own] death'. Therefore, this sacrifice is [meant] for him who, knowing this, wishes to attain to heaven. This has been expressed by [Bhartṛ-] hari with the words 'desirous of the main thing (i.e. heaven) by means of death they cause the sacrifice to proceed'."

Pārthasārathi's quotation does not only cast light on the form and meaning of Bhartṛhari's remark; it also indicates that Pārthasārathi (10th century C.E. according to Ramaswami Sastri, 1937) had no (longer?) access to the sources from which Bhartṛhari drew his example.

1.4. We turn to another passage where Bhartṛhari to all appearances draws upon the tradition of the Maitrāyaṇīyas. It occurs in his comments on the line *prayājāḥ savibhaktikāḥ kār-yāḥ* of the Mahābhāṣya (I.3.10). Bhartṛhari is here clearly influenced by the Mānava Śrauta Sūtra (5.1.2.6) which reads:

> *punar ādheye prayājānuyājānāṁ purastād vopariṣṭād vā vibhāk-tīḥ kuryāt / ye yajāmahe 'samiuhaḥ samidho'gnā ājyasya vyantv' agnir agnis 'tanūnapād-agnā ājyasya vetv' agnim agnim 'iḍo'gnā*

ājyasya vyantv' agner agner 'barhir agnā ājyasya vetv' agner agner iti |

"When [fire] is to be lit again one should recite the vibhaktis before or after the preliminary and final offerings, as follows: *ye yajāmahe* etc".

The first and introductory sentence of this passage is included in Bhartṛhari's remarks on the subject, which however go beyond the Mānava Śrauta Sūtra in giving some kind of justification for the choice of 'vibhaktis' (i.e. *agnir agniḥ* etc.) and even lead to an outcome that is different in one point; he also gives an alternative. Bhartṛhari's Mahābhāṣya Dīpikā reads (AL 12.25-13.4; Sw. 15.21-16.1; Ms 5a2-5; CE I 11.10-14):

vibhaktīnām api sarvāsāṁ prayoge prāpte yā dvyakṣarā vā satyaś caturakṣarā vā bhavantīti vacanād agnināgnineti na prayujyate | tathā na śabdajāmi kuryāt | śabdajāmi hi tad bhavati yat pañcamyantam | tasmād agner agner ity anena rūpeṇa ṣaṣṭhyantaṁ prayujyate | punarādhyeye prayājānuyājānāṁ purastād vopariṣṭād vā vibhaktīḥ kuryāt | narāśaṁso agnim agnim iti vā ubhayathā dṛṣṭatvāt |

"Although it would follow (from what precedes in Bhartṛhari's commentary) that all case-endings be used, the form *agnināgninā* is not used because it has been stated 'which have two syllables or four syllables'. Similarly one should not use *śabdajāmi. Śabdajāmi* is that which has an ablative ending. Therefore it is the genitive which is used in the form *agner agneḥ*, [not the ablative]. When [fire] is to be lit again one should recite the vibhaktis before or after the preliminary offerings. Or *narāśaṁso . . . agnim agnim* [is used instead of *tanūnapād . . . agnim agnim*] because it is seen both ways".

This shows that according to Bhartṛhari the following four 'vibhaktis' are to be used: *agnir agniḥ* (nom.), *agnim agnim* (acc.), *agner agneḥ* (gen.), *agnāv agnau* (loc.).

The essential correctness of the above reading of Bhartṛhari's Mahābhāṣya Dīpikā is confirmed by Śivarāmendra Sarasvatī's

Ratnaprakāśa, a subcommentary on the Mahābhāṣya. It says in this connection (p. 56-57):

> *tatrāpi sambuddhiṭāṅe'ntānāṁ na prayogaḥ, 'āvṛttyā dvyakṣarāḥ santaś caturakṣarā bhavanti' iti vacanāt / sambuddhyantasya dvyakṣaratve'pi dvirvacanottaraṁ pūrvarūpe sati 'agne'gne' iti tryakṣaratvāt / ṭāṅe'ntayor ādita eva dvyakṣaratvābhāvāc ca/ tathā ṅasyantam api na prayoktavyam, 'na śabdajāmi kuryāt, śabdajāmi hi tad bhavati yat pañcamyantam' iti vacanāt/ . . . / evaṁ ca caturṣv avaśiṣṭaprayājamantreṣu yathākramaṁ prathamādvitīyāṣaṣṭhīsaptamyekavacanāntānām agniśabdaprakṛtikānāṁ padānāṁ prayogaḥ kartavyaḥ / . . . / tathā cāyaṁ purastātprayogaḥ: 'ye yajāmahe agnir agniḥ samidhaḥ samidho'gna ājyasya vyantu vauṣaṭ' / 'ye yajāmahe agnim agniṁ tanūnapād agna ājyasya vetu vauṣaṭ' / 'ye yajāmahe agner agner iḍo'gna ājyasya vyantu vauṣaṭ' / 'ye yajāmahe agnāv agnau barhir agna ājyasya vetu vauṣaṭ' iti / paścātprayogas tu 'ye yajāmahe samidhaḥ samidho'gna ājyasya vyantu agnir agniḥ vauṣaṭ' ityādiḥ /*

It is true that Śivarāmendra refers immediately after this to Viṣṇumiśra's Kṣīroda, a now lost commentary on the Mahābhāṣya, for further elucidation. It is also true that he then mentions Bhartṛhari's commentary (*hariṭīkā*) and quotes from it a passage which clearly belongs to Bhartṛhari's subsequent treatment of 'vibhaktis' in accordance with the Āśvalāyana Śrauta Sūtra (see Bronkhorst, 1981:174). Yet there can be no doubt that also the above passage was composed under the direct or indirect influence of Bhartṛhari's Mahābhāṣya Dīpikā.

We return to Bhartṛhari's passage. It shows relationship with the Mānava Śrauta Sūtra, as we have seen. It further quotes a line that has close affinity with MS 1.7.3, KS 9.1, KapS 8.4[5] in order to justify that only 'vibhaktis' with two or four syllables are acceptable. Then however it deviates from any known text by quoting a remarkable rule: One should not use *śabdajāmi*; *śabdajāmi* is that which has an ablative ending. Subsequently Bhartṛhari observes that *tanūnapād* is sometimes replaced by *narāśaṁso*. Something similar was noted by the commentator Gārgya Nārāyaṇa on ĀśvŚS 2.8.6 (see Rau, 1980:176) and by Śivarāmendra Sarasvatī (see Bronkhorst, 1981:174), both in connection with the Āśvalāyana version of the 'vibhaktis'.

1.5. What is the source from which Bhartṛhari derived his detailed knowledge on ritual matters? The most likely answer is that he used Prayoga manuals belonging to the Maitrāyaṇīyas. Few old Prayogas have survived and their study has hardly begun. Yet the suspicion could be voiced that "some sort of Prayogas must have been in vogue even before the composition of the Śrautasūtras proper" (Śrautakośa Vol. I, English section, Part I, Preface, p. 7; see already Hillebrandt, 1879: XV; 1897: 38). Bhide (1979:150f.) studied two extant Prayogas of the Cāturmāsya sacrifices and compared them with the Hiraṇyakeśi Śrauta Sūtra, under which they resort. Interestingly, the older of these two Prayogas, by Mahādeva Somayājin, deviates a number of times from the Hiraṇyakeśi Śrauta Sūtra. This shows that Bhartṛhari may indeed have used Prayoga manuals belonging to his Vedic school, and that the few deviations from the Mānava Śrauta Sūtra which we noticed above do not prove that these manuals belonged to another school than that of the Mānavas.

2.1. We conclude from the above that Bhartṛhari was not a Mīmāṁsaka. Yet he was acquainted with Mīmāṁsā. He uses the word 'Mīmāṁsaka' several times in his commentary on the Mahābhāṣya. The line *siddhā dyauḥ siddhā pṛthivī siddham ākāśam iti* (Mbh I.6.18-19) is elucidated by Bhartṛhari's remark (AL 22.23; Sw 27. 19; Ms 8a4; CE I 19.11): *ārhatānāṁ mīmāṁsakānāṁ ca naivāsti vināśaḥ eṣām* "According to the Jainas and Mīmāṁsakas there is no destruction of these", i.e. of sky, earth and ether. At another place (AL 29.10-11; Sw 35.2; Ms 9d7; CE I 24.15) Bhartṛhari quotes the words *darśanasya parārthatvāt* in a discussion concerning the eternality of words. This must be a reflection of PMS 1.1.18 *nityas tu syād darśanasya parārthatvāt*. Note however that Bhartṛhari's quote does not only lack the initial words of the sūtra, it also has an additional word at the end, probably *viprapravṛttatvāt* which is absent from the sūtra.

The following quotation in the Dīpikā seems to throw more light on Bhartṛhari's relationship with Mīmaṁsā. In the third Āhnika Bhartṛhari proclaims (AL 96.3-4; Sw 113.14-15; Ms 31b4-5; CE III.3.19-20):

nānantaryaṃ sambandhahetuḥ / evaṃ hy ucyate / arthato hy asamarthānām ānantaryam akāraṇam /

"[Mere] contiguity is no cause of relationship. Thus, verily, it is said: 'contiguity is no cause of relationship between [words] which are not semantically connected'."

The quotation in this passage had to be reconstructed to some extent, and this could be done with the help of PMS 4.3.11 (*api vāmnānasāmarthyāc codanārthena gamyetārthānāṁ hy arthavattvena vacanāni pratīyante'rthato hy asamarthānām ānantarye'py asambandhas tasmācchrutyekadeśaḥ saḥ*), as pointed out by Palsule (Notes p. 66 of his edition; cf. Swaminathan, 1961:314). What is more, the quoted line occurs in precisely that form in a verse cited in Vaidyanātha's *Chāyā* (p. 160, 162) and which reads:

yasya yenābhisambandho / -ārthasambandho dūrasthasyāpi tena saḥ / arthato hy asamarthānām ānantaryam akāraṇam //

This suggests that Bhartṛhari knew a Mīmāṁsā work which contained this verse.

This impression is strengthened by another quotation in the Mahābhāṣya Dīpikā. on P. 1.1.46, in the context of sequential order. Here Bhartṛhari cites the following verse (AL 274.1-2; Ms 95b1-2 CE VII 5.16-17):

śruter arthāc ca pāṭhāc ca pravṛtteś ca manīṣiṇaḥ /
sthānān mukhyāc ca dharmāṇām āhuḥ kramavidaḥ kramān //

"Those sages who know about sequential order say that the sequential order of things (?) [is determined] on the basis of scriptural assertion, meaning, [order of] text, commencement, place and [order of] the principal".

This verse is close to PMS 5.1.1-15, as already observed by Swaminathan (1961:317). All its elements occur there: *śruti* in PMS 5.1.1 (*śrutilakṣaṇam ānupūrvyaṃ tatpramāṇatvāt*),[6] *artha* in 5.1.2 (*arthāc ca*), *pāṭha* is the subject-matter of 5.1.4, even though not called by this name, *pravṛtti* appears in 5.1.8 (*pravṛttyā tulyakālānāṃ tadupakramāt*), *sthāna* in 5.1.13 (*sthānāc cotpattisaṃyogāt*), *mukhyakrama* finally in 5.1.14 (*mukhyakrameṇa vā'ṅgānāṃ tadarthatvāt*). Again we are left with the impression that Bhartṛhari was acquainted with a work on Mīmāṁsā which contained verse.

2.2. The fact that the work on Mīmāṁsā used by Bhartṛhari appears to have contained verses may help us in identifying its author. Only one author on Mīmāṁsā is thought to have written an early work on this subject which contained verses; this is Bhavadāsa. Sucaritamiśra's commentary Kāśikā on Kumārila's Ślokavārttika quotes a half verse from Bhavadāsa[7] (Kane, 1929: esp. 153 fn. 3). It seems clear that Bhavadāsa preceded Śabara (Kane, 1929; Mishra, 1942:16-17; Frauwallner, 1968: 100f., 107, 112f.)[8]

The assumption that Bhartṛhari used Bhavadāsa's work does not conflict with anything in the Mahābhāṣyadīpikā, nor in the Vākyapadīya, as far as I know. It may be noted that on one occasion, where we seem to know the definition used by Bhavadāsa, Bhartṛhari does not quote Bhavadāsa but gives a definition of his own. Śabara on PMS 12.1.1 quotes a definition of the word *prasaṅga*: *prasaṅgaśabdārtho 'nyair uktaḥ, evam eva prasaṅgaḥ syād vidyamāne svake vidhāv iti*. The quoted line is half a śloka, the whole of which is given on PMS 11.1.1; it is plausible that it derives from Bhavadāsa. Bhartṛhari gives an own definition of this technical Mīmāṁsā term in his commentary (AL 45.4-5; Sw 54.2-3; Ms 14b4-5; CE I 37.11-12): *yady arthī prayojako anyadvāreṇārthaṁ pratipadyate sa prasaṅga ity ucyate*. A closer investigation shows however that Bhartṛhari's definition agrees contentwise with Bhavadāsa's śloka, whereas Śabara has changed the interpretation of the verse so as to make it suit his own ideas. See Bronkhorst, 1986.

2.3. If indeed we can accept that Bhartṛhari used a text on Mīmāṁsā different from Śabara's Bhāṣya we may be in a position to understand a passage that occupied Yudhiṣṭhira Mīmāṁsaka (1973:I:385 fn. 1). It reads (AL 31.2-3; Sw 36.19-21; Ms 10b7-8; CE I 25.24-26):

dharmaprayojano veti mīmāṁsakadarśanam / avasthita eva dharmaḥ / sa tv agnihotrādibhir abhivyajyate / tatpreritas tu phalado bhavati /

"[The words in the Mahābhāṣya (I.8.5-6)] *dharmaprayojano vā* . . . 'bringing about dharma'[9] [express] the view of the Mīmāṁsakas. [According to them] dharma is eternal. It is however manifested by [such sacrifices as] Agnihotra etc. Instigated by these [dharma] produces result".

Mīmāṁsaka contrasts this statement with a passage from Jayanta Bhaṭṭa's Nyāyamañjarī which reads (p. 664):

vṛddhamīmāṃsakāḥ yāgādikarmanirvartyam apūrvaṃ nāma dharmam abhivadanti yāgādikarmaiva śābarā bruvate |

"The old Mīmāṁsakas declare dharma, [also] called apūrva, to be produced by ritual activities such as sacrifices. The followers of Śabara say that the ritual activities such as sacrifices are themselves [dharma]."[10]

The two passages combined seem to indicate that the Mīmāṁsakas known to Bhartṛhari were older than Śabara. Mīmāṁsaka goes further and concludes that Bhartṛhari himself is much earlier than Śabara. This need not be true. In fact, Bhartṛhari's commentary contains an indication that its author knew a view according to which the constituents of the sacrifice are dharma. This indication consists in the twice quoted phrase *dadhimadhvādayo dharmaḥ* 'curds, honey, etc. constitute dharma'. The phrase is quoted (twice) in a difficult and corrupt passage, which may however be reconstituted as follows (Ms 11b3-5; AL 34.8-12; Sw 40.21-25; CE I 28.17-20):

yathā pūrvakālaṁ prayuktāni dīrghasattrāṇī idānīm aprayujyamānāny api dadhimadhvādayo dharma iti karmatādiviṣayaḥ sidhyata evam anyaiḥ prayuktānāṁ sarvakālam idānīm aprayujyamānānām apy anuvidhānaṁ yuktaṁ | ye tu dadhimadhvādayo dharma iti teṣāṃ vyākaraṇe'yam artho na sambhavati | na hi iha śabdoccāraṇāt dharma iti |

This may tentatively be translated:

Just as long Soma sacrifices were used formerly, and even

> though they are not used now, the aim of sacrificial activity is attained since curds, honey etc. constitute dharma; so the laying down of rules for things which have been used by others all the time is proper, even though these things are not used now. But this is not possible in grammar for those who [hold] that curds, honey etc. constitute dharma. For no dharma comes forth from uttering sound.

Much is unclear in this passage. But it shows that we do not have to conclude that Bhartṛhari lived much before Śabara. It seems more appropriate to conjecture that Bhartṛhari used a text on Mīmāṁsā older than Śabara's Bhāṣya, most probably Bhavadāsa's Vṛtti. We are however fully justified in thinking that Bhartṛhari cannot have lived long *after* Śabarà.

3. The above observations, if correct, allow us to draw the following conclusions. Bhartṛhari was acquainted with Mīmāṁsā, but did not use it where we would expect him to use it. In the context of ritual details he rather draws upon another tradition, most probably on the traditional manuals current in his Vedic school, that of the Maitrāyaṇīyas. And where he makes references to Mīmāṁsā, it is never to Śabara's Bhāṣya, but rather to a Mīmāṁsā work in verse, or containing verse, which has not survived, but may have been Bhavadāsa's Vṛtti. He may have known the Pūrva Mīmāṁsā Sūtra, or a part of it, but this is not certain.

Abbreviations

AiB	*Aitareya Brāhmaṇa*
AL	Abhyankar and Limaye's edition of Bhartṛhari's *Mahābhāṣya Dīpikā*
ĀśvŚS	*Āśvalāyana Śrauta Sūtra*
CE	'Critical Edition' of Bhartṛhari's *Mahābhāṣya Dīpikā*
KS	*Kāṭhaka Saṁhitā*
KapS	*Kapiṣṭhala Saṁhitā*
Mbh	*Mahābhāṣya*
Ms	Manuscript of Bhartṛhari's *Mahābhāṣya Dīpikā*
MS	*Maitrāyaṇī Saṁhitā*
MŚS	*Mānava Śrauta Sūtra*

PMS	*Pūrva Mīmāṁsā Sūtra*
ŚŚS	*Śāṅkhāyana Śrauta Sūtra*
Sw	Swaminathan's edition of Bahrtṛhari's *Mahābhāṣya Dīpikā*
TB	*Taittirīya Brāhmaṇa*
TS	*Taittirīya Saṃhitā*

Notes

1. MS 4.13.4; KS 16.21; AiB 6.6–7 (2.6–7); TB 3.6.6; AśvŚS 3.3; ŚŚS 5.17.

2. Bhartṛhari's independence from the influence of Mīmāṁsā when dealing with ritual details makes this a more likely assumption than that this stanza belonged to the Mīmāṁsā work in verse with which he appears to have been acquainted. See section 2, below.

3. Helārāja on Vākyapadīya 3.14.591 (590), p. 413 l. 24-25, quotes the same stanza and calls it 'tradition of the knowers of *ūha*' (*ūhavidām āmnāyaḥ*).

4. The Ms reading has been emended with the help of the quotation by Pārthasārathi Miśra; see below.

5. All these texts have *yad dvyakṣarāḥ satīś caturakṣarāḥ kriyant* [*e*].

6. Bhartṛhari's example of *śruti* is *hṛdayasyāgre'vadyati, atha jihvāyāḥ, atha vakṣasaḥ*. The same example is given by Śabara under PMS 5.1.5.

7. *bhavadāsena coktam: athāta ity ayaṁ śabda ānantarye prayujyate.*

8. Frauwallner (1968: 101) places him in the first half of the 5th century.

9. We must assume that Bhartṛhari considers *prayojana* here synonymous with *prayojaka* 'bringing about' for the following reasons: (i) otherwise *tatpreritas* makes no sense; (ii) a few lines further down we find the explanation *dharmasya....prayojaka*[*ḥ*]. Joshi and Roodbergen (1973: 82 fn. 326) explain this meaning as follows: "The word *prayojana* is formed by adding the suffix *LyuṬ* (i.e. *ana*, p. 7.1.1) to the stem *prayuj*, in the sense of *karaṇa:* 'instrument' (P. 3.3. 117). Thus the meaning of *prayojana* can be analyzed as *prayujyate anena tat prayojanam:* 'that by which something is regulated is (called) *prayojana*'. Taken in this sense, *prayojana* comes to mean *prayojaka:* 'regulator'. " It seems however more correct to account for *prayojana* in this sense by P. 3.3.113 (*kṛtyalyuṭo bahulam*). This is done, e.g., by Bhaṭṭoji Dīkṣita in his *Śabdakaustubha* (vol. I, p. 11): *atra prayujyate pravartyate 'neneti karaṇalyuḍantaḥ prayojayatīti kartṛvyutpattyā bāhulakāt kartṛlyuḍanto vā ubhayathāpi pravartakavidhiparaḥ puṁliṅgaḥ prayojanaśabda ekaḥ / phalaparaḥ klībo'paraḥ /.*

10. Cf. Śabara's Bhāṣya on PMS 1.1.2: *yo hi yāgam anutiṣṭhati taṁ dhārmika iti samācakṣate / yaś ca yasya kartā sa tena vyapadiśyate / yathā pācako lāvaka iti /.*

REFERENCES

Bhartṛhari: *Mahābhāṣyadīpikā*

1. Edited by K.V. Abhyankar and V.P. Limaye. Poona: Bhandarkar Oriental Research Institute. 1970. (Post-Graduate and Research Department Series No. 8).
2. Partly edited by V. Swaminathan under the title *Mahābhāṣya Ṭīkā*. Varanasi: Banaras Hindu University. 1965. (Hindu Vishvavidyalaya Nepal Rajya Sanskrit Series Vol. 11).
3. Manuscript reproduced. Poona: Bhandarkar Oriental Research Institute. 1980.
4. 'Critical edition'. Poona: Bhandarkar Oriental Research Institute. Āhnika 1 by J. Bronkhorst (1987), Āhnika 2 by G.B. Palsule (1988), Āhnika 3 by G.B. Palsule (1983), Āhnika 4 by G.V. Devasthali and G.B. Palsule (1989), Āhnika 5 by V.P. Limaye, G.B. Palsule and V.B. Bhagavat (1984), Āhnika 6 part 1 by V.B. Bhagavat and Saroja Bhate (1986), Āhnika 6 part 2 by V.B. Bhagavat and Saroja Bhate (1990), Āhnika 7 by G.B. Palsule and V.B. Bhagavat (1991).

Bhaṭṭoji Dīkṣita: *Śabdakaustubha*. Vol. I, Fasc. I to IV. Edited by Pandit Sri Mukund Sastri Puṇtamkar. Benares: Chowkhamba Sanskrit Series Office. 1933.

Bhide, V.V. (1979): *The Cāturmāsya Sacrifices*. With special reference to the Hiraṇyakeśi Śrautasūtra. Pune: University of Poona. (Publications of the Centre of Advanced Study in Sanskrit, Class B, No. 5).

Bronkhorst, Johannes (1981): 'On some Vedic quotations in Bhartṛhari's works.' *Studien zur Indologie und Iranistik* 7, 173–75.

Bronkhorst, Johannes (1986): 'Tantra and Prasaṅga.' *Aligarh Journal of Oriental Studies* 3, 77–80.

Bronkhorst, Johannes (1987): 'Further remarks on Bhartrhari's Vedic affiliation.' Studies in Indian culture. S. Ramachandra Rao Felicitation Volume. Bangalore, pp. 216–23.

Frauwallner, Erich (1968): *Materialien zur ältesten Erkenntnislehre der Karmamīmāṁsā* Wien: Österreichisc he Akademieder Wissenchaften. (Philosophisch-historische Klasse, Sitzungsberichte, 259. Band, 2. Abhandlung; Veröffentlichungen der Kommission für Sprachen und Kulturen Süd- und Ostasiens, Heft 6).

Garge, Damodar Vishnu (1952): *Citations in Śabara-Bhāṣya*. Poona: Deccan College. (Deccan College Dissertation Series, 8).

Helārāja: *Prakīrṇaprakāśa*. In: *Vākyapadīya of Bhartṛhari with the commentary of Helārāja*, edited by K.A. Subramania Iyer. 2 parts. Poona: Deccan College. 1963–73.

Hillebrandt, Alfred (1879): *Das altindische Neu- und Vollmondsopfer*. Jena: Gustav Fischer.

Hillebrandt, Alfred (1897): *Ritual-Litteratur. Vedische Opfer und Zauber*. Strassburg: Karl J. Trübner. (Grundriss der Indo-Arischen Philologie und Altertumskunde, III. Band, 2. Heft.)

Jayanta Bhaṭṭa: *Nyāyamañjarī*. Vol. I. Edited by K.S. Varadacharya. Mysore: Oriental Research Institute.

Jha, Ganganatha (tr.) (1933–36): *Śabara-Bhāṣya*. 3 vol. Baroda: Oriental Institute.

Jha, Ganganatha (1942): *Pūrva-Mīmāṁsā in its Sources*. Benares: Benares Hindu University.

Joshi, S.D., and Roodbergen, J.A.F. (1973): *Patañjali's Vyākaraṇa-Mahābhāṣya. Tatpuruṣāhnika* (P. 2.2.2–2.2.23). Poona: University of Poona. (Publications of the Centre of Advanced Study in Sanskrit, Class C, No. 7)

Kane, P. V. (1929): 'Bhavadāsa and Śabarasvāmin.' *Annals of the Bhandarkar Oriental Research Institute* 10, 153-54.

Kumārila Bhaṭṭa: *Tantravārttika*. See under 'Śabara'.

Mīmāṁsaka, Yudhiṣṭhira (1973): *Saṃskṛta Vyākaraṇa-Śāstra kā Itihāsa*. Parts I–III. Sonipat: Rāma Lāl Kapūr Trust. Saṃvat 2030.

Mishra, Umesha (1942): 'Critical bibliography.' Appendix to Jha 1942.

Pārthasārathi Miśra: *Śāstradīpikā*. Edited by P.N. Pattabhirama Sastri. New Delhi: Śri Lāla Bahādura Śāstri Kendriya Saṃskṛta Vidyāpīṭham. Part II. 1980-81. (Saṃskṛta Vidyāpīṭha Granthamālā 38.)

Patañjali: *Vyākaraṇa-Mahābhāṣya*. Edited by F. Kielhorn. Third Edition by K.V. Abhyankar. Poona: Bhandarkar Oriental Research Institute. 1962–72.

Ramaswami Sastri, K.S. (1937): 'Date of Pārthasārathimiśra and sequence of his works.' *Indian Historical Quarterly* 13, 488–97.

Rau, Wilhelm (1980): 'Bhartṛhari und der Veda'. *Studien zur Indologie und Iranistik* 5/6 (Festschrift Paul Thieme), 167–80.

Śabara: *Mīmāṁsā Bhāṣya*. In: *Mīmāṁsādarśana*. Edited by Kāśīnātha Vāsudevaśāstri Abhyaṃkara and Pt. Gaṇeśaśāstrī Jośī. Poona: Ānandāśrama. 1973–84. (Ānandāśrama Saṁskṛtagranthāvali 97.)

Śrautakośa. Vol. I, English section, Part I. By R.N. Dandekar; preface by C.G. Kashikar. Poona: Vaidika Saṁśodhana Maṇḍala. 1958.

Śivarāmendra Sarasvatī: *Ratnaprakāśa*. In: *Mahābhāṣya Pradīpa Vyākhyānāni*. Adhyāya I Pāda 1 Āhnika 1-4. Edited by M.S. Narasimhacharya. Pondichéry: Institut Français d'Indologie. 1973. (Publications de l'Institut Français d'Indologie No. 51, 1).

Swaminathan, V. (1961): 'Bhartṛhari and Mīmāṁsā.' *Proceedings of the All India Oriental Conference* 20 (1959), Vol. II, part 1, pp. 309–17.

Swaminathan, V. (1963): 'Bhartṛhari's authorship of the commentary on the Mahābhāṣyā.' *Adyar Library Bulletin* 27, 59–70.

Vaidyanātha: *Chāyā*. In: *Patañjali's Vyākaraṇa Mahābhāṣya*, edited by Raghunath Kāshīnāth Shāstrī and Sīvadatta D. Kudāla. Bombay: Nirṇayasāgar Press, 1932.

van Gelder, Jeanette M. (tr.) (1963): *The Mānava Śrautasūtra*. New Delhi: International Academy of Indian Culture. (Śata-Piṭaka Series, Indo-Asian Literatures, Vol. 27.)

24

BĀDARI AND PRABHĀKARA

Kiyotaka Yoshimizu

The edition of Prabhākara's Bṛhatī in the Madras University Sanskrit Series was completed in 1967. But since then philosophical concepts of Prabhākara expounded in this work have been little researched. In this paper[1] I would like to make clear Prabhākara's basical position on the question about what is the purpose of performing a Vedic sacrifice and how it can be ascertained from a Vedic injunction (*vidhi*) with reference to his remarks on an early Mīmāṁsaka, Bādari.[2]

The third Adhyāya of the Mīmāṁsāsūtra deals with the relation of a subordinate to its principal (*śeṣaśeṣibhāva*) among various ritual factors of which a Vedic sacrifice consists. The first Sūtra of the first Pāda '*athātaḥ śeṣalakṣaṇam*' declares this subject matter. The second Sūtra '*śeṣaḥ parārthatvāt*' shows the general ground for subordination, namely, having the other as its own aim (*parārthatva*). The third Sūtra '*dravyaguṇa-saṁskāreṣu bādariḥ*' informs about Bādari's opinion on what can be subordinate. The fourth Sūtra '*karmāṇy api jaiminiḥ phalārthatvāt*' shows Jaimini's opinion that even the act of sacrificing can be subordinated, namely, to the result.

According to the commentator Śabara, Bādari not only admitted that the substance (*dravya*) used as material for an oblation, its quality (*guṇa*) appropriate for an oblation and preparatory act (*saṁskāra*) to make an oblation are subordinated to the act of sacrificing, but also restricted subordination to these three kinds of ritual factors by adding the particle '*eva*' after the enumeration of them.[3] He maintained that the act of sacrificing (*yāga*) cannot be a means to any other ends because there remains nothing to be done (*kartavya*), once the act of sacrificing has been performed.[4] Even the result (*phala*) is not the purpose of the act of sacrificing because once it has been performed the result will issue automatically; for the act of sacrificing itself is the aim of human being (*puruṣārtha*).[5,6] This opinion of Bādari seems to be very akin to Prabhākara's theory of *niyoga* which has been regarded by many scholars as prompting one to act, regardless of any result.

The relation of Prabhākara to Bādari seems to have been examined so far only by two scholars: the first is the editor of the second edition of the Tantrarahasya, K.S. Ramaswami Sastri, who collected Bādari's views on Vedic sacrifice from the Mīmāṁsāsūtra and Śabara's Bhāṣya in his Introduction and drew a conclusion mainly from the above cited Śabara's report on JS 3.1.3 that Prabhākara followed the path of Bādari and attempted to establish his doctrines against Jaimini and Śabara.[7] As far as I know, no one has stated his own view on this assumption except A. Subrahmanya Sastri, who refused each evidence mentioned by K.S. Ramaswami Sastri in his Bhūmikā on his edition of the Prakaraṇapañcikā.[8] Concerning the Sūtra 3.1.3, he maintained that it is admitted not only by the Bhāṭṭa school but also by Prabhākara's that the act of sacrificing is subordinated (*śeṣa*) to the result, namely, heaven (*svarga*).[9] But he did not explain thoroughly how Prabhākara derives this subordination from a Vedic injunction, but simply named this method of interpretation '*vākya*' (syntactical unity)[10] and characterised it as *ārthika* or *aupādānika*.[11]

In Prabhākara's commentary on JS 3.1.3 we cannot find any statement which would determine whether he is for or against the opinion of Bādari. However he criticizes it in his commentary on the fourth Adhyāya as follows:

(*i*) *ata eva bādarer eṣā bhrāntiḥ dravyaguṇasaṁskāreṣv eva śeṣatvam iti*/ (Bṛh iv, p. 978, *ll.* 2-3)

But how does he criticize it here? At first we have to examine some technical terms of the Mīmāṁsā exegesis which are used in this criticism.

I. *Viniyoga*

First, the term '*viniyoga*' means the application of a ritual factor as a means to produce something else on the basis of the relation between an act and its factor (*kriyākārakasaṁbandha*) expressed in an injunction. The third Adhyāya of the Mīmāṁsā-sūtra enumerates the six kinds of linguistic *pramāṇa* which ascertain such an application: direct expression (*śruti*), indirect reference (*liṅga*), syntactic unity (*vākya*), contextual unity (*prakaraṇa*), order (*krama*) and etymological meaning (*samākhyā*).[12]

The term '*śruti*' can mean in general the direct meaning of any component of any word. But so far as *viniyoga* is concerned, it is restricted to the denotation of a case suffix (*kārakavibhakti*) which directly expresses the relation of a means to its end. For example, in the injunction of purchasing Soma-plant:

> *aruṇayā piṅgākṣyaikahāyanyā somaṁ krīṇāti.*[13] ("One purchases Soma with a tawny-colored yellow-eyed one-year-old cow.")

the instrumental suffix of the noun '*aruṇayā*' denotes that the meaning of the nominal stem, tawny color, is a means (*karaṇa*)[14] to the act of purchasing expressed by verbal stem '*krīṇā-*'.[15]

The second term '*liṅga*' can mean in general a sign which refers to something else while it expresses its own meaning. But as far as *viniyoga* is concerned, it means the meaning of word stem which indirectly refers to the relation of a means to its end. This pramāṇa *liṅga* is especially applied to ascertain the purpose of reciting a *mantra* on the basis of its component words. For example, the *mantra*:

> *kadācana starīr asi nendra saścasi dāśuse.*[16] ("Never art thou barren, O Indra, Never dost thou fail thy worshipper."[17])

which contains the word '*indra*' can be regarded as a means of praising the deity Indra on the basis of this word. In such a case, however, one should assume a corresponding injunction which makes it known that one should praise Indra by means of reciting this *mantra.*[18] Even when the relation of a means to its end is ascertained from any of the other remaining *pramāṇas*, a corresponding injunction with a suitable *śruti* should be assumed.[19] Therefore we can say: If one ascertains the relation of a subordinate to its principal on the basis of the case suffix of a noun in an existing injunction or in an assumed one, this process is named '*viniyoga*' in Śabara's commentary.

This process, however, cannot be completed within one single injunction of application. If a ritual factor should be subordinated to another one on the basis of the injunction of its application, there should be another injunction which prescribes that the latter factor should be actualized in the sacrifice. The hearer of a *viniyogavidhi* cannot understand that he should actualize a subordinate factor as a means to its end in the course of sacrifice unless he knows already that this end is required in the sacrifice and therefore should be actualized. Prabhākara draws our attention to this point as follows:

(*ii*) [Objection:] But in case of the injunction "*vrīhīn prokṣati*" it should be considered which one is subordinate and which one is principal between the meanings of words [in this single sentence].
[Reply:] Here it should be criticized that you do not hear [what I say about subordination]. The consideration of subordinate and principal in this (injunction) should be carried out together with [another injunction] "*vrīhibhir yajeta.*" (Bṛh iv, p. 626, *ll.*10, -p. 627, *ll.*3)[20]

(*iii*) [A ritual factor] which is applied to be done (*kārya*) has the latter only as its end. Therefore [the subordination] was characterized [in JS 3.1.2] as "on the ground that it has the other as its own aim." (*Ibid.* p. 628, *ll.* 6-7)[21]

Because the accusative case suffix means that the referent of its stem is the object (*karman*) which the agent most desires to gain through his action,[22] it is confirmed by the injunction "*vrīhīn prokṣati*" that besprinkling should be done for the sake of rice, but it is only on condition that it has already been confirmed by the injunction "*vrīhibhir yajeta*" that rice is to be done (*kārya*), namely, should be employed as material for the oblation. The linguistic *pramāṇa* which proves the application of a subordinate factor cannot operate without the superior injunction which enjoins to actualize its principal in the sacrifice.[23]

II. *Upādāna*

According to Prabhākara, application (*viniyoga*) is nothing more than one kind of ascertaining process of subordination, for which there exists another method too, called "association" (*upādāna*) by him. The fourth Adhyāya of the Mīmāṁsāsūtra deals with motivation (*prayojana*) of a ritual act or that of employing a ritual factor in the sacrifice. The first Sūtra[24] of the first Pāda declares that it will be examined in this Adhyāya whether the Vedic text in question prescribes a ritual act or factor for the sake of the sacrifice (*kratvartha*) or for the sake of the person (*puruṣārtha*). In reply to an objection[25] that the notion of *kratvartha* has already been examined in the preceding third Adhyāya, Prabhākara says:

(*iv*) [Reply:] You would be right if [the fourth Adhyāya] would deal with [the fact that a ritual factor has the other as its own aim (*tādarthya*)] which is derived from application. Here (in the fourth Adhyāya), however, [the author of JS] brings forward only [the having the other as its own aim] which is derived from *upādāna*.
[Question:] What is named *upādāna*?
[Answer:] *Upādāna* is the secondary indication of obligation (*niyogākṣepa*). (Bṛh iv, p. 956, *ll*. 4-5.)[26]

The verbal suffix (e.g. optative) in the injunction of an act issues an obligation (*niyoga*) which urges the hearer to perform the act. Prabhākara maintains here that the obligation indicates indirectly (*ākṣepa*) that something else is subservient either to the sacrifice or to the person, i.e. the sacrificer (*yajamāna*) who organizes the sacrifice. This function of obligation is named *upādāna*. The commentator Śālikanātha explains that the word '*niyogākṣepa*' means indicating something without which the obligation itself would not be fulfilled:

(*v*) It is generally acknowledged in worldly usage[27] that the meaning which has been made known by a word indicates indirectly something else without which it will not be completed. . . . In Veda also it is surely possible that the obligation which has been made known by a word indicates indirectly something else for the sake of its own fulfillment. (ṚP iv, p. 956, *ll.* 18-20)[28]

It will be examined later whether this explanation is based on Prabhākara's notion of *upādāna*.

Prabhākara admits here that both the third and fourth Adhyāya deal with the process of ascertaining that a ritual factor is subordinated to something else. But he distinguishes the aspect of subordination argued in the fourth Adhyāya from that in the preceding one.

(*vi*) [In case of the injunction "*vrīhīn prokṣati*"] it is ascertained on the basis of it (i.e. *upādāna*) that the besprinkling etc. are subservient to the sacrifice. On the basis of application, however, it is ascertained that it has rice as its own aim. (Bṛh iv, p. 956, *ll.* 6)[29]

In case of the injunction "One should besprinkle rice." (*vrīhīn prokṣati*) it is ascertained by means of *upādāna* of the obligation that this act of besprinkling subserves the sacrifice. But by means of *viniyoga* expressed by the accusative suffix of '*vrīhīn*' it is ascertained that this act subserves a particular ritual factor, namely, rice.

But how can it be ascertained whether the factor in question is *kratvartha* or *puruṣārtha*? Prabhākara gives a brief answer in his commentary on JS 4.1.2:

(*vii*) The desire of undertaking something upon which the happiness of the person follows[30] is characterized by the purpose on account of [that person's] inseparability [from that purpose].[31] (*yasmin prītiḥ puruṣasya tasya lipsā 'rthalakṣaṇā' aṇā' i-vibhaktatvāt.*)

The first half of this Sūtra '*yasmin prītiḥ puruṣasya*' defines what is *puruṣārtha*. If a person procures happiness after he has performed an act, this act is called '*puruṣārtha*'. The second half of the Sūtra '*tasya lipsā 'rthalakṣaṇā 'vibhaktavāt*' lays down in a very abridged style how to ascertain that an act is *puruṣārtha*. It says that human desire of undertaking a *puruṣārtha*-act is characterized by "purpose" (*artha*). Prabhākara comments on this word '*artha*' as follows:

(*viii*) And the fulfillment of obligation is [called] "purpose" [in JS 4.1.2]. Furthermore it was said [by me] that the [ground for the subservience of such an act to the person] is *upādāna*. (Bṛh iv, p. 958, *ll.* 2-3)[32]

'*Artha*' means here[33] the purpose of Veda which is nothing but the fulfillment of obligation (*niyogasiddhi*). The Veda which was believed by Mīmāṁsakas to exist as transcendental authority independent of human society lays an obligation in the form of injunctions on their hearers so that the sacrifice continues to be performed by them successively. The real interest of the Veda lies in the continual tradition of Vedic sacrifice. Only the act by means of which the obligation from Vedic injunction is definitely fulfilled subserves the sacrificer by causing him happiness and is thus *puruṣārtha*.

But how can one ascertain from a Vedic text that only such an act deserves to be called '*puruṣārtha*' though the sacrificer wishes his own happiness, not the obedience to the obligation of injunction? Prabhākara answers to this question scarcely by referring to the *upādāna* which he identified previously (*iv*) with the indirect indication of obligation (*niyogākṣepa*).

Instead of further explanation of the function called *upādāna* Prabhākara now allows the objector to point out that in the preceding passage (*vi*) he has admitted that it can also be ascertained by means of this *upādāna* that an act or a ritual factor is *kratvartha*. In reply to this objection, he distinguishes the process of ascertaining that an act is *puruṣārtha* from that in case of *kratvartha*.

(*ix*) [Objection:] But it was said [by you] that the subservience to the sacrifice too can be ascertained by means of the same *upādāna*.

[Reply:] [I] said that [a ritual factor can be ascertained by means of *upādāna* to be subservient to sacrifice] on condition that application (*viniyoga*) is present [in the injunction]. For it makes the difference [between *puruṣārtha* and *kratvartha*] that the subservience to the person is derived only from the purpose [of injunction, namely, the fulfilment of obligation]. (Bṛh iv, p. 958, *ll*.3-4)[34]

Whether a ritual factor is *kratvartha* or *puruṣārtha* depends on whether the injunction not only urges one to fulfill the obligation through it, but also ascertains its application to its principal or not. But how can it be the condition of its subservience to the sacrifice that the application is prescribed in the injunction? Here we should pay attention to some passages in other portions of the Bṛhatī in order to understand the function of obligation called *upādāna* more concretely.

In his commentary on JS 2.2.13-16 (Adhikaraṇa 5),[35] Prabhākara determines the relation of *upādāna* to the factor which is enjoined by injunction.

(*x*) What [the injunction] obligates [a person] to, is to be done (*kārya*). What is required to be associated [with it] (*upādīyate*) so as to fulfill it, is to be associated (*upādāna*).[36] (Bṛh iii, p. 456, *ll*. 5-6)[37]

Any material, quality or act which is prescribed in an injunction is to be done (*kārya*) because the injunction obligates the hearer to actualize it. In addition to it, it is also made known by this injunction that even some other factors should be realized if they are necessary for the realization of the directly enjoined factor. They have to be associated with the object of the injunction by the obligation so as to put its actualization into practice although they are not directly prescribed by it. This is the general meaning of the indirect indication of injunction (*niyogākṣepa*) with which Prabhākara identified the *upādāna*. It can be also confirmed by this passage[38] that Śālikanātha's explanation (cf. *v*) of the word '*niyogākṣepa*' is based on the original idea of Prabhākara.

It has already been mentioned (cf. I. *viniyoga*) that by means of an injunction of application it is ascertained that a subordinate factor should be actualized for the purpose of another principal one which has already been recognized as to be done from another injunction. In terms of the superior injunction which prescribes the principal we can rewrite this connection between a subordinate injunction and its superior as follows: Whereas the injunction "*vrīhibhir yajeta*" directly obligates the hearer to use rice as the material for oblation, it also requires more detailed prescription how to prepare the oblation from rice, without which this obligation would not be carried out; in order to satisfy this requirement of the preceding obligation, new injunctions of application "*vrīhīn prokṣati*" etc. come to be associated with it. Thus, as Prabhākara asserted in (*ix*), it is ascertained that besprinkling etc. are subservient to the sacrifice (*kratvartha*) because they supply the demand of the preceding obligation for a more detailed procedure of preparation in so far as they are prescribed in an injunction of application (*viniyoge sati*).[39]

Even within the content of a single injunction of application there can be some factors which are to be associated with the object of the application so as to put this application into practice. For example, the injunction "*yo dīkṣito yad agnīṣomīyaṁ paśum ālabhate*"[40] prescribes that one who has been consecrated to the Jyotiṣṭoma sacrifice should slaughter cattle as an oblation for Agni and Soma. But this slaughter can be carried out only on condition that the number of requisite head of cattle has been determined. Until one knows how many victims should be slaughtered, one cannot begin to sacrifice.

(*xi*) [Reply:] It [can be confirmed] not only on the ground of application that [a ritual factor] is auxiliary means to the act.

[Question:] How then?

[Answer:] The subordination results in fact on the ground of association too; for only [a substance] which has become the means [prescribed by this injunction] can be associated [with the act prescribed by the superior injunction], and in the same manner [a substance] furnished with singularity can be associated [with it]. For it is impossible to associate something which neither is any factor nor has any number. (Bṛh iv, p. 971, *l.* 9-p. 972, *l.* 3)[41]

The singularity of requisite head is determined in this injunction by the singular accusative suffix of the noun '*paśum*', which also denotes that the meaning of the nominal stem, namely, cattle, is the means[42] of the act of slaughter. Although this singularity is not prescribed by this injunction,[43] it must be regarded as the distinguishing feature (*viśeṣaṇa*)[44] of the cattle without which it is impossible to perform the slaughter of it.[45] Therefore the singularity of the requisite head subserves the sacrifice, namely, it is *kratvartha* because it is required by the injunction of slaughter in order to put the application of cattle in practice. In this case also the singularity is recognized as subserving the sacrifice (*kratvartha*) because the cattle which it distinguishes is prescribed to be applied as the oblation in an injunction of application (*viniyoge sati*).

Now we are going to consider how the subservience to the sacrificer (*puruṣārtha*) can be ascertained.

III. *Adhikāra*

All the injunctions of preparation of oblations, subsidiary and main offerings in a sacrifice construct many channels of command woven into an intricate hierarchy,[46] on the top of which the Mīmāṁsakas settled an injunction of qualification which prescribes who is qualified to organize the sacrifice, e.g.:

> One desiring heaven, should perform the new and fullmoon sacrifice. (*darśapūrṇamāsābhyāṁ svargakāmo yajeta*).[47]

Just as many narrow streams meet each other to form a tributary joining a large river which runs into the sea, each successive series of subordination of a means to its end can be theoretically traced back to a fundamental injunction which prescribes only the qualification for organizing the sacrifice without any application.

According to Śabara, JS 6.1.1-3 form one section called '*svargakāmādhikaraṇa*', in which it is discussed that the heaven mentioned in the subject '*svargakāmaḥ*' in the injunctions of qualification as cited above is the aim of performing the sacrifice for which they qualify the sacrifice. At the beginning of his commentary Prabhākara formulates in his own terminology the problem presented by Śabara.

(*xii*) [If the referent of a word is] already accomplished, [it] aims at the other. But if it is to be accomplished, it aims at itself. Now, concerning this (injunction) we do not know whether [this injunction] associates [the referent of the word '*svarga*'] as something already accomplished [with the act of sacrificing] for the sake of the other, (i.e. the act of sacrificing), or it (i.e. *svarga*) is associated [with the act of sacrificing] as something to be accomplished. (Bṛh v, p. 8, *ll.* 6-7)[48]

Taking into account the relation of *upādāna* to *kārya* mentioned in (*x*), we can understand this formulation as follows: In the injunction "*darśapūrṇamāsābhyāṁ svargakāmo yajeta*" the verb '*yajeta*' tells us by means of its optative ending that the act of a Vedic sacrifice[49] should be done (*kārya*), because it is the object (*viṣaya*) of the obligation; the word '*darśapūrṇamāsābhyām*' denotes the name of this sacrifice; The Bahuvrīhi[50] compound '*svargakāmaḥ*' is the subject which prescribes who is qualified for organizing this sacrifice. So, the meanings of these latter two words are associated with the *kārya*, i.e. the act of sacrificing because they play their own role necessary for accomplishing it.

Now it is asked in this Adhikaraṇa how the heaven can be associated with the act of sacrificing to be done: Does the qualifying word of the subject '*svarga*' characterize the heaven as the aim which is to be accomplished by means of the sacrifice or as a certain means which helps in some way its accomplishment? Prabhākara answers: If someone who has heard an injunction of qualification comes to understand that he is the person to be obligated (*niyojya*), i.e. comes to be aware of his duty to perform the sacrifice, he must have understood the relation of this act to his desired aim too. The injunction cannot urge a person desiring heaven to meet with the obligation to sacrifice without letting him know that by means of the sacrifice he can attain the desired heaven.

(*xiii*) But the awareness that one is the person to be obligated results from something else [than the obligation]. It is said that this (awareness) results from the relation [of the act] to the desired object. (Bṛh v, p. 38, *ll.* 2-3)[51] (*xiv*) But otherwise, namely, if the desire would not be realized by means of the sacrifice, it would be impossible that [the heaven is mentioned in the injunction as] something desired [by the qualified person]. (Bṛh v, p. 41, *l.* 6)[52]

Prabhākara maintains further that this relation between the heaven and the sacrifice is implied in the syntactical relation between the subject '*svargakāmaḥ*' and the verb '*yajeta*' in the injunction.

(*xv*) It is said [by the subject '*svargakāmaḥ*'] that the heaven qualifies a person in so far as it is desired [by him]. It is also said [by the verb '*yajeta*'] that there is an obligation concerning an action. Since [the subject and the verb denote respectively] the person to be obligated and the object of [the same] obligation, [both words] form one sentence... The meaning of the sentence is the fulfillment of obligation. (Bṛh v, p. 42, *ll.* 3-6)[53]

The subject '*svargakāmaḥ*' indicates that any person qualified by desiring heaven is the person to be obligated (*niyojya*) by an obligation; the verb '*yajeta*' indicates that the act of sacrificing is the object (*viṣaya*) of the same obligation. In this way the subject and the verb form one sentence (*ekavākyatā*) through their relation to one and the same obligation, and then the obligation comes to be understood in a concrete sense. Now, if the subject and the verb form one sentence, the desired object and the act of sacrificing should be related to each other so as to be related to one and the same obligation. Prabhākara examines this relation as follows:

(*xvi*) First, if only the act of sacrificing were to be done, the meaning [of the subject] which is the person to be obligated would not be related to the obligation. Or, if [only] the desired object [were to be done], the object of obligation would not be related to the person to be obligated. Therefore [in both cases] the awareness of one and the same obligation would be hindered. It has already been said[54] which failure would follow if the act of sacrificing were principal. Therefore [the desired object and the act of sacrificing] are related to one and the same obligation only because the desired object is principal. (Bṛh v, p. 42, *ll.* 6-9)[55]

(*xvii*) Therefore it is right [to understand from the injunction of qualification] that one should realize the heaven by means of the act of sacrificing. (Bṛh v, p. 43, *l.* 6).[56]

Prabhākara concludes here that the act of sacrifice is subordinated to the desired object. He insists that the act of sacrificing cannot but be subordinated to the desired object, namely, the heaven, because otherwise the noun '*svargakāmaḥ*' and the verb '*yajeta*' could not be related to one and the same obligation so as to form one sentence. Although the subordination of the act of sacrificing to the heaven is not directly expressed by any single word of this sentence, it is necessarily required by both the noun and the verb. The noun '*svargakāmaḥ*' does not only assert that wishing the heaven is the condition of the qualification (*adhikāra*) for organizing the sacrifice but also indicates indirectly that there must be some means to achieve heaven; the verb '*yajeta*' does not only oblige the hearer to organize the sacrifice but also indicates indirectly (*niyogākṣepa*) that there must be some result which he can achieve by means of sacrificing.[57] When both of them are put together to form one sentence, they cooperate to make it known by their indirect indication that the heaven is the result of the act of sacrificing, or in other words, that the latter is the means to achieve the former. In this way, it comes to be ascertained within the injunction of qualification without recourse to any case suffix proving the application of a subordinate factor —as Prabhākara asserted in (*ix*)—that the act of sacrificing subserves the sacrificer (*puruṣārtha*) by bringing him the desired result.

IV. *Prabhākara's criticism of Bādari*

Through a somewhat long and winding road, we have come back to our starting point. Prabhākara's criticism of Bādari pointed out in (*i*) is included in his commentary on ŚBh on JS 4.1.21[58] which declares that the subject matter from now is the 'equality' (*sāmya*) and 'unequality' (*vaiṣamya*) among substances and actions with regard to the purpose (*artha*). When two substances are produced or two acts are performed simultaneously right after an act during the ritual procedure, both substances or acts are said to be equal (*sama*) if both of them are the purpose (*artha*=*prayojana*) of the foregoing act; but they are unequal (*viṣama*) if only one is the purpose of it while the other is only an incidental byproduct.

At the beginning of his commentary on this Sūtra, Śabara states that the treatment of the subject matter of the third Adhyāya, namely, subordination (*śeṣabhāva*), has been already finished by this Sūtra.[59] But here arises a doubt why he can say so although the Sūtras from 4.1.22 on deal with a kind of subordination as before because one can say that the subject matter declared in JS 4.1.21 is to consider to which of two following substances or acts the foregoing act is subordinated as its means. Prabhākara vindicates Śabara's statement by distinguishing the field of investigation (*viṣaya*) from the valid means of investigation (*pramāṇa*) treated in the third Adhyāya: According to Prabhākara's interpretation, Śabara admits that the field of investigation which will be discussed from now is surely a kind of subordination as before, but he insists that the problems of subordination will be examined from now only by means of association (*upādāna*)[60] without recourse to application (*viniyoga*) ascertained by the direct expression (*śruti*) etc. which have been employed as *pramāṇa* in the third Adhyāya including JS 4.1. up to the Sūtra 20.

(*xviii*) This is the object of investigation of the third Adhyāya, but it cannot be recognized by the valid means of investigation treated in the third Adhyāya. Therefore it is examined in the fourth Adhyāya that it is only based upon the injunction (i.e. the obligation) that it (i.e. the ritual factor which will be examined from now) has the other as its own aim. It is also explained that [the six kinds of means ascertaining application, namely] direct expression etc. cannot always make it known that a factor has the other as its own aim. This is indeed what is explained here (in the fourth Adhyāya). And also [Śabara] will say [in the *svargakāmādhikaraṇa*] that it is based upon qualification that the act of sacrificing and the result have the other as their own aim. (Bṛh iv, p. 977, *l.* 8-p. 978, *l.* 1)[61]

As we have examined in III. *adhikāra,* it can be ascertained within an injunction of qualification that the act of sacrificing is subordinated to the result. One can prove the subordination even outside of injunctions of application which prescribe the subordination of a ritual factor to the act of sacrificing at the highest level in the ritual hierarchy. But then, one must refuse the view held by Bādari that the act of sacrificing itself is the aim of human being and the result is not the purpose which one can attain by means of sacrifice. Here Prabhākara begins to offer a criticism of Bādari. Taking the notions of '*viniyoga*', '*upādāna*' and '*adhikāra*' into account, we can now translate it as follows:

(*xix*) Therefore it is delusion of Bādari that subordination would lie only in substance, quality and preparatory act, because [he] restricted [the subordination to substance, quality and preparatory act] on account of the possibility of direct expression etc. in case of these substance etc. while he overlooks the capability of association and of qualification [to make the subordination known in case of the act of sacrificing and of result]. (Bṛh iv, p. 978, *ll.* 2-5)[62]

Although Prabhākara insists that the fulfilment of obligation (*niyogasiddhi*) is the real interest of the Vedic injunctions,[63] he also admits like Jaimini and Śabara and unlike Bādari[64] from the viewpoint of the human motivation that the act of sacrificing is a means to and therefore subordinated to the desired result.

ABBREVIATIONS AND TEXTS

ASK Arthasaṁgrahakaumudī : *Arthasaṁgrahaḥ . . . Mīmāṁsārthasaṁgrahakaumudīvyākhyāyutaḥ.* Nirnayasagar, Bombay 1950.

ĀpŚ Āpastambaśrautasūtra: *The Śrauta Sūtra of Āpastamba belonging to the Taittirīya Saṁhitā with the*

	commentary of Rudradatta. Ed. by R. Garbe, revised ed. by C.G. Kashikar, the second ed., New Delhi 1983.
ṚP	Ṛjuvimalāpañcikā: See Bṛh.
ṚV	Ṛgvedasaṁhitā: *Die Hymnen des Ṛgveda.* Ed. by Th. Aufrecht, Indische Studien, vol. VI-VII, 1877.
KP	Kāvyaprakāśa: *The Poetic Light, Kāvyaprakāśa of Manmata.* Ed. & tr. by R.C. Dwivedi, Delhi 1966.
JS	Mīmāṁsāsūtra: See ŚBh.
TS	Taittirīyasaṁhitā: *Die Taittirīya-Saṁhitā.* Ed. by A. Weber, Indische Studien vol. XI-XII, repr., Hildesheim 1973.
NRM	Nyāyaratnamālā: *Nyāyaratnamālā of Pārthasārathi Miśra with the Commentary Nāyakaratnam by Śrī Rāmānujācārya.* Ed. by A. Subrahmanya Shastri, Library Rare Texts Publication Series No. 4, Varanasi 1982.
Pāṇ	Aṣṭādhyāyī: *Aṣṭādhyāyī of Pāṇini.* Ed. & tr. by S.M. Katre, Texas Linguistics Series, Austín 1987.
PP	Prakaraṇapañcikā: *Prakaraṇa Pañcikā of Śālikanātha Miśra with the Nyāyasiddhi of Jaipuri Nārāyaṇa Bhatta.* Ed. by A. Subrahmanya Sastri, Banaras Hindu University Darśana Series No. 4, Varanasi 1961.
Bṛh iii	Bṛhatī: *Bṛhatī of Prabhākara Miśra with the Ṛjuvimalā Pañcikā of Śalikanātha.* Ed. by S. Subrahmanya Sastri, Madras University Sanskrit Series No. 24, Madras 1962.
Bṛh iv	Bṛhatī: *Ibid.*, No. 25, 1964.
Bṛh v	Bṛhatī: *Ibid.*, No. 26, 1967.
BS	Brahmasūtra: *Brahmasūtraśāṅkarabhāṣyam.* Nirnayasagar, Bombay 1927.
MBh	Mahābhāṣya: *The Vyākaraṇa=Mahābhāṣya of Patañjali.* Ed by Kielhorn, vol. I, the fourth ed., Poona 1985.
MS	Maitrāyaṇīsaṁhitā: *Maitrāyaṇī Saṁhitā.* Ed. by L. von Schroeder, Leipzig 1881-83-85-86.

ŚD Śāstradīpikā: *Śāstradīpikā Prabhāsahitā*. Ed. by Paṭṭābhirāma Śāstrī, pt. 1, Saṁskṛtavidyāpīṭhagranthamālā vol. 25, New Delhi 1978.

ŚBh ii Śābarabhāṣya: *Mīmāṁsādarśana*. Rev. ed., Ānandāśrama-saṁskṛtagranthāvali vol. 97, pt. 2, Poona 1981.

ŚBh iii Śābarabhāṣya: *Ibid*., pt. 3, 1971.

ŚBh iv Śābarabhāṣya: *Ibid*., pt. 4, 1972.

ŚBh v Śābarabhāṣya: *Ibid*., pt. 5, 1973.

ŚBh vii Śābarabhāṣya: *Ibid*., pt. 7, 1974.

NOTES

1. This paper, completed on July 1991, originates in my manuscript read at the VIIIth World Sanskrit Conference, Vienna 1990. I would like to express my sincere thanks to Dr. Irene Wicher who has carefully read this paper and corrected my English expression with valuable suggestions.

2. Bādari's views on the Pūrva- and Uttara-mīmāṁsā are recorded in JS 3.1.3; 6.1.27; 8.3.6; 9.2.33; BS 1.2.30; 3.1.11; 4.3.7; 4.4.10.

3. *bādarir ācāryo 'tra dravyaguṇasaṁskāreṣv eva śeṣaśabda iti mene na yāgaphalapuruṣeṣu.* (ŚBh iv, p. 17, *ll*.1-2.)

4. *yāgas tāvat kartavyaḥ puruṣasya. na hi tasmin (=yāge) nirvartite kiṃcid aparam asti kartavyam. sa (=yāgaḥ) hi puruṣārthaḥ.* (*Ibid*., *ll*. 10-12)

5. The term '*puruṣārtha*' is employed in the Mīmāṁsā school in one of the following two senses according to the context: It can mean the aim of human being which one is supposed to gain through one's act as in the common usage of this term (cf. JS 3.1.5:*phalaṃ ca puruṣārthatvāt*). On the other hand, it can also mean the direct means to this aim of human being or its prescription in Veda in contrast with '*kratvartha*' (cf. this paper II. *upādāna*). Bādari characterized the act of sacrificing as *puruṣārtha* in the former sense.

6. *phalam api na tena (=yāgena) kriyate. tasmiṁs (=yāge) tu kṛte svayam eva tad (=phalam) bhavati.* (ŚBh iv, p. 17, *ll*. 13-14)

7. "Prabhākara, on the other hand, has followed in his works Bādari's school condemned by both Jaimini and Śabara and has stated that duty alone is imposed by injunction on the functionary, who should perform it without any expectation of the result." (*Tantrarahasya A Primer of Prābhākara Mīmāṁsā* by *Rāmānujācārya*. Second Edition, Gaekwad's Oriental Series 24, 1956, Introduction, XXI-XXII.) K.S. Ramaswami Sastri repeated this assumption in his 'Bādari: A forgotten Mīmāṁsā Philosopher', *Viśveshvaranand Indological Journal*, vol. II, pr. i, 1964, pp. 96–100.

8. PP pp. (8)–(10).

9. *yat tu tṛtīyādhyāyaprathamapāde 'dravyasaṁskārakarmasu*(*sic.*) *bādariḥ' 'karmaṇy api jaiminiḥ phalārthatvād' ity atra dravyaguṇasaṁskārāṇām eva mukhyam aṅgatvam iti bādarimatam. yac ca karmaṇo 'pi svargaśeṣatvam, tad idam ubhayam api bhāṭṭaprābhākarayor avipratipannam.* (*Ibid.*, p. (8), *ll.*31-33)

10. *vākya* is the third linguistic *pramāṇa* of application (*viniyoga*) (cf. this paper I. *viniyoga*), which consists in the expectation (*ākāṅkṣā*) of a word by another within one or between two sentences. (Cf. ŚBh iv, p. 259, *ll.* 13-14: *vākya ekaikaṁ padaṁ vibhajyamāṇaṁ sākāṅkṣaṁ bhavati, kṛtsnaṁ paripūrṇaṁ bhavati.*) JS 3.3.1–10 deal with the cases of application by means of this *pramāṇa*, and its relative validity compared with other linguistic *pramāṇa*s is discussed in ŚBh on JS 3.3.14. But Prabhākara does not mention the relation between *yāga* and *svarga* in his *Bṛhati* on them. In the *svargakāmādhikaraṇa*, however, Śabara asserts that it is recognised by means of *vākya* that the desired object (*kāma*) is to be realized (*kartavya*) and the act of sacrificing is the means to it: *tatra vākyād avagatasya kāmasya kartavyatāvagamyate yāgasya ca karaṇatā.* (ŚBh v, p.183, *ll.* 5-6) Because, as we will see later, the basical viewpoint of Prabhākara concerning the relation of the act of sacrificing to the desired result corresponds precisely to that of Śabara, it seems to be based on this assertion of Śabara that A. Subrahmanya Sastri named Prabhākara's method of exegesis on this problem '*vākya*'.

11. *idam ato 'vagamyate svargakāmādivākye dvitīyāntadena svargasyānāmnāne 'pi yāgasvargasamabhivyāhāravaśāt* vākyena *śeṣaśeṣibhāvo 'vagamyate. dravyaguṇādiṣv iva sākṣāc chrutyā viniyogābhāve'pi śrautam aṅgatvaṁ dravyaguṇasaṁskārāṇām,* ārthikam aupādānikaṁ *vāṅgatvaṁ yāgaphalayoḥ.* (*Ibid.*, PP. p. 19, *ll.* 11-14)

12. *śruti*. JS 3.1.7–27; *liṅga:* 3.2; *vākya:* 3.3.1–10; *prakaraṇa:* 3.3.11; *krama* (=*sthāna*): 3.3.12; *samākhyā:* 3.3.13.

13. Cf. TS IV.1.6.7: *ekahāyanyā krīṇāti,. . . .aruṇayā piṅgākṣyā krīṇāti.*

14. Pāṇ 1.4.42: *sādhakatamaṁ karaṇam;* 2.3.18: *kartṛkaraṇayos tṛtīyā.*

15. ŚBh iv, p. 40, *ll.* 1-3: "For in this case the word (*aruṇayā*) refers to the quality, tawney colour, as a means of act, though it is shapeless, because it denotes 'by means of [something] tawney', joined with the third case suffix which denotes instrument." (*iha hi guṇam aruṇimānam amūrtaṁ santaṁ kriyāyāḥ karaṇam iti śabda upadiśati, yat karaṇābhidhāyinyā tṛtīyāvibhaktyā saṁyujya nirdiśati aruṇayeti.*)

16. ṚV VIII.51.7.

17. Translated by A.B. Keith: *The Veda of the Black Yajus School entitled Taittirīya Saṁhitā, Part I: Kāṇḍas I-III*, Harvard Oriental Series vol. 18, repr 1967, p. 75.

18. However it is prescribed as follows in some *brāhmaṇa* texts that one should utter this mantra when he pays reverence to the *gārhapatya*-fire. Cf. TS 1.5.6.4: *kādācana starīr asi nendra saścasi dāśuṣe;* TS I.5.8.4-5: *kadā cana starīr asīty āha, na starī rātriṁ vasati, ya evaṁ vidvān agnim upatiṣṭhate.* (Concerning the other vedic texts than TS, see J. Gonda: *The Mantras of the Agnyupasthāna and the Sautrāmaṇī*, 1980, pp. 43-44.)

In this case there arises a conflict of exegesis between the *śruti* based on the word '*agnim*' in the *brāhmaṇa* and the *liṅga* based on '*indra*' in the *mantra*. So as to resolve this conflict, the *liṅga* gives way to the *śruti* because revering the *gārhapatya* by this *mantra* is directly prescribed in the existing injunction, whereas revering Indra by it can be recognised as prescribed only if one assumes here a not existing injunction: '*aindryā indram upatiṣṭhati*'. Cf. ŚBh iv, p. 248, *ll.*8-10; p. 250, *ll.* 2-4.

19. Because each one of the above enumerated six *pramāṇas* for application presupposes all the preceding ones, each succeeding one is less authoritative than its preceding ones on account of the relative remoteness from *śruti* and therefore set aside in case of conflict with one of them. Cf. JS 3.3.14: *śruti-liṅga-vākya-prakaraṇa-sthāna-samākhyānāṁ samavāye pāradaurbalyam artha-viprakarṣāt*.

20. *nanu vrīhīn prokṣatīti padārthānāṁ śeṣaśeṣicintā. aśravaṇam atrāparādhyate bhavataḥ. vrīhibhir yajetety anena sahāsya śeṣaśeṣicintā na punar vrīhipadārthamātratayaiva.*

21. *yasya kārye viniyogaḥ sa tadartha eva bhavati. ataḥ parārthatvāditi lakṣitam.*

22. Pāṇ 1.4.49: *kartur īpsitatamaṁ karma;* 2.3.2: *karmaṇi dvitīyā.*

23. Bṛh iv, p. 626, *ll.* 7-8: "But this (application) which is considered in the third (Adhyāya of JS) is based on something to be done." (*yas tv ayaṁ tṛtīye cintyate sa kāryanimittakaḥ*).

Ibid., p. 631, *ll.* 3-4: "But the direct expression etc. cannot accomplish subordination if they are wanting for the obligation [to the principal] because [in this case] there is nothing to be done [to which the subordinate should be applied]. It is namely said [above] that having the other as its own aim is based on [the condition that the other] is to be done." (*na ca niyogaśūnyāni śrutyādīni śeṣatām āpādayituṁ śaknuvanti. kāryābhāvāt. kāryanimittaṁ ca pārārthyam* (ṚP iv, p. 631, *l.* 11 corrects Bṛh: *parārtham*) *ity uktam.*)

Cf. ASK p. 35, *ll.* 9-10: *aṅgānāṁ dravyadevatādilakṣaṇānāṁ pradhānair vākyāntaravihitaiḥ saha saṁbandhasya śeṣatvalakṣaṇasya bodhako vidhir ity arthaḥ*. H. Kuroda refers us to this definition of *viniyogavidhi* by Rāmeśvara when he explains that a *viniyogavidhi* applies a sacrificial factor to another one which has been prescribed by another *vidhi*. Cf. Kuroda, Hiroshi: "Kyū Prabhākara-ha (*Jaratprābhākarāḥ*) ni tsuite" (*Indo Shisōshi Kenkyū*, vol. 6, 1989, pp. 77–94), note (11).

24. JS 4.1.1: *athātaḥ kratvarthapuruṣārthayor jijñāsā.*

25. Bṛh iv, p. 956, *l.*3.

26. *bhaved etad evaṁ, yadi vainiyogikam ucyate. iha tu upādānanibandhanam eva pratijānāti. kim upādānaṁ nāma. niyogākṣepa upādānam.*

27. This type of indirect indication (*ākṣepa*) is regarded as a kind of *lakṣaṇā* and even named '*upādāna*' in the Alaṅkāra. *Cf.* KP p. 28, *ll.*1-4: "Assumption of another (i.e. secondary meaning) to establish itself (i.e. the primary meaning)...are *inclusive indication*...In cases like 'Lances enter' and 'Staffs enter' the (words) lances and others point to persons connected with themselves in order to make possible their own entrance. Therefore, this

indication is by inclusion (of the primary meaning)." (tr. by R.C. Dwivedi) (*svasiddhaye parākṣepaḥ...upādānaṁ...*(KP 2.10) *kuntāḥ praviśanti yaṣṭayaḥ praviśantītyādau kuntādibhir ātmanaḥ praveśasiddhyarthaṁ svasaṁyoginaḥ puruṣā ākṣipyante. tata upādāneneyaṁ lakṣaṇā.*) According to K.K. Raja it is *ajahallakṣaṇā* that Manmaṭa calls here *upādānalakṣaṇā*. Cf. K. Kunjunni Raja: *Indian Theories of Meaning*. The Adyar Library Series, vol. 91, The Second Edition, repr. 1977, p. 250.

28. *śabdena pratipādito 'rtho yenārthāntareṇa vinā na nirvahati tad ākṣipatīti sāmānyatas tāval loke prasiddhir asti...vede ca niyogaś śabdena pratipādito 'rthāntaraṁ svanirvāhāya ākṣipatīti nānupapattiḥ.*

29. *tatkṛtaṁ ca prokṣaṇādeḥ kratvarthatvam. viniyogāt punaḥ vrīhyarthataiva.*

30. This translation of the relative clause *'yasmin prītiḥ puruṣasya'* follows Śabara's commentary: "If happiness comes to a person after something has been done [by him], this thing is named *'puruṣārtha'*." (*yasmin kṛte padārthe puruṣasya prītir bhavati sa puruṣārthaḥ padārthaḥ*. ŚBh v, p. 2, *ll.* 6-7)

The term *'puruṣārtha'* refers in this context not to something desirable which pleases a person, but to something which causes him happiness so as to include even the laborious act of sacrifice. Prabhākara has no objection to this part of Śabara's commentary.

31. This and the immediately preceding parentheses follow Prabhākara's interpretation of the word *'avibhaktatvāt'* (in his quotation: *'avibhāgāt'*). Cf. Bṛh iv, p. 958, *l.* 5: "[Question:] What does the word 'on account of inseparability' means? [Answer:] It means 'because a person is not separated [from the purpose of Veda] by [any] relation to sacrifice.' "(*kim idam avibhāgād iti. puruṣasya kratusaṁbandhāvibhāgād ity arthaḥ.*) This interpretation accords with his commentary on *'artha'* (see below) while it opposes Śabara's following commentary on *'avibhaktatvāt'*: "[The thing (*padārtha*) which] subserves a person is not separable from happiness. Whatever is the means to happiness is subservient to the person." (*avibhakto hi puruṣārthaḥ prītyā. yo yaḥ prītisādhanaḥ sa puruṣārthaḥ*. ŚBh v, p. 2, *ll.* 9-10)

32. *arthaś ca niyogasiddhiḥ. tac copādānam ity uktam.*

33. Śabara maintains as follows that this *'artha'* means the purpose or interest of human being which one knows of himself without the instruction of Vedic text in contrast to the *kratvartha*:"The desire of undertaking that is caused by the purpose but not by Vedic text, whereas the subservience to the sacrifice is recognised only from Vedic text, not otherwise." (*tasya lipsārthenaiva bhavati na śāstreṇa. kratvartho hi śāstrād avagamyate nānyathā*. ŚBh v, p. 2, *ll.* 8-9)

But Prabhākara argues against Śabara because he insists that the knowledge of *puruṣārtha* is impossible without any kind of Vedic text, and then he restricts deliberately the meaning of the term *'śāstra'* in Śabara's comment only to the Vedic text of relation (*sambandhaśāstra*), i.e. the text of application (*viniyogaśāstra*, cf. ṚP iv, p. 958, *l.* 7), so that there remains the possibility of making the *puruṣārtha* known in case of another kind of Vedic text, i.e. that of qualification (*adhikāraśāstra*, cf. *ibid.*, *l.* 8): "It was contradictory said [by Śabara] that the desire of undertaking that is caused by the purpose, but not by Vedic text. Without [any] Vedic text it is neither recognized that the heaven should be realised [by a sacrifice], nor that it will come to its performer. [But in fact,] this was said with regard to the Vedic text of relation." (Bṛh iv, p. 957, *l.* 6-p. 958, *l.* 2) (*tasya lipsārthenaiva bhavati na śāstreṇa iti viruddham uktam. na śāstrād ṛte svargaḥ sādhyatayā pratīyate, kartṛgāmitayā ca. saṁbandhaśāstram aṅgīkṛtyaitad uktam.*) Cf. Ito, Michiya: 'Mīmāṁsāgakuha no Puruṣārtha', *Journal of Indian and Buddhist Studies*, vol. 32, pt. 2, 1984, pp. 138-139.

34. *nanu ca kratvarthatāpy upādānenaivoktā. viniyoge satīty uktam. arthād eva hi puruṣārtha iti viśeṣaḥ.*

35. In this Adhikaraṇa it is discussed that the injunctions *'āghāram āghārayati'* (TS II.5.11.6) or *'agnihotraṁ juhoti'** are not summarizing reference (*samudāyānuvādau*) to the detailed injunctions such as *'ūrdhvam āghārayati'***, *'saṁtatam āghārayati'* (TS II.5.11.7), *'ṛjum āghārayati'* (TS II.5.11.7) etc. or *'dadhnā juhoti'*, *'payasā juhoti'* etc., but distinct injunctions (*apūrvayor vidhī*) independent of them. (Cf. ŚBh iii, p. 48, *l.* 4-p.49, *l.* 3; Pūrvapakṣa: JS 2.2.13-15; Uttarapakṣa: JS 2.2.16)

*Cf. MS I.8.1 (p. 116, *l.* 5): *tān evāvarunddhe ya evaṁ vidvān agnihotraṁ juhoti*; I.8.6 (p. 124, *l.* 19): *sarvān yajñakratūn avarunddhe ya evaṁ vidvān agnihotraṁ juhoti.*

**Cf. ĀpŚ II.14.7: *ūrdhvam āghāraṁ svargakāmasya bhūyiṣṭam āhutīnāṁ juhuyāt.*

36. According to Śālikanātha (ṚP iii, p. 456, *ll.* 16-17) this *'upādāna'* means the object of the verb *'upādā'* (*upādīyata ity upādānam iti.*) because the LyuṬ suffix *'ana'* is variously introduced after a verbal stem (Pāṇ 3.3.113) and it can also mean the object (*karman*) (Pāṇ 3.3.116). Cf. ṚP iii, p. 456, *l.* 18: *tad upādānam tad upādeyam ity arthaḥ.*

37. *yatra niyuṅkte tat kāryam. tatsiddhaye yad upādīyate tad upādānam.*

38. Although the passage (*x*) is included in the Pūrvapakṣa (Bṛh iii, p. 450, *l.* 3-p. 459, *l.* 22), Prabhākara does not argue against this definition of *upādāna* in his Uttarapakṣa (*ibid.*, p.459, *l.* 22-p.465, *l.* 18). Therefore there is no reason to hesitate to regard (*x*) as forming Prabhākara's own definition of *upādāna.*

39. Because the obligation which precedes an injunction of application can be traced back to the injunction of qualification (cf. this paper III. adhikāra), Śālikanātha explains Prabhākara's statement cited in (*vi*) "*tatkṛtaṁ ca prokṣaṇādeḥ kratvarthatvam*" as follows:

> The association is, indeed, the indirect indication of obligation. On the basis of it, it is ascertained that besprinkling etc. are subservient to the sacrifice. If besprinkling etc. were not contributive to the means belonging to that (obligation of qualification)*, how could the cognition of the obligation connected with that (means) be completed in any other way? Therefore, in so far as the obligation is recognized as

connected with that (means), this obligation makes one suppose that besprinkling etc. are contributive to the means, so that it indicates indirectly that they have the means as is own aim. Thus it is ascertained on the basis of it that besprinkling etc. are subservient to sacrifice. (PP p. 466, *ll.* 10-14) (*niyogākṣepo hy upādānam, tat-kṛtaṁ prokṣaṇādeḥ kratvarthatvam. yadi tadīyakaraṇopakārakatā prokṣaṇāder na syāt tadā kenāpareṇa prakāreṇa tadanvitaniyogapratītir nirvahatīti, niyoga eva tadanvitaḥ pratipannas tasya karaṇopakāraka-tāṁ kalpayan karaṇaidamarthyam ākṣipatīti, tatkṛtam eva prokṣaṇādeḥ kratvarthatvam.*)

*'Means' (*karaṇa*) means here the act of sacrificing which is the direct means to fulfilment of the obligation and is made up of creativity (*bhāva*, which is referred to by '*bhāvārthāḥ*' in JS 2.1.1 and characterised by Prabhākara as 'causing something else' (*anyotpādakatva*) in Bṛh iii, p. 288, *l.* 9; p. 289, *l.* 6) and forms the object (*viṣaya*) of the obligation of qualification. Cf. PP p. 453, *ll.* 11-12; *tatra sa eva bhāvārtho viṣayībhūtaḥ karaṇam ity avasīyate; ibid.*, p. 466, *ll.* 8-9: "On the basis of association [it is ascertained that a sacrificial factor] has the act of sacrificing which has come to be the means of [fulfilment of] the obligation of qualification as its own aim." (*upādānataś cādhikāraniyogakaraṇībhūtayāgādyaidamarthyam.*)

40. This is the *viṣayavākya* cited* in ŚBh on JS 4.1.11-16 (Adhikaraṇa 5), in which it is discussed that the singularity of the requisite head is intended (*vivakṣita*) by the injunction. The exegetical rule presented in this Adhikaraṇa is called "*paśvekatvanyāya*". Cf. G.V. Devasthali: *Mīmāṁsā, Vākya—Śāstra of Ancient India*, Bombay 1959, p. 124: the *vacana* is *vivakṣita* if it belongs to a word which is not *uddeśya*, i.e. if the word is *vidhigata* or *upādeya*. See also J.M. Verpoorten: "Le nombre grammatical et son incidence sur l'injonction rituelle. une discussion de Śabara et Kumārila à Mīmāṁsā-Sūtra III 1 13, 14, 15", Orientalia J. Duchesne—Guillemin emerito oblata, Leiden 1984, pp. 519-42.

*Cf. TS VI.1.11.6: *purā khalu vāvaiṣa medhāyātmānam ārabhya carati yo dīkṣito. yad agnīṣomīyam paśum ālabhata ātmaniṣkrayaṇa evāsya sa.* (Cf. A.B. Keith: *op. cit.*, *Part 2: Kāṇḍas IV-VII*, vol. 19, repr. 1967, p. 500: "Now the consecrated person has for long been holding himself ready for the sacrifice. In that he offers an animal to Agni and Soma, that is a buying-off of himself;") Thus, this *viṣayavākya* is composed of two relative clauses of the two contiguous sentences.

41. *na viniyogād eva kriyāṅgatā. kiṁ tarhi. upādānād api hi śeṣatā bhavati. yathaiva hi karaṇībhūtasyaivopādānaṁ evam ekatvayuktasyāpi. na hy akārakasyopādānam asaṅkhyāyuktasyāpi saṃbhavati.*

42. In spite of Pāṇ 2.3.2 Prabhākara insists that the accusative suffix of the noun '*paśum*' in this injunction denotes that the meaning of the stem is means instead of object. Cf. Bṛh iv, p. 971, *ll.* 4-5: *tasmād ekatvaṁ karaṇatvaṁ ca prātipadikasyārthasyaiva.*

43. The singularity is not prescribed because it is not the meaning of the nominal stem '*paśu-*' i.e. *paśutva*. The application is concerned only with

the essential characteristic of substance expressed by the stem.

44. Cf. Bṛh iii, p. 455, *ll.* 1-2: "The association [of a ritual factor with the object of injunction], however, is only preceded by the recognition that [the former] is the distinguishing feature (*viśeṣaṇatva*, cf. ṚP iii, p. 455, *l.*12) [of the latter] just like the singularity of [the requisite head of] cattle in [the injunction] 'One should make sacrifice by means of one head of cattle (*paśunā*)'." (*upādānaṁ punaḥ viśeṣaṇatvāvagamapūrvakam eva yathā paśvekatvasya paśunā yajeta.*)

45. Cf. Bṛh iii, p. 455, *ll.* 6-8: "Because a substance which lacks its number and gender cannot be associated [with its principal factor to be done] even if it has been applied [to its principal factor], the singularity etc.* are associated [with the substance]." (*dravya[ṁ] saṁkhyāliṅgaśūnyaṁ viniyuktam api nopādātuṁ śakyata ity ekatvādaya upādīyante.*)

*Namely, the gender. Cf. JS 4.1.17: *tathā ca liṅgam.*

46. In a Vedic sacrifice there are many kinds of oblations which are made from different kinds of material. The whole process of preparing each oblation is prescribed systematically in detailed injunctions of application (cf. ŚBh on JS 3.1.7). Following these injunctions in order, one can complete the oblations, some of which one offers into the sacrificial fire following the injunctions of the main offerings (e.g. *āgneya*-cake, *upāṃśuyāja*-ghee and *aindrāgna*-cake or *sāṃnāyya*-milkproduct in the new moon sacrifice (*darśa*); *āgneya*-cake, *upāṁśuyāja*-ghee and *agnīṣomīya*-cake in the full moon sacrifice (*pūrṇamāsa*)), whereas the other oblations are offered at the subsidiary offerings (*prayāja*, *anuyāja* etc.) according to their respective injunctions (cf. ŚBh on JS 4.4.29; 34). All the main offerings are lumped together under the name of the sacrifice, e.g. *'darśapūrṇamāsau'* (cf. ŚBh vii, p. 6, *ll.* 8-9 on *'ekaśabdābhisaṁyogāt'* in JS 11.1.1).

47. According to G.V. Garge this oft-quoted injunction is "not found in this form, in any of the extant vedic texts" except an approximate text of ĀpŚ III.14.8: *svargakāmo darśapūrṇamāsau.* (D.V. Garge: *Citations in Śabara-Bhāṣya*, Deccan College Dissertation Series: 8, 1952, p. 128.) Rudradatta, the commentator on ĀpŚ, adds to it: *kuryād iti śeṣaḥ.*

48. *siddhārthas tu parārtho bhavati. atha sādhyārthaḥ tadā svārtho bhavati. tatredānīṃ na vidmaḥ kiṁ siddhārthasyopādānaṁ parārthatayā uta sādhyatayopadīyata iti.*

49. Namely, the main offerings named *'darśapūrṇamāsa'*. Cf. Note 46.

50. Cf. Bṛh v, p. 7, *l.* 4-p. 8, *l.* 5.

51. *niyojyāvagatis tv anyataḥ eva. sā ceyam iṣṭasaṃbandhād ity uktam.*

52. *nanu ceṣṭatvaṁ nānyathopapadyate yadi na yāgāt kāmasiddhiḥ.*

53. *kāmyamānatvena svargaḥ puruṣaṁ viśinaṣṭīty uktam. bhāvārthe ca niyoga ity etad apy uktam. seyaṁ niyoganiyojyaviṣayatayaikavākyatā... niyogasiddhiś ca vākyārthaḥ.*

54. Cf. Bṛh v, p. 37, *l.* 6-p. 38, *l.*3; p. 38, *l.* 9-p. 39, *l.* 8.

55. *tatra tāvad yadi yāgasyaiva kartavyatā, na niyojyārtho 'nveti niyoge. atha kāmaḥ, ananvito viṣayaḥ syāt niyojyena. tataś caikaniyogāvagatiḥ*

pīḍyeta. yāgaprādhānye cokto doṣaḥ. tasmāt kāmapradhānatayaivaikaniyogasaṃbandhaḥ.

56. *tasmāt yāgena svargaṁ sādhayed iti yuktam.*

57. Śabara referred to the mutual expectation between the noun *'svargakāmaḥ'* and the verb *'yajeta'* in the injunction of qualification. Cf. ŚBh (on JS 2.1.1) ii, p. 341, *ll.* 1-4:

> [It is expected by the verb *'yajeta'*] that something should be realized by means of its meaning, namely, the creativity, whereas [it is expected by the noun *'svargakāmaḥ'*] that the desire for heaven should be realized by some means; [In this way, both words] are combined together (*saṁprayoga*) just as one whose horse has been lost and another whose chariot has been burnt* [harness the remaining horse to the remaining chariot in order to journey together]. The verb 'should sacrifice' (*yajeta*) etc. which have the expectation: "For what, by which means and how one should sacrifice?" fulfill the expectation [regarding 'for what'] by means of this motivation, [namely, the heaven expressed in the noun] 'One desiring heaven'. (*bhāvārthaiḥ kim api bhāvayitavyaṁ svargakāmasya ca kenāpi bhāvyateti. tayor naṣṭāśvadagdharathavat saṁprayogaḥ. yajetety evamādayaḥ sākāṅkṣā yajeta kiṃ kena katham iti, svargakāma ity anena prayojanena nirākāṅkṣāḥ.*)

Commenting on this (Bṛh iii, p. 299, *l.* 6-p. 302, *l.* 2), Prabhākara denies the possibility of ascribing the denotation of the relation between the act of sacrificing and the heaven to any case suffix and thus to any application (*viniyoga*), while he maintains that this indication is characterized by the qualification (*ibid.*, p. 300, *l.* 6: *adhikāralakṣaṇaḥ*) expressed by the noun *'svargakāmaḥ'* as well as the nature of creativity (*ibid.*, p. 301, *l.* 7: *bhāvasvabhāvo*) expressed by the verb *'yajeta'*.

*Cf. Kātyāyana's Vārttika 16 on Pāṇ 1.1.50 (MBh p. 125, *l.* 4, cf. *ibid.*, *ll.* 5-6): *saṁprayogo vā naṣṭāśvadagdharathavat.*

58. *arthe samavaiṣamyam ato dravyakarmaṇām.*

59. ŚBh v, p. 18, *l.* 13: *atikrāntas tṛtīyaviṣayaḥ.*

60. Bṛh iv, p. 977, *ll.* 3-4: *idānīṁ punaḥ sthite pārārthye kevalam upādānam eva cintyate, kena prayojanenopādānaṁ kena neti.*

But Pārthasārathi Miśra refuses to acknowledge that the fourth Adhyāya employs any other *pramāṇa* of subordination than *śruti* etc. (ŚD pt. 1, p.400, *l.* 13-p.401, *l.* 2) Pārthasārathi denies even the possibility that *upādāna* is a distinct *pramāṇa* of subordination (NRM p. 208, *l.* 12-p. 211, *l.* 5). In reply to Śālikanātha's view that the obligation of qualification indicates indirectly that besprinkling etc. are contributive to the means, i.e. the act of sacrificing (NRM p. 209, *ll.* 7-8 = PP p. 466, *ll.* 12-13, cf. Note 39), he insists that this function of obligation is nothing but the contextual unity (*prakaraṇa*), namely the fourth *viniyogapramāṇa*, which, for example, subordinates *prayāja* etc. to the main offering (NRM p. 210, *ll.* 1-3).

61. *tṛtīyasyāyaṁ viṣayaḥ na punaḥ tārtīyair pramāṇaiḥ śakyate 'vagantum. ato vidhinimittakam evāsya pārārthyam iti caturthe cintitam. etac ca vyākhyā-*

tam na śrutyādibhiḥ sarvasya parārthyaṁ śakyate pratipādayitum iti. etad evātra kathyate. tathā ca yāgaphalayor adhikārāt pārārthyaṁ vakṣyati.

62. *ata eva bādarer eṣā bhrāntiḥ dravyaguṇasaṁskāreṣv eva śeṣatvam iti, śrutyādīnāṁ tatra dravyādau saṃbhavāt upādānādhikārayoḥ sāmarthyam apaśyato 'vadhāraṇāt.*

63. Cf. This paper (*viii*) and Bṛh v, p. 50, *l.* 5: "But who would not acknowledge that with regard to the fulfillment of obligation all (the ritual factors including the person desiring the heaven (*kāmin*, cf. *ibid. ll.* 2-3)) are subsidiary to it?" (*niyogasiddhau tu sarvaṁ tadanuguṇam iti kena neṣyate.*)

64. In addition, I will quote two other phrases from the Bṛhatī in which Prabhākara rejects Bādari's opinion on subordination. According to Prabhākara, the reason why Bādari enumerated only substance, quality and preparatory act as subordinate ritual factors is that the obligation is fulfilled through the completion of the act of sacrificing and it is these three that are contributive to the act of sacrificing (cf. Bṛh iv, p. 637, *ll.* 2-3). But Prabhākara emphasizes that the contribution (*upakāra*) to the act of sacrificing cannot be the general character of all subordinate factors because it is prescribed only in injunctions of application (but not in that of qualification):

> But the reference to Bādari [in JS 3.1.3] was done for the purpose of showing the contribution to the act of sacrificing [in case of substance, quality and preparatory act], but not for the purpose of denying the reason for subordination [mentioned in JS 3.1.2:] "having the other as its own aim". [Question:] Why? [Answer:] For with regard to the application that ("having the other as its own aim") was mentioned. [Objection:] But Bādari also mentioned this (contribution to the act of sacrificing) only with regard to the application. [Reply:] That is why it was refused. (Bṛh iv, p. 960, *ll.* 2-5) (*bādarigrahaṇaṁ punar upakārapradarśanārtham. na punaḥ parārthatvād iti śeṣahetunivṛttyartham. katham. viniyoge hi sa uktaḥ. nanu bādariṇāpi viniyoga evāsāv upanyastaḥ. ata evāsau nirākṛtaḥ.*)

The next criticism is found in Bṛh on the *svargakāmādhikaraṇa*. Because the awareness of the hearer of an *adhikāravidhi* that he is the person to be obligated (*niyojya*)presupposes his knowledge that the act of sacrificing is the means to the result desired by him, the opponent (i.e. some grammarians *vaiyākaraṇāḥ kecit*) insists that the person qualified for a sacrifice (*adhikārin*) is not a person who has awared that he is to be obligated, but simply the agent of the sacrifice (*kartṛ*) (cf. Bṛh v, p. 14, *ll.* 1-3). Prabhākara remarks that this position of the opponent corresponds with the view of Bādari:

> This is nothing but the view of Bādari, who thinks that the relation [namely, the subordination,] can be recognized as lying in substance, quality and preparatory act, but not in act of sacrificing, in result or in person. (Bṛh v, p. 14, *ll.* 5-6) (*ayam eva cāsau bādaripakṣaḥ, dravyaguṇasaṁskāreṣv ity evaṁ saṁbandhāvagamaṁ manyate, na yāgaphalapuruṣeṣv iti.*)

25

ŚRĪ ŚAṄKARA AND PURVAMĪMĀṀSĀ

K.T. Pandurangi

Both Pūrvamīmāṁsā and Vedānta derive their tenets from Vedas. Pūrvamīmāṁsā derives its tenets mostly from Brāhmaṇa portions while Vedānta derives from Upaniṣads. Therefore, both are interested in the interpretation of Vedas. Pūrvamīmāṁsā has evolved certain guidelines for the interpretation of Vedas. These are mostly accepted by Vedānta. However, their central doctrine and the goal are different. Pūrvamīmāṁsā is concerned with *Dharma*, i.e. ritual programmes, while Vedānta is concerned with Brahman. Therefore, they differ in respect of their goal and the means to achieve it.

Śaṅkara refers to Pūrvamīmāṁsā by the name *Prathamatantra*, *Pūrvakāṇḍa*, *Pramāṇa-lakṣaṇa* etc. He refers to Śabarasvāmin and Upavarṣa. He utilises the Pūrvamīmāṁsā guidelines of interpretation such as *Upakrama*, *Upasaṁhāra* etc. and also *śruti*, *liṅga* etc. He quotes Pūrvamīmāṁsā *Nyāyas*. Brahmasūtrakāra himself refers to Jaimini. Many Pūrvamīmāṁsā terms and the names of sacrifices like *Agnihotra*, *Dvādaśāha* etc. are referred to in Brahmasūtra. But in respect of the central doctrine and the goal Vedānta differs from Pūrvamīmāṁsā. Some of their differences are fundamental in the areas of epistemology, metaphysics, and ethics. Śaṅkara discusses these in his Brahmasūtrabhāṣya and Upaniṣad-bhāṣyas. It is not possible to collect the entire material in this respect in one paper and analyse the same. Therefore, some crucial points that deserve special attention are noticed in this paper.

In the very introduction to his Brahmasūtrabhāṣya, i.e. Adhyāsabhāṣya Śrī Śaṅkara raises the question as to what is the scope of the authority of Vedic injunctions, prohibitions etc. that constitute the source of authority for the *Dharma* of Pūrvamīmāṁsā.[1]

He clearly states that these are authoritative within the field of *Avidyā* as in the case of perception, inference and other *pramāṇas*. The knowledge of *Dharma*, i.e. ritual programmes, given by Vedic injunctions, prohibitions etc. is not helpful to achieve *Brahmajñāna*; on the contrary it is opposed to *Brahmajñāna* as it involves the differentiation of agent, object, results etc. The ritual programme of Pūrvamīmāṁsā falls within the field of *Avidyā* and therefore, that portion of Veda that conveys this has authority only within that field.

The question of the difference in the scope and the objective of Pūrvamīmāṁsā and Vedānta is again raised under the first Sūtra while discussing the import of *atha*[2] (अथ).

Atha means after. This raises the point after what? Śrī Śaṅkara clearly states that it cannot be taken as 'after *karmajñāna* or *dharmajñāna*'. In support of this stand he gives three reasons:

(1) The object of enquiry of Pūrvamīmāṁsā and Vedānta are different and unrelated. *Dharma* and *Brahman*[3] constitute the objects of enquiry of these two respectively. These are not related as main and subordinate so as to warrant a consideration of one after the other. No such sequence is warranted on any other ground also. One can undertake the enquiry of *Brahman* before *Dharmajñāna* or after it, or even without it, since *Dharmajñāna* is irrelevant for *Brahmajñāna*. In fact, it is opposed to it.

(2) The goals of the two are different. *Dharma* is meant for the prosperity within the field of *avidyā* while *Brahmajñāna* is intended to cross over *avidyā*.

(3) The nature of *Dharma* is such that it has to be performed while that of *Brahman* is to be realised. Further, *Dharma* has to be accomplished in future while *Brahman* is ever present. Therefore, the two are totally different and unrelated. Thus Śrī Śaṅkara clearly demarcates the areas of Pūrvamīmāṁsā and Vedānta.

Under *Janmādhikaraṇa* (I.1-2) another interesting point is mentioned in respect of *Dharma* and *Brahmajñāna*. *Śruti* is the source and it communicates *Dharma*. Whatever *śruti* informs us as *Dharma* that has to be taken as *dharma* and performed. But in case of *Brahman śruti* has to lead to the experience.[4] It is the experience or the realisation of *Brahmanhood* that is important. As *Dharma* is communicated through verbal communication, the classification of communicated matter as injunction, prohibition, etc. is possible and meaningful. The arrangement as general, exception, and alternate is also possible and meaningful. But in case of *Brahmajñāna* the process of communication does not end by mere verbal communication, it has to lead to the experience and realisation.[5] Therefore, *Brahmajñāna* is definitive. Further, *Dharmajñāna* is of the nature of *Parokṣajñāna* (mediate knowledge) while *Brahmajñāna* is *aparokṣajñāna.* (immediate knowledge).

Here an important epistemological point is made. According to Advaita Vedānta, even verbal communication can lead to direct perception. The example that is generally quoted to bring home this point is "*daśamaḥ tvam asi.*" The *śruti* passage "*tat tvam asi*" leads to such direct perception. Thus *śruti* helps to obtain the experience or realisation of *Brahman*. As soon as *śruti* leads one to such an experience its purpose is over. This is how the *śruti* that belongs to the field of *Avidyā* enables one to cross over *Avidyā.*

It is in the *Samanvaya-adhikaraṇa* (I.1-4) that an issue on which Pūrvamīmāṁsā and Vedānta fundamentally differ is discussed.

The Mīmāṁsā holds that the Vedas communicate only in terms of injunction. No passage that does not communicate an injunction or something that is connected with it can be considered authoritative. Therefore, *Brahman* as such cannot be communicated by Vedas. However, if the passages that refer to *Brahman* are construed as injunctions of meditation, then, *Brahman* can be treated as communicated as an object of an injunction. Another way of getting Brahman communicated through Vedic passages is to treat these passages as conveying a deity connected with the rituals. In any case Brahman alone cannot be communicated without relating it with an injunction.[6] No Vedic passage is meaningful or authoritative unless it conveys an injunction.

This position of Mīmāṁsā is not acceptable to Vedānta. Śrī Śaṅkara refers to a number of *śruti* passages that refer to *Brahman* but do not contain any injunction. From this it is clear that *Brahman* as such can be communicated without injunction.[7]

Śrī Śaṅkara also rejects the plea that *Brahman* can at least be treated as an object of the injunction to know it. The contention of those who somehow want to bring the communication of *Brahman* within the scope of an injunction is that the Vedic communication should lead to either *Pravṛtti* or *Nivṛtti*—that is to say, either prompting to undertake something or to withdraw from something. This can be managed only by injunctions and prohibitions. Descriptive passages do not prompt either undertaking or withdrawing. Therefore, the passages that describe *Brahman* have to be treated as injunctions to know *Brahman*.[8] In some of the passages that deal with *Brahman* injunctive verbs and potential participles are employed.

This contention is not acceptable to Vedānta. It is not necessary that every passage should lead to *Pravṛtti* or *Nivṛtti*. Nor it is necessary that either *upādeya* or *heya* be communicated. *Brahman* is neither *upādeya* nor *heya*. *Brahmanhood* is ever present. It neither needs obtaining nor rejecting. It has to be only realised. Therefore, mere communication of it so as to enable to realise it is sufficient.[9] No injunction to know it is necessary. Knowledge is not an activity.[10] For instance, the knowledge of the fire as fire is not an activity. Therefore, it cannot be enjoined. It can only arise. The verbs in potential mood, and potential participles in some of the Vedic passages that communicate *Brahman* are intended to communicate the withdrawal from other objects rather than enjoining to know *Brahman*.[11] It is the cessation of all activity that is a precondition of *Brahmajñāna*. As regards the statement of Jaimini to the effect that no Vedic passage that does not communicate an injunction is meaningful or authoritative, it applies only to such passages as do not communicate *Brahman*. In conclusion Śrī Śaṅkara remarks that if Brahman were also to be communicated through *codanā* or an injunction, it would have been a sub-topic of *Dharma* and no separate treatment of *Brahman* enquiry would have been necessary.

The above discussion makes it clear that Mīmāṁsā and Vedānta fundamentally differ on the issue of the mode of verbal communication. Their respective stands are very vital to their respective doctrinal positions. This issue of the mode of verbal communication has been a major issue in Indian epistemology. These two theories of verbal communication are known as *kārya-vyutpatti* and *siddhavyutpatti* theories. Apart from Advaita Vedānta a few other systems also go by *siddhavyutpatti* theory. But the special point of Advaita in verbal communication is that it can lead to direct experience or immediate experience. The passages like '*tat tvam asi*' lead to immediate experience or realisation of *Brahman* according Advaita.

The problem of the relative position of *Karma* and *Jñāna* in achieving human goal has been a matter of controversy between Mīmāṁsakas and Vedāntins. Mīmāṁsakas are reluctant to give an independent position to *jñāna* in this respect while Vedāntins consider *karma* only a *sahakārin* for *jñāna* but not a direct means for achieving final goal. This point is raised under many *adhikarṇas* of *Brahmasūtras* and Vedāntin's position is made clear by Śrī Śaṅkara.

Under *Kartradhikaraṇa* and *Takṣādhikaraṇa* (II.3.33-40 and II.3.40) the very basic question whether *Jīva* is Agent or not, and if he is an Agent, whether his Agency is real or super-imposed is raised. Śrī Śaṅkara agrees that *Jīva* is agent but he states that this agency is not real but it is super-imposed.[12] *Jīva* is Agent within the field of *Avidyā*. When he crosses the bound of *Avidyā* he has no separate identity and therefore, there is no question of any Agency.

The Vedas issue injunctions and prohibitions. These will be meaningful only when there is an Agent to translate them into action. Therefore, *Jīva* has got to be an Agent. At the same time, his true nature is, i.e. he is *nityaśuddhabuddhamuktasvabhāva*. Therefore, there cannot be any real Agency on the part of *Jīva*. These two positions can be reconciled only by envisaging super-imposed agency on the part of *Jīva*. This stand of Vedānta naturally relegates the entire sacrificial activity of Mīmāṁsakas to the field of *Avidyā*.

That the Vedic injunctions are meant for *avidvān*, while the Vedic teachings of *Brahman* or *Ātmaikya* are meant for *vidvān* is another way of putting the same thing.

Śrī Śaṅkara points out that the Vedic injunctions do not cause the real Agency but only enjoin certain duties with reference to the Agency that is there.[13] It is irrelevant for this purpose whether such an Agency is real or super-imposed.

Under *Puruṣārthādhikaraṇa* (III.4.1-17) the question whether *jñāna* is an independent and direct means of *puruṣārtha* or subordinate to *karma* is specifically raised. Mīmāṁsakas naturally take the view that it is subordinate to *karma*. *Ātman* is the agent to perform *karmas*. Therefore, he is connected with *karma*. Hence, *Ātmajñāna* is also connected with the *karma*. Therefore, whatever it achieves that is achieved through *karma* only.[14] It has no independent goal. The results of *Ātmajñāna* such as freedom from sorrow etc. that are mentioned over and above the results of *karma* are only of *Arthavāda* nature. That is why it is found that even *brahmajñānins* like Janaka took to *karma*. It is specifically stated in *śruti* passages like "*yadeva vidyayā karoti tadeva vīryavattaraṁ bhavati.*" This clearly shows only the supporting role of *jñāna*. Passages like "*kurvanneveha karmāṇi*" make the performance of *karma* obligatory. Therefore, the Mīmāṁsakas argue that *jñāna* is not an independent means of *Puruṣārtha*.

This contention of Mīmāṁsakas is opposed in *Puruṣārthādhikaraṇa*. By Ātman the Mīmāṁsakas have understood *saṁsārī Ātman* here. He is, no doubt, connected with *karma* as Agent. But when *śruti* talks of *Ātmajñāna* it is *Paramātman* who is bereft of Agency etc. who is meant. He is not connected with *karma* and not subordinate to *karma*. Therefore, *Ātmajñāna* in the sense of *Brahmajñāna* is not subordinate to *karma*. It is an independent means of *Puruṣārtha*.[15]

Here, by *Puruṣārtha* Mīmāṁsakas understand, *svarga* etc., while Vedāntin understands liberation. Therefore, for Mīmāṁsaka *karma* is the means for *svarga* etc., while *jñāna* may support *karma* to some extent. For Vedāntin it is *jñāna* that is the real means for liberation. *Karma* that involves the Agent, the object etc. i.e. *bheda-prapañca*, is actually opposed to liberation.

However, *Vedāntins* do accept *karma* as *sahakārin* to *jñāna*. This question is raised in *Sarvāpekṣādhikaraṇa*[16] (III.26-27). It is true that *jñāna* is an independent and direct means to liberation. *Karma* does not directly contribute to this end but *karma* assists in obtaining knowledge through *cittaśuddhi*. Performance of *Āśramakarmas* and *Nityakarmas* does help to obtain *cittaśuddhi* and knowledge. This point is also discussed under *Āśramakarmādhikaraṇa*[17] (III.4.32-36) particularly under the *sūtra* '*sahakāritvena ca*' (III.4.33). Even *kāmyakarma* when performed bereft of *kāma* does assist *jñāna*. *Agnihotra* and other *nityakarmas* are stated to be *Ārādupakāraka* to liberation under the *Sūtra*[18] IV.1.16.

Vedāntins do not reject the utility of *karma* within the field of *Avidyā*. In fact they defend sacrifice within this field. Under the *sūtra* "*aśuddhamiti cet na śabdāt*" performance of sacrifice and offering *paśu* in a sacrifice is defended.[19] The results to be obtained by sacrifice are accepted as valid within the field of *Avidyā*. But *karmas* cannot lead to liberation. These also cannot prevent liberation once the knowledge is obtained. The knowledge will nullify the effects of the *karmas*. This point is discussed under *Tadadhigamādhikaraṇa* and *Itarāsaṁśleṣādhikaraṇa* (IV.1.13-14). The point raised here is: How can *karmas* remain without producing their results simply because one has obtained *jñāna*? *Karmas* have the potency to produce their results and, therefore, they must lead to the respective results irrespective of one obtaining *Ātmajñāna*. This line of argument is not acceptable to Vedāntins. According to them *Ātmajñāna* cuts the very roots of *karma*. The notions of *Kartṛtva* and *Bhoktṛtva* are the basis of *karma*. *Ātmajñāna* cuts these very notions and hence the effects of *karma* are nullified by *jñāna*.

Finally, the Vedāntins do not accept the Mīmāṁsaka's contention that *karma* leads to its results through *Apūrva*. The very concept of *Apūrva* is not acceptable to Vedāntins.

This question is raised under *Phalādhikaraṇa* (III.2.38-41). Here, the question whether *karma* leads to its results or *Īśvara* bestows the results of *karma* is raised. Mīmāṁsakas take the view that *karma* produces *Apūrva* which ultimately leads to the results. This view is rejected here. *Apūrva* being *jaḍa* (non-intelligent) cannot lead to the results by itself. The concept of *apūrva* in between *karma* and its results is not warranted since Īśvara bestows the results taking into account the *karmas* of *jīvas*.[20] This is probably the biggest blow to the Mīmāṁsakas. Though early Mīmāṁsakas are silent about *Īśvara*, later Mīmāṁsakas like Kumārila do accept *Īśvara*. Therefore, they cannot argue that since there is no *Īśvara*, *Apūrva* is necessary.

Under *Devatādhikaraṇa* (I.3.26-33) an interesting point on which Vedānta and Mīmāṁsā differ is raised. Mīmāṁsakas are of the opinion that the deities have no *vigraha* or form. Mīmāṁsakas do not accept *vigraha* or form to the deities for two reasons:

(1) Many persons will be performing the same sacrifice at diffe-

rent places at the same time. It would be difficult for Indra and other deities to be present at all places if they have *vigraha* or form.

(2) The forms of the deities, if any, will be perishable. The deities are mentioned in Vedas. The Vedic words and their meanings are eternally connected. However, if one of them, say, meaning is perishable, then the very relation between the Vedic word and its meaning will be perishable. This will ultimately affect the very doctrine of *Vedanityatva*.

This line of argument is not acceptable to Śrī Śaṅkara. One and the same deity can assume many forms and be present at all sacrifices wherever he is involved at the same time. Further, it is not their physical presence that is necessary. The offerings are meant for them wherever they are.[21]

As regards the second reason, Śrī Śaṅkara makes it clear that the meaning of words is not *vyakti* but *ākṛti*.[22] *Ākṛti* is *nitya*. Therefore, even if *indravyakti* is perishable Ākṛti is not perishable. Hence, neither the *nityatva* of the relation between word and meaning is affected nor *vedanityatva* is affected.

Incidentally Śrī Śaṅkara discusses two other important questions here:

(1) Whether there is any need to accept the doctrine of *sphoṭa* or *varṇas* constituting a word.

(2) What is exactly meant when it is stated that the whole world arises from *Śabda*? He rejects the concept of *sphoṭa* and subscribes to the Mīmāṁsā view that *varṇas* constitute word. In this connection, he quotes the views of Upavarṣa who had commented on both *Mīmāṁsāsūtras* and *Vedāntasūtras*. As regards the second point, Śrī Śaṅkara points out that when it is stated that the world arises from '*śabda*', it is not intended to convey their *upādāna-upādeya-bhāva* (relation) as in the case of *Brahman* and the world but it only means that words connote objects. The problems of *Vedanityatva* and *Vedāpauruṣeyatva* are also discussed under this *Adhikarṇa*. Vedānta supports Pūrvamīmāṁsā on these two issues.

The Pūrvamīmāṁsā guidelines to determine the purport of a *śruti* passage viz. *Upakrama*, *Upasaṃhāra* etc. *tātparyaliṅgas* are fully utilised by Śrī Śaṅkara all along his *Brahmasūtrabhāṣya* and *Upaniṣadbhāṣyas*. Sūtrakāra himself mentions these in his *sūtras*. In many cases the agreement between *Upakrama* and

Upasaṁhāra is utilised to determine the purport of a passage. *Abhyāsa* and *Apūrvatā* are shown to determine the purport in a few cases.

Śruti, Liṅga, Vākya etc., the guidelines for determining the meaning, are also utilised. The Jaimini-Sūtra that states the relative priority of these is quoted in *Liṅgabhūyastvādhikaraṇa* (III. 3.44). But there is one important difference in the application of these between Mīmāṁsā and Vedānta. In Mīmāṁsā these are *aṅgatvanirṇāyaka* while in Vedānta these are *arthanirṇāyaka.*

Mīmāṁsā guidelines of *Karmabheda* are utilised to decide *saguṇopāsanā vidyābheda.* The Jaiminisūtra that lays down these guidelines is quoted in *Śabdādibhedādhikaraṇa* (III.3.58). The guidelines for determining some *vidyās* that are mentioned in more than one *śākhā* as one *vidyā*, and shifting the material from one *śākhā* to another *śākhā* in case of such *vidyās* are also utilised. It is stated that just as *Dravya* and *Devatā* constitute the central point of a sacrifice the object to be meditated upon constitutes the central point of a *saguṇopāsanā vidyā.* The passages that describe *upāsanās* like *Udgīthopāsanā* are treated as injunctions. Even the distinctions like *yajamānakarma* and *Ṛtvikkarma* are introduced in case of some *saguṇopāsanās.* Thus, the Mīmāṁsā technique and terminology are considerably utilised in Vedānta. So far as the field of *Avidyā* is concerned the Pūrvamīmāṁsā programme is a respectable field of activity. But when it comes to the stage of *Brahmajñāna* and realisation of *Ātmaikya* the ritual programme stands rejected.

Notes

1. तमेतमविद्याख्यमात्मानात्मनोरितरेतराध्यासं पुरस्कृत्य सर्वे प्रमाणप्रमेयव्यवहाराः लौकिकाः वैदिकाश्च प्रवृत्ताः। सर्वाणि च शास्त्राणि विधिप्रतिषेधमोक्षपराणि।

   शास्त्रमविद्यावद्विषयत्वं नातिवर्तते। तथाहि 'ब्राह्मणो यजेत' इत्यादीनि शास्त्राणि आत्मनि वर्णाश्रमवयोऽवस्थादि विशेषाध्यासमाश्रित्य प्रवर्तन्ते।

   (अध्यासभाष्यम्)

2. अथशब्दः आनन्तर्यार्थः ... यत्पूर्ववृत्तं नियमेन अपेक्षते। न नु इह कर्मव-

बोधानन्तर्यविशेषः। न। धर्मजिज्ञासायाः प्रागपि अधीतवेदान्तस्य ब्रह्मजिज्ञासोपपत्तेः। न इह क्रमः विवक्षितः शेषशेषित्वे अधिकृताधिकारे वा प्रमाणाभावात् धर्मब्रह्मजिज्ञासयोः। (SB I.1.1)

3. अभ्युदयफलं धर्मज्ञानं निश्रेयसफलं तु ब्रह्मज्ञानम्। (SB I.1.1)

4. भव्यञ्च धर्मः भूतं ब्रह्म। या हि चोदना धर्मस्य लक्षणं सा स्वविषये नियुञ्जानैव पुरुषमवबोधयति। ब्रह्मचोदना तु पुरुषमवबोधयत्येव केवलम्। (SB I.1.1)

5. न धर्मजिज्ञासायामिव श्रुत्यादय एव प्रमाणं ब्रह्मजिज्ञासायाम्। किन्तु श्रुत्यादयः अनुभवादयश्च यथासम्भवमिह प्रमाणं अनुभवावसानत्वात् भूतवस्तुविषयत्वाच्च ब्रह्मज्ञानस्य। (SB I.1.2)

6. कथं पुनः ब्रह्मणः शास्त्रप्रमाणकत्वमुच्यते। यावता 'आम्नायानां क्रियार्थत्वादानर्थक्यमतदर्थानाम्' इति क्रियापरत्वं शास्त्रस्य प्रदर्शितम्। अतः वेदान्तानामानर्थक्यं अक्रियार्थत्वात्। कर्तृ देवतादिप्रकाशनार्थत्वेन वा क्रियाविधिशेषत्वं उपासनादिक्रियान्तरविधानार्थत्वं वा। न हि परिनिष्ठितवस्तु प्रतिपादनं संभवति। (SB I.1.4)

7. यद्यपि अन्यत्र वेदवाक्यानां विधिसंस्पर्शमन्तरेण प्रमाणत्वं न दृष्टं तथापि आत्मविज्ञानस्य फलपर्यन्तत्वात् न तद्विषयस्य शास्त्रस्य प्रामाण्यं शक्यं प्रत्याख्यातुम्। (SB I.1.4)

8. अत्र अपरे प्रत्यवतिष्ठन्ते यद्यपि शास्त्रप्रमाणकं ब्रह्म तथापि प्रतिपत्तिविधिविषयतयैव शास्त्रेण ब्रह्म समर्प्यते। कुत एतत् प्रवृत्तिनिवृत्तिप्रयोजनपरत्वात् शास्त्रस्य...कर्तव्यविध्यननुप्रवेशे वस्तुमात्र कथने हानोपादानासंभवात्। (SB I.1.4)

9. यदपि अकर्तव्यप्रधानमात्मज्ञानं हानोपादानाय न भवतीति तत्तथैव अभ्युपगम्यते। अलंकारो हि अयमस्माकं यद् ब्रह्मात्मावगतौ सत्यां सर्वकर्तव्यताहानिः कृतकृत्यता च। (SB I.1.4)

10. ज्ञानं केवलं वस्तुतन्त्रमेव न चोदनातन्त्रं नापि पुरुषतन्त्रम्।...या तु प्रसिद्धे अग्नौ अग्निबुद्धिः न सा चोदनातन्त्रा नापि पुरुषतन्त्रा। (SB I.1.4)

11. 'आत्मा वा अरे द्रष्टव्यः श्रोतव्यः' इत्यादीनि विधिच्छायानि वचनानि स्वाभाविकप्रवृत्तिविमुखीकरणानीति ब्रूमः। (SB I.1.4)

12. एवं तावत् शास्त्रार्थवत्त्वादिभिः हेतुभिः कर्तृत्वं शारीरस्य प्रदर्शितम्।... तत्पुनः स्वाभाविकं कर्तृत्वमात्मनः न संभवति अनिर्मोक्षप्रसङ्गात्।...नित्यशुद्धबुद्धात्मप्रतिपादनात् मोक्षसिद्धिरभिमता। तादृगात्मप्रतिपादनं च न स्वाभाविक कर्तृत्वे अवकलपेत। तस्मात् उपाधिधर्माध्यासेनैव आत्मनः कर्तृत्वं न स्वाभाविकम्। (SB II.3.40)

13. विधिशास्त्रं तावत् यथा प्राप्तं कर्तृत्वमुपादाय कर्तव्यविशेषमुपदिशति न कर्तृत्वमात्मनः प्रतिपादयति ।...अविद्याकृतं कर्तृत्वमुपादाय विधिशास्त्रं प्रवर्तिष्यते । (SB II.3.40)

14. कर्तृत्वेन आत्मनः कर्मशेषत्वात् तद्विज्ञानमपि कर्मसंबन्ध्येव इत्यतः तस्मिन्नवगतप्रयोजने आत्मज्ञाने या फलश्रुतिः सा अर्थवाद इति जैमिनिः आचार्यः मन्यते । (SB III.4.2)

15. यदि संसारी एव आत्मा शारीरः कर्ता भोक्ता च शरीरमात्रव्यतिरेकेण वेदान्तेषु उपदिष्टः स्यात् ततो फलश्रुतेः अर्थवादत्वं स्यात् । अधिकः तावत् शारीरादात्मनः असंसारी ईश्वरः कर्तृत्वादि संसारिधर्मरहितः परमात्मा वेद्यत्वेन उपदिश्यते वेदान्तेषु । (SB III.4.8)

16. यज्ञादीनि शमदमादीनि च यथाश्रमं सर्वाण्येव आश्रमकर्माणि विद्योत्पत्तौ अपेक्षितानि । (SB III.4.27)

17. उत्पन्ना हि विद्या फलसिद्धिं प्रति न किञ्चित् अन्यदपेक्षते उत्पत्तिं प्रति तु अपेक्षते । (SB III.4.26)

18. यत् नित्यं कर्म वैदिकमग्निहोत्रादि तत् तत्कार्यायैव भवति ।... ननु ज्ञानकर्मणोः विलक्षणकार्यत्वात् कार्यैकत्वानुपपत्तिः । नैषः दोषः । ज्वरमरणकार्ययोः दधिविषयोरपि गुडमंत्रसंयुक्तयोः तृप्तिपुष्टिकार्यदर्शनात् । (SB IV.1.10)

19. यत्पुनरुक्तं पशुहिंसादियोगात् अशुद्धमाध्वरिकं कर्म तस्य अनिष्टमपि अवकल्पते इति । तत्परि ह्रियते ।...शास्त्राच्च हिंसानुग्रहात्मकः ज्योतिष्टोम धर्म इत्यवधारितः स कथं अशुद्ध इति शक्यते वक्तुम् । (SB III.1.25)

20. अथोच्येत माभूत् कर्मानन्तरं फलोत्पादः । कर्मकार्यात् अपूर्वात् फलमुत्पत्स्यत इति । तदपि नोपपद्यते । अपूर्वस्य अचेतनस्य चेतनेन अप्रवर्तितस्य प्रवृत्त्यनुपपत्तेः । तदस्तित्वे च प्रमाणाभावात् । अर्थापत्तिः प्रमाणमिति चेत् । न । ईश्वरसिद्धेः अर्थापत्तिः क्षयात् । (SB III.2.38)

21. स्यादेतत् यदि विग्रहवत्त्वाद्यभ्युपगमेन देवादीनां विद्यासु अधिकारो वर्ण्येत, विग्रहवत्त्वात् ऋत्विगादिवत् इन्द्रादीनामपि स्वरूपसन्निधानेन कर्मांगभावो अभ्युपगम्येत तदा च कर्मणि विरोधः स्यात् । न हि इन्द्रादीनां स्वरूपसन्निधानेन यागे अंगभावः दृश्यते । न च संभवति बहुषु यागेषु युगपदेकस्य इन्द्रस्य स्वरूपसन्नि धानतानुपपत्तेः इति चेत् । नायमस्ति विरोधः । कस्मात् । अनेकप्रतिपत्तेः । एकस्यापि देवतात्मनः युगपदनेकस्वरूपप्रतिपत्तिः संभवति । (SB I.3.27)

22. आकृतिभिश्च शब्दानां सम्बन्धः न व्यक्तिभिः । (SB I.3.28)

DR. MANDAN MISHRA

āścaryavatpaśyati kaścidan-
māścaryavadvadati tathaiva cānyaḥ /
āścaryavaccainamanyaḥ śṛṇoti
śrutvāpyenaṁ veda na caiva kaścit //

Bhagavad Gītā II.29

Dr. Mandan Mishra, presently the Vice-Chancellor of the Lal Bahadur Shastri Rashtriya Sanskrit Vidyapeetha (a deemed to be University), is undisputed leader of Sanskrit world in India. Whatever be the formal history and outfit, he is in reality an architect of many central organisations like the Rashtriya Sanskrit Vidyapitha, Rashtriya Veda-Vidya Pratisthana and two central deemed to be Universities of Sanskrit. In promoting traditional Sanskrit education he has no match. He is aptly described as the Madan Mohan Malaviya of Sanskrit Vidyapithas. He is in the centre of many literary and cultural activities in the national capital of India and some of the States, more particularly his home state of Rajasthan. His distinction as a scholar of Sāhitya, Mīmāṁsā and many other traditional śāstras is testified both by written and oral words in Sanskrit. Virtues of friendship and sincere gratitude, sweetness of disposition and *karmayoga* (*yogaḥ karmasu kauśalam*) for the cause of Sanskrit have made him friend, philosopher and guide of older and younger generations of Sanskritists.

I have had unique distinction of being closely associated for more than a quarter of a century with this great crusader of Sanskrit. I have always felt like many others deep and profound bond of brotherliness (*saubhrātra*) with him. This volume in his honour is a humble offering in recognition of his qualities of head and heart to the brother (*bandhu*) and friend (*kalyāṇamitra*) of Sanskrit. His biodata given here contains certain details of this *mahāpuruṣa* of our times.

—Editor

BIODATA

1. Full Name — DR. MANDAN MISHRA

2. Age, Date of Birth and Birth Place — 64 Years, 7th June, 1929 Village Hanutia, 50 Km. from Jaipur.

3. Name of Parents — Shri Kanhiya Lal Mishra—Father. Shrimati Manni Devi Mishra—Mother.

4. Name of Gurus — Studied Mīmāṁsā Philosophy and Vyākaraṇa under the able guidance of Acharya Shri Pattabhiram Shastri, and late Shri Rameshwar Prasad Shastri Dadhimatha in Jaipur.

5. Present Post — Vice-Chancellor, Shri Lal Bahadur Shastri Rashtriya Sanskrit Vidyapeetha, New Delhi.

6. Academic Qualifications

No.	*Exam. Passed*	*Subject*	*University/ Board*	*Remarks*
1.	Acharya	Mimamsa	Rajasthan Govt.	1st Division
2.	Acharya	Sahitya	Darbhanga Skt. University, Darbhanga	1st Class Ist Gold Medalist
3.	M.A.	Sanskrit	Gurukul Kangri University, Haridwar	1st Class Ist
4.	Ph.D.	Mimamsa	Rajasthan University, Jaipur	

7. Positions held:

No.	*Name of the Organisation*	*Position held*	*Period*
1.	Maharaja Sanskrit College	Teacher, Lecturer, Professor	1948-1962
2.	Sanskrit Vidyapeetha, Delhi	Founder, Director & Principal	1962-1973
3.	Kendriya Sanskrit Vidyapeetha Tirupati (Andhra Pradesh)	Principal	Jan. 1973 to August 1973
4.	Ganga Nath Jha Kendriya Sanskrit Vidyapeetha, Allahabad (U.P.)	Principal	Sept. 1973 to June, 1974
5.	Kendriya Sanskrit Vidyapeetha, New Delhi	Principal	July, 1974 to Sept. 1978
6.	Ranbir Kendriya Sanskrit Vidyapeetha, Jammu (J & K)	Principal	Oct. 1978 to March, 1979
7.	Shri Lal Bahadur Shastri Kendriya Sanskrit Vidyapeetha, New Delhi	Principal	April, 1979 to 22-6-1989
8.	Rajasthan Sanskrit Academy	Chairman (Honorary)	1981 to 1990
9.	Rashtriya Sanskrit Sansthan, New Delhi	Director	25-1-1982 to 22-5-1982
10.	Rashtriya Sanskrit Sansthan, New Delhi	Director	30th July 1983 to 31-12-1989
11.	Shri Lal Bahadur Shastri Rashtriya Sanskrit Vidyapeetha, New Delhi	Vice-Chancellor	23rd June, 1989 to date.

8. *Research and Publications*:

(a) Mimamsa Darshan—Original Work.

(b) Worked out a comprehensive scheme of Vishwa Sanskrit Shatabdi Grantha and planned its publication. Worked as Chief Editor and Director of Voluminous Work. In 'Vishwa-Shatabdi-Grantha' Scheme edited three volumes pertaining to Jammu-Kashmir, Andhra and Rajasthan States (these three volumes are published by the All India Sanskrit Sahitya Sammelan, New Delhi). In this scheme the matter pertaining to Bihar, Assam, Gujarat, Kerala, England, America, Russia etc. was collected (more than 5000 pages) and edited.

(c) Edited Shodha Prabha, a Research Journal published by Shri Lal Bahadur Shastri Sanskrit Vidyapeetha.

(d) Edited the Research Journal 'Vimarsha' of Rashtriya Sanskrit Sansthan.

(e) Member, Editorial Board of the 'Sanskrit' Abhinandan Grantha of Aditya Nath Jha.

(f) Chief Editor—Shri Pattabhiram Shastri Felicitation Volume which was released and presented by Honourable Smt. Indira Gandhi, Prime Minister of India.

(g) Edited 'Sanskrit Ratnakar' (including several special numbers)—a periodical (monthly) publication of the All India Sanskrit Sahitya Sammelan, New Delhi from 1959 to 1968.

(h) Edited 'Swar Mangala', Research Journal of Rajasthan Sanskrit Academy, Jaipur.

(i) Member—Editorial Board of Dr. Raghavan Abhinandan Grantha.

(j) Member—Editorial Board of Shri Lal Bahadur Shastri Smarak Grantha named 'Dharti-ke-lal'.

(k) Editor, Shri Chinna Swami Shatabdi Granth.

(l) Guided more than ten Research students for Ph.D. Degree on different aspects of Sanskrit and Indian Culture. Out of these 9 have been conferred Ph.D. degrees.

(m) Contributed more than 30 Research Articles in different Journals and had about 50 talks in All India Radio.

(n) The following works have been edited and published:

1. Prameya Parijata, 1964.
2. Purana Parijata, 1965.
3. Vaidika-Vijnanam, 1965.
4. Kasmiretihasah, 1968.
5. Giti-Kadambari, 1968.
6. Pancamrtam, 1968.
7. Annual Bibliography of Indology, 1969.
8. Adhvara Mimamsa-Kutuhala Vrtti, 1969-70.
9. Panini, Katyayana and Patanjali (English), 1969.
10. Nityakarmaprakash, 1970.
11. Rgveda-Kavi-Vimarsah, 1971.
12. Shri Mahavir ParinirvanSmriti Grantha, 1971.
13. Shri Mahavira Caritamrtam, 1971.
14. Rtu in Sanskrit Literature, 1972.
15. Sanskrit Sahitya Mein Shabdalankar, 1972.
16. Chalukyaraja Ayyanavamsa Caritam.
17. Jiwana-parimala, 1974.
18. A Critical Study of Chandra Vyakarana-Vrtti, 1974.
19. Anveshana, Research Journal, 1974.
20. Devi Puranam, 1976.
21. Vyakhayan Vallari, 1976-77.
22. Citrabandhavatarika, 1977.
23. Brought out G.N. Jha Kendriya Sanskrit Vidyapeetha Research Journal.
24. Krsna Yajurvediya Taitiriya Samhita, 1981, 89 (Two Parts).
25. Sri Mahatripura Sundari Khadgamala.
26. Manashcikitsa Vijnana Bhumika, 1981.
27. Chaturveda Charita Champur, 1982.
28. Abhinava-Krida-Tarangini, 1982.
29. Subhagodaya Stuti, 1982.
30. Katyayana-Shrauta-Sutram (Two Parts) 1982-83.
31. Agama Mimamsa, 1982.
32. Mimamsa-Nyaya-Prakasha, 1983.
33. Ashavalayana-Shrauta-Sutra, 1984.
34. Ajatashatru, 1984.
35. Shabara-Bhashyam, 1984.

36. Rajendra-Chandrodaya-Champur, 1985.
37. Kabiravani (Two Parts), 1985.
38. Shabdalankara Sahitya ka Samikshatmaka Sarvekshana, 1985.
39. Shrimad Bhagavatiyam Samkhyam, 1986.
40. Indira-Kirti-Kaumudi, 1986.
41. Sanskara Prakasha, 1986.
42. Gayatri Varivasya, 1986.
43. Shri Bahurupa-Garbha-Stotra, 1986.
44. Shodha Prabha:
    (i) M.M. Giridhar Sharma Chaturveda-Shatabdi Smriti Visheshanka.
    (ii) Vishva Sanskrit Sammelan Visheshanka.
    (iii) Dr. Rajendra Prasad Janma Shatabdi Smritigrantha.
    (iv) Smt. Indira Gandhi Shraddhanjali Visheshanka.
45. Atharva-Samhita-Vidhana, 1988-89.
46. Vidyapeetha-Panchanga.
47. Nehru-Charitam, 1991.

9. *Membership of Academic Institutions*:

1. General Secretary, All India Sanskrit Sahitya Sammelan, Delhi, 1959 to 1967.
2. Member, Advisory Committee on Sanskrit Programmes of All India Radio, New Delhi.
3. Member, Executive Committee, Delhi Sanskrit Academy.
4. Member, Executive Council of Dr. Sampoornanand Sanskrit University, Varanasi—appointed by Govt. of U.P. (about 8 years).
5. Member, Reorganisation Committee of the College of Oriental Learning, Banaras Hindu University, Banaras.
6. Member, Academic Council and Faculty of Oriental Learning, Rajasthan University, Sanskrit University, Banaras Hindu University and Kashi Vidyapeetha Varanasi.
7. Member, Survey Committee of All India Kashi Raj Trust of the Project of Puranas (Nominated by the Govt. of India, Ministry of Education and Social Welfare).

8. General Secretary, Akhil Bharatiya Sanskrit Shiksha Sammelan, New Delhi.
9. Member of the Governing Body of the Sankara Academy of Sanskrit Culture and Shankar Vidya Kendra, New Delhi.
10. Convenor, All India Vedic Convention held with the assistance of the Ministry of Education (1981).
11. President, Fifth All India Sanskrit Maha Mandal Convention (Pandarpur, Maharashtra) held at New Delhi (May, 1977) and Tirupati (May, 1978).
12. Organised Conference of the Intellectuals on National Integration which was inaugurated by Prime Minister, Smt. Indira Gandhi on 7th November, 1983.
13. Presided valedictory function of International Conference on Translation organised by Jawaharlal Nehru University, New Delhi.
14. Member, Rashtriya Veda Vidya Pratisthan, Govt. of India, New Delhi.
15. Member of the Indian Council for Cultural Relations.
16. Convenor, Classical Languages Group for VIII Five Year Plan (Ministry of Human Resource Development), Govt. of India.
17. Member, National Committee, Adi Shankaracharya Jayanti Celebrations, Govt. of India under the Chairmanship of Shri Rajiv Gandhi.

10. *Distinctions/Awards received*:

1. President's Certificate of Honour in 1983 with lifelong honorarium of Rs. 10000 per annum.
2. All India Shankaracharya Award of Rs. 10000 for best book on Philosophy by U.P. Sanskrit Academy.
3. International Sanskrit Award of Rs. One Lakh from Uttar Pradesh Sanskrit Academy, Govt. of U.P.
4. Award of Rs. 1100, Shawl and Saraswati statue by Sahitya Kala Parishad, Delhi Administration, for contribution to Sanskrit Studies.
5. 'Vidyabhaskar' title and Gold Medal by His Holiness Jagad Guru Shankaracharya of Sringeri.

6. B.H.U. honoured by special felicitations for his efforts in getting the status of deemed to be University for Delhi Vidyapeetha.
7. Haareet Award of Rs. 5000 from Mewar Foundation, Udaipur, for best work in the field of Sanskrit and Indian Culture.
8. Rajasthan Sanskrit Academy (Govt. of Rajasthan) awarded Rs. 5000 for his special services in the field of Sanskrit.

11. *Contribution towards the Development and Propagation of Sanskrit Studies in India*

1. Worked as General Secretary of the All India Sanskrit Sahitya Sammelan from 1959 to 1967. During the period State level Sanskrit Associations were organised all over the country and thus the status of the Sammelan raised up to such extent that two Prime Ministers (First late Shri Lal Bahadur Shastri and later on Hon'ble Smt. Indira Gandhi) adorned the Presidentship of the Sammelan.
2. Founded Delhi Sanskrit Vidyapeetha. Now this Vidyapeetha is named as Shri Lal Bahadur Shastri Sanskrit Vidyapeetha. During his tenure as Director the annual budget of the Vidyapeetha has increased from 10 thousand to more than one crore, eleven acres of land was procured on which the first and second phase of construction of building is completed. U.G.C. pay scales implemented and the Vidyapeetha has been given the status of 'Deemed to be University' w.e.f. 16-11-1987.
3. Gave up the permanent post held in the Rajasthan Govt. at the instance of Shri Lal Bahadur Shastri, the then Prime Minister of India, to serve the cause of Sanskrit Development in this country in a better way. Shri Lal Bahadur Shastri appointed and confirmed Dr. Mandan Mishra as Director of the Delhi Vidyapeetha.
4. Founder, Rajendra Sanshrit Pustakalaya, Delhi.
5. Secretary, Shastra Charcha Parishad of International Sanskrit Conference organised by the Govt. of India, Ministry of Education and Social Welfare in 1972 (New Delhi) and 1981 (Varanasi).

6. Secretary and Joint Convenor of the Rajasthan Bharat Sewak Samaj and Rajasthan Bharat Sadhu Samaj (5 years).
7. President (thrice), Rajasthan Sanskrit Shikshak Sammelan.
8. Founder of the following Sanskrit Institutions and remained their Founder-Chairman:
   1. Sanskrit College, Manoharpur (Rajasthan).
   2. Sanskrit Vidyapeetha, Mainpuri (Rajasthan).
   3. Sanskrit College, Mahapura (Rajasthan).
   4. Sanskrit Vidyalaya, Meda, Jaipur (Rajasthan).
9. Convinced the State Governments and authorities of Delhi Administration regarding the parity of pay scales of Sanskrit Teachers and pursuaded Delhi Administration to sanction 95% financial aid towards the salary of Sanskrit teachers in Sanskrit Pathasalas of Delhi.
10. It was due to his efforts that an atmosphere of awakening for Sanskrit was created in the capital and the Govt. of India, Delhi Administration and the State Governments paid their attention towards this aspect and as a consequence Vidyapeethas and other Sanskrit Institutes were established in different parts of the country.
11. Attended as Convenor (Leader of the Delegation) of the Govt. of India Delegation in World Sanskrit Conference at University of Philadelphia, U.S.A.
12. During his tenure, Tirupati and Shri Lal Bahadur Shastri Kendriya Sanskrit Vidyapeetha, New Delhi declared 'Deemed to be University' w.e.f. 16-11-1987.
13. Dr. Mandan Mishra's services for the cause of Sanskrit were highly praised and appreciated by the great lovers of Sanskrit viz. late Dr. Rajendra Prasad, Dr. Radhakrishnan, Shri Lal Bahadur Shastri, Smt. Indira Gandhi, Shri N.V. Gadgil, Dr. Sampoornanand, Justice Shri C.P. Ramaswamy Ayyar, Justice P.B. Gajendragadkar and Dr. Aditya Natha Jha etc.

CONTRIBUTORS TO THE VOLUME

R.C. Dwivedi*

Dr. R.C. Dwivedi, Professor of Sanskrit and Dean, Faculty of Sanskrit Studies, University of Rajasthan, Jaipur, is author of a number of books and research papers covering various aspects of Sanskrit Studies including Alaṅkāraśāstra, Buddhism, Jainism and Kashmir Śaivism. He has visited a number of countries for academic programmes. Dr. Dwivedi is a member of the Central Sanskrit Board, Rashtriya Sanskrit Sansthan, Rashtriya Veda Vidya Pratisthan and also of the Executive Councils of a number of Universities. An astoundingly able administrator, Dr. Dwivedi has been awarded Certificate of Honour by the President of India in recognition of his contribution to Indological Studies.

G.P. Bhatt

Dr. G.P. Bhatt is Editor of the Serial *Ancient Indian Tradition and Mythology* projected and published by MLBD and author of *The Basic Ways of Knowing*, a research work on Kumārila's contribution to Indian Epistemology.

John Taber

John Taber is Associate Professor of Philosophy at the University of New Mexico. He is author of *Transformative Philosophy: a Study of Śaṅkara, Fichte, and Heidegger* and various articles on Mīmāṁsā and Indian philosophy in such publications as *Philosophy East and West*, *Journal of the American Oriental Society* and *Journal of Indian Philosophy*.

Sarveswara Sharma Peri

Dr. Sarveswara Sharma Peri, Vyākaraṇācārya, M.A. (Sanskrit), Sahitya Ratna (Hindi), Dr. Phil. (Marburg), taught Indian languages, Telugu, Hindi and Sanskrit at Marburg. He has

*We regret to announce the sad and untimely, passing-away of Dr. Dwivedi on 27th September 93. —Publishers

written books, articles and book reviews and read papers in oriental conferences.

Lars Göhler

Lars Göhler studied Philosophy and Indology in Leipzig. After writing a doctoral thesis on 'Philosophical Aspects of Vedic Ritual' at present he turns his interest to Mīmāṁsā.

Shlomo Biderman

Dr. Shlomo Biderman is Senior Lecturer in the Department of Philosophy of Tel-Aviv University. He has served as Chairman of the Department of Philosophy (1987-91) and at present is Head of the Shirley and Leslie Porter School of Cultural Studies at Tel-Aviv University. His fields of interest are Indian Philosophy, Philosophy of Religion, and Scepticism. His publications are predominantly in these fields. He is co-editor (with Ben Ami Scharfstein) of a series *Philosophy and Religion*—comparative year-books, published by Brill.

Tomoyasu Takenaka

Tomoyasu Takenaka is Professor of Indian Philosophy in the Faculty of Foreign Studies, Tokohagauen University, Shizuoka, Japan. He did his M.A. and Doctoral Course in Indian Philosophy at Kyoto University. He published a number of articles on the epistemology and the *Sāmānyavāda* of Mīmāṁsā, Nyāya and Mahāyāna schools.

J.M. Verpoorten

J.M. Verpoorten teaches classical languages (Greek-Latin) in a Belgian college. He has written many papers, reviews and lectures on varous subjects (Vedism, classical Indian philosophy) and is a contributor to the French collection 'La Pléiade" (Callimard, Paris) for the Indian theater (Bhāsa) and philosophy (Nyāya-Vaiśeṣika-Mīmāṁsā).

P.T. Raju

P.T. Raju (1904-93), Ph.D. from Calcutta in 1935, author of hundreds of articles in Indian and Western journals and twelve books with translations into eight languages, received a Padma

Bhushan in 1958. He was honoured by the American Philosophical Association by holding a Seminar on his thought, was Professor of Philosophy and Psychology at the University of Rajasthan, and was Emeritus Professor of Philosophy and Indian Studies at the college of Wooster, U.S.A.

HAJIME NAKAMURA

Hajime Nakamura D. Lit., is Professor Emeritus at the University of Tokyo and a member of Japan Academy of Sciences. Currently Director of the Eastern Institute, Tokyo, he is a recipient of the Imperial Prize from the Japan Academy of Sciences (1957) and of the Cultural Order from the Emperor of Japan (1977). Among his works in the English language are *Ways of Thinking of Eastern Peoples: India, Tibet, Japan* (1964), *A Comparative History of Ideas* (1975), *Indian Buddhism* (1980), *A History of Early Vedānta Philosophy* (1983).

PURUSHOTTAMA BILIMORIA

Purushottama Bilimoria Ph.D., edits a journal 'SOPHIA' in philosophy of religion and theology, and is currently Managing Editor for two monograph series: *Indian Thought* with E.J. Brill, and *Studies in Indian Traditions* (Delhi). He is Associate Professor at Deakin University in Australia where he teaches East-West Philosophy, Sanskrit and Philosophy of Religion. He is a co-editor for the Mīmāṁsā project within the Encyclopaedia of Indian Philosophies.

K. KUNJUNNI RAJA

Dr. K. Kunjunni Raja, Director Adyar Library and Research Centre and formerly Professor and Head of the Department of Sanskrit, University of Madras, was educated at Trichur, Madras and London. Publications include: *The Contribution of Kerala to Sanskrit Literature*, *Indian Theories of Meaning*, *Encyclopaedia of Indian Philosophies*, *Vol.* 5 (ed. with H. Coward), *New Catalogue Catalogarum* (Vols. III-XI) (ed.), *Naiṣadhānanda* (ed. with A.K. Warder). He is a recipient of President's award of Honour for Sanskrit.

HAROLD COWARD

Dr. Harold Coward is Director, Centre for Studies in Religion and Society, University of Victoria, Canada. With K. Kunjunni Raja, he edited *The Philosophy of the Grammarians*. Other recent books include *Derrida and Indian Philosophy*, *Hindu Ethics*, and *Sacred Word, Sacred Text: Scripture in World Religions*.

ALBRECHT WEZLER

Albrecht Wezler is Professor and Chairman, Department of Indology. Hamburg University and has several books and articles to his credit.

P. SRI RAMACHANDRUDU

Professor P. Sri Ramachandrudu, was Professor and Head, Department of Sanskrit, Osmania University. For three years he was Emeritus Fellow (U.G.C.) in the same department, Honorary Director of Sanskrit Academy, Osmania University for eleven years, and Honorary Professor in the University of Hyderabad. He made special study of Vyākaraṇa, Vedānta and Alaṅkāraśāstra. He translated the *Gītāñjali* of Rabindranath Tagore into Sanskrit and wrote a political drama (in Sanskrit) *Susaṁhatabhāratam* in six acts. These two works were awarded prizes by the Government of Uttara Pradesh. He has written several books in Telugu and edited fourteen books of general interest in Sanskrit. His work *The Contribution of Paṇḍitarāja to Sanskrit Poetics* has won a prestigious prize.

PATTABHIRAM SHASTRI

Shri Pattabhiram Shastri (1908-92). After receiving the degree of Ācārya in Mīmāṁsā, Sāhitya and Nyāya, Shri Shastri was appointed as Assistant Professor and subsequently as Professor in the Banaras Hindu University. He joined as Principal of Maharaja Sanskrit College, Jaipur in the year 1945. Shri Shastri was invited by Calcutta University to grace the chair of Mīmāṁsā Ācārya in 1952. Thereafter, he was appointed as Head of the Department of Sāhitya, Mīmāṁsā and Tantra, in Varanaseya Sanskrit University, from were he retired in January, 1975.

President of India honoured him by awarding him Padmabhushan in 1985.

N.S. RAMANUJATATACHARYA

Dr. N.S. Ramanujatatacharya Vidyāvāridhi, formerly a Reader and then a Professor at Kendriya Sanskrit Vidyapitha, Tirupati, is currently Vice-Chancellor of the same Institute raised to the status of a Deemed University. He was awarded a prize by the President of the Indian Union and also by the Sanskrit Academ U.P.

FRANCIS X. CLOONEY S.J.

Francis X. Clooney S.J. (Roman Catholic) is an Associate Professor of comparative theology in the Theology Department at Boston College, and Director of Graduate Studies since 1991. His first book, *Thinking Ritually*, was published in 1990 and his *Theology After Vedānta* in early 1993. His articles have appeared in *History of Religions*, the *Journal of Religion*, the *Journal of the American Oriental Society*, the *Journal of the American Academy of Religion*, and *Theological Studies*, and in Indian journals, including *Prabuddha Bharata*, *Sriramanujavani*, and the *Journal of Oriental Research*.

KUNIO HARIKAI

Kunio Harikai (born 1942) M.A. (1969), Ph.D. (1987 Kyūshū University) is an Associate Professor (Philosophy and Ethics) at Saga Medical School, Japan.

BATUK NATH SHASTRI KHISTE

Prof. Batuk Nath Shastri Khiste is a former Professor of Sampurnananda Sanskrit University, Varanasi and a recipient of several Gold Medals and prestigious awards. He is a specialist of Āgamaśāstra and author/editor of several publications including an original work in Hindi on the life and work of Bhāskararāya Dīkṣita.

YUDHISHTHIRA NIMAMSAKA

Yudhishthira Mimamsaka has taught Sanskrit Grammar,

Nirukta, Veda and Pūrva Mīmāṁsā in a number of institutions and contributed a large number of research articles to various journals in sanskrit and Hindi. He is author of a book in Hindi on the History of Sanskrit Grammar in three parts and several others including a few yet unpublished. He has won a number of prizes for his writings.

HARUO KURATA

Haruo Kurata studied philosophical systems of Mīmāṁsā and Vedānta under the guidance of Prof. Hajime Nakamura and Prof. Sengaku Mayeda at the University of Tokyo, and studied at Madras University with the advice of Prof. T.M.P. Mahadevan.

He translated the Mīmāṁsā Chapter of the *Sarvadarśanasaṅgraha* into Japanese with notes and indices in collaboration with Prof. Mayeda, and published some papers on Mīmāṁsā philosophy especially on problems of *jñāna* and *karma*.

JOHANNES BRONKHORST

Johannes Bronkhorst is a Professor since 1987, of Sanskrit and Indian Studies at the University of Lausanne, Switzerland. His main interests are indigenous Sanskrit grammar, history of asceticism and meditation, Indian thought. His publications include: *The Two Traditions of Meditation in Ancient India* (Wiesbaden, 1986; Second, MLBD Delhi); *Tradition and Argument in Classical Indian Linguistics* (Dordrecht, 1986); *Three Problems Pertaining to the Mahābhāṣya* (Poona, 1987); *The Two Sources of Indian Asceticism* (Bern, forthcoming); numerous articles.

KIYOTAKA YOSHIMIZU

Kiyotaka Yoshimizu is a Ph.D. student at the Institute of Indology, the University of Vienna. He has a special interest in theories of sacrifice and exegetics, especially from Śrautasūtra/Mīmāṁsāsūtra to Kumārila/Prabhākara/Maṇḍana.

K.T. PANDURANGI

Prof. K.T. Pandurangi, currently President of Mythic Society and Upakulapati of Poornaprajna Vidyapeetha, was educated at Mysore Sanskrit College. Annamalai University and Banaras Hindu University. He worked as Professor at Karnatak College at Dharwad, Government College in Bangalore and Bangalore University from 1948-80. He has twenty books to his credit on Vedānta, Mīmāṁsā and Sāhitya. *Contribution of Pūrva-mīmāṁsā*, *Essentials of Dvaita Vedānta* are his philosophical works.

INDEX

Mango Mood

Mango Mood

Sharmila Kamat

Rupa . Co

Published 2011 by
Rupa Publications India Pvt. Ltd.
7/16, Ansari Road, Daryaganj,
New Delhi 110 002

Sales Centres:
Allahabad Bengaluru Chandigarh Chennai
Hyderabad Jaipur Kathmandu
Kolkata Mumbai

Inside illustrations by Naguesh Sardessai

Typeset in Adobe Caslon by
Mindways Design
1410 Chiranjiv Tower
43 Nehru Place
New Delhi 110 019

Printed in India by
Nutech Photolithographers
B-240, Okhla Industrial Area, Phase-I,
New Delhi 110 020, India

To

My Parents

Contents

Foreword

I HAVE GONE THROUGH, WITH GREAT PLEASURE, THIS beautiful collection of 'tongue-in-cheek' pieces on Goa, and the rest of India, by Sharmila Kamat.

The great French dramatist, Pierre Augustin Caron de Beaumarchais once wrote, 'I hasten to laugh at everything, for fear of being obliged to weep.' On going through this book, one gets the impression that Sharmila, too, subscribes to the same philosophy.

Sharmila has an inborn flair for light satire. She has wielded her pen with ease to depict the foibles and weaknesses of human nature without hurting the feelings of the subjects of her pieces. From her writings, one gets the impression that she would like to see a change for the better from those entrusted with the destiny of the common man.

Her pieces on our society are lighthearted on the surface but, on closer observation, serve as pertinent comments on the way of life in our country. Besides making us chuckle, they arouse our conscience, and set us thinking about what we would have dismissed as everyday realities.

From her articles, one concludes that human behaviour is the same everywhere. The vagaries of human nature are, and will continue to be, a fertile ground for humorous pieces by persons like Sharmila who possess an observant eye and a witty turn of phrase.

Today's world is full of turmoil and tensions. A casual glance at a newspaper makes us realise that murder and mayhem reigns supreme across the globe. Internecine conflicts, regional tensions and the threat of terrorism have combined to make world peace a distant dream. We are fortunate, therefore, to have writers like Sharmila Kamat who, through their witty writings, make us laugh despite all these depressing realities.

Jean de la Bruyere, a seventeeenth century French essayist and moralist, once wrote, 'One must laugh before one is happy, or one may die without ever laughing at all.' Those who will read Sharmila's pieces need not have this fear..

I, therefore, recommend this collection of essays to the reading public.

Dr Kashinath Mahale
Former Vice Chancellor, Manipur University, Imphal
And former Rector, Jawaharlal Nehru University,
New Delhi

Preface

THIS BOOK BRINGS TOGETHER VARIOUS TONGUE-IN-cheek pieces on Goa and the rest of India that I contributed to national and international publications over the past years.

It takes a lighthearted look at Goa – its culture and society, its people and their peculiarities. It takes a detour to comment on events that grabbed national headlines, using them as a peg to highlight what makes the average Indian tick.

This book has two sections with a total of forty-two 'pieces,' as we refer to them in a journalistic vein. The collection of vignettes of life as it is lived in our land is titled *Mango Mood*.

Why *Mango Mood*, one may well ask? The reader may be forgiven for mistaking this volume as a treatise on that king of all fruits who reigns supreme over Goa in the second quarter of the year. They may believe that contained within the covers is a mouthwatering collection of recipes featuring the *aam* as the main ingredient.

The reader would not be alone in presuming thus. When the first edition of this book was released, many a bookseller came to a similar conclusion.

I came to realise this when I found my book displayed in the culinary section of bookstalls, rubbing shoulders with such delights as '*Balchão de porco and other adventures in Gastronomy*' and '*Neureos, Sannas* and *Kulkuls*: My travels across Goa armed with a sweet tooth and an open mouth.'

The title *Mango Mood* was chosen based on the belief that my writings resemble the King of Fruits. They aim at being soft on the outside but with a hard core at its centre. The tongue-in-cheek nature of the prose forms the soft, sweet casing that conceals within its confines pertinent observations on hard realities of our society.

Besides, this book has, as its centerpiece, a collection of stories on Goa. What better symbol can there be for Goa than the luscious, mouth-watering mango?

Why opt for a second edition of stories first published some years back? Quite simply because these tales never lost their topicality or relevance!

Some time back I had observed that commuting by public bus in Goa made one appreciate the predicament of a sardine packed tightly in a can with so many of its ilk. Can we honestly say that the intervening years have lent us more legroom?

Then, I had commented on the entry of casinos and the public disapproval of this government-sanctioned gambling.

Mindful of the people's scorn, the casinos had remained tucked away discreetly in five star resorts. Today, casinos not only flourish in the state but are also found floating on the River Mandovi, thumbing a nose at the populace.

Then I had written a wry commentary on how Goa was being denuded of its greenery by real estates sharks. Today, these creatures have, if anything, sharpened their bite.

The nexus between drugs, booze and crime remains as strong as ever, the urge to legalise illegalities has not lost its appeal and the fine tradition of passing off '*O malhão, malhão*' as an authentic Goan folk tune continues apace.

In the good old days, the Wagles, TV's ubiquitous average middle class family, had been outraged at the goings-on on Goan beaches. Now, thanks to the Scarlett Keeling scandal and other lurid tales, most Indians feel the same way.

As for the *piece de resistance* of my book – the endless toppling games that pass for democracy in Goa. Can we truly, madly, deeply, claim things are *different* now?

An earlier story on Gandhiji revisiting modern India had commented on how he would have looked askance at the juxtaposition of designer togs with the rags covering the 28% or so of the population that still crouches below the poverty line. Today, India shines brighter but in the parts of the country yet to benefit from this lustre, the *aam aadmi* follows the path adopted by the Mahatma in the tale – investing in Hope.

I would like to express my gratitude to the editors and publishers of *The Times of India*, Mumbai, *The Sunday*

Observer, Mumbai, *Gomantak Times*, Panaji, *Goa Today*, Panaji, and *The Navhind Times*, Panaji, for permitting me to publish the articles in this book. Some of these stories had first appeared in these publications.

My gratitude to the late Professor Kashinath Mahale, former Vice-Chancellor of Manipur University, for having written the *Foreword* to the first edition of this book.

To Naguesh Sardessai, for embellishing my articles with his most appropriate illustrations, my sincere thanks.

This book would not have been possible had it not been for the support of my family.

This book would not have been possible had it not been for the support of my family:

My parents, Prabhakar Kamat and Janvrubai Kamat, for their unwavering support and guidance (not to mention their constant prodding during the slack periods).

My sister, Pratima, for suggesting the title of the book and the significance behind the same and for painstakingly going through the manuscript and identifying proofreading mistakes that had escaped my observation.

My brother, Prashant, who pitched in with his help when I needed it.

If this book brings a smile on the faces of readers even as it provokes them to think about the issues discussed in it, then its purpose would have been served.

Sharmila Kamat

Introduction

SERVED SUNNY SIDE UP

THINK OF GOA AND THE FOLLOWING IMAGES SPRING TO the mind: miles upon miles of sun-kissed beaches, palm trees swaying gently in the mid-morning breeze, narrow country lanes weaving their way through vast stretches of lush green paddy fields, the sun, the sand and the surf.

However, there is more to Goa than a well-thumbed set of picture postcards offering tantalising glimpses of 'An Untouched Corner of Paradise.' It goes beyond the lilting, lyrical prose that flows out of the pens of copywriters engaged in selling dreams at the rate of Rs 500 per column centimetre of newsprint.

Goa has more to offer than just Latin tempers and lotus-eaters, beaches and Bohemians, fun and *feni*. For 'a place that has not changed since the world began,' to quote the aforementioned wordsmiths, the state has come a long way since its creation, eons ago, at the hands of Parashurama.

As legend has it, the sixth *avatar* of Lord Vishnu was in search of a place to unwind after completing the task of dispatching twenty-one generations of *Kshatriyas* to that great battlefield in the sky.

On reaching the West Coast, he shot an arrow into the sea. The prudent Sea God immediately took a step backwards, thus creating the ultimate holiday resort – Goa!

Parashurama was the first to head for Goa in search of rest and relaxation. Centuries later, the hoary tradition continues with battle-weary warriors trooping into the state to recharge their batteries for the next round.

Only now, the blood and gore has been replaced by boardroom bouts and Terminators by corporate Fat Cats.

From being, 'Tired Nature's Sweet Restorer' to reuniting sundered hearts is but a small step. It was one that Goa had no hesitation in taking.

As legend also has it, a rift in the matrimonial lute resulted in Lord Shiva storming out of his abode atop Mount Kailash. Determined not to return home, at least not until tempers had cooled down, the Lord decided to set up residence in Goa.

A penitent Goddess Parvati, meanwhile, traced her husband's whereabouts to the state and followed him there. The timeless beauty of the Gomant cast its spell on the warring couple. Recriminations turned to regrets. Angry utterances gave way to terms of endearment. It was sweetness and light once again at the old homestead.

The Lord and his consort led the way. Ever since then, couples have been making a beeline for Goa whenever there is an outbreak of hostilities on the marital front.

Goa never fails to work its charm on them.

The idyllic surroundings do the needful, as does the bracing sea air. In no time at all, everything is forgiven and forgotten. The love light returns to shine brightly from the estranged ones' eyes.

Those with rings on their fingers are not the only ones to benefit from Goa's ability to smoothen the path of true love. Lovers who have dispensed with the formality of a marriage license have also not returned empty-handed.

Since time immemorial, Goa has played host to couples whose union fell foul of caste, creed and parental disapproval. Goa sees a steady inflow of eloping couples throughout the year, with the traffic registering a slight increase in the winter months.

The runaways come followed, after a decent interval, by outraged parents and relatives. The latter make the scene with the sole purpose of dragging the straying sheep, kicking and screaming, back into the fold.

However, they reckon without Goa's romantic nature. The sun, sand and salubrious clime swing into action. A change of heart follows. A happy conclusion is affected in the distinctly unromantic interiors of the Town Police Headquarters, under the benign gaze of the Police Inspector, the two Sub-Inspectors and the four constables assigned to the case.

The scenario outlined above is adhered to in ninety percent of the love-and-run cases recorded in Goa. In the remaining ten percent, however, the script takes an entirely different turn.

The grim-faced continue to present a grim visage. The entreaties of the errant duo are ignored. The persuasive skills of the Police Inspector, the Sub-Inspectors and four constables go unrewarded. The slogan, 'Say No to Marriage,' retains its appeal.

With the chance of a happy union being remote in this life, the lovers decide to try their luck in the next. Adopting a course of action favoured by countless Hindi films, the star-crossed sweethearts throw themselves off the Dona Paula cliff into the placid waters of the Arabian Sea.

They leave behind parents assailed by regrets and a police force burdened with yet another statistic to add to the growing number of suicides in the state.

The passage of time has seen Goa take on yet another role – that of providing the setting for not just the closing chapters of innumerable love stories, but the opening chapters as well.

We have it on the authority of the ancient texts that Lord Krishna left home to pay a brief visit to the state. He immediately fell in love with the beautiful locale and the damsels inhabiting it.

A special mention has been made of the time when the Lord stumbled upon a group of young girls enjoying a leisurely bath even as their cows grazed peacefully in the nearby fields. He stopped. He saw. He was conquered.

Members of the Lord's entourage may have carried back reports of the comeliness of the Goan girls. Perhaps it may have been that other visitors were also lucky enough to stumble upon the 'Gorgeous Girls commune with nature' scene.

Whatever be the reason, *Goparashtra*, as it was so christened by Krishna, had discovered its Unique Selling Proposition – Eden and Eve. Like Dublin fair city, here, too, the girls were so pretty.

The U.S.P. has proved to be one that has withstood the ravages of time. As the centuries rolled on, the territory's name changed from *Goparashtra* to *Goa Dourada* (Golden Goa) and finally to Goa, the twenty-fifth state of the Indian Union.

To its publicists, however, it is as if the era of Krishna and the cowgirls has never ended. They steadfastly refuse to budge from the tried and tested path. The 'Beauty and the Belle' motif persists, as do images featuring 'the countryside and the cowgirls' and 'the sunshine and the *senoritas*.'

The combination of beaches and bikinis continues to retain its appeal, making this the longest running campaign in advertising history.

Strange as it may seem, the formula continues to work to date. From period unknown, BC to AD 2010, the response from the target audience has been overwhelming.

They have come in their thousands – city slickers and country yokels, *Bambai ka babus* and *Bihari bhaiyyas*, *Punjab da puttars* and Tamil tigers, all looking for a little romance.

However, unlike the Lord, these latter-day Romeos do not stop at the *dekko*.

They ogle, they stare.
The lasses object, their menfolk glare.
Before long, vile abuse fills the air.

This only goes to show that even a palatable dish like romance, if served in excess, can give you indigestion.

The coming of the Portuguese, in 1510, gave new direction to Goa's quest for fame. Like all colonial rulers, the Portuguese came uninvited, and then proceeded to dig themselves into the woodwork for the next 451 years.

When measured on the geological time scale, 451 years does not amount to much. However, it provided time enough for the Iberian influence to touch all aspects of the Goan culture.

From the *pork vindaloo* on the dining room table to the cashew apple on the tree, and Carnival on the streets, the Lusitanians made sure that they left their mark on everything before the Indian Army gave them the royal order of the boot.

The Portuguese chapter in Goan history is not one that has suffered from want of attention. The Lusitanian link has been discussed at length in research journals and history texts, and more importantly, in travel guides, tourist brochures and countless advertisements issued by the Department of Tourism, inviting the world and his wife to 'Come, partake of the pleasures of India's beach paradise!'

The travel world's version of the Portuguese rule may not be the most authentic account available, but it is by far the most original. Sometimes, startlingly so.

The Portuguese are credited with the establishment, in Goa, of the first printing press in Asia. They were also responsible for introducing *papayas* and chillies into the country. As also the cashew tree.

Considering that the cashew apple is the main ingredient of that all-abiding symbol of Goa, the cashew *feni,* this may or may not have been a good thing.

However, the most important achievement of the colonial regime was introducing, in the common man's lexicon, a word that soon came to symbolise Goa – *soçegado* (relaxed).

Opinions differ as to who made whom *soçegado.* One school of thought firmly believes that the Lusitanians caused the Goans to adopt a more leisurely life-style. The rival body contests this claim, subscribing instead to the viewpoint that contact with Goa led a once-mighty sea power to retire to the sidelines.

This debate, like all others, is conducted in what is undoubtedly Goa's most popular forum for such discussions – the 'Letters to the Editor' columns of the local newspapers.

The ball is set rolling by Ermelinda da Cunha Rivara, a resident of Betalbatim village in South Goa. In a missive to the Editor, and hence to the readers of the daily, the lady asserts that the colonial rulers were indeed the culprits. The Lusitanian influence led an otherwise hardworking Goan people to put up their feet and relax.

Untrue, protests Charmaine de Menezes e Furtado in the next day's edition. The Goan tendency to take things easy rubbed off on the imperialists. That is the reason why, once

settled in Goa, the Portuguese chose to take a backseat and let Britannia rule the waves.

The last observation causes M.L. Mhapsekar, from the village of Salvador-do-Mundo, to step into the fray. His observations elicit contributions from Fr. X. de Souza, N.B. Kalangutkar and a 'Name withheld on request.'

By now, the decencies of debate have been abandoned in favour of an unrestrained fistfight. Charges and counter-charges are traded. Words like neo-colonialist, lap dog of the imperialists and quisling feature prominently in the columns.

Several other readers join issue with the combatants. Several thousands more rush off to buy the subsequent issues of the paper.

Cunha Rivara sharpens her pencils, preparatory to releasing yet another stinker to the press. Menezes e Furtado, 'Name withheld on request' *et al* follow suit. The stage is set for a grand confrontation.

Unfortunately, it never materialises. The editor, until then content to stand by and watch tempers and circulation rise, chooses to blow the whistle on the scrimmage.

The 'Letters' column in the next day's edition of the paper carries a terse, 'Correspondence on this subject is closed.'

A cease-fire is enforced on the war of the missives.

Rival warriors are reluctantly compelled to replace their newly sharpened pencils in their stationery boxes and return to being model members of their respective village communities, at least until the next controversy appears on the horizon.

From 'Readers Fight,' it is back to being 'Readers Write' for the response columns. After heaving a collective sigh of disappointment, the reading public of the state moves off in search of fresh sources of entertainment.

Goa's justly deserved reputation of being one of the finest watering holes in the country dates back to the Portuguese era. The Goan's love for liquor is as old as time itself.

It is a truth often told that the Lusitanians gave wings to this romance. Their enthusiasm for the role of Cupid's assistant was so pronounced that it had led a prominent

Goan freedom fighter, T. B. Cunha, to accuse the imperial power of turning Goa into one big *taverna licenciada* (public house) where the Portuguese regime handed out drinks as the *taverneiro* (bartender).

Following Liberation, the dispensation of drinks has become even more liberal. Where once there was just one *taverna*, there is now a bar, two bar-cum-restaurants, a wine store and three wine marts, all rubbing shoulders on a single street.

In the land of milk and honey, Goa boasts of an overflowing casket of *feni.*

The high spirits have the blessings of not just the powers-that-be but the divine powers as well. The leading lights of the liquor trade are, like all Goans, a deeply religious people, preferring to carry out their activities under the benign gaze of a favourite deity or patron saint.

It is a common sight to see *Shri Krishna* Bar-n-Restaurant cheek by jowl with *Menino Jesus* Wine Mart ('Genuine Scotch Whisky sold here'). Often, we find St. Anthony's Pub provide relief to parched throats in the company of *Sai* Liquors.

Thirst is a dangerous thing. The wise men that throng the corridors of power are aware of this fact. It is no wonder then that they have never stinted when it comes to issuing licenses to those engaged in the noble task of slaking the common man's thirst.

Far from it. There has been certain open-handedness in their approach. Licenses have been issued freely, liberally. They may have fallen short of 'There is one for everyone.' No matter, they are close. There is one for every 200 residents of the state.

This abundance of riches has led to an influx of Distinguished Visitors, eager to sample the liquid delights of Goa. They come armed with invitations from the Who's Who of the travel world.

'Come,' urge quarter-page advertisements in the local dailies, 'and learn the subterfuge of *feni*, that venerable Goan spirit that lulls as it excites.' Can they help but accede to such a request? Especially in view of the fact that acquisition of knowledge has become a fad in the present times?

The conditions are right for the learning process. The tourists, too, are quick learners.

However, too much knowledge can sometimes lead to pitfalls in the form of an overdose of high spirits. It becomes necessary to unlearn some of the things imbibed with such enthusiasm not so long ago. The authorities' decision to set up Alcoholics *Ashrams* in the state is a step in that direction.

Colonisation brought evangelisation and evangelisation led to a change in the name of those converted to the new faith. The Lusitanians subscribed to the dictum: A rose by any other name would smell just as sweet.

This was the reason why they had no hesitation in giving a dozen different names to their little roses. For, when it comes to naming their offspring, Portuguese parents are generous to a fault. There is nothing miserly in their approach. A Lusitanian lass may go through life with many disadvantages. Lack of appellations is not one of them.

Goans who had adopted the faith of the conquerors displayed the same munificence. It is not uncommon to meet a Goan woman who answers to the name of Maria Clara Philomena Thelma Theresa Goretti do Carmo da Araujo Mascarenhas e Menezes. Quite a mouthful, would you say? Not at all! It is on the shorter side in fact.

Goans are nothing, if not innovative, when it comes to naming their babies. The Jovitos and Pedros of yore have long since made way for more imaginative appellations.

The patriotic types prefer Gandhi Diniz and Tagore Mesquita. The statesmanlike plumb for Churchill Dias and Kennedy de Souza. The business-friendly favour Onassis Afonso. Sports fans gravitate towards Steffi Mascarenhas and Rafael de Sa Coutinho.

Besides this, there are also the mamas and papas with an inclination for custom-made names that are a happy mix of Mom and Dad's Christian names. The new arrival in José and Mariana Figuereido's little home goes through life as Josmar. The flights of fancy often soar to such heights that it requires the intervention of a parish priest to bring the high-fliers back to ground level.

Those drawn into the Christian fold may have given up their religion but not their castes. A *Brahmin* or a *Sudra* remained so in the new faith. The only difference was that now the words Roman Catholic preceded the caste designation.

Like their Hindu counterparts, the Catholics, too, put Correct Caste at the top of the list when specifying conditions necessary for the selection of a life partner.

Even today, matrimonial advertisements in Sunday newspapers read as follows: 'Wanted a bride for a tall, handsome, fair-complexioned US-returned Roman Catholic *Brahman*. Sub-castes no bar.' The last statement is the only concession made to modern times.

The start of the 1960s saw Goa finally break free from the clutches of the imperialists. The closing years of the decade, however, were witness to its falling prey to yet another power – Flower Power. The flower children of the West discovered the unspoilt beaches of the Rome of the East and spread the good word around.

Followed the deluge. Beatniks, longhaired iconoclasts and rebels with a thousand causes poured in, determined to drink their fill of the untouched beauty before crowds and crass commercialisation caused Goa to go the Florida and Hawaii way.

They were the Wild Ones, the non-conformists. Acceptable modes of behaviour were unacceptable to them. They cast aside their inhibitions – and their clothes!

While the locals could only stare, they dared to lay their assets bare.

The Goan beaches became the venue of a unique kind of fashion parade, unique because the range on display consisted entirely of birthday suits. The Natural look was back in vogue since the days of Adam and Eve.

News of the free show reached the ears of Peeping Toms from across the nation. This led to another influx, this time of oglers armed with binoculars and lewd looks.

The hippies had come to feast their eyes on the virgin sands of Goa. These latter-day arrivals came to feast their eyes on the not-so-virgin expanses of bare white flesh stretched out on the selfsame sands.

A corresponding movement in the reverse direction – Goans leaving the security of home in search of petrodollars in the Gulf – matched the inflow of sightseers and the sights-worth-seeing.

In the bygone days, a Goan had few ambitions – to have his own home, lead a happily married life and enjoy his fish curry and rice for dinner each evening. Now, all his hopes and desires were sought to be fulfilled by that magic formula – finding a job in the Gulf.

The unimaginable riches that poured in by way of remittances altered forever the Goan landscape. Ramshackle houses in sleepy little hamlets were transformed into country mansions and villas. The modern-day palaces more than made up for in ostentation for what they lacked in aesthetics.

Every couple of years, the purveyor of these riches would return from Kuwait or Abu Dhabi, flashily dressed, doused with scent and laden with electronic goods of all kinds.

The stated purpose of the trip was to pay a visit to the folks back home. The unstated purpose was to revel in the looks of envy directed at him by his less fortunate brethren.

The Gulfies got into the serious business of making pots of money. The Goan political class entered the equally serious business of spending lots of it.

At the time of Liberation, intellectuals had despaired over Goa's ability to catch up with the rest of India, given the latter's fourteen-year head start over the former.

The situation is the reverse nowadays. Analysts doubt whether leaders from other regions of India can maintain the scorching pace of their Goan counterparts.

Rumour has it that potential *Aya Rams* and *Gaya Rams* are taking a break from their rabble-rousing routines to fly to Goa for a crash course in politicking. These masters are the ones to approach for all that you wanted to know about disqualifications, party hopping and horse trading but were afraid to ask.

The Goan political class can be classified under two categories – those filing disqualification notices and those facing such notices. The latter are sub-divided in those who have been disqualified, those disqualified but subsequently re-qualified, and a small minority of politicians who went through the arduous process of disqualification, re-qualification and subsequently re-disqualification.

The Goan politician, it is said, makes more turns than a Ferris wheel.

However, it is not all fun and toppling games for our beloved leaders. They are also busy inaugurating newly constructed bridges across one of Goa's many rivers.

They open a spanking new bridge on one of Goa's rivers. Subsequently, they return to lay the foundation stone for a second bridge on the selfsame river.

Why this abundance of riches? The answer is simple! A gregarious soul, a Goan abhors solitude. This holds for the bridges in his land as well. Besides, Goan bridges have a distressing tendency to cave in at the most inopportune moments.

A standby is naturally called for.

This shows that not only is the state blessed with a surfeit of Nature's bounties, but it is pretty well equipped with the munificence of humankind as well.

The passage of time has seen the land of sun-kissed sands undergo a great deal of changes. In the old days, the Gods were the visitors. Now, the not-so-godly types include it in their itinerary.

The notorious felon, Charles Sobhraj, included a visit to the state on his AWOL tour following his jailbreak. Philoo Khan, a conspirator in the Mumbai blasts, is said to have stopped by here *en route* to safer climes in South-East Asia.

Police intelligence has it that many suicide bombers-cum-*jihadis*, bred in terrorist hotbeds further north, head here for Rest and Recreation before undertaking another vile act of villainy prior to their hot date with those 72 virgins.

Back in the mists of antiquity, the state was known as *Gomant* – a land blessed with acres of rich pastureland and virgin forests. Now, the pastures are making way for '*Gomant* Housing Society' ('Two and three bedroom flats available. Complex includes a swimming pool and sauna facilities. Panoramic view of the countryside. Last few units left.')

As for the jungle, the wood is slowly making way for the concrete.

However, some things in life never change. The Goan's love for fish is one of them. Eons ago, the first Goan had turned to his life-partner and asked, 'Darling, what kind of fish-curry is there for dinner tonight?'

Centuries later, his descendants pose the same query to their helpmeets.

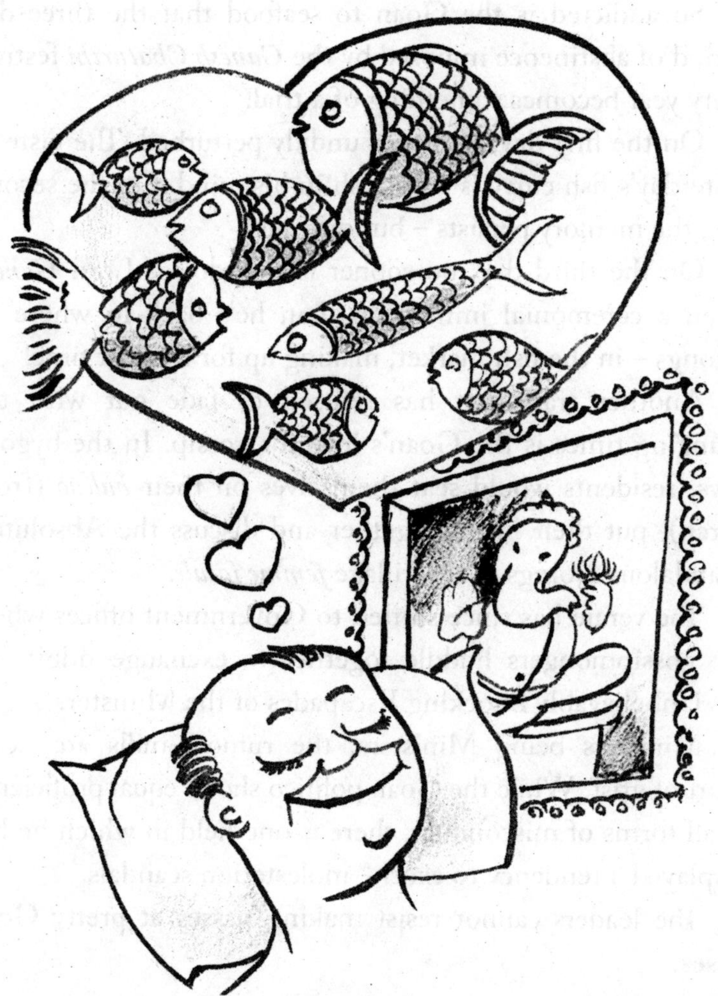

To a Goan, buying fish for the midday meal is the single most important chore of the day. It is too important a task to be left to the kitchen help. The householder himself goes to the fish market to inspect the day's catch, haggle over the price and return home with the buy.

So addicted is the Goan to seafood that the three-day period of abstinence imposed by the *Ganesh Chaturthi* festival every year becomes something of a trial.

On the first day, he is not unduly perturbed. The taste of yesterday's fish curry is still fresh in his mind. On the second day, the memory persists – but only just.

On the third day, no sooner is the idol of Lord *Ganesh* given a ceremonial immersion than he's back to where he belongs – in the fish market, making up for the lost time!

Another trait that has refused to fade out with the changing times is the Goan's love for gossip. In the bygone days, residents would seat themselves on their *balcão* (front porch), put their heads together and discuss the Absolutely Scandalous Doings of the village *femme fatale.*

The venue has since shifted to Government offices where the gossipmongers huddle together to exchange tidbits on the Unbelievably Shocking Escapades of the Minister.

Ministers being Ministers, the rumour-mills are never short of grist. While the Goan politico shows equal proficiency in all forms of misconduct, there is one field in which he has displayed a tendency to excel – molestation scandals.

The leaders cannot resist making passes at pretty Goan lasses.

The leader asks, 'Yes?' The lady says, 'No!'
'Monstrous behaviour!' the dailies bellow.
And the public sits back to enjoy the show.

The Goan's passion for music is also something that has shown no signs of diminishing over the years. Goa began its journey through time as a land that laughed with song – and it hasn't stopped guffawing since!

The rhythm of the *Gomant* resounds in every nook and corner of the state. From the classical music that flourished in the shadows of the pillars and domes of the temples to the rap and reggae beats that thrive on television screens in family living rooms, Goa has nurtured, nourished and sustained every possible form of music.

This includes the somewhat discordant notes arising from the petty squabbles of minor politicians.

This, then, is Goa – a land of silvery sands and sunny smiles.

Fun and frolic, music and dance.

Fish and *feni*, a little romance.

Where life is *soçegado*, the pace is sedate.

And every bridge has a duplicate.

Where the past and the present mix-n-match, co-existing in harmony.

Goa – served sunny side up!

Goa - Redux

SECOND HELPINGS

GOA HAS UNDERGONE TREMENDOUS CHANGES SINCE the publication of the first edition of *Mango Mood.* Like the rest of India, the state has been dragged, kicking and screaming into a new century where the world is less of a globe and more of a flat, interconnected global village.

In this spanking new world, there is much more of everything. There are many more cars on the streets. Hundreds more people populate the pavements, spilling over, ever so often, onto much wider roads. Thousands more tourists clog the beaches and spill over, even more often, onto lurid headlines in the national dailies and 24/7 television news channels.

The days when Graham Bell's invention was the only means of communication are *passé.* Cell phones are as ubiquitous as undergarments. Blogs are *de rigueur*. The old style matchmaker has been put out to pasture with cyber-dating the rage.

Everyone is cued in on the Internet, even old-timers for whom a mouse once meant a marauder of the night and not the gizmo handled effortlessly by little Nikhil or baby Neha while playing Space Invaders on their Papa's desktop.

There is more asphalt, and fewer potholes, on the highways. Power problems are less frequent than in the earlier days. Lifestyles are flashier than they were in the yesteryears.

Yet, as the French would not fail to say – *plus ça change, plus c'est la même chose.*

The more things change the more they stay the same.

The medium may be different. The message has shown little variation.

Back then, newspapers in Goa served a double role. Usually, they carried staid news items of a robbery here and the toppling bid on the Government there. Every now and then, their pages would break out in a rash of photographs to celebrate the birthday of Our Beloved Minister, Leader of the Masses and Succour to the Great Unwashed.

Today, most pages of the city's dailies carry the day's news except for that one page that breaks out in a rash of photographs celebrating the nightly activities of Goa's party animals and the ever-increasing list of jet-setters heading for the state for another noisy round of Rest and Recreation.

Then, the Letters to the Editor columns of newspapers were the preferred forum for spewing bile on neighbours, colleagues and sundry bystanders. Today, the online blogs are where aspersions are cast, insults traded and newer, more innovative cuss-words tested in the public arena.

Tourism reigns supreme, the one change being that the British offensive of yore has since yielded place to a Russian invasion.

Then, the haberdasher from Hounslow haggled over the price of bananas with roadside vendors on the streets of Panaji. Today, the store clerk from St. Petersburg bargains over kitschy souvenirs with *lamani* hawkers in Morjim and Agonda.

In a more innocent age, all we had to worry about when venturing out on a beach was chancing upon hippies communing with the sun in the altogether.

In later years, there was the risk of bumping into duty-free traders with a quaint predilection for conducting their commerce in the dead of the night, far from the intruding gaze of a Customs Officer.

Still later, there was the fear of rubbing shoulders with representatives of international drug cartels that had set retail outlets on the silver sands, dispensing pocket-sized packets of illusion and delusion to an ever-expanding clientele.

As terrorism began rivalling tourism as an international pastime, the drug barons jostled for space with gunrunners and illegal weapons traffickers.

Add to the mix, an upsurge in hedonistic revellers a.k.a. tourists, unscrupulous locals and a constabulary whose presence is more the exception than the rule and today, a pleasant day out on the beach qualifies for a scene worthy of its own 'We, the People,' on NDTV, with Barkha Dutt bemoaning the fall of Eden.

This leads us to another constant in Goan life – public protest.

Goans continue to exercise their birthright – to contest a perceived wrong in loud and indignant style.

Around the time of the first edition of this book, they were out on the streets protesting against the second-class treatment meted out to the mother tongue of most Goans – Konkani. No sooner was this grave error rectified than the protestors were back on the streets – to hyperventilate over the first class treatment meted out to Konkani.

Today, they voice their disapproval over the manner in which the lush green of Goa is fast making way for the dull grey of concrete and the dirty brown of construction material.

They wax eloquent on the builder – politician nexus and the free ride given to the construction lobby in the corridors of power.

They turn apoplectic with rage at Goa being sold to the highest bidder – except, of course, when they are a party to the sale.

The voice of protest against the rape of Goa has led to a remarkable phenomenon – an explosion of experts in things Goan. Suddenly, every second person you encounter is an authority on Goan culture. Every third person is a noted historian from Goa.

There are more chroniclers of Goa's past today than had possibly existed throughout its journey from the *Aparant* of yore to AD 2010.

In the good old days, senior citizens would sit on park benches and watch the world go by; homemakers would gather on porches to gossip about the neighbourhood *femme fatale* and Government servants congregate in the fish market to squabble about local politics.

Life was more easy-paced, more *soçegado.*

Not any more. To a man, and a woman, they are all hard at work – crouched over their laptops penning the Great Goan novel.

For Goa sells nowadays. And how!

Part 1

A Goan Potpourrie

Must See In The Universe:
Goa, Earth

Mango Mood

EVERYONE IS TALKING MANGOES THESE DAYS. Conversation nowadays centres solely on the King of Fruits in its various incarnations. Eavesdrop on two householders chatting, and you can be sure to count four *Alphonsos*, three *Mancurados*, and even a *Mussarado,* popping up in the discussion, all within the space of two minutes.

The Mango season has arrived.

At the start of the season, the man staying next door went to the market and bought mangoes worth five hundred rupees.

How many would that make? All of one single golden yellow specimen.

Extravagant, would you say? Not at all! For this was no ordinary fruit, but one of the first crop to arrive at the stalls, captured after a no-holds barred fight with six other hopefuls in the marketplace.

He took it home and cut it in three pieces, a slice apiece for himself and his wife, and the central portion for his seven-year-old daughter.

For a while, silence reigned as five hundred rupees' worth of fruit paused for long moments in the mouth, then made its way down the gullet to find temporary residence in the stomach.

The last morsel having completed its downward journey, the man leaned back and declared that this season's fruit was definitely sweeter than that of last year. True, it did not hold a candle to the crop of the year before, but it was a good attempt.

The little girl wiped her mouth on her mother's sari and asked, 'Papa, can I have another?'

As mango prices descended a little in the following weeks, more and more fruit changed hands. Mangoes of all shapes and sizes found their way into serious discussions, casual conversations and desultory small talk.

Street-side chatter could well be summed up in a single word – *ammo* (mango). Even gossip became mango ripe!

The bank officer would go *gaga* over the taste of yesterday's fruit. The insurance agent would grimace over the previous week's selection. The lower division clerk would relate gleefully how he beat down the price of a delicious dozen by fifteen rupees. Meetings would disperse on the hope that today's buy would, by far, be the most pleasing to the palate.

It is Mango talk in Government offices, nowadays. From Monday to Friday, bureaucrats exchange hot words on the relative merits of the *Fernandine* and the *Pairi*.

The discussions are terminated only when a colleague charges into the room, eyes ablaze. 'Guess what?' he cries, opening his shoulder bag to empty a dozen mangoes on the file-laden table. 'I got them for just Rs 500. Rush, before they are all sold out!'

Disbelief, excitement and commotion follow. Soon, the office starts discharging its occupants, purses and wallets clutched to their frames, making a beeline for the market.

It's time for yet another mango break!

Curious onlookers have been heard to wonder whether the seat of Government has shifted to the marketplace. Never before has there been such a profusion of Secretaries and Under Secretaries among the fruit vendors. There are more bureaucrats facing the fruit than facing the files.

The mango madness has taken its toll on the other occupants of the market. Nobody wants vegetables any more. Potatoes lie forlornly in their jackets. Tomatoes shrivel in their skins for want of a buyer.

Shrimps and clams have lost their charms with even fishwives deserting them to pay obeisance to the King of Fruits.

At home, the lemonades have made way for mango shakes. Chocolate sundaes have yielded place to ice-cold confections featuring the King of Fruits. Puddings and *shrikhands* have surrendered before the onslaught of that bane of calorie-watchers – the *aamras*.

Mango magic has once again captivated the state.

(First published in *The Navhind Times,* Panaji.)

Commuting By Omnibus

I STOOD AT THE BUS STAND, AWAITING THE ARRIVAL OF a bus to take me to the city. It was 2:20 p.m. I had been waiting almost twenty minutes for a conveyance.

Wiping the sweat from my brow, I stepped onto the road and peered into the distance. Not a vehicle could be seen. Sighing loudly, I returned to my post.

The girl on my left checked the time on her wristwatch and clicked her tongue impatiently. She adjusted her skirt, smoothed down her hair, and then re-checked her watch. She was obviously getting very late.

The man at her side banged his fist against a telephone pole and muttered, 'Lousy buses!'

Just then, there was a loud wailing sound, a cross between a factory siren and the noisy protest of a pig bulldozed, against his wishes, into being the *entrée* of the Sunday afternoon meal.

Esmeralda (or was it *Joaquinha*?) came charging towards us.

Brakes screeching, tyres squealing with indignation at the treatment meted out to them, Esmy halted a few metres from us.

A lean, mean and hungry-looking individual jumped out of the vehicle and began calling out to us. 'Come along! Come along!'

It was the conductor. He made an impatient gesture with his right hand, holding out his left hand to receive the fare from passengers who were dismounting from the bus.

I was the 223rd passenger in the bus. No, I exaggerate! I was merely the 201st.

The conductor planted his hand on the small of my back and gave me a hefty shove.

'Get to the rear!' he growled. 'There is plenty of space inside.'

I lost myself in the mass of pushing, shoving bodies – until the pointed heel of a shoe descended firmly on my unprotected toes.

I tapped the shoulder of the woman by my side. 'Excuse me!' I gasped. 'You're stepping on my feet.'

In reply, she bent down and appeared to be searching for something. Three minutes later, she resurfaced with a smile on her face. 'It's not my foot,' she informed me. 'I finally located the missing appendage. It's three sandals, two galoshes and one pair of rain slippers away from yours.'

The bus was still at the stand. The conductor was signalling to a speck in the distance.

'Come along! Come along!' he yelled.

A teenager tapped his arm. 'We are full up. Can't we move on?'

'The engine has been idling for fifteen minutes,' added a stout gent. 'No wonder, private transportation in the state runs into huge losses.'

'That's why we raised the fares.' The conductor held out his hand for the raised fare.

'Where is my ticket?' asked the commuter as he handed over the amount.

The conductor inclined his head to one side, and eyed the other like a bacteriologist peering into a suspect culture. 'Are you feeling well?' he inquired courteously.

'I thought a fare increase was to be accompanied by a compulsory issuance of tickets and conductors in uniforms,' insisted the stout passenger. 'Where is yours, by the way?'

'I forgot to stitch it,' the conductor observed, amused. 'Sue me!'

'What, here?' countered the other. 'There's no place for that.'

The speck in the distance materialised into a little old lady. Four or five heads popped out of the windows to cheer her on. The conductor joined the chorus.

Agonising minutes later, she reached near the back end of the bus. Just as she was about to step inside, I pushed my way to the door and dismounted from the vehicle.

'What's the matter?' asked the conductor. 'Did you forget something?'

'Yes,' I replied. 'I forgot to say, "Thank You," to the Transport Minister.

Better bus services promised in exchange for increased fares – News Item.

(First published in the *Gomantak Times,* Panaji.)

Monsoon Madness

EVERY YEAR, THE DEPARTMENT OF METEOROLOGY KEEPS the nation in suspense until it pronounces its verdict – the monsoons will be normal this year. As the weatherman prophesies that the Rain God will once again favour the nation with His Munificence, India erupts in joy and trepidation.

Joy at the prospect of a bountiful harvest, trepidation at the thought of the floods that will follow and the mayhem they will spawn in their wake.

No sooner is the official announcement made than the corporate sector swings into action. The tyre companies take out quarter page ads in the leading dailies predicting the exact date of the arrival of the showers.

The Municipalities gear up for some last minute, or should one call it last second, repair work guaranteed to be reduced to naught by the first week of the monsoons.

The public girds its loins preparatory to wading through knee-length slush, dragging two-wheelers whose engines have stalled from waterlogging through flooded streets, and generally waiting for the skies to clear before venturing out in the open.

Sometimes, the Rain God, in a tearing hurry to make his Presence felt, spreads the cheer a fortnight ahead of schedule. May, the month of sweltering heat, sees daylong showers and nights that resound with the clap of thunder. All those raincoats and umbrellas that had been waiting for June to take centre-stage find themselves pressed in service two weeks in advance.

As the Monsoon advances and overcast skies become the norm, the daily weather report becomes monotonously familiar: 'It will rain all day, today.'

Soon, the only sound that reverberates on eardrums is the staccato tapping of raindrops on rooftops and the swooshing sound made by a thousand droplets sliding down windowpanes in a mad rush to be the first to make it to the ground.

Sure, a good monsoon is excellent news for a parched land and manna from Heaven for the farming community.

It is in this season that rural Goa is at its most verdant, cloaked in a green and shining shawl, even as urban Goa almost chokes under an equally thick blanket of muddy water.

Still, as day follows day of unceasing showers, the cry goes out: Where, oh where, has the Sun gone? With our resident star in vacation mode offering no more than fleeting appearances to remind folks of its existence, maybe it is time to warble those famous lines from the song, 'Raindrops keep falling on my head':

> 'So, I just did some talking to the Sun.
> Said I did not like the way he got things done.
> Sleeping on the job....'

It is time the Boss got a wake-up call.

The rains are a very welcome bounty but, oh, for a little sunshine...!

(First published in the *Gomantak Times*, Panaji.)

Freeze Frame

HOW DOES ONE DESCRIBE LIVING IN A STATE – BETTER known as the beach paradise of India, the Bahamas of the East no less, in a compact little piece that seeks to entertain, amuse and elevate?

Simple! Take the help of the alphabet! Just as the Government trots out a series of R's – Right to Information, Right to Education and the Right to be right – when asked to enlist its achievements, so can I requisition the services of another letter – C – when waxing lyrical on the Hawaii of the Indian subcontinent.

Any description of the state must necessarily begin with the first C – Confusion, a.k.a. what passes for traffic on city roads.

Now, I understand that most residents must own two cars and at least one two-wheeler ('How else can one keep up with the Sardesais and the Souzas?') but is it necessary to bring them out on the streets all at the same time?

If they must do so, must they treat the potholed wonders that pass for our roads as daredevil arenas where every manoeuvre known to man and stuntman is executed under the benign gaze of the friendly neighbourhood policeman? Favourite feats include jumping the red light, overtaking from the left and entering one-way streets the wrong way around, prior to making a mad dash for the fish market.

This brings me to the second C – Conversation. If ever there is a place where Goans congregate at noon to debate over who is seeing whom and which discontented Minister is plotting the next round of Operation Topple, it is the Municipal Fish Market in the main towns.

As pomfrets, shrimps and mackerels change hands, so does gossip change tongues. A sure-fire solution for depression, an outing to the market offers the best of the day's catch, from both the sea and the rumour mills.

If the blues refuse to budge, it's time to fall back on the other C – Consumerism. The right addresses for jeans and jackets, shoes and shades, jostle for space in the shops lining the capital city's main arteries. Swanky showrooms with goods sporting even swankier price tags.

They make you wish you had pots and pots of that other C – Cash!

The arrival of the monsoons signals the entry into the popular lexicon of another C – Canal. I am not alluding to the Grand Canal of Venice but its little brothers and sisters who run riot every time there is a moderate to heavy downpour.

Streets metamorphose into quaint little inland waterways. Roads turn into gently flowing streams. Pavements become waterways and street corners disappear.

You can no longer walk to the Printing Press or the Police station. You wade up to it.

As you plough your way determinedly through the knee-deep water that swirls around you, the thought comes to your mind.

Can living somewhere else make for a more challenging experience?

(First published in the *Gomantak Times*, Panaji.)

On The Standby

THE GOVERNMENT PLANS TO START WORK IMMEDIATELY on the new bridge across the River Zuari in Goa so that it is ready for use by the time the present bridge collapses.

An eminently sensible move indeed!

In the uncertain world of today, standbys are the need of the hour. One never fails to regret that the foresight and vision, seen in such abundance today, was woefully lacking in the predecessors of this Government.

Had they been equally farsighted, the present chaos across the River Mandovi could have been avoided. At the first sign of a crack, a wise government would have issued tenders for a new bridge.

This would have ensured that a standby was there, at hand, and ready to take over, when the first bridge met its premature death.

In its infinite wisdom, the Government has planned for any eventuality. Nowadays, materials used in construction projects masquerade under various aliases. Cement, especially, is remarkable for its ability to don different disguises. Sometimes, it makes an entry as sand. Too often, it sneaks in as mud.

The bridges, unable to bear the strain of such deceptions, cave in. A standby, therefore, becomes essential.

However, if cement is not cement in the original, could it be so in the standby? It does not seem likely! Hence, the chances of the reserve making it to that great building site in the sky becomes brighter.

What do the authorities do in such a case? Why, build a standby for the standby, of course! Should it also collapse, no problem! By the time the standby's standby is ready, the original would have been reconstructed, returning the construction process to Square One.

Standbys make their presence felt in many fields, as in the construction of new buildings, for example.

Bridges let a decent interval pass before throwing in the towel. Buildings, on the other hand, are in a tearing hurry to tear themselves down. The collapse can occur even before the construction is officially complete. This makes it necessary for a second building to come up as a standby for the first, and a third to be ready to stand in for the second. Thus, by continuously building standbys for each previous standby, Goa could well be on target for the crown of the most developed state in India by AD 2020.

With buildings and bridges accounted for, can roads be far behind? Recently, most roads in the main cities of the territory received a much-deserved face-lift. Side-by-side with the repair work, however, the Municipalities were careful to issue fresh tenders for the repaving work that would be necessary two months hence.

Farsighted? Yes! Unfortunately, it was not enough. The Roads Division of the Municipality failed to account for the activities of the Drains Division. In the fortnight following the repaving, the latter decided to inspect some drains they had missed in the earlier rounds. Now, repaving is necessary, but no standby is available.

With the profusion of standbys, construction sites have multiplied. Fresh labour is being imported from the neighbouring states as standbys for construction workers collapsing from overwork. Fresh accounts have been opened in banks as standbys for the overflowing accounts of the contractors and their political patrons.

The wafer-thin majority enjoyed by the ruling party has sent it scurrying for standby M.L.A.s from the Opposition camp. As for the Ministers, except for those already in the Cabinet, the remaining legislators are, naturally, standbys for berths in that much-desired formation.

The Opposition is on standby, ready to assume charge in case the present incumbent is forced to hand in its papers.

Considering the people's anger over the slipshod originals, chances are that the standbys may be needed much sooner than later.

Government to build a standby for the Zuari Bridge – News Item.

(First published in *The Navhind Times*, Panaji.)

Come As You Are – Leave Different

The Wagles' Goan Jaunt

THE WAGLES WERE GOING ON A VACATION. NO, NOT to the city zoo. This time, Mr Wagle had made elaborate inquiries before choosing a particular holiday retreat.

'Why don't you go down to Goa?' suggested a friend. 'You'll love the golden beaches fringed by softly-swaying palm trees and the many picturesque cottages.'

Ten days later, Mr and Mrs Wagle, Raju and Manoj, arrived in Panaji, eager to experience the holiday of a lifetime.

The tourist guide read out their itinerary.

'On the first day, you will see the churches. On the second day, you do the temples. On the third day, you relax on the beach.'

Three days later found the Wagles stretched out on one of Goa's famed beaches. A young man sporting dark glasses and an 'I love Goa' T-shirt came and sat next to Wagle.

Turning sideways, he offered him a wide, friendly grin. Surprised, Wagle could only offer a weak smile in return.

Sometime later, Radhika went off with the kids to buy ice cream. Wagle continued to gaze at the sea.

The youth slithered up to Wagle. Bending forward, he gave him a sharp prod in the ribs. 'Want some stuff?' he asked in a hoarse whisper.

'What stuff?' Wagle was confused.

'You know,' smirked the stranger. 'Smack! Coke!'

'Of course not!' Wagle went rigid with shock.

'Okay, just asking.' The man raised his hands in a mock gesture of surrender and left.

'Guess what?' Radhika came charging up to Wagle, her eyes shining. 'I have been offered first dibs from a batch of contraband goods. The prices are quite reasonable.'

'But that is wrong,' protested Wagle. 'Dealing with contraband is against the law.'

'Who cares?' she retorted. 'The Deshpandes did not when they made a killing. Why should I worry?'

Raju and Manoj came back to their parents, leisurely licking the ice-cream cones they had just bought. 'Mummy, look!' cried Manoj. Two bronzed hippy belles, clad in the barest minimum, ran lightly across the sands in front of them.

Drawing her breath in sharply, Radhika grabbed little Raju and quickly covered the innocently wide-open eyes. 'Outrageous!' she fumed.

'Yes, yes!' muttered Wagle in embarrassment.

'Hey!' called out a voice. Wagle looked up warily.

Three young men, sporting T-shirts and huge straw hats, came running up to him. 'Which way did the dames go?' they asked him.

Speechless, Wagle could only point in the right direction.

'Thanks, man!' The youth raised their hands in a mock salute. 'Want to come?'

'No, thanks!' Wagle shook his head fiercely, his cheeks red.

There was an urgent tap on his shoulder. An agitated Radhika looked beseechingly at him. 'Can we please go back to the zoo?'

(First published in *The Navhind Times*, Panaji.)

Wagle ki Duniya was a popular television serial on Doordarshan before the advent of cable and the 100 plus alternatives to Chitrahaar and Amchi Mati Amche Manse. The serial followed the adventures of Mr Wagle, a.k.a. The Common Man, his long-suffering wif, Radhika, and their sons, Raju and Manoj, as they coped with the trials and tribulations that is life in Mumbai. This piece transports the Wagles to Goa, in particular to one of its famed beaches. The cocktail of uncontrolled tourism, drug trafficking and minimal law enforcement holding fort here helps them appreciate why sections of the Goan coastline have become no-go zones for respectable middle class folk like the Wagles. Is the situation better today? Ask the mother of Scarlett Keeling, the British teenager found murdered in Anjuna. Ask the mother of the nine-year-old Russian girl molested at Arambol. Ask the participants of last weekend's rave party in Palolem. Ask ... Never mind. You get the message.

The *Corredinho* Conundrum

SUPER SLEUTH SAM D' SILVA RAN A FINGER THROUGH HIS unruly locks and paused, a thoughtful expression on his face.

His faithful sidekick, Gopi, who had been dodging his footsteps, came to a halt. The two detectives had left *Kala Academy,* Goa's best-known centre for music, dance and the theatrical arts, after attending a discussion titled, 'Whither Goan Culture?'

'Is something wrong, Boss?' asked Gopi.

Sam nodded his head. 'We have a new problem to be investigated.'

'But Boss,' Gopi scratched his baldpate. 'Are we not investigating the case of the missing *Jihadi*? We are neck deep in coded messages, IEDs and fake currency rackets.'

'Never mind all that,' replied his chief. 'The National Investigation Agency can handle that matter. We need to focus on a problem exercising the minds of all Goans.'

'What is that problem?' asked Gopi.

'The discussion at the seminar centred around the fact that the *corredinho*, a popular Portuguese folk dance, pops up like a bad penny in every cultural offering on Goa when it has no business being there. It even sneaked into Goa's Republic Day float.'

'Sneaked?' Gopi was puzzled. 'Do you mean to say it walked into the programme on its own, without even a well-administered shove in the right direction?'

'Not even a nudge,' asserted Sam. 'The Minister disclaimed all responsibility for the gatecrash. He asserted that most Goans knew not what the *corredinho* is. Yet, there it was, bold as brass, claiming to be an authentic folk dance of Goa.'

'It is there in all the tourism brochures,' said the sidekick. 'It is the main attraction of cultural programmes on river cruises on the Mandovi. What is all the fuss about?'

'The fuss, my dear Gopi, is about how it has come to symbolise Goa. The locals contend that the Latin touch in Goan culture has been overemphasised while the Indian core has been given short shrift. The politicians are outraged. The civil servants are distressed. The artistic community is dismayed.'

'If everyone who matters is against it, how does it inveigle its way into every presentation on Goa?' Gopi remained perplexed.

'Exactly!' cried Sam. 'That is the mystery we must solve. The local bigwigs maintain that their hands are clean. Clearly, an unknown hand is at work, doing the damage.'

'The foreign hand?' Gopi hazarded a guess.

'Gopi, you are a genius!' Sam looked approvingly at his sidekick. 'The dreaded Foreign Hand is up to its usual mischief. Those tasked with promoting Goa are needlessly blamed for this erroneous depiction. The culprit is elsewhere.'

'The Foreign Hand is like the Home Minister of India, is it not?' observed Gopi. 'In both cases, the truism holds true: The Buck Stops Here.'

(First published in the *Gomantak Times*, Panaji.)

An *Ashram* For Every *Taverna*

IT WAS THE OPENING OF THE FIRST *ASHRAM* (REFUGE) set up by the Government for the rehabilitation of severe alcoholics in Goa. The hall booked for the inaugural function was packed to capacity with tipsy old men, sozzled youth and victims of the Demon Rum.

At the entrance, a white-haired senior citizen, already in an advanced state of inebriation, was having a quick one before staggering towards his seat. A little further on, a well tanked-up gentleman was practising his proposed vote of thanks to the Government in front of a crowd of equally blotto colleagues.

A bottle of Scotch Whisky was making its way along the second row of seats, pausing every now and then to be relieved of its contents.

The door opened and a reporter of a local TV channel entered. He was covering the inaugural function of the *Ashram* and hoped to interview some of its likely occupants.

He went up to a relatively sober individual. 'Good morning!' he greeted him.

The man fished out a bottle from his coat pocket, uncorked it and held it out to the reporter. 'Have a sip,' he offered.

The scribe pushed aside the bottle. 'Some other time, thanks.' He looked at his companion with interest. 'Am I addressing a likely resident of the *Ashram*?'

'It looks like it,' the other grimaced. 'My wife threatens to divorce me if I don't sober up. Not fair really, given that it is she who led me into this state in the first place.'

The scribe eyed him with disbelief.

'Fact, I assure you,' asserted the drunk. 'There I was, a God-fearing man with a grocery store on a lane with five other stores. Naturally, it wasn't doing well. One-by-one, my neighbours abandoned selling soaps and suds in favour of running bars. They were soon raking it in sackfuls. My wife watched enviously as a drab middle class existence was junked for *nouveau riche* life worthy of an art paper pullout in a celebrity rag.'

'Unable to bear it any longer, she badgered me to apply for a liquor license. Soon, 'Mercy Stores' became 'Mercy Bar – Genuine Scotch Sold Here'. From the owner of a public house to a sampler of its contents is a small step. It was one I took with ease. The result – my present condition.'

The reporter moved to a tourist in a shocking pink T-shirt and Bermuda shorts.

'You should be ashamed of yourself,' he reprimanded the visitor. 'Reducing yourself to this state in someone else's home. How would you have liked it if a Goan had made a similar exhibition of himself in your state?'

The drunken visitor thought over the observation, then shook his head. 'Not likely!' he concluded. 'Back home our Department of Tourism does not invite folks to visit the state to try its wonder brew. It is rarely that we have a street with two bars, a bar-n-restaurant, three wine stores and a liquor shop.'

'It is harder to get sozzled back home,' the man frowned.

The scribe turned to the person beside him and did a double take.

'You, too?' he demanded of the bureaucrat. 'What are you doing at the *ashram*?'

The *babu* sighed. 'I have fallen prey to the charms of the Demon Rum.'

'But how? Why?'

'Every day, my office is inundated with applications for licenses to open bars and wine stores. Uncles, colleagues and friends, all desire that I rush through their proposals. Remarkably, the Government seems to give the matter top priority.'

'True!' agreed the scribe. 'It is quite enthusiastic about issuing bar licenses.'

'I read somewhere that there is a bar for every forty males in Goa,' added the bureaucrat. 'I was intrigued. How did this molten liquid so captivate the people?'

'I sampled some of it,' he continued, 'a gift from the owner of a public house whose application I had expedited. I liked it.'

The officer directed a sheepish look at the reporter and continued. 'No, let me confess. I loved it! I wanted more – and more. So, here I am, one more candidate for the Government sponsored Alcoholics *Ashram*.'

Goa Government proposes to open ashrams for alcoholics – News Item.

(First published in the *Gomantak Times*, Panaji.)

Double Take

'EIGHTY-TWO MILES OF COASTLINE, WITH THE SILVERY sands of some of the world's most beautiful beaches...'

I looked up from the tourist brochure and glanced at the clock on the wall.

Oh, my God! It was 5:45 a.m. already.

I would have to set off on my morning walk right away if I was to make it to the Beach and back before the heat became unbearable. The scintillating prose could wait. Better still, I could take the brochure and read it during my walk.

Thirty-five minutes later found me near the public bus stop at Miramar, the principal beach of the capital, Panaji. To my surprise, I saw that, even at this early hour, the stop was packed to capacity. I went closer and saw that it was indeed packed, but with a difference.

The crowd was not upright, as are commuters waiting for a bus. Instead, everyone had adopted a horizontal position. How strange, I said to myself, and moved forward.

The mystery was solved. Tourists were using the stand as a makeshift dormitory. Men, women and children lay inside the stand and around it, fast asleep.

I went up to one of the sleeping men and tapped his shoulder. The blankets were thrown back to reveal a groggy-eyed individual staring balefully at me.

'Couldn't you get accommodation anywhere?' I asked him.

'All the affordable hotels were full,' replied the tourist. 'The rest, which incidentally make up the majority, were beyond our limited means. Paying guest accommodation was out of question as Goans prefer to rent out rooms to foreigners.'

I walked on, flipping the pages of my brochure. 'Goa,' I read, 'has accommodation for various classes of tourists. Hotel charges, here, are moderate.'

The sound of someone splashing about in water made me raise my head. Some tourists were bathing in the fountain at the traffic circle near the beach. Outraged, I stormed up to the offenders.

'This is not a public bathhouse,' I stormed.

'I agree,' said one of the visitors. 'But we have no choice. We decided to visit Goa on an impulse while driving down to Belgaum. New Year's Eve is a fun affair here.'

'Do you call this fun?' I shook my head in disbelief and walked on.

'In sun-kissed Goa,' said the guide, 'the water is clean and warm.' I looked back and watched as the youth transferred the grime from their bodies to the clean and warm waters of Goa.

'Watch out!' I was about to sit down on a bench when a voice stopped me. A stocky individual was stretched out on the aforementioned place.

Another tourist? This was persecution.

I put my hands on my hips and glared down at him. 'This is a beach for heaven's sake, not a makeshift motel.'

'Tell that to your Tourism Department which invites more and more people to visit Goa without checking to see if there is enough accommodation,' shot back the tourist.

I looked at my brochure. 'Goa,' continued the guide, 'is serious business for the tourist who is looking for the holiday of a lifetime.'

'Discover Goa!' it added. 'May you never lose it!'

(First published in *The Gomantak Times*, Panaji.)

Chronicles Of A State, Often Told

IT HAD BEEN DAYS SINCE I HAD SEEN POORVI. I HAD NOT seen her holding court at the fancy coffee shop sipping an even fancier-priced cappuccino. I had missed passing her on my evening walks. There had been nary an email or an SMS from her for some time.

I decided to call on her to make sure that she was not sick. The look of barely concealed irritation on her face when she opened her front door suggested that mine was not a welcome visit.

'Where have you been?' I inquired. 'I haven't seen you in ages.'

'I have been crazy busy,' she revealed as she led the way to her study.

The room was in a mess. There were books piled all over the table, on the couch and on the floor. Seven books of the coffee-table variety surrounded her laptop. A yellow highlighter was being used liberally to underscore portions of the text in these tomes.

'I'm writing a book on the history of Goa,' she informed me.

I was surprised. To my knowledge, Poorvi was neither a historian nor someone with an inclination towards things ancient.

'Good heavens!' she said testily when I commented on the same. 'You do not need to be a historian to write about Goan history. Far better to start with little to no knowledge. That way, you approach the subject with an uncluttered mind. It makes for a more fascinating presentation.'

'Surely you need some framework....'

'Facts are an optional extra,' she insisted. 'They just get in the way. They stem the free flow of the creative juices. What's critical is having the gift of the gab, a passable felicity with words and a Rolodex of Who's Who in the publishing business.'

She paused to tap her finger on one of the books. 'If I need facts, I can always get them from here.'

'Are you focusing on a particular period?' I picked up the marker that presumably channelled those selfsame creative juices.

'The Portuguese colonial rule, of course. The brand name sells. You must gear your product to the demands of the market.'

I had hated history in school, linking it with the need to memorise an endless array of dates and names of dynasties.

However, this talk of brand positioning made me recognise that I had misjudged its appeal.

'How is it going?' I directed my gaze at the laptop screen.

'I just finished the chapter on Goan music.' Her eyes took on a faraway look. 'It has been great going so far. I have almost caroled my way through the discussion on the sonorous rhythms of the *ghumot*, the juxtaposition of the *desi* and *videshi* elements in the *mando*, the plaintive wail of the *fado*....'

'Isn't the *fado* a Portuguese musical style?' I was a little surprised. Perhaps, this is what she meant while referring to the untrammelled flow of creative juices.

'I suppose so,' she conceded. 'I was running short of my quota of 15 Portuguese words per page so I slipped it in.'

She eyed me with defiance. 'It was President Andrew Jackson who observed that 'It's a damn poor mind that can only think of one way to spell a word.' It is an impoverished imagination that balks at embellishing otherwise drab historical facts.'

Damn it! Had I realised history was such fun, I would have become a historian myself. Maybe, even penned my own history of Goa.

'When do you have to submit the manuscript?' I asked.

'I promised to deliver it by, like, yesterday,' she frowned. 'It is a race for time. A rival publisher has commissioned a similar book by a leading culture vulture. Another coffee-table publication is due for release in a couple of months. At least two prominent heritage sharks are circling the pond, waiting for me to miss the deadline before swooping in to grab my advance....'

'Golly!' This was war. I checked to see if the highlighter retained its ink. All weapons had to be kept in battle-ready mode at each stage of the war.

'I'll leave you to your *magnum opus*,' I informed her, heading for the door.

'Facts confuse me,' I sighed. 'Dates bore me. When it comes to Goa, all I remember is that it was liberated in 1961 – or was it 1962?'

'The ideal candidate,' pronounced Poorvi. She thrust a business card in my hand. 'Here is the name of my publisher. Give him a call.'

Possibilities, Endless

Communal Arithmetic

THE MEMBERS OF THE RULING PARTY HAD GATHERED TO discuss the composition of the Council of Ministers.

'As you are aware,' said the Chairman, 'two-thirds of our legislators are Catholics while the rest are Hindu. The present Cabinet has six members, four Catholic, two Hindus, exactly replicating the communal fraction. The difficulty arises in the choice of the four new Ministers.'

'We must ensure that each community gets proper representation in the Council of Ministers,' asserted a member.

'Quite right,' nodded the Chairman. 'I asked our statistician to tabulate all possible permutations and combinations for a well-balanced Council.'

The statistician came forward. 'To maintain the present ratio, we need two Hindu and two Catholic members. However, if we make it 3:1 in favour of the Hindus, each community gets fifty percent representation in the Cabinet. If it is 1:3....'

'Wait a minute!' yelled a backbencher. Let us get the arithmetic clear. Who gets the Cabinet ranks?'

'If we allot one Cabinet and one Minister of state per community,' the statistician punched a few keys on his calculator, 'that makes it 5:3 in favour of the Catholics in the Cabinet.'

An honourable member stood up. 'I feel a member of the minority community must be made the Chief Minister. That would be a truly secular move.'

'Nonsense.' His rival dismissed the suggestion. 'As the majority community is in a minority in the legislative wing of our party, we reassert our secular credentials by retaining their man in the Chair.'

'What about the Chairmanships of the Corporations?' shouted another backbencher.

'I think the Hindus should get the lion's share this time,' suggested the Secretary.

'Are we not over-emphasising the religious angle?' interrupted a member. 'We must be seen giving weight to ability and experience also.'

'That's impossible!' A frontbencher shook his head vigorously. 'If we choose men on the basis of merit alone, we may not be able to do justice to all the communities.'

'We will be accused of widening the chasm between various groups,' said another.

'We may even be charged with ... communalism,' said a third party member, shaken.

'One mistake like that and the entire edifice of secularism tumbles down,' agreed a senior member, nodding his head gravely.

'We dare not disturb the delicate communal balance in the state,' said the Chairman, striking out the suggestion.

'Reverting back to our discussion, as regards the percentage of Catholics for Chairmanships....'

(First published in *The Navhind Times,* Panaji.)

Toppling Games

THE SPLIT IN THE RULING PARTY, AND THE SUBSEQUENT formation of the new governing front, has changed forever the social landscape of Goa.

All of a sudden, people are appreciating the worth of words like secularism and nationalism. Means have been provided to stem the rising tide of communalism in the country. Deepening fissures between the two major communities in Goa had compelled the dissenting faction to break away from the party.

This move, declared the rebels, will forever end the scourge of communalism.

Now, every time there is an increase in the communal temperature in the state, there is no need to make an urgent call to the Centre asking for police reinforcements. Instead, one-third of the ruling party M.L.A.s should immediately make tracks for the Opposition benches and trigger a sharp fall in the thermometer level.

The people have come to appreciate how precariously secularism is positioned in the Republic. Every time a group of M.L.A.s is denied Ministerial berths, the secular fabric is dangerously stretched. This necessitates immediate moves and counter-moves on the part of those who rule the destinies of the people.

It is only when the legislators join as Ministers, in a rival front, that secularism can breathe freely again.

A small step for an M.L.A. A giant step for humankind.

Patriotism has become a much-feared word today, especially for incumbent Chief Ministers. The dissident faction that toppled the Government claimed to have done so in the larger interests of the nation.

Now, every time a legislator angles for a Ministership, he need not approach the High Command on bended knees. All he need do is look long and hard at the tricolour instead.

Ministers of State, desirous of a rise in their status, need only to talk of the national honour to gain a Cabinet berth.

The people are bursting with pride. Never before in the history of democracy has there been a more dedicated set of M.L.A.s.

Citizens speak in hushed whispers of the fourth split necessitated by an urge to bury communalism, the fifth split triggered by the need to satisfy the aspirations of the masses, and the tenth split that was a reaction to the seventh split.

Babes are being brought up on the heroic tales of sacrifice of their M.L.A. Grandmas put their grandchildren to sleep on the heart-rending tale of the supreme sacrifice made by the legislator who forsook a Ministership, settling for a Chairmanship of a Corporation, for the sake of national unity.

The frequent changes of Government have had their side effects too. Nowadays, newspaper offices put out 'Today's special' boards to keep the public informed on 'Today's C.M' and 'Today's party in power.'

Raj Bhavan correspondents are on the alert for unscheduled swearing-in ceremonies.

Party-naming contests are organised each week, inviting the people to suggest names for newly-formed coalitions. The political class is showing keen interest in the results.

The sordid world of gambling has entered in the fray, with handsome wagers being laid on who will be the next C.M. and how long he will last.

An unfortunate fall-out of the continuous comings and goings has been the need to replace the Assembly carpet every three months. The frequent floor-crossings have taken a heavy toll of its services.

Citizens no longer contact the Secretariat with requests for an audience with the Chief Minister.

'Be precise,' they are told. 'Which C.M. are you talking about? Yesterday's CM, today's Chief Executive or tomorrow's Big Boss?'

The Secretariat plans to issue notices celebrating 'Twenty days in office' on the lines of cinema posters claiming likewise for the new blockbuster in town.

Ex-Ministers and members of the Opposition are producing racy accounts of the fast-paced political developments in the state.

A former Chief Minister is writing his memoirs, tentatively titled '*Thirty Days in the Hot Seat*'. His immediate successor is bringing out '*No Bed of Roses*', an account of his month in office. A neck and neck tussle is on to be the first off the publishing block.

The residents of the state are congratulating themselves for having finally found the key to lasting communal harmony in Goa – make all the M.L.A.s, Ministers.

They are also patting themselves on the backs for having discovered an even more revolutionary path to lasting peace and stability – making all these Ministers, Chief Ministers.

Once that is done there will be no cause for strife anymore!

Ruling party splits. New Formation takes office – News Item.

(First published in The *Gomantak Times*, Panaji.)

'Watch Out, We're Shooting!'

BLOOD HOUND, THAT INTREPID STAR REPORTER OF THE daily, *Scandal Bag* ('Any scandal, big or small, cross our hearts, we uncover them all.') was summoned by his editor.

'I have an assignment for you,' said his boss. 'An Honourable M.L.A. threw a missile at another M.L.A. during Question Hour in the Legislative Assembly. I want a follow-up report on the incident.'

'Right, boss!' The reporter clicked his heels and withdrew from the room.

His first stop was the home of the M.L.A. who had launched the missile attack.

Hound entered the house and did a double check at the sight that met his eyes. What had once been a pleasantly decorated living room resembled a hunter's den. There were guns everywhere – machine guns, automatics, rifles and shotguns.

PRESS

In the midst of this firepower stood the sharpshooter himself, lovingly stroking the barrel of the gun in his hand.

'What is this?' gasped Hound, his eyes nearly popping out of their sockets. 'Did I stray into a set of a *Masala* Western? Are you essaying the role of Quick Gun Murugan?'

The gunman put his rifle down and beamed at the scribe. 'You must have heard about my target practice in the House.'

'I don't think anybody failed to hear of it,' observed Hound.

'Well then, you must have heard of how the missile slipped out of my hands and hit my *bête noire* on the head. If I could score a bull's-eye even when I was not aiming at anything, just imagine what I could achieve with a little practice. I may even bag an Olympic Gold in shooting like Abhinav Bindra.'

Hound's next stop was the home of a veteran politician. He wanted the leader's views on the legislators turning the floor of the House into a shooting range.

'Deplorable behaviour,' said the long-time observer in a shocked tone. 'If this conduct persists, we may soon hear 'Here's aiming at you' instead of 'Will the Honourable member please oblige,' in the House. Perhaps, it will be Duck, Minister instead of Yes, Minister soon.'

The scribe's last stop was the home of the Member who had been the target in the shoot-out.

'Come on in!' beamed the M.L.A. 'I have something to show to you.'

He led Hound to his study where a suit of armour stood next to a glass-topped table.

'It's a new uniform that I have designed for all the Members of the House. No M.L.A. should think of entering the Assembly building without it. It is a must wear for debates.'

Throwing a loving glance in the direction of the suit, he revealed, 'I plan to market it on a large scale. Hopefully, I will make a fortune from it.'

(First published in the *Gomantak Times*, Panaji.)

A Damsel In Distress

'PSST, PSST!' CALLED OUT A VOICE. THE WAITER WHO WAS walking by the poolside looked around in surprise.

'Up here!' called the voice. The waiter looked up to see a beautiful woman leaning down from the balcony of her room.

'Can I help you, ma'am?' inquired the waiter.

'They are holding me under duress in this room. My kidnapper stepped out of the room for a smoke, so I rushed to the balcony for help. Can you rescue me, please?'

'I'll have you out in a jiffy.' The waiter assured her. Walking briskly, he made his way into the building and towards the lobby.

Just then, there was a tap on his shoulder. He turned to see a smartly dressed gent by his side.

'Can I trust you to be discreet?' The newcomer wanted to know. 'I have a task for you. There's good money in it if you do as you are told without any fuss or bother.'

The steward watched him impassively. His not to reason why. He had no objection to making a little money on the side provided nothing illegal was involved.

'I have some visitors in my room upstairs,' said the newcomer. He mentioned his room number. 'They are Legislative Assembly members from my party. I am in the running for the post of Legislature Party Chief. I'm working on them to cast their votes in my favour.'

'They are all my strong supporters,' continued the guest. 'However, circumstances compel me to keep them confined to my suite to guard against their being sneaked away by the rival camp.'

The hotel employee continued to maintain an impassive front.

'I want you to make sure that they are well fed and attended to without revealing their location to any interested party,' instructed the man. 'If someone asks, point him or her to another floor, another hotel. Do you follow me?'

The waiter nodded his head and moved on. He still had to rescue his damsel in distress.

As he was passing the men's washroom, a hand emerged and grabbed him by the arm. The door of the washroom opened and a red-faced man stepped out.

'I have learnt that some of our party legislators are holed up in this resort,' he said. 'If you lead me to them, Diwali and Christmas will come early for you this year.'

The waiter listened but kept his counsel. If there was going to be a bidding war, it was best to ascertain the highest offer before concluding the transaction.

'By the way,' added the newcomer. 'Can you check if there is a room vacant in the premises? I may need it if I find the fugitives and persuade them to change places.'

The steward muttered something unintelligible and shook free from the other's grasp. On reaching the room where the damsel in distress was confined, he inserted the master key in the lock and threw open the door.

The woman came running up to him, gratitude written on her face.

'Who are you and why were you locked up in this room?' The waiter was understandably curious.

'My so-called guardians believe that I am incapable of exercising my free will and need to be constantly under watch. For my own protection, I was told that I must be kept under lock and key.'

'I am sorry to hear that,' said the waiter sympathetically. 'I hope you will feel better now, Miss ... er ... I am sorry I missed your name.'

'They call me Democracy,' sighed the woman.

Ringside View Of A Farce

THERE WAS A TIME, NOT SO LONG AGO, WHEN I WAS A political novice. At that time, hectic consultations meant little more to me than the part to be skipped in a news report on the election of a Chief Minister.

I would be hard put to imagine how an emissary of the High Command succeeded in papering over the cracks in the state unit. In those days, what I knew about daylong deliberations and all-night confabulations could have been written, with ease, on the back of a postage stamp.

Such is not the case any more—not since I had the privilege of bagging a ringside seat for the 'Bout of the Year' in Goa—the battle for the Chief Ministership of the state.

For the theatre in which the political drama accompanying the selection of Goa's Top Gun unfolded, the Government-owned Circuit House, happens to be the house next door to mine.

Thanks to this vantage point, I was transformed, within minutes, from one who wouldn't have been able to recognise a consensus even if it came and bit her, to one who could predict, to the very second, when conflicting claims for the Chair would be abandoned in favour of a 'unanimous' choice.

The curtain rose on the first Act, a little after midday, with the news of the resignation of the incumbent Chief Minister. Almost immediately, all rumour mills in the capital went into top gear.

Panaji came to resemble a football field, as members of the public went into the huddle formation to speculate over the identity of the successor.

By mid-afternoon, the word had gone around that the two rival contenders were engaged in a fight to the finish for the crown. The representatives of the ubiquitous High Command were, it seems, making weak, ineffectual attempts to bring about a cease-fire.

As dusk fell, the scene of action shifted to the Circuit House. Vehicles of all kinds, from the staff cars of Government functionaries to the motorcycles and scooters of the curious citizenry, started converging on the road in front of the building.

While their owners represented all shades of political opinion in the state, the vehicles served as a cross-section of the industry, with almost every leading brand represented at the venue.

Eight o'clock came, bringing with it the news that, as the earlier rounds were inconclusive, the last and final round in the Championship Bout would be fought within the portals of the Circuit House.

The procession of cars now became a veritable motorcade. Every couple of minutes, an official car would screech to a halt in front of the entrance, disgorge its occupants and wander off in search of a parking place.

The task completed, the driver of the vehicle would head for the nearby kiosk where fellow drivers, cheerleaders of the various factions and curious bystanders had gathered to enjoy a quiet cigarette or *paan* and mull over the day's events.

Every now and then, a man would come running out of the Circuit House and make his way to the kiosk. The crowd would pounce on him and bombard him with queries. The air would be full of '*Kidein re*?' ('Well?') and '*Konn zallo*?' ('Who made it?')

A sudden hush would descend on the crowd as the man would first pause for effect, and then, with a flourish, give a blow-by-blow account of the latest developments.

The minutes ticked by. Ministers, M.L.A.s and M.P.s drove up, dismounted and disappeared. The High Command arrived and stood revealed -- as three harassed souls who looked as if they would rather be anywhere else but here.

Each new arrival attracted a fresh round of spectators. They included Ministerial confidants who claimed to have inside knowledge about the way in which the vote was likely to go and the residents of the locality who had by now abandoned all pretence of being disinterested in the proceedings.

Sensing an excellent opportunity, an enterprising group began accepting bets on the likely outcome of the battle for power.

Time passed by. Within the Circuit House, the deliberations to choose Goa's new Chief Minister continued. Endless rounds of tea were served.

Outside, the crowds became restive. Cigarettes and sweets were passed around.

Two stray dogs paused in front of the building to look curiously at the crowd. The junior member of the duo turned an inquiring face towards his partner and asked him something in a few, short barks. (Probably '*Konn zallo*?' in doggie language.)

Every now and then, the High Command was put on hold as someone went to answer a more pressing call of nature in the rest rooms of the Circuit House. The onlookers, meanwhile, availed of the great open spaces adjacent to the building.

At half past ten, the whisper went around that the legislators had finally come to a decision on the choice of their Chief. In the time-honoured tradition of the party, bitter enemies suddenly turned loyal party workers.

The display of fisticuffs made way for the need to present a united front to the public. The election was 'unanimous' with the other contenders sheathing their claws, for the moment, and agreeing to propose their rival's name.

Democracy, Indian style, had triumphed again!

New Leader elected after marathon Congress Legislature Party meeting – News Item.

(First published in *The Times of India*, Mumbai.)

Time passed by. Within the Circuit House the deliberations to choose Goa's new Chief Minister continued. Endless rounds of tea were served.

Outside, the crowds became restive. Cigarettes and sweets were passed around.

Two stray dogs paused in front of the building to look curiously at the crowd. The junior member of the duo turned an inquiring face towards his partner and asked him something in a few short barks. (Probably '*Kaun aaya?*' in doggie language.)

Every now and then, the High Command was put on hold as someone went to answer a more pressing call of nature in the rest rooms of the Circuit House. The onlookers, meanwhile, swarmed the great open spaces adjacent to the building.

At half past two, the whisper went around that the legislators had finally come to a decision on the choice of their Chief. In the time-honoured tradition of the party, the premises suddenly turned loyal party workers.

The display of [illegible] made way for the need to present a united front to the public. The election was unanimous with the other contenders sheathing their claws for the moment, and agreeing to propose their rival's name.

Democracy, Indian style, had triumphed again!

[illegible] elected after marathon [illegible] Party meeting – News Item.

(First published in *The Times of India*, Mumbai)

You've Come A Long Way, Baby

Legalising Illegalities

SON: DADDY?

Father: Yes, son?

Son: Are you aware that Goa has a flourishing business in *matka*?

Father (wearily): Who is not aware of this? The police force ignores the racket even as the State Government wrings its hands in despair.

Son: Not any more, Daddy. The Big Chief has come up with a brilliant new way of tackling the menace.

Father: Are there any plans to come down heavily on the offenders?

Son: Trying to put curbs on their operations is an exercise in futility. The Big Chief has come to realise this. The authorities have chosen a more pragmatic course of action. They are studying proposals to legalise the menace.

Father: Well, it certainly is an original way of tackling the problem.

Son: Does this mean that, henceforth, *matka* bookies will be termed as small-scale entrepreneurs? Will the kingpins be designated as captains of industry? Are the gullible folk who place their bets to be labelled as investors?

Father: I don't know, son.

Son: And, Daddy?

Father: Yes, son?

Son: If *matka* is made legal, there is nothing to stop other so-called illegal activities from switching over to the right side of the law.

Father: That's right, son. Perhaps, in the future, streetwalking will no more be an offence. The women plying this trade will metamorphose into industrialists of the night.

Son: What about larceny, Daddy? Will that be legal as well? The police has not had much success in curbing this menace either.

Father: If they do not legalise it, the bandit kings and queens of Goa will raise a howl of protest against this discrimination. There may even be allegations of human rights violations.

Son: Under what trade can they be registered?

Father: Considering that they specialise in decamping with people's belongings, I would say furniture movers, son.

Son (bewildered): I do not understand, Daddy. If gambling, prostitution and similar offences are made legal, what happens to the state police? It will no longer be able to apprehend confidence tricksters and other racketeers as no such penal action will exist.

Father: That is right, son. Conventional definitions of law and order may have to go in for an overhaul.

Son: Does that mean that conventional policing will now be an illegal activity, Daddy?

Father: I do not know, son!

Government may legalise matka – News Item.

(First published in the *Gomantak Times*, Panaji.)

Casino Capers

'HEY, MOTHER!' CALLED OUT FOURTEEN-YEAR-OLD NAVIN from his place by the window. 'Come and take a look at this!'

His mother abandoned her pots and pans and came scurrying into the room.

'Look!' said Navin, pointing to a kiosk located on the street below.

It was late evening and the shadows were lengthening. With the exception of the owner who was fiddling with a notebook and pencil, the kiosk wore a deserted look.

Deserted? The lady pushed her glasses on her nose and peered down. Hold it! There seemed to be a figure there, lurking in the shadows by the side of the kiosk.

'Why, that's our neighbour down there!' exclaimed the boy's mother. 'What is he doing at the kiosk at this time of the night?'

'Observe his actions,' advised her son.

The man seemed undecided about whether to go to the kiosk or not. He would glance over his shoulder, take two steps forward, then three steps back.

'I get it!' smiled the woman as realisation dawned. 'He doesn't want any witnesses for whatever he plans to do. If somebody passes by as he is heading for the kiosk, he scrambles back into the shadows. I wonder what forbidden item he hopes to buy there.'

Navin had an explanation for his conduct. 'He wants to place a bet on a number.'

'On a number?'

'*Matka*, Mother,' explained Navin. 'He is gambling.'

'Gambling!' his mother was shocked. 'Why, that's the devil's own pastime!'

'It is now our neighbour's, too,' added the teenager cheekily. 'Be with it, Mother. Gambling is in. The poor labourers play cards, the middle class buys lotteries and everyone else plays *matka*. Now, even the Richie rich have their own slot machines.'

'A casino?' The mater frowned.

'Entertainment centre,' clarified Navin. 'Not a casino. It recently opened at a five-star resort in Goa and boasts of twenty entertainment machines and eighteen slot machines. The Government will issue licenses for operating several such centres.'

'What do these machines do?' asked his mother, fascinated.

'They hold the promise of unbelievable riches. You can win Rs 50,000, perhaps even Rs 5,00,000, if the Gods are smiling at you. Of course, the Gods rarely do smile at you. The owners of the Entertainment Centres ensure that.'

'Is this get-rich-quick scheme available at a local hotel?'

'Uh, huh! It is the first such centre in the country. A bit of Las Vegas in *Amchem Goem* (our Goa).'

'Where are you going?' called Navin as his mother rushed out of the room.

'To check my bank passbooks. First thing tomorrow, I go to the bank to withdraw cash. I have this urge to play the slot machines. Who knows, I may be the lucky winner.'

'Mother,' Navin reeled back in mock surprise. 'Gambling! Why, it is the devil's own pastime! What will the Almighty say?'

'Not much,' replied his mater shortly. 'It's none of his business anyway. Besides, what relevance does the Almighty have in Goa today?'

Casino opens in Goa hotel – News Item.

(First published in the *Gomantak Times*, Panaji.)

The Midas Touch

THE GLEAMING BLACK MERCEDES BENZ CAME TO A HALT on National Highway 17. The rear doors of the vehicle opened and two men stepped out.

'This is it, Your Highness!' The first man, a property developer, waved his hand to indicate the surroundings.

There was a pause as King Midas, for it was he, surveyed the lush green paddy fields stretching out in front of him.

The King turned to his companion. 'Is this what you were referring to when you spoke of an untapped gold mine on my land?'

'Nothing less, I assure you. Look around you, Your Highness. Today there is nothing here but paddy fields.' He spat out the words 'paddy fields'. 'Of what use are the fields to anyone? If Your Highness converted this land for non-agricultural use, in eight months it will cease to be an eyesore to the motorists traversing this route every day.'

'What do you propose to do with the land?' asked Midas.

The builder's face took on a dreamy look. 'For starters, I plan to build a housing society here. I will add a shopping mall, a basketball ground and a car park. You will, of course, get a hefty percentage of the profit from the sale of the units.'

Satisfied with the offer, King Midas returned to the palace. The Prime Minister was summoned and informed about the plan.

The Prime Minister was aghast. 'That would mean the destruction of hundreds of square metres of land growing paddy.'

'Think of the money we stand to make,' argued the builder.

'Exactly,' agreed the King. 'Think of the money.'

A year later, the King sat in his treasury counting his money. The land conversions had proved to be a good investment, contributing handsomely to his treasury. Emboldened by the initial success, the King had authorised the conversion of more and more land for 'non-agricultural' purposes.

The King patted his stomach. Counting all that money had made him hungry. He summoned his pageboy and bade him instruct the Palace kitchen to prepare his lunch.

The table was set in the dining room. The King went to inspect the meal – and gasped. Not a single dish was edible. For the main course, there was a brick and a lump of clay. For dessert, there was a bundle of currency notes.

'Explain this outrage!' The King thundered at the cook. 'Where is my *pulao*, my vegetable curry and my salad?'

'I am helpless, Sire,' said the chef, wringing his hands. 'There are no vegetables for the curry, no rice for the *pulao*.'

'No vegetables, no rice?' asked Midas. 'How is that so?'

'You should know why, Your Highness,' replied his subject. 'Did you not order the destruction of all the paddy fields and cultivable area in the state? Now, there are no fields to grow paddy, no plots in which to cultivate vegetables. All that remains are housing societies and hard cash. It's time we learnt to satisfy our hunger with them.'

(First published in the *Gomantak Times*, Panaji.)

The Car Chase

THREE MEN WERE STANDING BY THE SIDE OF THE Dayanand Bandodkar Marg, the tree-lined street that follows the River Mandovi in Panaji, discussing the price of kingfish in the Municipal Fish Market.

Just then, a jet black *Sumo Grande* raced past, barely missing one of the bystanders. If his friend had not pulled him back in time, the oldest member of the group would have had the side of his face and arm full of unexpected Multi Utility Vehicle.

Just as he was about to send a prayer heavenwards for the presence of mind shown by his friend, two more vehicles, a maroon coloured *Qualis* and a dark blue *Scorpio*, followed in the wake of the first car.

The friend went through the same Grab, Hold and Pull Back routine.

'What was that?' asked the twice-rescued man as he righted himself with difficulty. He stared, mouth agape, in the direction in which the cars had disappeared.

'I have no idea,' said the other. 'Maybe they are shooting a chase sequence from a Hindi film. They have a film unit here almost every other day. Maybe, they have reached the part where the villain has the heroine in his clutches and the hero is trying desperately to save her *izzat* and her life.'

'I did not see any cameramen.' The third member of the group entered the discussion. 'It may be a real car chase. Somebody has a massive grudge against someone else and wants to settle the issue with the world as his witness.'

'Who could be chasing whom?' His companion wondered.

'It could be one of those cops and gangsters' routines played out in alarming frequency on the streets of Mumbai. Maybe, the D-company has opened a retail outlet here,' guessed the senior member.

'That would be terrible!' exclaimed his friend. 'We are full up with undesirables in the state. Add the D-company underlings and the mix would be too strong for us.'

'I may be mistaken,' said the older man. 'There may be a harmless explanation for this daylight car chase. It is possible that irate householders fed up of endless 'dry days' in the water supply are pursuing a Public Works Department Official. It could be a Valentine Day's couple being hounded into an early marriage by the Moral Police. Maybe, the T.V channels are chasing an outed Molester about his last transgression.'

He looked up and stepped back hurriedly. 'Look, here they come again.'

Sure enough, the three cars raced past in the reverse direction, accompanied by squealing brakes and raised voices of the occupants of the vehicles. It seemed they had picked up additional baggage en route as three other cars, moving at an equally brisk pace, followed them.

'Did you see who they were?' asked his friend.

'I sure did,' said the youngest member of the group. He had the sharpest eyes and the quickest reflexes of the trio. 'Those chasing the first were an assortment of the Usual Suspects polluting the Goan landscape. I distinctly saw Drug-runner and Extortionist in one of the cars. Child Molester was in the second vehicle, egging Corrupt Cop, who was driving, to go faster.'

'I don't get it,' said his friend. 'Who were they after?'

'I did not actually see her but I can guess.' His colleague made a face. 'Who else but the once peaceful, easy-going state of Goa?'

Sun, Sand and Scandals

ONCE UPON A TIME THERE WAS A LAND BLESSED WITH miles upon miles of sun-kissed beaches, a countryside of verdant splendor and a people who wanted nothing more from life than 'a homely home and simple pleasures, enough to eat and enough to wear.'

That was Goa, before the advent of the tourists.

They came in waves – the conquering hordes, eager to stake their claim to the virgin sands that hugged the coastline, hungry to explore the coconut tree-lined winding lanes that snaked their way through a countryside ensconced in a gorgeous cloak of foliage.

The initial invasion was driven by Flower Power. Roused into anger by the Vietnam War, propelled into protest by the student uprising in Europe, the rebellious youth headed east in search of Shangri La.

As Mao's armies had already overrun the original, they took a detour to newly liberated Goa.

For the flower children, Civilisation was a twelve-letter word. Its trappings were shunned. Its rules were rejected. Its social mores were discarded.

The visitors' needs were simple. All they wanted was to commune directly with Nature. In their natural garb.

The news of this novel form of protest reached the ears of Lotharios from Ludhiana and Casanovas from Calicut, ushering in a fresh wave of arrivals keen on revelling in the natural abundance, far from the disapproving gaze of their mothers and wives.

The iconoclasts populating the silver sands had cast aside their clothes, adopting instead the embrace of a drug-fuelled state of bliss. Maintaining this happy state of affairs meant that the layers of delusion needed to be replenished constantly with fresh infusions of stimulants.

Satisfying this demand required commerce to rear its ugly head in this corner of paradise by setting up retail outlets offering tantalising glimpses of Heaven in exchange for cold hard cash.

The secluded nature of the beaches meant that smuggling, an activity carried out in gay abandon during the Portuguese regime, continued abated. In the old days, gold had been the undisputed favourite of the duty-free merchants. With the passage of years, foreign spirits, electronic appliances and even snakeskins were traded briskly on this midnight exchange.

With Goa catapulting into the honours league of smuggling havens, it was but natural that the Mumbai Underworld would sit up and take notice.

This was back in the good old days when mafia dons carried out acts of murder and mayhem in the hope of securing an obscenely lavish lifestyle in this life, and not the promise of 72 virgins in the next.

Traffic to Goa's famed coastline registered a sharp upswing as gunrunners and weapon traffickers rushed here to explore tie-ups with the bullion traders. Area Commanders of Liberation Armies made flying visits to the territory to sample the wares on display on the silver and gold-en sands. Arms dealers across the borders began to fret as orders were cancelled and armanents went unsold.

As Goan beaches became veritable hives of activities, mostly undesirable, where were the law-enforcing agencies one may well ask. Contary to the caustic observation of one Disgruntled Tourist in the Letters to the Editor column of the local newspaper, the cops were not Missing in Action.

They were hard at work doing the following:

Walking along the sea front stretching their arms, bracing their shoulders and taking deep breaths of the clean, invigorating sea breeze.

Forming teams of twos and threes to snicker as groups of male tourists from Bhatinda and Baroda ogled at the expanse of exposed white limbs laid out on the sands.

Collecting *haftas* from the peddlers of delusion and the gypsy hawkers selling trinkets on the beaches.

Harassing motorcycle pilots for taking more than one pillion rider.

Hounding shack owners into offering them endless servings of the molten liquid.

With such a packed schedule, it is little wonder that not much time was left at the end of the day to attend to the other activities on the beaches.

As the years passed, there were a few changes among those who came to savour the sun, sand and surf.

The flower children of the sixties made way for bargain hunting Britishers. They arrived in numbers robust enough to overcome wave after wave of a German offensive which received reinforcements from the Scandinavian nations.

This was followed by an Israeli invasion with one Goan shoreline even being christened Tel Aviv in honor of the West Asian legions.

When the Israeli contingent began thinning with several members leaving for home, feet first, felled by substance abuse and related issues, it was time to find a replacement population. This came in the form of the Russian offensive.

The new breed of tourists today are as far removed from the visitors of old as the hippies were removed from the constraints of civilization. The flower children may have traded the riches of this world for life on a higher plane. The Muskovites are firm about operating on this plane, complete with makeshift commercial enterprises that blur the distinction between Visitor's visa and Business Visa.

Russian novelists like Dostoevsky and Gogol may have agonized about the soul. His present-day compatriots focus solely on the human body and its material needs.

A visit to a Goan beach today allows one to meet the following cast of characters:

A large contingent of foreign sunbathers, overwhlemingly female, moving around 'with hardly any dress on them' to quote a Goan Member of Parliament. Among them, one may come across a white skinned girl of tender years with very little clothing on her and even fewer friends and relations around her.

An equally robust deputation of male, mainly *desi*, tourists, with plenty of dress and eyes that refuse to veer from this sight. This includes a couple of oglers not content to merely look lasciviously.

Follows the inevitable grope, maybe more, and the quiet of the beach is shattered by cries of 'Molestation'.

This is the cue for the arrival of the other members of the ensemble:

A posse of cops who arrive on the scene – late as usual.

Print, television and cable news reporters, mikes and cameras poised to get sound bytes from everyone and his grandmother.

Socio-psychologists wearing grave looks on their faces.

'Local experts' wearing angry looks, surreptitiously crafting one-liners bemoaning the moral degradation of the state.

Celebrity anchors putting together hardhitting questions even as their teams put together a studio audience for the next episode of 'We, the People' and others of its ilk on the fall of Eden.

Part II

With a Dash of Garam Masala

Keep Walking

Moments In Time

THE CREAM-COLOURED TABBY SUNNING ITSELF ON THE front porch throws a languid glance in my direction. Our eyes meet – mine beckoning invitingly, his sizing me up with an impassive stare.

I am matched against some unknown standard in feline fraternisation – and pass the test.

With slow deliberate movements, he rises, stretches himself, and then, with a gait that would do a royal proud, walks up to me. He arches his back invitingly. Correctly interpreting his action as a command to caress, I lean down to scratch him behind the ears and run my fingers down his soft, furry body.

It is late evening hour and I am on my way home from my evening walk. Around me, the shadows lengthen as joggers loosen their stride in anticipation of the hot bath and dinner awaiting them back home. The streetlights begin to come on.

However, the road stretches ahead invitingly. I decide to walk on, following a stretch of road that weaves its way through picture-postcard pretty homes. No noisy crowds. None of the characteristic sights, sounds, and smells associated with the march of civilisation. Just the clean fresh smell of Nature's bounties on a long, weaving lane.

It is said that there is nothing like a walk to put new vigour in tired muscles and weary minds. Doctors speak highly of its therapeutic effects. Fitness experts swear by its body-toning abilities.

For some, walking is more than just an exercise; it is a means of communion with Nature. It is the time of the day when the mind is uncluttered by the baggage of incomprehensible problems. When the imagination explores uncharted territory even as the feet tread long familiar paths. When ideas germinate into stories even as the legs take a detour to a different street, another lane.

The woman with the duffel bag passes me by. I see her every day, running around a stretch of trees, bag slung over her shoulder. Each day she makes the rounds of the foliage, a pinched expression on her face, sweat flowing freely down her T-shirt.

I wonder about the bag. Is the choice of the shoulder burden dictated by a New Age exercise popular among the with-it set? Is it a Zen thing? Or, just a fun thing?

My attention is diverted by sounds of barking. A jogger and his dog pass by. The jogger nods his head in greeting. The dog pauses to sniff inquiringly at me.

For some reason, I offend his sensibilities. Suspicions fully aroused, he gives a low, threatening growl. I back off. He growls some more. This time it draws the attention of its owner, who, with an apologetic smile, pulls the animal away from temptation.

I step out of harm's way and make tracks for home. En route, I pass the park bench that is a favourite with old-timers of the locality. There are two senior citizens sitting on it, a little old woman with a face that seems to have survived a thousand calamities and a rather stout individual with a discontented look on his face.

Darkness is falling as I make tracks for home. A quick shower and I am ready to join my friends for coffee and some light shopping at the mall. It is time to trade the peace and quiet of the evening for the bustle and noise of that shrine to Mammon.

Nature may whisper in soft gentle tones but money – it talks. And how!

Street Smart

'EVERYTHING IS HAPPENING ON THE ROADS. PEOPLE EAT, sleep, cook and fight on it. Cows, too, live on the roads.' – Tennis legend Boris Becker on the streets of India.

I chanced on this quote from Becker as I was on my way to the city to attend to some chores. It seemed a good time to test the veracity of his observation.

My four-wheeler joined the principal street that runs through the heart of the town. It was a little hard navigating past pedestrians who had spilled onto the road from the sidewalks. The pavements were choc-a-bloc with hawkers, street-criers, panhandlers and rashes of tourists stumbling out of travel agencies lining the street.

As I came to the crossroads, I noticed three cows stretched out on the asphalt near the traffic island, contentedly chewing their cud. The cop on duty seemed supremely unconcerned with the cows turning a busy street into a bovine base.

As I watched, the cows continued to look glassily into space. The cars, scooters and rickshaws milled around them. I turned into a side road, swerving sharply to avoid a couple of pedestrians who had chosen the middle of the street to conduct, going by their facial expressions, a conversation of great import.

Manoeuvring past them, I drove on to find that I had strayed into a tense moment in a neighbourhood cricket match. The street ahead had been converted into a makeshift *maidan* by a group of youngsters. A block of wood in the centre served as the wickets.

As the bowler prepared to toss another yorker at the batsman, I wondered whether I should read the riot act to the future Sachins and Dhonis. Really, is it that hard for parents to teach their kids the basic difference between a busy street and a cricket field?

I decided against advancing their education on this front.

Three stray dogs crossed the road suddenly, forcing me to step on the brakes. A buffalo followed them in leisurely pursuit. I tried to turn into a less occupied lane and found my way blocked. Somebody had parked his car on the curve, limiting my visibility.

Becker was right! There is more to an Indian street than just the vehicles on it.

(First published in the *Gomantak Times*, Panaji.)

One For The Road

DRIVING, AS AN ART, HAS ALWAYS FASCINATED WRITERS the world over. Put a man behind the wheel of a station-wagon or a sedan, and you will find hundreds of potential authors crawling out of the metalwork, pen and paper in hand, ready to immortalise, in scintillating prose, his valiant attempts to smash the speed barrier, chronicle the vehicle's many arguments with pedestrians of varied shapes and denominations, and click a reproving tongue or two at the lamentable lapses into porcine behaviour exhibited by the chief navigator.

George Mikes, in several slim volumes, touched on Italians with an irresistible urge to overtake, Flying Finns who left Paavo Nurmi gasping for breath and other star attractions of the European roads.

P.G. Wodehouse tales are peppered with accounts of daughters of earls and sons of baronets having a determined bash at the world record for driving from Shropshire to London in a two-seater.

Indians, too, have not hesitated in participating in this literary pastime. Taxi drivers stand next only to politicians as the most widely written about class in the media.

The Indian tendency to overtake from the wrong side of the road has agitated countless in-house psychologists of high society periodicals. Bestsellers have been written on the roadside manners of the sons, sons-in-law and nephews-twice-removed of the State and Central Ministers.

Sadly, it is often the motorist who comes out the worse for wear in this literary exercise. He is the chief villain in every version of Road Wars, sowing death and destruction on what was once a bustling city lane.

The natural human tendency to root for the underdog paints him in all shades of black, with a forked tongue and a tail to boot, in his confrontation with pedestrians.

No doubt, a good many decent, sensible persons go berserk when placed behind a wheel. But, more often than not, it is the folk surrounding the vehicle who behave peculiarly once it becomes mobile.

Old women, until then content to swat flies on the sidewalk, venture out on the great, gravelled surfaces, with or without the assistance of the street's resident Boy Scout.

Cricket balls, followed in quick succession by pint-sized batsmen, make the scene in large numbers. Otherwise, staid cyclists develop an urge to practise the death-defying routine that they have perfected for the forthcoming circus trials.

A long time ago, Indian roads were characterised by the resemblance that they bore to a snail dozing in the mid-morning sun. Both appeared to have little to do with the frenetic pace of modern civilisation.

Foot power, whether of man or beast, was the main form of transportation, with only the odd bus or two making an appearance to justify the expense of laying out the asphalt.

With increased modernisation, the number of cars multiplied, effectively dividing the available road space. This signalled the advent of demolition squads masquerading as the telephone department, the water works division, and the craftiest of them all, the Road Repairs Wing of the Municipalities.

Concerted investigations by a team of underground cable men and drainage experts led to the discovery of that horror of the Indian motorways – the pothole. 'Men at Work' signs sprouted up like mushrooms after the first monsoon shower.

To add to these woes were the speed breakers. There were the stone-and-rubble edifices guaranteed to turn a car turtle and lead a driver to avail, feet first, of the services of the local Emergency Ward.

In close competition were bovine versions of the same, four-legged brigades that brought highway traffic to a halt with military precision. Car drivers had to wait, engines running, thumbs twiddling, as an entire herd wandered down the street, sniffing interestedly at every pothole in its path.

The few reckless ones who sought to hasten matters by following the animals' rear ends were stunned into a coronary thrombosis when they collided, head on, wiht a solitary cow, who, in the finest traditions of her sex, had changed her mind at the last minute.

Completing the bump and grind triumvirate were the rubble heap, the gravel mountain and the cement pile, surprise gifts for motorists left at street corners and narrow side lanes by the construction lobby.

Speedometer readings dropped to single figures as cars met wooden beams taking a breather before the next day's schedule. Strategically positioned nails helped reduce speeding by deflating the tyres (and the egos) of high flying Street Hawks.

The last two decades have seen another addition to the list of highway horrors – fast cars driven hard by charged drivers. Speed limits, slowing down at turns and other golden rules of civilisation matter little to the low-flying squad.

The Road Transport Authorities and the Traffic Police had better scour around for new guinea pigs on whom to pin the blame every time the accident curve shows an upward spiral, instead of forever pouncing on the hapless motorist.

The man behind the wheel is far more the wronged against than the wrongdoer.

(First published in *The Times of India*, Mumbai.)

Fear Of Flying

'IN THE MIDDLE AGES PEOPLE WERE TOURISTS BECAUSE of their religion, whereas now they are tourists because tourism is their religion' – Robert Runcie, Archbishop of Canterbury.

With millions of adherents, and the numbers inching up each day, tourism has indeed become the fastest growing religion in the modern world, eclipsing the reach of the more conventional faiths.

For Goans, the former Archbishop's words are particularly relevant given that their state continues to be one of the pre-eminent shrines of this faith.

The vehicle of transport for an overwhelming number of its adherents is the commercial airline. True, there are some folks, principally in the US, who 'summer' using their cars. Europeans also tend to favour the railways.

There are also the Richie Richs who have a weakness for pleasure cruises in ocean liners that serve as floating five star resorts.

However, for a very large part of the world, at least the part undertaking journeys longer than heading for the neighbouring district or state, travel by air is the way to go.

It is not tourism alone that depends on this mode of transport. The business world would be greatly handicapped if planes failed to convey jetsetters from one end to the other of the interdependent village that is today's world.

Despite having the two flourishing industries of tourism and the global economy depend so heavily on it, the airline business is in a bad shape today.

It is not just the rising fuel costs that have led to this situation. Nor are faulty management practices or the sorry tendency of rival carriers to resort to price gouging the reason for this state of affairs. A principal cause for the decline is the spectacular rise of another global industry – terrorism.

It does not help a bit when you are perceived as the destination of choice for terrorists, suicide missionaries and other seekers of the three minutes of fame that comes through Breaking News banner headlines on television.

As it is, one used to board a plane waiting in trepidation to see what the journey had in store – being near a bawling infant or having to occupy an aisle seat next to two unfortunate souls who need to visit the restroom every 15 minutes, and not simultaneously.

Now, one has to worry that the quiet stranger in the seat next to you will rise as the plane reaches cruising altitude and announce a last minute change in the flight plan.

Having taken various intercontinental flights over the last several years, I have been witness to the havoc wrought by the world's burgeoning population of extremists, fanatics and malcontents on the psyche of the international air traveller.

The paranoia attacks commence long before one is even airborne. The notion that this is a dangerous world is brought home to passengers once they join the queue for a security clearance to board the plane.

Depending on the port of departure, the bunker mentality manifests itself in different ways. At European stopovers like Paris and Amsterdam, it shows up in a determined effort to separate the passenger from any carry on bottle containing more than the allotted 100 ml of liquid.

At New York and other US venues, it appears in the form of a long line of weary individuals assiduously removing shoes, socks and boots under the hawkeyed gaze of the TSI official.

At London, it achieves hysterical proportions when the airport security officer calls out, in increasingly strident tones, begging passengers to, 'Please, please, PLEASE, do not remove your footwear!' Unlike those across the pond, the Brits do not want to see your toes protruding out of the holes in your socks.

As a frequent airline passenger, I, too, have had my share of episodes of near panic involving air travel. It is bad enough being confined to a giant metal container for over 14 hours at a stretch with nary an escape route in sight.

The endless press reports of foiled terrorist plots and failed attempts to hijack a plane just serve to heighten the nervousness.

I was sitting at Mumbai airport waiting for my international flight when a forty-something man, nattily dressed and sporting a well-trimmed goatee, occupied the seat next to me.

He parked his mid-sized black suitcase in front of him. Minutes later, he got up and left the hall, leaving his luggage behind.

Ordinarily, I would not have even noticed it. However, these are extraordinary times.

Five minutes passed, and then seven. I glanced at the name-tag on the bag. Uh, oh! I know it is politically incorrect to think of racial profiling but my heart started beating faster. I eyed the suitcase and looked away. It seemed to be staring menacingly at me.

Another ten minutes passed. By now, I was perspiring quite freely. My hands were trembling. The suitcase had sprouted horns and seemed all set to do the first movement of the *Danse Macabre*.

I could not take it any more! I stopped a passing police officer and laid my troubles on his shoulder. I was panicking. He panicked even more and then – the owner returned.

Apparently, there had been a very long line in front of the men's restroom.

Schiphol airport, Amsterdam. I was waiting in line to be asked the usual meaningless drivel about suitcases being packed while being in your, and only your, custody.

A family of nine, count them, nine, boisterous members brazenly cut the line in front of me. Outraged, I appealed to the airline official for justice. One of the queue-cutters walked up to the airline agent and began talking to her in Dutch.

Soon, an animated conversation followed in which, going by the smiles and laughter, little mention was made of bad manners. I was upset and agitated. I was boiling mad with anger.

In the eyes of the airline personnel, I had morphed into a 'suspicious character'.

Suffice to say that a painful interrogation followed in which I was asked all kinds of questions, even those I had not known existed.

It is only when the security officer retired hurt out of sheer exhaustion that I was allowed to board. Never again, I promised myself. I would remain calm even if the whole airport cut in front of me.

Like Woody Allen in *Scoop*, the flight crew, the passengers and the airport security, anyone remotely connected to the industry seems to have taken up anxiety as a form of aerobics. Not as a pastime but as a vocation, given the vigorous nature of the work-out.

Thomas Friedman was right. The world is flat.

Paranoia is everywhere.

Making Twice The Noise

Petrified Provocations

THE PIGEON DID A DOWNWARD SWOOP AND LANDED on the statue of the Great National Leader that stood majestically in the town square. It was taking a well-deserved rest after spending some quality time in the skies.

It flapped its wings in a desultory fashion and then surveyed the ground around the statue. It hoped that the nice old man who came each evening to feed it would not be late today.

'I would advise you to be careful about how you sit on me,' said a deep voice.

Nearly scared out of its wits, the bird looked around trying to trace where the sound was coming from.

'Look to your right,' advised the Voice. The pigeon did as directed.

Incredible! The statue was speaking.

'What do you mean?' The bird was affronted. 'I've been assuming this position for a long time now and you never complained earlier.'

'I do not mind how you sit on me,' said the Great Leader, for it was he who was speaking through his stone image. 'I worry that your actions may be misinterpreted by my admirers. I would not like your wings broken because you failed to observe the basic protocol in dealing with my image.'

'These are sensitive times,' continued the Leader. 'My fans are quick to register outrage if anyone is found disrespecting my image. Last week, one of my statues was found garlanded with footwear.'

'Why would anyone do a nasty thing like that?' The pigeon was puzzled.

'God knows why,' the Leader sighed. 'My admirers were terribly affronted and made public their ire by rioting. According to them, I had been grossly insulted.'

'Why would they believe that you were insulted by this act? Your greatness comes from your deeds not your multiple images. It is just a stone edifice that was vandalised.'

'They contended that an insult to my statue was an insult to me.'

'Isn't that a greater insult?' the bird asked. 'To hold that a silly little effort to grab notoriety somehow lowered your standing in society. Surely, your legion of devotees cannot believe that your image is so fragile that it can be harmed by such acts.'

'I'd like to think that my contribution to this nation was so substantial that pin-pricks cannot affect my standing in the society,' agreed the Leader. 'My fans subscribe to an opposing viewpoint.'

He sighed and continued, 'The nation seems to have become more intolerant since I passed away. This is why I am cautioning you just in case one of my followers objects to your performing a bodily function on my shoulder and vents his ire by tossing a hefty stone in your direction.'

'I'd better leave,' said the pigeon hurriedly. It flapped its wings preparatory to taking flight.

'I little knew,' observed the bird to itself, 'that greatness must be secured with stones. The more fragile an admirer considers his leader, the greater is his perceived esteem for him.'

A Bigger Share For The Better Half

THE CONSTITUTIONAL AMENDMENT BILL SEEKING TO reserve 33% of seats in Parliament for women has drawn a mixed reaction from our political class.

There are women Members of Parliament who are die-hard supporters of the Bill and cannot countenance any change to the draft that has been circulated. All that is left now, they say, is for Parliament to pass the Bill in its present form.

There are male MPs, keen on burnishing their bleeding heart liberal credentials, who see no harm in allowing the Bill to become a law.

Then there is the Yadav trio who worry that a female invasion, of the bob-cut and bobby pins variety, will force them to vacate their seats and, consequently, the limelight.

Due to the diversity of views on the Bill, it was decided to call a meeting of political leaders to discuss how best to ensure its smooth passage.

'The question is not how but when,' said a well-known women legislator. 'Women have been discriminated against for centuries. It is only fair that there is affirmative action in their favour.'

'Hear! Hear!' Her colleagues in gender cried.

A male politician stood up. 'There is not a soul in this country,' he said grandly, 'who will raise his or her voice in protest when we help our mothers and sisters. Reservation for women is necessary. Our party has always been in its favour. It has been on our manifesto for the last three general elections.'

'Then why the reluctance to translate the Act into fact?' Another woman parliamentarian sought to know.

'There are wheels within wheels. We must heed the call of our mothers and sisters but we cannot remain deaf to the entreaties of our backward brothers and our minority uncles. If the best seats are taken by women alone, what will happen to our spurned relatives?'

'This will require reserving seats for OBCs and religious minorities in the entire House, not just among the women's quota,' said a woman MP. 'This cannot be done easily. It needs a national debate to study the consequences, deliberate over the change in the complexion of the House. That will take ages to become law.'

'Exactly,' smiled the male MP.

'We are not trying to stall the issue,' said a member of the Yadav brigade. 'We are merely registering our disapproval of the likely influx of short-haired, well-groomed women from India who will grab a major chunk of the reserved seats.

What will happen to the long-haired 'Look Ma, No Face Cream' females of *Hamara Bharat*?'

'May I interject at this point?' An attractive young person stood up. 'Our friends are beating the wrong end of the stick. In the quota for women, what we will need are not sub-reservations but sub-non-reservations.'

The gathering looked at her in surprise. Non-reservations? What did she mean?

'If reservations of seats for women become a reality,' continued the lady, 'we must ensure that 50% of this quota is spared the invasion of the *bahu, biwi* and *beti* crowd. At least, half the women should make it on their own merit without the crutch of a prominent male member of the family.'

She glanced at her male counterparts. 'You are right. All of us want reservations for our mothers and sisters. But, please, specifically not just for your mothers and sisters.'

The Slim And Trim Force

'IT'S TOUGH BEING A COP THESE DAYS,' GRUMBLED MY friendly neighbourhood police officer.

'What's the matter?' I was surprised. He had always seemed content with his job. 'Are you fed up of the power and the glory associated with your job?'

'Power and glory? Ha!' My companion snorted. 'I call it impotence and ignominy. The cop is everybody's favourite whipping boy.'

'Have our politicians been twisting your arm again?'

'Not more than usual,' was the reply. 'We recognise that maintaining law and order sometimes entails releasing outlaws due to pressure from the higher-ups. It is a cross that we must bear. Pressure on the arms I can handle. However, when it comes to pressure on the stomach....'

I was confused. 'The stomach?'

'It's these damn Hindi films that are the culprits. Earlier, they made us appear as bumbling fools. Facing the

TRIM
GYM

moustached dacoit chief or the politician-cum-ganglord was a rotund, shorts-clad incompetent called Pandu Hawaldar who doubled up as the film's comic act. However, those films had one saving grace. Pot-bellied heroes.'

'That's a plus point?' I was amazed.

'Yes, if you are a cop. With our heroes exhibiting their portly forms, the common folk did not get agitated about the excess weight on the frames of the screen cops. Unfortunately, this happy state did not last. Fitness soon became something of a religion for the New Age hero.'

'What has that to do with your predicament?'

'Our politicians are great fans of Hindi films. When the rest of the cast slimmed down, the plump cop stood out like a sore thumb. This led the powers-that-be to peer closely at our figures, not only on reel but in real life.'

The policeman paused to pat his belly. 'The police force, it was concluded, had become a little too fleshy. It needed to shed the excess flab.'

'By making exercising compulsory?'

'Worse! Strict instructions were issued regarding our diet. Oily foods were a no-no, as were sweetmeats. A daily exercise regime was prescribed.'

'You must admit that your figure could do with some improvement,' I could not help commenting.

'That's not all. The talk is that increments in pay will match decrements in flab.'

'I don't blame them!' I replied. 'A lean, mean hungry Force is the best guarantee for internal security in our country. However, there is a silver lining to your problem.'

'Is there?' The cop leaned forward eagerly.

'Now that the polls have been announced, the politicians are likely to go slow on the slimming drive. A slim-n-trim police officer is a thing of beauty. However, when it comes to tackling booth capturers, criminal gangs and anti-social elements, a few additional pounds are the need of the hour.'

(First published in the *Gomantak Times*, Panaji.)

Headline Hardsell

A TWENTY-SECOND COMMERCIAL FEATURING A DETERGENT soap and the Chief Executive who had recently been released in exchange for two Red Terrorists is taking the advertising industry by storm.

In the 20 second spot, the kidnap victim returns to the scene of his capture. Only to find himself followed in a dimly lit alley in the dead of the night. As he turns around to confront his pursuer, he finds his way blocked by a dubious individual in regulation villain gear, complete with a kerchief covering his face.

Conscious of the paucity of quality militants available for future swap deals by the Government, the industrialist does not hesitate. Confronting his would-be assailant, he demands an explanation.

'Mercy!' bleats the Dubious One, clutching the other's ankles. 'But I needed to know. How are your clothes so extra white? What laundry do you patronise?'

'Laundry nothing,' smiles the magnate, beaming down at the cowering individual. 'Just washed at home with this,' and, with a flourish, he holds up a detergent bar.

Cue for housewives across India who abandon their TV sets to race to the nearest general store and stock up on the Ultras-resistant bar.

Besides winning rave reviews for pulling off the casting coup of the year, the advertisement comes as manna from heaven for agencies hard put to find tempting new morsels with which to bait the advertising hook.

News headlines and brand names – a potent combination! Celebrity advertising is no more the preserve of tinsel town. Current Topics has muscled its way in with a vengeance.

Page Three beauties find their charms waning when compared to the leading lights of Page One even as the only vital statistics that matter are the number of inches typeset in the banner headlines. Advertising executives are working overtime drawing up exhaustive lists of Area Commanders of Liberation Armies and district commander of Naxalite platoons as they finalise the cast for their next commercial offering.

Songwriters are composing catchy little jingles on the troubled Vale of Kashmir. (Neighbour's Envy. Owner's Pride!) Tunesmiths are drawing inspiration from the latest 'hits' of heavy metal groups like the *Lashkar-e-Toiba* and *Jaish-e-Mohammed.*

Hot-shot photographers are scouting for exotic settings for next year's Spring Collection in Sopore and Baramulla.

The endlessly squabbling political class features as the lead player in a 15 second soft drink commercial. Just as insults are flying fast and furious across the hall in Parliament, an upper limb of unknown parentage makes the scene, holding out the drink. Follows a mad grab for the proffered delight and, hey presto, the glares and the frowns are replaced by beatific smiles. 'Shady dealer,' says one member to another but in a voice dripping with honey. 'Morally challenged,' counters the other in an equally saccharine tone.

The most ambitious venture yet is the sixty-second commercial celebrating Incredible India. Featuring close-ups of Naxal hotbeds in Chhattisgarh, Indian Mujahideen cells in Pune and terrorist hideouts in Kashmir, it is a celebration of the coming together of an age-old culture and twenty-first century molten passions.

The past and the present like nowhere else.

Look no further!

Kidnap victim to feature in detergent ad – News Item.

(First published in the *Gomantak Times*, Panaji.)

No Rules. Just Right

A Profile Of Our Beloved Leader

ON THE FORTIETH BIRTH ANNIVERSARY OF OUR BELOVED Leader, his legion of loyal followers and sundry back-scratchers would like to present before the public a brief profile of this dynamic personality.

This voice of the masses was born to humble and god-fearing parents in a small village in the heart of rural India. Almost immediately, he began to exhibit the leadership qualities that he is famed for today.

His statesman-like nature stood revealed even before he soiled his first diaper. No sooner had he begun stringing words together to form a sentence than he had given voice to his innermost feelings.

'All Indians are one,' had lisped the two-year-old toddler.

Secularism has been a way of life for our leader since his primary school days. While still in Nursery, he had made it a point not to discriminate while making friends

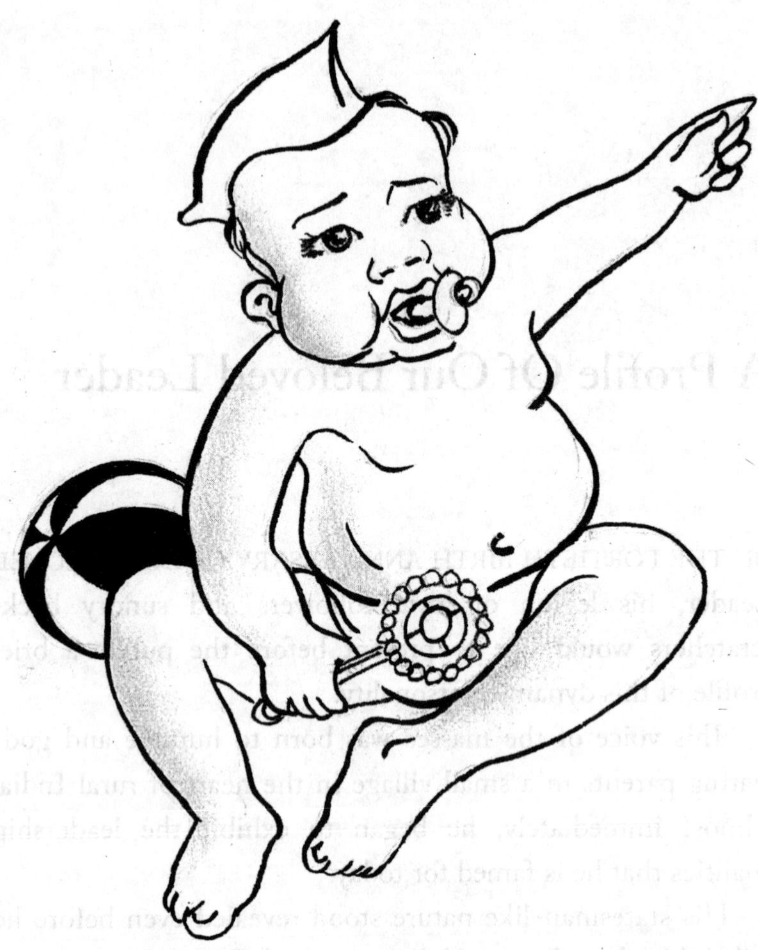

with youngsters belonging to different castes, sub-castes and communities.

By the time he was promoted to Lower Kindergarten, the young boy was already exercised about the rising tide of communalism in the country. His play hour, and often his naptime, would be spent pondering over the dangers that this would entail to the future of the nation.

'Of what use are the fruits of development if we cannot live together as brothers and sisters?' he would ask his class teacher.

The welfare of his fellow citizens has always been a subject close to our leader's heart. His boyhood and teenage years, were spent serving the cause of the Common Man. In school, he made it a point to spend two years in one class to get adequate time to address himself to the problems faced by the Indian tween and the Indian teen.

In college, he was in the forefront of all the agitations organised by the student community. He burnt his first bus at sixteen, and exchanged blows with his first police officer two years later.

By the time he was eighteen, he had familiarised himself with the insides of the major jails of his district whose wardens looked forward to his periodic visits to their fiefdoms.

Even before he made the transition to the twenties, his bruised and battered visage had made it to the front pages of leading dailies – another victim of Police Brutality.

It was but natural that such an individual would opt for a career in public service. He took to politics as a *hawaldar* (police constable) takes to a *lathi* charge, or as a Member of the Opposition takes to molded leather suitcases twelve hours before the tabling of a 'No Confidence Motion' in Parliament.

Soon, he was knee-deep in campaigns aimed at wiping the teardrops from the faces of the poor and the forsaken.

When the polls were announced, our leader was the party's automatic choice as candidate for the Lok Sabha seat.

He vindicated the trust reposed in him by the party bosses. He drew heavily on the support-base built up during his days in the slammer – and slammed the door of Parliament in the face of his opponents.

His unconventional methods of making friends and influencing people attracted the notice of the High Command that rightly concluded that his formidable muscle power was better used at the national level. Within no time, he had the ear of the Prime Minister who came to rely on him for all matters pertaining to the state.

However, our leader's rising fortunes did not cause him to lose touch with his people. He hired a top interior designer to redecorate his Ministerial cabin so that visitors from the backwaters of his constituency could acquaint themselves with the latest advances in office comforts when they paid him a visit.

He regularly toured the length and breadth of the land – using an Air Force plane in times of drought, a helicopter in times of floods.

He also made sure that every such visit received wide coverage in the official media so that his constituents were assured of seeing a familiar face when they gathered around the community television set in the village every evening.

However, our leader's work is far from complete. There are still so many hungry mouths to feed, so many naked torsos to clothe. A visionary's work is never done.

Here's wishing Our Beloved Leader many more years of selfless service to the nation!

(First published in the *Gomantak Times*, Panaji.)

Politics Redefined

THE FAST-PACED POLITICAL DEVELOPMENTS IN VARIOUS parts of the country in the past few weeks have left most Indians bewildered and more than a little confused.

Many a citizen has confessed to feeling hopelessly outdated when confronted with the new breed of politicians and their innovative style of politicking. The changing political fashions have led to the re-defining of oft-repeated words like secularism, communal harmony and social equity to suit emerging trends in nation building.

A group of political enthusiasts have come together to compile a political dictionary for the public. This book will help nonprofessionals interpret the statements of their politicians and give them a clear picture of modern-day Indian politics.

Here is a choice selection of old political favourites and their new definitions:

Social justice: Investing in a section of society with the just hope of harvesting a record number of votes from them in the next elections.

Social discord: Revolt by the leftover sections on being denied a share of the reservation cake.

Social transformation: Rich returns from the aforementioned investments.

Socially backward classes: Politically forward classes.

Reservations: Booking a seat in the next Lok Sabha.

Communalism: A serious threat of being dislodged from the seat of power.

Combating communalism: A life-and-death struggle to combat the threat.

Communal amity: Emerging successful from the trial of strength. (See also, Burying the ghost of communalism.)

Need of the hour: Crossing the floor to the other side.

Need of the nation: A split in the party.

Vote of confidence: Free-for-all.

People's wishes: That their Member of Parliament be awarded with a Ministership.

People's interests: That he (or she) explores all possible means of obeying this directive from his (or her) constituents.

Honouring the mandate: Joining the Cabinet.

Betrayal of the people: Denying one's son, daughter or nephew a share of the spoils.

Unconditional support: Until the supporting group is denied its next extravagant demand by the Government.

Invitation to form the Government: Successful completion of a life-long struggle.

Oath of office: Dreams come true!

Forming the Cabinet: Rewarding old faithful.

Responsibility without power: Power without responsibility.

Shunning public office: Rejecting mere Ministerships for the Prime Ministership.

Broad-based Council of Ministers: Gargantuan Ministries.

Nation: An eternal vote-bank.

Democracy: A system that offers every politician an opportunity to aim for a Ministership, a Chief Ministership or a Prime Ministership.

And finally,

People: A forgotten commodity.

(First published in *The Times of India*, Mumbai.)

The ABC Of Candidate Selection

WITH POLLING DAY A MERE TWENTY-FOUR HOURS AWAY, I decided to survey the candidates in the fray before pledging my support to one of them. I had planned to go around town, to seek them out, but this being poll time, each hopeful landed at my front door, right hand extended, with an ingratiating smile on his, or her, face.

The first arrival was the representative of ABC party. 'We offer stability, prosperity and peace,' said the politician.

He launched into a list of things he would do if elected. He also launched into a list of things his opponents would not do if elected. I was impressed.

I would have pledged my vote for him but for a niggling doubt.

'Were you not part of DE Front some time back?' I asked.

'Indeed I was,' agreed my visitor. 'I left it when I realised it could not help me address the aspirations of the poor.

Subsequently, I joined the FGH combine but resigned when it became a threat to secularism. Till a few weeks ago, I was part of IJ.'

'Did IJ challenge your vision of democracy?' I was curious.

'It did worse. It denied me the party ticket for this position. That caused me to come home to ABC. You may recall I was part of this group a couple of years ago.'

The next candidate belonged to LMN party. He had a unique reason for seeking my support. 'If you choose me,' I was informed, 'you get two for the price of one. I am contesting here as a candidate of LMN and in the next constituency as an Independent.'

'Is that permitted?' I asked surprised.

'Everything *chalega*,' he announced grandly. 'I have a bonus in store for you. In case I am elected but LMN fails to make it to the Government, I am amenable to change loyalties to OP, QRS, TU or even the VW group. I promise to do it for your benefit.'

'Thank you!' I said gratified. It was nice to know that someone somewhere *cared*.

The parade continued until all the candidates had met me and sought my support.

'So, which party will you choose?' asked my friend. 'Choose with care,' he advised. 'Don't just plumb for any X, Y or Z.'

'Who will get the X stamp of approval?' I mused. 'Y, it is quite clear what I plan to do. It matters not what party I choose as the candidate will inevitably shift to a rival formation once the results are in. I will play it safe. My vote will go for Z.'

'Z?' The neighbour looked at me inquiringly.

'Z as in Zzzzz,' I smiled.

Special Topics in Calamity Physics

INDIA'S LONG-DRAWN GENERAL ELECTION IS FINALLY ending. In a few days from now, the rich electoral stew of regional demands, caste combines and egoistical satraps will bubble over with what will be, one hopes, a relatively stable Federal Government.

In democracies the world over, people vote to decide who will run the nation. In India, this is the first rung in the ladder of Government formation. To attain power in New Delhi, political groups must cobble together post-poll alignments, indulge in horse-trading and conduct ruthless negotiations for plum Ministries in exchange for Members of Parliament (MPs).

Come Counting Day and the scramble up the remaining rungs begins in earnest.

In India, we subscribe to Democracy 2.3, customised for local tastes.

A vote cast for Party A may well morph into support for Party B, be used to snub CD even as it flirts with EFG while cocking a snook at HIJK, traversing the entire length of the alphabet soup of political formations as counting begins. A solid punch of the button for a party can evolve into a fluid alliance with its rival, transcend into an amorphous mass traversing the political space, filling out any ideological size or shape of container into which it is tossed with impunity, in the name of political expediency.

The world may rhapsodise over that marvel of political science that is an Indian Election. What are astounding are the parallels it bears to that other great science celebrating Uncertainty and Indeterminism – Quantum Mechanics.

Consider the central premise of a science that drew a derisive, 'God does not play dice' from Einstein in 1926: Nature is inherently random and unpredictable.

Fast-forward to the Indian political theatre circa 2009. With the ruling Congress making overtures to the Communist Party at dawn only to snub it by evening and the Opposition Bharatiya Janata Party burying a regional heavyweight at breakfast only to praise him by tea-time, can there be a better illustration of the fickle nature of, well, Nature, than the results of an Indian Election?

Unpredictable? Check. Uncertainty? You cannot get chancier than this.

On the very small scale, says quantum physics, it is impossible to know the exact position and speed of an object at the same time – the famous Heisenberg's Uncertainty

Principle. With the prospects of a hung Parliament looming large, majorities will be cobbled together on the very smallest scale – at the level of a single MP.

Now, confide in me – Do you have the foggiest idea of what will be the exact location of your representative on Counting Day?

Would you be able to hazard a guess at the speed at which he (or she) will zigzag from one political front to another once the numbers are in?

Try to pin down one's MP to a political formation and there is a certain possibility that you may find him there.

Hold it. He has moved somewhere else. He could be here, there, anywhere, the probability of his presence increasing the closer a formation is to the half-way mark of the House of Representatives.

His behaviour resembles that of an electron in an atom – his location a matter of chance, unfettered by the inconveniences of party ideology or voter preference.

This ability to turn up in unexpected places is shared by MPs – and objects on the microscopic scale.

In quantum physics, we call it tunnelling. In electoral politics, it goes under the sobriquet of Look Ma, No Hands!

There is always a tiny possibility that a particle confined to this side of a high wall can magically materialise on the other side, seemingly able to tunnel through what seemed an impenetrable barrier.

So, when a political group vanishes from the ranks of the Left to rematerialise on the Right side once the latter appears closer to the finish line, it won't be the lure for power that guides this decision.

Just the plain simple rules that govern the fascinating world of Quantum Physics.

A Style For Every Story

Strike Out!

THE EMPLOYEES OF THE CENTRAL GOVERNMENT ARE troubled over the long delay in receiving their pay arrears and have decided to go on strike to register their disapproval over the wait.

After a brief period when a lull persisted in worker – manager disputes, it is back to grievance season in Labour Land.

The season of strikes has returned. Suddenly, everybody seems to have acquired a set of grievances that necessitates the suspension of his or her day-to-day activities.

Transport operators remain firm about not occupying the driver's seat until their demands are met. Bank employees take the day off from work to remind the Finance Minister of what is still pending as unfulfilled demands in their current accounts.

Airlines pilots refuse to soar into the skies while their monthly pay packets stay grounded. Workers belonging to all the remaining industries are abandoning their posts to express their solidarity with other striking colleagues.

Going on strike seems to be a popular pastime of not just the human race, but the plant and the animal world as well. Even Mother Nature, that indefatigable worker, seems to have resolved to protest against her exploitation by resorting to a few stalling techniques of her own.

Inanimate objects, long considered ignorant of twentieth century labour legislation, are proving to be as intransigent as the average worker on protest.

The monsoons are on strike. The South-West monsoons have suspended operations for a fortnight and appear likely to continue their agitation for some time to come.

Rumour has it that Mother Nature, upset with the unsatisfactory conclusion of climate change negotiations, is making her feelings known through one of her faithful deputies.

My vehicle has been on strike for some time now. Though I conceded its demands by fitting new tyres, giving it a tune-up and throwing in an unscheduled servicing, it refuses to step out of the garage.

Our telephone has struck work since the middle of last month. As the Government now permits subscribers to carry the instrument with you wherever you go, I picked it up and carried it – to the nearest trashcan.

It remained perched on the neighbourhood refuse for three days until I realised that the garbage collectors, too, were on strike. Fearful that my environment-conscious neighbour would resent the dumping of a non-biodegradable, non-functional object in the rubbish heap, I buried it by the side of the road.

It surfaced the next day, as one of the treasures unearthed by the Road Repairs wing of the Municipality. Why does it not ever go on strike?

Obviously, influenced by all the protests, little Raju decided to go on a one-man strike. The immediate provocation – the incessant nagging from his mother to do his homework.

'Enough is enough!' shouted the little boy. 'As of now, I'm on an indefinite strike. I refuse to do my homework, clean my room or put away my toys until the following demands are met: No vegetables for dinner, relaxed bedtime hours and regular gifts of chocolates.'

However, like protestors the world over, Raju was careful to leave room for a compromise. 'I'm open to negotiations,' he announced grandly.

Raju's mother was not similarly inclined. She picked up her son and placed him face down on her knee.

Strike! Strike! The palm of her hand came firmly down on the seat of his pants.

The strike was withdrawn unconditionally.

'You would make a terrible modern-day employer,' sobbed the little boy. 'You don't know the basics of dealing with the workforce.'

(First published in *The Times of India*, Mumbai.)

The Artful Dodgers

IT IS EXAMINATION TIME ONCE AGAIN! THE TIME OF THE year when diehard slackers turn into bookworms, and long-forgotten textbooks are dug out, dusted and delved into as part of a last minute cramming session.

Exams also signal a last-minute cramming session. The path to a good grade is a long and arduous one. It is a rare soul who can stick to the straight and narrow path. Most of the others opt for the numerous short cuts along the route.

Cheating in examinations these days is no longer the rush job of the yesteryears. No more is copying restricted to sneaky sideway glances into the neighbour's answer sheets when the supervisor's back is turned. Today's students frown on such pedestrian efforts. The clumsy cribbers of yesterday have given way to the Artful Dodgers of today.

Modern cheating techniques can well be compared to present-day warfare, so meticulous is the planning and so aggressive the implementation.

Training begins in right earnest at least three months before the exams.

Scouts are dispatched to the concerned Board or University and particulars of the likely examiners are obtained. The supervisor's family history is studied and contacts established.

Side-by-side, hawkers in seedy localities are assiduously cultivated. They can be relied upon to offer a sneak preview of the question papers – for a price. Also courted are obliging academics, willing to decipher the same – also for a price.

Discreet inquiries into the past practices of supervisors follow. Should the man be a sporting type, offering not to see all that he must not see, all preparations are suspended forthwith. A walkover is assured.

If indications point to a tough egg, the training resumes with added vigour.

Come examination eve and it is time for the advance guard to move in. Armed with pencils and penknives, the recruits penetrate the exam halls.

Two hours of swift and silent labour later, the highlights of the year's syllabus find themselves reproduced on desktops and all over the walls. Does the 'integration by parts' formula elude you? No problem! Turn sideways and the wall to your right will refresh your memory.

The D-day dawns. The bell sounds the start of the three-hour ordeal. For the first ten minutes, inactivity reigns supreme. Soon, well-informed sources of paper make the scene in large numbers. They appear from under the waistbands of skirts, down socks and up shirtsleeves.

As if on cue, rows upon rows of blank faces are suddenly suffused with knowledge. Hitherto empty sheets start filling rapidly with the fruits of enlightenment. For some candidates, the human body is the best medium. Paper crinkles, skin does not. So, salient features of the main topics of study are painstakingly written on the upper arm.

Exam time also witnesses the launch of a range of user-friendly garments. Pockets are back in fashion, the more spacious the better. Windcheaters and large-sized hiking boots become the rage on campuses.

Inanimate objects are not the only ones recruited for the task. The services of the animate ones, too, are solicited. Favoured with a window seat, one master strategist enlisted the services of a feathered friend to airdrop relief supplies dispatched by an accomplice standing outside the examination hall.

Unfortunately, the frequent appearances of the bird made the supervisor suspicious, and all further flights were immediately suspended.

Once the exams are over, the mopping up operations commence. The aforementioned contacts are once again prodded, this time to ensure that the marks are awarded freely, generously.

If, despite all this, the candidate fails to make the grade, then what he had long suspected has finally come true.

The examination system has gone to the dogs!

(First published in *The Sunday Observer*, Mumbai.)

Austerity Measures

EVER SINCE THE *ENFANT TERRIBLE* OF THE COUNCIL OF Ministers, Shashi Tharoor, wrote snarkily about flying cattle class in solidarity with the holy cows of Indian politics, it has become fashionable to be poor.

Or, unrich to use a more palatable alternative. The word 'poor' still has the tendency to conjure up images of starving babies, emaciated mothers and 'The City of Joy.' Unrich has a nice, clinical ring to it.

Poverty is in. Ostentation is definitely out. Flaunt your finery at a society do and you will draw the wrath of society matrons, celebrities and the usual contingent of *jholawallas* and those whose hearts bleed for the *aam aadmi*.

A ride down the street in your brand new Multi Utility Vehicle will no longer fetch you admiring glances and envious stares. Pedestrians are more likely to turn their heads in disgust, passing uncomplimentary remarks on taunting and flaunting.

The economic crisis facing our nation has affected its political class, too. Elected representatives, for whom penury featured more in the preaching than the practising, are discovering the virtues of austerity measures.

Cabinet Ministers are threatening to behave like the commoners they were before power corrupted them absolutely. The Chief Minister makes an appearance on the front pages of newspapers to keep the people informed of every step taken in the glorious march of austerity.

An early move was to enforce a ten percent cut in the salaries of Cabinet Ministers. For some time, Ministers revelled in their newfound poverty.

They soon came to the realisation that the cut had had no impact on their pockets. They could take a 100 % cut and still not feel the pinch. The benefits alone helped maintain a high standard of living. Obviously, measures that were more effective had to be found.

'How about a blanket ban on air travel?' suggested the Chief Minister.

There were loud protests against this suggestion. One minister wondered how he could attend to his duties if he was grounded for an indefinite period.

Another colleague threatened to join the dissidents if the measure was enforced. The rebel leader sat back, salivating at the prospect of his rival being felled by an own goal.

'I have a suggestion,' said another Minister. 'Curbing air travel or restricting furniture allowances are just cosmetic changes. What we need is an in-depth study of the problem, a committee to explore the entire gamut of governmental spending. It should not be a rush job. Let them deliberate on finding ways and means of reducing expenses. Let them study the pros and cons of each austerity measure.'

'What is the time frame of this committee?' asked the Chief Minister.

'At least six months,' came the prompt reply. 'Hopefully, the country would have sorted out its economic problems by then.'

(First published in the *Gomantak Times*, Panaji.)

Page Three And All That

SOCIALITE SIMI PACED THE ROAD IMPATIENTLY. IT WAS seven am and the newspaper boy had still not made an appearance.

Did he have to be late today of all days? She could hardly breathe, so excited was she at the thought of grabbing hold of the paper and turning its pages to....

Up the street and round the corner, Wannabe Wanda looked out of the window for the fiftieth time. This was just too bad. The paperboy was late AGAIN, for the third time in seven days.

The sound of a horn made her rush to the window. False alarm! It was a passing motorist, not the delivery boy honking to let her know he had thrown the newspaper outside her porch.

The suspense was unbearable. When, when would she be able to lay her hands on the paper and turn the page to...?

The delivery boy was not far from her house. If you went further up the street, down an incline and made a sharp turn rightwards, you reached Jet-set Javed's home. It was here that the newspaper deliveryman's scooter was parked as he handed five different dailies to the head of the household.

As the last daily changed hands, Mrs Javed came rushing out of the house, eager anticipation written all over her face.

'Well?' she demanded as Javed turned the pages over until he came to that all-important page – the cluster of snapshots chronicling the adventures of the rich and the famous on the previous evening.

'Nothing.' Javed's voice was thick with disappointment.

'That's impossible!' cried the missus. 'You must not have looked properly. Give me the paper.' She seized it from his hand.

Nouveau Riche Nina had made it to the page, despite having forgotten most of her clothes at home. As had Mover Mikhail while joining hips with Shaker Sasha even as With-it Waman watched, a silly grin and 'This is the life' written all over his face.

In another photo, Lion hunter Lazarus beamed. Not only had he snagged the coveted spot next to the Celebrity-in-Chief but also he had dispatched his bitter adversary, Upstart Uday, to the outer reaches of the frame.

'Nothing in the second paper, *nada* in the third,' observed Javed bitterly.

There was a pinched look on Mrs Javed's face as she scanned the photographs in the fourth publication. What was that D-lister Nancy doing on Page Three? There she was, cool as can be, seated at a table with what appeared to be her extended family.

It was bad enough that B and C graders sneaked their way into the newsprint. Now this outrage! Did the unwashed masses have to muscle their way into everything? Was nothing sacred anymore?

'I hosted the event in the Club of the moment. The band was hot, the guest list hotter. I even added some *goras* and *goris* for that all-important *phoren* look. The copy spoke of how "the music hit the right notes" and how "all in all, a good time was had by all". Why did we not make the cut?' Javed was distraught.

Down the road, Wannabe Wanda agonised over the same question. Five evenings in a row, she had graced the most-happening event in town. Her outfits were the last word in glamour; her dance moves the final step in seduction. She had spared no effort in her drive to join the ranks of the Bold and the Beautiful.

All for nothing. It was enough to make her howl with rage.

Three houses along the street, the newspaperman watched as Socialite Simi scanned her sheet. 'This is a news-hungry street,' he remarked. 'Folks can't wait to read the latest headlines.' He peered over her shoulder at the open pages of the newspaper. 'Have there been more bomb blasts? Did another Government fall?'

'Who knows? Who cares?' Simi cast a scornful glance at the newspaperman. 'You are behind the times. People no longer read the newspaper to find out what is happening in the world. They read it to make sure the world knows what is happening in their lives.'

Some Things Money Can't Buy

The Great Freedom Run

IT WAS THE START OF THE GREAT FREEDOM RUN. AT THE venue, thousands of people waited impatiently for the start of the race. Fresh-faced youngsters, bored adolescents, jaded old men—they had all gathered there to run for their country—to run for freedom!

Bang! The starter's gun sounded its solitary note and we were off! Running by my side was a reporter who was covering the event for his newspaper.

We had begun to gain momentum when a police officer raced past us.

'What are the cops doing at a fun race?' I wondered.

'He is a member of the Central Reserve Police Forces,' explained the scribe. 'He's off to New Delhi to inform the Centre of the latest law and order situation in the Red Corridor. There have been 62 cases of extortion, 14 shoot-outs, 13 kidnappings and 43 other unsavoury incidents, I

think, at the last count. The Naxalites are keeping him very busy indeed.'

'Making arrests?'

'No. Keeping count.'

We jogged on. Just as we were completing the first lap, two well-built individuals elbowed their way through the crowds and dashed past us.

'Goodness!' I exclaimed. 'Did you notice the speed at which they were moving? They must be professional runners.'

'The one on the left is Inflation,' said the scribe. 'He's always been a fast mover. Besides, he has had intensive training in the last few months. The other man is Corruption. He always runs side-by-side with Inflation.'

As we moved ahead, we passed a sad-faced youth in full running gear on our way.

'How strange!' I commented. 'He appeared to be moving in the opposite direction.'

'That's Indian sport,' replied my companion. 'It tends to move in the reverse direction.'

We had reached the halfway mark of the race. Suddenly, there was a commotion behind us. Turning around, we saw three roughnecks elbow their way through the crowd, rudely pushing aside all those who happened to come in their way.

'What an uncouth lot!' I was appalled by their behaviour.

'Sssh!' The scribe put a warning finger on his lips. 'Those are Money-launderer, Briber and Blackmarketeer. Watch how they shove aside the old woman who comes in their path. She is Moral Values. Poor woman! She always gets a beating from the trio.'

Just then, there was a commotion and a motley group of runners overtook us. They made up in speed what they lacked in manners, with one of the participants almost knocking me into the wayside ditch in his hurry to get ahead.

As I pursed my lips preparatory to making a caustic observation about their uncouth behaviour, the lead runner veered sideways and took a detour away from the main track. Even more remarkably, every one of the team changed tracks and followed him off the course.

'What was that about?' I looked at my companion, bewildered.

'That's the 24/7 News Hound,' he explained. 'He must have taken off for a restroom break.'

'Why did the others follow him?' I inquired.

'They are the rival channels. They probably thought he had found something juicier on the sidelines and followed him off the field in search of higher TRP ratings.'

There was a short pause and then the reporter spoke up once more.

'Well, well!' he observed, amused. He was watching a short, stocky man who was running ahead of us, his face a deep hue of red, thanks to his exertion. Every now and then, he would pause to look fearfully over his shoulder.

Behind him followed a set of out-of-shape runners, puffing and panting, as they tried to overtake him.

'The man in front,' explained the reporter, 'is the Chief Minister. He is racing ahead to check if he still occupies the Chair. Those hard at his heels are the dissidents. They are as eager to ascertain if they succeeded in dislodging him.'

'Why are they here?' I wondered. 'Whom do they expect to meet at this race?'

The scribe directed an amused glance at me. 'Look in front of you,' he advised.

I did as I was told and nearly did a double take.

The track ahead was swarming with security men. Black Cat commandos, Central Reserve Police personnel and the local constabulary – all the law-enforcing agencies seemed to have sent their representatives here.

'That's Z+++ security,' explained the scribe. 'Do you see that speck in the distance? That is the High Command. They are trying to catch up with the One in Authority.'

We were a hundred metres from the finish. Ahead of us ran a small boy, the Indian tricolour clutched tightly in his hand. Wearing a determined look on his face, the lad trotted resolutely towards the finishing line.

Suddenly, there was a loud roar. Turning behind, we saw Gunrunner, Inflation, Corruption and all our old friends come charging towards the finishing line, each one determined to get there first.

In the stampede that followed, the youngster was pushed to the ground and his flag thrown a few feet away from him.

The lad waited until the mob moved away. Then slowly getting up, he picked up the flag. Gently dusting it, he resumed running, the tricolour fluttering proudly in his hand.

Agonising minutes later, he had crossed the finishing line.

'That,' said my companion, his voice choked with emotion, 'is Hope for the Future.'

(First published in *The Navhind Times*, Panaji.)

Quo Vadis, Democracy

INDIA IS TOUTED AS THE WORLD'S LARGEST DEMOCRACY. As a people, we remain wedded to a system of governance of the people, for the people and by the people.

Democracy is the way to go in the New Millennium. Communism is passé, though Putin and his polonium posse may argue that it is days away from its expiration date. Dictatorships are looked at askance, unless their interests converge with ours, in which case we do not look in that direction at all. Fascism is on the decline, like tuberculosis, except when a high profile case brings it flaring back to life, again like tuberculosis.

Anarchy occasionally thrusts itself into the limelight, notably in Iraq, but it is the considered opinion of most people that this is not *kosher*.

India hollers from the rooftops every time it has a general election. One billion strong for democracy! The US trolls the globe marketing democracy with missionary zeal. If the pill sometimes gags in the throat, the fault lies not with the doctor but the ingrate patient too dumb to swallow what is best for him.

Yes, democracy is the ideal form of governance.

Nevertheless, is it? Is democracy all that it is cracked up to be?

I come from a small state in India – Goa. In the 1960s, it was the preferred destination of the psychedelically inclined. These worthies promoted self-rule in its purest form by abjuring rules, regulations, even clothing. Sort of like Democracy – Super Sized.

Since the 1990s, however, its governance has become a showcase of all that can go wrong with democracy. Ideally, the public votes in a government for a fixed term – five years in India, five in the UK, four in the US, after which it returns to the polls either to renew the incumbent's lease or demand a change.

In the interim period, governments do what they supposedly do best – keep the economy afloat and ensure that main-artery bridges do not collapse during rush hour.

In reality, governments are formed on razor-thin majorities and tremendous energy is expended in evolving ways of toppling them via floor crossing and horse-trading.

When Goa became a state, it got a 40-member Assembly. Then, cynics had drawn parallels with Ali Baba and the forty thieves. Little did they realise their prescience.

Parliamentary democracy in India requires that the party gaining a majority in the House forms the Government. In a

40 member House, this means the group with 21 members gets the spoils.

Unfortunately, the last several polls left the House evenly divided between the two main coalitions, give or take a couple of seats. If Team 1 had 21 members and Team 2 had 19, it was easy for the Opposition to persuade some ruling party members to defect. Easy pickings lay among the disgruntled folk who missed the choice cuts of pork – Ministerships and Directors of Corporations.

Soon, floor crossings became rampant. The asking price for a legislator raced past that of a dowry-seeking groom in the marriage market – 'not even in the same galaxy' as Rick Hilton had crowed to Barbara Walters. The complexion of the House changed several times over the next five years.

Parliament passed the Anti-Defection law to curb this practice with at least one-third of a group required to change sides. Independents could not change their allegiance. Period. Violate these rules and you lost your membership of the Assembly.

This changed things, not necessarily for the better. Now, instead of the solitary malcontent, teams traded places. Legislators who did the switcheroo on their ownsome lonesome were disqualified. Polls were announced and the same faces returned to represent their rival formations in the Assembly.

In the last 20 years, Goa has seen 19 elected Chief Ministers. Legislators have waltzed from Party A to Party B, resigned, been re-elected, moved to C, resigned, been re-elected … well you get the drift.

On each occasion, a weary population makes another trip to the polling booths, asking one another, 'Tell me again, why are we lucky that we do not live under a dictatorship?'

The *New York Times* columnist Nicholas Kristof believes China has a better chance to outpace India as the powerhouse of the world economy by AD 2100. It makes sense.

The single party governing China can focus on growth with little concern for the outcome of the next polls. In India, market forces revving up the economic engine must contend with democracy's foot being placed firmly on the brake.

Fractious coalitions jostling for the spoils of office. Governments teetering on the edge until the next election releases them from the misery. Can double-digit growth ever hope to be single-minded focus of any country in the face of such competing challenges?

Remind me again, why is democracy the Holy Grail of Governance?

A Bonfire Of The Vanities

595 MADISON AVENUE, MANHATTAN. I STOOD OUTSIDE the headquarters of Antiquorum Auctioneers, venue of the auction of the personal items of Mahatma Gandhi. They included his trademark spectacles, a pair of sandals, a pocket watch, a plate and a bowl.

Not an impressive list for one of the tallest leaders of the twentieth century. Then, Gandhi believed in eschewing material wealth in favour of strength of character.

There was chaos all around me. Reporters jostled with news anchors in search for sound bites, photographers butted heads with television camera operators, and business tycoons elbowed aside rivals sneaking into their picture frames as they held forth on peace and non-violence.

Clearly, the passions aroused in India over the sale of Gandhi's belongings had spilled out on the East side of Manhattan.

I glanced at the pocket book of quotes by Gandhi in my hand and read, 'I believe in equality for everyone except reporters and photographers.' Bolstered by this pithy reflection, I sidestepped the microphone thrust under my nose and entered the building.

I was immediately greeted by the smell of incense and the soft strains of *Vaishnava Janato*, the leader's favourite hymn.

Ahead of me, seated in the lotus position, with eyes closed and a gentle smile on his face, was James Otis, the owner of the Gandhi memorabilia. He was taking a break to cleanse his mind before the start of the auction.

Some sixth sense, maybe the click of a microphone being turned on, alerted him of further publicity to be had. He opened his eyes.

'No more interviews,' he waved a weary hand. 'I've spent the last 72 hours negotiating with the Indian Government on how they must allocate their finances. It's been brutal.'

He turned to beam at a passing TV camera. '5% is my absolute last offer on Anti-poverty programmes. The Mahatma would never have settled for less.'

'It seems a little sordid haggling thus over Gandhi's possessions,' I observed. 'Why not just donate them to the Indian people?'

In answer, I received a withering look. 'Talk sense,' said the champion of the oppressed.

I walked ahead and came across two men, an Indian politician and an industrialist, in the midst of a heated conversation.

'The auction ends at 3:15 p.m.,' said the politician. 'At 4:00 p.m., I have scheduled a press conference to announce to the Indian people that the Mahatma is coming home.'

'If I put in the money, I get to tell the world I saved Gandhi,' insisted the executive.

'Nothing doing,' the politician was adamant. 'The general elections are in April. This is worth at least a five percentage point rise in polling numbers.'

'We are in the midst of a recession,' countered the other. 'For this kind of publicity, I would have to shell out cash to cover 100 hours of prime-time advertising.'

I stepped forward, hoping to end the impasse.

Suddenly, something solid struck the back of my head. Tottering, I realised that I had collided with a humongous backpack attached to a young man. He was clad in cargo pants, T-shirt and sneakers, an AK-47 assault rifle dangling nonchalantly from one shoulder. It was Ajmal Kasab, the surviving gunman from the Mumbai terror attacks.

I was stunned. True, sauntering about in broad daylight in a frank, there-are-no-secrets-between-us manner was the signature style of these *jihadis* but even brazenness has to draw the line somewhere.

'No reruns here,' Kasab reassured me. 'There's way too much mayhem here already.' He reached into his backpack to pull out an energy bar, an apple and a paddle. 'I plan to bid for the spectacles. Gandhi said they gave him the vision to realise his dream of a free India. I am hoping they show me the way to my promised land.'

Just then, Lot No. 364, the Gandhi items, came up for bidding. After a frenetic few minutes, they were sold for 1.8 million dollars to a high-flying liquor baron from India.

He promised to donate the items to the Indian people. The room erupted with joy. Bidders joined hands to do a little celebratory gig in the middle of the room.

'The Mahatma would have found it passing strange,' I said bemused, 'that a flamboyant playboy, known as the King of Good Times, restored the assets of a leader synonymous with austerity and sobriety.'

The man near me interrupted his fifth 'Jai Ho' to shrug his shoulders. 'The bottom line is that Gandhi's things are back in India.'

'A fortune made selling liquor financed the purchase of the personal effects of a man who spent a lifetime preaching temperance,' I frowned. 'The Mahatma always maintained that alcohol was not the answer to life's questions.'

'It sure provided the solution to this one.' The other man grinned.

I looked down at my book of Gandhi's quotes. 'They say the means are after all just means,' I read. 'I would say means are after all everything. As the means, so the end.'

I shut the book and went forward to join the celebrations.

The Mahatma's Account

A FRAIL BESPECTACLED OLD MAN ENTERED THE BANK OF India at Pune and walked up to the counter.

'Excuse me,' he said to the clerk. 'I would like to withdraw all the money from my account.'

'Name, please?' inquired the bank employee.

'Mohandas Karamchand Gandhi.'

The clerk looked up, startled. '*Bapuji*!' He joined his hands in a *namaste*. 'Please wait. I'll bring the money right away.'

Minutes later, he was back. 'Here you are, *Bapu*. Rs 248.'

Thanking him, the *Mahatma* stood up to leave.

'Please, *Bapu*! May I ask you a question? You were the unrivalled leader of our people for nearly thirty years, yet your savings total a mere Rs 248. How is that so?'

'You expected more, perhaps?'

'Pardon me, *Bapu*, but the amount is laughable. A peon earns several times as much today. Nowadays, a doctor or an engineer is practically a *lakhpati*. As for our leaders, they have entire sections reserved for them in the Swiss banks.'

The *Mahatma* shook his head sadly. 'They were wise men. They banked all their savings. I invested mine.'

'That's a great way to make money,' agreed his companion.

'Not so in my case,' came the forlorn reply. 'All my investments were colossal failures. I had placed a great deal of faith in a fresh new concern called "Free India." It had just started operations then, and had been full of exciting new schemes. It had offered a promising one called "Non-Violence," recommended by wise men like the Buddha and the Shankaracharya. Unfortunately, it was a resounding flop. Terrorists, insurgents and anti-social elements ganged up to destroy it. A parallel issue on violence was a sell-out. Unfortunately, I had backed the wrong horse.'

Gandhiji sighed and continued, 'Our age-old traditions led me to invest in secularism. That was another disaster. They surreptitiously diverted its funds into an issue called Communalism. Even the offices were burnt down during the last riot.'

'I'm so sorry, *Bapu*,' said the bank employee.

'Truth,' mused Gandhi. 'Now, that was billed to be a winner. I especially rooted for that one.'

'It's no longer a catchword then?'

'Catchword?' The *Mahatma* gulped down a sob. 'It's unparliamentary language.' He was silent for some time and then continued. 'I had invested a major part of my funds in Economic Equality,' he continued.

'Surely, that must have fetched you some returns?'

'Yes! Designer *khadi* and naked bodies. Imported caviar alongside empty bellies. I'd rather have done without such returns,' said *Bapu*, burying his face in his hands.

'You appear to have been singularly unlucky in your financial transactions,' commented the clerk, shaking his head.

The *Mahatma* did not hear him. 'As for my favourite, the *Harijan* uplift scheme, that was the cruellest cut of all.'

'Did it fold up, too?'

'It never took off. They kept on reserving it every ten years for future consideration.' Two great tears rolled down the old man's cheeks.

'I'm so sorry, *Bapu*!' cried the clerk. 'But why are you withdrawing your savings?'

The Father of the Nation patted his companion's shoulder. 'You may think me foolish, but I'm an eternal optimist. Today, Free India is offering something new – Hope for the Future. I'm investing all that is left in it.'

Mahatma's account still in Pune Bank – News Item.

(First published in *The Times of India*, Mumbai.)